# CONTEMPORARY
# SOCIOLOGICAL
# THEORY

# Other Authored Books by Jonathan Turner:

*Patterns of Social Organization* (1972)

*American Society: Problems of Structure* (1972)

*The Structure of Sociological Theory* (1974)

*Inequality: Privilege and Poverty in America* (1976, with Charles Starnes)

*Social Problems in America* (1977)

*Sociology: Studying the Human System* (1978)

*Functionalism* (1979, with Alexandra Maryanski)

*The Emergence of Sociological Theory* (1981, with Leonard Beeghley)

*Societal Stratification: A Theoretical Analysis* (1984)

*Oppression: A Socio-History of Black-White Relations in America* (1985, with Royce Singleton and David Musick)

*Herbert Spencer: A Renewed Appreciation* (1985)

*American Dilemmas: A Sociological Interpretation of Enduring Social Issues* (1985, with David Musick)

*Sociology: A Student Handbook* (1985)

*Sociology: The Science of Human Organization* (1986)

*A Theory of Social Interaction* (1988)

*The Impossible Science: An Institutional History of American Sociology* (1990, with Stephen P. Turner)

*The Social Cage: Human Nature and the Evolution of Society* (1992, with Alexandra Maryanski)

*Classical Sociological Theory: A Positivist's Perspective* (1992)

*Sociology: Concepts and Uses* (1993)

*Socjologia Amerykansa W. Posukiwaiou Tazamosci* (1993, with Stephen P. Turner)

*American Ethnicity: A Sociological Analysis of the Dynamics of Discrimination* (1994, with Adalberto Aguirre)

*Macrodynamics: Toward a Theory on the Organization of Human Populations* (1995)

*The Institutional Order* (1997)

*On the Origins of Human Emotions: A Sociological Inquiry into the Evolution of Human Affect* (2000)

*Face-to-Face: Toward a Sociological Theory of Interpersonal Behavior* (2002)

*Human Institutions: A Theory of Societal Evolution* (2003)

*The Sociology of Emotions* (2005, with Jan E. Stets)

*Incest: The Origins of the Taboo* (2005, with Alexandra Maryanski)

*Sociology* (2006)

*On the Origins of Society by Natural Selection* (2007, with Alexandra Maryanski)

*Human Emotions: A Sociological Theory* (2008)

*Theoretical Principles of Sociology, Volume 1 on Macrodynamics* (2010)

*Theoretical Principles of Sociology, Volume 2 on Microdynamics* (2010)

*Theoretical Principles of Sociology, Volume 3 on Mesodynamics* (2012)

*The Problem of Emotions in Societies* (2011)

*Theoretical Sociology: 1830 to the Present* (2012)

*Ten Theoretical Perspectives in Sociology* (2012)

# Edited Books by Jonathan Turner:

*Theory Building in Sociology* (1988)

*Social Theory Today* (1987, with Anthony Giddens)

*Handbook of Sociological Theory* (2001)

*Handbook of the Sociology of Emotions* (2007, with Jan E. Stets)

*Handbook of Neurosociology* (2012, with David Franks)

# CONTEMPORARY
# SOCIOLOGICAL
# THEORY

### Jonathan H. Turner
*University of California, Riverside*

Los Angeles | London | New Delhi
Singapore | Washington DC

Los Angeles | London | New Delhi
Singapore | Washington DC

FOR INFORMATION:

SAGE Publications, Inc.
2455 Teller Road
Thousand Oaks, California 91320
E-mail: order@sagepub.com

SAGE Publications Ltd.
1 Oliver's Yard
55 City Road
London EC1Y 1SP
United Kingdom

SAGE Publications India Pvt. Ltd.
B 1/I 1 Mohan Cooperative Industrial Area
Mathura Road, New Delhi 110 044
India

SAGE Publications Asia-Pacific Pte. Ltd.
3 Church Street
#10-04 Samsung Hub
Singapore 049483

Acquisitions Editor:   David Repetto
Editorial Assistant:   Caitlin Crandell
Production Editor:   Eric Garner
Copy Editor:   Lana Todorovic-Arndt
Typesetter:   C&M Digitals (P) Ltd.
Proofreader:   Laura Webb
Indexer:   Sheila Bodell
Cover Designer:   Gail Buschman
Marketing Manager:   Erica DeLuca
Permissions Editor:   Karen Ehrmann

Printed in the United States of America

*Library of Congress Cataloging-in-Publication Data*

Turner, Jonathan H. Contemporary sociological theory / Jonathan H. Turner, University of California, Riverside.

pages cm
Includes index.

ISBN 978-1-4522-0344-7 (hbk. : alk. paper) —
ISBN 978-1-4522-0345-4 (pbk. : alk. paper)
1. Sociology—History. 2. Sociology—Philosophy. I. Title.

HM435.T97 2013
301—dc23          2012031491

This book is printed on acid-free paper.

12 13 14 15 16 10 9 8 7 6 5 4 3 2 1

# Brief Contents

# Detailed Contents

**To David B. Thordarson, M.D.**

and the Staff in the Department of Orthopaedic Surgery,
University of Southern California

*With gratitude for putting me back together again*

## CHAPTER 1

# The Nature of Sociological Theory

## Theories Invite Controversy

Theories seek to explain things. And thus, sociological theory attempts to explain how the social world operates. This social world consists of the behaviors, interactions, and patterns of social organization among humans, although some would argue that a sociology of nonhuman animals that organize is also possible. As we will see, sociological theory tends to focus on interaction and organization more than behavior per se, but interactions are interpersonal behaviors, and patterns of social organization are ultimately built from interactions among individuals. And so, even though interaction and organization are the subject matter of most theories, there are almost always implicit theories of human behavior tagging along with this emphasis on interaction and social organization.

Theorizing about the social world is, of course, hardly new. Humans have always sought to explain the social world around them from their very beginnings, and today, each of us is a kind of "folk sociological theorists" offering explanations for why people behave and interact with others in a particular manner. We all are social critics of society, and in so being, we are also folk sociologists of patterns of social organization. Moreover, people generally do not see their folk theorizing as highly speculative; in fact, they typically think that have captured the essential reason for why and how people behave, interact, and organize. And yet, people often consider the theories of others, even scientists, to be speculation or "just a theory," as when someone argues that the modern synthesis that produced the biological theory of evolution is "just a theory," or a matter of speculation that has "yet to be proven." But, theory is more than just speculation; the goal of articulating theories is to assess them *against the facts of the empirical world* to see if they are plausible.

And so, most theories in science that have been around for some time are much more than idle speculation. They are explanations for why and how social processes operate the way they do. They are generally backed up by considerable evidence and data; and still, they are often doubted, just as the modern theory of biotic evolution is doubted by many in some societies, particularly in the United States but elsewhere as well.

Thus, people often chose not to believe a theory, even one that is well supported, because it violates their perceptions of how the world really works or their beliefs that are important to them. And people tend to have strong beliefs about human nature, appropriate behaviors and interpersonal demeanors, and how societies should be organized. These beliefs can be more powerful than a clearly stated theory in science, even one supported by evidence. And such is most likely to be the case for sociological theories because our theories are about what people often experience in their daily lives, leading them to assume that they understand the social world and, thereby, do not need sociologists to tell them about "their" world. There is, then, always a problem in developing sociological explanations that contradict people's folk theorizing.

Even within the discipline of professional sociologists, there are many who reject even the possibility that sociology can develop theory like that in the natural sciences. Sociological theorists must, therefore, confront not only a skeptical lay public but also professional colleagues who would argue that scientific theorizing about human behavior, interaction, and organization is not possible. People are different, these critics argue, because they have the capacity for agency that can change the fundamental nature of the social universe, thereby obviating any proposed laws about the fundamental properties and processes of the social universe. Other critics take a different stance and argue that scientific theory is too value neutral, dispassionate, and detached from the problems of societies; instead of standing on the sidelines, sociology should be moral, exposing social problems and proposing solutions to these problems. Sociology must advocate and not sit back as dispassionate and cold scientists. Indeed, science and formal theories are often seen by these moralizing sociologists as "part of the problem" in societies.

As will become clear, my bias is toward scientific theorizing in sociology—even if it is necessary to endure the distain of critical sociologists. I not only believe that there can be a natural science of society,[1] but that sociology is far along in explaining the fundamental dynamics of the social universe. The skeptics within and outside sociology are, I would argue, simply wrong in their challenge to theoretical sociology. Still, we cannot ignore the critics, and in the pages to follow, I will outline the principle theories in sociology of how the social world operates *and* the critiques of, and challenges to, such theories.

---

[1] I have taken this phrase from A. R. Radcliffe-Brown's, *A Natural Science of Society* (Glencoe, IL: Free Press, 1948).

From its very beginnings, when Auguste Comte proclaimed in 1830 that there could be a "social physics," immediate controversy arose over whether or not there could be scientific sociology built around explanatory theories of the social universe.[2] This controversy persists to the present day and, no doubt, will persist well into the future. One way to put the controversy into a broader perspective is to outline the fundamental beliefs of scientific theory in a broader context of other belief systems. Science is a belief system, but it is obviously not the only set of beliefs that influence people perceptions and judgments. There are different types of knowledge possessed by humans, and science is only *one of several types*, which means, inevitably, that science as a way of knowing about the world will sometimes clash with knowledge generated by other belief systems.

# Science as a Belief System

Social scientific theories begin with the assumption that the universe, including the social universe created by acting human beings, reveals certain basic and fundamental properties and processes that explain the ebb and flow of events in specific contexts. Because of this concern with discovering fundamental properties and processes, scientific theories are always stated abstractly, rising above specific empirical events and highlighting the underlying *forces that drive these events* in all times and places. In the context of sociological inquiry, for example, theoretical explanations are not so much about the specifics of a particular economy as about the underlying dynamics of production and distribution as social forces that drive the formation and change of economies. Similarly, scientific theories are not about a particular form of government but about the nature of power as a basic social force. Or, to illustrate further, scientific theories are not about particular behaviors and interactions among actual persons in a specific setting as about the nature of human interpersonal behavior in general, and hence, the forces that are always operative when people interact with each other. The goal, then, is always to see if the underlying forces that govern particulars of specific empirical cases can be discovered and used to explain the operation of these empirical cases. To realize this goal, theories must be about generic properties and processes transcending the unique characteristics of any one situation or case. Thus, scientific theories always seek to transcend the particular and the time bound. Scientific theories are therefore about the generic, the fundamental, the timeless, and the universal.

Another characteristic of scientific theories is that they are stated more formally than ordinary language. At the extreme, theories are couched in

---

[2]Auguste Comte, *System of Positive Philosophy*, vol. 1 (Paris: Bachelier, 1830). Subsequent portions were published between 1831 and 1842. For a more detailed analysis of Comte's thought, see Jonathan H. Turner, Leonard Beeghley, and Charles Powers, *The Emergence of Sociological Theory*, 7th ed. (Newbury Park, CA: Sage).

another language, such as mathematics, but more typically in the social sciences and particularly in sociology, theories are phrased in ordinary language. Still, even when using regular language, an effort is made to speak in neutral, objective, and unambiguous terms so that the theory means the same thing to all who examine it.

Terms denoting properties of the world and their dynamics are defined clearly so that their referents are clear, and relationships among concepts denoting phenomena are stated in ways such that their inter-connections are understood by all who examine the theory. At times, this attention to formalism can make theories seem stiff and dull, especially when these formalisms are couched at higher levels of abstraction. Yet, without attention to what terms and phrases denote and connote, a theory could mean very different things to diverse audiences.

A final characteristic of scientific theories is that they are designed to be systematically tested with replicable methods against the facts of particular empirical settings. Despite being stated abstractly and formally, scientific theories do not stand aloof from the empirical. Useful theories all suggest ways that they can be assessed against empirical events.

All scientific fields develop theories. For in the end, science seeks (1) to develop abstract and formally stated theories and (2) to test these theories against empirical cases to see if they are plausible. If the theory seems plausible in light of empirical assessment, then it represents *for the present time* the best explanation of events. If a theory is contradicted by empirical tests, then it must be discarded or revised. If competing theories emerge to explain the same phenomena, they too must be empirically assessed, with the better explanation winning out.

Science is thus a rather slow process of developing theories, testing them, and then rejecting, modifying, or retaining them, at least until a better theory is proposed. Without attention to stating theories formally and objectively, while assessing them against the empirical world, theory would become self-justifying and self-contained, reflecting personal biases, ideological leanings, or religious convictions.

Our biases and personal ideologies about what should occur, or our commitments to other belief systems such as those articulated by religion, are, in essence, belief systems; these stand in contrast to science as a belief system. These differences between scientific theory and other types of knowledge are presented in Figure 1.1.

The typology asks two basic questions:[3] (1) Is the search for knowledge to be evaluative or neutral? (2) Is the knowledge developed to pertain to actual empirical events and processes, or is it to be about non-empirical realities? In other words, should knowledge tell us what *should be* or *what is?* And should it refer to the observable world or to other, less observable,

---

[3]I am borrowing the general ideal from Talcott Parsons' *The Social System* (New York: Free Press, 1951).

**Figure 1.1**   Types of Knowledge

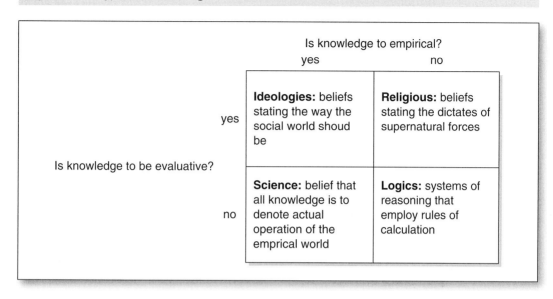

realms? If knowledge is to tell us what should exist (and, by implication, what should not occur) in the empirical world, then it is *ideological knowledge*. If knowledge informs us about what should be and does not pertain to observable forces but to hypothesized supernatural force, then the knowledge is *religious* and, hence, about forces and beings in another realm of existence. If knowledge is neither empirical nor evaluative, then it is a formal *system of logic*, such as mathematics, for developing other forms of knowledge, particularly science. And if it is about empirical events and is non-evaluative, then it is *science*.

   This typology is crude, but it makes the essential point: there are different ways to look at, interpret, and develop knowledge about the world. Science is only one way. In its most developed form, science is based on the pre-sumptions that theoretical knowledge (1) can be value free, (2) can explain the actual workings of the empirical world in all times and place, and (3) can be revised as a result of careful observations of empirical events. These characteristics distinguish science from other beliefs about how we should generate understanding and insight about the world.[4]

---

[4]It is very difficult to find recent works in sociology on formal theory building because these kinds of works have fallen out of favor. There is some justification for this because these works tended to have an overly idealized view of how theories are built. Still, it is useful to read one or two such works, just to get an idea of the issues involved in developing formal theory. Though necessarily old, because no new works have been written, I have found the following useful references over the years: Paul Davidson Reynolds, *A Primer in Theory Construction* (Indianapolis: Bobbs-Merrill, 1971, now in its 21st printing by Macmillan); Arthur L. Stinchcombe, *Constructing Social Theories* (New York: Harcourt, Brace & World,

The boundaries among these types of knowledge are often open, or at least permeable. Logics can be the language of science, as is the case when mathematics is used to state important relationships among forces driving the universe. The boundaries between these forms of knowledge can also be confrontational, as is evident today in the controversy between religious and scientific explanations for the evolution of humans. Within sociology proper, the most contentious and controversial relationship is between ideology and science. Many sociologists believe that theory must contain an ideological component; it must criticize undesirable conditions and advocate alternatives. Beliefs about "what should be" thus dominate the analysis of the social universe. This view of sociology contradicts the value-neutrality of science, where ideologies and other evaluative beliefs are not to contaminate analysis of social conditions. As noted earlier, the debate between those who advocate a scientific approach and those who argue for the infusion of ideology into sociology has been present for most of the history of sociology, and today, this debate still rages. In the last section of this book, I devote several chapters to *critical theory* where the goal is to criticize existing conditions and to advocate potential alternatives.

These critical theories make a number of arguments. One is that no matter how hard scholars try to exclude ideology from their work, ideology will slip in. Every analyst is located at a particular position in society and will, therefore, have certain interests that guide both the problems selected for analysis and the mode of analysis itself. Inevitably, what people think should occur will enter their work, and so, it is only an illusion that statements about the operation of the social world are free of ideology. Another line of criticism is that when scientists study what exists, they will tend to see the way the social world is currently structured as the way things must be. As a result, theories about the world as it exists in the present can become ideologies legitimating the status quo and blinding thinkers to alternative social arrangements.[5] And, a third line of attack on the value-neutrality of

---

1968), pp. 3–56; Karl R. Popper, *The Logic of Scientific Discovery* (New York: Harper & Row, 1959); David Willer and Murray Webster, Jr. "Theoretical Concepts and Observables," *American Sociological Review* 35 (August 1970): pp. 748–57; Hans Zetterberg, *On Theory and Verification in Sociology*, 3rd ed. (Totowa, NJ: Bedminister Press, 1965); Jerald Hage, *Techniques and Problems of Theory Construction in Sociology* (New York: John Wiley & Sons, 1972); Walter L. Wallace, *The Logic of Science in Sociology* (Chicago: Aldine Publishing, 1971); Robert Dubin, *Theory Building* (New York: Free Press, 1969); Jack Gibbs, *Sociological Theory Construction* (Hinsdale, IL: Dryden Press, 1972); Herbert M. Blalock, Jr., *Theory Construction: From Verbal to Mathematical Formulations* (Englewood Cliffs, NJ: Prentice Hall, 1969); Nicholas C. Mullins, *The Art of Theory: Construction and Use* (New York: Harper & Row, 1971); Bernard P. Cohen, *Developing Sociological Knowledge: Theory and Method* (Chicago: Nelson-Hall, 1989).

[5]For example, there is a growing conviction among some sociologists that science is much like any other thought system in that it is devoted to sustaining a particular vision, among a community of individuals called scientists, of what is "really real." Science simply provides one interesting way of constructing and maintaining a vision of reality,

science is that humans have the capacity to change the very nature of their universe; therefore, there can be no immutable laws of human social organization because humans' capacity for agency allows them to alter the very reality described by these laws. As a result, a natural science of society is not possible because the very nature of social reality can be changed by the will of actors.

Those who advocate a scientific approach reject these arguments by critical theorists. While they see ideological bias as a potential problem, this problem can be mitigated, if not obviated, by careful attention to potential sources of bias. And even if one's position in the social world shapes the questions asked, it is still possible to answer these questions in an objective manner. Moreover, the notion that the objective study of the social world ensures that inquiry will support the status quo is rejected by those committed to science. Real science seeks to examine the forces driving the current world, and theories are about these underlying forces that, in the very best theories, have operated in all times and places. Thus, science does not just describe the world as it presently is, but rather, it tries to see how forces operating in the past, present, and future work to generate the empirical world. These forces will thus change the present, just as they transformed the past into a new present and will eventually bring about a new future. There is no reason, therefore, for theories to legitimate a status quo; indeed, theories are about the dynamic potential of the forces that change social arrangements. And finally, the contention of critics that humans can change the very nature of the forces driving the social world is rejected by scientists. Humans can, of course, change the social world as it exists, but this is very different from changing the generic and basic forces that shape the organization of the social universe. Agency is thus constrained by the underlying forces that drive the social universe; indeed, for agency to be successful, it must be directed at changing the valences of the forces that drive the social universe. In fact, when people's concerted efforts to change certain arrangements consistently fail, this failure is often an indicator that they are fighting against a powerful social force. For example, humans can change the way they produce things, but they cannot eliminate production as a basic force necessary for the survival of the species; people can change political regimes, but they cannot eliminate the operation of power in social relations.

---

but there are other, equally valid views among different communities of individuals. Obviously, I do not accept this argument, but I will explore it in more detail in various chapters. For some interesting explorations of the issues, see Edward A. Tiryakian, "Existential Phenomenology and the Sociological Tradition," *American Sociological Review* 30 (October 1965): pp. 674–88; J. C. McKinney, "Typification, Typologies, and Sociological Theory," *Social Forces* 48 (September 1969): pp. 1–11; Alfred Schutz, "Concept and Theory Formation in the Social Sciences," *Journal of Philosophy* 51 (April 1954): pp. 257–73; Harold Garfinkel, *Studies in Ethnomethodology* (Englewood Cliffs, NJ: Prentice Hall, 1967); George Psathas, "Ethnomethods and Phenomenology," *Social Research* 35 (September 1968): pp. 500–520.

The debate over whether or not sociology can be a natural science will, no doubt, rage into the future.[6] For our purposes, we simply must recognize that commitments to science vary among theorists in sociology. Yet, in the pages to follow, emphasis is on the contribution of theories to the science of sociology. Of course, those theories rejecting this orientation are also examined, but these alternatives will always be examined in terms of how they deviate from scientific sociology.

# The Elements of Theory

Theory is a mental activity revolving around the process of developing ideas that explain how and why events occur. Theory is constructed with several basic elements or building blocks: (1) concepts, (2) variables, (3) statements, and (4) formats. Although there are many divergent claims about what theory is or should be, these four elements are common to all of them. Let me examine each of these elements in more detail.

## Concepts: The Basic Building Blocks of Theory

Theories are built from concepts. Most generally, concepts denote phenomena; in so doing, they isolate features of the world that are considered, for the moment at hand, important. For example, notions of atoms, protons, neutrons, and the like are concepts pointing to and isolating phenomena for certain analytical purposes. Familiar sociological concepts would include production, power, interaction, norm, role, status, and socialization. Each term is a concept that embraces aspects of the social world that are considered essential for a particular purpose.

Concepts are constructed from definitions.[7] A *definition* is a system of terms, such as the sentences of a language, the symbols of logic, or the notation of mathematics, that inform investigators as to the phenomenon denoted by a concept. For example, the concept *conflict* has meaning only when it is defined. One possible definition might be the following: *Conflict is interaction among social units in which one unit seeks to prevent another from realizing its goals.* Such a definition allows us to visualize the phenomenon that is denoted by the concept. It enables all investigators to see the same thing and to understand what it is that is being studied.

Thus, concepts that are useful in building theory have a special characteristic: they strive to communicate a uniform meaning to all those who use them. However, since concepts are frequently expressed with the words

[6]For my views on these controversial issues, see Jonathan H. Turner, "In Defense of Positivism," *Sociological Theory* 3 (Fall 1985): pp. 24–30 and Stephan Fuchs and Jonathan H. Turner, "What Makes a Science Mature?" *Sociological Theory* 4 (Fall 1986): pp. 143–50.

[7]For more detailed work on concept formation, see Carl G. Hempel, *Fundamentals of Concept Formation in Empirical Science* (Chicago: University of Chicago Press, 1952).

of everyday language, it is difficult to avoid words that connote varied meanings—and hence point to different phenomena—for varying groups of scientists. It is for this reason that many concepts in science are expressed in technical or more neutral languages, such as the symbols of mathematics. In sociology, expression of concepts in such special languages is sometimes not only impossible but also undesirable. Hence the verbal symbols used to develop a concept must be defined as precisely as possible so that they point to the same phenomenon for all investigators. Although perfect consensus may never be attained with conventional language, a body of theory rests on the premise that scholars will do their best to define concepts unambiguously.

The concepts of theory reveal a special characteristic: *abstractness*.[8] Some concepts pertain to concrete phenomena at specific times and locations. Other, more abstract, concepts point to phenomena that are not related to concrete times or locations. For example, in the context of small-group research, *concrete concepts* would refer to the persistent interactions of particular individuals, whereas an *abstract* conceptualization of such phenomena would refer to those general properties of face-to-face groups that are not tied to particular individuals interacting at a specified time and location. Whereas abstract concepts are not tied to a specific context, concrete concepts are. In building theory, abstract concepts are crucial, although we will see shortly that theorists disagree considerably on this issue.

Abstractness, then, poses a problem: how do we attach abstract concepts to the ongoing, everyday world of events that we want to understand and explain? Although it is essential that some of the concepts of theory transcend specific times and places, it is equally critical that there be procedures for making these abstract concepts relevant to observable situations and occurrences. After all, the utility of an abstract concept can be demonstrated only when the concept is brought to bear on some specific empirical problem encountered by investigators; otherwise, concepts remain detached from the very processes they are supposed to help investigators understand. Thus, just how to attach concepts to empirical processes, or the workings of the real world, is an area of great controversy in sociology. Some argue for very formal procedures for attaching concepts to empirical events. Those of this persuasion contend that abstract concepts should be accompanied by a series of statements known as *operational definitions,* which are sets of procedural instructions telling investigators how to go about discerning phenomena in the real world that are denoted by an abstract concept.

Others argue, however, that the nature of our concepts in sociology precludes such formalistic exercises. At best, concepts can be only sensitizing devices that must change with alterations of social reality, and so we can only intuitively and provisionally apply abstract concepts to the actual flow

---

[8]For a useful and insightful critique of sociology's ability to generate abstract concepts and theory, see David and Judith Willer, *Systematic Empiricism: Critique of Pseudoscience* (Englewood Cliffs, NJ: Prentice Hall, 1973).

of events. Moreover, among those making this argument, emulating the natural sciences in an effort to develop formal operations for attaching concepts to reality is to ignore the fact that social reality is changeable; it does not reveal invariant properties like the other domains of the universe.[9] Thus, to think that abstract concepts denote enduring and invariant properties of the social universe and to presume, therefore, that the concept itself will never need to be changed is, at best, naive.[10]

And so the debate rages, taking many different turns. We need not go into detail here since these issues will be brought out again and again as the substance of sociological theory is examined in subsequent chapters. For the present, it is only necessary to draw the approximate lines of battle.

## Variables as an Important Type of Concept

When used to build theory, two general types of concepts can be distinguished: (1) those that simply label phenomena and (2) those that refer to phenomena that differ in degree.[11] Concepts that merely label phenomena would include such commonly employed abstractions as *dog, cat, group, social class,* and *star.* When stated in this way, none of these concepts reveals the ways in which the phenomena they denote vary in terms of such properties as size, weight, density, velocity, cohesiveness, or any of the many criteria used to inform investigators about differences in degree among phenomena.

Those who believe that sociology can be like other sciences prefer concepts that are translated into variables—that is, into states that vary. We want to know the variable properties—size, degree, intensity, amount, and so forth—of events denoted by a concept. For example, to note that an aggregate of people is a group does not indicate what type of group it is or how it compares with other groups in terms of such criteria as size, degree of differentiation of roles, and level of cohesiveness. And so, some concepts of scientific theory should denote the *variable* features of the world. To understand events requires that we visualize how variation in one phenomenon *is related to*

---

[9]For examples of this line of argument, see Herbert Blumer, *Symbolic Interaction: Perspective and Method* (Englewood Cliffs, NJ: Prentice Hall, 1969) or Anthony Giddens, *New Rules of Sociological Method* (New York: Basic Books, 1977). For a more recent advocacy, see John Martin Levy, *The Explanation of Social Action* (New York: Oxford University Press, 2011).

[10]For the counterargument, see Jonathan H. Turner, "Toward a Social Physics: Reducing Sociology's Theoretical Inhibitions," *Humboldt Journal of Social Relations* 7 (Fall/Winter 1979–80): pp. 140–55; "Returning to Social Physics," *Perspectives in Social Theory,* vol. 2 (1981); "Some Problematic Trends in Sociological Theorizing," *The Wisconsin Sociologist* 15 (Spring/Summer 1978): pp. 80–88; and *Theoretical Principles of Sociology,* vol. 1, 2, and 3 (New York: Springer, 2010–2012).

[11]Reynolds, *Primer in Theory Construction,* p. 57; see also Stinchcombe, *Constructing Social Theories,* pp. 38–47 for a discussion of how concepts not only point to variable properties of phenomena but also to the interaction effects of interrelated phenomena. For an interesting discussion of the importance of variable concepts and for guidelines on how to use them, see Hage, *Techniques and Problems of Theory Construction.*

variation in another. Others, who are less enamored by efforts to make sociology a natural science, are less compulsive about translating concepts into variables. They are far more interested in whether or not concepts sensitize and alert investigators to important processes than they are in converting each concept into a metric that varies in some measurable way. They are not, of course, against the conversion of ideas into variables, but they are cautious about efforts to translate each and every concept into a metric.

## Theoretical Statements and Formats

To be useful, the concepts of theory must be connected to one another. Such connections among concepts constitute *theoretical statements*. These statements specify the way in which events denoted by concepts are interrelated, and at the same time, they provide an interpretation of how and why events should be connected. When these theoretical statements are grouped together, they constitute a *theoretical format*. There are, however, different ways to organize theoretical statements into formats. Indeed, in sociological theory, there is relatively little consensus over just how to organize theoretical statements; in fact, much of the theoretical controversy in sociology revolves around differences over the best way to develop theoretical statements and to group them together into a format. Depending on one's views about what kind of science, if any, sociology can be, the structure of theoretical statements and their organization into formats differ dramatically. Let us review the range of opinion on the matter.

There are five basic approaches in sociological theory for generating theoretical statements and formats: (1) meta-theoretical schemes, (2) analytical schemes, (3) discursive schemes, (4) propositional schemes, and (5) modeling schemes. Figure 1.2 summarizes the relations among these schemes and the basic elements of theory.

Concepts are constructed from definitions; theoretical statements link concepts together; and statements are organized into five basic types of formats. However, these five formats can be executed in a variety of ways. So, in reality, there are more than just five strategies for developing theoretical statements and formats. Moreover, these various strategies are not always mutually exclusive, for in executing one of them, we are often led to another as a kind of next step in building theory. Yet—and this point is crucial—these various approaches are often viewed as antagonistic, and the proponents of each strategy have spilled a great deal of ink sustaining the antagonism. Moreover, even within a particular type of format, there is constant battle over the best way to develop theory. This acrimony represents a great tragedy because in a mature science—which, sad to say, sociology is not—these approaches are viewed as highly compatible. Before pursuing this point further, we need to delineate in more detail each of these approaches.

(1)  **Meta-Theoretical Schemes**. This kind of theoretical activity is more comprehensive than ordinary theory. Meta-theoretical schemes are

**Figure 1.2** The Elements of Theory in Sociology

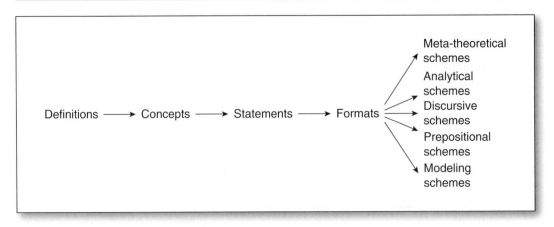

not, by themselves, theories that explain specific classes of events; rather, they explicate the basic issues that a theory must address. In many socio-logical circles, meta-theory is considered an essential prerequisite to ade-quate theory building,[12] even though the dictionary definition of *meta* emphasizes "occurring later" and "in succession" to previous activities.[13] Furthermore, in most other sciences, meta-theoretical reflection has occurred *after* a body of formal theoretical statements has been developed. It is typically after a science has used a number of theoretical statements and formats successfully that scholars begin to ask: what are the underlying assumptions about the universe contained in these statements? What strate-gies are demanded by, or precluded from, these statements and their organization into formats? What kind of knowledge is generated by these statements and formats, and conversely, what is ignored? In sociological theory, however, advocates of meta-theory usually emphasize that we can-not develop theory *until* we have resolved these more fundamental episte-mological and metaphysical questions.

For those who emphasize meta-theory, several preliminary issues must be resolved. These include the following: (1) What is the basic nature of human activity about which we must develop theory? For example, what is the basic nature of human beings? What is the fundamental nature of society? What is the fundamental nature of the bonds that connect peo-ple to one another and to society? (2) What is the appropriate way to develop theory, and what kind of theory is possible? For instance, can we build highly formal systems of abstract laws, as is the case in physics, or must we be content with general concepts that simply sensitize and

---

[12]For a review of different types of meta-theorizing, see George Ritzer, *Metatheorizing in Sociology* (Lexington, MA: Lexington Books, 1991).

[13]*Webster's New Collegiate Dictionary* (Springfield, MA: G & C Merriman, 1976).

orient us to important processes? Can we rigorously test theories with precise measurement procedures, or must we use theories as interpretative frameworks that cannot be tested by the same procedures as in the natural sciences? (3) What is the critical problem on which social theory should concentrate? For instance, should we examine the processes of social integration, or must we concentrate on social conflict? Should we focus on the nature of social action among individuals, or on structures of social organization? Should we stress the power of ideas, like values and beliefs, or must we focus on the material conditions of people's existence?

A great deal of what is defined as sociological theory in sociology involves trying to answer these questions. The old philosophical debates—idealism versus materialism, induction versus deduction, causation versus association, subjectivism versus objectivism, and so on—are re-evoked and analyzed with respect to social reality. At times, meta-theorizing has been true to the meaning of *meta* and has involved a re-analysis of previous scholars' ideas in light of these philosophical issues. The idea behind re-analysis is to summarize the metaphysical and epistemological assumptions of the scholars' work and to show where the schemes went wrong and where they still have utility. Furthermore, on the basis of this assessment, there are some recommendations for re-analyses as to how we should go about building theory and what this theory should be.

Meta-theorizing often gets bogged down in weighty philosophical matters and immobilizes theory building. The enduring philosophical questions persist because they are not resolvable—which is the reason they are philosophical in the first place. One must just take a stand on the issues and see what kinds of insights can be generated. But meta-theory often stymies as much as stimulates theoretical activity because it embroils theorists in inherently unresolvable and always debatable controversies. Of course, many sociologists reject this assertion, and so, for our present purposes, the more important conclusion is that a great deal of sociological theory is, in fact, meta-theoretical activity.

Yet, not all meta-theorizing gets bogged down in unresolvable issues. Some meta-theorists, and I must include myself in this group, examine theories that have been stated in one format and try to convert it to another format. For example, a theory stated discursively in just words and texts might be converted to more formal propositions so that the key theoretical ideas are highlighted, or the theory might be converted into an analytical model, where the variables or forces in play are visually arranged so as to highlight their causal relations to each other. Thus, as George Ritzer has emphasized, there are several different types of meta-theorizing, with one being the analysis of existing theories to make the theories more formal and precise.[14]

---

[14]Alexander's work is more in this tradition. See also Richard Münch, *Theory of Action: Reconstructing the Contributions of Talcott Parsons, Émile Durkheim, and Max Weber* (Frankfurt: Suhrkamp, 1982).

(2)   **Analytical Schemes.** Much theoretical activity in sociology consists of concepts organized into a classification scheme that denotes the key properties, and interrelations among these properties, in the social universe. There are many different varieties of analytical schemes, but they share an emphasis on classifying basic properties of the social world. The concepts of the scheme chop up the universe; then, the ordering of the concepts gives the social world a sense of order. Explanation of an empirical event comes whenever a place in the classificatory scheme can be found for an empirical event.

There are, however, wide variations in the nature of the typologies in analytical schemes, although there are two basic types: (1) *naturalistic schemes,* which try to develop a tightly woven system of categories that is presumed to capture the way in which the invariant properties of the universe are ordered,[15] and (2) *sensitizing schemes,* which are more loosely assembled congeries of concepts intended only to sensitize and orient researchers and theorists to certain critical processes. Figure 1.3 summarizes these two types of analytical approaches.

Naturalistic/positivistic schemes assume that there are timeless and universal processes in the social universe, just as there are in the physical and biological realms. The goal is to create an abstract conceptual typology that is isomorphic with these timeless processes. In contrast, sensitizing schemes are sometimes more skeptical about the timeless quality of social affairs. As a consequence of this skepticism, concepts and their linkages must always be provisional and sensitizing because the nature of human activity is to change those very arrangements denoted by the organization of concepts into theoretical statements.[16] Hence, except for certain very general conceptual categories, the scheme must be flexible and capable of being revised as circumstances in the empirical world change. At best, then, explanation is simply an interpretation of events by seeing them as an instance or example of the provisional and sensitizing concepts in the scheme.

Often it is argued that analytical schemes are a necessary prerequisite for developing other forms of theory. Until one has a scheme that organizes the properties of the universe, it is difficult to develop propositions and models about specific events. For without the general analytical framework, how can a theorist or researcher know what to examine? There is some merit to this position, but if the scheme becomes too complex and elaborate, it is not easily translated into other theoretical formats. Thus, analytical schemes can represent a useful way to begin theorizing, unless they are too rigid and elaborate to stimulate theorizing outside the parameters imposed by the scheme itself.[17]

---

[15]Talcott Parsons' work is of this nature, as we will see in the next chapter.

[16]Anthony Giddens' work represents this alternative. See his *The Constitution of Society* (Berkeley, CA: University of California Press, 1984).

[17]For my best effort to use sensitizing schemes, see Jonathan H. Turner, *A Theory of Social Interaction* (Stanford, CA: Stanford University Press, 1988).

**Figure 1.3**  Types of Analytical Schemes

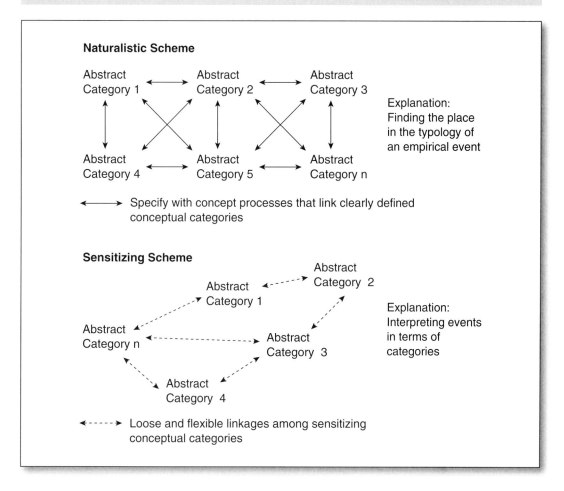

(3)  **Discursive Schemes**. Many theories are simply stated in words that are not highly formalized or ordered into propositions or other structured formats. They simply outline in everyday language key variables and forces, discursively suggesting the ways in which they affect each other. Indeed, it may be that the majority of sociological theories are stated in this way because their authors often think of formalization as overly contrived and, hence, unnecessary. Such theories are, of course, often subject to meta-theorizing as theorists try to extract the key arguments and formalize them in some manner, as I will do for various theories reviewed in the chapters to follow.

The great strength of discursive schemes is that they are typically easier to understand than those that are more formal, but the great weakness can be that the variables and forces highlighted and the dynamic relations among them are vague and imprecise. Such is often the case with meta-theorizing and analytical schemes discussed above, and indeed, these may present more difficulty than discursive schemes in figuring out the causal connections or even the basic relationships among the forces theorized to operate. For example, a theory may be illustrated with so much historical detail that it is difficult to figure out what the more generic forces in play might be. Or, the forces may be defined as a typology in which variations in the values and valences of the forces are not emphasized; as a result, it is difficult to understand how variations in typologically defined forces cause variation in other forces. Yet, when the theory is powerful, a meta-theorist can often make reasonable inferences about the range of variation in forces and thus connect them in analytical models or propositional schemes. When, however, the variables are not clearly defined and are used loosely in rambling text, meta-theorizing may not be able to isolate them and then connect their operation to other forces driving the social world. For example, of the founding theorists of sociology—say, Auguste Comte, Herbert Spencer, Karl Marx, Max Weber, Georg Simmel, Émile Durkheim, and George Herbert Mead—it is relatively easy to convert their arguments into propositions or laws, even if they themselves would not have agreed with such a meta-theoretical exercise. Some are particularly easy because, like Spencer, Simmel, and Durkheim, they presented their discursive arguments in close-to-proposition formats, whereas a scholar like Weber did not. Still, it is not difficult to convert Weber's arguments, for all of their embeddedness in historical analysis and typologies (his "ideal types"), into causal models and propositions. For, when a theorist is being a "good theorist," attention is paid to isolating key variables and forces and, in discursive text, connecting them to other forces. Even with a certain vagueness in language, it is still possible to discern the basic theoretical argument and convert it—if one is so disposed—into a more formal format like an analytical model or propositions scheme, as is outlined below.

(4) **Propositional Schemes.** A proposition is a theoretical statement that specifies the connection between two or more variables. It tells us how variation in one concept is accounted for by variation in another. For example, the propositional statement "group solidarity is a positive function of external conflict with other groups" says that, as group conflict increases, so does the internal sense of solidarity among members of the respective groups involved in the conflict. Thus, two properties of the social universe denoted by variable concepts, "group solidarity" and "conflict," are connected by the proposition that, as one increases in value, so does the other.

Propositional schemes vary perhaps the most of all theoretical approaches. They vary primarily along two dimensions: (1) the level of abstraction and (2) the way propositions are organized into formats. Some are highly abstract and contain concepts that do not denote any particular case but all cases of a type (for example, group solidarity and conflict are abstract because no particular empirical instance of conflict and solidarity is addressed). In contrast, other propositional systems are tied to empirical facts and simply summarize relations among events in a particular case (for example, as World War II progressed, nationalism in America increased). Propositional schemes vary not only in terms of abstractness but also by virtue of how propositions are laced together into a format. Some are woven together by very explicit rules; others are merely loose bunches or congeries of propositions.

By using these two dimensions, several different types of propositional schemes can be isolated: (a) axiomatic formats, (b) formal formats, and (c) various empirical formats. The first two (axiomatic and formal formats) are clearly theoretical, whereas various empirical formats are simply research findings that might be useful to test more abstractly stated theories. But, these more empirical types of propositional schemes are often considered theory by practicing sociologists, and so they are included in our discussion here.

(a) An *axiomatic* organization of theoretical statements involves the following elements. First, it contains a set of concepts. Some of the concepts are highly abstract; others, more concrete. Second, there is always a set of existence statements that describe those types and classes of situations in which the concepts and the propositions that incorporate them apply. These existence statements make up what are usually called the *scope conditions* of the theory. Third—and most nearly unique to the axiomatic format—propositional statements are stated in a hierarchical order. At the top of the hierarchy are *axioms,* or highly abstract statements, from which *all* other theoretical statements are logically derived. These latter statements are usually called *theorems* and are logically derived in accordance with varying rules from the more abstract axioms. The selection of axioms is, in reality, a somewhat arbitrary matter, but usually they are selected with several criteria in mind. The axioms should be consistent with one another, although they do not have to be logically interrelated. The axioms should be highly abstract; they should state relationships among abstract concepts. These relationships should be law-like in that the more concrete theorems derived from them have not been disproved by empirical investigation. And the axioms should have an intuitive plausibility in that their truth appears to be self-evident.

The end result of tight conformity to axiomatic principles is an inventory or set of interrelated propositions, each derivable from at least one axiom and usually more abstract theorems. There are several advantages to this form of theory construction. First, highly abstract concepts, encompassing a broad range of related phenomena, can be employed. These abstract concepts do not have to be directly measurable since they are logically tied to more specific and measurable propositions that, when empirically tested, can indirectly subject the more abstract propositions and the axioms to empirical tests. Thus, by virtue of this logical interrelatedness of the propositions and axioms, research can be more efficient since the failure to refute a particular proposition lends credence to other propositions and to the axioms. Second, the use of a logical system to derive propositions from abstract axioms can also generate additional propositions that point to previously unknown or unanticipated relationships among social phenomena.

There are, however, some fatal limitations on the use of axiomatic theory in sociology. In terms of strict adherence to the rules of deduction (the details of which are not critical for my purposes here), most interesting concepts and propositions in sociology cannot be legitimately employed because the concepts are not stated with sufficient precision and because they cannot be incorporated into propositions that state unambiguously the relationship between concepts. Axiomatic theory also requires controls of all potential extraneous variables so that the tight logical system of deduction from axiom to empirical reality is not contaminated by extraneous factors. Sociologists can create such controls, although in many situations, this kind of tight control is not possible.[18] Thus, axiomatic theory can be used only when precise definitions of concepts exist, when concepts are organized into propositions using a precise calculus that specifies relations unambiguously, and when the contaminating effects of extraneous variables are eliminated.

These limitations are often ignored in propositional theory building, and the language of axiomatic theory is employed (axioms, theorems, corollaries, the like); but these efforts are, at best, pseudo-axiomatic schemes.[19] In fact, it is best to call them *formal propositional* schemes[20]—the second type proposition strategy listed earlier.

  (b) *Formal* theories are, in essence, watered-down or loose versions of axiomatic schemes. The idea is to develop highly abstract propositions that are used to explain some empirical event. Some highly abstract propositions are seen as higher-order laws, and the goal of explanation is to visualize empirical events as instances of this *covering law*. Deductions from the laws are made, but they are much looser, rarely conforming to the strict rules of axiomatic theory. Moreover, there is a recognition that extraneous variables cannot always be excluded, and so the propositions

---

[18]For more details of this argument, see Lee Freese, "Formal Theorizing," *Annual Review of Sociology* 6 (1980): pp. 187–212 and Herbert L. Costner and Robert K. Leik, "Deductions from Axiomatic Theory," *American Sociological Review* 29 (December 1964): pp. 19–35.

[19]See, for example, Peter Blau's *Structural Context of Opportunities* (Chicago: University of Chicago Press, 1994) and *Inequality and Heterogeneity: A Primitive Theory of Social Structure* (New York: Free Press, 1977).

[20]See Freese.

usually have the disclaimer "other things being equal." That is, if other forces do not impinge, then the relationship among concepts in the proposition should hold true. For instance, our earlier example of the relationship between conflict and solidarity might be one abstract proposition in a formal system. Thus a formal scheme might say "Other things being equal, group solidarity is a positive function of conflict." Then we would use this law to explain some empirical event—say, for example, World War II (the conflict variable) and nationalism in America (the solidarity variable). And we might find an exception to our rule or law, such as America's involvement in the Vietnam War, or more recently the wars in Iraq and Afghanistan, that contradict the principle, forcing its revision or the recognition that "all things were not equal." In this case, we might revise the principle by stating a condition under which it holds true: when parties to a conflict perceive the conflict as a threat to their welfare, then the level of solidarity of groups is a positive function of their degree of conflict. Thus, in the end, the Vietnam War nor the wars in Iraq and Afghanistan did not produce internal solidarity in America because, eventually, they were not defined as a threat to America's general welfare (whereas, for the North Vietnamese or Taliban, the threat posed by the American military did produce solidarity of the enemy, which in turn made the wars not only costly but difficult to win).

The essential idea here is that, in formal theory, an effort is made to create abstract principles. These principles are often clustered together to form a group of laws from which we make rather loose deductions to explain empirical events. Much like axiomatic systems, formal systems are hierarchical, but the restrictions of axiomatic theory are relaxed considerably. Most propositional schemes in sociological theorizing are, therefore, of this formal type.

(C) Yet, much of what is defined as theory in sociology is more empirical. These *empirical formats* consist of generalizations from specific events, in particular empirical contexts. For example, Golden's Law states that "as industrialization increases, the level of literacy in the population increases." Such a proposition is not very abstract; it is filled with empirical content—industrialization and literacy—which have not existed in all times and places of human social organization. Thus, the law is not about a timeless process, since industrialization is only a few hundred years old and literacy emerged, at best, only 6,000 years ago. There are many such generalizations in sociology that are considered theoretical. They represent statements of empirical regularities that scholars think are important to understand. Indeed, most substantive areas and subfields of sociology are filled with these kinds of propositions.

Strictly speaking, however, these are not theoretical. They are too tied to empirical contexts, times, and places. In fact, they are generalizations that are *in need of a theory to explain them*. Yet, many scholars working in substantive areas see their empirical generalizations as theory; and so, once again, it is clear that there is no clear consensus in sociology as to what constitutes theory.

There are other kinds of empirical generalizations, however, that raise fewer suspicions about their theoretical merits. These are often termed *middle-range theories,* because they are more abstract than a research finding and because their empirical content pertains to variables that are also found in other domains of social reality.[21] For example, a series of middle-range propositions from the complex organization's literature might be stated: "(a) Increases in the complexity (differentiation) of its structure, (b) reliance on formal rules and regulations, (c) decentralization of authority, and (d) span of control for each center of authority of a bureaucracy is a positive function of a bureaucracy's size and rate of growth."[22] These principles (the truth of which is not an issue here) are more abstract than Golden's Law because they denote a whole class of phenomena—organizations. They also deal with more generic variables—size, differentiation, centralization of power, spans of control, rules, and regulations—that have existed in all times and all places. Moreover, these variables could be stated more abstractly to apply to *all* organized social systems, not just bureaucratic organizations. For instance, a more abstract law might state: "(a) Increases in levels of system differentiation, (b) codification of norms, (c) decentralization of power, and (d) spans of control for each center of power is a positive function of the size of the system and its rate of growth." The truth or falsity of these propositions is not being asserted here; rather, these are illustrations of how empirical generalizations can be made *more abstract* and, hence, theoretical. The central point is that some empirical generalizations have more theoretical potential than others. If their variables are relatively abstract and if they pertain to basic and fundamental properties of the social universe that exist in other substantive areas of inquiry, then it is more reasonable to consider them theoretical.

In sum, there are three basic kinds of propositional schemes: axiomatic, formal, and various types of empirical generalizations. These propositional schemes are summarized in Figure 1.4. Although axiomatic formats are elegant and powerful, sociological variables and research typically cannot conform to their restrictions. Instead, we must rely upon formal formats that generate propositions stating abstract relations among variables and then make loosely structured "deductions" to specific empirical cases.

---

[21]See Chapter 5 on Robert K. Merton's work. In particular, consult his *Social Theory and Social Structure* (New York: Free Press, 1975).

[22]I have borrowed this example from Peter M. Blau's "Applications of a Macrosociological Theory" in *Mathematizche Analyse von Organisationsstrukktaren und Prozessen* (Internationale Wissenschaftliche Fachkonferenz, vol. 5, March 1981).

**Figure 1.4**   Types of Propositional Schemes

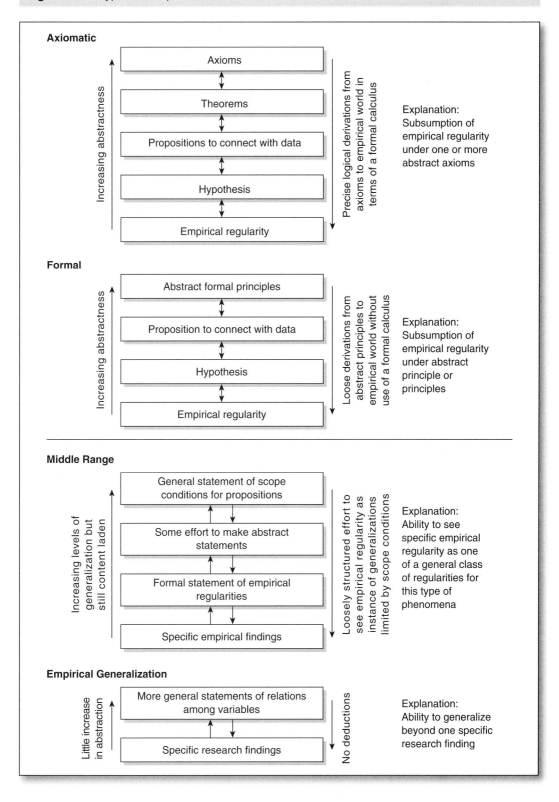

Finally, there are empirical formats that consist of generalizations from particular substantive areas, and these are often considered theories of that area. Some of these theories are little more than summaries of research findings that require a theory to explain them. Others are more middle range and have more potential as theory because they are more abstract and pertain to more generic classes of variables.

(5) **Analytical Modeling Schemes.** At times, it is useful to draw a picture of social events. Some models are drawn with neutral languages such as mathematics, in which the equation is presumed to map and represent empirical processes.[23] In reality, such equations are propositions (formal statements of relations among variables) *unless* they can be used to generate a picture or some form of graphic representation of processes. There is no clear consensus on what a model is, but in sociological theory, there is a range of activity that involves representing concepts and their relations as a picture that arrays in visual space what are considered the important elements of a social process.

A model, then, is a diagrammatic representation of social events. The diagrammatic elements of any model include: (1) concepts that denote and highlight certain features of the universe; (2) the arrangement of these concepts in visual space so as to reflect the ordering of events in the universe; and (3) symbols that mark the connections among concepts, such as lines, arrows, vectors, and so on. The elements of a model may be weighted in some way, or they may be sequentially organized to express events over time, or they may represent complex patterns of relations, such as lag effects, threshold effects, feedback loops, mutual interactions, cycles, and other potential ways in which properties of the universe affect one another.[24]

In sociology, most diagrammatic models are constructed to emphasize the *causal connections* among properties of the universe. That is, they are designed to show how changes in the values of one set of variables are related to changes in the values of other variables. Models are typically constructed when there are numerous variables whose causal interrelations an investigator wants to highlight.

Sociologists generally construct two different types of models, which can be termed *analytical* models and *causal* models. This distinction is somewhat

---

[23]Actually, these are typically *regression equations* and would not constitute modeling as I think it should be defined. A series of differential equations, especially as they are simulated or otherwise graphically represented, would constitute a model. Computer simulations represent, I think, an excellent approach to modeling. See, for example, Robert A. Hanneman, *Computer-Assisted Theory Building: Modeling Dynamic Social Systems* (Newbury Park, CA: Sage, 1988).

[24]Good examples of such models are in my *Theoretical Principles of Sociology, Volume 1 on Macrodynamics* (New York: Springer, 2010). For examples of more empirical, yet still analytical, models, see Gerhard and Jean Lenski, *Human Societies* (Boulder, CO: Paradigm Press, 2011). See also the numerous analytical models in Randall Collins, *Theoretical Sociology* (San Diego, CA: Harcourt Brace Jovanovich, 1988).

arbitrary, but it is a necessary one if we are to appreciate the kinds of models that are constructed in sociology. The basis for making this distinction is two-fold: First, some models are more abstract than others in that the concepts in them are not tied to any particular case, whereas other models reveal concepts that simply summarize statistically relations among variables in a particular data set. Second, more abstract models almost always reveal more complexity in their representation of causal connections among variables. That is, one will find feedback loops, cycles, mutual effects, and other connective representations that complicate the causal connections among the variables in the model and make them difficult to summarize with simple statistics. In contrast, the less abstract models typically depict a clear causal sequence among empirical variables.[25] They typically reveal independent variables that effect variation in some dependent variable; furthermore, if the model is more complex, it might also highlight intervening variables and perhaps even some interaction effects among the variables.

Thus, analytical models are more abstract: they highlight more generic properties of the universe, and they portray a complex set of connections among variables. In contrast, causal models are more empirically grounded; they are more likely to devote particular properties of a specific empirical case; and they are likely to present a simple lineal view of causality. These modeling strategies are summarized in Figure 1.5.

Causal models are typically drawn in order to provide a more detailed interpretation of an empirical generalization. They are designed to sort out the respective influences of variables, usually in some temporal sequence, as they operate on some dependent variable of interest. At times, a causal model becomes a way of representing the elements of a middle-range theory so as to connect these elements to the particulars of a specific empirical context. For example, if we wanted to know why the size of a bureaucratic organization is related to its complexity of structure in a particular empirical case of a growing organization, we might translate the more abstract variables of size and complexity into specific empirical indicators and perhaps try to introduce other variables that also influence the relationship between size and complexity in this empirical case. The causal model thus becomes a way to represent with more clarity the empirical association between size and complexity in a specific context.[26]

Analytical models are usually drawn to specify the relations among more abstract and generic processes. Often they are used to delineate the processes that operate to connect the concepts of an axiomatic or, more likely, a formal theory.[27] For example, we might construct a model that tells us

---

[25]The "path analysis" that was so popular in American sociology in the 1970s is a good example of such modeling techniques.

[26]For an example of a model for these variables, see Peter M. Blau's "A Formal Theory of Differentiation in Organizations," *American Sociological Review* 35 (April 1970): pp. 201–18. See also Chapter 12.

[27]Ibid. is a good example.

**Figure 1.5** Types of Modeling Schemes

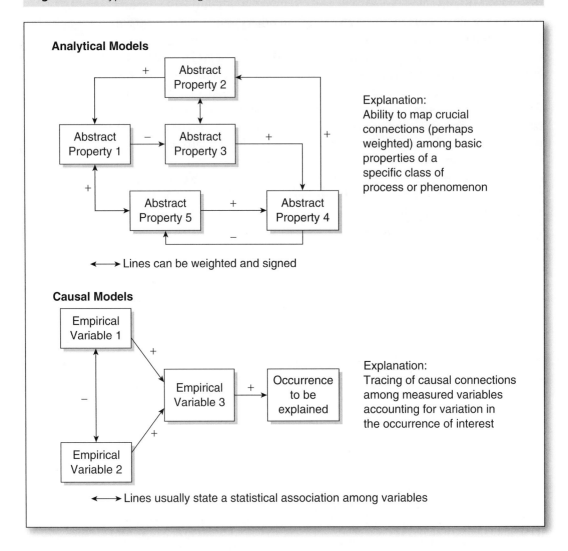

more about the processes that operate to generate the relationship between conflict and solidarity or between size and differentiation in social systems. Additional concepts would be introduced, and their weighted, direct, indirect, feedback, and cyclical, lagged, and other patterns of casual effect on one another would be diagrammed. In this way, the analytical model tells us more about how and why properties of the universe are causally connected. In addition to specifying processes among formal propositions, analytical models can be used to describe processes that connect variables in the propositions of a middle-range theory. For example, we might use a model to map out how organization size and complexity are connected by virtue of other processes operating in an organization.

Of course, we can construct analytical models or causal models for their own sake, without reference to an empirical generalization, a middle-range theory, or a formal/axiomatic theory. We may simply prefer modeling to propositional formats. One of the great advantages of modeling is that it allows the presentation of complex relations among many variables in a reasonably parsimonious fashion. To say the same thing as a model, a propositional format might have to write complex equations or use many words. Thus, by itself, modeling represents a tool that many theorists find preferable to alternative theoretical schemes.

# Assessing Diverse Theoretical Approaches

My belief is that theory should be abstract. That is, the less substantive content in the concepts, the better they are. For if theories are filled with empirical referents, they are tied to specific contexts and, hence, are not as useful as those that view specific empirical contexts as instances or examples of a more basic underlying process. Most theorists in sociology, however, would disagree with me on this score; I will return to this point of contention shortly.

I also believe that theory should be such that it can be proven wrong by empirical tests. As a general platitude, few would disagree with this statement. But as a more practical matter of how we should construct theories to be proven wrong, there is enormous disagreement. Theories must be sufficiently precise in the definitions of concepts and in the organization of concepts into statements that they can be, in principle, measured and tested. It is only through the generation of precise theoretical statements and efforts at their refutation that scientific knowledge can be generated. What distinguishes good theoretical statements from the bad ones is that they *are created to be proven wrong*. A theory that, in principle, cannot be proven wrong is not very useful. It becomes a self-sustaining dogma that is accepted on faith. A theory must allow for understanding of events, and hence, it must be tested against the facts of the world. If a theoretical statement is proven wrong by empirical tests, science has advanced. When a theory is rejected, then one less possible line of inquiry will be required in search of an answer to the question, Why? By successively eliminating incorrect statements, those that survive attempts at refutation offer, for the present at least, the most accurate picture of the real world. Although having one's theory refuted may cause professional stigma, refutations are crucial to theory building. It is somewhat disheartening, therefore, that some scientists appear to live in fear of such refutation. For in the ideal scientific process, just the opposite should be the case, as Karl Popper has emphasized:

Refutations have often been regarded as establishing the failure of a scientist, or at least of his theory. It should be stressed that this is an inductive error. Every refutation should be regarded as a great success; not merely as a success of the scientist who refuted the theory, but also of the scientist who created the refuted theory and who thus in the first instance suggested, if only indirectly, the refuting experiment.[28]

Even statements that survive refutation, and hence bring professional prestige to their framers, are never fully proven. It is always possible that the next empirical test could disprove them. Yet, if statements consistently survive empirical tests, they have high credibility and are likely to be at the core of a theoretical body of knowledge. As I have now phrased the issue, however, many sociological theorists would disagree. Moreover, most philosophers of science would argue that this process of refutation is idealized and, in fact, rarely occurs in the actual operation of science.

Despite these reservations, it is perhaps best to proceed *as if* we can develop theoretical statements that are highly abstract and, at the same time, sufficiently precise so as to be testable. Again, as will be evident in the chapters to come, many social theorists disagree with this position. I have injected my personal views because it is important to understand the biases with which I approach the review and analyses of social theory. Moreover, these biases are the central issue around which the debate over the best approach to developing theory and knowledge rages. So, let me elaborate on them by assessing the merits of various approaches that were outlined in this chapter.

From my point of view, empirical generalizations and causal models of empirically operationalized variables are not theory at all. They are useful summaries of data that need a theory to explain them. Some would argue that theory can be built from such summaries of empirical regularities. That is, we can induce from the facts the more general properties that these facts illustrate. Yet, induction is not a mechanical process of making empirical variables more abstract; often, a creative leap of insight is necessary, and so, theory building by total immersion in the empirical facts is, I believe, a barrier to rising above these facts and producing more abstract theory. Still, there are many instances in science where scholars have been able to make inductions, and so, we should not be too quick to reject this approach out of hand. Still, there is almost always a creative leap here as one moves from empirical generalizations to more generic and abstract concepts, propositions, and models that can explain these facts.

At the other extreme, meta-theory is like empirical facts in that it often becomes difficult to move onto producing real theory. It is easy to get bogged down in enduring philosophical issues when producing meta-theory, with the result that scholars never get around to developing theory. Again, such is not always the case, but there is a clear tendency for theorists in sociology who practice meta-theorizing to remain meta-theorists and indeed to become hostile to formal theories and models or, if not hostile,

[28]Karl R. Popper, *Conjectures and Refutations* (New York: Basic Books, 1962), p. 243.

to think of these as premature and as not fully exploring their implicit assumptions.

Analytical schemes often suffer from the same problems as meta-theory. Naturalistic schemes have a tendency to become overly concerned with their architectural majesty. In an effort to construct an orderly scheme that mirrors at an abstract level the empirical world in all its dimensions, naturalistic schemes get ever more complex; as new elements are added to the scheme, efforts to reconcile new portions with the old take precedence over making the scheme testable. Moreover, the scheme as a whole is impossible to test because relations among its elements cover such a broad range of phenomena and are rarely stated with great precision. And when imprecision is compounded by the abstractness, then empirical tests are infrequent because it is not clear to researchers how to test any portion of the scheme. Yet, despite these problems, creators of analytical schemes view them as a necessary prerequisite for developing testable theoretical statements, and in this sense, they are much like meta-theoreticians.

In contrast, sensitizing schemes are typically constructed as a loose framework of concepts to interpret events and to see if they yield greater understanding of how and why these events occur. Even if such schemes are not considered science, they can be very insightful. Yet, much like naturalistic approaches, sensitizing schemes also become self-reinforcing because they are so loosely structured and so often vague (albeit suggestive and insightful) that the facts can always be bent to fit the scheme. Hence, the scheme can never be refuted or, I suspect, revised on the basis of actual empirical events. Sensitizing schemes are most useful, then, when they are used to orient us to important phenomena and, then, are elaborated upon with propositions and analytical models.

Discursive schemes vary in how useful they can be in generating explanations. If there is precision in the writing—that is, variables are clearly defined and their connection and effects on other variations are unambiguously stated—then a discursive format can offer a sound explanation. But, if variables do not vary but are typologized in categories, and if causal statements say things like "sometimes has an effect on," "tends to influence," "is known to have an effect on," and the like, then the theory will lack precision, and it will be difficult to isolate the forces in play and their relation to each other. Unfortunately, much discursive theorizing is imprecise; even when highly provocative and interesting, the use of informal languages is filled with vagueness. As a result, a meta-theorist interested in formalizing the theory will have to make many inferences and, in the process, not capture the discursive argument intended by the theorist. This weakness in much discursive theorizing is immediately noticeable once the reader seeks precise definitions of the concepts and causal relations among the properties of the social universe supposedly denoted by these concepts.

Let me now turn to axiomatic/formal propositional formats, analytical models, and middle-range propositions. As already indicated, axiomatic theorizing is, for the most part, impractical in sociology. In my view, formal theorizing is the most useful approach because it contains abstract concepts that are linked with sufficient precision so as to be testable. Analytical models can be highly insightful, but they are hard to test as a whole. They contain too many concepts, and their linkages are too diverse to be directly tested. And so, it is reasonable to ask: in what sense can they be useful for sociological theorizing? My view is that an analytical model can best be used to specify the processes by which concepts in a formal proposition are connected.[29] For example, if a proposition states that the "degree of differentiation" is a function of "system size," the model can tell us why and how size and differentiation are connected. That is, we can get a better sense for the underlying processes by which size increases differentiation (and perhaps vice versa). Alternatively, analytical models can also be a starting point for formal theorizing. By isolating basic processes and mapping their interconnections, we can get a sense for the important social processes about which we need to develop formal propositions. And although the model as a whole cannot be easily tested (because it is too complex to be subject to a definitive test), we can decompose it into abstract propositional statements that are amenable to definitive tests.

Thus, analytical models are much more abstract, and thus, they can be the basis for developing formal propositional statements (in rare case, perhaps even axiomatic), or they can specify at an abstract level the robust causal connections among the abstract variables stated in a formal proposition. Moreover, both analytical models and formal propositional schemes cover a wide range of phenomena without being too broad as to become difficult to test empirically. Let me illustrate further with the proposition presented earlier that conflict promotes increased solidarity. While this proposition specifies a fundamental relationship in the social universe, it does not tell us just *how* threat and conflict translate into solidarity. What are the processes by which conflict and threat generate solidarity? The answer to this question can often be stated in an abstract model that outlines the causal sequences—direct, indirect, and reverse—of events that move parties to conflict to form more cohesive structures revealing high solidarity. In fact, introducing the notion of threat (as I did earlier) could have come from an analytical model as a variable that is critical to transforming conflict into high levels of prolonged solidarity. And, one might add other variables, such as (1) leader who can frame the issues and articulate ideologies highlighting threat and (2) entrepreneurs who can mobilize resources (including material and symbolic resources), to sustain the sense of threat and keep members of the conflict party mobilized and focused. Thus, an analytical model can fill in information that makes the basic relationship between conflict and solidarity more robust. One gets a better sense for why and through what processes conflict leads to solidarity, and of course, when it would not. Thus, there can be a synergy between formal propositional schemes and analytical models: the propositional scheme

---

[29]I have tried to illustrate this strategy in my *Theoretical Principles of Sociology.*

indicates the nature of the fundamental relationship (e.g., the basic relationships between conflict and solidarity), while the analytical model indicates how and through what basic processes this relationship is produced. Moreover, the key processes discovered in the analytical model can be converted into a propositional scheme. For instance, a proposition like the following (no claim about its accuracy or exhaustiveness): the degree to which conflict generates solidarity among conflict parties is a positive and additive function of the level of threat posed, the availability of leaders to frame and formulate ideologies about the threat, and the capacity to mobilize symbolic, organizational, and material resources to pursue conflict.

Analytical schemes are less likely to have this synergetic effect, even though they may be highly abstract and incorporate a wide range of phenomena. Because they categorize phenomena rather than seeing them as variables and because they do not specify causal relations among these phenomena within categories, they are often difficult to convert to propositional schemes or analytical models. They describe, albeit at a very abstract level, the organization of a broad range of phenomena in terms. Sensitizing schemes have the same problem. They are abstract, which is useful in building theory, but they do not specify in great detail the fundamental relations among phenomena. Rather, they denote phenomena, suggest how they might be related without great precision, and always hold out the possibility that the categories and variables in the scheme may be obviated by the agency of actors.

Middle-range propositions are, I feel, less useful as places to begin theory building. They tend to be too filled with empirical content, much of which does not pertain to the more basic, enduring, and generic features of the social universe.[30] For example, a "theory of ethnic antagonism" is often difficult to translate into a more general proposition or model on conflict. Moreover, scholars working at this middle range tend to become increasingly empirical as they seek to devise ways to test their theories in specific empirical contexts. Their propositions become, I have found, ever more like empirical generalizations as more and more research content is added. There is no logical reason why substantive and empirical referents cannot be taken out of middle-range theories and the level of abstraction raised, but such has infrequently occurred.

In Figure 1.6, I have summarized these conclusions in the right column. Meta-theory and naturalistic analytical schemes are interesting philosophy but poor theory. Sensitizing analytical schemes, formal propositional statements and analytical models offer the best place to begin theorizing, especially if interplay among them is possible. Middle-range theories have rarely realized their theoretical potential, tending to move toward empirical generalizations as opposed to formal propositions. Causal models and empirical generalizations are useful in that they give theorists some sense of

---

[30]I doubt if this was Merton's intent when he formulated this idea, but my sense is that his advocacy became a legitimization for asserting that empirical generalizations were "theory."

**Figure 1.6**  Theoretical Formats and Potential for Building Testable Theory

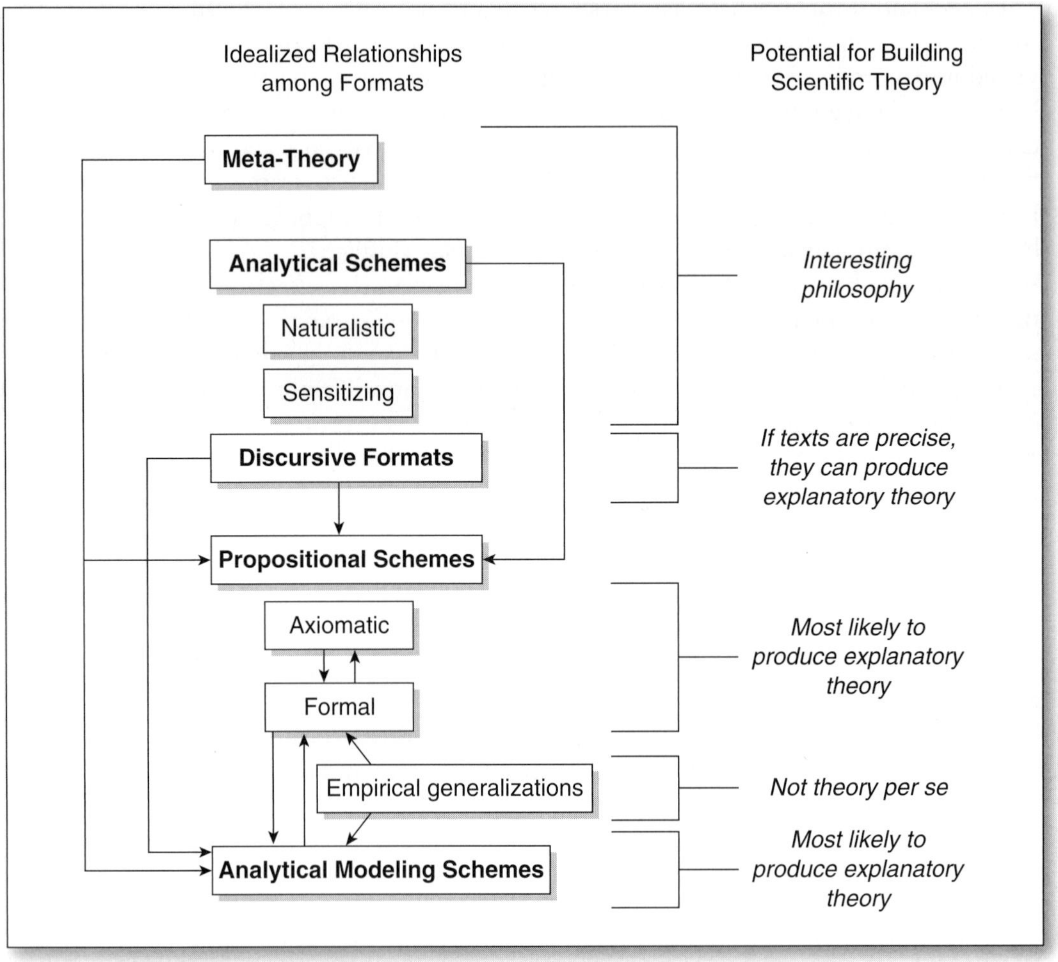

empirical regularities, but by themselves and without creative leaps in scope and abstraction, they are not theoretical. They are usually data in need of a theory.

In the left column, I have presented my idealized view of the proper place of each theoretical approach for generating knowledge.[31] If we begin to accumulate bodies of formal laws (perhaps on the basis of leads provided by a sensitizing scheme), then it is desirable to extract out the key concepts and look at these as the basic sensitizing and orienting concepts of sociology (much as magnetism, gravity, relativity, and the like were for early twentieth-century physics). We may even want to construct a formal analytical scheme and ponder on the meta-theoretical implications of these. In turn, such

---

[31]I should emphasize that this is not how things actually work in sociology; the diagram represents my *wish* for how sociological theory should be developed.

pondering can help reformulate or clarify analytical schemes, which can perhaps help construct new, or reverse old, formal propositions. But without a body of formal laws to pull meta-theory and analytical schemes back into the domain of the testable, they become hopelessly self-sustaining and detached from the very reality they are supposed to help clarify.

For building theory, the most crucial interchange is, I believe, between formal propositions and analytical models. There is a creative synergy between translating propositions into models and vice versa. Theories that begin with analytical models or propositions will help improve each other. Analytical models will add robustness that can be incorporate into propositions, whereas propositions will specify the beginning and end states of two phenomena—say conflict, as the beginning state, leads to solidarity, the end state. They will inevitably lead theorists to ask the question: how and why does this beginning state lead to the end state? And once this question is asked, an analytical model can specify the flow of causality and, in this specification, can introduce additional variables that are in play. In turn, these variables can be, if theorists are so disposed, converted into propositional schemes.

# Going Forward

I have introduced a great deal of material in this first chapter that will, I believe, make more sense after studying various theories outlined in the pages to follow. Thus, the outline of theoretical approaches presented above may seem somewhat confusing, but if the basic types of schemes are kept in mind, it will be clear as to which one is being practiced by a particular theorist. For example, in Chapter 3 on Talcott Parsons, it will be evident that he is developing an analytical scheme, or system of categories, and as I will comment, this scheme is suggestive and indeed even intriguing, but it is difficult to translate into propositions or analytical models that would make the scheme testable. The same could be said of Anthony Giddens sensitizing scheme outlined in Chapter 28. Other theorists, such as Ralf Dahrendorf, Lewis Coser, and Jonathan Turner generate propositions in their effort to explain the dynamics of conflict, and for Turner and Dahrendorf, these propositions reflect engagement with analytical models on conflict that were initially generated from the discursive theories of Max Weber, Karl Marx, and Georg Simmel. Other theories, such as those on urban communities and organizations are stated abstractly and, yet, they have the flair of middle range theory because they are about urban communities and organizations in the present, although it would be relatively easy to make the theories for abstract and general, as will be evident in Amos Hawley's analysis in Chapter 7.

Thus, reading this chapter *after* the end of the book might provide instructive to readers—after, as it were, absorbing the range of theories presented in varying formats that now constitute theoretical sociology. For the present, I will begin with sociology's first and most enduring theoretical perspective—functionalism. Functionalism emerged with Auguste Comte and then was solidified as a theoretical approach by Herbert Spencer and Émile Durkheim. For the first half of the twentieth century, functionalism virtually disappeared from sociology but was carried to the century's mid-point by anthropologists such as A. R. Radcliffe-Brown and Bronislaw Malinowski (whose work is briefly examined in the next chapter on the rise of functional theory). In the 1950s, however, functional theory reemerged with Talcott Parsons, whose work is examined in Chapter 3, and became the dominant theoretical approach in sociology for several decades. Then, after ruthless and sometimes unfair criticism, it seemingly disappeared, but as we will see in Chapter 5 where criticisms of the perspective are reviewed, functionalism has reemerged in new guises that often hide their functionalist origins.

**PART I**

# Functional Theorizing

## CHAPTER 2

# The Rise of Functionalist Theorizing

Auguste Comte (1798–1857) is usually credited as being the founder of sociology. Philosophizing about humans and society had, of course, long been a preoccupation of lay people and scholars alike, but Comte advocated a "science of society" and coined the term *sociology*. Although Comte's work soon fell into neglect and obscurity—leading him to live out his later years in frustration and bitterness—it profoundly influenced social thought. It is regrettable that few recognize this influence, even today, but despite Comte's current obscurity, the emergence of the functionalist perspective began with his work.[1] Comte created functionalism by comparing societies to biological organisms—a point of emphasis that remained for the entire nineteenth century.

## The Organismic Analogy

### Auguste Comte and the Organismic Analogy

Comte felt that human evolution in the nineteenth century had reached the positive stage in which empirical knowledge could be used to understand the social world and to create a better society. Comte thus advocated applying the scientific method to the study of society—a strategy that, in deference to Comte, is still termed *positivism* in the social sciences. This application of the scientific method gave birth to a new science, sociology.

---

[1]Auguste Comte, *The Course of Positive Philosophy* (1830–1842). References are to the more commonly used edition that Harriet Martineau condensed and translated, *The Positive Philosophy of Auguste Comte*, vols. 1, 2, and 3 (London: Bell & Sons, 1898; originally published in 1854).

Comte's entire intellectual life represented an attempt to legitimate sociology. His efforts on this score went so far as to construct a "hierarchy of the sciences," with sociology as the "queen" of the sciences. Although this hierarchy allowed Comte to assert the importance of sociology and thereby separate it from social philosophy, his most important tactic for legitimating sociology was to borrow terms and concepts from the highly respected biological sciences. Sociology was thus initiated and justified by appeals to the biological sciences—which helps explain why functionalism was sociology's first and, until the 1970s, most dominant theoretical orientation. Seeing the affinity between sociology and biology as residing in their common concern with organic bodies, Comte divided sociology into *social statics*, or morphology, and *social dynamics*, or social growth and progress. But Comte was convinced that, although "Biology has hitherto been the guide and preparation for Sociology . . . Sociology will in the future . . . [provide] the ultimate systematization of Biology." Comte visualized that, with initial borrowing of concepts from biology and later with the development of positivism in the social sciences, the principles of sociology would inform biology. Thus, sociology must first recognize the correspondence between the individual organism in biology and the social organism in sociology:

> We have thus established a true correspondence between the Statistical Analysis of the Social Organism in Sociology, and that of the Individual Organism in Biology. . . . If we take the best ascertained points in Biology, we may decompose structure anatomically into elements, tissues, and organs. We have the same things in the Social Organism; and may even use the same names.[2]

Comte then began to make clear analogies between specific types of social structures and the biological concepts:

> I shall treat the Social Organism as definitely composed of the Families which are the true elements or cells, next the Classes or Castes which are its proper tissues, and lastly, of the cities and Communes which are in real organs.[3]

In Comte's hands, the organismic analogy was rough and crude, but it provided a model for legitimating sociology under the mantra of the more respected biological sciences as well as a strategy for conducting sociological inquiry. Yet, Comte never followed through on his advocacy; it was left to the British sociologist Herbert Spencer to develop more fully the implications of the organismic analogy.

---

[2]Auguste Comte, *System of Positive Polity or Treatise on Sociology* (London: Burt Franklin, 1875; originally published in 1851), pp. 239–40.

[3]Ibid., pp. 241–42.

## The Analytical Functionalism of Herbert Spencer

Herbert Spencer (1820–1903) was a broad-based philosopher who, before writing on sociology, had produced multivolume treatises on ethics,[4] biology,[5] and psychology.[6] All were a part of his Synthetic Philosophy, which was to unify the diverse realms of the universe under a common set of abstract principles.[7] In writing his major work on sociology, *The Principles of Sociology*,[8] Spencer developed an organismic analogy that systematically compared society to organisms:[9]

1. As organic and superorganic (societal) bodies increase in size, they increase in structure. That is, they become more complex and differentiated.

2. Such differentiation of structures is accompanied by differentiation of functions. Each differentiated structure serves distinctive functions for sustaining the "life" of the systemic whole.

3. Differentiated structures and functions require in both organic and superorganic bodies integration through mutual dependence. Each structure can be sustained only through its dependence on others for vital substances.

4. Each differentiated structure in both organic and superorganic bodies is, to a degree, a systemic whole by itself (that is, organs are composed of cells, and societies are composed of groupings of individuals); thus the larger whole is always influenced by the systemic processes of its constituent parts.

5. The structures of organic and superorganic bodies can "live on" for a while after the destruction of the systemic whole.

---

[4]Herbert Spencer, *Social Statics* (New York: D. Appleton, 1870; originally published in 1850) was only one volume, but it became a much larger work near the end of Spencer's career when he wrote *The Principles of Ethics* (New York: D. Appleton, 1879–1893).

[5]Herbert Spencer, *The Principles of Biology* (New York: D. Appleton, 1864–1867).

[6]Herbert Spencer, *The Principles of Psychology* (New York: D. Appleton, 1898; originally published in 1855).

[7]These are contained in his *First Principles* (New York: A. C. Burt, 1880; originally published in 1862).

[8]Herbert Spencer, *The Principles of Sociology* (1874–1896). This work has been reissued in varying volume numbers. References in this chapter are to the three-volume edition (the third edition) issued by D. Appleton, New York, in 1898. When you read this long work, it is much more critical to note the parts (numbered I through VII) than the volumes, because pagination can vary with editions.

[9]See Jonathan H. Turner, *Herbert Spencer: Toward a Renewed Appreciation*, Chap. 4 (Beverly Hills, CA: Sage, 1985). See also Spencer's *Principles of Sociology*, vol. 1, part II, pp. 449–57. The bulk of Spencer's organism is on these few pages of a work that spans more than 2,000 pages; yet this is what we most remember about Spencer.

These points of similarity between organism and society, Spencer argued, must be qualified for their points of "extreme unlikeness":[10]

1. There are great differences in the degree of connectedness of the parts, or structures, in organic and social wholes. In superorganic wholes, there is less direct and continuous physical contact and more dispersion of parts than in organic bodies.

2. There are differences in the modes of contact between organic and superorganic systems. In the superorganic, there is much more reliance on symbols than in the organic.[11]

3. There are differences in the levels of consciousness and voluntarism of parts in organic and superorganic bodies. All units in society are conscious, goal seeking, and reflective, whereas only one unit can potentially be so in organic bodies.

As Spencer continued to analogize the points of similarity between organicism and societies, he began to develop what can be termed *requisite functionalism*. That is, organic and superorganic bodies reveal certain universal requisites that must be fulfilled for these bodies to adapt to an environment. Moreover, these same requisites exist for all organic and superorganic systems. To quote Spencer on this point:

> Close study of the facts shows us another striking parallelism. Organs in animals and organs in societies have internal arrangements framed on the same principle. Differing from one another as the viscera of a living creature do in many respects, they have several traits in common. Each viscus contains appliances for conveying nutriment to its parts, for bringing it materials on which to operate, for carrying away the product, for draining off waste matters; as also for regulating its activity.[12]

It is not hard to see the seeds of an argument for universal functional requisites in this passage. Indeed, on the next page from this quote, Spencer argued "it is the same for society" and proceeded to list the basic functional requisites of societies. For example, each superorganic body

> [h]as a set of agencies which bring the raw material . . . ; it has an apparatus of major and minor channels through which the necessities of life are drafted out of the general stocks circulating through the

---

[10]*Principles of Sociology*, part II, pp. 451–62.

[11]Spencer's theory of symbolism is commonly ignored by contemporary sociologists who simply accept Durkheim's critique. Part I of *Principles of Sociology* contains a very sophisticated analysis of symbols.

[12]*Principles of Sociology*, part II, p. 477.

kingdom ...; it has appliances ... for bringing those impulses by which the industry of the place is excited or checked; it has local controlling powers, political and ecclesiastical, by which order is maintained and healthful action furthered.

Even though these universal requisites are not so clearly separated as they were to become in modern functional approaches, the logic of the analysis is clear. First, there are certain universal needs or requisites that structures function to meet. These revolve around (a) securing and circulating resources, (b) producing usable substances, and (c) regulating and integrating internal activities through power and symbols. Second, each system level—group, community, region, or whole society—reveals a similar set of needs. Third, the important dynamics of any empirical system revolve around processes that function to meet these universal requisites. Fourth, the level of adaptation of a social unit to its environment is determined by the extent to which it meets these functional requisites.

Thus, by recognizing that certain basic or universal needs must be met, analysis of organic and superorganic systems is simplified. One examines processes to determine needs for integrating differentiated parts, needs for sustaining the parts of the system, needs for producing and distributing information and substances, and needs for political regulation and control. In simple systems, these needs are met by each element of the system, but when structures begin to grow and to become more complex, they are met by distinctive types of structures that specialize in meeting one of these general classes of functions. As societies become highly complex, structures become even more specialized and meet only specific subclasses of these general functional needs.

The logic behind this form of requisite functionalism guided much of Spencer's substantive analysis and is the essence of functional analysis today. The list of basic needs to be met varies among theorists, but the mode of the analysis remains the same: Examine specific types of social processes and structures for the needs or requisites that they meet.

## Functionalism and Émile Durkheim

We should not be surprised that, as the inheritor of a long French tradition of social thought, especially Comte's organicism, Émile Durkheim's (1858–1917) early works were heavily infused with organismic terminology. Although his major work, *The Division of Labor in Society*, was sharply critical of Herbert Spencer, many of Durkheim's formulations were clearly influenced by the nineteenth-century intellectual preoccupation with biology.[13] In addition to the extensive use of biologically inspired terms,

---

[13]Émile Durkheim, *The Division of Labor in Society* (New York: Macmillan, 1933; originally published in 1893). Durkheim tended to ignore the similarity between Spencer's organismic

Durkheim's basic assumptions reflected those of the organicists: (1) Society was to be viewed as an entity in itself that can be distinguished from and is not reducible to its constituent parts. In conceiving society as a reality, *sui generis,* Durkheim in effect gave analytical priority to the social whole. (2) Although such an emphasis by itself did not necessarily reflect organismic inclinations, Durkheim, in giving causal priority to the whole, viewed system parts as fulfilling basic functions, needs, or requisites of that whole. (3) The frequent use of the notion *functional needs* is buttressed by Durkheim's conceptualization of social systems as "normal" and "pathological" states. Such formulations, at the very least, connote the view that social systems have needs that must be fulfilled if "abnormal" states are to be avoided. (4) When we view systems as normal and pathological, as well as by functions, the additional implication is that systems have equilibrium points around which normal functioning occurs.

Durkheim recognized the dangers in this kind of analysis and explicitly tried to deal with several of them. First, he was clearly aware of the dangers of teleological analysis—of implying that some future consequence of an event causes that very event to occur. Thus he warned that the causes of a phenomenon must be distinguished from the ends it serves:

> When, then, the explanation of a social phenomenon is undertaken, we must seek separately the efficient cause which produces it and the function it fulfills. We use the word "function" in preference to "end" or "purpose," precisely because social phenomena do not generally exist for the useful results they produce.[14]

Thus, despite giving analytical priority to the whole and viewing parts as having consequences for certain normal states, and hence, meeting system requisites, Durkheim remained aware of the dangers of asserting that all systems have "purpose" and that the need to maintain the whole causes the existence of its constituent parts. Yet Durkheim's insistence that the function of a part for the social whole always be examined sometimes led him, and certainly many of his followers, into questionable teleological reasoning. For example, even when distinguishing cause and function in his major methodological statement, he leaves room for an illegitimate teleological interpretation: "Consequently, to explain a social fact, it is not enough to show the cause on which it depends; we must also, at least in most cases,

---

analogy and his own organic formulations as well as the close correspondence between their theories of symbols. For more details on this line of argument, see Jonathan H. Turner, "Émile Durkheim's Theory of Social Organization," *Social Forces* 68, no. 3 (1990): pp. 1–15 and "Spencer's and Durkheim's Principles of Social Organization," *Sociological Perspectives* 27 (January 1984): pp. 21–32.

[14]Émile Durkheim, *The Rules of the Sociological Method* (New York: Free Press, 1938; originally published in 1895), p. 96.

show its function in the establishment of social order."[15] In this summary phrase, the words *in the establishment of* could connote that the existence of system parts can be explained only by the whole, or social order, that they function to maintain. From this view, it is only a short step to outright teleology: The social fact in question is caused by the needs of the social order that the fact fulfills. Such theoretical statements do not necessarily have to be illegitimate, for it is conceivable that a social system could be programmed to meet certain needs or designated ends and thereby have the capacity to cause variations in cultural items or *social facts* to meet these needs or ends. But if such a system is being described by an analyst, it is necessary to document how the system is programmed and how it causes variations in social facts to meet needs or ends. As the previous quotation illustrates, Durkheim did not have this kind of system in mind when he formulated his particular brand of functional analysis; thus, he did not want to state his arguments teleologically.

Despite his warnings to the contrary, Durkheim appears to have taken this short step into teleological reasoning in his substantive works. In his first major work on the division of labor, Durkheim went to great lengths to distinguish between cause (increased population and moral density) and function (integration of society). However, the causal statements often become fused with functional statements. The argument goes, generally, like this: Population density increases moral density (rates of contact and interaction); moral density leads to competition, which threatens the social order; in turn, competition for resources results in the specialization of tasks as actors seek viable niches in which to secure resources; and specialization creates pressures for mutual interdependence and increased willingness to accept the morality of mutual obligation. This transition to a new social order is not made consciously, or by "unconscious wisdom"; yet, the division of labor is necessary to restore the order that "unbridled competition might otherwise destroy."[16] Hence, the impression is left that the threat or the need for social order causes the division of labor. Such reasoning can be construed as an illegitimate teleology, because the consequence or result of the division of labor—social order—is the implied cause of it. At the very least, then, cause and function are not kept as analytically separate as Durkheim so often insisted.

In sum, then, despite Durkheim's warnings about illegitimate teleology, he often appears to waver on the brink of the very traps he wanted to avoid. The reason for this failing can probably be traced to the organismic assumptions built into this form of sociological analysis. In taking a strong sociologistic position on the question of emergent properties—that is, on the irreducibility of the whole to its individual parts—Durkheim separated

---

[15]Ibid., p. 97.

[16]Ibid., p. 35. For a more detailed analysis, see Jonathan H. Turner and Alexandra Maryanski, *Functionalism* (Menlo Park, CA: Benjamin/Cummings, 1979). See also Percy S. Cohen, *Modern Social Theory* (New York: Basic Books, 1968), pp. 35–37.

sociology from the naive psychology and anthropology of his day.[17] However, in supplementing this emphasis on the social whole with organismic assumptions of function, requisite, need, and normality/pathology, Durkheim helped weld organismic principles to sociological theory for nearly three-quarters of a century. The brilliance of his analysis of substantive topics, as well as the suggestive features of his analytical work, made a functional mode of analysis highly appealing to subsequent generations of sociologists and anthropologists.

# Functionalism and the Anthropological Tradition

Functionalism might have died with Durkheim except that anthropologists began to find it an appealing way to analyze simple societies. Indeed, functionalism as a well-articulated conceptual perspective was perpetuated in the first half of the twentieth century by the writings of two anthropologists, Bronislaw Malinowski and A. R. Radcliffe-Brown.[18] Each of these thinkers was heavily influenced by the organicism of Durkheim, as well as by their own field studies among preliterate societies. Despite the similarities in their intellectual backgrounds, however, the conceptual perspectives developed by Malinowski and Radcliffe-Brown reveal many dissimilarities.

## The Functionalism of A. R. Radcliffe-Brown

Recognizing that "the concept of function applied to human societies is based on an analogy between social life and organic life" and that "the first systematic formulation of the concept as applying to the strictly scientific study of society was performed by Durkheim," Radcliffe-Brown (1881–1955) tried to indicate how some problems of organismic analogizing might be overcome.[19] Radcliffe-Brown believed the most serious problem with functionalism was the tendency for analysis to appear teleological. Noting that Durkheim's definition of function pertained to the way in which a part fulfills system needs, Radcliffe-Brown emphasized that, to

---

[17]Robert A. Nisbet, *Émile Durkheim* (Englewood Cliffs, NJ: Prentice Hall, 1965), pp. 9–102.

[18]For basic references on Malinowski's functionalism, see his "Anthropology," *Encyclopedia Britannica*, supplementary vol. 1 (London and New York, 1936); *A Scientific Theory of Culture* (Chapel Hill: University of North Carolina Press, 1944); and *Magic, Science, and Religion and Other Essays* (Glencoe, IL: Free Press, 1948). For basic references on A. R. Radcliffe-Brown's functionalism, see his "Structure and Function in Primitive Society," *American Anthropologist* 37 (July–September 1935): pp. 58–72; *Structure and Function in Primitive Society* (Glencoe, IL: Free Press, 1952); and *The Andaman Islanders* (Glencoe, IL: Free Press, 1948). See also Turner and Maryanski, *Functionalism* (cited in note 16).

[19]Radcliffe-Brown, "Structure and Function in Primitive Society," *American Anthropologist* 37 (July–September 1935), p. 68. This statement is, of course, incorrect, because the organismic analogy was far more developed in Spencer's work.

avoid the teleological implications of such analysis, it would be necessary t "substitute for the term 'needs' the term 'necessary condition of existence. In doing so, he felt that no universal human or societal needs would t postulated; rather, the question of which conditions were necessary for survival would be an empirical one, an issue that would have to be discovered for each given social system.

Furthermore, in recognizing the diversity of conditions necessary for the survival of different systems, analysis would avoid asserting that every item of a culture must have a function and that items in different cultures must have the same function. Once the dangers of illegitimate teleology were recognized, functional or (to use his term) structural analysis could legitimately proceed from several assumptions: (1) One necessary condition for survival of a society is minimal integration of its parts. (2) The term function refers to those processes that maintain this necessary integration or solidarity. (3) Thus, in each society, structural features can be shown to contribute to the maintenance of necessary solidarity. In such an analytical approach, social structure and the conditions necessary for its survival are irreducible.

In a vein similar to that of Durkheim, Radcliffe-Brown saw society as a reality in and of itself. For this reason, he usually visualized cultural items, such as kinship rules and religious rituals, as explicable through social structure—particularly social structure's need for solidarity and integration. For example, in analyzing a lineage system, Radcliffe-Brown would first assume that some minimal degree of solidarity must exist in the system. Processes associated with lineage systems would then be assessed to determine their consequences for maintaining this solidarity. The conclusion was that lineage systems provided a systematic way of adjudicating conflict in societies where families owned land because such a system specified who had the right to land and through which side of the family it would always pass. The integration of the economic system—landed "estates" owned by families—is thus explained.[20]

This form of analysis poses a number of problems that continue to haunt functional theorists. Although Radcliffe-Brown admitted that "functional unity [integration] of a social system is, of course, a hypothesis," he failed to specify the analytical criteria for assessing just how much or how little functional unity is necessary for testing this hypothesis. As subsequent commentators discovered, without some analytical criteria for determining what is and what is not minimal functional integration and societal survival, the hypothesis cannot be tested, even in principle. Thus, what is typically done is to assume that the existing system is minimally integrated and surviving because it exists and persists. Without carefully documenting how various

---

[20]Radcliffe-Brown, *Structure and Function in Primitive Society* (Glencoe, IL: Free Press, 1952), pp. 31–50. For a secondary analysis of this example, see Arthur L. Stinchcombe, "Specious Generality and Functional Theory," *American Sociological Review* 26 (December 1961): pp. 929–30.

cultural items promote instances of both integration and malintegration of the social whole, such a strategy can reduce the hypothesis of functional unity to a tautology: If one can find a system to study, then it must be minimally integrated; therefore, lineages that are a part of this system must promote its integration. To discover the contrary would be difficult, because the system, by virtue of being a surviving system, is already composed of integrated parts, such as a lineage system. There is a non sequitur in such reasoning, because it is quite possible to view a cultural item as a lineage system as having both integrative and malintegrative (and other) consequences for the social whole. In his actual ethnographic descriptions, Radcliffe-Brown often slips inadvertently into a pattern of circular reasoning: The fact of a system's existence requires that its existing parts, such as a lineage system, be viewed as contributing to the system's existence. Assuming integration and then assessing the contribution of individual parts to the integrated whole lead to an additional analytical problem. Such a mode of analysis implies that the causes of a particular structure—for example, lineages—lie in the system's needs for integration, which is most likely an illegitimate teleology.

Radcliffe-Brown would, of course, have denied this conclusion. His awareness of the dangers of illegitimate teleology would have seemingly eliminated the implication that the needs of a system cause the emergence of its parts. His repeated assertions that the notion of function "does not require the dogmatic assertion that everything in the life of every community has a function" should have led to a rejection of tautological reasoning.[21] However, much like Durkheim, what Radcliffe-Brown asserted analytically was frequently not practiced in the concrete empirical analysis of societies. Such lapses were not intended but appeared to be difficult to avoid with functional needs, functional integration, and equilibrium as operating assumptions.[22]

Thus, although Radcliffe-Brown displayed an admirable awareness of the dangers of organicism—especially of the problem of illegitimate teleology and the hypothetical nature of notions of solidarity—he all too often slipped into a pattern of questionable teleological reasoning. Forgetting that integration was only a working hypothesis, he opened his analysis to problems of tautology. Such problems were persistent in Durkheim's analysis, and despite his attempts to the contrary, their specter haunted even Radcliffe-Brown's insightful essays and ethnographies.

---

[21]See, for example, Radcliffe-Brown, *Structure and Function in Primitive Society* (cited in note 20).

[22]A perceptive critic of an earlier edition of this manuscript provided an interesting way to visualize the problems of tautology:

When do you have a surviving social system?
When certain survival requisites are met.
How do you know when certain survival requisites are met?
When you have a surviving social system.

## The Functionalism of Bronislaw Malinowski

Functionalism might have ended with Radcliffe-Brown because it had very little to offer sociologists attempting to study complex societies. Both Durkheim and Radcliffe-Brown posited one basic societal need—integration—and then analyzed system parts to determine how they meet this need. For sociologists who are concerned with differentiated societies, this is likely to become a rather mechanical task. Moreover, it does not allow analysis of those aspects of a system part that are not involved in meeting the need for integration.

Bronislaw Malinowski's (1884–1942) functionalism removed these restrictions; by reintroducing Spencer's approach, Malinowski offered a way for modern sociologists to employ functional analysis.[23] Malinowski's scheme reintroduced two important ideas from Spencer: (1) the notion of system levels and (2) the concept of different and multiple system needs at each level. In making these two additions, Malinowski made functional analysis more appealing to twentieth-century sociological theorists.

Malinowski's scheme has three system levels: the biological, the social-structural, and the symbolic.[24] At each level, we can discern basic needs or survival requisites that must be met if biological health, social-structural integrity, and cultural unity are to exist. Moreover, these system levels constitute a hierarchy, with biological systems at the bottom, social-structural arrangements next, and symbolic systems at the highest level. Malinowski stressed that the way in which needs are met at one system level sets constraints on how they are met at the next level in the hierarchy. Yet he did not advocate a reductionism of any sort; indeed, he thought that each system level reveals its own distinctive requisites and processes meeting these needs. In addition, he argued that the important system levels for sociological or anthropological analysis are the structural and symbolic. And in his actual discussion, the social-structural level receives the most attention. Table 2.1 lists the requisites or needs of the two most sociologically relevant system levels.

In analyzing the structural system level, Malinowski stressed that institutional analysis is necessary. For Malinowski, institutions are the general and relatively stable ways in which activities are organized to meet critical requisites. All institutions, he felt, have certain universal properties or "elements" that can be listed and then used as dimensions for comparing different institutions. These universal elements are

1. *Personnel*: Who and how many people will participate in the institution?

2. *Charter*: What is the purpose of the institution? What are its avowed goals?

---

[23]Don Martindale, *The Nature and Types of Sociological Theory* (Boston: Houghton Mifflin, 1960), p. 459.

[24]Bronislaw Malinowski, *A Scientific Theory of Culture and Other Essays* (London: Oxford University Press, 1964), pp. 71–125; see also Turner and Maryanski, *Functionalism* (cited in note 16), pp. 44–57.

| **Table 2.1**   Requisites of System Levels |
| --- |

---

#### Cultural (Symbolic) System Level

1. Requisites for systems of symbols that provide information necessary to adjust to the environment

2. Requisites for systems of symbols that provide a sense of control over people's destiny and over chance events

3. Requisites for systems of symbols that provide members of a society with a sense of a communal rhythm in their daily lives and activities

#### Structural (Instrumental) System Level

1. The requisite for production and distribution of consumer goods

2. The requisite for social control of behavior and its regulation

3. The requisite for education of people in traditions and skills

4. The requisite for organization and execution of authority relations

---

3. *Norms*: What are the key norms that regulate and organize conduct?

4. *Material apparatus*: What is the nature of the tools and facilities used to organize and regulate conduct in pursuit of goals?

5. *Activity*: How are tasks and activities divided? Who does what?

6. *Function*: What requisite does a pattern of institutional activity meet?

By describing each institution along these six dimensions, Malinowski believed that he had provided a common analytical yardstick for comparing patterns of social organization within and between societies. He even constructed a list of universal institutions as they resolve not just structural but also biological and symbolic requisites.

In sum, Malinowski's functional approach opened new possibilities for sociologists who had long forgotten Spencer's similar arguments. Malinowski suggested to sociologists that attention to system levels is critical in analyzing requisites; he argued that there are universal requisites for each system level; he forcefully emphasized that the structural level is the essence of sociological analysis; and, much like Spencer before him and Talcott Parsons a decade later (see Chapter 3), Malinowski posited four universal functional needs at this level—economic adaptation, political authority, educational socialization, and social control—that were to be prominent in subsequent functional schemes. Moreover, he provided a clear method for analyzing institutions as they operate to meet functional requisites. It is fair to say, therefore, that Malinowski drew the rough contours for modern sociological functionalism.

# Conclusion

Functionalism was sociology's first coherent theoretical perspective. It addressed an interesting question: what is necessary for a society or any social system to survive in its environment? The question appealed to Auguste Comte, Herbert Spencer, and Émile Durkheim within the first generations of sociologists. And then, after it died in sociology with the demise of evolutionary thinking in the first decade of the twentieth century, functional theorizing was taken over by anthropologists like A. R. Radcliffe-Brown and Bronislaw Malinowski. At about the time that functionalism was declining in anthropology in the 1950s and early 1960s, sociologists began to revive it, and for a decade or so, functionalism became the dominant theoretical perspective in sociology under the advocacy of Talcott Parsons, whose work is examined in the next chapter.

## CHAPTER 3

# Talcott Parsons' Analytical Functionalism

Talcott Parsons was probably the most prominent theorist of his time, and it is unlikely that any one theoretical approach will so dominate sociological theory again. In the years between 1950 and the late 1970s, Parsonian functionalism was clearly the focal point around which theoretical controversy revolved. Even those who despised Parsons' functional approach could not ignore it. Even now, years after his death and more than four decades since its period of dominance, Parsonian functionalism is still the subject of controversy.[1] To appreciate Parsons' achievement in bringing functionalism to the second half of the twentieth century, it is best to start at the beginning, in 1937, when he published his first major work, *The Structure of Social Action*.[2]

## The Structure of Social Action

In *The Structure of Social Action*, Parsons advocated using an "analytical realism" to build sociological theory. Theory in sociology must use a limited number of important concepts that "adequately 'grasp' aspects of the external world. . . . These concepts do not correspond to concrete phenomena,

---

[1]Although few appear to agree with all aspects of Parsonian theory, rarely has anyone quarreled with the assertion that he has been the dominant sociological figure of the last century. For documentation of Parsons' influence, see Robert W. Friedrichs, *A Sociology of Sociology* (New York: Free Press, 1970) and Alvin W. Gouldner, *The Coming Crisis of Western Sociology* (New York: Basic Books, 1970).

[2]Talcott Parsons, *The Structure of Social Action* (New York: McGraw-Hill, 1937); the most recent paperback edition (New York: Free Press, 1968) will be used in subsequent notes.

but to elements in them that are analytically separable from other elements."[3] Thus, theory must involve the development of concepts that abstract from empirical reality common analytical elements that capture the essence and generic properties underlying all of the empirical world. In this way, concepts will isolate phenomena from their embeddedness in the complex relations that constitute social reality.

The unique feature of Parson's analytical realism is the insistence about how these abstract concepts are to be employed in sociological analysis. Parsons did not advocate the immediate incorporation of these concepts into theoretical statements but rather advocated their use to develop a "generalized system of concepts." This use of abstract concepts would involve their ordering into a coherent whole that would reflect the important features of the "real world." What is sought is an organization of concepts into analytical systems that grasp the salient and systemic features of the universe without being overwhelmed by empirical details. This emphasis on systems of categories represents Parsons' application of Max Weber's ideal-type strategy for analytically accentuating salient features of the world. Thus, much like Weber, Parsons believed that theory should initially resemble an elaborate classification and categorization of social phenomena that reflects significant features in the organization of these social phenomena. This strategy was evident in Parsons' first major work where he developed the "voluntaristic theory of action."[4]

Parsons believed that the voluntaristic theory of action represented a synthesis of the useful assumptions and concepts of utilitarianism, positivism, and idealism. In reviewing the thought of classical economists, Parsons noted the excessiveness of their utilitarianism: unregulated and atomistic actors in a free and competitive marketplace rationally attempting to choose those behaviors that will maximize their profits in their transactions with others. Parsons believed such a formulation of the social order presented several critical problems: Do humans always behave rationally? Are they indeed free and unregulated? How is order possible in an unregulated and competitive system? Yet Parsons saw as fruitful several features of utilitarian thought, especially the concern with actors as seeking goals and the emphasis on the choice-making capacities of human beings who weigh alternative lines of action. Stated in this minimal form, Parsons felt that the utilitarian heritage could indeed continue to inform sociological theorizing.

In a similar critical stance, Parsons rejected the extreme formulations of radical positivists, who tended to view the social world in terms of observable cause-and-effect relationships among physical phenomena. In

---

[3]Ibid., p. 730.

[4]For useful analyses of Parsons' work in relation to the issues he raised in *The Structure of Social Action*, see Leon Mayhew, "In Defense of Modernity: Talcott Parsons and the Utilitarian Tradition," *American Journal of Sociology* 89 (1984): pp. 1273–306 and Jeffrey C. Alexander, "Formal and Substantive Voluntarism in the Work of Talcott Parsons: A Theoretical Reinterpretation," *American Sociological Review* 13 (1978): pp. 177–98.

so doing, he felt, they ignored the complex symbolic functioning of the human mind. Furthermore, Parsons saw the emphasis on observable cause-and-effect relationships as too easily encouraging a sequence of infinite reductionism: groups were reduced to the causal relationships of their individual members; individuals were reducible to the cause-and-effect relationships of their physiological processes; these were reducible to physico-chemical relationships, and so on, down to the most basic cause-and-effect connections among particles of physical matter. Nevertheless, despite these extremes, radical positivism draws attention to the physical parameters of social life and to the deterministic impact of these parameters on much—but of course not all—social organization. Finally, in assessing idealism, Parsons saw the conceptions of "ideas" to circumscribe both individual and social processes as useful, although all too frequently, these ideas are seen as detached from the ongoing social life they were supposed to regulate.

The depth of scholarship in Parsons' analysis of these traditions is impossible to communicate. More important than the details of his analysis is the weaving of selected concepts from each of these traditions into a voluntaristic theory of action. At this starting point, in accordance with his theory-building strategy, Parsons began to construct a functional theory of social organization. In this initial formulation, he conceptualized voluntarism as the subjective decision-making processes of individual actors, but he viewed such decisions as the partial outcome of certain kinds of constraints, both normative and situational. Voluntaristic action therefore involves these basic elements: (1) Actors, at this point in Parsons' thinking, are individual persons. (2) Actors are viewed as goal seeking. (3) Actors also possess alternative means to achieve the goals. (4) Actors are confronted with a variety of situational conditions, such as their own biological makeup and heredity as well as various external ecological constraints, that influence the selection of goals and means. (5) Actors are governed by values, norms, and other ideas such that these ideas influence what is considered a goal and what means are selected to achieve it. (6) Action involves actors making subjective decisions about the means to achieve goals, all of which are constrained by ideas and situational conditions.

Figure 3.1 represents this conceptualization of voluntarism. The processes diagrammed are often termed *the unit act*, with social action involving a succession of such unit acts by one or more actors. Parsons chose to focus on such basic units of action for at least two reasons. First, he felt it necessary to synthesize the historical legacy of social thought about the most basic social process and to dissect it into its most elementary components. Second, given his position on what theory should be, the first analytical task in the development of sociological theory is to isolate conceptually the systemic features of the most basic unit from which more complex processes and structures are built.

Once these basic tasks were completed, Parsons began to ask: How are unit acts connected to each other, and how can this connectedness be

**Figure 3.1**   The Units of Voluntaristic Action

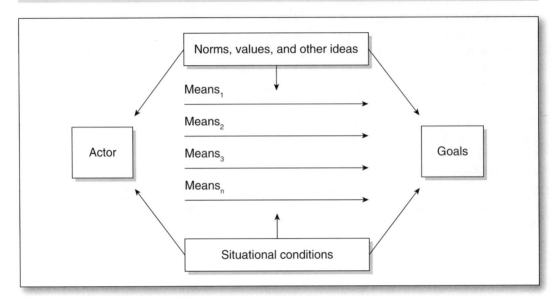

conceptually represented? Indeed, near the end of *The Structure of Social Action*, he recognized that "any atomistic system that deals only with properties identifiable in the unit act . . . will of necessity fail to treat these latter elements adequately and be indeterminate as applied to complex systems."[5] However, only the barest hints of what was to come were evident in those closing pages.

## The Social System

Figure 3.2 summarizes the transition from unit acts to social system.[6] This transition occupies the early parts of Parsons' next significant work, *The Social System*.[7] Drawing inspiration from Weber's typological approach to this same topic,[8] Parsons viewed actors as "oriented" to situations in terms of motives (needs and readiness to mobilize energy) and values (conceptions about what is appropriate). There are three types of motives: (1) cognitive

---

[5]Parsons, *The Structure of Social Action* (cited in note 2), pp. 748–49.

[6]See also, Jonathan H. Turner, "The Concept of 'Action' in Sociological Analysis," in *Analytical and Sociological Theories of Action*, eds. G. Seeba and Raimo Toumea (Dordrecht, Holland: Reidel, 1985).

[7]Talcott Parsons, *The Social System* (New York: Free Press, 1951).

[8]Max Weber, *Economy and Society*, vol. 1 (Totowa, NJ: Bedminster, 1968), pp. 1–95.

(need for information), (2) cathectic (need for emotional attachment), and (3) evaluative (need for assessment). Also, there are three corresponding types of values: (1) cognitive (evaluation by objective standards); (2) appreciative (evaluation by aesthetic standards); and (3) moral (evaluation by absolute rightness and wrongness). Parsons called these modes of orientation. Although this discussion is somewhat vague, the general idea seems to be that the relative salience of these motives and values for any actor creates a composite type of action, which can be one of three types: (1) instrumental (action oriented to realize explicit goals efficiently); (2) expressive (action directed at realizing emotional satisfactions); and (3) moral (action concerned with realizing standards of right and wrong). That is, depending on which modes of motivational and value orientation are strongest, an actor will act in one of these basic ways. For example, if cognitive motives are strong and cognitive values most salient, then action will be primarily instrumental, although the action will also have expressive and moral content. Thus the various combinations and permutations of the modes of orientation—that is, motives and values—produce action geared in one of these general directions.

Unit acts therefore involve motivational and value orientations and have a general direction as a consequence of what combination of values and motives prevails for an actor. Thus far, Parsons had elaborated only on his conceptualization of the unit act. The critical next step was only hinted at in the closing pages of *The Structure of Social Action*: As variously oriented actors (in the configuration of motivational and value orientations) interact, they develop agreements and sustain patterns of interaction, which become "institutionalized." Such institutionalized patterns can be, in Parsons' view, conceptualized as a social system. Such a system represents an emergent phenomenon that requires its own conceptual edifice. The

**Figure 3.2**   Parsons' Conception of Action, Interaction, and Institutionalization

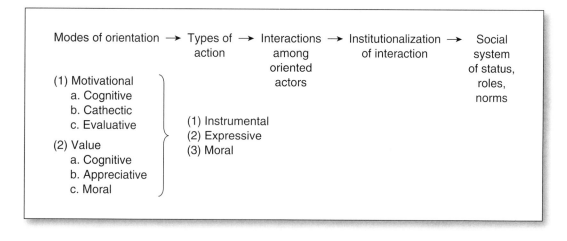

normative organization of status-roles becomes Parsons' key to this conceptualization; that is, the subject matter of sociology is the organization of status, roles, and norms.

Yet, Parsons recognized that the actors who are incumbent in status-roles are motivationally and value oriented; thus, as with patterns of interaction, the task now becomes one of conceptualizing these dimensions of action in systemic terms. The result is the conceptualization of action as composed of three "interpenetrating action systems": the cultural, the social, and the personality. That is, the organization of unit acts into social systems requires a parallel conceptualization of motives and values that become, respectively, the personality and cultural systems. The goal of action theory now becomes understanding how institutionalized patterns of interaction (the social system) are circumscribed by complexes of values, beliefs, norms, and other ideas (the cultural system).

Later Parsons added the organismic (subsequently called behavioral) system, but let me not get ahead of the story. At this stage of conceptualization, analyzing social systems involves developing a system of concepts that, first, captures the systemic features of society at all its diverse levels and, second, points to the modes of articulation among personality systems, social systems, and cultural patterns.

In his commitment to developing concepts that reflect the properties of all action systems, Parsons was led to a set of concepts denoting some of the variable properties of these systems. Termed *pattern variables,* they simultaneously allow the categorization of the modes of orientation in personality systems, the value patterns of culture, and the normative requirements in social systems. The variables are phrased as polar dichotomies that, depending on the system under analysis, allow a rough categorization of decisions by actors, the value orientations of culture, or the normative demands on status-roles.

1. *Affectivity/affective* neutrality concerns the amount of emotion or affect that is appropriate in a given interaction situation. Should a great deal or little affect be expressed?

2. *Diffuseness/specificity* denotes the issue of how far-reaching obligations in an interaction situation are to be. Should the obligations be narrow and specific, or should they be extensive and diffuse?

3. *Universalism/particularism* points to the problem of whether evaluation of others in an interaction situation is to apply to all actors, or should all actors be assessed by the same standards?

4. *Achievement/ascription* deals with the issue of how to assess an actor, whether by performance or by inborn qualities, such as sex, age, race, and family status. Should an actor treat another on the basis of achievements or ascriptive qualities that are unrelated to performance?

5. *Self-collectivity* denotes the extent to which action is to be oriented to self-interest and individual goals or to group interests and goals. Should actors consider their personal or self-related goals over those of the group or large collectivity in which they are involved?[9]

Some of these concepts, such as self-collectivity, were later dropped from the action scheme, but others, such as universalism-particularism, assumed greater importance. The intent of the pattern variables remained the same: to categorize dichotomies of decisions, normative demands, and value orientations. In *The Social System*, however, Parsons was inclined to view them as value orientations that circumscribe the norms of the social system and the decisions of the personality system. Thus the structure of the personality and social systems reflects the dominant patterns of value orientations in culture. This implicit emphasis on the impact of cultural patterns on regulating and controlling other systems of action became ever more explicit in his later work.

By 1951, Parsons had already woven a complex conceptual system that emphasizes the process of institutionalization of interaction into stabilized patterns called social systems, which are penetrated by personality and circumscribed by culture. The profile of institutionalized norms, of decisions by actors in roles, and of cultural value orientations can be typified by concepts—the pattern variables—that capture the variable properties in each of these action components.

Having built this analytical edifice, Parsons then returned to a question, first raised in *The Structure of Social Action*, that guided all his subsequent theoretical formulations: How do social systems survive? More specifically, why do institutionalized patterns of interaction persist? Such questions raise the issue of system imperatives or requisites. Parsons was asking how systems resolve their integrative problems. The answer is provided by the elaboration of additional concepts that point to how personality systems and culture are integrated into the social system, thereby providing assurance of some degree of normative coherence and a minimal amount of commitment by actors to conform to norms and play roles. Figure 3.3 delineates the key ideas in Parsons' reasoning.

Just how are personality systems integrated into the social system, thereby promoting equilibrium? At the most abstract level, Parsons conceptualized two mechanisms that integrate the personality into the social system: (1) mechanisms of socialization and (2) mechanisms of social control.

1. Mechanisms of socialization are the means through which cultural patterns—values, beliefs, language, and other symbols—are internalized into the personality system, thereby circumscribing its need structure.

---

[9]These pattern variables were developed in collaboration with Edward Shils and were elaborated in *Toward a General Theory of Action* (New York: Harper & Row, 1951), pp. 76–98, 183–89, 203–4. Again, Parsons' debt to Max Weber's concern with constructing ideal types can be seen in his presentation of the pattern variables.

**Figure 3.3** Parsons' Early Conception of Integration among Systems of Action

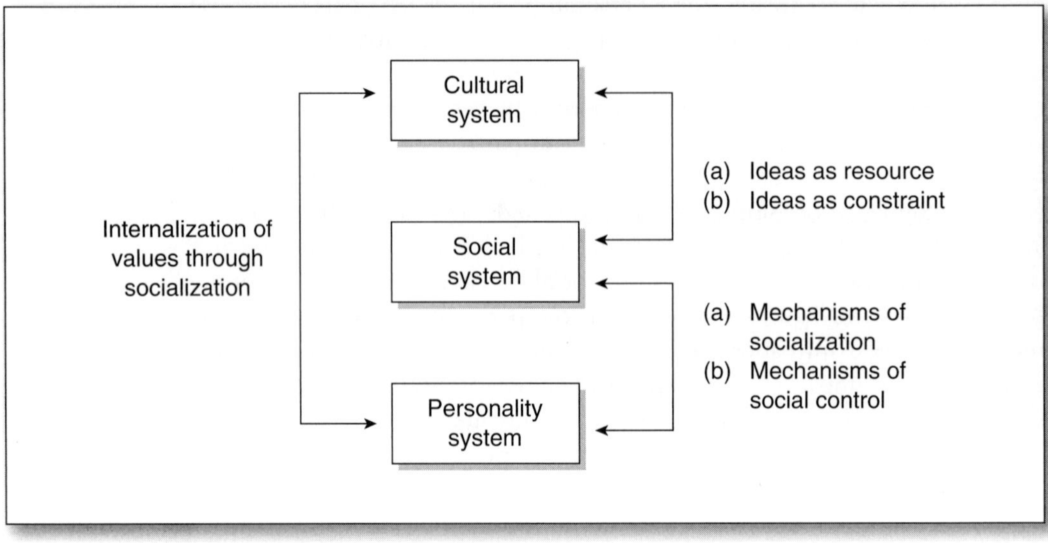

Through this process, actors are made willing to deposit motivational energy in roles (thereby willing to conform to norms) and are given the interpersonal and other skills necessary for playing roles. Another function of socialization mechanisms is to provide stable and secure interpersonal ties that alleviate much of the strain, anxiety, and tension associated with acquiring proper motives and skills.

2. Mechanisms of social control involve those ways in which status-roles are organized in social systems to reduce strain and deviance. There are numerous specific control mechanisms, including (a) institutionalization, which makes role expectations clear and unambiguous while segregating in time and space contradictory expectations; (b) interpersonal sanctions and gestures, which actors subtly employ to mutually sanction conformity; (c) ritual activities, in which actors act out symbolically sources of strain that could prove disruptive while they reinforce dominant cultural patterns; (d) safety-valve structures, in which pervasive deviant propensities are segregated in time and space from normal institutional patterns; (e) reintegration structures, which are specifically charged with bringing deviant tendencies back into line; and finally, (f) institutionalizing the capacity to use force and coercion into some sectors of a system.

These two mechanisms resolve one of the most persistent integrative problems facing social systems. The other major integrative problem facing social systems concerns how cultural patterns contribute to the maintenance of social order and equilibrium. Again at the most abstract level, Parsons visualized two ways in which this occurs: (1) Some components of culture, such as language, are basic resources necessary for interaction to occur. Without symbolic resources, communication and, hence, interaction would not be possible. Thus, by providing common resources for all actors, interaction is made possible by culture. (2) A related but still separable influence of culture on interaction is exerted through the substance of ideas contained in cultural patterns (values, beliefs, ideology, and so forth). These ideas can provide actors with common viewpoints, personal ontologies, or to borrow from W. I. Thomas, a common "definition of the situation." These common meanings allow interaction to proceed smoothly with minimal disruption.

Naturally, Parsons acknowledged that the mechanisms of socialization and social control are not always successful, hence allowing deviance and social change to occur. But clearly, the concepts developed in *The Social System* weigh analysis in the direction of looking for processes that maintain the integration and, by implication, the equilibrium of social systems.

## The Transition to Functional Imperativism

In collaboration with Robert Bales and Edward Shils, Parsons published *Working Papers in the Theory of Action* shortly after *The Social System*. In *Working Papers*, conceptions of functional imperatives dominated the general theory of action,[10] and by 1956, with Parsons and Neil Smelser's publication of *Economy and Society*, the functions of structures for meeting system requisites were well institutionalized into action theory.[11]

During this period, systems of action were conceptualized to have four survival problems, or requisites: adaptation, goal attainment, integration, and latency. *Adaptation* involves securing sufficient resources from the environment and then distributing these throughout the system. *Goal attainment* refers to establishing priorities among system goals and mobilizing system resources for their attainment. *Integration* denotes coordinating and maintaining viable interrelationships among system units. *Latency* embraces two related problems: pattern maintenance and tension management. Pattern maintenance pertains to how to ensure that actors in the social system display the appropriate characteristics (motives, needs, role playing, and so forth). Tension management concerns dealing with the internal tensions and strains of actors in the social system.

All these requisites were implicit in *The Social System*, but they tended to be viewed under the general problem of integration. In Parsons' discussion of integration within and between action systems, problems of securing

---

[10]Talcott Parsons, Robert F. Bales, and Edward A. Shils, *Working Papers in the Theory of Action* (Glencoe, IL: Free Press, 1953).

[11]Talcott Parsons and Neil J. Smelser, *Economy and Society* (New York: Free Press, 1956). These requisites are the same as those enumerated by Malinowski. See Chapter 2 in this work, Table 2.1.

facilities (adaptation), allocation and goal seeking (goal attainment), and socialization and social control (latency) were conspicuous. Thus, the development of the four functional requisites—abbreviated A, G, I, and L—was not so much a radical departure from earlier works as an elaboration of concepts implicit in *The Social System.*

With the introduction of A, G, I, and L, however, a subtle shift away from the analysis of structures to the analysis of functions occurs. Structures are now evaluated explicitly by their functional consequences for meeting the four requisites. Interrelationships among specific structures are now analyzed by how their interchanges affect the requisites that each must meet.

As Parsons' conceptual scheme became increasingly oriented to function, social systems are divided into sectors, each corresponding to a functional requisite—that is, A, G, I, or L. In turn, any subsystem can be divided into these four functional sectors. Then, each subsystem can be divided into four functional sectors, and so on. This process of functional *sectorization*, to invent a word to describe it, is illustrated for the adaptive requisite in Figure 3.4.

Of critical analytical importance in this scheme are the interchanges among systems and subsystems. It is difficult to comprehend the functioning of a

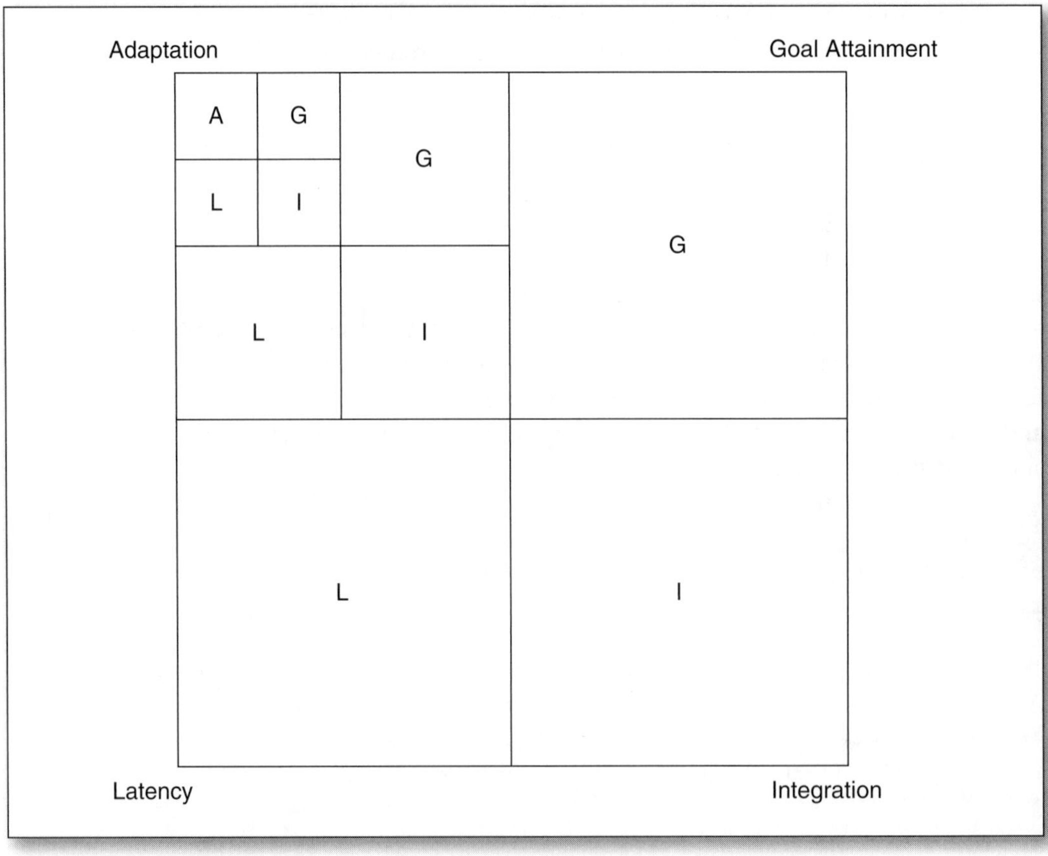

**Figure 3.4**   Parsons' Functional Imperativist View of Social Systems

designated social system without examining the interchanges among its A, G, I, and L sectors, especially because these interchanges are affected by exchanges among constituent subsystems and other systems in the environment. In turn, the functioning of a designated subsystem cannot be understood without examining internal interchanges among its adaptive, goal attainment, integrative, and latency sectors, especially because these interchanges are influenced by exchanges with other subsystems and the more inclusive system of which it is a subsystem. Thus, at this juncture, as important interchanges among the functional sectors of systems and subsystems are outlined, the Parsonian scheme begins to resemble an elaborate mapping operation.

# The Informational Hierarchy of Control

Toward the end of the 1950s, Parsons turned his attention toward interrelationships among (rather than within) what were then four distinct action systems: culture, social structure, personality, and organism. In many ways, this concern represented an odyssey back to the analysis of the basic components of the unit act outlined in *The Structure of Social Action*. But now each element of the unit act is a full-fledged action system, each confronting four functional problems to resolve: adaptation, goal attainment, integration, and latency. Furthermore, although individual decision making is still a part of action as personalities adjust to the normative demands of status-roles in the social system, the analytical emphasis has shifted to the input/output connections among the four action systems.

At this juncture, Parsons began to visualize an overall action system, with culture, social structure, personality, and organism composing its constituent subsystems.[12] Each of these subsystems is seen as fulfilling one of the four system requisites—A, G, I, L—of the overall action system. The organism is considered to be the subsystem having the most consequences for resolving adaptive problems because it is ultimately through this system that environmental resources are made available to the other action subsystems. As the goal-seeking and decision-making system, personality is considered to have primary consequences for resolving goal-attainment problems. As an organized network of status-norms integrating the patterns of the cultural system and the needs of personality systems, the social system is viewed as the major integrative subsystem of the general action system. As the repository of symbolic content of interaction, the cultural system is considered to have primary consequences for managing tensions of actors and ensuring

---

[12]Talcott Parsons, "An Approach to Psychological Theory in Terms of the Theory of Action," in *Psychology: A Science*, ed. S. Koch, vol. 3 (New York: McGraw-Hill, 1958), pp. 612–711. By 1961, these ideas were even more clearly formulated; see Talcott Parsons, "An Outline of the Social System," in *Theories of Society*, eds. T. Parsons, E. Shils, K. D. Naegele, and J. R. Pitts (New York: Free Press, 1961), pp. 30–38. See also Jackson Toby, "Parsons' Theory of Social Evolution," *Contemporary Sociology* 1 (1972): pp. 395–401.

that the proper symbolic resources are available for the maintenance of institutional patterns (latency).

After viewing each action system as a subsystem of a more inclusive, overall system, Parsons explored the interrelations among the four subsystems. What emerged is a hierarchy of informational controls, with culture informationally circumscribing the social system, with the structure of the social system informationally regulating the personality system, and with personality informationally regulating the organismic system. For example, cultural value orientations would be seen as circumscribing or limiting the range of variation in the norms of the social system; in turn, these norms, as translated into expectations for actors playing roles, would be viewed as limiting the kinds of motives and decision-making processes in personality systems; these features of the personality system would then be seen as circumscribing biochemical processes in the organism.

Conversely, each system in the hierarchy is also viewed as providing the "energic conditions" necessary for action at the next higher system. That is, the organism provides the energy necessary for the personality system, the personality system provides the energic conditions for the social system, and the organization of personality systems into a social system provides the conditions necessary for a cultural system. Thus the input/output relations among action systems are reciprocal, with systems exchanging information and energy. Systems high in information circumscribe the utilization of energy at the next lower system level, and each lower system provides the conditions and facilities necessary for action in the next higher system. This scheme has been termed a *cybernetic hierarchy of control* and is diagrammed in Figure 3.5.

## Generalized Media of Exchange

Until his death, Parsons maintained his interest in the intra- and intersystemic relationships of the four action systems. Although he never developed the concepts fully, he had begun to view these relationships as generalized symbolic media of exchange.[13] In any interchange, generalized media are employed—for example, money is used in the economy to facilitate the buying and selling of goods. What typifies these generalized media, such as money, is that they are really symbolic modes of communication. The money is not worth much by itself; its value is evident only for what it says symbolically in an exchange relationship.

---

[13]Parsons' writings on this topic are incomplete, but see "On the Concept of Political Power," *Proceedings of the American Philosophical Society* 107 (1963): pp. 232–62; "On the Concept of Influence," *Public Opinion Quarterly* 27 (Spring 1963): pp. 37–62; and "Some Problems of General Theory," in *Theoretical Sociology: Perspectives and Developments*, eds. J. C. McKinney and E. A. Tiryakian (New York: Appleton-Century-Crofts, 1970), pp. 28–68. See also Talcott Parsons and Gerald M. Platt, *The American University* (Cambridge, MA: Harvard University Press, 1975).

**Figure 3.5**   Parsons' Cybernetic Hierarchy of Control

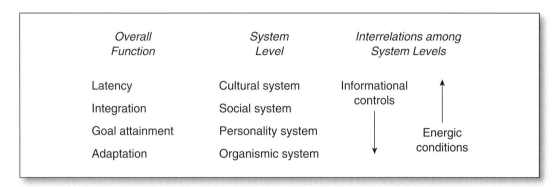

Thus, what Parsons proposed is that the links among action components are ultimately informational. This means that transactions are mediated by symbols. Parsons' emphasis on information is consistent with a cybernetic hierarchy of control. Informational exchanges, or cybernetic controls, are seen as operating in at least three ways. First, the interchanges or exchanges among the four subsystems of the overall action system are carried out by different types of symbolic media—that is, *money, power, influence,* or *commitment*s. Second, the interchanges within any of the four action systems are also carried out by distinctive symbolic media. Finally, the system requisites of adaptation (A), goal attainment (G), integration (I), and latency (L) determine the type of generalized symbolic media used in an inter- or intra-systemic exchange.

Within the social system, the adaptive sector uses *money* as the medium of exchange with the other three sectors; the goal-attainment sector employs *powe*r—the capacity to induce conformity—as its principal medium of exchange; the integrative sector of a social system relies on *influence*—the capacity to persuade; and the latency sector uses commitments—especially the capacity to be *loyal.* The analysis of interchanges of specific structures within social systems should thus focus on the input/output exchanges using different symbolic media.

Among the subsystems of the overall action system, a similar analysis of the symbolic media used in exchanges should be undertaken, but Parsons never clearly described the nature of these media.[14] What he appeared to be approaching was a conceptual scheme for analyzing the basic types of symbolic media, or information, linking systems in the cybernetic hierarchy of control.[15]

---

[14]For his first attempt at a statement, see Parsons, "Some Problems of General Theory" (cited in note 13), pp. 61–68.

[15]For a more readable discussion of these generalized media, see T. S. Turner, "Parsons' Concept of Generalized Media of Social Interaction and Its Relevance for Social Anthropology," *Sociological Inquiry* 38 (Spring 1968): pp. 121–34.

# Parsons on Social Change

In the last decade of his career, Parsons became increasingly concerned with social change. Built into the cybernetic hierarchy of control is a conceptual scheme for classifying the locus of such social change. What Parsons visualized was that the information and energic interchanges among action systems provide the potential for change within or between the action systems. One source of change can be excesses in either information or energy in the exchange among action systems. In turn, these excesses alter the informational or energic outputs across systems and within any system. For example, excesses of motivation (energy) would have consequences for the enactment of roles and perhaps ultimately for the reorganization of these roles or the normative structure and eventually of cultural value orientations. Another source of change comes from an insufficient supply of either energy or information, again causing external and internal readjustments in the structure of action systems. For example, value (informational) conflict would cause normative conflict (or anomie), which in turn would have consequences for the personality and organismic systems. Thus, inherent in the cybernetic hierarchy of control are concepts that point to the sources of both stasis and change.[16]

To augment this new macro emphasis on change, Parsons used the action scheme to analyze social evolution in historical societies. In this context, the first line of *The Structure of Social Action* is of interest: "Who now reads Spencer?" Parsons then answered the question by delineating some of the reasons why Spencer's evolutionary doctrine had been so thoroughly rejected by 1937. Yet, after some forty years, Parsons chose to reexamine the issue of societal evolution that he had so easily dismissed in the beginning. And in so doing, he reintroduced Spencer's and Durkheim's evolutionary models back into functional theory.

In drawing heavily from Spencer's and Durkheim's insights into societal development, Parsons proposed that the processes of evolution display the following elements:

1. Increasing differentiation of system units into patterns of functional interdependence

2. Establishment of new principles and mechanisms of integration in differentiating systems

3. Increasing adaptive capacity of differentiated systems in their environments

---

[16]For a fuller discussion, see Alvin L. Jacobson, "Talcott Parsons: A Theoretical and Empirical Analysis of Social Change and Conflict," in *Institutions and Social Exchange: The Sociologies of Talcott Parsons and George C. Homans*, eds. H. Turk and R. L. Simpson (Indianapolis: Bobbs-Merrill, 1970).

From the perspective of action theory, then, evolution involves (a) increasing differentiation of the personality, social, cultural, and organismic systems from one another; (b) increasing differentiation within each of these four action subsystems; (c) escalating problems of integration and the emergence of new integrative structures; and (d) the upgrading of the survival capacity of each action subsystem, as well as of the overall action system, to its environment.

Parsons then embarked on an ambitious effort to outline the pattern of evolution in historical systems through primitive, intermediate, and modern stages in two short volumes.[17] In contrast with *The Social System,* where he stressed the problem of integration between social systems and personality, Parsons drew attention in his evolutionary model to the inter- and intra-differentiation of the cultural and social systems and to the resulting integrative problems. Each stage of evolution is seen as reflecting a new set of integrative problems between society and culture as each of these systems has become more internally differentiated as well as differentiated from the other. Thus, the concern with the issues of integration within and among action systems, so evident in earlier works, is not abandoned but applied to the analysis of specific historical processes.

Even though Parsons was vague about the causes of evolutionary change, he saw evolution as guided by the cybernetic hierarchy of controls, especially the informational component. In his documenting of how integrative problems of the differentiating social and cultural systems have been resolved in the evolution of historical systems, the informational hierarchy is regarded as crucial because the regulation of societal processes of differentiation must be accompanied by legitimization from cultural patterns (information). Without such informational control, movement to the next stage of development in an evolutionary sequence will be inhibited.

Thus, the analysis of social change is an attempt to use the analytical tools of the general theory of action to examine a specific process, the historical development of human societies. What is of interest in this effort is that Parsons developed many propositions about the sequences of change and the processes that will inhibit or accelerate the unfolding of these evolutionary sequences. It is of more than passing interest that tests of these propositions indicate that, on the whole, they have a great deal of empirical support.[18]

---

[17]Talcott Parsons, *Societies: Evolutionary and Comparative Perspectives* and *The System of Modern Societies* (Englewood Cliffs, NJ: Prentice Hall, 1966, 1971, respectively). The general stages of development were first outlined in Talcott Parsons, "Evolutionary Universals in Society," *American Sociological Review* 29 (1964): pp. 339–57.

[18]See Gary L. Buck and Alvin L. Jacobson, "Social Evolution and Structural-Functional Analysis: An Empirical Test," *American Sociological Review* 33 (June 1968): pp. 343–55; A. L. Jacobson, "Talcott Parsons: Theoretical and Empirical Analysis" (cited in note 16).

# Parsons on "The Human Condition"

Again in a way reminiscent of Spencer's grand theory, Parsons attempted to extend his analytical scheme to all aspects of the universe.[19] In this last conceptual addition, it is ironic that Parsons' work increasingly resembled Spencer's. Except for the opening line in *The Structure of Social Action*—"Who now reads Spencer?"—Parsons ignored Spencer. Indeed, he may not have realized how closely his analyses of societal evolution and his conceptualization of the "human condition" resembled Spencer's effort of one-hundred years earlier. At any rate, this last effort was more philosophy than sociology. Yet it represents the culmination of Parsons' thought. Parsons began in 1937 with an analysis of the smallest and most elementary social unit, the act. He then developed a requisite functionalism that embraced four action systems: the social, cultural, personality, and what he called "the behavioral" in later years (he had earlier called this the *organismic*). Finally, in this desire to understand basic parameters of the human condition, he viewed these four action systems as only one subsystem within the larger system of the universe. This vision is portrayed in Figure 3.6.

As can be seen in Figure 3.6, the universe is divided into four subsystems, each meeting one of the four requisites—that is, A, G, I, or L. The four action systems resolve integrative problems, the organic system handles goal-attainment problems, the physico-chemical copes with adaptation problems, and the telic ("ultimate" problems of meaning and cognition) deals with latency problems.

Each subsystem employs its own media for intra- and inter-subsystem activity. For the action subsystem, the distinctive medium is symbolic meaning; for the telic, it is transcendental ordering; for the organic, it is health; and for the physico-chemical, it is empirical ordering (law-like relations of matter, energy, and so forth). There are double interchanges of these media among the four A, G, I, L sectors, with "products" and "factors" being reciprocally exchanged. That is, each subsystem of the universe transmits a product to the others, while it also provides a factor necessary for the operation of other subsystems. This can be illustrated with the L (telic) and I (action) interchange. At the product level, the telic system provides "definitions of human responsibility" to the action subsystems and receives "sentiments of justification" from the action subsystem. At the factor level, the telic provides "categorical imperatives" and receives "acceptance of moral obligations." These double interchanges are, of course, carried out with the distinctive media of the I and A subsystems—that is, transcendental ordering and symbolic meaning, respectively.

The end result of this analysis was a grand metaphysical vision of the universe as it impinges on human existence. Parsons' analysis represents an

---

[19]Talcott Parsons, *Action Theory and the Human Condition* (New York: Free Press, 1978). See the last chapter in this book and my analysis in "Parsons on the Human Condition," *Contemporary Sociology* 9 (1980): pp. 380–83.

**Figure 3.6**   The Subsystems of the Human Condition

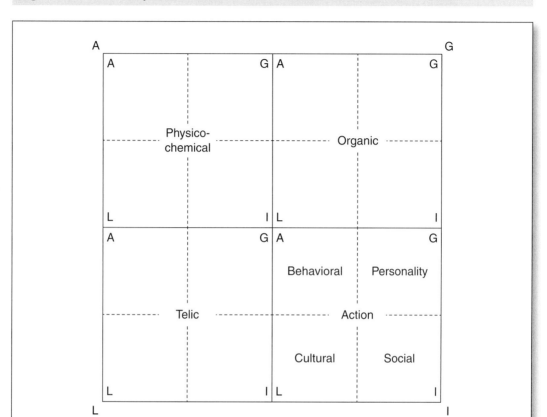

effort to categorize the universe into systems, subsystems, system requisites, generalized media, and exchanges involving these media. As such, this analysis is no longer sociology but philosophy or, at best, a grand meta-theoretical vision. Parsons had indeed come a long way since the humble unit act made its entrance in 1937.

## CHAPTER 4

# Niklas Luhmann's Systems Functionalism

The grand architecture of the Parsonian functional scheme, as it evolved over a forty-year period at the midcentury, inspired a great amount of criticism, both inside and outside the functionalist perspective. Within the functionalist camp, the Parsonian conceptual edifice was heavily criticized for being too abstract and detached from empirical reality. Yet, other functionalists were not so willing to abandon high-level abstractions. Rather, the alternative was to reduce the complexity and rigidity of the conceptual edifice, while maintaining a broad scheme at a high level of abstraction. Still, others continued to build on Parsons' approach, focusing on the same substantive questions as Parsons, and sustaining a commitment to analyzing these problems within the four-functions paradigm.[1]

In this chapter, I will examine the work of Niklas Luhmann, who took the criticisms about the analytical complexity of Parsons' four-functions approach seriously and dropped many particulars of this scheme itself but not the goal of producing abstract frameworks for analyzing social reality. Luhmann studied for a time with Parsons, but he eventually criticized Parsonian action theory for being "overly concerned with its own architecture." Luhmann considered himself a systems theorist more than a functionalist, and the last years of his life, the systems aspects of his scheme have been given increasing emphasis.[2] But he is still a functionalist because he

---

[1]For the best of these efforts, see Richard Münch's work: *Theory of Action: Towards a New Synthesis Going Beyond Parsons* (London: Routledge, 1988); *Die Struktur der Moderne* (Frankfurt am Main: Suhrkamp, 1984).

[2]See, for example, Niklas Luhmann, *Systems Theory* (Stanford, CA: Stanford University Press, 1995).

tends to analyze system processes by how they meet one master functional requisite: reduction of environmental complexity.[3]

# Luhmann's General Systems Approach

## System and Environment

Luhmann employs a general systems approach to stress that human action becomes organized and structured into systems. When the actions of several people become interrelated, a social system can be said to exist. The basic mechanism by which actions become interrelated to create social systems is communication via symbolic codes, such as words and other media. All social systems exist in multidimensional environments, posing potentially endless complexity with which a system must deal. To exist in a complex environment, therefore, a social system must develop mechanisms for reducing complexity, lest the system simply merge with its environment. These mechanisms involve selecting ways and means for reducing complexity. Such selection creates a boundary between a system and its environment, thereby allowing the system to sustain patterns of interrelated actions.

The basic functional requisite in Luhmann's analysis is thus the need to reduce the complexity of the environment in relation to a system of interrelated actions. All social processes are analyzed with respect to their functions for reducing complexity in relation to an environment. Processes that function in this way are typically defined as mechanisms in a manner reminiscent of Talcott Parsons' early discussion in *The Social System*[4] (see pp. 55–56 in Chapter 3). Indeed, the bulk of Luhmann's sociology revolves around discussions of such mechanisms—differentiation, ideology, law, symbolic media, and other critical elements of his scheme.

## Dimensions of the Environment

There are three basic dimensions along which the complexity of the environment is reduced by these mechanisms: (1) a temporal dimension, (2) a material dimension, and (3) a symbolic dimension. More than most social theorists, Luhmann is concerned with time as a dimension of the social universe. Time always presents complexity for a system because it reaches into the past, because it embodies complex configurations of acts in the present, and because it involves the vast horizons of the future. Thus a social system must develop mechanisms for reducing the complexity of time. The

---

[3]Luhmann has published extensively, but most of his work is in German. The best sample of his work in English is *Systems Theory* and *The Differentiation of Society*, trans. S. Holmes and C. Larmore (New York: Columbia University Press, 1982).

[4]Talcott Parsons, *The Social System* (New York: Free Press, 1951).

system must find a way to order this dimension by developing procedures to orient actions to the past, present, and future.[5]

Luhmann is also concerned with the material dimension of the environment—that is, with all the possible relations among actions in potentially limitless physical space. Luhmann always asks these questions: What mechanisms are developed to order interrelated actions in physical space? What is the structure and form of such ordering of relations?

Luhmann visualizes the third dimension of human systems as the symbolic. Of all the complex symbols and their combinations that humans can conceivably generate, what mechanisms select some symbols over others and organize them in some ways as opposed to the vast number of potential alternatives? What kinds of symbolic media are selected and used by a social system to organize social actions?

Thus the mechanisms of a social system that reduce complexity and thereby maintain a boundary between the system and the environment function along three dimensions: the temporal, material, and symbolic. The nature of a social system—its size, form, and differentiations—will be reflected in the mechanisms that the system uses to reduce complexity along these dimensions.

## Types of Social Systems

A social system exists any time the actions of individuals are "meaningfully interrelated and interconnected," thereby setting them off from the temporal, material, and symbolic environment by virtue of the selection of functional mechanisms. From such processes come three basic types of social systems: (1) interaction systems, (2) organization systems, and (3) societal systems.[6]

**Interaction Systems.** An interaction system emerges when individuals are co-present and perceive each other. The very act of perception is a selection mechanism that sorts from a much more complex environment, creating a boundary and setting people off as a system. Such systems are elaborated by the use of language in face-to-face communication, thereby reducing complexity even further along the temporal, material, and symbolic dimensions. For example, Luhmann would ask the following type of question: How does the language and its organization into codes shape people's perceptions of time? Who is included in the conversation? And what codes and agreements guide conversation and other actions?

Interaction systems reveal certain inherent limitations and vulnerabilities, however. First, only one topic can be discussed at a time, lest the system collapse as everyone tries to talk at once (which of course frequently occurs). Second, the varying conversational resources of participants often

---

[5]Luhmann, *The Differentiation* (cited in note 3), Chap. 12.

[6]Ibid., pp. 71–89.

lead to competition over who is to talk, creating inequalities and tensions that can potentially lead to conflict and system disintegration. Third, talk and conversation are time-consuming because they are sequential; as a result, an interaction system can never be very complex.

Thus, interaction systems are simple because they involve only those who can be co-present, perceived, and talked to; they are vulnerable to conflict and tension; and they consume a great deal of time. For a social system to be larger and more complex, additional organizing principles beyond perceptions of co-presence and sequential talk are essential.

**Organizational Systems**. These systems coordinate the actions of individuals with respect to specific conditions, such as work on a specific task in exchange for a specific amount of money. Organizational systems typically have entry and exit rules (for example, come to work for this period of time and leave with this much money), and their main function is to "stabilize highly 'artificial' modes of behavior over a long stretch of time" to resolve the basic problem of reconciling the motivations and dispositions of individuals and the need to get certain tasks done. An organization does not depend on the moral commitment of individuals, nor does it require normative consensus. Rather, the entrance and exit rules specify tasks in ways that allow individuals to do what is required without wholly identifying with the organization.

Organization systems are thus essential to a complex social order. They reduce environmental complexity by organizing people (1) in time by generating entrance and exit rules and by ordering activities in the present and future; (2) in space by creating a division of labor, which authority coordinates; and (3) in symbolic terms by indicating what is appropriate, what rules apply, and what media, such as money or pay, are to guide action. In his delineation of organization systems, Luhmann stresses that complex social orders do not require consensus over values, beliefs, or norms to be sustained; they can operate quite effectively without motivational commitments of actors. Their very strength—flexibility and adaptability to changing environmental conditions—depends on delimited and situational commitments of actors, along with neutral media of communication, such as money.[7]

**Societal Systems**. These systems cut across interaction and organization systems. A societal system is a "comprehensive system of all reciprocally accessible communication actions."[8] Historically, societal systems have been limited by geopolitical considerations, but today Luhmann sees a trend toward one world society. Luhmann's discussion on the societal system is

---

[7]In making this assertion, Luhmann directly attacks Parsons. Luhmann, *The Differentiation* (cited in note 3), Chap. 3.

[8]Ibid., p. 73.

rather vague, but the general idea can be inferred from his analysis of more specific topics: Societal systems use highly generalized communication codes, such as money and power, to reduce the complexity of the environment. In so doing, they set broad limits on how and where actions are to be interrelated into interaction and organization systems. These systems also organize how time is perceived and how actions are oriented to the past, present, and future.

## System Differentiation, Integration, and Conflict

These three systems—interaction, organization, and societal—cannot be totally separated because "all social action obviously takes place in society and is ultimately possible only in the form of interaction."[9] Indeed, in very simple societies, they are fused together, but as societies become larger and more complex, these systems become clearly differentiated from and irreducible to one another. Organizations become distinctive with respect to (1) their functional domains (government, law, education, economy, religion, science); (2) their entrance and exit rules; and (3) their reliance on distinctive media of communication (money, truth, power, love, and so on). As a consequence, they cannot be reduced to a societal system. Interaction systems follow their own laws, for rarely do people strictly follow the guidelines of organizations and society in their conversations.

The differentiation of these systems poses several problems for the more inclusive system. First is the problem of what Luhmann calls "bottlenecks." Interaction systems are slow, sequentially organized patterns of talk, and they follow their own dynamics as people use their resources in conversations. As a result, interaction systems often prevent organizations from operating at high levels of efficiency. As people interact, they develop informal agreements and take their time, with the specific tasks of the organization going unperformed or underperformed. Similarly, as organization systems develop their own structure and programs, their interests often collide, and they become bottlenecks to action requirements at the societal level. Second is the problem of conflict in differentiated systems. Interactants may disagree on topics; they may become jealous or envious of those with conversational resources. And because interaction systems are small, they cannot become sufficiently complex "to consign marginals to their borders or to otherwise segregate them." At the organizational level, diverse organizations can pursue their interests in ways that are disruptive to both the organization and the more inclusive societal system.

Yet, countervailing these disruptive tendencies are processes that maintain social integration. One critical set of processes is the nesting of system levels inside each other. Actions within an interactive system are often nested within an organization system, and organizational actions are conducted within a societal system. Hence the broader, more inclusive system

---

[9]Ibid., p. 79.

can promote integration in two ways: (1) It provides the temporal, material, and social premises for the selection of actions, and (2) it imposes an order or structure on the proximate environment around any of its subsystems. For example, an organizational system distributes people in space and in an authority hierarchy; it orients them to time; it specifies the relevant communication codes; and it orders the proximate environment (other people, groupings, offices, and so on) of any interaction system. Similarly, the functional division of a society into politics, education, law, economy, family, religion, and science determines the substance of an organization's action, while it orders the proximate environment of any particular organization. For example, societal differentiation of a distinctive economy delimits what any economic organization can do. Thus a corporation in a capitalist economy will use money as its distinctive communications media; it will articulate with other organizations concerning market relations; it will organize its workers into bureaucratic organizations with distinctive entrance and exit rules ("work for money"); and it will be oriented to the future, with the past as only a collapsed framework to guide present activity in the pursuit of future outcomes (such as profits and promotions).

In addition to these nesting processes, integration is promoted by the deflection of people's activities across different organizations in diverse functional domains. When many organizations exist in a society, none consumes an individual's sense of identity and self because people's energies are dispersed across several organization systems. As a consequence of their piecemeal involvement, members are unlikely to be emotionally drawn into conflict among organization systems, and when individual members cannot be pulled emotionally into a conflict, its intensity and potential for social disruption are lessened. Moreover, because interaction systems are distinct from the more inclusive organization, any conflict between organizations is often seen by the rank and file as distant and remote to their interests and concerns; it is something "out there" in the environment of their interaction systems, and hence it is not very involving.

Yet another source of conflict mitigation is the entrance and exit rules of an organization. As these become elaborated into hierarchies, offices, established procedures, salary scales, and the like, these rules reduce the relevance of members' conflicts outside the organization—for example, their race and religion. Such outside conflicts are separated from those within the organization, and as a result, their salience in the broader societal system is reduced.

Finally, once differentiation of organizations is an established mechanism in a society, specific social control organizations—law, police, courts—can be easily created to mitigate and resolve conflicts. That is, the generation of distinct organizations that are functionally specific represents a new "social technology"; once this technology has been used in one context, it can be applied to additional contexts. Thus the integrative problems created by the differentiation and proliferation of organizations create the very conditions that can resolve these problems—the capacity to create organizations to mediate among organizations.

And so, although differentiation of three system levels creates problems of integration and conditions conducive to conflict, it also produces countervailing forces for integration. In making this argument, Luhmann emphasizes that, in complex systems, order is not sustained by consensus on common values, beliefs, and norms. On the contrary, there is likely to be considerable disagreement about these, except perhaps at the most abstract level. This point of emphasis is an important contribution of Luhmann's sociology, for it distinguishes his theoretical approach from that of Talcott Parsons, who overstressed the need for value consensus in complex social systems. In addition, Luhmann stresses that individuals' moral and emotional attachment to the social fabric is not essential for social integration. To seek a romantic return to a cohesive community, as Émile Durkheim, Karl Marx, and others have argued, is impossible in most spheres of a complex society. And, rather than viewing this as a pathological state—as concepts like alienation, egoism, and anomie connote—the impersonality and neutrality of many encounters in complex systems can be seen as normal and analyzed less evaluatively. Moreover, people's lack of emotional embeddedness in complex systems gives them more freedom, more options, and more flexibility.[10] This also liberates them from the constraints of tradition, the restrictions of dependency on others, and the indignities of surveillance by the powerful that are so typical of less complex societies.

## Communications Media, Reflexivity, and Self-Thematization

Luhmann's system theory stresses the relation of a system to its environment and the mechanisms used to reduce its complexity. All social systems are based on communication among actors as they align their respective modes of conduct. Because action systems are built from communication, Luhmann devotes considerable attention to communications theory, as he defines it. He stresses that human communications become reflexive and that this reflexiveness leads to self-thematization. Luhmann thus develops a communications theory revolving around communication codes and media as well as reflexiveness and self-thematization. Each of these elements in his theory will be explored briefly.

**Communication and Codes**. Luhmann waxes philosophically and metaphorically about these concepts, but in the end he concludes that communication occurs through symbols that signal actors' lines of behavior, and such symbols constitute a code with several properties.[11] First, the organization of symbols into a code guides the selection of alternatives that reduce

---

[10]Here Luhmann takes a page from Georg Simmel's *The Philosophy of Money*, trans. T. Bottomore and D. Frisby (Boston: Routledge & Kegan Paul, 1978).

[11]Luhmann, *The Differentiation* (cited in note 3), p. 169.

the complexity of the environment. For example, when someone in an interaction system says that he or she wants to talk about a particular topic, these symbols operate as a code that reduces the complexity of the system in an environment (its members will now discuss this topic and not all the potential alternatives). Second, codes are binary and dialectical in that their symbols imply their opposite. For example, the linguistic code "be a good boy" also implicitly signals its opposite—that is, what is not good and what is not male. As Luhmann notes, "language makes negative copies available" by its very nature. Third, in implying their opposite, codes create the potential for the opposite action—for instance, "to be a bad boy." In human codes, then, the very process of selecting lines of action and reducing complexity with a code also expands potential options (to do just the opposite or some variant of the opposite). This makes the human system highly flexible because the communications codes used to organize the system and reduce complexity also contain implicit messages about alternatives.

**Communications Media.** Communication codes stabilize system responses to the environment (while implying alternative responses). Codes can organize communication into distinctive media that further order system responses. As a society differentiates into functional domains, distinctive media are used to organize the resources of systems in each domain.[12] For example, the economy uses money as its medium of communication, which guides interactions within and among economic organizations. Thus, in an economy, relations among organizations are conducted in money terms (buying and selling in markets), and intra-organizational relations among workers are guided by entrance and exit rules structured by money (pay for work at specified times and places). Similarly, power is the distinctive communications medium of the political domain; love is the medium of the family; truth, the medium of science; and so on for other functional domains.[13]

Several critical generalizations are implicit in Luhmann's analysis of communications media. First, the differentiation of social systems into functional domains cannot occur without the development of a distinctive medium of communication for that domain. Second, media reduce complexity because they limit the range of action in a system. (For example, love as a medium limits the kinds of relations that are possible in a family system.)[14] Third, even in reducing complexity, media imply their opposite and thus expand potential options, giving systems flexibility (for instance, money for work implies its opposite, work without pay; the use of power implies its opposite, lack of compliance to political decisions).

---

[12]Obviously, Luhmann is borrowing Parsons' idea about generalized media. See Chapter 3.

[13]Much like Parsons, this analysis of communications media is never fully explicated or systematically discussed for all functional domains.

[14]We will see shortly, however, that money is the sole exception here.

**Reflexivity and Self-Thematization**. The use of media allows for reflexivity, or the capacity to examine the process of action as a part of the action itself. With communications media structuring action, we can use these media to think about or reflect on action. Social units can use money to make money; they employ power to decide how power is to be exercised; they can analyze love to decide what is true love; they can use truth to specify the procedures to get at truth; and so on. Luhmann sees this reflexivity as a mechanism that facilitates adaptation of a system to its environment. Reflexivity does so by ordering responses and reducing complexity, while providing actors in a system with the capacity to think about new options for action. For example, it becomes possible to mobilize power to think about new and more adaptive ways to exercise power in political decisions, as is the case when a society's political elite create a constitutional system based on a separation of powers.

As communications media are used reflexively, they allow for what Luhmann terms *self-thematization*. Using media, a system can conceptualize itself and relations with the environment as a "perspective" or "theme." Such self-thematization reduces complexity by providing guidelines about how to deal with the temporal, material, and symbolic dimensions of the environment. It becomes possible to have a guiding perspective about how to orient to time, to organize people in space, and to order symbols into codes. For example, money and its reflexive use for self-thematization in a capitalist economy create a concern with the future, an emphasis on rational organization of people, and a set of codes that emphasize impersonal exchanges of services and commodities. The consequence of these self-thematizations is that economic organizations reduce the complexity of their environments and, thereby, coordinate social action more effectively.

## Luhmann's Basic Approach

In sum, Luhmann's general systems approach revolves around the system versus environment distinction. Systems need to reduce the complexity of their environments in their perceptions about time, their organization of actors in space, and their use of symbols. Processes that reduce complexity are conceptualized as functional mechanisms. There are three types of systems: interaction, organization, and societal. All system processes occur through communications that can develop into distinctive media and allow reflexivity and self-thematization in a system.

# Luhmann's Conception of Social Evolution

Because Luhmann's substantive discussions are cast into an evolutionary framework, it is wise to begin by extracting from his diverse writings the key elements of this evolutionary approach. Like other evolutionary theorists,

Luhmann views evolution as the process of increasing differentiation of a system in relation to its environment.[15] Such increased differentiation allows a system to develop more flexible relations to its environment and, as a result, to increase its level of adaptation. As systems differentiate, however, there is the problem of integrating diverse subsystems; as a consequence, new kinds of mechanisms emerge to sustain the integration of the overall system. But, unlike most evolutionary theorists, Luhmann uses this general image of evolution in a way that adds several new twists to previous evolutionary approaches.

## The Underlying Mechanisms of Evolution

Luhmann is highly critical of the way traditional theory has analyzed the process of social differentiation.[16] First, traditional theories—from Marx and Durkheim to Parsons—all imply that there are limits to how divided a system can be, so they all postulate an end to the process, which, in Luhmann's view, is little more than an evaluative utopia. Second, traditional theories overstress the importance of value consensus as an integrating mechanism in differentiated systems. Third, these theories see many processes, such as crime, conflict, dissensus about values, and impersonality, as deviant or pathological; however, they are inevitable in differentiated systems. Fourth, previous theories have great difficulty handling the persistence of social stratification, viewing it as a source of evil or as a perpetual conflict-producing mechanism.

Luhmann's alternative to these evolutionary models is to use his systems theory to redirect the analysis of social differentiation. Like most functionalists, he analogizes to biology but not to the physiology of an organism; rather, his analogies are to the processes delineated in the theory of evolution. Thus he argues for an emphasis of those processes that produce (1) variation, (2) selection, and (3) stabilization of traits in societal systems.[17] The reasoning here is that sociocultural evolution is like other forms of biological evolution. Social systems have mechanisms that are the functional equivalents of those in biological evolution. These mechanisms generate variation in the structure of social systems, select those variations that facilitate adaptation of a system, and stabilize these adaptive structures.[18]

---

[15]This is essentially Parsons' definition (see Chapter 3). It was Spencer's and Durkheim's as well (see Chapter 2).

[16]Luhmann, *The Differentiation* (cited in note 3), pp. 256–57.

[17]Luhmann's interpretation of the synthetic theory of evolution in biology is, at best, loose and inexact.

[18]Luhmann, *The Differentiation* (cited in note 3), p. 265. Luhmann seems completely unaware that Herbert Spencer in his *The Principles of Sociology* (New York: D. Appleton, 1885; originally published in 1874) performed a similar, and more detailed, analysis a hundred years ago.

Luhmann argues that the "mechanism for variation" inheres in the process of communication and in the formation of codes and media. All symbols imply their opposite, and so there is always the opportunity to act in new ways (a kind of "symbolic mutation"). The very nature of communication permits alternatives, and at times people act on these alternatives, thereby producing new variations. Indeed, compared with the process of biological mutation, the capacity of human systems for variation is much greater than in biological systems.

The "mechanism for selection" can be found in what Luhmann terms *communicative success*. The general idea behind this concept is that certain new forms of communication facilitate increased adjustment to an environment by reducing its complexity while allowing more flexible responses to the environment. For example, the creation of money as a medium greatly facilitated by adaptation of systems and subsystems to the environment, as did the development of centralized power to coordinate activity in systems. And, because they facilitated survival and adaptation, they were retained in the structure of the social organism.

The "stabilization mechanism" resides in the very process of system formation. That is, new communication codes and media are used to order social actions among subsystems, and in so doing, they create structures, such as political systems and economic orders, that regularize for a time the use of the new communications media. For example, once money is used, it creates an economic order revolving around markets and exchange that, in turn, feeds back and encourages the extension of money as a medium of communication. From this reciprocity ensues some degree of continuity and stability in the economic system.

## Evolution and Social Differentiation

Luhmann believes that sociocultural evolution involves differentiation in seven senses.

1. Evolution is the increasing differentiation of interaction, organization, and societal systems from one another. That is, interaction systems increasingly become distinct from organization systems, which in turn are more clearly separated from societal systems. Although these system levels are nested in each other, they also have their unique dynamics.

2. Evolution involves the internal differentiation of these three types of systems. Diverse interaction systems multiply and become different from one another (for example, compare conversations at work, at a party, at home, and at a funeral). Organization systems increase in number and specialize in different activities (compare economic with political organizations, or contrast different types of economic organizations, such as manufacturing and retail organizations). And the societal system becomes differentiated from the organization and

interaction systems that it comprises. Moreover, there is an evolutionary trend, Luhmann claims, toward a one world society.

3. Evolution involves the increasing differentiation of societal systems into functional domains, such as economy, polity, law, religion, family, science, and education. Organization subsystems within these domains are specialized to deal with a limited range of environmental contingencies, and in being specialized, subsystems can better deal with contingencies. The overall result for a societal system is increased adaptability and flexibility in its environment.

4. Functional differentiation is accompanied by (and is the result of) the increasing use of distinctive media of communication. For example, organization systems in the economy employ money, those in the polity or government exercise power, those in science depend on truth, and those in the family domain use love.

5. There is a clear differentiation during evolution among the persons, roles, programs, and values. Individuals are entities separated from the roles and organizations in which they participate. One plays many roles, and each involves only a segment or part of a person's personality and sense of self; many roles are played with little or no investment of oneself in them. Moreover, most roles persist whether or not any one individual plays them, thereby emphasizing their separation from the person. Such roles are increasingly grouped together into an ever-increasing diversity of what Luhmann calls programs (work, family, play, politics, consumption, and so on) that typically exist inside different kinds of organization systems operating in a distinctive functional domain. In addition, these roles can be shuffled around into new programs, emphasizing the separation of roles and programs. Finally, societal values become increasingly abstract and general, with the result that they do not pertain to any one functional domain, program, role, or individual.[19] They exist as very general criteria that can be selectively invoked to help organize roles into programs or to mobilize individuals to play roles; however, their application to roles and programs is made possible by additional mechanisms such as ideologies, laws, technologies, and norms. For, by themselves, societal values are too general and abstract for individuals to use in concrete situations. Indeed, one of the most conspicuous features of highly differentiated systems is the evolution of mechanisms to attach abstract values to concrete roles and programs.

6. Evolution involves the movement through three distinctive forms of differentiation: (a) segmentation, (b) stratification, and (c) functional

---

[19]Luhmann is borrowing here from Émile Durkheim's analysis in *The Division of Labor in Society* (New York: Free Press, 1949; originally published in 1893) as well as from Talcott Parsons' discussion of value generalization. See Chapter 3.

differentiation.[20] That is, the five processes outlined earlier have historically created, Luhmann believes, only three distinctive forms of differentiation. When the simplest societies initially differentiate, they do so segmentally in that they create like and equal subsystems that operate very much like the ones from which they emerged. For example, as it initially differentiates, a traditional society will create new lineages, or new villages, that duplicate previous lineages and villages. But segmentation limits a society's complexity and, hence, its capacity to adapt to its environment. And so, alternative forms of differentiation are selected during sociocultural evolution. Further differentiation creates stratified systems in which subsystems vary in their power, wealth, and other resources. These subsystems are ordered hierarchically, and this new form of structure allows for more complex relations with an environment but imposes limitations on how complex the system can become. As long as the hierarchical order must be maintained, the options of any subsystem are limited by its place in the hierarchy.[21] Thus pressures build for a third form of differentiation, the functional. Here communication processes are organized around the specific function to be performed for the societal system. Such a system creates inequalities because some functions have more priority for the system (for example, economics over religion). This inequality, however, is fundamentally different from that in hierarchically ordered or stratified systems. In a functionally differentiated society, the other subsystems are part of the environment of any given subsystem—for example, organizations in the polity, law, education, religions, science, and family domains are part of the environment of the economy. And although the economy might have functional priority in the society, it treats and responds to the other subsystems in its environment as equals. Thus inequality in functionally differentiated societies does not create a rigid hierarchy of subsystems; as a consequence, it allows more autonomy of each subsystem, which in turn gives them more flexibility in dealing with their respective environments. The overall consequence of such subsystem autonomy is increased flexibility of the societal system to adjust and adapt to its environment.

7. Evolutionary differentiation increases the complexity of a system and its relationship with the environment. In so doing, it escalates the risks, as Luhmann terms the matter, of making incorrect and maladaptive decisions about how to relate to an environment. With increased complexity comes an expanded set of options for a system, but there is a corresponding chance that the selection of options will be dysfunctional for a system's relationship to an environment. For

---

[20]Luhmann, *The Differentiation* (cited in note 3), pp. 229–54.

[21]Ibid., p. 235.

example, any organization in the economy must make decisions about its actions, but there are increased alternatives and escalated unknowns, resulting in expanded risks. In Luhmann's view, the ever-increasing risk level that accompanies evolutionary differentiation must be accompanied by mechanisms to reduce risk, or at least by the perception or sense that risk has been reduced. Thus evolution always involves an increase in the number and complexity of risk-reducing mechanisms. Such mechanisms also decrease the complexity of a system's environment because they select some options over others. For example, a conservative political ideology is a risk-reducing mechanism because it selects some options from more general values and ignores others. In essence, an ideology assures decision makers that the risks are reduced by accepting the goals of the ideology.[22]

Before proceeding further, we should review these elements of Luhmann's view of evolution and how they change a society's and its constituent subsystem's relation to the temporal, material, and symbolic dimensions of the environment. Temporally, Luhmann argues that social evolution and differentiation lead to efforts at developing a chronological metric, or a standardized way to measure time (clocks, for example). Equally fundamental is a shift in people's perspective from the past to the future. The past becomes highly generalized and lacks specific dictates of what should be done in the present and the future. For, as systems become more complex, the past cannot serve as a guide to the present or future because there are too many potential new contingencies and options. The present sees time as ever-more scarce and in short supply; thus people become more oriented to the future and to the consequences of their present actions. Materially, social differentiation involves (1) the increasing separation of interaction, organization, and societal systems; (2) the compartmentalization of organization systems into functional domains; (3) the growing separation of person, role, program, and values; and (4) the movement toward functional differentiation and away from segmentation and stratification. And, symbolically, communication codes become more complex and organized as distinctive media for a particular functional domain. Moreover, they increasingly function as risk-reducing mechanisms for a universe filled with contingency and uncertainty.

Luhmann has approached the study of specific organizational systems from this overall view of sociocultural evolution and differentiation. As he has consistently argued, an analytical framework is only as good as the insights into empirical processes that it can generate. Luhmann's framework is much more complex than he contends such a framework should be, and it is often more metaphorical than analytical. Yet, it allows him to analyze political, legal, and economic processes in functionally differentiated societies in very intriguing ways.

---

[22]Ibid., p. 151.

# The Functional Differentiation of Society

## Politics as a Social System

As societies grow more complex, new structures emerge for reducing complexity. Old processes, such as appeals to traditional truths, mutual sympathy, exchange, and barter, become ever more inadequate. A system that reaches this point of differentiation, Luhmann argues, must develop the "capacity to make binding decisions." Such capacity is generated from the problems of increased complexity, but this capacity also becomes an important condition for further differentiation.

To make binding decisions, the system must use a distinctive medium of communication: power.[23] Power is defined by Luhmann as "the possibility of having one's own decisions select alternatives or reduce complexity for others." Thus, whenever one social unit selects alternatives of action for other units, power is being employed as the medium of communication.

The use of power to make binding decisions functions to resolve conflicts, to mitigate tensions, and to coordinate activities in complex systems. Societies that can develop political systems capable of performing these functions can better deal with their environments. Several conditions, Luhmann believes, facilitate the development of this functional capacity. First, there must be time to make decisions; the less time an emerging political system is allowed, the more difficulty it will have in becoming autonomous. Second, the emerging political system must not confront a single power block in its environment, such as a powerful church. Rather, it requires an environment of multiple subsystems whose power is more equally balanced. So, the more the power in the political subsystem's environment is concentrated, the more difficult is its emergence as an autonomous subsystem. Third, the political system must stabilize its relations with other subsystems in the environment in two distinctive ways: (1) at the level of diffuse legitimacy, so that its decisions are accepted as its proper function, and (2) at the level of daily transactions among individuals and subsystems.[24] That is, the greater the problems of a political system are in gaining diffuse support for its right to make decisions for other subsystems and the less salient the decisions of the political system are for the day-to-day activities, transactions, and routines of system units, then the greater will be its problems in developing into an autonomous subsystem.

Thus, to the extent that a political system has time to develop procedures for making decisions, confront multiple sources of mitigated power, and achieve diffuse legitimacy as well as relevance for specific transactions, then the more it can develop into an autonomous system and the greater will be

---

[23]Ibid.

[24]Ibid., pp. 143–44.

a society's capacity to adjust to its environment. In so developing, the political system must achieve what Luhmann calls structural abstraction or the capacity to (1) absorb multiple problems, dilemmas, and issues from a wide range of system units and (2) make binding decisions for each of these. Luhmann sees the political system as "absorbing" the problems of its environment and making them internal to the political system. Several variables, he argues, determine the extent to which the political system can perform this function: (1) the degree to which conflicts are defined as political (instead of moral, personal, and so forth) and therefore in need of a binding decision; (2) the degree of administrative capacity of the political system to coordinate activities of system units; and (3) the degree of structural differentiation within the political system itself.

This last variable is the most crucial in Luhmann's view. In response to environmental complexity and the need to absorb and deal with problems in this environment, the political system must differentiate along three lines: (1) the creation of a stable bureaucratic administration that executes decisions, (2) the evolution of a separate arena for politics and the emergence of political parties, and (3) the designation of the public as a relevant concern in making binding decisions. Such internal differentiation increases the capacity of the political system to absorb and deal with a wide variety of problems; as a consequence, it allows greater complexity in the societal system.

This increased complexity of the political and societal systems also increases the risks of making binding decisions that are maladaptive. As complexity increases, there are always unknown contingencies. Therefore, not only do political systems develop mechanisms such as internal differentiation for dealing with complexity, but they also develop mechanisms for reducing risk or the perception of risk. One mechanism is the growing reflexiveness of the political process—that is, its increased reflection on itself. Such reflection is built into the nature of party politics where the manner and substance of political decisions are analyzed and debated. Another mechanism is what Luhmann calls the positivization of law, or the creation of a separate legal system that makes "laws about how to make laws" (more on this in the next section). Yet another mechanism is ideology or symbolic codes that select which values are relevant for a particular set of decisions. A related mechanism is the development of a political code that typifies and categorizes political decisions into a simple typology.[25] For example, the distinction between progressive and conservative politics is, Luhmann argues, an important political code in differentiated societies. Such a code is obviously very general, but this is its virtue because it allows very diverse political acts and decisions to be categorized and interpreted with a simple dichotomy, thereby giving political action a sense of order and reducing perceptions of risk. Luhmann even indicates that it is a system's capacity to develop a political code, more than consensus of values, that leads to social order. For in interpreting actions in terms of the code, a

---

[25]Ibid., pp. 168–89.

common perspective is maintained, but it is a perspective based on differences—progressive versus conservative—rather than on commonality and consensus. Thus, complex social orders are sustained by their very capacity to create generalized and binary categories for interpreting events rather than by value consensus.

Still another mechanism for reducing risks is arbitrary decision making by elites. However, although such a solution achieves order, it undermines the legitimacy of the political system in the long run because system units start to resent and to resist arbitrary decision making. And a final mechanism is invocation of a traditional moral code (for example, fundamentalistic religious values) that, in Luhmann's terms, "remoralizes" the political process. But when such remoralization occurs, the political system must de-differentiate because strict adherence to a simple moral code precludes the capacity to deal with complexity (an example of this process would be Iran's return to a theocracy from its previously more complex political system).

In sum, then, it is fair to say that Luhmann uses his conceptual metaphor to analyze insightfully specific institutional processes, such as government. Yet he does not use his scheme in a rigorous deductive sense; much like Parsons before him, he employs the framework as a means for denoting and highlighting particular social phenomena. Although much of his analysis of political system differentiation is old wine in new bottles, there is a shift in emphasis and, as a result, some intriguing but imprecise insights. In a similar vein, Luhmann analyzes the differentiation of the legal system and the economy.

## The Autonomy of the Legal System

As discussed earlier, Luhmann visualizes social evolution as involving a separation of persons, roles, programs, and values. For him, differentiation of structure occurs at the level of roles and programs. Consequently, there is the problem of how to integrate values and persons into roles organized into programs within organization systems. The functional mechanism for mobilizing and coordinating individuals to play roles is law, whereas the mechanism for making values relevant to programs is ideology.[26] Thus, because law regulates and coordinates people's participation in roles and programs and because social differentiation must always occur at the roles level, it becomes a critical subsystem if a society is to differentiate and evolve. That is, a society cannot become complex without the emergence of an autonomous legal system to specify rights, duties, and obligations of people playing roles.[27]

A certain degree of political differentiation must precede legal differentiation because there must be a set of structures to make decisions and enforce

---

[26]Ibid., pp. 90–137.

[27]This is essentially the same conclusion Parsons reached in his description of evolution in *Societies: Evolutionary and Comparative Perspectives* and *The System of Modern Societies* (Englewood Cliffs, NJ: Prentice Hall, 1966 and 1971, respectively).

them. But political processes often impede legal autonomy, as is the case when political elites have used the law for their own narrow purposes. For legal autonomy to emerge, therefore, political development is not enough. Two additional conditions are necessary: (1) "the invocation of sovereignty," or references by system units to legal codes that justify their communications and actions, and (2) "lawmaking sovereignty," or the capacity of organizations in the legal system to decide just what the law will be.

If these two conditions are met, then the legal system can become increasingly reflexive. It can become a topic unto itself, creating bodies of procedural and administrative law to regulate the enactment and enforcement of law. In turn, such procedural laws can themselves be the subject of scrutiny. Without this reflexive quality, the legal system cannot be sufficiently flexible to change in accordance with shifting events in its environment. Such flexibility is essential because only through the law can people's actions be tied to the roles that are being differentiated. For example, without what Luhmann calls the "positivization of law," or its capacity to change itself in response to altered circumstances, new laws and agencies (for example, workers' compensation, binding arbitration of labor and management disputes, minimum wages, health and safety) could not be created to regulate people's involvement in roles (in this case, work roles in a differentiating economy).

Thus, positivization of the law is a critical condition for societal differentiation. It reduces complexity by specifying relations of actors to roles and relegating cooperation among social system units. But it reduces complexity in a manner that presents options for change under new circumstances; thus it becomes a condition for the further differentiation of other functional domains, such as the economy.

## The Economy as a Social System

Luhmann defines the economy as "deferring a decision about the satisfaction of needs while providing a guarantee that they will be satisfied and so utilizing the time thus acquired."[28] The general idea seems to be that economic activity—production and distribution of goods and services—functions to satisfy basic or primary needs for food, clothing, and shelter, as well as derived or secondary needs for less basic goods and services. But this happens in a way not fully appreciated in economic analysis: The economic activity restructures humans' orientation to time because economic action is oriented to the satisfaction of future needs. Present economic activity is typically directed at future consumption; so, when a person works and a corporation acts in a market, they are doing so to guarantee that their future will be unproblematic.

Luhmann's definition of the economic subsystem is less critical than his analysis of the processes leading to the creation of an autonomous

---

[28]Luhmann, *The Differentiation* (cited in note 3), p. 194.

economic system in society. In traditional and undifferentiated societies, Luhmann argues, only small-scale solutions are possible with respect to doing something in the present to satisfy future needs. One solution is stockpiling of goods, with provisions for the redistribution of stocks to societal members or trade with other societies.[29] Another solution is mutual assistance agreements among individuals, kin groups, or villages. But such patterns of economic organization are very limited because they merge familial, political, religious, and community activity. Only with the differentiation of distinctly economic roles can more complexity and flexibility be structured into economic action. The first key differentiation along these lines is the development of markets with distinctive roles for buyers and sellers.

A market performs several crucial functions. First, it sets equivalences or the respective values of goods and services. Second, it neutralizes the relevance of other roles—for instance, the familial, religious, and political roles of parties in an exchange. Value is established by the qualities of respective goods, not by the positions or characteristics of the buyers and sellers.[30] Third, markets inevitably generate pressures for a new medium of communication that is not tied to other functional subsystems. This medium is money, and it allows quick assessments of equivalences and value in an agreed-on metric. In sum, then, markets create the conditions for the differentiation of distinctly economic roles, for their separation and insulation from other societal roles, and for the creation of a uniquely economic medium of communication.

Money is a very unusual medium, Luhmann believes, because it "transfers complexity." Unlike other media, money is distinctive because it does not reduce complexity in the environment. For example, the medium of power is used to make decisions that direct activity, thereby reducing the complexity of the environment. The medium of truth in science is designed to simplify the understanding of a complex universe. And the medium of love in the family circumscribes the actions and types of relations among kindred and, in so doing, reduces complexity. In contrast, money is a neutral vehicle that can always be used to buy and sell many different things. It does not limit; it opens options and creates new opportunities. For example, to accept money for a good or for one's work does not reduce the seller's or worker's options. The money can be used in many different ways, thereby preserving and even increasing the complexity of the environment. Money thus sets the stage for—indeed it encourages—further internal differentiation in the economic subsystem of a society.

In addition to transferring complexity, Luhmann sees money as dramatically altering the time dimension of the environment. Money is a liquid resource that is always "usable in the future." When we have money, it can

---

[29]Ibid., p. 197.

[30]Luhmann fails to cite the earlier work of Georg Simmel on these matters. See Simmel's *The Philosophy of Money* (cited in note 10).

be used at some future date—whether the next minute or the following year. Money thus collapses time, because it is to be used in the future, hence making the past irrelevant, and the present is defined by what will be done with money in the future. However, this collapsing of time can come about only if (1) money does not inflate over time and (2) if it is universally used as the medium of exchange (that is, if barter, mutual assistance, and other traditional forms of exchange do not still prevail).[31]

Like all media of communication, money is reflexive. It becomes a goal of reflection, debate, and action itself. We can buy and sell money in markets; we can invest money to make more money; we can condemn money as the root of evil or praise it as a goal that is worth pursuing; we can hoard it in banks or spread it around in consumptive activity. This reflexive quality of money, coupled with its capacity to transfer complexity and reorient actors to time, is what allows money to become an ever more dominant medium of communication in complex societies. Indeed, the economy becomes the primary subsystem of complex societies because its medium encourages constant increases in complexity and growth in the economic system. As a consequence, the economy becomes a prominent subsystem in the environment of other functional subsystems—that is, science, polity, family, religion, and education. The economy becomes something that must always be dealt with by these other subsystems.

This growing complexity of the economic subsystem increases the risks in human conduct. The potential for making a mistake in providing for a person's future needs or a corporation's profits increases because the number of unknown contingencies dramatically multiplies. Such escalated risks generate pressures, Luhmann argues, for their reduction through the emergence of specific mechanisms. The most important of these mechanisms is the tripart internal differentiation of the economy around (1) households, (2) firms, and (3) markets.[32] There is a "structural selection" for this division, Luhmann believes, because these are structurally and functionally different. Households are segmental systems (structurally the same) and are the primary consumption units. Firms are structurally diverse and the primary productive units. And markets are not as much a unit as a set of processes for distributing goods and services. Luhmann is a bit vague on this point, but it seems that there is strength in this correspondence of basically different structures with major economic functions. Households are segmented structurally and are functionally oriented to consumption; firms are highly differentiated structurally and are functionally geared to production; and markets are processually differentiated by their function to distribute different types of goods and services. Such differentiation reduces complexity, but at the same time, it allows flexibility: Households can change consumption patterns, firms can alter production, and markets can expand or contract. And, because they are separated from one another, each

---

[31]Luhmann, *The Differentiation* (cited in note 3), p. 207.

[32]Ibid., p. 216.

has the capacity to change and redirect its actions, independent of the others. This flexibility is what allows the economic system to become so prominent in modern industrial societies.

Yet, Luhmann warns, the very complexity of the economy and its importance for other subsystems create pressures for other risk-reducing mechanisms. One of these is intervention by government so that power is used to make binding decisions on production, consumption, and distribution as well as on the availability of money as a medium of communication. The extensive use of this mechanism, Luhmann believes, reduces risk and complexity in the economy at the expense of its capacity to meet needs in the future and to make flexible adjustments to the environment.

## CHAPTER 5

# Efforts to Revitalize Functionalism

Sociological functionalism died in the first decade of the twentieth century, not so much because of the functionalism per se, but because functional theories were evolutionary. Whether Herbert Spencer's more detailed stage model or Émile Durkheim's simple dichotomy between "mechanical" and "organic" solidarity, functionalists conceptualized the long run of societal development as movement from simple to more complex stages of development. Unfortunately, in many lay and academic circles, this progressive movement was also seen as evolution from "primitive" to "civilized" stages of development, a distinction ripe for ethnocentrism by Europeans about their own superiority and somewhat racist-sounding portrayals of people in simple societies. Sociologists were not so guilty here, but the eventual reaction against such racist and ethnocentric portrays led to a general abandonment of evolutionary theories by the end of the second decade in the twentieth century. Near the end of the third decade into the twentieth century, Talcott Parsons, who was eventually to become the preeminent functional theorist, was moved to proclaim: "Who now reads Spencer?" He attributed this fate to Spencer not because of his functionalism, which he was to adopt two decades later, but Spencer's evolutionism.

When functional theory reemerged in the 1950s, primarily under the influence of Parsons, it would eventually reintroduce stage-model evolutionary theories back into functionalism. Yet, at first, it was the functionalism of the early masters that came back into sociology. Ironically, the reintroduction of stage-model evolutionary theory was a response to the increasingly loud chorus criticisms of functionalism as unable to account for social change, which prompted Parsons to introduce stage-model evolutionism into his later works. This effort only ramped up additional criticism of functionalism.

Still, as we will see in Part II of this book, the criticism of evolution did not stick. Even as functionalism began to die once again, stage-model evolution that has been a part of functional approaches since their inception survived the attacks on functionalism and, today, still exists as a prominent theoretical approach in sociology. In contrast, the critique of functional theory was successful, and by the end of the twentieth century, only a small handful of theorists could be recognized as functionalists.

The criticism had started in the works of Robert K. Merton a few years before Parsons' first functional works appeared. Merton began by criticizing the anthropologists, such as A. R. Radcliffe-Brown and Bronislaw Malinowski, but the constant reprinting of the chapter, originally written in 1949, for the next two decades in Merton's *Social Theory and Social Structure*, was clearly intended to be a critique of Parsons as well. Merton's critique hit home and, indeed, highlighted some of the basic problems with functionalist logic. Yet, Merton did not advocate the abandonment of functionalism but rather its redirection. Between the late 1950s and early 1980s, the criticism of Parsonian functionalism in particular, but also functionalism in general, continued—seemingly driving it out of sociology. However, as I will explore shortly in some of my own work, Parsons' functionalism disappeared not so much for being functional but for being insufficiently theoretical. As emphasized in Chapter 1, analytical schemes like those developed by Parsons are, in reality, category systems that do not conceptualize adequately social processes and structures as variables and do not develop propositions explaining their dynamic properties. Let me first begin with Merton's early critique and then move to my views on how to retain the important characteristics of functionalism without its liabilities.

# Robert K. Merton's Critique of Functionalism

## The Critique of Functional Analysis

As a contemporary of Talcott Parsons, Robert K. Merton was a persistent critic of analytical functionalism that sought to explain the social world with a grand analytical scheme (see Chapter 1 and Figure 1.6). Whether Émile Durkheim, A. R. Radcliffe-Brown, Bronislaw Malinowski, or Talcott Parsons (and, no doubt, Niklas Luhmann as well), Merton saw fundamental flaws in their collective approaches to theorizing. He saw functional theorizing as potentially embracing three questionable postulates: (1) the functional unity of social systems, (2) the functional universality of social items, and (3) the indispensability of functional items for social systems.[1] Each of these is examined below.

---

[1]Robert K. Merton, "Manifest and Latent Functions" in his *Social Theory and Social Structure* (New York: Free Press, 1968), pp. 45–61. See also Merton's "Discussion of Parsons' 'The Position of Sociological Theory,'" *American Sociological Review* 13 (1948): pp. 164–68. For a more comprehensive review and critique of functional theorizing, see Jonathan Turner and Alexandra Maryanski's, *Functionalism* (Menlo Park, CA: Benjamin-Cummings, 1979).

**1. The Functional Unity Postulate**. As emphasized in Chapter 2, A. R. Radcliffe-Brown, following Émile Durkheim's lead, frequently transformed the hypothesis that social systems reveal social integration into a necessary requisite or need for social system survival. Although it is difficult to argue that human societies cannot persist without some degree of integration—otherwise they would not be systems—Merton viewed the *degree of integration* in a system as an issue to be *empirically* determined. To assume, however subtly, that a high degree of functional unity must exist in a social system is to define away the important theoretical and empirical questions: What levels of integration exist for different systems? What various types of integration can be discerned? Are varying degrees of integration evident for different segments of a system? And, most importantly, what variety of processes leads to different levels, forms, and types of integration for different spheres of social systems? Merton believed that beginning analysis with the postulate of "functional unity" or system integration can divert attention away not only from these questions but also from the varied and "disparate consequences of a given social or cultural item (usage, belief, behavior pattern, institutions) for diverse social groups and for individual members of these groups."[2]

Instead of the postulating functional unity, analysis should be on varying types, forms, levels, and spheres of social integration and the varying consequences items for integrating various segments of social systems. In this way, Merton sought to direct functional analysis away from concern with total systems and toward an emphasis on how different patterns of social organization within more inclusive social systems are created, maintained, and changed, not only by the requisites of the total system but also by interaction among sociocultural items within systemic wholes.

**2. The Issue of Functional Universality.** One result of emphasis on functional unity was for some early anthropologists to assume that if a social item exists in an ongoing system, it *must* therefore have positive consequences for the integration of the social system. This assumption tended to result in tautologous statements: A system exists; an item is a part of the system; therefore, the item is positively functional for the maintenance of the system. How do we know this item has positive functional consequences? Because the social system exists.

Merton reasoned that, if an examination of empirical systems is undertaken, it is clear that there is a wider range of empirical possibilities. First, items can be not only positively functional for a system or another system item but also dysfunctional for either particular items or the systemic whole. Second, some consequences, whether functional or dysfunctional, are intended and recognized by system incumbents and are thus manifest, whereas other consequences are not intended or recognized and are therefore

---

[2]Merton, *Social Theory and Social Structure* (1968), cited in note 1, pp. 81–82.

latent. Thus, in contrast to Malinowski and Radcliffe-Brown, Merton proposed the analysis of diverse consequences or functions of sociocultural items—whether positive or negative, manifest or latent—"for individuals, for subgroups, and for the more inclusive social structure and culture."[3] In turn, the analysis of varied consequences requires calculating a "net balance of consequences" of items for each other and more inclusive systems. In this way, Merton visualized contemporary functional thought as compensating for the excesses of earlier forms of functionalism that only examined parts of a system that were functional for the system as a whole. For Merton, then, contemporary functionalism should be more open to examining diverse functional consequences of sociocultural forms, whether for positive or negative effects and whether for their consequences on each other or the systemic whole.

**3. The Issue of Indispensability.** Somewhat out of context and unfairly, Merton quoted Malinowski's assertion that every cultural item "fulfills some vital function, has some task to accomplish, represents an indispensable part within a working whole"[4] as simply an extreme statement of two interrelated issues in functional analysis: (1) Do social systems have functional requisites or needs that must be fulfilled? (2) Are certain crucial structures indispensable for fulfilling these functions?

In response to the first question, Merton provided a tentative "yes," but with an important qualification: The functional requisites must be established empirically for specific systems. For actual groups or whole societies, it is possible to ascertain the "conditions necessary for their survival," and it is of theoretical importance to determine which structures, through what specific processes, have consequences for these conditions. But to assume a system of universal requisites adds little to theoretical analysis. To stress that certain functions must be met in *all* systems pushes observers to describe only those processes in social systems that meet these presumably universal system requisites. For Merton contended, it is more desirable to describe cultural and social patterns as a whole and, then and only then, assess their various consequences in meeting the specific needs of different segments of concrete empirical systems.

Merton's answer to the second question is emphatic: Empirical evidence makes the assertion that only certain structures can fulfill system requisites obviously false. Examination of the empirical world reveals quite clearly that alternative structures can exist to fulfill basically the same requisites in both similar and diverse systems. This led Merton to postulate the importance in functional analysis of concern with various types of "functional alternatives,"

---

[3]Ibid., p. 84.

[4]This quote is from an article in the *Encyclopaedia Britannica* in which Malinowski argued against ethnocentrism. His more scholarly work (see Chapter 2) is much less extreme. See also Turner and Maryanski, *Functionalism* (cited in note 1), for a more balanced analysis of Malinowski's work.

or "functional equivalents," and "functional substitutes" within social systems. In this way, functional analysis would not view the social items of a system as indispensable and thereby would avoid the tautological trap of assuming that items must exist to ensure the continued existence of a system. Furthermore, in looking for functional alternatives, analytical attention would be drawn to questions about the range of items that could serve as functional equivalents. If these questions are to be answered adequately, analysts should then determine why a particular item was selected from a range of possible alternatives, leading to questions about the "structural context" and "structural limits" that might circumscribe the range of alternatives and account for the emergence of one item over another.

Merton believed examining these interrelated questions would thus facilitate the separate analysis of the causes and consequences of structural items. By asking why one particular structure, instead of various alternatives, had emerged, analysts would not forget to document the specific processes leading to an item's emergence as separate from its functional consequences. In this way, the danger of assuming that items must exist to fulfill system needs would be avoided.

In questioning the basic assumptions of early functionalism and, by extension, the functionalism of Talcott Parsons, Merton formulated alternative postulates that advocate a concern for the multiple consequences of sociocultural items for one another and for more inclusive social wholes, without assumptions of functional needs or imperatives. Rather, functional analysis must specify (1) the social patterns under consideration, whether a systemic whole or some subpart; (2) the various types of consequences of these patterns for empirically established survival requisites; and (3) the processes whereby some patterns rather than others exist and have the various consequences for one another and for systemic wholes.

## An Alternative Protocol for Functional Analysis

To ascertain the causes and consequences of particular structures and processes, Merton insisted that functional analysis begin with "sheer description" of individual and group activities. In describing the patterns of interaction and activity among units under investigation, we can discern clearly the social items to be subjected to functional analysis. Such descriptions can also provide a major clue to the functions performed by such patterned activity. For these functions to become more evident, however, additional steps are necessary.

The first step is for investigators to indicate the principal alternatives that are excluded by the dominance of a particular pattern. Such description of the excluded alternatives indicates the structural context from which an observed pattern first emerged and is now maintained—thereby offering further clues about the functions or consequences the item might have for other items and perhaps for the systemic whole. The second analytical step beyond sheer description involves an assessment of the meaning, or mental and emotional significance, of the activity for group members. Description of these meanings can offer some indication of the motives behind the activities of the individuals involved and thereby shed some tentative light on the manifest functions of an activity. These descriptions require a third analytical step of discerning some array of motives for conformity or for deviation among participants, but these motives must not be confused with either the objective description of the pattern or the subsequent assessment of the functions served by the pattern. Yet by understanding the configuration of motives for conformity and deviation among actors, an assessment of the psychological needs served (or not served) by a pattern can be understood—offering an additional clue to the various functions of the pattern under investigation. But focusing on the meanings and motives of those involved in an activity can skew analysis away from unintended or latent consequences of the activity. Thus, a final analytical step describing the patterns under investigation reveals regularities not recognized by participants but appearing to have consequences for both the individuals involved and other central patterns or regularities in the system. In this way, analysis will be attuned to the latent functions of an item.

Merton assumed that, by following each of these steps, it would be possible to assess the net balance of consequences of the pattern under investigation, as well as to determine some of the independent causes of the item. These steps ensure that a proper functional inquiry will ensue because postulates of functional unity, assumptions of survival requisites, and convictions about indispensable parts do not precede the analysis of social structures and processes. On the contrary, attention is drawn only to observable patterns of activity, the structural context in which the focal pattern emerged and persists despite potential alternatives, the meaning of these patterns for actors involved, the actors' motives for conformity and deviation, and the implications of the particular pattern for unrecognized needs of individuals and other items in the social system. Thus, with this kind of preliminary work, functional analysis will avoid the logical and empirical problems of previous forms of functionalism. And in this way, functional analysis can provide an understanding of the causes and consequences of system parts for one another and for more inclusive system units.[5]

Figure 5.1 recapitulates the essential elements of Merton's strategy. First, only empirical units are to be analyzed, and the part and the social context of the part must be clearly specified. Then the task is to establish the particular survival requisites of the empirical system—that is, what is necessary for this particular empirical system to survive. By assessing the functions or consequences of an item's meeting or not meeting these needs, we can achieve insight into the nature of a part and its social contexts. In addition to this structural analysis must come an analysis of the meaning for participants, particularly the psychological needs served or not served by participation in

---

[5]Ibid., p. 136.

**Figure 5.1**   Merton's Net Functional Balance Analysis

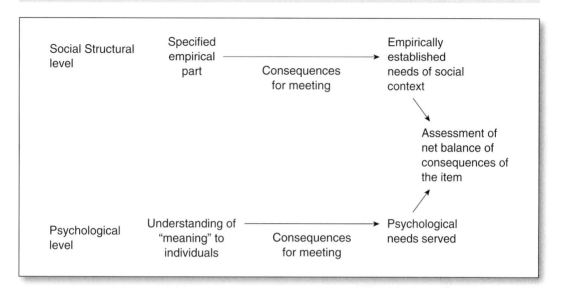

a structure. In this way, we can assess the net balance of consequences of an item at diverse levels of social organization.

## The Call for Theories of the "Middle Range"

In Merton's view, theories of *the middle range* offer more theoretical promise than do grand functional schemes. These middle-range theories are couched at a lower level of abstraction and reveal clearly defined and operationalized concepts that are incorporated into statements about a limited range of phenomena. Although middle-range theories are abstract, they are also connected to the empirical world, thus encouraging the research so necessary for the clarification of concepts and reformulation of theoretical generalizations. Without this interplay between theory and research, Merton contended, analytical theoretical schemes like those in functionalism (see Chapter 1 and Figure 1.6) will remain suggestive congeries of concepts, which are incapable of being refuted, whereas, on the other hand, empirical research will remain unsystematic, disjointed, and of little utility in expanding a body of sociological knowledge. Thus, by following a middle-range strategy, the concepts and propositions of sociological theory will become more tightly organized as theoretically focused empirical research forces clarification, elaboration, and reformulation of the concepts and propositions of each middle-range theory.

From this growing clarity in theories directed at a limited range of phenomena and supported by empirical research can eventually come the more encompassing theoretical schemes. Merton reasoned that, although it is necessary to concentrate energies on constructing limited theories that inspire research, theorists must also be concerned with "consolidating the special theories into a more general set of concepts and mutually consistent propositions."[6] The special theories of sociology must therefore be formulated with an eye toward what they can offer more general sociological theorizing. However, just how these middle-range theories should be formulated to facilitate their eventual consolidation into a more general theory poses a difficult analytical problem, for which Merton had a ready solution: A form of functionalism should be used in formulating middle-range theories.

Such functional theorizing should take the form of a paradigm that allows easy specification and elaboration of relevant concepts, while encouraging systematic revision and reformulation as empirical findings would dictate. Conceived in this way, Merton believed that functionalism could build not only middle-range theories but also the grand theoretical schemes that would someday subsume such middle-range theories. Thus, for Merton, functionalism represents a strategy for ordering concepts and for sorting significant from insignificant social processes.[7]

In the end, functional theorists ignored Merton's protocol, and some began to call for a neo-functionalism where the notion of functional requisites was abandoned, but not the focus on macro-level phenomena.[8] Instead, Merton's protocol was used to criticize all functionalist theory, and this criticism has followed general theories per se for the last fifty years. Unlike Merton, this criticism of grand theories is also used as an indictment of scientific theorizing in sociology—as we will see many points in the chapters to come.

## Jonathan Turner's Critique of Grand Functional Theorizing

While some sociologists still employ a functionalism that invokes notions of system requisites and, like Parsons, seeks to build a grand analytical scheme,[9]

---

[6]Merton, *Social Theory and Social Structure* (1957), p. 10

[7]See Turner and Maryanski, *Functionalism* (cited in note 1), pp. 65–68 for details.

[8]For example, see *Neofunctionalism*, edited by Paul Colomy (Brookfield, VT: Edward Elgar, 1990). See also Jeffrey C. Alexander, ed., *Neofunctionalism* (Beverly Hills, CA: Sage, 1985); Jeffrey C. Alexander and Paul Colomy, "Toward Neofunctionalism," *Sociological Theory* 3, no. 2 (Fall 1985): pp. 11–23; "Neofunctionalism Today: Restructuring a Theoretical Tradition," in *Frontiers of Social Theory*, ed. George Ritzer (New York: Columbia University Press, 1990); and Paul Colomy, ed., *Functionalist Sociology: Classic Statements* (London: Edward Elgar, 1990). Alexander along with Paul Colomy argued for a neofunctionalsim that, in essence, abandoned the notion of functional requisites—which are the hallmark of this perspective. Instead, focus should be on structural differentiation and culture, which tended to be the empirical referents of most functionalist schemes, as is evident in both Parsons' and Luhmann's approaches summarized in Chapters 3 and 4, respectively. There is some merit for this call to abandon requisites because they are the source of many of the problems with functional analysis.

[9]The predecessors of this book were the seven editions of *The Structure of Sociological Theory* (Homewood, IL: Dorsey Press, 1974 being the first edition with subsequent editions published by Wadsworth and Cengage). In this first edition, pp. 46–58, I have a much more

this form of functional analysis has virtually disappeared over the last few decades. Some might argue that functional analysis itself has disappeared since this perspective is defined by invoking notions of functional needs and requisites necessary for social system survival. Indeed, most of the criticisms leveled at functionalism tended to follow from of the overemphasis in all functional approaches on the needs or requisites that elements of social systems meet or fulfill. If such is in fact the case, then Merton's call for a more empirical and middle range analysis of functional requisites was not likely to quell the criticisms of *any* form of functionalism. As a result, Merton's famous (for the time) protocol for a "new" empirically based form of functional analysis was never really followed. There are, of course, many researchers and theorists engaged in middle-range theorizing, but these efforts do not evidence functionalist trappings. Merton was correct in some of his criticisms, but let me cast them in a somewhat different light that reflects the consensus of opinion among critics during the last decades of the last century. Then, we can see if there is a way to get around these criticisms.

## The Codification of Criticisms of Functional Theorizing

Like Merton, but with a different emphasis, there were three overlapping criticism of functional theorizing. First, functional theories often become an illegitimate teleology where consequences cause the emergence of those processes that bring about these consequences. That is, end states cause the creation of those very structures and processes that lead to these end states. Second, these theories are also tautological and engage in circular reasoning. And third, they connote an overly orderly social world that underanalyzes conflict and contradiction in societies. Each of these three mainstream criticisms is discussed below.

1. **Illegitimate Teleologies**. An illegitimate teleology exists when the outcome or end state causes the very processes that bring about this end state. For example, Émile Durkheim often implied that the need for integration inevitably created the structural and cultural forces that brought about this integration. Or, Parsons implicitly argued that a functional requisite, such as adaptation, somehow causes the very sociocultural formations that meet needs for systemic adaptation. When such statements are made, they are not an illegitimate teleology per se, but when the processes and mechanisms by which functional outcomes cause the structures that bring about these outcomes are not specified, then the argument becomes an illegitimate teleology. Without some specification of the processes involved, it is reasonable to ask: How can what occurs at $time_2$ create the structures at $time_1$? Thus, many functionalist explanations bordered on being an illegitimate teleology and hence were highly suspect.

---

detailed analysis with full references to the relevant philosophical works, and so, it might be useful to consult this 1974 edition, which is in most research libraries on college campuses.

2. **Tautologies**. As Merton noted, many functional explanations become circular, and hence tautological. Social structures within a larger system are said to be functional for the system, and how do we know that such is the case? Because the system exists and is functioning. Or, how do I know that a system part is meeting needs for, say, adaptation? Because the system is surviving, and hence its needs for survival are being met. Without a clearer understanding of what would, and would not, constitute survival, or what would be adaptive, it is difficult to determine if a structure or part is meeting needs for adaptation and hence system survival. Moreover, it is also necessary to know just how, through what causal processes, a part meets needs for survival. Simply assuming that, if a part exists, it *must* promote survival and adaptation explains little. Such arguments bypass concern with how the part came into existence and how it operates. To assert that a part meets a functional requisite thus bypasses the kinds of explanations necessary in sociological analysis of a sociocultural formation. Moreover, the tendency of many functional explanations to posit not only tautologies but also illegitimate teleologies made functional explanations to seem politically conservative and supportive of the status quo.

3. **The Image of Social Reality.** As early as 1958, Ralf Dahrendorf[10] codified the growing criticism Parsons' functionalism into an argument that the image of society connoted by functionalism is like all "utopian" arguments: not real and, hence, a gross distortion of how social reality actually operates. Dahrendorf accused Parsons of portraying a world that (a) reveals no developmental history, (b) displays a high degree of integration among its components, (c) reveals consensus over values, ideologies, and norms, and (d) operates smoothly because of mechanisms that sustain the status quo. Like all utopian thought, the world is and will be perfect. Harmony, consensus, cooperation, and integration will prevail for all times and places. Conflict, change, exploitation, suppression, contradictions, deviance, discord, and other disintegrative states are not given conceptual prominence. Structures are emphasized for what they do to sustain the system rather than how they might tear this system apart—as is so evident in human affairs and history.

This criticism struck a responsive cord throughout sociology, and even when Parsons sought to address criticism (a) above, he was pilloried for presenting a stage model of evolution in which societies were seen as marching toward the Western democratic ideal. Some of these criticisms were overdrawn, but they did have some merit, and in the 1960s—a period of conflict and change in many societies—they were effective in sending many otherwise functional theorists into hiding, with the consequence that with Parsons' death in the late 1970s, functional theorizing appeared dead, except for a few strongholds in the United States and Europe. But, was the essence of functional theorizing really gone forever? Or, had it simply changed its vocabulary and added a few conceptual refinements?

---

[10]Ralf Dahrendorf, "Out of Utopia: Toward a Reorientation of Sociological Analysis," *American Journal of Sociology* 64 (1958): pp. 115–27.

## The Rebirth of Functional Theory in New Guises

As Figure 1.6 in Chapter 1 emphasizes, analytical schemes are typically more philosophical than explanatory. They give an image of reality, highlighting some of its key properties without explaining how they came about or how they work. For an abstract analytical scheme to become more theoretical, it needs to be converted into propositions and analytical models that explain how the social world operates. When I first encountered functionalism, ignorant initially of the many criticisms, I found it fascinating because everything had its place in the larger system of categories denoting the essence of social reality. I have found, as an aside, that students all over the world, when first learning about functionalism, reacted much as I did. For example, a decade ago, I asked a class of Chinese students to whom I had given a set of lectures on various theories the following question: Which theory do you like the best? They were almost in complete agreement that functional theorizing was their favorite.

Even as I began to accept some of the criticisms of Parsons analytical scheme as a big category system, I still found many elements of this scheme intriguing, particularly the notion of *generalized symbolic media* and the exchanges among functional sectors in Talcott Parsons' AGIL scheme (see pp. 60–62 and Figure 3.4 on page 58); I could describe the structure and dynamics of social institutions in a society by simply laying out the interchanges among institutions at different locations in the AGIL scheme. Each institutional system—e.g., economy and polity—had its respective place in one of the four quadrants (e.g., economy and polity in, respectively, the adaptive and goal-attainment sectors of a society), and their basic relationship involved exchanges of symbolic media. No one has ever noticed in the three books[11] that I have written on institutions that I am using Parsons' AGIL scheme to trace the structure and inter-connections among institutions during the course of societal evolution from simple to more complex forms. I have gotten away with this subterfuge because, by the time I was writing, evolutionary theory was no longer stigmatized—in fact, it had made a big comeback in the late 1960s and 1970s—and because I never mention or even suggest that there are universal functional requisites.

To overcome the inherent problems in functional analysis, it is critical to drop the notion of functional requisites. Doing so, however, removes what makes functional analysis so intriguing: an emphasis of what it takes for a social system to survive in its environment. Once the notion of requisites is taken away, one of the most interesting features of functionalism is lost. Thus, we need to see how we can restore, in a less problematic way, some idea of what it takes for a social system to survive in its environment, without invoking the problems enumerated by Merton and me above.

---

[11]Jonathan H. Turner, *Patterns of Social Organization* (New York: McGraw-Hill, 1972); *The Institutional Order* (New York: Longman, 1997); *Human Institutions: A Theory of Societal Evolution* (Boulder, CO: Rowan and Littlefied, 2002).

We also need to change the mode of theorizing from an analytical scheme, as summarized in Chapter 1. One important change is to reduce the amount of categorizing; the best way to do this is to have a minimalist conceptual scheme that classifies the relatively few basic dimensions and domains of the social universe. For, one of many of the problems with Parsons' scheme is that he kept *adding* categories as he tried to explain ever-more phenomena, including the course of societal evolution and the place of human action within the larger biological, physico-chemical, and telic universes (see Figure 3.6 on page 65).

Finally, without using a complex analytical scheme as the explanatory tool, it is necessary to develop (a) analytical models that trace causal connections among basic social forces and (b) systems of propositions or laws about the fundamental and timeless properties and processes of the social universe. When all of these tasks are undertaken, it becomes possible to obviate the inherent problems in functional theory and convert it to a true scientific theory, as will be more fully outlined in Chapter 9 where I lay out in more detail the evolutionary theory that I have developed on macrodynamic processes in the social world.

## An Outline of What Is Needed to Reinvigorate Functional Theorizing

**Getting Around the Problems of Functional Needs/Requisites.** Functional analysis is used in other fields, particularly in physiology and medicine, where it is commonplace to talk about the function of this or that organ and system for the maintenance of health in the human body. Indeed, functional analysis in sociology was born from the organismic analogy proposed by Comte (see pp. 35–36 in Chapter 1) and later carried forward by Spencer (see pp. 37–39 in Chapter 2). What is implicit in all uses of the notion *function* in medicine and biology are the *dynamics of selection*. The implicit argument goes like this: In the distant past as species were evolving, natural selection and the other forces of evolution (mutations, gene flow, and genetic drift; see Chapters 6 and 8) operated to transform physiology of organisms because these changes increased the fitness or level of adaptation of populations of organisms to their environment. These mechanisms were not known when Comte was still writing, and Spencer with his famous phrase "survival of the fittest" hinted at the notion of natural selection almost a decade before the publication of Charles Darwin's *On The Origin of Species.* And Durkheim explicitly adopted Darwin's ideas and emphasized that large, densely-settled populations would reveal considerable conflict for resources that, in turn, would cause differentiation. Durkheim, however, just assumed that the need or requisite for integration among differentiated social units would cause the mechanisms of integration to evolve—an illegitimate teleology because Durkheim did not specify how and through what processes the mechanism resulting in integration actually evolved from the need for integration.

It turns out that the resolution to the problems in Durkheim's and most functional analyses can be found, at least implicitly, in Spencer's functional approach. For Spencer, the functional requisites he posited for production, distribution, reproduction, and regulation (through power) generate a different kind of selection than just natural selection fueled by competition for resources among social and biological organisms under conditions of density in an ecological niche (see Chapters 6 and 7 for theories developed using the idea of natural selection in the biological sense). There is another kind of selection that, at various times, I have called *functional selection* or *Spencerian selection* (as is emphasized in Chapter 9, I sometimes call applications of Darwinian natural selection in the social sciences *Durkheimian selection* because he was the first sociologist to use this notion as a basic force driving social organization). What Spencer implicitly argued is that production, distribution, reproduction, and regulation generate "selection pressures" on a population to find solutions to problems associated with production, distribution, reproduction, and regulation. Rather than seeing these as functional requisites, a subtle but critical redirection of emphasis is required. These are fundamental forces of the social universe, and their valences vary. When their valences are high, they pose problems of producing enough and distributing resources, problems of reproducing social structures and humans occupying them, or problems in coordinating and control through power (regulations) members of a population. These problems can be viewed as *selection pressures* that force individual and collective actors to search for solutions to these problems by borrowing, by planning and innovation, or by virtue of trial and error. These solutions almost always involve developing new sociocultural formations that will reduce the valences and hence selection pressures from these forces—that is, production, reproduction, distribution, and regulation—on members of a population. Thus, what were once functional requisites are converted into basic forces of the social universe that, like gravity in the physical universe, drive the formation of structures. These forces push on actors to find solutions to problems, often in the absence of density among actors or the existence of any sociocultural formations that can deal with these problems. As their valences increase, these forces individually or collectively generate selection pressures to which actors try to respond since their survival or the survival of their cultures and social structures depends upon finding new sociocultural formations that can meet these selection pressures. There is no guarantee, however, that actors will be successful in creating new structures or cultural systems that effectively respond to these selection pressures, as the history of societal collapse so readily documents.

Thus, what I have done is put the notion of *selection* back at the center of analysis, and selection is a powerful force in human social organization. Older notions of requisites give a sense for what the fundamental forces pushing on actors are; however, we do not need to see these as needs or end states but simply as part of the social universe. There are a limited number of such forces; in my scheme, there are only five: population (growth or decline), production, distribution, regulation, and reproduction. These are always present when humans organize, but with population growth, they all increase and exert pressures on individual and collective actors to discover and build up new kinds of sociocultural units or formations that can deal with rising valences and selection pressures from these forces. Figure 5.2 summarizes in broad contours my argument.

Now let me turn to how to build a simple analytical scheme denoting the fundamental properties of the social universe, at least for the purposes of sociological analysis. This scheme is outlined in Figure 5.3. The social universe unfolds at the macro, meso, and micro levels. These are more than analytical distinctions; the three levels of reality are ways the social world actually unfolds. The macro and micro universes are formed by distinctive forces that push on actors who build up corporate units and categoric units at the meso level; these meso-level units are, in turn, the building blocks of the macro realm. Thus, as actors respond to selection pressures from population growth and decline as these potentially generate problems of production, distribution, regulations, and reproduction, they seek to build corporate units (I am ignoring categoric units for my purposes here) that can meet these selection pressures. These actors must be entrepreneurial, but there is no guarantee that they will succeed. They are simply under Spencerian selection pressures to create these new kinds of corporate units that can be linked together to form institutional domains such as economy, polity, kinship, education, religions, law, and so on.

Figure 5.3 tells us the basic properties of the social universe, when stripped to the barest number. This category scheme is not a theory; rather, the theory is about the dynamics of each of the sociocultural formations outlined in Table 5.3. At the meso level, the dynamics of corporate and categoric units need to be explained as responses to forces driving actors at the macro and micro levels of social organization. At the macro level, the dynamics of institutional domains, stratification systems, societies, and inter-societal systems need to be explained. And, at the micro level, the forces and dynamics driving encounters and the relations among these, need to be explained by a theory of interpersonal processes. Complexity in the theory does not inhere in the typology in Figure 5.3 but in the propositions that describe the dynamics of the basic dimensions and structures of the social universe that are portrayed in the diagram.

Theory will thus be a series of sociological laws on macro and micro forces, on the selection pressures that they generate, and on the emerging dynamics of encounters, corporate and categoric units, institutional domains, stratification systems, societies, and inter-societal systems. The result is a theory that articulates a series of sociological laws (and analytical models) that can be tested, a theory that covers all of the basic structures that organize the micro, meso, and macro realms of the social universe, a theory that makes linkages among these levels, a theory that is evolutionary without being locked into stages but only change over time, a theory that still captures what made the notion of requisites so appealing, and most significantly, a theory that is explanatory (via propositions and analytical models) rather than classificatory. For more details, see my three-volume *Theoretical Principles of Sociology*[12] and Chapter 9. Functionalism can, in a

---

[12]Jonathan H. Turner, *Theoretical Principles of Sociology* (New York: Springer 2010–2013),

**Figure 5.2**    Turner's Analysis of Macrodynamic Forces and the Evolution of Sociocultural Formations

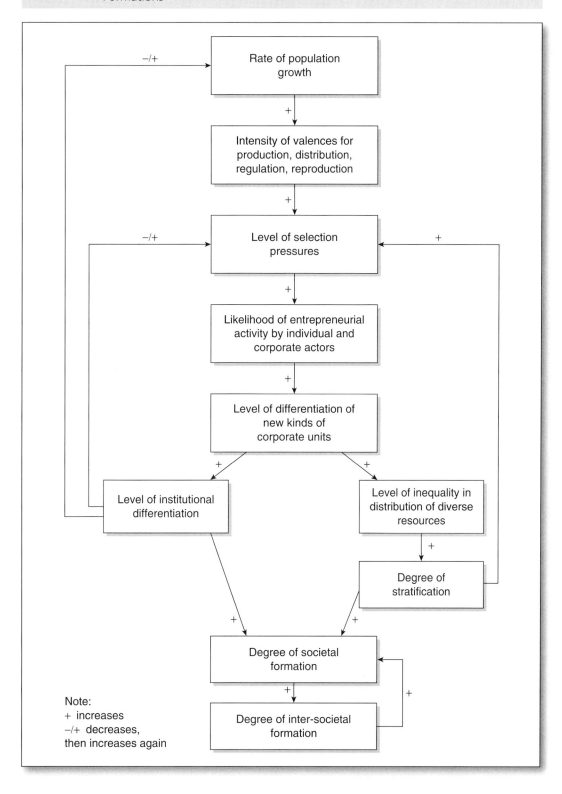

**Figure 5.3**   A Simple Conceptual Scheme

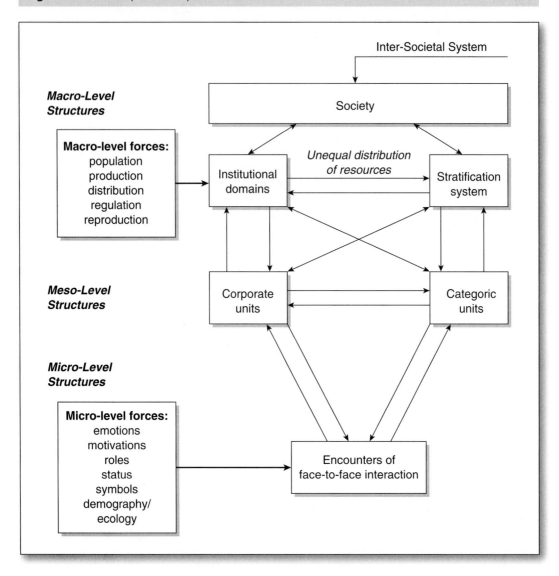

manner, be saved from itself, but it no longer looks like most functionalist schemes that build up a complex analytical (Parsons) scheme or a suggestive but vague discursive (Luhmann) scheme.

---

three volumes on macro, meso, and micro dynamic processes. Note the emphasis on *principles* or laws that explain the dynamics of each of the three realms of the universe. It is a theory inspired by functionalism, at least for the macrodynamic realm, but a theory that jettisons the baggage of functionalism while trying to retain in a new form the very things that made functionalism an intriguing approach.

# PART II

# Evolutionary and Ecological Theorizing

## CHAPTER 6

# The Rise of Evolutionary and Ecological Theorizing

S ociology was born in the nineteenth century when biology was fast becoming the dominant science. The idea of evolution was in the air, and despite the power of religious orthodoxy to repress nonbiblical speculation about the origins of humans, the Age of Science had its own powerful momentum. Thoughts about the mechanisms accounting for the great diversity of species on earth, including humans, were not going to be repressed, whatever the risks. Indeed, one key mechanism was staring scholars in the face because, after all, animal and plant breeders had been engaged in unnatural selection for centuries.

When Charles Darwin, under pressure of being scooped by Alfred Wallace, finally published his decades-old conclusions in *On the Origin of Species*,[1] biology was changed forever. The idea of evolution by natural selection not only provided a simple explanation for speciation of life forms, but it also led to a search for other mechanisms creating the variations on which natural selection works—mechanisms already discovered by Gregor Mendel[2] that had to be rediscovered decades later. Equally significant, theorizing in sociology began to borrow ideas from biology for a field that eventually became known as ecology.

This borrowing still occurs, and indeed, there is even more excitement today about the prospects for a biologically informed evolutionary sociology

---

[1]Charles Darwin, *On the Origin of Species* (New York: New American Library, 1958; originally published 1859).

[2]Gregor Mendel, "Versuche über pflanzen-hybriden," translated into English in the *Journal of the Rural Horticulture Society* 26 (1901); originally published in 1865.

than there was at the end of the nineteenth century.[3] The central figure in evolutionary theory was, of course, Darwin, but closer to home, Herbert Spencer and Émile Durkheim more directly inspired evolutionary sociology in two senses. First, each posited a stage model of societal evolution, with the level of differentiation from simple to more complex forms being the general direction of societal evolution. Second, each brought into sociology ideas from bio-ecology that were essential to the emergence of ecological analysis in sociology at the turn into the twentieth century and that anticipated the incorporation of Darwinian evolutionary theory into the social sciences over the last three decades. Let us see what each contributed to what is now reemerging as an important new form of theorizing in sociology.

# Herbert Spencer's Contribution to Evolutionary Sociology

## Stage Models of Evolution

Herbert Spencer used his ideas about functional requisites to also build a model of the stages of societal evolution over the long course of human development from hunter-gatherers to industrial societal formations.[4] As outlined in Chapter 2 on the rise of functional theorizing, Spencer posited four basic requisites for the survival of a population: production, reproduction, distribution, and regulation. In order for societies to survive, they must be able to produce goods and services; reproduce members of the population and the structures organizing their activities; distribute information, resources, and members of the population around territories through markets and infrastructures; and regulate members of a population and the structures organizing their activities so as to maintain coordination and control. As stressed in the last chapter, Spencer implicitly saw these needs or requisites of survival of a population in its environment as generating "selection pressures" on actors to create social structures that would meet these needs and thus increase the fitness of a population and the society organizing its members' lives.

Because meeting these functional requisites was so essential to survival of a population and a society, evolution of a society could be traced by patterns

---

[3]See, for example, a coordinated series of essays by diverse theorists in Peter Weingart, Sandra D. Mitchell, Peter J. Richerson, and Sabine Maasen, eds., *Human by Nature: Between Biology and the Social Sciences* (New York: Lawrence Erlbaum, 1997).

[4]Herbert Spencer, *The Principles of Sociology* (New York: Appleton-Century, [1874–96]1898). For a recent reprint and long introduction by me, see *Principles of Sociology*, four volumes (New Brunswick, NJ: Transaction Publishers, 2002). This multivolume work is, in essence, an analysis of the mechanisms of societal evolution from simple to complex societies, and it was certainly the most detailed of all stage models well into the twentieth century in both its empirical detail and theoretical sophistication.

of sociocultural differentiation within and between these four requisites. That is, the movement from a simple, homogeneous society has been a process of differentiation of members in a society and the structures organizing their activities along four great axes: production, reproduction, distribution, and regulation. By differentiating new structures as these functional needs generated selection pressures, a population and the society in which this population lives becomes more fit and, hence, able to sustain itself in its biophysical and sociocultural environments. Figure 6.1 communicates Spencer's vision of societies evolving through various stages along three great axes—which is really four axes because Spencer included production and reproduction under the heading "operative." Thus, selection pressures from regulatory, distributive, and operative (production and reproduction combined) push upon individuals and collective actors to build new structures so as to meet these need states. This pressure came from the master variable in Spencer's scheme: population growth. Thus, the more a population grows and the greater its rate of growth and its diversity, the greater will be selection pressures emanating from production, reproduction, distribution, and regulation. Members of a society will be under pressures to produce more; to reproduce more members in more complex and diverse social structures; to find new ways to distribute resources across territories and among larger numbers and more diverse peoples; and to regulate the larger population and the new, differentiated structures organizing their activities. The empirical detail offered by Spencer was extensive and remarkably accurate, and the conceptualization of stages corresponds to what most subsequent stage models developed decades later, although we would need to add the current post-industrial (some would say postmodern; see Chapter 32) stage of societal development as arising out of trebly compound societies.

Like all evolutionary theorists, Spencer's star had faded dramatically by the time of his death in 1903, and with it went his functionalism, which was only revived in sociology at the midpoint of the twentieth century. When stage model theories of societal evolution began to reemerge in sociology in the 1960s,[5] they looked very much like that developed by Spencer, although few ever gave Spencer much credit because sociologists had stopped reading Spencer by the end of the second decade of the last century.

Yet, Spencer analysis of societal evolution was the best of all among both sociologists and anthropologists at the end of the nineteenth century; thus, he can be credited with providing a model of how to build a stage model of societal evolution. In many implicit ways, this model was highly modern because it had a set of mechanisms driving evolution: population growth as it generates selection pressures with respect to production, reproduction, distribution, and regulation. Spencer also added a conflict theory to this

[5]See, for example, Talcott Parsons, *Societies: Evolutionary and Comparative Perspectives* and his *The System of Modern Societies* (Englewood Cliffs, NJ: Prentice Hall, 1966 and 1971, respectively); Gerhard Lenski, *Power and Privilege* (New York: McGraw Hill 1966, reprinted by the University of North Carolina Press).

**Figure 6.1**   Spencer's Stage Model of Societal Evolution

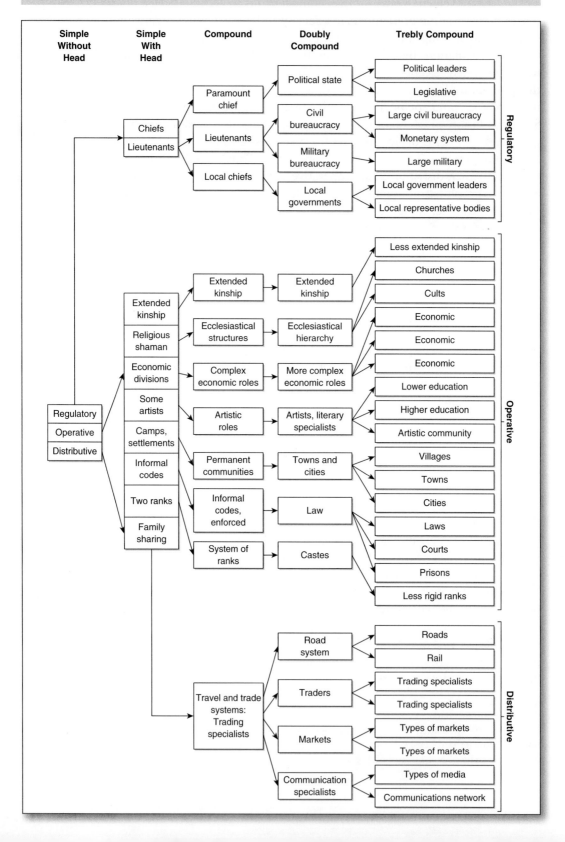

theory, arguing that war had been prime mover of evolution because, as populations grow, they are more likely to come into conflict over resources, and when they go to war, the better organized society generally wins and incorporates members of conquered into its sociocultural formations. The net result is that war had driven much of the movement from simple to ever-more complex societal formations, although Spencer argued that once societies industrialize and develop dynamic markets and infrastructures, war is no longer necessary. Instead, markets and infrastructural development should drive evolution more than war, which, Spencer had contended, destroyed the dynamism of markets.

## Anticipating the Darwinian Evolution

Almost a decade before Darwin published *On the Origin of Species*, Spencer coined the phrase *survival of the fittest*.[6] He used this phrase in a moral and philosophical sense, arguing that the best forms of social organization emerge with unregulated competition among humans, which allows the most fit to survive, thereby elevating the level of society. Obviously, this moral philosophy is highly flawed, but it became a significant argument in the nineteenth and early twentieth century; what became known as *Social Darwinism*[7] was actually more Spencerian in tone. Indeed, Darwin would have turned over in his grave if he knew the extremes to which Spencer's moral philosophy had gone under his name. Yet, in Spencer's more sociological writings, the notion of survival of the fittest is used more to explain war—as a kind of competitive struggle between societies—with the more fit society surviving and the less fit being vanquished or incorporated into the structure of the more fit society, thereby ratcheting up the size and complexity of human societies as they evolved.

Darwin acknowledged Spencer in the preface to his famous book, in which the basic idea of natural selection as the driving force of speciation is developed, but this acknowledgment was perhaps only a courtesy to a well-known social philosopher who was friends with many of Darwin's supporters. Thus, even though Spencer's original conception of evolution as survival of the fittest preceded Darwin's formulation, at least in print, it had little direct impact on the reemergence of biologically inspired thinking in the second half of the twentieth century. Yet, Spencer had made the connection between biology and sociology.

Of course, we must remember that twenty years before Spencer's publication of his moral philosophy, and more than forty years before Spencer

---

[6]Herbert Spencer, *Social Statics: or the Conditions Necessary for Human Happiness Specified, and the First of Them Developed* (New York: Appleton, 1888; originally published in 1852).

[7]Richard Hofstader, *Social Darwinism in American Thought* (Boston: Beacon, 1955).

published his first sociological treatises, Auguste Comte[8] had allied sociology with biology, arguing that in the hierarchy of the sciences sociology would emerge from biology and become the "queen science." Comte was the key figure in reintroducing organismic analogies to sociology. He sought to find the counterparts of cells, tissues, and organs of biological organisms in the structure of society. As we saw in Chapter 2, this argument evolved into functionalism, where theory focuses on the consequences of a social phenomena for the larger "body social" in which they operate. Much later in the 1870s, when Spencer finally turned to sociology[9] (after writing treatises on morals,[10] physics,[11] biology,[12] and psychology),[13] he made the comparison between social and biological organisms more explicit. But Spencer did more than make superficial analogies between biological and social bodies; he proclaimed that sociology was to be the study of *superorganic organisms*[14]— that is, relations among living organisms—and he included more than human organisms in this definition. All species that organize are superorganic and, thus, can be the subject matter of scientific sociology—an idea that has been rediscovered just recently. In making these analogies and assertions about sociology's subject matter, Spencer also developed several modes of analysis that influenced sociological theory in the nineteenth and early twentieth century. In turn, these lines of thinking—though often not acknowledged—anticipated and, to a limited extent, shaped the reemergence of biologically oriented sociological theory.

Another point of emphasis in Spencer's work, but one that was more fully developed by Émile Durkheim twenty years later in 1893, is the Darwinian analogy: Social differentiation, or *social speciation,* is the result of competition among actors for resources; from such competition comes differentiation as those most fit to secure resources in a niche win out, whereas those actors who are less fit change (or die) and seek resources in

---

[8]Auguste Comte, *The Course of Positive Philosophy* (originally published in serial form between 1830 and 1842). More accessible is Harriet Martineau's translation and condensation, published under the title *The Positive Philosophy of August Comte,* 3 volumes (London: Bell and Sons, 1898; originally published in 1854).

[9]Herbert Spencer, *The Principles of Sociology,* 3 volumes (New York: Appleton-Century-Crofts, 1898; originally published in serial form between 1874 and 1896). For a review of Spencer's theoretical principles, see Jonathan H. Turner, *Herbert Spencer: A Renewed Appreciation* (Beverly Hills, CA and London: Sage, 1985).

[10]Herbert Spencer, *Social Statics, or the Conditions Essential to Human Happiness Specified, and the First of Them Developed* (New York: Appleton-Century-Crofts 1888; originally published in 1881)

[11]Herbert Spencer, *First Principles* (New York: A. L. Burt, 1880; originally published in 1862).

[12]Herbert Spencer, *The Principles of Biology,* 2 volumes (New York: Appleton, 1897; originally published in serial form between 1864 and 1867).

[13]Herbert Spencer, *The Principles of Psychology,* 2 volumes (New York: Appleton, 1898; originally published in 1855).

[14]Spencer, *The Principles of Biology* and *The Principles of Sociology* (cited in notes 12 and 13).

other resource niches.[15] This process of seeking resource niches is, then, the driving force of social differentiation and, hence, of societal evolution. For Spencer, as emphasized earlier, growth in size of a population increases competition for resources—an idea that Spencer borrowed from Thomas Malthus' famous essay on population[16]—and sets into motion the selection processes that cause social differentiation and societal evolution.

What we see in Spencer's work, then, is a concern with biological modes of thinking that were emerging throughout the nineteenth century. Spencer himself had, of course, written a multivolume treatise on biology, but far more important for sociological theory was his incorporation of biological analogies and metaphors into thinking about the dynamics of society. Thus, where Comte had been a bit vague in his pronouncements about the connection between biology and sociology, Spencer added considerably more substance and detail to how sociological and biological theories could be blended together.

# Émile Durkheim's Bio-Ecological Analogy

Today, we tend to forget how important a figure Spencer was, not just in the nineteenth-century Europe but in America as well. In the present day, Durkheim is considered the far more imposing figure, and we often give him credit for ideas that, in reality, come from Spencer.[17] But Durkheim made the connection between the Darwinian idea of evolution by natural selection and societal evolution more explicit than Spencer. Thus, as bio-ecological theorizing and evolutionary theory were developing in the early twentieth century, Durkheim became as significant a contributor as Spencer was.

Durkheim's first major work was *The Division of Labor in Society* and, as we saw in Chapter 2, it served as an inspiration for functional theorizing. In analyzing the causes of the division of labor—that is, what forces increase specialization of activities (or social speciation)—Durkheim began to draw from his reading of Darwin:

> Thus, Darwin says that in a small area, opened to immigration, and where, consequently, the conflict of individuals must be acute, there is always to be seen a very great diversity in the species inhabiting it.[18]

---

[15]Émile Durkheim, *The Division of Labor in Society* (New York: Free Press, 1933; originally published in 1893).

[16]Thomas R. Malthus, *An Essay on the Principle of Population as It Affects the Future Improvement of Society* (London: Oxford University Press, 1798).

[17]Durkheim, *The Division of Labor in Society* (cited in note 15).

[18]Ibid., p. 266.

Durkheim then noted that such diversity made the survival of each species less problematic and, indeed, contributed to the well-being of each species. And so, Durkheim posited:

> Men submit to the same law. In the same city, different occupations can coexist without being obliged mutually to destroy one another, for they pursue different objects. The soldier seeks military glory, the priest moral authority, the statesman power, the businessman riches, the scholar scientific renown. Each of them can attain this end without preventing the others from attaining theirs. [19]

Durkheim was seeking an answer to a question that had vexed all social theory since the time of Adam Smith (who, in the eighteenth century, created the basic utilitarian ideas that so dominate economics today): If societies are differentiating, what force is to hold them together? Durkheim's answer became part of his functionalism, but in the previous passage, we can see his effort to paint the division of labor in a benign light. For our purposes, Durkheim's ecological model on the causes of the division of labor is more important than his ultimate answer about what holds society together. Figure 6.2 presents his basic model. In this model, Durkheim argues that those forces that increase the material density of a population—forces such as immigration, population growth, and ecological barriers—and those that reduce the "social space" between individuals—forces like improved transportation and communication technologies—all increase competition. Such competition, in turn, leads to social speciation or the division of labor, which, Durkheim felt, reduced competition and increased cooperation as individuals in different social niches went their own way while exchanging resources with each other.

In a manner more explicit than Spencer, Durkheim argued that population density increases competition for resources, which then leads to social differentiation, but like Spencer, Durkheim argued that this mechanism is ultimately what is responsible for social evolution of society from simple to more complex forms. That is, as populations grow or the social space among members is reduced by new technologies, competition escalates; from competition comes social differentiation and increased societal complexity. Thus, social speciation follows a kind of Darwinian route, except for Durkheim individuals do not die (a possibility held out by Spencer, in contrast). Instead, they seek a new resource niche, and in the process, they differentiate themselves and the structures and culture organizing their activities. Natural selection in the social world is less brutal than for Spencer and Darwin. The key point in all this overlap with Darwin is that sociologists, early on, had seen some of the relationships between biological and sociological models. These were carried forward in sociology by ecological theorizing that began in the early decades of the twentieth century and has

---

[19]Ibid., p. 267.

**Figure 6.2**   Durkheim's Ecological Model of Social Differentiation

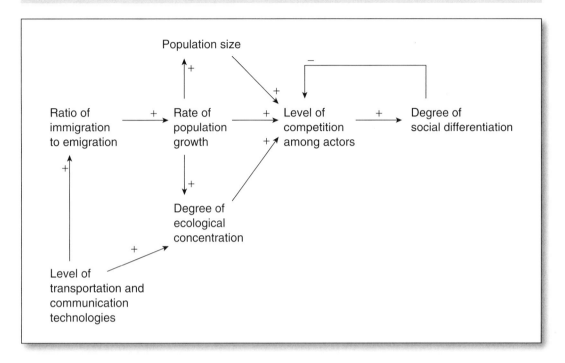

continued to the present, as we will see in Chapter 7. In the second half of the twentieth century, more purely Darwinian ideas began to filter into the social sciences, and so, before examining these more Darwinian movements, it would be wise to pause and highlight the critical insights of Darwin himself.

## Charles Darwin and Natural Selection

I have alluded to Darwin, but let me review how his ideas set the framework not only for nineteenth-century evolutionary theorizing but, more significantly, for the revival of evolutionary theory in the twentieth century. Like Spencer, Darwin was greatly influenced by Malthus' essay on population, especially Malthus' "notion of a natural elimination mechanism." In his early notebooks,[20] for example, Darwin considered the power of the Malthusian force when he wrote that "no structure will last . . . without it[s] . . . adaptation to whole life . . . it will decrease and be driven outwards in the grand crush of population," and "there is a contest . . . and a grain of

———————
[20]Charles Darwin's *Notebooks, 1836–1844: Geology, Transmutation of Species, Metaphysical Enquiries. Notebook E,* transcribed and edited by David Kohn (British Museum, New York: Cornell University Press), p. 395.

sand turns the balance." Coupled with Darwin's observations as the naturalist on the famous voyage of the *Beagle*, where it became clear to him that somewhat different environments create new variants of species, Darwin was led to the concept of natural selection. This was to be the title of his book, but he later settled on the more controversial title *On the Origin of Species*. Darwin held the idea of natural selection for twenty years before he published his treatise; only when Alfred Wallace,[21] who had also been inspired by Malthus, came up with a similar idea to explain evolution did Darwin begin to publish his ideas. Darwin's and Wallace's initial papers were read jointly at the Royal Society, and both argued that the natural world reveals a "struggle" among species and that this competition "selects" for survival those organisms that are better equipped to adapt to the conditions imposed by an environment. As a result, these organisms are more likely than less fit organisms to produce offspring. Thus, the basic assumptions of Darwin's (and Wallace's) model are as follows:

1. Members of any given species reveal variations in their physical and behavioral traits.

2. Members of any given species tend to produce more offspring than can be supported by an environment.

3. Members of any given species must therefore compete with one another and with other species for resources in an environment.

4. Members of a given species revealing those traits that enable them to compete and secure resources will be more likely to survive and produce offspring, whereas those members evidencing traits that are unsuited to competition or ability to secure resources will be less likely to survive and have offspring.

Thus the environment selects those traits of organisms that enable them to compete, secure resources, survive, and reproduce. Evolution is driven by this process of natural selection, as those varying traits of organisms are successively selected by the environment. In this line of argument, an important distinction must be emphasized: Selection operates on an individual organism, whereas evolution involves a population of organisms. That is, the individual organism survives and reproduces, or fails to do so, but it is the population as a whole that evolves. This population consists of all those individual organisms that possess those traits that enable them to survive and reproduce. This distinction is critical for understanding modern evolutionary theory. We must remember, then, that as different individual organisms revealing varying traits are "selected for" by the conditions of the environment, the overall composition of the population of organisms changes, or evolves.

---

[21]See Charles Darwin and Alfred Russell Wallace, *Evolution by Natural Selection* (Cambridge, England: Cambridge University Press, 1958).

We can see an affinity of these ideas to Spencer's famous phrase *survival of the fittest*, but the most direct source of inspiration for modern evolutionary theory in the social sciences was the blending of Darwin's discovery of the mechanism of natural selection with Mendel's overlooked insights into the mechanisms of inheritance. For, despite the power of the concept of natural selection to explain evolution, Darwin's portrayal could not answer some basic questions: What is the source of those variations in organisms that are the objects of natural selection? How are traits passed on from one organism to another? What is the mechanism of inheritance? The answers to these questions sat for thirty-five years in dusty academic journals in the form of Mendel's short manuscripts on the inheritance of characteristics in garden peas.[22] But not until 1900 was the science of genetics born with the rediscovery of Mendel's work and its independent confirmation by Karl Correns in Germany, Hugo de Vries in Holland, and Erich Tschermak in Austria. This synthesis of the notions of natural selection and genetic variation was coupled with additional insights into the forces of evolution in what is called the Modern Synthesis. This initial synthesis was, as we will see, crucial to reconnecting biology and sociology in the twentieth century.

# The Modern Synthesis in Biology[23]

Within biology, Gregor Mendel's insights into the mechanism of inheritance were being developed at about the same time that ecological ideas were being downsized into analyses of urban areas by sociologists. The word *genetics* was coined in 1906 to denote the new discoveries about how inheritance operates. Although these discoveries occurred over a number of decades, they are discussed together here. What is critical is the recognition that an increasing understanding of the mechanisms of inheritance would provide the basis for the Modern Synthesis of evolutionary theory and recent efforts to bring biology back into sociological theory. What, then, were the new insights from genetics? Let us divide them into two types: (1) those pertaining to individual organisms and (2) those dealing with populations of organisms.

## The Genetics of the Individual

Genes[24], or what Mendel[25] had termed *merkmals*, are the basic units of inheritance. The information regarding the transmission of characteristics is

---

[22]Gregor Mendel, "Versuche über pflanzen-hybriden" (cited in note 2).

[23]This section is authored with Alexandra Maryanski.

[24]The term genetics was coined by William Bateson in 1906 as the basic construct to describe individual heredity and variation.

[25]Gregor Mendel, "Versuche über pflanzen-hybriden."

stored here. Genes can be dominant or recessive, and the various combinations of these—as worked out by Mendel—determine what traits will be visible for an organism. Yet, even when not visible, information can still be in the genes and, as a result, emerge in subsequent generations. Genes are strung along thread-shaped bodies, or chromosomes, within the nuclei of cells. Alleles are the alternative or variant forms of a gene that affect the same trait in different ways—for example, potential variations in eye color are alleles (because they affect the variation of the same basic trait). Genotype is the sum of all the alleles making up an individual, including those that are visible and those that are stored in the genes but not manifest. Phenotype refers to the visible traits of an organism that are regulated by genes.

Thus, at the level of the individual, inheritance is regulated by genes. Those genes of an individual that are visibly expressed are its phenotype, whereas the complete collection (both expressed and invisible) of genes and alleles of an individual are its genotype. Differences in the characteristics of individuals result from the information on discrete genes that provide the fund of variation; hence, natural selection is the mechanism by which genetic material is preserved or lost.

## The Genetics of the Population

Selection works on the individual and its phenotype and, as a result, an organism's more inclusive genotype, but the breeding population as a whole evolves. From a genetic point of view, however, it is not so much a population of individual organisms that evolves but, rather, it is a cluster of genotypes. Individual organisms come and go, but what is passed on and remains is their genetic information. Those genes that produce traits facilitating individual organisms' survival in an environment will increase the likelihood that such organisms will survive and produce offspring. From a genetic perspective, then, the genes that survive with the living organisms are simply temporary vessels, carrying a most interesting cargo—genotypes.

As this perspective developed, the concept of *gene pool* was introduced to characterize this shift in emphasis from the individuals who carry the genes to the sum total of their different alleles. A gene pool is thus the pooled sum of all the genotypes in a population of organisms. A species as a whole is the most inclusive gene pool because it contains all the genetic information for those genotypes that have survived, whereas a less inclusive gene pool would be a breeding population in a particular area or region.

What causes changes in the composition of genes in the pool? One obvious force—which, surprisingly, was not initially recognized—is *natural selection.* As some individual organisms (and their phenotypes and genotypes) survive and reproduce, others are selected out, leading to a shift in the composition of the gene pool. Another force changing the gene pool composition is *random mutations,* which add new DNA (the actual codes of information on genes) to the gene pool. A third force is *gene flow,* which results from the movement of individuals to and from different breeding populations (say, for example, intermarriage and offspring among Asians and Caucasians). Yet another force is *genetic drift*, or random changes in gene frequencies in the pool stemming from the fact that a smaller breeding population will be less likely to evidence over time as many duplicate alleles as a larger population. The overall degree of variation in the gene pool is related to the interactions among these forces. Mutations and gene flow increase variation within a breeding population because they add new genetic material. Natural selection normally reduces variation because it weeds out those phenotypes (and genotypes) less suited to an environment. Similarly, genetic drift reduces variation through the random loss of genetic variance available to a small breeding population.

This shift to conceptualizing populations as pools of genes rather than individuals emerged in the twentieth century, although the actual term gene pool was a midcentury formulation.[26] As early as 1907, for instance, G. H. Hardy and W. Weinberg applied the new discoveries about particulate inheritance to the population level.[27] Hardy and Weinberg believed evolution could be conceptualized as "changes in gene frequencies" (later conceptualized as the gene pool). In what became known as the Hardy-Weinberg equilibrium model for assessing the degree of evolution, Hardy and Weinberg presented a decisive argument. If we know the allele frequencies in a population (that is, all the dominant and recessive genes relevant to various traits), we can predict the genotypic frequencies in the next generation, but to do so, we must assume the following: No natural selection is operating; no mutations are produced; no gene flow resulting from migrations of breeding populations is evident; no genetic drift is to be found; no bias in mating can be observed (it is random); and no limits on population size exist (it is infinite). Obviously, such assumptions do not correspond to natural populations in real environments, but they allow us to compute the

---

[26]The term *gene pool* was coined by Dobzhansky in 1950 and became the fundamental construct of population genetics. See Theodosius Dobzhansky, "Mendelian Populations and Their Evolution," *American Naturalist* 14 (1950): pp. 401–18. For further readings on the history of genetics, see Theodosius Dobzhansky, *Genetics and the Origin of Species,* 3rd rev. ed. (New York: Columbia University Press, 1951) and *Mankind Evolving* (New York: Bantam, 1962). See also Mark B. Adams, "From 'Gene Fund' to 'Gene Pool': On the Evolution of Evolutionary Language," *History of Biology* 3 (1979): pp. 241–85 and "The Founding of Population Genetics: Contributions of the Chetvevikov School 1924–1934," *Journal of the History of Biology* 1 (1968): pp. 23–39; Alfred Sturtevant, *A History of Genetics* (New York: Harper & Row, 1965); and James Crow, "Population Genetics History: A Personal View," *Annual Review of Genetics* 21 (1987): pp. 1–22.

[27]Extending Mendel's Laws by deducing the mathematical consequences of a nonblending system of heredity (that is, genes are discrete and do not blend), G. H. Hardy and W. Weinberg laid the cornerstone for population genetics; in turn, the modern science of statistics was born in the study of quantitative genetics. G. H. Hardy, "Mendelian Proportions in Mixed Populations," *Science* 28 (1908): pp. 49–50; W. Weinberg, "Über den Nachweis der Vererbung beim Menschen," *Jh. Ver. Vaterl. Naturk. Wurttemb* 64 (1908): pp. 368–82.

expected distribution of genotypes in the next generation if none of these forces of change in the gene pool is operating. Then, by comparing this idealized computation of gene frequencies with the actual frequencies, we get some indication of how much change or evolution is occurring. If not much difference occurs between the idealized prediction and the actual genotypes in the population, then not much evolution is evident, but if there is a large difference, then the degree of evolution can be measured (by comparing the predicted and actual gene frequencies). What is important about the Hardy-Weinberg Law is that it states that evolution (or a change in gene frequencies) can occur only when variations exist in a population on which selection forces can act. These selective differences among genotypes are what change the gene frequencies.

In the first decade of the twentieth century, this revolution in population genetics was not well integrated with Darwinian views of natural selection as the mechanism of evolution. Curiously, as concepts in genetics emerged, they were often considered to represent an alternative explanation to Darwinian natural selection. Indeed, during the first part of this century, a major anti-Darwinian movement rejecting natural selection as the force behind evolution emerged with opposition so negative that one noted scholar could write, "We are now standing at the deathbed of Darwinism." By the 1920s, even major textbooks on evolution carried forth an anti-selectionist position. And for many scholars, it was already a foregone conclusion that the Darwinian revolution had passed and that "a new generation has grown up that knows not Darwin."[28]

The modern synthetic theory of evolution began to emerge from the revival of Darwinian notions of natural selection and their eventual coupling with genetics. At this point, the basic ideas of sociobiology were first articulated. And sociobiology was the first of the Darwinian-inspired approaches, after human ecology, to begin to penetrate the social sciences, although as we will see, sociologists reacted violently to the contention that biology could explain sociocultural phenomena.

# The Rise of Ecological Theory in Sociology

The period between World Wars I and II cannot be noted for great theoretical progress in sociology. Even as the last works of the early masters began to appear or be translated into English, theoretical sociology did not develop in the same way as it had during sociology's first one hundred

---

[28]See Eberhart Dennert, *At the Deathbed of Darwinism*, trans. E. G. O'Hara and John Peschges (Burlington, Iowa: German Literary Board, 1904), p. 4. Also see J. H. Bennett, *Natural Selection, Heredity, and Eugenics* (Oxford: Clarendon, 1983), p. 1; Garland Allen, "Hugo de Vries and the Reception of the Mutation Theory," *Journal of the History of Biology* 2 (1969): pp. 56–87; and Sewall Wright, "Genetics and Twentieth-Century Darwinism," *American Journal of Human Genetics* 12 (1960): pp. 24–38.

years. Part of the reason for this dearth of theoretical activity resides in the efforts to make sociology a more rigorous research discipline, especially in America where sociologists concentrated on ethnographic studies or on developing quantitative survey techniques. As a consequence, theoretical ideas developed during this interwar period were almost always connected to empirical work on particular topics. One of the most famous efforts to blend theory and research was in what is often termed the "Chicago School," which derives its name from the activities of a group of sociologists at the University of Chicago.

One facet of the Chicago School was its study of urban problems; the city of Chicago became the laboratory for conducting research on these problems. Louis Wirth was perhaps the key figure in developing a more theoretically informed analysis of urban Chicago, and he reintroduced ideas that had been at the center of Durkheim's and Spencer's analyses of social differentiation. But in Wirth's approach, these big ideas about society and human evolution were downsized to study the dynamics of urban areas. Wirth believed urban development could be understood by studying the size and density of urban populations because these influence the diversity and heterogeneity of the population. For example, in his famous essay "Urbanism as a Way of Life,"[29] Wirth argued that a dense population of a certain size inevitably leads to the proliferation of secondary groups, a lessening of the intensity of personal interaction, and increased cultural heterogeneity. These events, he continued, lead to a weakening of family ties and to a subversion of traditional bases of social control, such as religion, common folklore, and shared cultural heritage. There was, then, a social problem bias in Chicago School research, but within this tradition, Wirth and others brought ecological theorizing into the twentieth century and, in essence, kept it alive and available to succeeding generations.

## Borrowing from the Science of Ecology

Thinkers in the Chicago School[30]—Ernest Burgess, Chauncy Harris, Homer Hoyt, Roderick McKenzie, Robert Park, Edward Ullman, Louis

---

[29]Louis Wirth, "Urbanism as a Way of Life," *American Journal of Sociology* 44 (1938): pp. 46–63.

[30]See, for examples, Ernest W. Burgess, "The Growth of the City" in *An Introduction to Sociology*, ed. R. E. Park and E. W. Burgess (Chicago: University of Chicago Press, 1921); Robert E. Park, "Human Ecology," *American Journal of Sociology* 42 (1936): pp. 1–15; Homer Hoyt, *The Structure and Growth of Residential Neighborhoods in American Cities* (Washington, DC: Federal Housing Authority, 1939); Robert E. Park, Ernest Burgess, and Roderick D. McKenzie, *The City* (Chicago: University of Chicago Press, 1925); Chauncy D. Harris and Edward L. Ullman, "The Nature of Cities," *Annals of the American Academy of Political and Social Science* (1945): pp. 789–96; Robert Ardrey, *African Genesis* (New York: Delta, 1961) and *The Territorial Imperative* (New York: Atheneum, 1966).

Wirth, and their students—borrowed quite self-consciously from the emerging subfield of ecology in biology. As Amos Hawley noted:

> In their search for order in the turbulent urban centers of America ... sociologists were stimulated by work then being done by bioecologists. ... Those researchers showed that plant species adapt to their environment by distributing themselves over a localized area in a pattern which enables them to engage in contemporary uses of habitat and resources. That idea opened a vista to an understanding of what was occurring in the burgeoning industrial city. For then it was apparent that various subpopulations were jostling for spatial positions from which they could perform their diverse functions in an unfolding division of labor.[31]

Chicago School ecologists thus began to view urban areas as a kind of sociocultural ecosystem in which different zones, sectors, and nuclei became differentiated by virtue of competition for resources.

A variety of models on the growth of urban areas were proposed, but the general model underlying Chicago School thinking is better represented in Figure 6.3. For the Chicago School, urban growth was related to production and population growth because these aggregated people and the various corporate units, such as family housing and business structures, that people used to survive in space. As aggregation intensified, population density increased, which, in turn, led to a competition for resources, including urban space, governmental resources, retail markets, and virtually any resource that could be used to facilitate the survival of individuals and corporate units. Real estate markets greatly accelerated this competition for resources. For once a market exists, price becomes the gateway to individuals' and corporate actors' ability to gain access to the resources in an urban area and, thereby, to survive in a particular spatial niche that, to Chicago School theorists, was the counterpart of a niche in a biotic system. From this competition came the differentiation of urban areas by the kinds of residents they had, the nature of the productive and business activity evident, and the cultural symbols associated with these. As competition increased, urban areas expanded as actors sought resource niches further from those areas where the competition was too intense, and the market-driven price for living or doing business was simply too high.

Because they relied too heavily on data from Chicago, the models that these early urban ecologists developed were too simplistic and, indeed, rather parochial. But these models made an important connection between biological thinking about selection processes arising out of competition for urban space and resources, on the one hand, and sociocultural dynamics, on the other. Because of the dominance of the University of Chicago's Department of

---

[31]Amos H. Hawley, "Human Ecology: Persistence and Change," *American Behavioral Science* 24 (January 1981): p. 423.

**Figure 6.3** How Early Urban Ecologists Saw Urban Growth

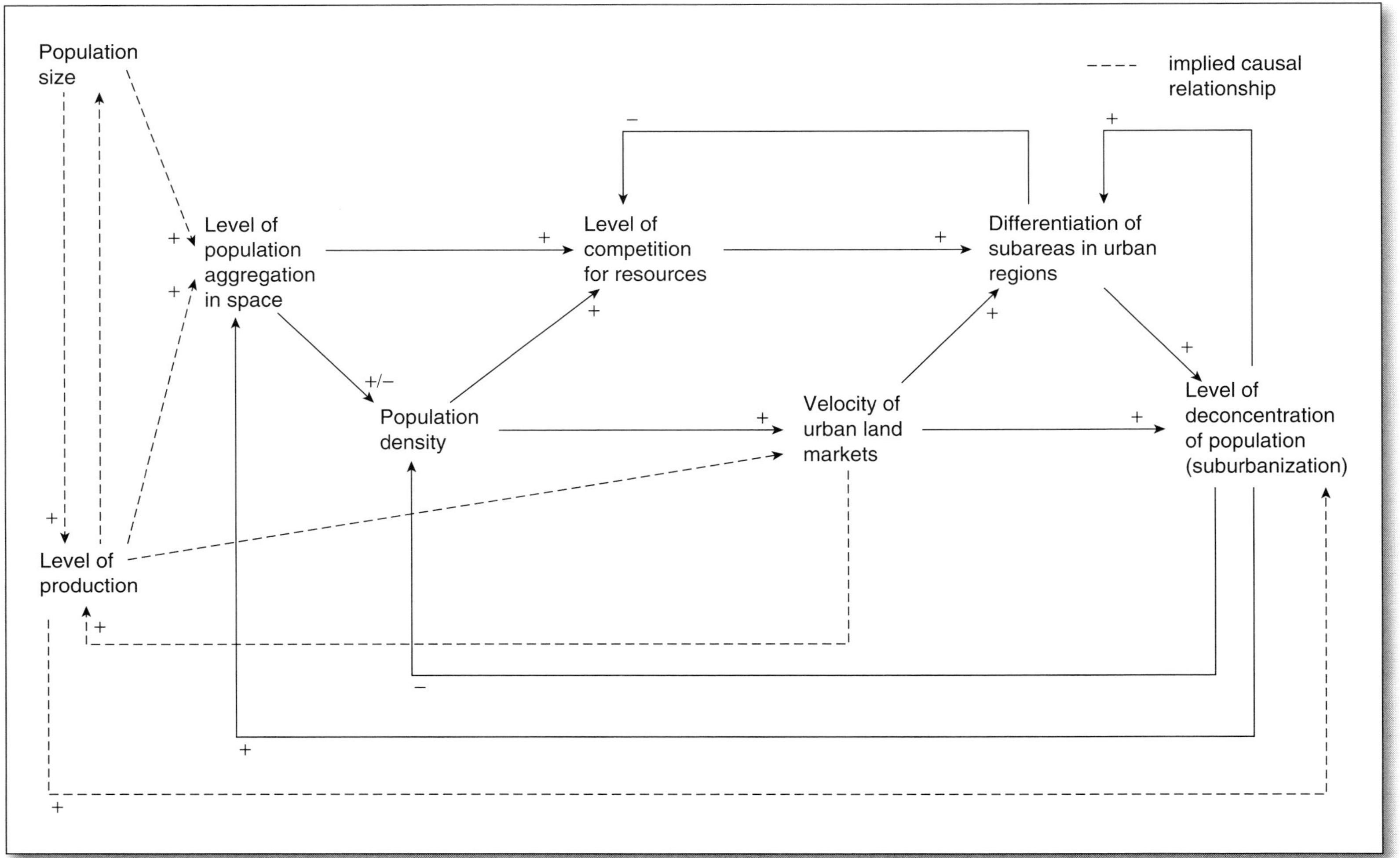

Sociology, this connection could not be ignored, and as we will see in the next chapter, during the last sixty years, it has become transformed into one of the more sophisticated theoretical approaches in sociology. Thus, taking a cue from Spencer and Durkheim but, equally so, from biology proper, the most important orientation to emerge from the theoretically fallow years between World Wars I and II was human ecology. In biology, however, these years proved decisive in establishing the broad contours of the Modern Synthesis where the ideas of Darwin were linked to genetics; from this synthesis, it was not long before dramatic revival of Darwinian ideas moved into the social sciences, eventually penetrating sociological theorizing.

# The New Darwinism in the Social Sciences

In *The Genetical Theory of Natural Selection*, R. A. Fisher was the first to recognize the implications of synthesizing genetics and Darwinian selection.[32] Fisher's first task was to refute the main competitor to natural selection as the force behind evolution. This competitor was *mutation theory*, which argued that large mutations are the driving force behind evolution. Fisher demonstrated with elegant mathematical equations that the vast majority of mutations are harmful and doomed to extinction by natural selection. In particular, Fisher demonstrated that those large mutations that were posited as the key force behind evolution would be harmful and, hence, selected out of the gene pool. Instead, only small mutations offering slight advantages in promoting the fitness of organisms to an environment could be involved in evolution, but these modest mutations could not by themselves alter the gene pool. Rather, the power of natural selection to favor such mutations drives evolution.

With this argument, Fisher welded population genetics and natural selection, while introducing an important concept: *fitness*. This concept was as old as Malthus, Spencer, and Darwin, but it took on new meaning in Fisher's hands. The mean fitness of a population, Fisher argued, will usually be proportional to some component of its genetic variance. That is, gene pools revealing considerable variation provide a greater range of options for selection to work on, thereby increasing the mean fitness of that population to survive. Moreover, even with small variations in a gene pool, selection will still remain the significant force in determining gene frequencies.

---

[32]R. A. Fisher, *The Genetical Theory of Natural Selection* (Oxford: Clarendon, 1930). For an overview of Fisher's contribution, see J. H. Bennett, *Natural Selection, Heredity, and Eugenics* (Oxford: Clarendon, 1983). J. B. S. Haldane and Sewall Wright also laid the foundation for the reconciliation of Mendelian heredity and Darwinian selection, but Fisher's work triggered this revitalization. Fisher was primarily interested in how an organism can increase its fitness—however it is achieved. This emphasis on fitness is summarized in his fundamental theorem: "The rate of increase in fitness of any organism at any time is equal to its genetic variance in fitness at that time." Fisher, *The Genetical Theory of Natural Selection*, p. 35.

In this way, the concepts of selection, genetic variation, and fitness were linked together. Others in the 1930s extended this argument, but what is crucial for our purposes is the view of evolution as revolving around the power of natural selection to promote fitness by selecting those variations in genes that promote adaptation.

In the 1940s, all these leads were crystallized in the Modern Synthesis, with natural selection hailed as the only directional force in evolution. But before this synthesis had fully emerged, Fisher had set the stage for modern human sociobiology. In the last one-third of *The Genetical Theory of Natural Selection*, Fisher quoted Herbert Spencer and turned to an analysis of "Man and Society," stressing the need for forms of eugenics to promote the "survival of the fittest genes." And although Fisher's ideas on eugenics are not now important, they firmly planted in the minds of some biologists that human behavior and organization might be understood through the same natural processes affecting other species—that is, variation in genes, natural selection, and fitness as the adaptive value of genes.

# The Rise of Sociobiology

## Early Instinct Theories

The first sociobiologists were, curiously, not those working in the tradition established by Fisher and the synthesis of population genetics and natural selection. Rather, the initial thrust for a biological view of humans and society was a group of scholars who were throwbacks to the older instinct theories that had always existed in sociology and social philosophy. Perhaps the most influential figure was the father of ethology, Konrad Lorenz. In particular, Lorenz investigated the "aggression instinct," which he saw as becoming channeled by rituals (presumably through natural selection) to space members of an animal species for food gathering, mating, and mitigation of violent encounters.[33] Lorenz viewed human aggression as maladaptive, however, because natural selection had not equipped humans' early ancestors with ritualized mechanisms for inhibiting aggression in high-density situations. Other speculation on human instincts for aggression and domination followed—for example, Robert Ardrey's portrayal of the "killing instinct" in *African Genesis* and *The Territorial Imperative*,[34] Desmond Morris' "naked ape,"[35] Lionel Tiger's and Robin Fox's "imperial animal,"[36] and the

---

[33]Konrad Lorenz, *On Aggression* (New York: Harcourt Brace Jovanovich, 1960).

[34]Robert Ardrey, *African Genesis* (New York: Delta, 1961) and *The Territorial Imperative* (New York: Atheneum, 1966).

[35]Desmond Morris, *The Naked Ape* (New York: Dell, 1967).

[36]Lionel Tiger and Robin Fox, *The Imperial Animal* (New York: Holt, Rinehart & Winston, 1971).

early sociobiological work of Pierre van den Berghe on age, sex, and domination.[37]

## Group Selection and the Early Codification of Sociobiology

Like their predecessors in the nineteenth century, these instinct speculations passed into obscurity, although newer approaches along these lines have emerged in the last decades of the twentieth century (see pp. 197–202 of Chapter 9). In the place of crude instinct approaches came sociobiology. Sociobiology also emerged partly in response to what is known as the *group selectionist* argument. Perhaps V. C. Wynne-Edwards is the scholar most closely associated with this group selection perspective.[38] Wynne-Edwards saw the basic problem as this: How is altruistic behavior in animals to be explained? That is, how does natural selection, with its emphasis on the individual organism's effort to survive and reproduce, explain cooperative behavior in which organisms sacrifice their own fitness for the good of the group? Despite being a competitive world, Wynne-Edwards argued in 1962, "the members of social groups cooperate in civilizing it and, so far as the competition is concerned, they act according to rules. Everything the social code decrees is done for the common good."[39] Thus it might be that, in higher animals, the group is often the unit of selection rather than the individual, as Spencer had recognized a hundred years earlier.[40] Variations in group structures are selected for because of their capacity to adapt and survive in an environment. Such an argument was not terribly different from Spencer's view that social groups, especially whole societies, often compete for existence in a given area, with the better organized society surviving (usually as a result of its superior military ability); so, evolution had, in Spencer's view, involved the successive competition and survival of ever-more fit societies.[41] Whether the author was a Spencer or a Wynne-Edwards, the idea was that the individual organism is not the only unit of selection; groups or, in Spencer's terms, "superorganic" units composed of

---

[37]Pierre van den Berghe, *Age and Sex in Human Societies: A Biosocial Perspective* (Belmont, CA: Wadsworth, 1973). A comparison of this work with later works hints at the changes that van den Berghe was to make. See *Human Family Systems: An Evolutionary View* (New York: Elsevier, 1979).

[38]V. C. Wynne-Edwards, *Evolution through Group Selection* (Oxford: Blackwell, 1986) and *Animal Dispersion in Relation to Social Behavior* (New York: Hafner, 1962). For a review of the controversy surrounding group selection arguments, see David Sloan Wilson, "The Group Selection Controversy: History and Current Status," *Annual Review of Ecological Systems* 14 (1983): pp. 159–87.

[39]Wynne-Edwards, *Evolution through Group Selection* (cited in note 38), p. 9, outlining his original ideas in the course of writing *Animal Dispersion*.

[40]Herbert Spencer, *The Principles of Sociology* (cited in note 4).

[41]Ibid.

interacting and mutually dependent organisms can also constitute a "body" or "social organism" subject to selection pressures.

Sociobiology emerged as a reaction against such group selection arguments;[42] therefore, it is not surprising that sociologists would recoil against this approach because, to any sociologist and certainly ecologists, group selection seem much more viable than concern with selection on individuals. We will review the rise of sociobiology here, even though our discussion will takes us well into the modern period of theorizing, but all of the founders of this approach were not sociologists—another bone of contention as they sought to explain the phenomena studied by sociologists. However, except for a few sociologists, this approach was not seriously considered by sociology until well into the modern period of sociological theorizing; and so, it is better to review these founders now before turning to the modern period of theory in sociology.

George C. Williams launched the most influential critique of group selection, arguing that the real unit of selection is not the group or even the individual organism.[43] Rather, the unit of selection is *the gene*, leading Williams to posit the concept of genic selection. Those genes temporarily housed in individuals and groups that promote survival and reproduction in an environment—that is, *fitness*—will be retained. Whatever the effects of selection for promoting *groupness*, selection at the gene level is the operative mechanism. For "group-related adaptations do not, in fact, exist"; instead, the characteristics of groups—altruism, reciprocity, and exchange, for example—are the result of natural selection on individuals because "simply stated, an individual who maximizes his friendships and minimizes his antagonisms will have an evolutionary advantage, and selection should favor those characters that promote the optimization of personal friendship."[44] Thus, particular genes that promote those traits in individuals facilitating groupness will, in certain environments, promote fitness—that is, survival and reproduction. It is not necessary, Williams argued, to explain group processes using group selection; "genic selection" can explain such group processes, for "the fitness of a group will be high as a result of [the] summation of the adaptations of its members."[45]

---

[42]For an effort to extend group selection arguments, especially those developed by Spencer but also Durkheim, see Jonathan H. Turner, *Theoretical Principles of Sociology*, vol. 1, *Macrodynamics* (New York: Springer, 2010). See also Jonathan H. Turner, *Macrodynamics: Toward a Theory on the Organization of Human Populations* (New Brunswick, NJ: Rutgers University Press for Rose Book Series, 1995).

[43]George C. Williams, *Adaptation and Natural Selection: A Critique of Some Current Evolutionary Thought* (Princeton, NJ: Princeton University Press, 1966). For his defense of reductionism away from the group level, see "A Defense of Reductionism in Evolutionary Biology," in *Oxford Surveys in Evolutionary Biology* 2, eds. R. Dawkins and M. Ridley (Oxford: Oxford University Press, 1985), pp. 1–27.

[44]Williams, *Adaptation and Natural Selection*, p. 95.

[45]Ibid.

W. D. Hamilton took this kind of reasoning a step further by introducing the important concept of inclusive fitness.[46] This concept was intended to account for cooperation among relatives, and the argument goes something like this: Natural selection promotes *kin selection* in the sense that those who share genes will interact and cooperate to promote one another's fitness—or capacity to pass on their genes. Self-sacrifice for a biological relative is, in reality, not altruism at all but the selfish pursuit of fitness because, in helping a relative to survive and reproduce, one is passing on one's own genetic material (as stored in relatives' genotypes). Thus, from this point of view, self-sacrifice for, and cooperation with, relatives will be greater as the amount of shared genetic material increases. So, altruistic behaviors among parents and offspring or among siblings can be understood as behaviors that were selected for as a way to pass on one's genetic material, or to keep it in the gene pool. This is the process of inclusive fitness—inclusive in the sense that one shares identical genes with others, and fitness in the sense that, in helping these others, one is also ensuring that shared genetic material will remain in the gene pool. This kind of argument takes the altruism out of altruism among family members and sees such behaviors as simple matters of self-interest: to maximize the amount of one's genetic material that stays in the gene pool. Hence the goal of genes is to preserve themselves, and it is rational for them to help preserve the bodies of those individuals who carry common genetic material. Of course, genes do not think, but blind natural selection has operated in the distant past to promote behaviors in organisms, such as altruism among relatives, that increased fitness in ways that maximize the passing on of particular sets of genes.

Although Hamilton's notions of kin selection and inclusive fitness might be seen to account for cooperation among relatives, the question was soon raised: How can such arguments explain altruism and cooperation among nonrelatives who do not share genetic material? Robert Trivers sought to overcome this objection with the concept of reciprocal altruism.[47] In a series of modeling procedures, he presented the following scenario: Natural selection can produce organisms that will incur the "costs" of helping a nonrelative because at some later time this nonrelative can "reciprocate" and help "altruistic" organisms (thereby increasing the latter's fitness, or ability to survive and pass on genes). Thus, for species that live a long time and congregate, natural selection can promote reciprocal altruism and increase all

[46]W. D. Hamilton, "The Evolution of Altruistic Behavior," *American Naturalist* 97 (1963): pp. 354–56; "The Genetical Theory of Social Behavior I and II," *Journal of Theoretical Biology* 7 (1964): pp. 1–52; "Innate Social Aptitudes of Man: An Approach from Evolutionary Genetics," in *Biosocial Anthropology*, ed. R. Fox (New York: Wiley, 1984), pp. 135–55; "Geometry for the Selfish Herd," *Journal of Theoretical Biology* 31 (1971): pp. 295–311.

[47]Robert L. Trivers, "The Evolution of Reciprocal Altruism," *Quarterly Review of Biology* 46, no. 4 (1971): pp. 35–57; "Parental Investment and Sexual Selection," in *Sexual Selection and the Descent of Man, 1871–1971*, ed. B. Campbell (Chicago: Aldine, 1972); and "Parent-Offspring Conflict," *American Zoologist* 14 (1974): pp. 249–64.

individuals' fitness, whereas those that would cheat and fail to reciprocate others' altruism will be selected out (because eventually, without signs of reciprocity, others would not come to their aid). And so, once again what seems like altruism is, in reality, selfishness by the individual organisms, each of which is trying to maximize its capacity to keep genes in the pool.

The last major conceptual development in sociobiology has been the use of *game theory* to describe the process of fitness. Here the key figure has been J. Maynard-Smith,[48] although Trivers had started his analysis with the classic "Prisoner's Dilemma" game to show how selfish individuals can cooperate to increase their fitness beyond what it would be without cooperation.[49] In game theory, it is assumed that, under particular conditions imposed by the game, rational decision-making actors seek the best possible payoff by adopting a particular behavioral strategy. The payoffs in game theory are typically some unit of subjective value. In contrast, unlike classical utilitarianism, in which actors are assumed to be conscious, rational, and payoff maximizing, game theory as it is applied to evolutionary theory cannot assume rational consciousness of its players (genes), and the payoffs are always a measure of fitness (capacity to pass on genes). The process of selection is presumed to have decided (unconsciously) the strategy that maximizes fitness in a given environment; the investigator's task is then to determine what behavioral strategy for a particular species in an environment would best ensure maximal payoffs of fitness, or the capacity to survive, reproduce, and pass on genes. This is what Hamilton did with the concept of inclusive fitness: Helping one's biological relatives is the best strategy, as decided by the forces of natural selection, for passing on one's genetic material.

Maynard-Smith went a step further and developed the concept of an *evolutionary stable strategy* (ESS) to describe the stabilization of behavioral strategies among the individuals of a population. Without outlining the mathematical and statistical details, the ESS enabled Maynard-Smith to calculate an equilibrium point, around which the relative amounts of various behaviors, or strategies, for fitness will stabilize. In this way, it is possible

---

[48]J. Maynard-Smith, "The Theory of Games and the Evolution of Animal Conflicts," *Journal of Theoretical Biology* 47 (1974): pp. 209–21; "Optimization Theory in Evolution," *Annual Review of Ecological Systems* 9 (1978): pp. 31–56; *Evolution and the Theory of Games* (London: University of Cambridge Press, 1982). See also Susan E. Riechert and Peter Hammerstein, "Game Theory in the Ecological Context," *Annual Review of Ecological Systems* 14 (1983): pp. 377–409.

[49]The basic format for the "Prisoner's Dilemma" is this: Two criminals are caught together and accused of a crime; they are taken to separate rooms for questioning, with each being offered leniency in prosecution for telling on the other. If both refuse to talk, the police have no real evidence; yet, if one talks and the other does not, then the latter is at a disadvantage. Thus the dilemma is to talk or keep quiet under conditions in which each partner in crime does not know what the other will do. The maximizing strategy is for both to keep quiet, but each can get less than the maximum benefit (and far more than the worst outcome) by telling on the other.

to show that all members of a population do not have to adopt the same strategy; rather, each potential strategy affects the payoffs of the others, and over time, the relative frequencies of various strategies for survival will, as a result of natural selection, reach equilibrium, or the ESS.

This application of game theory gave sociobiologists a well-developed and powerful set of mathematical tools for making predictions about how natural selection will produce behavioral strategies maximizing fitness and how varying configurations of such strategies can reach equilibrium. Such configurations can, sociobiologists argued, explain patterns of social organization.

Richard Dawkins popularized this emerging sociobiological approach in his well-known work *The Selfish Gene*.[50] His argument is that genes are "replicator" or "copy" machines that try to reproduce themselves. Natural selection favored those replicators that could find a "survival machine" to live in—initially, in the distant past, a cell wall, then a grouping of cells, then an organism, and eventually a grouping of organisms. As Dawkins notes:

> What weird machines of self-preservation would the millennia bring forth. . . . They (replicators) did not die out, for they are past masters of the survival arts. . . .Now they swarm in huge colonies, safe inside gigantic lumbering robots, sealed off from the outside world, communicating with it by tortuous indirect routes, manipulating it by remote control. They are in you and me; they created us, body and mind; and their preservation is the ultimate rationale for our existence. They have come a long way, those replicators. Now they go by the name of genes, and we are their survival machines.[51]

Such a rich metaphor captures the essence of modern sociobiology because the unit of selection becomes the gene, and evolution is the result of genes competing and adopting strategies that allow them to leave their DNA in the gene pool. Evolution is not an effort of individuals or species to survive; these are only vehicles for the real driving force of evolution: genes that are "ruthlessly selfish" in adopting strategies to maximize their fitness. At times, it serves the genes' interest to foster limited forms of altruism and other social behaviors that are often considered to be the exclusive domain of the social sciences. But from a sociobiological perspective, many of the behaviors, strategies, and organizational traits of animals, including humans, are simply the genes' way of coping with an unpredictable environment. Indeed, even the human capacity for thinking and learning, Dawkins avers, can be viewed as the genes' way to construct a better survival machine; cooperation can similarly be seen as one survival machine making use of another survival machine in an effort to further assure its fitness; and

---

[50]Richard Dawkins, *The Selfish Gene* (Oxford: Oxford University Press, 1976).

[51]Ibid., p. 21

various patterns of social organization can thus be conceptualized as nothing more than more complex and inclusive survival machines for genes.

Yet, Dawkins hedged in his last chapter, as have many contemporary sociobiologists in recent years. Dawkins posits a "new replicator," which he terms *memes*. The basic tenets of sociobiology—genic selection, inclusive fitness, and reciprocal altruism, all producing strategies and survival machines for genes—can explain how humans came to exist, but culture begins to supplement and supplant biology as the major replicating mechanism. Memes are those new cultural units that exist inside brains and that, via socialization, are passed on and preserved in a "meme pool." Meme evolution will now begin to accelerate, for "once genes have provided their survival machines with brains which are capable of rapid imitation, the memes will automatically take over." And it might even be possible for memes to rebel against their creators, the selfish genes. Similarly, other sociobiologists now talk of "co-evolution," operating at both the genetic and the cultural levels.

Although these metaphors are colorful, sociobiology is highly technical—involving extensive use of mathematics, game theory, and computer simulations. It changes the image of natural selection as a process working on passive individuals and posits, instead, active actors driven by their genes to maximize their reproductive success by any strategy available (which can be modeled and simulated with various game-theoretic approaches). The challenge of this perspective is that many processes considered by sociologists to be explicable only by sociological laws are seen by sociobiologists to be understandable as biological processes derived from the laws of the synthetic theory of evolution.

# Conclusion

Biological ideas have been part of sociological theorizing since its beginning in the work of Herbert Spencer and Émile Durkheim. These biological ideas began to penetrate the social sciences along two fronts: (1) the analysis of ecosystems and how concepts from this branch of biology could be used to understand competition and selection processes in the units of sociocultural systems and (2) the analysis of genetics and how notions of fitness, inclusive fitness, and reciprocal altruism could be employed to explain human behavior and social organization as survival machines for the real driving force of society—genes. The third branch of biological thinking about the long-term evolution of complexity reemerged after its demise in the early twentieth century in not only functional theories but other theoretical traditions as well. These will be examined in Chapter 9.

As we will explore in the next chapter, the ecological front of biologically inspired theory became the more prominent application of biological ideas in the latter half of the twentieth century. Amos Hawley, for example, not only continued the urban ecology approach (of his early work), but more significantly, he trained the theorists who would found a new ecological perspective—organizational ecology. And, perhaps more surprising, he also moved ecological analysis back to the macro level where both Spencer and Durkheim had originally employed ecological ideas. These will be the focus of the next chapter.

The genetic front of theory became translated into rather extreme socio-biological arguments about behavior and social organization as driven by genes trying to maximize their fitness—arguments that became, to say the least, highly controversial and especially so in sociology. Yet, as we will see in Chapter 9, the reaction against these extreme arguments has proven to be healthy because it led to efforts to tone down the extremes of sociobiology and, more importantly, to reintegrate biological arguments in genetics, ecology, and even social evolution into more general theoretical arguments. Still, arising from sociobiology came evolutionary psychology, which has been more successful than sociobiology in penetrating the social sciences, but like sociobiology, it has encountered a hostile reception in sociology, even as some sociologists take up its banner. For the present, the place of biological ideas in sociology is in flux, but one thing is clear: sociology will not be able to reject all ideas from biology. And so, as we will explore in Chapter 9, it is time for an assessment of what biological ideas will be useful in sociology. These will be examined in Chapter 9 on Darwinian-inspired theorizing of evolutionary dynamics.

## CHAPTER 7

# Ecological Theories

Ecological theorizing has a clear lineage from Herbert Spencer to Émile Durkheim and to early twentieth-century Chicago School sociology, where it spread to early centers of ecological theorizing such as the University of North Carolina at Chapel Hill. During this time frame, human ecology became a more general interdisciplinary field, but ecological theorizing in sociology followed a particular trajectory. First, theorizing was downsized from the macro level of Spencer and Durkheim to the meso level of social organization, with an emphasis on the ecology of urban areas. Then, ecological theorizing in sociology was extended to the study of complex organizations in which populations of organizations seeking resources in a particular niche became the unit of analysis. Finally, ecological theorizing was taken back up to the macro-societal level by the key figure connecting the Chicago School to North Carolina. At the same time, many other types of macro theories, from world systems analysis (see Chapter 13) to stage-model theories of evolution (see next chapter) also began adding more ecological elements to their theories. Thus, even though the number of free-standing ecological theories remains comparatively small, the perspective has penetrated many other theoretical traditions.

In this chapter, I will begin by outlining the continuation of urban ecology to the present, then review the rise of organizational ecology, and then trace the movement of these meso-level theories on urban and organizational dynamics back to the macro level, where ecological theorizing began in the works of Spencer and Durkheim.

## Theorizing on Urban Ecology

Even after the decline of ecological work at the University of Chicago, urban ecology remained a viable and vibrant meso-level theoretical approach. Recast as the study of spatial processes, theorists sought to explain such variables as the size of settlements, the concentration of populations within these settlements, the rate and form of geographical expansion of settlements, and the nature of connections among settlements. Much of what is termed *urban sociology* has sought to examine specific cases empirically, just as the original Chicago School once used the city of Chicago for its laboratory. But, at a more purely theoretical level, an effort was made to conceptualize urban processes generically as fundamental processes influencing patterns of organizing a population in space. This latter theoretical thrust can properly be seen as ecological, and the kinds of models developed by these spatial theorists owe a great deal to early Chicago School ecologists.

This debt can be best appreciated by examining Figure 7.1, which presents a composite and abstracted model of various approaches in urban ecology.[1] This model does not represent any one theorist's ideas but, rather, communicates the general thrust of various approaches combined.[2] As can be seen on the left of the model, technology and demographics influence two important variables, evident in Spencer's and Durkheim's respective theories. These two variables are (1) the level of development in communication and transportation technologies and (2) the level of production of goods and services. Population size and technology both determine the level of production directly, and as can be seen by the arrows flowing into production, other forces made possible by expanded production feedback and increase production even more. Similarly, transportation and communication technologies set into motion many urban processes, and these also provide feedback, especially via production, to increase the level of these technologies and, in turn, the store of a population's technology in general.

Both technology and production increase the scale of the material infrastructure of a population—that is, its roadways, canals, ports, railroads, airports, subways, buildings, and all other physical structures built in space. The scale of this infrastructure gets an extra boost as the distributive capacities of a population increase—that is, the capacity to move information, materials, goods, and services about space. As can be seen along the bottom of the model in Figure 7.1, the volume and velocity of markets is important in this process; among populations with well-developed market systems,

---

[1]For a more detailed analysis, see Jonathan H. Turner, "The Assembling of Human Populations: Toward a Synthesis of Ecological and Geopolitical Theories," *Advances in Human Ecology* 3 (1994): pp. 65–91 and *Macrodynamics: Toward Theory on the Organization of Human Populations*, Chap. 6 (New Brunswick, NJ: Rutgers University Press for Rose Book Series, 1995).

[2]In particular, the model summarizes ideas from Parker W. Frisbie, "Theory and Research in Urban Ecology," in *Sociological Theory and Research: A Critical Approach*, ed. H. M. Blalock (New York: Free Press, 1980); Parker W. Frisbie and John D. Kasarda, "Spatial Processes," in *Handbook of Sociology*, ed. N. J. Smelser (Newbury Park, CA: Sage, 1988); Mark Gottdiener, *The Social Production of Urban Space* (Austin: University of Texas Press, 1985); Amos H. Hawley, *Urban Society: An Ecological Approach* (New York: Ronald, 1981); John D. Kasarda, "The Theory of Ecological Expansion: An Empirical Test," *Social Forces* 51 (1972): pp. 165–75.

**Figure 7.1** The Abstracted Urban Ecology Model

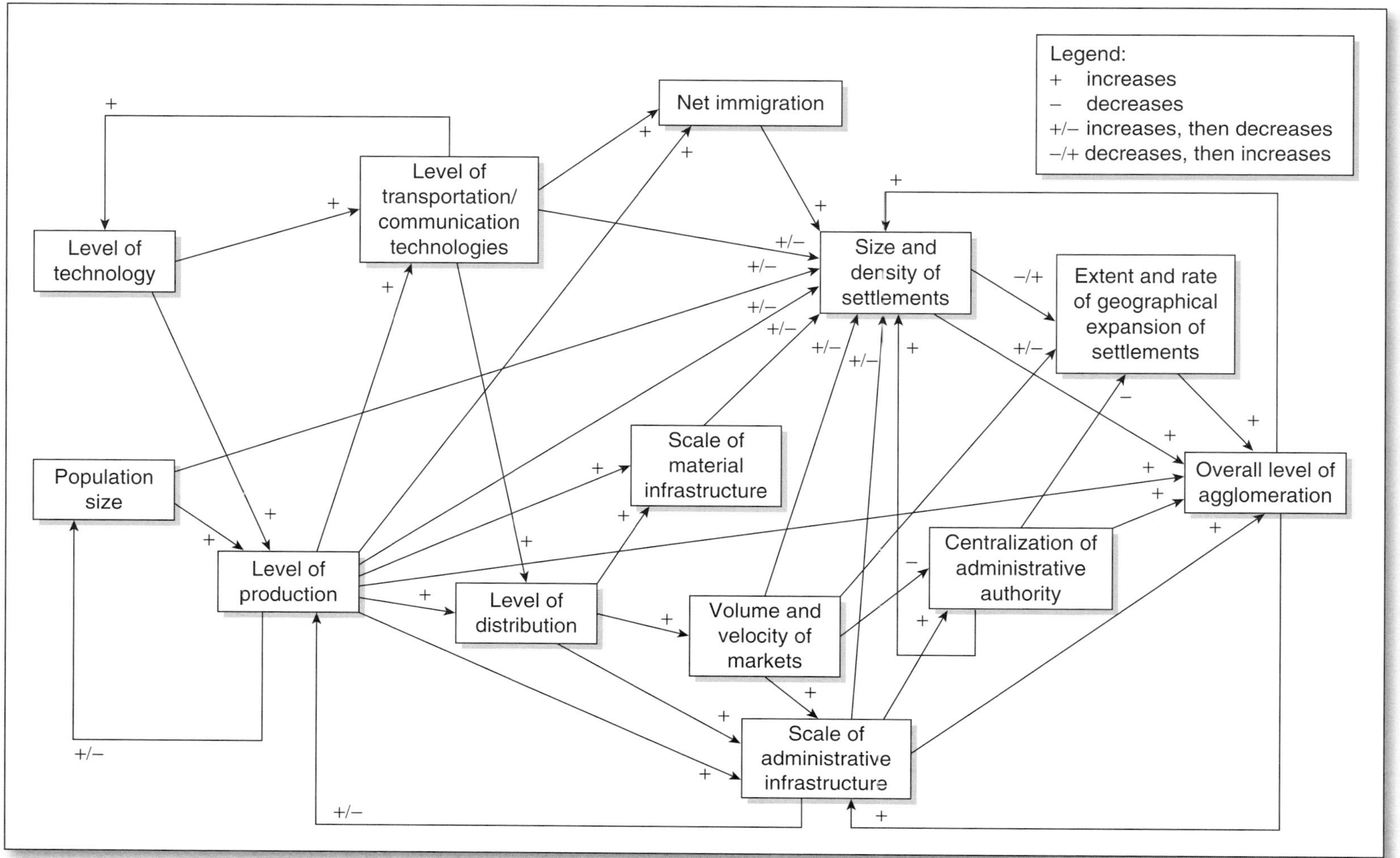

Legend:
+ increases
− decreases
+/− increases, then decreases
−/+ decreases, then increases

135

distributive activities increase. They do so because markets create new kinds of administrative and authority systems—banks, governmental agencies, insurance, sales, advertising, services, wholesale and retail outlets, and all the organizational structures required to sustain high volume markets. These are labeled, respectively, *scale of administrative infrastructure* and *centralization of administrative authority* in the model, and they have important effects on not only increasing the level of distribution but also on settlement patterns.

These latter effects are most noticeable on the size and density of settlement patterns. Administrative infrastructures and authority systems directly influence the size and density of settlements by concentrating activities and, thereby, pulling a population to urban areas. These administrative variables also operate indirectly on density by increasing distribution and production, which, in turn, expands transportation and communication technologies and the scale of the material infrastructure that have their own effects on increases in the size and density of settlements.

Immigration patterns are influenced not only by transportation and technology but also by the level of production. When these are high, existing dense settlements become magnates for new immigrants, especially in settlements with dynamic market systems and administrative structures that offer opportunities to secure a living and other resources. Immigration, in turn, increases the size and density of settlements, particularly when previous waves of similar immigrants have already settled and can provide friends, relatives, and others of similar origins a place to house themselves and, perhaps, job opportunities.

As the size and density of settlements increase, these forces concentrate populations in ways that discourage geographical expansion of the urban area. But eventually, the population in urban cores must begin to move outward. Such movement is facilitated by markets, especially real estate markets but also markets that can distribute goods and services in new locations. Centralized authority, such as governmental functions, can for a time discourage movement too far from this center of administrative control, but in the end, the growing size and density of the population, coupled with real estate and other markets, enable or force some of the population to extend the boundaries of the settlement or to create new settlements.

The term on the far right of the model in Figure 7.1—*agglomeration*—is meant to connote what is evident all over the world today: Outward movement of settlements, even when this movement involves creating separate settlements, eventually leads to relative contiguous systems of dense settlements—often termed urban or suburban *sprawl*. That is, as movement out from the original urban core occurs, new settlements typically remain within physical proximity of this core; as new areas attract migrants from the older core or new immigrants from other urban areas, these areas also become larger and more dense. Eventually, they begin to bump into each other, creating high levels of agglomeration or the proximity of contiguous and relatively dense settlements spread across a comparatively large geographical space. Such agglomeration increases the scale of the administrative infrastructure, which, in turn, increases governmental functions and its administrative structure across the urban space. Via the reverse causal arrows in the model, agglomeration increases, indirectly, the level of distribution of goods, services, materials, and information around the agglomerated urban space, which affects the level of production and transportation and communication technologies.

Much urban sociology describes specific empirical cases within these general ecological dynamics. Yet, from these more specific empirical studies that began with the Chicago School (see Figure 6.3 on page 123) have emerged interesting generalizations that can supplement the processes outlined in the model presented in Figure 7.1. One older principle is that the density of settlements in an urban area declines exponentially (that is, at an accelerating rate) as the distance from the center of an urban area increases.[3] This idea follows from early Chicago School observations that high demand for space in the core of urban areas will raise market prices and force out those who cannot afford to live or do business in the core; these actors must now assume the additional mobility costs of settling in lower-cost, outlying areas.[4] Yet, as more recent studies indicate,[5] the recent technological and organizational changes, especially those associated with information technologies, have tended to change the nature of the connection between the central urban core and outlying areas.

In fact, there is a movement of material and administrative infrastructures from the core to less densely settled outlying regions, creating a more polycentric system across agglomerated settlement patterns. Thus, the densities of settlements in outlying areas can increase as the distance from the old settlement core increases, but eventually, the principle that settlement density decreases with distance from urban core or cores in a polycentric system will become operative.

A related principle is that the relative size of settlements or cities decreases as movement from the urban core or cores increases.[6] That is, as movement from the large cities occurs, the size and density of settlements will decrease in a pattern: Large urban cores will be surrounded by midsized cities, which, in turn, will be connected to smaller settlements.

---

[3]C. Clark, "Urban Population Densities," *Journal of the Royal Statistical Society*, Series A, 114 (1951): pp. 490–96.

[4]B. J. L. Berry and John D. Kasarda, *Contemporary Urban Ecology* (New York: Macmillan, 1977).

[5]Frisbie and Kasarda, "Spatial Processes" (cited in note 2).

[6]This idea was originally formulated by George Zipf, *Human Behavior and the Principle of Least Effort* (Reading, MA: Addison-Wesley, 1949) and expanded on in other studies: Hawley, *Urban Society* (see note 2); E. G. Stephan, "Variation in County Size: A Theory of Segmental Growth," *American Sociological Review* 36 (1979): pp. 451–61 and "Derivation of Some Socio-Demographic Regularities from the Theory of Time Minimization," *Social Forces* 57 (1979): pp. 812–23.

Another related principle is that the flow of resources across settlements will reflect the degree to which they constitute an integrated system, especially in their markets and hierarchies of governmental structures.[7] When settlements are connected by markets and governmental agencies, the flow of resources—information, goods, and services—will be more rapid and efficient.

These and other principles specify in more detail what is subsumed in the model in Figure 7.1 under the label of *agglomeration.* These kinds of principles, in essence, indicate the ways that settlements become connected to each other and form ever-larger settlement patterns in physical space. Many of these generalizations are time bound and relevant to particular empirical cases, but they do point to several more generic and fundamental forces that organize a population in physical space. Thus, the general intent of the early Chicago School of urban ecology has been retained in more recent work: to see the patterns of settlement of populations in physical space and, then, to develop more abstract generalizations describing these patterns.

# Theories of Organizational Ecology

One creative extension of theory during the last thirty years has been the analysis of organizational dynamics from an ecological perspective. In these theories, populations of organizations of a given type are viewed as competing for resources, with selection favoring those most fit in a given environment. Thus, the rise and fall in the numbers and proportions of various kinds of organizational forms in a society can be seen as a kind of Darwinian struggle in which organizations compete with each other in resource niches, dying out if they are unsuccessful or, if they can, moving to find a new resource niche in which they can survive. The first well-developed theory about the ecology of complex organizations was presented by Michael Hannan and John Freeman in the late 1970s[8]; others have extended their approach, typically by analyzing empirically specific populations of organizations. We will first examine Hannan and Freeman's general theory and then review a creative addition to theorizing on organizational ecology by Miller McPherson and various collaborators.

## Michael T. Hannan and John Freeman's Ecological Theory

Hannan and Freeman had an important insight:[9] Populations of organizations of various kinds can be viewed as competing for resources. For

---

[7]Frisbie and Kasarda, "Spatial Processes" (cited in note 2). See also Jonathan H. Turner, *Theoretical Principles of Sociology, vol.1, Macrodynamics* (New York: Springer, 2010).

[8]Michael T. Hannan and John Freeman, "The Population Ecology of Organizations," *American Journal of Sociology* 82 (1977): pp. 929–64.

[9]Ibid.

example, automobile companies, clothing outlets, newspapers, governmental agencies, service clubs, and just about any organized corporate unit depend on particular kinds and levels of resources from their respective environments. Thus, a population of organizations, such as automobile companies, can be seen as competing in the same resource niche; for automobile companies, the resource environment consists of those who can afford to buy cars. This basic situation is analogous to evolutionary processes in that organizations must compete with each other to secure resources, particularly as the number of organizations occupying a given niche increases; from such competition comes selection of those organizational forms that are most fit. With this basic insight, Hannan and Freeman extended the analogy, and Figure 7.2 attempts to summarize all the key variables in their theory, as it has developed during the last thirty years.[10]

Hannan and Freeman's basic question focused on why organizations of a given type die out and others increase in frequency.[11] The key dynamic is shown at the center of the model in Figure 7.2: competition within a population of organizations for resources. High levels of competition increase the selection pressures on organizations; those that can secure resources in this competition survive, and those that cannot will fail or move to another resource niche. The theory then examines the forces that increase competition and selection. One critical set of organizational forces is presented in the middle of the model, moving from left to right: the number of organizations of a given type increases the density of organizations in a niche, thereby increasing competition, selection, and rates of organizational failure.

Another force increasing competition is open and free markets. Such markets institutionalize competition, forcing ever-more organizations to compete with each other for customers, members, or any other resource. Thus, as the scale and scope of markets increase, the level of competition increases, especially when niche density is high. If monopolies can emerge or government regulates markets extensively, however, then the level of competition is reduced, thereby lowering selection pressures and rates of organizational failure.

---

[10]For an analysis of the more macrostructural implications of the variables delineated in Figure 7.2, see Jonathan H. Turner, *Macrodynamics*, Chap. 7 and "The Ecology of Macrostructure" (both cited in note 1).

[11]For representative works by Hannan and Freeman, see "Structural Inertia and Organizational Change," *American Sociological Review* 49 (1984): pp. 149–64; "The Ecology of Organizational Founding: American Labor Unions 1836–1985," *American Journal of Sociology* 92 (1987): pp. 910–43; "The Ecology of Organizational Mortality: American Labor Unions," *American Journal of Sociology* 94 (1988): pp. 25–52; *Organizational Ecology* (Cambridge, MA: Harvard University Press, 1989). See also M. T. Hannan, "Ecologies of Organizations: Diversity and Identity," *Journal of Economic Perspectives* 19 (2005): pp. 51–70; M. T. Hannan, L. Pólos and G. R. Carroll, *Logics of Organization Theory: Audiences, Codes, and Ecologies*, (Princeton University Press, 2007); M. T. Hannan and G. R. Carroll, *Dynamics of Organizational Populations: Density, Legitimation, and Competition*, (New York: Oxford University Press, 1992).

**Figure 7.2** Hannan and Freeman's Ecological Model

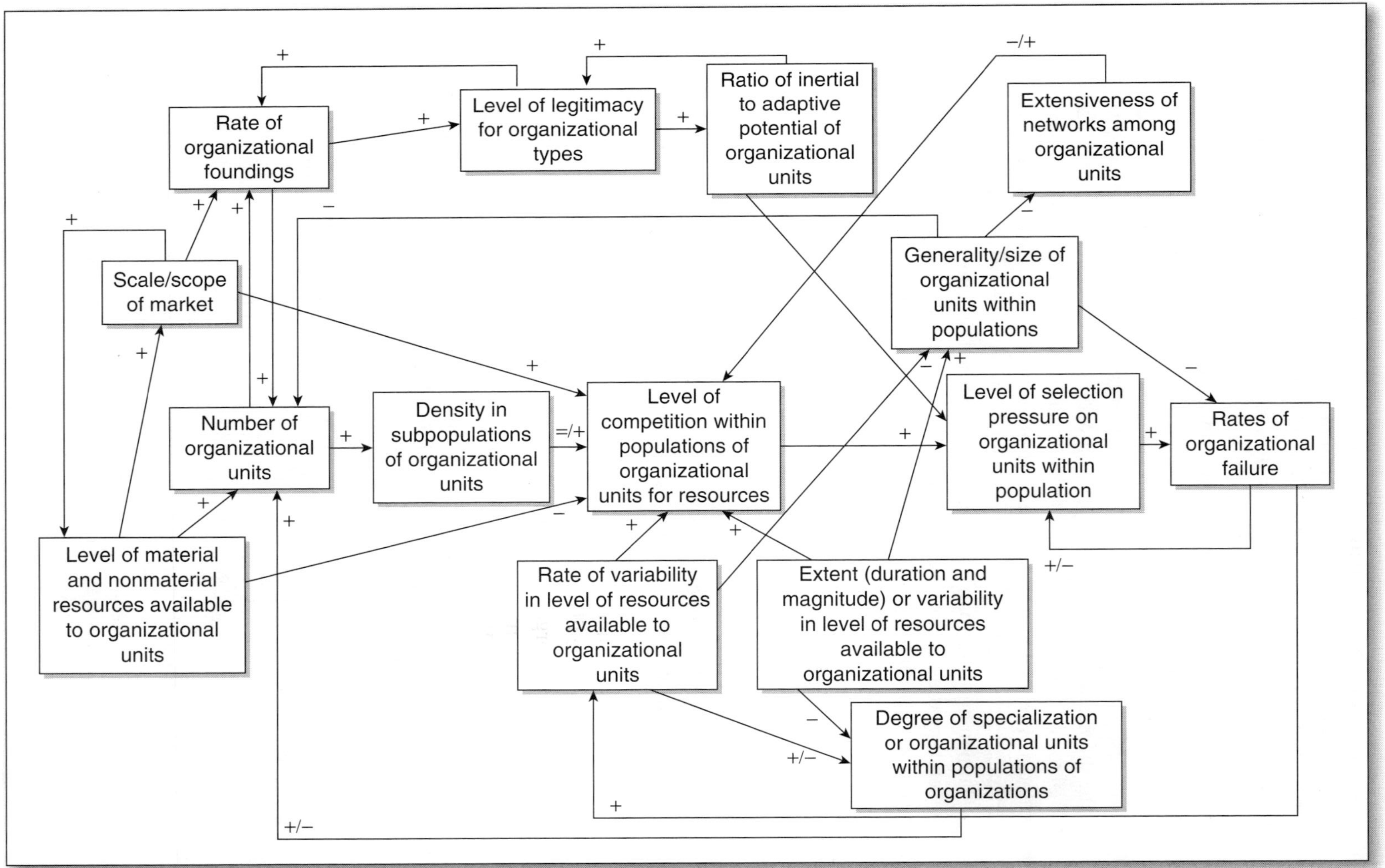

Still another set of variables moves across the top of the model, from left to right. When an organization of a given type first emerges in a niche, it must legitimate itself by surviving, and once it enjoys success, then the rate of organizational foundings, or the creation of new organizations of this type, will increase. These new foundings escalate niche density, competition, and selection, but they also do something else: They make organizations of a given type legitimate, which only encourages more foundings. With legitimization also comes what is phrased in the model as the ratio of inertial to adaptive tendencies in organizations. When organizations have structured themselves successfully in a particular manner and thereby achieved legitimacy, they can also develop structural rigidities or inertial tendencies. They become conservative, locked into the old ways of performing activity. These inertial tendencies give selection processes something to work on. As density in a resource niche increases or the level of resources declines, then those organizations that are too rigid or inertial are likely to be selected out of the population of organizations, whereas those that reveal flexibility or new and creative ways of organizing themselves in the pursuit of resources will be more likely to survive.

A third set of variables moves across the bottom portion of the model in Figure 7.2. The resources available to organizations will vary in several respects. One source of variation in resources is the rate of variability, or how often resources increase and decline. Are resources constantly shifting, or is the fluctuation gradual and slow? Another source of variation in the available resources is the magnitude and duration of variability, or the degree and length of fluctuation between high and low periods of resource availability. When there is rapid fluctuation in resources, specialized types of organizations are likely to emerge and be able to outcompete larger and more generalized organizational structures that, because of their inertial tendencies, cannot move fast enough to respond to rapid shifts in the resources available. When the magnitude of shifts is great and prolonged, however, the specialization of organizations is discouraged because larger and more generalized organizations can ride out the dramatic drop in the level of resources available more effectively than can smaller and highly specialized organizations; these larger organizations have other resource niches that they can pursue, and they typically have bigger resource reserves, whereas the more specialized organizations are likely to have too few reserves to survive large drops in the resources available.

As can be seen from the arrows in the model going into the competition variable, environmental change, whether rapid or severe, will increase the struggle among organizations. As Darwin noted, when the environment changes, the resource niches of species are disrupted, escalating competition and natural selection. When change occurs over longer periods and is of high magnitudes, selection favors larger, more generalized organizations that draw from more than one niche and can ride out fluctuations of high magnitude in any one niche. As organizations become large and general, they often create extensive networks of ties and agreements to reduce competition that could potentially select them out. Examples of these networks can include cartels, trade agreements, interlocking boards of directors in private corporations, liaisons with government, joint production agreements, price fixing among oligopolies, and many other mechanisms by which organizations seek to reduce competition. These networks in effect decrease the density among organizations and hence their competition, which, in turn, reduces their rates of organizational failure.

Hannan and Freeman's theory has thus taken Spencer's and Durkheim's down to a more meso level of analysis, but more directly, the theory adapts Darwinian ideas to the analysis of organizations. Thus, Hannan and Freeman inject a new meso-level phenomenon into ecological analysis: the dynamics within populations of complex organizations. Their approach has stimulated an entirely new branch of research and theory in sociology, and this branch has dominated ecological theorizing during the last two decades, although new, more macro approaches to ecology have also begun to rival the preeminence of theory and research on the ecology of organizations.

## J. Miller McPherson's Ecological Theory

J. Miller McPherson and various collaborators have developed a variant on Hannan and Freeman's model of organizational ecology.[12] McPherson's empirical work has been primarily on voluntary associations and organizations, and this emphasis has led to several additional insights into the dynamics of organizational ecology. McPherson begins with an idea that he adapted from Peter M. Blau's theory of macrostructure: The environment of organizations consists of members of a population who reveal a diversity of characteristics, such as age, sex, ethnicity, income, education, recreational interests, and so on. These characteristics distinguish individuals from each other and, often, become important markers of categorization (as is the case with sex and ethnicity) and inequality (as with income and years of education). These characteristics are also potential resource niches

---

[12]See J. Miller McPherson, "A Dynamic Model of Voluntary Affiliation," *Social Forces* 59 (1981): pp. 705–28; "An Ecology of Affiliation," *American Sociological Review* 48 (1983): pp. 519–32; "The Size of Voluntary Organizations," *Social Forces* 61 (1983): pp. 1044–64; "A Theory of Voluntary Organization," in Community Organizations, ed. C. Milofsky (New York: Oxford University Press, 1988), pp. 42–76; "Evolution in Communities of Voluntary Organization," in *Organizational Evolution*, ed. J. Singh (Newbury Park, CA: Sage, 1990); J. M. McPherson, P. A. Popielarz, and S. Drobnic, "Social Networks and Organizational Dynamics," *American Sociological Review* 57 (1992): pp. 153–70; J. M. McPherson and J. Ranger-Moore, "Evolution on a Dancing Landscape: Organizations and Networks in Dynamic Blau-Space," *Social Forces* 70 (1991): pp. 19–42; and J. M. McPherson and T. Rotolo, "Testing a Dynamic Model of Social Composition: Diversity and Change in Voluntary Groups," *American Sociological Review* 61 (1996): pp. 179–202; J. M. McPherson, "A Blau Space Primer: Prolegomenon to an Ecology of Affiliation," *Industrial and Corporate Change*, 13 (2004): pp. 263–80 and "Ecological Theory," *Handbook of Social Theory*, ed. G. Ritzer (Newbury Park, CA: Sage, 2003).

for organizations seeking members and clients. Thus, McPherson conceptualizes the diversity of characteristics among members of a population as *Blau-space* in deference to the theorist whose work gave him this idea. Blau-space is the environment of organizations, and the greater diversity of characteristics that differentiate members of a population, the greater is the number of resource niches in Blau-space available for organizations to recruit members and clients.

Figure 7.3 summarizes the model developed by McPherson in more general terms, giving us a way to visualize the causal relations among the variables in the theory. The size of the population is, as Spencer and Durkheim both recognized, an important determinant of the level of diversity of characteristics of individuals in Blau-space, as is indicated on the left of the model. The larger the population is, the more likely the characteristics of its members will be differentiated. Moreover, population size per se generates resources in the niches of Blau-space; that is, the more people there are, the more resources are available for organizational systems.

Population size also reduces the density of networks among members of a population; the more people there are to organize, the less likely individuals are to be connected to each other directly or indirectly (as summarized in Chapter 29 on networks, *network density* is a concept denoting the degree of connectedness among actors). With low density, or low rates of connectedness among members of a population, these members are more likely to develop distinctive characteristics because they do not have direct contact and the informal social control and conformity that such contacts generate. Thus, low network density among members of a large population increases the niches in Blau-space available that organizations can exploit.

As the number of niches in Blau-space increases, the number of organizational units in each niche will also tend to increase, and as their numbers grow, the level of competition among organizational units in a niche will begin to escalate. In turn, as niches become densely populated with organizational units, rates of organizational failure will increase, thereby lowering the number of units competing for resources in a particular niche in Blau-space.

Competition among organizations will increase the number of distinguishable organizational units for two reasons: First, each organization seeks to distinguish itself from competitors, thereby increasing the diversity of organizations in a niche. Second, as organizational units distinguish themselves, they create more niches in Blau-space because the members of organizations can reveal somewhat different characteristics. Indeed, as the model portrays, there is a mutually reinforcing cycle between number of niches and number of distinguishable types of organizations in Blau-space. Competition only accelerates these forces.

Organizations in Blau-space also become distinctive because they tend to recruit members with similar characteristics, or what is termed *rate of homophyly in the model*. Thus, for example, service organizations such as the

**Figure 7.3** McPherson's Ecological Model

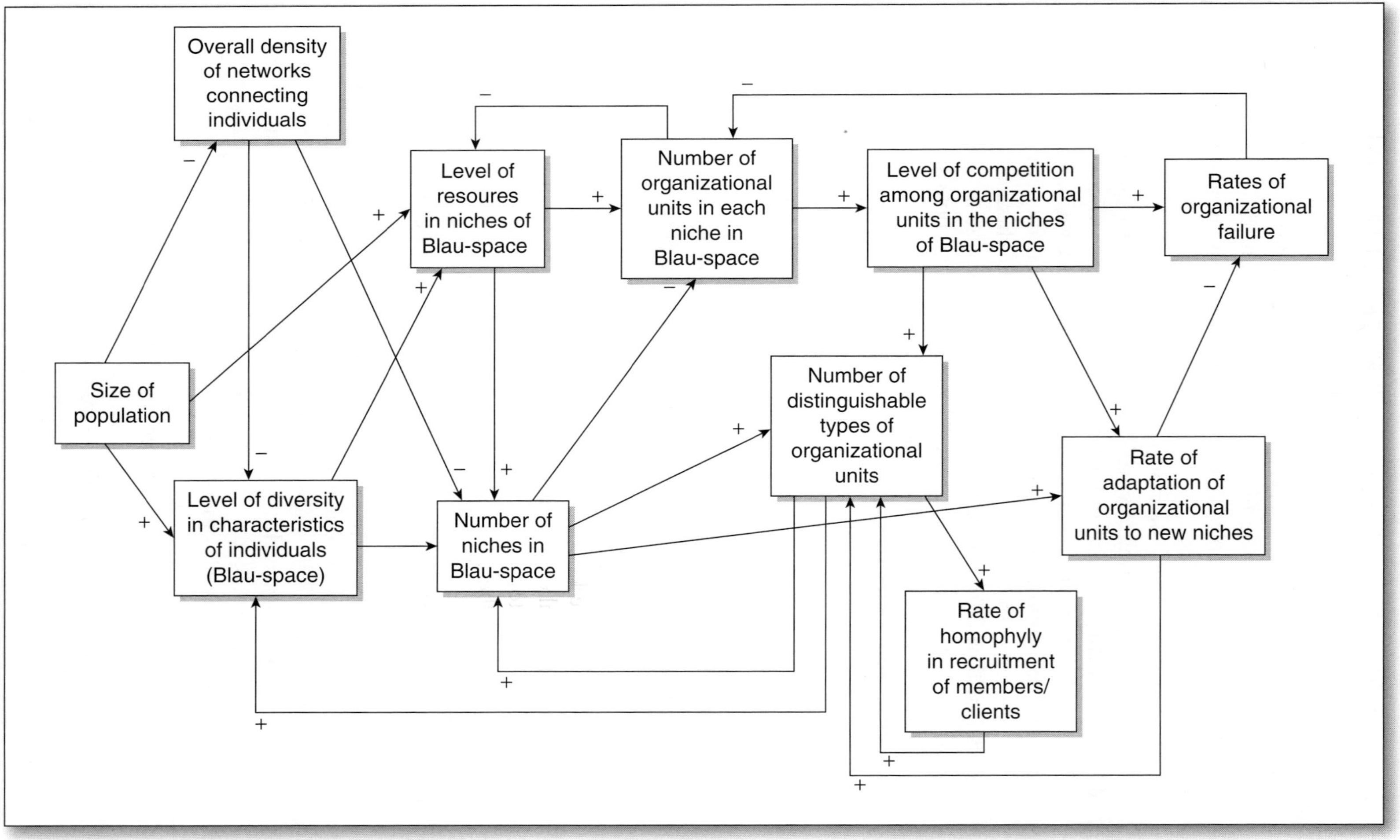

Lions, Kiwanis, Optimists, American Legion, and the like will seek members whose characteristics converge; as these organizations do so, they sustain their distinctiveness and, hence, the diversity of characteristics among members in a population and the corresponding niches in Blau-space. Competition for members or clients, however, places selection pressure on organizations, forcing them to adapt and change if they find themselves less able to compete in a niche. For example, in recent decades in America, service organizations have had great difficulty sustaining their memberships because the number of individuals in this niche has declined as the demographics and structure of the society have changed. Such competition has led to a decline in membership and some organizational failures, but it has also done something else: Some organizations have been forced to seek new niches in Blau-space. For example, a service organization might shift from a middle-income and high-education pool of members to lower-income and less-educated members because the competition is less intense. Rates of adaptation to new niches are influenced not only by the level of competition but also by the number of niches in Blau-space. If there are many niches, then an organization that is having trouble recruiting members and clients has options that would not be available if there were only a few niches in Blau-space. Adaptation to new niches is particularly likely when there are adjacent niches that do not require a complete restructuring of the organization. For example, when the polio vaccine was created, the March of Dimes lost its resource base because its cause for recruiting donations was obviated; to survive, the March of Dimes moved to a new but adjacent charity niche that still involved the basic structure of soliciting charitable contributions.

As is evident, the key idea of McPherson's model is much the same as other organizational ecological models:[13] competition and selection among organizations lead to organizational failure or movement of organizations to new niches. McPherson's most important addition is expansion of what constitutes the resource environment of organizations. Hannan and Freeman's model connoted a more money- and market-driven image of the resource environment, whereas McPherson's model expands the notion of what constitutes resources. Virtually any set of characteristics that distinguishes people in a population can become a resource niche for organizations that seek members, clients, or customers. The more varied the Blau-space is, the more diversity of organizational forms the environment can support and the more likely are less successful organizations in one niche to move to new, adjacent niches in efforts to survive.

---

[13]For some general overviews of research and theory on organizational ecology, see Glenn R. Carroll, ed., *Ecological Models of Organizations* (Cambridge, MA: Ballinger, 1988) and "Organizational Ecology," *Annual Review of Sociology* 10 (1984): pp. 71–93; Jitendra V. Singh and Charles J. Lumsden, "Theory and Research in Organizational Ecology," *Annual Review of Sociology* 16 (1990): pp. 161–95.

# Amos H. Hawley's Return to Macro-Level Ecological Theory

As noted earlier, the macro-level ideas of Herbert Spencer and Émile Durkheim about the ecology of human social organization were downsized in the first half of the twentieth century to the meso-level analysis of urban social processes. Amos Hawley, who was a direct descendant of the Chicago School tradition, continued this emphasis on the differentiation of urban space in his early work in the late 1940s and early 1950s,[14] and yet, he was becoming "increasingly disenchanted with the then received conception of human ecology. The prevailing preoccupation with spatial distributions, which had attracted me at first, seems to me a theoretical cul-de-sac."[15] By the 1980s, he had pushed ecological analysis back to the macro or societal level.[16]

## Production, Transportation, and Communication

Hawley's theory of ecological processes begins with three basic assumptions:

1. Adaptation to environment proceeds through the formation of a system of interdependencies among the members of a population.

2. System development continues, other things being equal, to the maximum complexity afforded by the existing facilities for transportation and communication.

3. System development is resumed with the introduction of new information that increases the capacity for movement of materials, people, and messages and continues until that capacity is fully used.

---

[14]Amos H. Hawley, *Human Ecology: A Theory of Community Structure* (New York: Ronald, 1950).

[15]Amos H. Hawley, "The Logic of Macrosociology," *Annual Review of Sociology* 18 (1992): pp. 1–14.

[16]The following list of titles from Hawley's work reviews this progression of thinking that culminated in the last reference at the end of this note. "Human Ecology," in *International Encyclopedia of the Social Sciences*, ed. D. C. Sills (New York: Crowell, Collier and Macmillan, 1968); *Urban Society: An Ecological Approach* (New York: Ronald, 1971 and 1981); "Human Ecology: Persistence and Change," *American Behavioral Scientist* 24, no. 3 (January 1981), pp. 423–44; "Human Ecological and Marxian Theories," *American Journal of Sociology* 89 (1984): pp. 904–17; "Ecology and Population," *Science* 179 (March 1973): pp. 1196–201; "Cumulative Change in Theory and History," *American Sociological Review* 43 (1978): pp. 787–97; "Spatial Aspects of Populations: An Overview," in *Social Demography*, eds. K. W. Taueber, L. L. Bumpass, and J. A. Sweet (New York: Academic, 1978); "Sociological Human Ecology: Past, Present and Future," in *Sociological Human Ecology*, eds. M. Micklin and H. M. Choldin (Boulder, CO: Westview, 1980); and most significantly, *Human Ecology: A Theoretical Essay* (Chicago: University of Chicago Press, 1986).

Hawley terms these assumptions, respectively, the *adaptive*, *growth*, and *evolution* propositions. These assumptions resurrect in altered form ideas developed by Herbert Spencer and Émile Durkheim. To survive and adapt in an environment, human populations become differentiated and integrated by a system of mutual interdependencies. The size of a population and the complexity of social organization for that population are limited by its knowledge base, particularly with respect to transportation and communication technologies. Populations cannot increase in size, nor elaborate the complexity of their patterns of organization, without expansion of knowledge about (1) communication and (2) movement of people and materials.[17] Hawley conceptualized the combined effects of transportation and communication technologies as *mobility costs*.

Linked to transportation and communication technologies is another variable, *productivity*. Curiously, in his most recent theoretical essay, this variable is somewhat subordinate, whereas it is highlighted in earlier statements. No great contradiction or dramatic change in conceptualization occurs in this more recent statement, so we can merely reintroduce the productivity variable in more explicit terms. Basically, a reciprocal set of relations exists between production of materials, information, and services, on the one side, and the capacity of a system to move these products to other system units, on the other side. The development of new transportation and communication technologies encourages expanded production, whereas the expansion of production burdens existing capacities for mobility and thereby stimulates a search for new technologies. There is also a more indirect linkage among productivity, growth, and evolution, because productivity "constitutes the principal limiting condition on the extent to which a system can be elaborated, on the size of the population that can be sustained in the system, and on the area or space that the system can occupy."[18] Thus, to support a larger, more differentiated, population in a more extended territory requires the capacity to (1) produce more goods and services and (2) distribute these goods and services through transportation and communication technologies. If productivity cannot be increased or if the mobility costs of transportation and communication cannot be reduced, then there is an upper limit on the size, scale, and complexity of the system.

## The Environment

An ecosystem is "an arrangement of mutual dependencies in a population by which the whole operates as a unit and maintains a viable environmental relationship."[19] The environment is the source of energy and materials for productivity, but the environment reveals more than a biophysical

---

[17]Hawley, *Human Ecology: A Theoretical Essay* (cited in note 16).

[18]Hawley, "Human Ecology" (cited in note 16).

[19]Hawley, *Human Ecology: A Theoretical Essay* (cited in note 16).

dimension. There is also an *ecumenical* dimension composed of the "ecosystems or cultures possessed by peoples in adjacent areas and beyond."[20] Moreover, in Hawley's view, ecological analysis "posits an external origin of change" because "a thing cannot cause itself";[21] thus, in examining a population as a whole in its physical, social, or biological environment, Hawley's approach emphasizes that change comes more from these environmental systems than from processes internal to organization of a population.

## Functions and Key Functions

In Hawley's approach, the arrangement of mutual dependencies of a population in an environment is conceptualized as classes or types of *units* that form *relations* with one another with respect to functions.[22] *Functions* are defined as "repetitive activity that is reciprocated by another or other repetitive activities." Of particular importance are *key functions*, which are repetitive activities "directly engaged with the environment." As such, key functions transmit environmental inputs (materials and information) to other "contingent functions" (or repetitive activities joining units in a relation).[23] Hawley visualizes that a relatively small number of key functions exists, and "to the extent that the principle of key functions does not obtain, the system will be tenuous and incoherent."[24] A system is thus composed of functional units, a few of which have direct relations with the environment and perform key functions. Most other units, therefore, must "secure access to the environment indirectly through the agency of the key function."[25]

For example, production is a key function, and in earlier essays, Hawley seemed to see productivity as the primary key function. Yet there are obviously other key functions—political, military, and perhaps ideological—that also influence the flow of resources to and from the environment. As a result, other functional units gain access to the environment only through their inter-connections with those units engaged in these various key functions. Thus the relations of units that form the structure of a population are conceptualized as functions and key functions, or classes of reciprocated repetitive activities that join units together. This is, of course, another way of denoting specialization and differentiation of various types in clusters of activity. Just why Hawley proposes this particular terminology is unclear, but in doing so, Hawley transforms the ecology perspective into a more functional form of analysis.

---

[20]Ibid., p. 13.

[21]Hawley, "Human Ecological and Marxian Theories" (cited in note 16).

[22]Hawley, "Human Ecology" and *Human Ecology: A Theoretical Essay*, p. 32 (both cited in note 16).

[23]Hawley, *Human Ecology: A Theoretical Essay* (cited in note 16), p. 34.

[24]Hawley, "Human Ecology" (cited in note 16), p. 332.

[25]Ibid.

**Table 7.1**   General Propositions on Functions in Ecosystems

1. The more a function (recurrent and reciprocated activity) mediates critical environmental relationships (key function), the more it determines the conditions under which all other functions are performed.

2. The more proximate is a function to a key function, the more the latter constrains the other, and vice versa.

3. The more a function is a key function, the greater is the power of those actors and units involved in this function, and vice versa.

4. The more differentiated are functions, the greater is the proportion of all functions indirectly related to the environment.

5. The greater the number of units using the products of a function and the less the costs of the skills used in the function, the greater is the number of units in the population engaged in this function.

6. The greater the mobility costs (for communication and transportation) associated with a function, the more stable are the number of, and the interrelations among, units implicated in this function.

7. The more stable the number of, and interrelations among, units implicated in functions, the more a normative order corresponds to the functional order.

Indeed, slipping into Hawley's analysis is a stronger version of the term function. In part, this stronger notion of function is implied by the concept of key function. A key function regulates inputs of energy, materials, and information into the system, and it is not hard to see how the next step on the road to functionalism is made: Certain key functions are necessary for adaptation and survival. Hawley himself takes this step when he notes:

> We might suppose, for purposes of illustration, that every instance of collective life is sustained by a mix of activities that produce sustenance and related materials, distribute the production among the participants, maintain the number of units required to produce and distribute the products, and exercise the controls needed to assure an uninterrupted performance of all tasks with a minimum of friction. [26]

Indeed, these requisites look very much like those proposed by Herbert Spencer—production, regulation, distribution, and reproduction.

Whatever the merits or defects in such functionalism, Hawley translated his ideas into a series of "hypotheses." Table 7.1 restates in somewhat modified form some of the most critical propositions that can be pulled from his

---

[26]Hawley, *Human Ecology: A Theoretical Essay* (cited in note 16), p. 32.

analysis thus far.[27] These propositions represent abstract "laws" from which Hawley's many hypotheses can be derived. The basic ideas in the propositions of Table 7.1 are the following: key functions, or those that mediate exchanges with the environment, disproportionately influence other functions and hold power over these other functions (for example, units involved in key economic or political functions in a society usually hold more power and influence than others, because they are engaged in interchanges, respectively, with the physical and social environment); the more proximate a function is to a key function, the greater this influence is; conversely, the more remote a function is from a key function, the less influence this function has on a key function. Differentiation of key functions decreases other functions' direct access to the environment, because such access is now mediated by units involved in key functions (for example, most people do not grow their own food or provide their own military defense in highly differentiated societies). As mobility costs for personnel and materials needed for functions increase, the functions' number and relations stabilize; under these conditions, a normative order can develop to regulate the internal relations of functions, as well as their interrelations.

## Equilibrium and Change

An ecosystem is thus a population organized to adapt to an environment, with change in this system being defined by Hawley as "a shift in the number and kinds of functions or as a rearrangement of functions in different combinations."[28] In contrast with change, growth is "the maturation of a system through the maximization of the potential for complexity and integration implicit in the technology for movement and communication possessed at a given point in time,"[29] whereas evolution is "the occurrence of new structural elements from environmental inputs that lead to synthesis of new with old information and a consequent increase in the scope of the accessible environment."[30] This series of definitions presents a picture of ecosystem dynamics as revolving around the following: (1) the internal rearrangement of functions; (2) the increase of complexity to the maximum allowed by an existent level of communication and transportation technologies; and (3) the receipt of environmental inputs, especially new information that expands transportation and communication (or capacity for mobility) and that, as a consequence, increases the scale and complexity of the ecosystem (to the limits imposed by the new technologies).

There is an image of a system in equilibrium that is then placed into disequilibrium by new knowledge about production as it influences

---

[27]Ibid., pp. 43–44.

[28]Ibid., p. 46.

[29]Ibid., p. 52.

[30]Ibid.

mobility (of people, materials, and information). Somewhat less clear is where this new information comes from. Must it be totally exogenous (from other societies, migrants, changes in biophysical forces that generate new knowledge)? Or can the system itself generate the new information through a particular array of functions? It would appear that both can be the source of change; yet the imagery of Hawley's model[31] connotes a system that must be disrupted from the outside if it is to evolve and develop new levels of structural complexity. Internal dialectical processes, or self-transforming processes that increase technology, seem to be underemphasized as crucial ecosystem dynamics. Table 7.2 summarizes the more abstract "laws" that can be culled from Hawley's hypotheses on these dynamics.[32]

These propositions reinforce the emphasis in human ecology that the source of change is exogenous, residing particularly in the ecumenical environment. From this environment, new knowledge will come and then become synthesized with the existing knowledge base. Such synthesized knowledge will then change production, transportation, and communication in ways that allow the system to increase its complexity, size, and territory. Yet,

**Table 7.2**  General Propositions, Change, Growth, and Evolution in Ecosystems

1. The greater the exposure of an ecosystem to the ecumenical environment (other societies or cultures of other societies), the greater is the probability of new information and knowledge penetrating the system and, hence, the greater is the probability of change, growth, and evolution.

2. The more new information increases the mobility of people, materials, and information, as well as production, the more likely that change will be cumulative, or evolutionary, to the limits of complexity allowed by the new information as it is translated into technologies for production, transportation, and communication.

3. The more new information improves various mobility and productive limits on the faster-changing technology.

4. The more a system approaches the scale and complexity allowed by technologies, the slower the rate of change, growth, and evolution is and the more likely the system is to achieve a state of closure (equilibrium) in its ecumenical environment.

---

[31]Ibid., p. 59. Hawley "boxes" lists of variables and then draws arrows among the boxes but not among the variables within each box. Hence, detailed causal arguments need to be inferred.

[32]Ibid., pp. 85–87.

new knowledge can introduce change only to a point. If some technologies lag behind others, the rate of change will be pulled down by the lower technology. And eventually the maximal size, scale, and complexity of the system will be reached, unless new technologies are inserted into the system from the environment. Thus systems that have grown to the maximum size, scope, and complexity allowed by production, transportation, and communication technologies will achieve equilibrium. New knowledge from the environment can disrupt the equilibrium when such knowledge is used to achieve increases in productivity and mobility. But each technology has limits on how much growth and evolution it can facilitate; when this limit is reached, the system will tend to re-equilibrate.

The concept of equilibrium is most problematic, although Hawley employs it only as a heuristic device. Hawley means the notion of equilibrium to connote "the balance of nature, denoting a tendency toward stabilization of the relative numbers of diverse organisms within the web of life and their several claims on the environment."[33] Yet Hawley recognizes that "equilibrium . . . is a logical construct"[34] and connotes that ecological systems tend toward stability, although Hawley also employs terms like *partial equilibrium* to connote only a tendency toward some degree of instability.

## Growth and Evolution

The most interesting portions of ecological theory are those dealing with growth and evolution—that is, increasing size, scale, scope, and complexity of the systematic whole in its environment. This analysis builds on the propositions in Tables 7.1 and 7.2, but it extends them in creative ways and, as a result, goes considerably beyond the early formulations of Spencer and Durkheim.

In Figure 7.4, Hawley's model is redrawn in a way that makes the causal dynamics more explicit. Starting on the far left of the model, Hawley believes that an expanded knowledge base must come from the ecumenical environment. As the model stresses, new knowledge causes growth and change when it increases the level of communication and transportation technologies, either directly or indirectly, through increasing production (which then causes expansion of these technologies). A critical variable in Hawley's scheme is mobility costs; for any given technology, a cost (time, energy, money, materials) is associated with the movement of information, materials, and people. As these costs reach their maximum—that is, the system cannot pay for them without degenerating—they impose a limit on the scale of the system: the size of its population, the extent of its territory, the level of its productivity, and the level of complexity. Conversely, as the feedback arrows in the model indicate, the size of territory and population

---

[33]Hawley, "Human Ecology" (cited in note 16), p. 329.

[34]Ibid., p. 334.

Figure 7.4 Hawley's Macro-Level Ecological Model

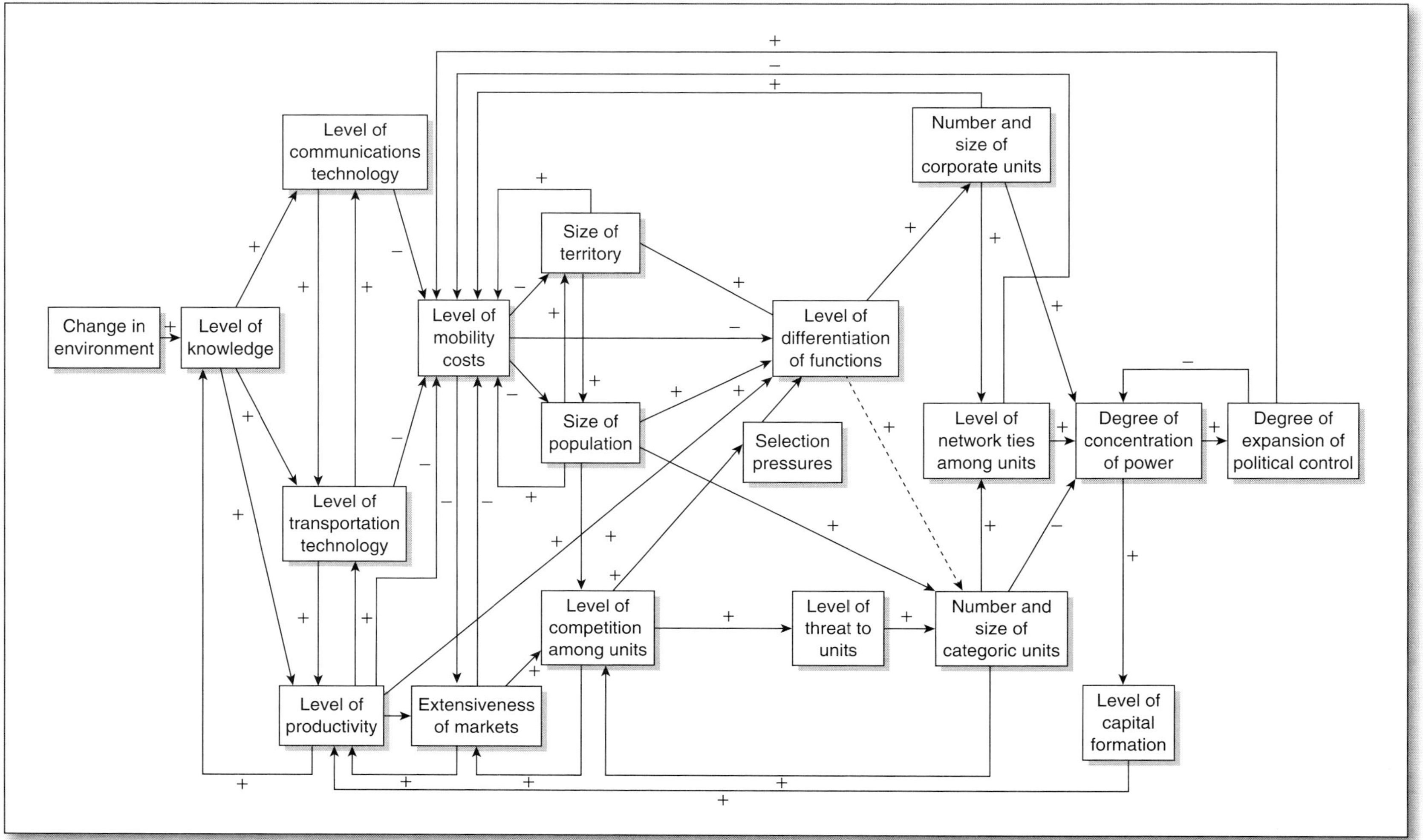

will, as they expand and grow, begin to impose higher mobility costs. Eventually these costs will increase to a point at which the population cannot grow or expand its territory—unless new communication and transportation technologies that reduce costs are discovered.

Much as Spencer and Durkheim argued, population and territorial size, because these are influenced by mobility costs, cause specialization of functions—what is termed *differentiation in the model.* As Hawley notes, however, the relationship between population size and differentiation is not unambiguous, but it does create "conditions that foster, if not necessitate, increases in the sizes of subsystems" and the number of such subsystems serving various functions. Thus, for Hawley, "the greater the size, the greater the probable support for units with degrees of specialization." And, as he adds, "Other pertinent conditions are the rate or volume of intersystem communications, scope of a market, and amount of stability in intersystem relations."[35]

These causal connections are not clearly delineated by Hawley, and so the model involves making many causal inferences. The causal paths moving from level of productivity through extensiveness of markets and level of competition to selection pressures and differentiation of functions represent the old Spencerian and Durkheimian argument: Expansion of markets increases the level of competitiveness among units and, at the same time, increases the capacity to distribute goods and services because these are constrained by mobility costs (note arrows connecting markets and mobility costs); competition under conditions of increased production and population size allows—indeed encourages—specialization as actors seek their most viable niche. Similarly, the causal arrows moving from communication and transportation technologies through mobility costs, size of territory, and size of population to level of differentiation of functions restate Spencer's, but more particularly Durkheim's, argument in a more sophisticated form: Changes in communication and transportation technologies reduce mobility costs and allow population growth and territorial expansion; all these forces together create selective pressures to adjust and adapt varying attributes and competencies, especially under conditions of intense competition for resources.

Hawley believed that differentiation of subunits engaged in various functions occurs along two axes: (1) corporate and (2) categoric.[36] *Corporate units* are constructed from *symbiotic relations* of mutual dependence among differentiated actors, whereas *categoric units* are composed of *commensalistic relations* among actors who reveal common interests and who pool their activities to adapt more effectively to their environments. Table 7.3 delineates these types of units along an additional dimension—their "unifying

[35]Hawley, *Human Ecology: A Theoretical Essay* (cited in note 16), pp. 80–81.

[36]Ibid., pp. 68–73 and "Human Ecology" (cited in note 16), pp. 331–32.

**Table 7.3**   A Typology of System Units

| Unifying Principle | Relational Structure | |
|---|---|---|
| | Corporate Units | Categoric Units |
| **Familial** | Household units | Clan, tribe, kin |
| **Territorial** | Village, city, ecumene | Polity, neighborhood, ethnic enclave, ghetto |
| **Associational** | Industry, retail store, school, government | Caste, class, guild, union, professional organization |

principle."[37] Thus, as differentiation increases, an ecosystem will represent a complex configuration of corporate and categoric units along various unifying principles: familial, territorial, associational. It is not clear if Hawley meant this typology to be exhaustive or merely illustrative. Nonetheless, the typology is provocative.

The dynamics of these two types of units are very different. Corporate units form around functions, or sets of related activities, and are engaged in interchanges with other corporate units. As a consequence of this contact, corporate units tend to resemble one another, especially those that engage in frequent interchanges or are closely linked to corporate units engaged in key functions (interchanges with the environment). Moreover, as they engage in interchanges, corporate units tend toward closure of structure and establishment of clear boundaries. The size and number of such corporate units depend, of course, on the size of the population, the inter- and intra-unit mobility costs associated with communication and transportation technologies, the capacity for production and distribution in markets (as constrained by mobility costs), and the level of competition among units.

In contrast, categoric units involve interdependencies that develop "on the basis of similarities among the members of a population"[38]; their number and size are related to the size of the population and territory as well as to the level of threat imposed by their environment. As Hawley noted, the nature of the threat can vary—a "task too large for the individual to accomplish in a limited time, such as the harvesting of a crop"; "losing land to an invader"; "possible destruction of a road or other amenity"; "a technological shift that might render an occupation obsolete"; and so on. If a threat is persistent, the actors in a categoric unit will form a more "lasting association," and if similar units are in competition (say, rival labor unions or ideologically similar political parties), the costs and destructiveness of such

---

[37]Hawley, *Human Ecology: A Theoretical Essay* (cited in note 16), p. 74.

[38]Ibid., p. 70.

competition will eventually lead to their consolidation into a larger categoric unit. Moreover, those categoric units that persist will develop a corporate core to sustain the flow and coordination of resources necessary to deal with the persisting or recurring threat. Categoric units can also get much larger than corporate units because their membership criteria—mere possession of certain characteristics (ethnic, religious, occupational, ideological)—are much more lax than those of corporate units, which recruit members to perform certain specialized and interdependent activities or functions. Of course, the size and number of categoric units are still circumscribed by the size and complexity of the ecosystem and, to a lesser extent than with corporate units, by the mobility costs associated with communication and transportation technologies.

As is indicated in the right portion of Figure 7.4, differentiation of categoric and leads corporate units to consolidate into networks, which create larger subsystems. This regularization of ties among units engaged in similar and symbiotic activities or functions reduces mobility costs. And, reduced mobility costs facilitate the growth of the ecosystem (note the feedback arrow to mobility costs).

Differentiation of units and their consolidation into larger networks also have consequences for the concentration of power. Categoric-unit formation and the consolidation of such units into larger networks and subsystems tend to reduce concentrations of power. The reason for this reduction of power is that various confederations of categoric units will pose a check on one another. In contrast, corporate units are more likely to cause the concentration of power. This concentration is directly related to the capacity of some units to perform key functions and thereby dictate the conditions under which interrelated functions must operate. This control is facilitated by consolidation of networks into subsystems because such networks connect outlying and remote corporate units, via configurations of successive network ties, to those engaged in key functions. Such connections among corporate units, as they facilitate the concentration of power, enable political control to expand to the far reaches of the ecosystem; political and territorial boundaries tend to become coterminous in ecosystems. Yet, centralization of power and extension of control can increase mobility costs as rules and regulations associated with efforts at control escalate, setting limits on how complex the ecosystem can become, without a change in communication and transportation technologies (hence the long feedback arrow at the top of Figure 7.4).

We can add a variable to the model that is implicit but crucial: capital formation. Hawley does not address this issue extensively, so we are clearly adding it to his model. Nonetheless, it is important to recognize that concentration of power also consolidates the flow of resources, facilitating capital formation. If not squandered on maintenance of control, defense, or offensive efforts at military expansion, this capital can be used to expand productivity and, indirectly, to change the knowledge and technological base of the system (note the long feedback arrows at the bottom of Figure 7.4).

**Table 7.4** Basic Propositions on Patterns of Ecosystem Differentiation

1. The greater is the size of a population and its territory and the greater is the selection pressure stemming from competition among members of this population, the greater will be the differentiation of functions and the number, as well as size of corporate units, to the maximum allowed by mobility costs.

2. The greater is the size of a population and the greater are the threats posed by competition and environmental change, the greater will be the number of categoric units, to the maximum allowed by mobility costs.

3. The greater are the number and size of both categoric and corporate units, the more will increases in number of relations occur at a geometric rate and the greater will be the amount of time and energy allocated to mobility.

4. The greater is the number of relations among units and the higher are the costs of mobility, the more likely are differentiated units to establish networks and combine into more inclusive subsystems, thereby reducing mobility costs.

5. The more concentrated in power, the more prominent will be networks and subsystems and the more extensive will be political regulation of units in the ecosystem.

As with Tables 7.1 and 7.2, Table 7.4 extracts the most crucial hypothesis from Hawley's many hypotheses. As territory and population size increase, because of new knowledge about production, transportation, and communication, it is possible and perhaps necessary to differentiate units around specific functions. This is particularly true for corporate units, which represent clusters of interdependencies revolving around a particular function. Categoric units form in response to threats, which ultimately stem from the competition that results from increases in population size, productivity, and markets. As the number of differentiated units in a system increases, the number of relations increases at an exponential rate, increasing mobility costs. Corporate and categoric units both tend to consolidate into larger networks, forming subsystems and reducing mobility costs. But the effects of corporate and categoric unit differentiation and consolidation on the concentration of power vary. Corporate units consolidate, centralize, and extend power and regulation, whereas categoric units form power blocks that diffuse power in a system of checks and balances.

As with the other propositions, the many specific hypotheses in Hawley's scheme can be deduced from these and from the scenario delineated.[39] Thus the propositions in Tables 7.1, 7.2, and 7.4 do not do full justice to the depth

[39]Ibid., pp. 106–108, 123–24.

and extent of Hawley's scheme. They are intended as more abstract statements rather than as the many "hypotheses" that punctuate Hawley's theory.

In sum, then, Hawley's ecological theory retains some important ideas of early sociology. One of these ideas is the obvious but often ignored view that society represents an adaptation of the human species to its environment. Another related idea is that it is not possible to understand human social organization without reference to the interchanges between environment and internal social structure. Yet another crucial idea is that the basic dynamics of a society revolve around (1) aggregation of actors in physical space, competition, and differentiation and (2) integration through subsystem formation and centralization of power. Still another useful point is the emphasis on population size, territory, productivity, communication and transportation technologies, and competition as important causes of those macrostructural processes—differentiation, conflict, class formation, consolidation of power, and the like—that have long interested sociologists. Finally, a significant, though problematic, idea is that the altered flow of resources—energy, information, materials—into the system is the ultimate source of social system growth and evolution.

# Conclusion

Ecological models in sociological theory have all represented an analogy to the forces of evolution, particularly natural selection through competition. Whether operating at the macro level or meso level, these theories seek to demonstrate that certain parallel processes operate in populations of collective actors within societies and populations of species in the biotic world. Ecological theorizing in sociology originally emerged in functionalist theorizing about stages of societal evolution, and as I have noted, functionalism initially disappeared because of its use of stage models of societal evolution from simple to complex forms. Functionalism reemerged in the 1950s, only to begin to decline in the 1970s and 1980s, but this time theorizing about stages and phases of evolution reemerged in the 1960s in sociology and, unlike functionalism, has remained a key form of evolutionary theorizing in the present day. It is these stage models of evolution that will be examined in the next chapter, but such models can also be seen in a number of diverse theoretical traditions, such as Marxist-inspired world systems (Chapter 13) analysis and critical theory (Chapter 31 and 32) as well as in functional theories that still persists (Chapters 3 and 4).

## CHAPTER 8

# Stage Theories of Societal Evolution

A s we saw in the last chapter, the most prominent form of biologically inspired theorizing in sociology has been ecological, where competition and selection processes are seen as the force behind social differentiation of whole societies, spatial arrangements in urban areas, and distributions among populations of complex organizations. Alongside ecological approaches, developmental theories of societal evolution from simple to ever-more complex forms have also persisted, arising with Herbert Spencer and Émile Durkheim and moving forward within a number of theoretical traditions in the second half of the twentieth century.

## Gerhard Lenski's Stage Model of Societal Evolution

In the mid-1960s, evolutionary theorizing about stages of societal evolution reemerged. I have already detailed Talcott Parsons' theory[1] in Chapter 3, but more influential at the time was Gerhard Lenski's work on societal evolution and stratification.[2] By outlining a stage theory of societal evolution, and at the same time, concentrating on power, inequality, and potential conflict, Lenski's model was more in tune with the times. Conflict theorizing was reemerging in the United States in the post-McCarthy era, where Marx could once again be examined in public places, and Lenski's model was received much better than Parsons' because it did not carry functionalist

---

[1]Talcott Parsons, *Societies: Evolutionary and Comparative Perspectives* and *The System of Modern Societies* (Englewood Cliffs, NJ: Prentice Hall, 1966 and 1971, respectively).

[2]Gerhard Lenski, *Power and Privilege: A Theory of Social Stratification* (New York: McGraw-Hill, reprinted by the University of North Carolina Press).

trappings and, instead, focused on conflict. Later, in association with Gene Lenski, and then, Patrick Nolan,[3] this early approach was broadened to a full macro-level theory of social organization; more recently, Lenski himself reconfigured his theory to emphasize the ecological dynamics woven into the stage model of societal-level evolution.[4]

## Power and Privilege During Societal Evolution

The basic argument developed in *Power and Privilege: A Theory of Stratification* is that the level of technology determines, along with other factors, the level of production in a society. The higher is the level of technology in a society, the greater will be the level of economic production; the higher is the level of production, the greater will be the amount of economic surplus in a society. And, as the level of economic surplus increases, the more it can be usurped by those consolidating power, thereby increasing inequality and the privilege of those with this power. This basic dynamics is outlined in Figure 8.1.

The fundamental relationship among technology, production, economic surplus, and inequality in a society is mediated by a number of factors. One is environmental or ecological conditions, such as available resources in the natural environment, available geographical space, and presence of other societies and the potential threats that they might pose. Another key factor is demographic, revolving around the size of a population and the profile of characteristics (e.g., age, ethnicity, class locations, religious affiliation, etc.). Still another set of factors is the nature of social organization generated, in particularly the form of polity and its degree of consolidation of power, but also other institutional systems such as the structure of kinship, religion, law, education, and science. Yet another is the geopolitical situation of a society revolving around competition for resources and warfare with other societies. Still another is the value and ideological cultural systems that emerge and constrain patterns of social organization and action.

These additional factors are all labeled in Figure 8.1, but as the bold arrows try to make clear, the primary factors in Lenski's model revolve around technology, production, productive surplus, consolidation of power, inequality, and system of stratification.

What made this analysis appealing in the 1960s is that Lenski used a stage model of evolution to explain variations in the primary influences affecting the forces generating stratification. Thus, the lower is the level of technology, the lower will be the level of production in a society, and hence, the less

---

[3]Gerhard Lenski, Patrick Nolan, and Jean Lenski, *Human Societies: An Introduction to Macrosociology*, 7th ed. (New York: McGraw-Hill, 1995). For the most recent edition, see Patrick Nolan and Gerhard Lenski, *Human Societies*, 11th ed. (Boulder, CO: Paradigm Press, 2009).

[4]Gerhard Lenski, *Ecological-Evolutionary Theory: Principles and Applications* (Boulder, CO: Paradigm Press, 2005).

**Figure 8.1** Lenski's Basic Model of Stratification

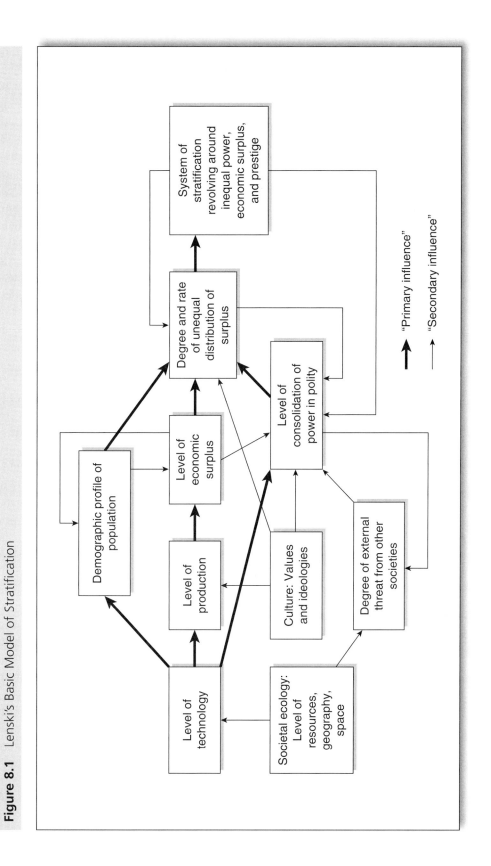

will be the size of the productive surplus, if any, generated. And, without surplus, there is nothing to usurp by those consolidating power; as a consequence, degree of stratification in a society will be low. The history of human societies, then, has revolved around a series of basic stages during which the level of technology, production, and surplus have all increased. The stages proposed by Lenski are very similar to those developed by Herbert Spencer (see Figure 6.1 on page 110): hunting and gathering without a head; hunting and gathering with a head (and hence, beginnings of polity); simple and advanced horticultural (gardening without animal power); simple and advanced agrarian (farming using animal power); and industrial (relying on inanimate power). Within each of these stages, there are variations in the degree of development, but each stage defines the basic mode of technology that is used to gather resources and produce material products. There are also fishing variants for nomadic hunting and gathering, as well as herding variants for horticultural and agrarian societies. Moreover, there is a marine variant for agrarian societies.

Lenski's analysis attempts to explain two forces. One is the goal of earlier functional stage models: the growing complexity of societies by virtue increases in the level of technology and production that, in turn, affect the number of people who can be supported in a society and, hence, a society's size. But this relationship is mediated by the consolidation of power in polity or government and, in turn, the degree to which power is used to usurp productive surplus to sustain elite privilege. So Lenski, like all functional theorists before him, sought to isolate the driving forces of evolutionary history—in his case, technology, production, and economic surplus (whereas functionalists like Spencer and Durkheim tended to emphasize increases in population size and rates of growth as what kick-starts the development of technologies and productive capacities). These demographic forces are also part of Lenski's model, as laid out in Figure 8.1, but they are given somewhat less significance than in early functional models outlining the stages of societal evolution.

The second goal is to use these same dynamics to explain the evolution and operation of stratification systems in human societies, with stratification hypothesized to increase with the level of technology, production, and surplus. In a very real sense, data assembled on societies at different stages of development are intended to assess the theory of inequality and stratification—thus making this kind of evolutionary theorizing more in tune with the conflict theories that were emerging at the same time.

The hypothesized relationship among technology, production, surplus, and inequality is portrayed by the straight line in Figure 8.2, but the actual empirical findings from data on all stages of societal development were found to be more like that portrayed in the curvilinear line in Figure 8.2. The hypothesized relationship held up until the industrial stage. From hunting and gathering forward, stratification increases as technology and production generate ever-more surplus that historically has led to the consolidation of power in polity and the usurpation of surplus—thereby

**Figure 8.2** Hypothesized and Actual Trend in Inequality during Societal Evolution

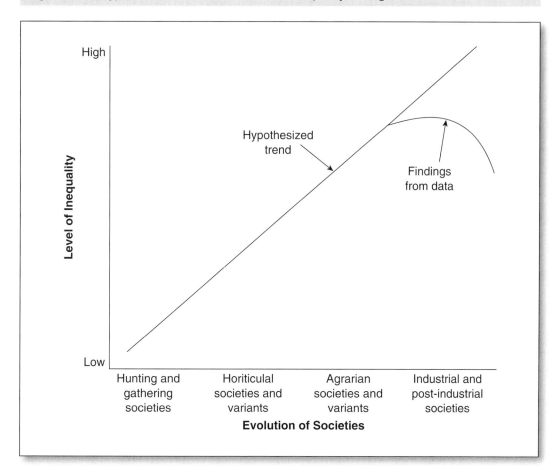

increasing the level of inequality in the stratification system. Going against this long-term evolutionary/historical trend, however, is a significant, though still rather modest, decrease in inequality in industrial societies. This reversal requires an explanation, and hence, Lenski introduces what he terms secondary variables—democratization of power, reliance on education and its extensions to the masses as an important criterion for resource distribution, and changes in societal ideologies toward advocating more equality or at least equality of opportunity. These variables become more highly valenced in industrial societies, and the result is a reversal of the long-term historical trend toward ever-more inequality and stratification in human societies.

The influence of Lenski's analysis cannot be underestimated. He made stage modeling of evolutionary sequences respectable outside of functional analysis because he emphasized forces—power, inequality, and stratification— at the core of conflict theory that was challenging functional theory in general and Talcott Parsons' version of functional and evolutionary theory in particular. And, over the last five decades, Lenski himself has continued to refine the model of societal evolution, but equally, if not more important, a large number of theorists began to follow the path opened up by Lenski's *Power and Privilege.*

## Gerhard Lenski, Patrick Nolan, and Jean Lenski's Evolutionary Theory

As Lenski continued to theorize on evolution, he increasingly added more biological and ecological forces to his analysis. Working with his wife before her early death and later with Patrick Nolan, Lenski began to include in his theory of societal development more Darwinian theoretic ideas as well as ideas form the Modern Synthesis in biology—perhaps a good indicator of how much biological theorizing was beginning to influence the social sciences in the 1970s and 1980s.

Both biological and social evolution are, first, "based on records of experience that are preserved and transmitted from generation to generation in the form of coded systems of information" and, second, on "processes that involve random variation and selection" of those traits that promote adaptation to the environment.[5] Yet, there are some important differences between biological and social evolution. One is that, in organic evolution, the genes are the preservers of the informational codes, whereas in social evolution, cultural "symbol systems are the functional equivalents of the genetic alphabet."[6] Another difference revolves around the way that information is transmitted. In biological evolution, genetic information can be transmitted only through the reproduction of new organisms; moreover, diverse species cannot interbreed, so the transmission of information is limited to one species. In contrast, cultural information is more readily and broadly transmitted, moving from one type of society to another. The end result is that in biological evolution, speciation leads to ever-new patterns of differentiation and diversification, whereas in social evolution, the movement of information across societal types "is likely to eventuate in ever fewer and less dissimilar societies than exist today."[7] A related difference is that in biological evolution, both simple and complex species can continue to exist in their respective resource niches, whereas in social evolution, simpler societal types tend to be extinguished by more complex types. Still another difference is that acquired traits can be transmitted through socialization, whereas in biological evolution, such Lamarckian processes do not occur. An outcome of this difference is that genetic change in biological evolution is slow (because selection processes have to sort out genes across many generations), whereas cultural evolution can be very rapid (because

---

[5]Lenski, Nolan, and Lenski, *Human Societies,* 7th ed. (cited in note 3), p. 75.

[6]Ibid.

[7]Ibid, pp. 75–76.

new traits can be created, learned, transmitted, and diffused within one generation).

These similarities and differences lead to the recognition that human societies are part of the natural world and subject to selection forces from both their biophysical and sociocultural environments, that humans like any other animal are influenced by their genetic heritage, and that only humans are the creators of their cultural heritage or the informational codes that guide behavior and social organization. A given society,[8] then, has social structural and cultural (symbolic) characteristics that, for analytical purposes, can be divided into the following: (1) its population size and characteristics; (2) its culture or systems of symbols, particularly technologies; (3) its material products generated by the application of its technology to productive processes; (4) its organizational forms that structure activities; and (5) its institutional systems that combine (1) through (4) into systems addressing basic problems of survival and adaptation for individuals and the society as a whole. These five components of a society influence, while being influenced by other forces—(1) a society's biophysical environment, (2) its social environment of other societies and their respective cultures, (3) the genetic heritage of humans as a species, namely an evolved ape, and (4) the prior social and cultural characteristics of a society as these—continue to influence its internal operation and its adaptation to the external environment.

In this more recent analysis, Lenski's earlier emphasis on technologies as the driving force of social evolution is retained, but the argument is recast into an evolutionary framework inspired by Darwin and the Modern Synthesis. As Lenski recently remarked, "It seems no exaggeration to say that advances in subsistence technology are functionally equivalent to adaptive changes in a population's gene pool; new energy resources and new materials enable populations to do things that they could not do before."[9]

Social evolution is a cumulative process in the sense that new technologies proving more adaptive alter the pattern of social organization, generally toward larger and more complex forms of organization. Two basic forces drive change in human societies:[10] (1) innovation where new information and social structural patterns are created, whether by chance or conscious intent and (2) extinction where old cultural and structural patterns are abandoned. Innovations in sociocultural evolution cause more rapid change than forces in biological evolution, because (a) humans have conscious capacities to develop new informational codes; (b) humans have "needs and desires" that are potentially "limitless" and, under certain conditions, drive them to make new discoveries as old needs are satisfied and new ones emerge; (c) humans

---

[8]Ibid., adapted from pp. 21, 23–55; see also Gerhard Lenski, "Societal Taxonomies: Mapping the Social Universe," *Annual Review of Sociology* 20 (1994): p. 33. See also, Lenski, *Ecoloigcal-Evolutionary Theory* (cited in note 4), p. 118.

[9]Lenski, "Societal Taxonomies" (cited in note 8), p. 23.

[10]Lenski, Nolan, and Lenski, *Human Societies,* 7th ed. (cited in note 3), pp. 57–58.

can adopt the information of other societies through diffusion; (d) humans can force another society to adopt their informational codes through conquest and repression of older cultural and structural patterns, especially when larger and more complex societies conquer or co-opt smaller and less complex ones; (e) humans can institutionalize innovation in such structural forms as science, thereby creating a set of cultural codes and social structures specifically geared to constant innovation; and (f) humans can create complex inter-connections among systems of information that force changes in other elements as changes in another occur.

Yet, Lenski, Nolan, and Lenski stress that there are also forces operating to sustain continuity in the cultural systems that guide the organization of a population.[11] One force for continuity is socialization, in which older patterns are transmitted to each new generation. Another force is ideology, which preserves cultural systems and guides the transmission of culture from one generation to another. Still another force is the systemic nature of human sociocultural systems, which resist change in one element because so many other elements will be forced to change (although, as noted earlier, once change in one element occurs, it has a cascading effect and actually accelerates change). Another force is vested interests, especially of the powerful in stratified societies who have the power to suppress innovations when changes threaten status quo interests. Yet another force is inertia, where past practices appear to promote adaptation and sufficient satisfaction for individuals to resist adopting new practices whose impact cannot be fully known.

Despite these forces promoting continuity, the long-term historical record confirms that societal evolution has involved change, fueled by technological innovations, toward larger and more complex societies. Societies vary, of course, in their rates of innovation; these rates vary because of several important forces. First, the amount of information already possessed by a society greatly influences its capacity to create and adopt more information. Second, the size of a population is another important factor because larger populations have more individuals who hold ideas and who can potentially generate new ideas. Third, the stability and nature of a society's environment, both social and biophysical, is another force of change; the more the environment changes, the more likely a society is to be innovative or adopt the innovations of another. Fourth, the nature of the innovations per se is a very significant factor; some innovations are fundamental and pave the way for additional innovations (for example, the discovery of metallurgy or new sources of energy stimulated even more innovations). And fifth, the ideology of a society greatly circumscribes the creation or adoption of innovations; powerful and conservative ideologies make it difficult for individuals to be innovative, while discouraging the diffusion of innovations from other societies.

Over the long course of societal development, however, productive technologies are the most important driving force of evolution.[12] In the end,

---

[11]Ibid.

[12]Ibid., p. 84.

technological innovations can overcome the forces promoting continuity, even the ideologies and the vested interests of the powerful. The reason for this significance of technology is that those societies that can better gather, produce, and distribute resources will generate an economic surplus that can support a larger population and its differentiation into new organizational forms and institutional systems. Eventually, their technologies diffuse to other societies, and particularly so when larger, more complex societies conquer, co-opt, or outcompete smaller and less complex societies. Thus, a kind of group selection operates in the history of human societies, as more powerful societies (with better technologies, productive capacities, and organizational forms) impose their cultural systems and structural patterns on others through conquest, provide models and incentives for less developed societies to adopt their cultural and structural systems, or take the resources on which less developed societies depend for their survival.[13] These last points echo Herbert Spencer's argument that survival of the fittest operates at the group level where the better organized society will prevail in war and in economic competition over the less organized. Indeed, selection processes have favored an emerging world system of societies.

# Jonathan Turner's Evolutionary Analysis

In my efforts to develop general theory on all fundamental social processes (see Figure 5.3 on page 104), I found myself using a stage model of evolution when examining the macro level of social reality. My goal has not been to theorize about the prime movers of stages in the same manner that Lenski in his latest works has done, but rather, my intent is to develop abstract principles that explain the dynamics of the macro realm in all times and places. This is what is often seen as *grand theorizing*, when the goal is to explain large sections of social reality, or even the entire social universe. For many, however, it is better to chop and dice up the social universe into small bits and pieces in order to develop very narrow and specialized theories on each of these bits and pieces. Such work is often important but, at some point, theories must be consolidated; the conceptual humpty dumpty needs to be put back together.

At the macro level of social organization, contemporary sociology reveals very active theorizing in world systems, or the analysis of inter-societal systems, which often posits stages and phases of development in inter-societal networks. The macrodynamics of institutions, however, has been relegated to the analysis of the organizational basis of institutions, but the notion of institutions themselves is left under-theorized, or even clearly defined, for

---

[13]Ibid., p. 54. This is an idea that was originally proposed by Herbert Spencer who emphasized that societies evolved from competition and war between societies, with the more complex, productive, and powerful society winning out in a struggle for the survival of the fittest.

that matter. The dynamics of stratification in general has virtually disappeared, but in the United States, it has been chopped up into ideologically driven critical theories about class, race, and gender, with stratification as a whole system being rather neglected. Even conflict processes generated by stratification have declined from their peak in the 1960s and 1970s where theories building on Marx, Weber, and Simmel were commonplace. There are no theories of societies as a distinctive macro-level unit, as was once a goal in sociology. When we retain a vision of societies as having evolved over a long period of time toward ever-more complex forms—as was once a vision shared by all sociologists before the twentieth century—the partitioning of even macro sociology, to say nothing of meso and micro sociology into many diverse and highly specialized theoretical research programs becomes glaringly apparent. This is why I set out two decades ago on my own theoretical crusade to bring grand theory back into sociology, ever since its last remnants were destroyed by critics of functional theory.

It is not necessary to bring functionalism back, however. If we seek out the fundamental properties and forces that have driven the macro realm of reality from the beginnings of human societies and, presumably, into all future societies, we need data on all types of societies that have ever existed. The goal is not to theorize about industrialism, agrarianism, or any past or future stage of evolution but, instead, to theorize about *the common dynamics of all societies* from their very beginning to the present day. This is what I have tried to do in my three volume *Theoretical Principles of Sociology,*[14] and somewhat to my surprise (before I thought about it), I found myself using the data that I had assembled on diverse societies from hunting and gathering to all subsequent stages of development to assess the plausibility of the models and propositions that I was developing. The more the dynamic forces outlined in these models and proposition seemed to operate in diverse societal types across the full range of societal and inter-societal formations that have ever been developed by humans, the more confident I became that, perhaps, I had formulated some of sociology's basic laws about the macro-level universe. Many of these laws represented only refinement of those implicitly articulated by the early masters of sociology, but others incorporate the data and conceptual work from highly specialized fields that have merged over the last fifty years. The critical point here is that using evolutionary models, and the data on which they are based, in developing general theory at the macro level is essential to assessing the plausibility of theories. And, I suspect, this is one of the reason that stage models of societal evolution made a comeback at mid-twentieth century; they were needed in macro-level theorizing because they provided a great array of data over the long-term evolutionary history of societal formations.

---

[14]Jonathan H. Turner, *Theoretical Principles of Sociology*, three volumes on macrodynamics (volume 1), microdynamics (volume 2), and mesodynamics (volume 3), (New York: Springer, 2010–2013). Volume 1 on macrodynamics is the relevant volume for this section.

As discussed in Chapter 5, I visualize the macrodynamic universe as driven by five fundamental forces—population, production, regulation, distribution, and reproduction.[15] These are not functional requisites but, instead, properties and contingencies of the social universe. They vary in their valences, and if these valences increase, then they generate selection pressures on human populations. These can be Darwinian or Durkheimian (competition among social units in resource niches), or what I call Spencerian, or pressures on actors to develop responses and solutions to selection pressures in the absence of any existing structures that can successfully respond to these pressures. For example, if populations grow, then this growth generates pressures of its own, but it does more: it raises the valences of the other forces. New kinds of social structures and new systems of culture will have to be developed to meet pressures for more production, distribution, regulation, and reproduction. If new adaptive responses cannot occur, then the population and the society (and the constituent sociocultural formations organizing its activities) will disintegrate. Thus, much selection in sociocultural systems is not Darwinian but rather Spencerian. Spencerian selection occurs under low density of structures, or the non-existence of any structures capable of solving new selection pressures from the five forces of the macrodynamic realm.

These selection pressures will often, but not always, cause the emergence of entrepreneurs who seek to mobilize cultural and organizational resources to meet new challenges posed by selection pressures (see Figure 5.2 on page 103). There is no guarantee that entrepreneurs will emerge or, if they emerge, will be successful in creating new kinds of corporate units (units with divisions of labor to achieve goals) that can deal with the problems posed by Spencerian selection pressures. The theory thus begins with an analysis of the conditions that increase the valences of macrodynamic forces, the conditions that increase the likelihood (or vice versa) that entrepreneurs will emerge, and the conditions under which they are more likely to be successful in consolidating resources and forming new kinds of corporate units and new systems of cultural symbols.

As entrepreneurs mobilize resources, they organize people into new kinds of divisions of labor within corporate units capable of responding to selection pressures. If these units prove successful, they will be copied by other actors—thereby setting off their reproduction. At the same time, entrepreneurs use symbolic resources to regulate activities and justify and legitimate their actions and the new sociocultural formations that these actions create. Functional theorists, like Talcott Parsons and Niklas Luhmann, conceptualized these symbol systems as *generalized symbolic media* that are articulated and exchanged among actors. Depending upon the symbolic media developed, these media become part of the culture of emerging institutional domains. For example, as Simmel first emphasized,

---

[15]Ibid. See also my earlier *Macrodynamics: Toward a Theory on the Organization of Human Populations* (New Brunswick, NJ: Rutgers University Press, 1995).

*money* is a symbol of value (rarely does the money itself—that is the paper on which value is expressed by numbers—have inherent value); similarly *power* as a symbolic media is a highly valued resource, as are other symbolic media such as *love, health, knowledge, learning, competition,* and *aesthetics.* These are symbols that are part of discourse among individuals and collective units engaged in particular kinds of activities that will eventually form a new, or change old, institutional domains. But, the media are more than symbolic; they are also valued resources that become unequally distributed and, hence, the basis of a stratification system.

As these symbolic media are used, they also carry evaluations of what is good/bad and appropriate/inappropriate. They become evaluative and, if in wide circulation, they are codified into *institutional ideologies* about what should, and should not, occur within particular institutional domains. For instance, the ideology of polity is built from the symbolic medium of *power*; the ideology of production, especially in a capitalist system, is built from the symbolic medium of *money*; the ideology of medicine is built from the symbolic medium of *health*; the system of law is constructed from symbols about *influence* and *justice*; the medium of kinship revolves around the medium of *love/loyalty*; the medium of religion is *sacredness/piety*; the medium of education is *learning*; and so on for all institutional domains.

As these symbolic media are used in the formation of new corporate units to address selection pressures, they become part of the culture of these organizational units, while framing and forming the basis of the *ideology* of the emerging institutional domain—e.g., economy, kinship, religion, polity, science, medicine, education, and so on. Thus, the evolution of institutional domains, whether entirely new domains or significant transformations of existing domains, is built from congeries of corporate units that are integrated by structural and cultural mechanisms codified into *ideologies* that specify what should and ought to occur within a domain.

Thus, a large part of the theory that I develop consists of propositions about how the structure and culture of domains evolves by virtue of linking corporate units and culturally legitimating these linkages with ideologies. Moreover, generalized symbolic media are also the terms of discourse among people in a domain—e.g., capitalists talk about money, incessantly; politicians about power; educators about learning; scientists about new knowledge; churches about sacredness and piety. From this discourse, the culture of the corporate units within a domain is built from its symbolic medium as it is translated into normative expectations in the division of labor of a corporate unit. And, moreover, the symbolic medium is inherently rewarding and thus it becomes the valued resource distributed by corporate units in an institutional domain.

Symbolic media circulate among corporate units within and between institutional domains; thus, many domains have multiple media circulating. For example, polity franchises to actors in the domain of education certain limited *rights to power* as authority to organize and run an educational system; the polity does the same for religion; most corporate units in most domains in modern societies pay their incumbents with money, so money also circulates. But some domains are more insulated, as is the case where kinship revolves around the medium of *love/loyalty*, and while some *money* (from the economic domain) and *authority* (from polity) circulate, its influence is less than in other domains because "love" should not be "tainted" by money (which is one of the basic tenets of the ideology of kinship in many societies). This circulation of media is often viewed critically, as is the case when academics bemoan the "corporatization" of university (that is, bemoan the influence of money). But, when media circulate, this can operate as a means of integrating highly differentiated societies because, as media circulate, so do the ideologies of a domain that have been built from these media. The result is that dominant institutional domains—say, economy, polity, education, science, and in some societies, religion—will have their media circulate to most other domains, and as the ideologies of these domains are piggybacked on the symbolic medium, they will often be consolidated into *meta-ideologies*, which are mergers of several ideologies. These meta-ideologies also provide a basis for cultural integration across differentiated institutional domains. I do not have the space to outline the propositions that describe the conditions under which media circulate, become dominant, and become codified into meta-ideologies, but these events can be theorized in ways that are testable—often with the data from the diverse types of societies portrayed in stage-model evolutionary schemes.

Since symbolic media are also valued resources, they are distributed unequally in corporate units—usually as an outcome of an incumbents place in the division of labor of a corporate unit. Thus, symbolic media are not only the symbolic building blocks of ideologies and norms; but they are also the valued resources that are distributed unequally. As such, they generate stratification systems. Historically, sociologists have focused on money and power (both of which are symbolic media) as the most important resource distributed unequally in a stratification system. Some schemes like Lenski's theory of stratification also note that *prestige*, as a generalized marker of social worth, is also part of the unequal distribution of a stratification system. But, in my view, *all* symbolic media are valued resources. And hence, the unequal distribution of resources involves *many more* resources than is typically conceptualized in sociological accounts of stratification. Not just *money* and *power* from economy and polity, respectively, but *love/loyalty* (family), *learning* (education), *knowledge* (science), *sacredness/piety* (religion), *aesthetics* (art), and all other symbolic media are distributed unequally by corporate units in an institutional domain. And, the more of these symbolic media as resources are possessed by people and families in a society, the more individuals can also enjoy rewards inherent in more generalized reinforces, such as prestige and positive emotions. Rewards of any kind bring positive emotions, and some like *knowledge* and *learning* can also bring prestige to those who possess large amounts of such valued resources.

What is important here is that some of these symbolic media are more equally distributed than other media. If emphasis is only on money and power, then inequality will be seen as greater in a society, whereas if other symbolic media as valued resources are also part of the assessment of the level of inequality, then individuals may not feel so deprived compared to their rich and powerful counterparts in other classes. Thus, inequalities in the distribution of money and power are, to some extent, countered by more equality in the distribution of, say, *love/loyalty, sacredness/piety, learning,* and perhaps *health.* And, this more equal distribution can reduce the sense of deprivation that individuals in the class system feel, and in fact, it can make the boundaries of the class system, except at the very top (rich, powerful) and very bottom (impoverished and powerless), rather mushy. As is evident in the middle classes of a post-industrial society, their boundaries are porous because members have some money, plus somewhat varying shares of other generalized symbolic media. As a result, class homogeneity will decline, and if it declines, so does the clear linear rank-ordering of moral worth since members have many additional symbolic media and the ideologies built from these media to measure favorably their moral worth, even if they do not have power or money.

Thus, part of a theory of macrodynamics requires propositions specifying the conditions under which symbolic media circulate to varying degrees; these propositions then become part of a general theory of stratification.[16] The tensions among classes and the potential for conflict generated by inequalities in the stratification system will be increased or mitigated depending upon *which* and *how many* symbolic media are distributed unequally in a society. Again, to test out propositions derived from this analysis often requires, as Lenski first realized, analysis of stratification in the types of societies that can be found in stage models of evolution.

Analysis of institutional domains and stratification systems as part of the macro-level social universe inevitably takes us back to the question of integration so central to early functional analysis. I make no assumptions about whether particular mechanisms of integration are good or bad; rather a theory predicts when various types of mechanisms of integration are likely to be activated, with what effect on what structures of the macro realm of social reality. As I approached the issue of integration, it became immediately apparent that a wide range of societies was needed to assess propositions, and so, once again, stage models of societal evolution provided useful data. There are a variety of structural mechanism of integration of corporate units within and between institutional domains; in my theory, I emphasize the following:[17] (1) *segmentation* (reproduction of structurally and culturally equivalent corporate units); (2) *structural differentiation*

---

[16]See Jonathan H. Turner, "The Stratification of Emotions: Some Preliminary Generalizations," *Sociological Inquiry* 80 (2010): pp. 168–99.

[17]Turner, *Theoretical Principles of Sociology*, vol. 1, *Macrodynamics* (cited in note 14), pp. 116–25, 184–86, 223, 225, 275.

(production of different units to manage complex selection pressures); (3) *structural interdependences* among differentiated units through (a) *exchanges,* (b) *structural inclusion* or embedded of smaller in larger corporate units, (c) *structural overlaps* among corporate units, and (d) *structural mobility* of incumbents across differentiated corporate units; (4) *structural domination* of corporate units by those with more power; and (5) *structural segregation* in time and space of corporate units with incompatible goals.

To illustrate how useful stage models can be in assessing the conditions under which one or the other of these mechanisms dominates, segmentation is the primary mode of integration among hunter-gatherers, as both Spencer and Durkheim recognized; structural interdependences must increase as differentiation of corporate units and institutional domains in which they are located occurs. Yet, historically, the consolidation of power and domination have also been responses to selection pressures generated by differentiation. Indeed, structural interdependences only increased dramatically in societal evolution when markets and other distributive mechanisms expanded. Thus, by looking at data from hunter-gatherers, horticulturalists (and variants of these), agrarian societies (and their maritime and herding variants), industrial, and post-industrial formations could I see the conditions under which one or the other of these various mechanisms dominate institutional integration and, hence, societal integration as well.

Similarly, mechanisms of cultural integration among texts, technologies, traditions, values, ideologies, and norms could only be assessed by looking at societies at different stages of evolution. For example, hunter-gatherers have only two basic units—bands and families—which means that they have differentiated only one institutional domain, kinship, although elements of religion are evident as is an incipient polity among settled hunter-gatherers. Thus, cultural integration had to be built around *love/loyalty* in nomadic hunter-gatherers since no other symbolic media had yet evolved. Indeed, the evolution of societies is, as the first functionalist emphasized, the successive differentiation of new institutional domains (built from new types of corporate units), and thus the only way to see the shift in modes of cultural integration is by examining how cultural systems change with (1) institutional differentiation and (2) emergence and then elaboration of the stratification system, which is also integrated by meta-ideologies built up from the ideologies of dominant institutional domains.

In turning to stratification-system integration, it increasingly became evident to me that very low and high degrees of stratification were well integrated (again, forms of integration are not evaluated; they are either effective or ineffective in sustaining a population in its environments). Systems of high stratification are sustained by domination at every level of society and at every linkage among corporate and categoric units. Low levels of stratification occur in societies where power is not consolidated because there is, as Lenski emphasized, a lack of economic surplus to distribute unequally. It is societies in-between these extremes that diverse patterns of structural and cultural integration can be found. For example, simple horticulturalists use structural embedding of nuclear kinship units in lineages, which are in turn embedded subclans inside of clans that are often moieties, and this system of embeddeding is legitimated by ideologies built from *love/loyalty* in kinship. Other mechanisms of integration are also part of this system. For example, even though kin units are differentiated, they tend to be reproduced across territories, and so, there are segmentation and structural equivalence processes in play; that is, nuclear units, lineages composed of nuclear units, and clans built from lineages are much the same in different villages and even in different horticultural societies. There is also a pattern of domination evident in these systems, a pattern that is also the same across territories of horticulturalists, with kin leaders of one clan often assuming dominance over those of others as a kind of "paramount chief." Once *powe*r as symbolic medium is introduced into the hierarchy of kin units, the ideology built from *love/loyalty* is supplemented by the ideology built of *power* as a symbolic medium, making authority an important cultural means of legitimating structures where domination is fast becoming structural mode of societal integration.

Compared to an agrarian system where kinship breaks down and polity is separated from kinship, but also where religion becomes a dominant institution, the basis of structural and cultural integration shifts to a new profile. Then, when markets as modes of structural interdependence evolve, the ideology built around *money* becomes more salient in the structural relations of corporate units not only in economy but other domains as well, and this ideology will be incorporated into the meta-ideology of dominant domains (typically polity and religion), legitimating new configurations of structural interdependencies and domination as the primary structural mechanisms of integration. These patterns of cultural and structural integration will also be affected by the changes in the stratification system and its modes of cultural and structural integrations. All of these highly dynamic processes can be theorized and assessed against the data that are available in diverse types of societies in stage models of societal evolution.

I have only touched the surface of the theory, which is expressed in twenty-three abstract propositions in volume 1 of *Theoretical Principles of Sociology.* Thus, by keeping the analytical scheme simple, as is outlined in Figure 5.3 on page 104, by isolating only those properties of the macro-level social universe that are generic and universal (a relatively small number when this criterion is applied), and by putting the complexity of the social universe in the principles (rather that the analytical scheme as Parsons did), a true explanatory theory inspired by functionalism can be developed. Moreover, as functionalists recognized, such a "grand" theory can only be assessed by data from a wide variety of societal formations, and the accumulated knowledge derived from stage models describing diverse societal types can be used to assess the plausibility of each theoretical principle. Moreover, by stating the theory as principles and by outlining key causal relations in analytical models, the grand theory can be decomposed to specific topics of interests to specialists. For example, I have not addressed here for lack of space how different configurations of stratification increase or decrease the potential for conflict in society, but the models developed and propositions listed for these dynamics can be easily extracted and imported into more specialized literatures on conflict and social movements. In fact, the models and principles that I eventually developed in *Theoretical Principles of Sociology* are very much like those outlined in my first effort, some thirty-plus years ago, in developing an analytical theory of conflict, as is outlined in Chapter 11. The new models are similar to the old, but significantly embellished and elaborated upon, in light of new data and theory, but I began with the old theory and then asked: How can it be improved in light of subsequent theorizing and by a broader view of stratification across the full range of societal types that humans have created over the last 200,000 years? So, models and propositions can be imported from specialized theories and then, once developed, exported back to these specialized theories. But, these exported theories will have the benefit of a broader database supporting their plausibility.

# Conclusion

Viewing societies as evolving through distinct stages does not mean that every society must go through these stages. Conquest, diffusion, borrowing of technologies, markets, and many forces can transform societies dramatically, allowing them to jump over various stages. The real utility of stage models of societal evolution is twofold. First, these models give us a sense of the history of human societies, from their beginnings as small bands of hunter-gatherers to the large-scale macro societies of the industrial and post-industrial world. Second, by emphasizing the characteristics of different societies at varying stages of development, we assemble a large database for developing and assessing macro theories of human social organization.

This second point is the most important. To theorize at the macro level of social organization, we need more than just industrial societies; instead, we need *all types* of societies as a data source for assessing plausibility of models and theories about societal dynamics. Otherwise, we would have theories of distinctive stages rather than societies and their dynamics more generally. For, scientific theory seeks to isolate the key properties and dynamics of the social universe that are *always* operative when humans form societies; and so, to assess whether or not a theory or model meets this criterion of universality, we need to be sure that they are assessed against the full range of sociocultural formations that humans have created over the last 200,000 years.

Once the ethnocentrism of some early theories of stages in societal development was abandoned, the revival of this form of theorizing could now provide a more robust database for assessing newer, value-neutral theories that seek to explain macrodynamic processes in societies. Moreover, evolutionary theories will, in the end, emphasize the dynamic forces that drive the formation, change, collapse, and reformation of societies; thus, new evolutionary theories will not have any of the connotations of being static and conservative that haunted functional analysis. They will be about the forces that drive societies across history, and hence, any point in the past or future as societies and inter-societal systems continue to evolve.

## CHAPTER 9

# Darwinian-Inspired Evolutionary Theories

D arwinian theorizing on the dynamics of natural selection as a force of evolution influenced Émile Durkheim's analysis in *The Division of Labor in Society* and early Chicago School urban ecology. This influence on urban and, later, organizational ecology has continued to the present day. As human ecology developed in sociology, the Modern Synthesis of evolutionary theorizing combined Darwin's emphasis on natural selection with newer understandings of other forces of evolution—namely, *mutation*, *gene flow*, and *genetic drift*. Closer to the present, many elements from the Modern Synthesis began to enter social science theorizing in general and, with some reluctance, sociology as well. The diversity of theories using Darwinian-inspired ideas, as they were blended into the Modern Synthesis, has grown considerably within sociology over the last two decades, but not without a great deal of criticism. In this chapter, several of these approaches, which have grown up alongside the revival of stage models of societal evolution and theories of human ecology, will be reviewed.

## Sociobiological Theorizing

In Chapter 6, the rise of sociobiology in the second half of the twentieth century is reviewed. None of the founders of this approach were sociologists, and indeed, the reaction to pronouncements by sociobiologists that their approach could explain the social world studied by sociologists was almost universally rejected. Still, some saw merit in this approach and began to apply the tenets—somewhat modified—of what J. H. Turner tends to call "hard-core" sociobiology.

---

*Sections of this chapter were coauthored with Alexandra Maryanski.

## Pierre van den Berghe's Approach

Pierre van den Berghe has been among the most prolific advocates of a biological perspective on human affairs. As Van den Berghe has consistently asserted for several decades, it "is high time that we seriously look at ourselves as merely one biological species among many." Until this shift away from what he calls "species-wide anthropocentrism" is accomplished, sociology will remain stagnant, for there can be no doubt that biological forces shape and constrain patterns of human organization.[1] In his early advocacy, van den Berghe proposed a biological approach that corresponded to the instinct approach of some early sociologists and several contemporary thinkers, whereas in his later works, van den Berghe fully embraced sociobiology and, since then, has consistently used sociobiological theory to interpret a variety of social behaviors among humans. Van den Berghe began his turn to sociobiology by posing the question: Why are humans "social" in the first place? His answer is that the banding of animals together in cooperative groups increases their reproductive fitness by (1) protecting them against predators and (2) providing advantages in locating, gathering, and exploiting resources. Such fitness allows the alleles of those who are social to stay in the gene pool.

Three sociobiological mechanisms produce the sociality that promotes reproductive fitness:[2] (1) *kin selection* (or what was termed *inclusive fitness* in Chapter 6); (2) *reciprocity* (or what was labeled *reciprocal altruism* in Chapter 6); and (3) *coercion.* Because each of these mechanisms promotes reproductive fitness of individuals, they lie at the base of sociocultural phenomena. Let me examine each mechanism separately and then see how van den Berghe generates theoretical explanations with them.

**Kin Selection.** In van den Berghe's view, kin selection (that is, a propensity to favor kin) is the oldest mechanism behind sociality. He sees this mechanism, as with all modern human sociobiological arguments, as operating at the genetic level, for "the gene is the ultimate unit of natural selection, [although] each gene's reproduction can be modified by cultural forces and, overall, is dependent on what Robert Dawkins terms its 'survival machine,' the organism in which genes happen to be located at any given time."[3]

---

[1]Pierre van den Berghe, *Age and Sex in Human Societies: A Biosocial Perspective* (Belmont, CA: Wadsworth, 1973), p. 2. See also his *Man in Society: A Biosocial View* (New York: Elsevier, 1975); "Territorial Behavior in a Natural Human Group," *Social Science Information* 16 (1977): pp. 421–30; "Bringing Beasts Back In: Toward a Biosocial Theory of Aggression," *American Sociological Review* 39 (1974): pp. 777–88; "Why Most Sociologists Don't (and Won't) Think Evolutionarily," *Sociological Forum* 5 (1990): pp. 173–85; "Genes, Mind and Culture," *Behavioral and Brain Sciences* 14 (1991): pp. 317–18.

[2]van den Berghe, "Bridging the Paradigms," *Society* 15 (1977–1978): pp. 42–49; *The Ethnic Phenomenon* (New York: Elsevier, 1981); and *Human Family Systems* (Prospect Heights, IL: Waveland, 1990), pp. 14ff.

[3]van den Berghe, "Bridging the Paradigms", p. 46

This survival machine carrying genetic material in its genotype need not be consciously aware of how natural selection in the distant past has created *replicators* or genes in its body that seek to survive and to be immortal. But selection clearly favored those replicators that could pass themselves on to new and better survival machines. One early survival machine was the body of individual organisms, and a later type of survival machine is cooperative arrangements among bodies sharing alleles in their genotypes. In van den Berghe's words:

> Since organisms are survival machines for genes, by definition those genes that program organisms for successful reproduction will spread. To maximize their reproduction, genes program organisms to do two things: successfully compete against . . . organisms that carry alternative alleles . . . and successfully cooperate with (and thereby contribute to the reproduction of) organisms that share the same alleles of the genes.[4]

So, in van den Berghe's terms, individuals are nepotistic and favor kin over nonkin, and close kin over distant kin, for the simple reason that close kin will share genetic material (in their genotypes):[5]

> Each individual reproduces its genes directly through its own reproduction and indirectly through the reproduction of its relatives, to the extent that it shares genes with them. In simple terms, each organism may be said to have a 100 percent genetic interest in itself, a 50 percent interest in its parents, offspring, and full-siblings, a 25 percent interest in half-siblings, grandparents, grandchildren, uncles, aunts, nephews, and nieces, a 12½ percent interest in first cousins, half-nephews, great-grandchildren, and so on.

The degree of altruism for kin, or nepotism, will vary with the amount of genetic material shared with a relative and with the ability of that relative to reproduce this genetic material. For van den Berghe, then, blood is thicker than water for a simple reason: reproductive fitness, or the capacity to help those machines carrying one's genetic material to survive and reproduce.

Van den Berghe is careful, however, to emphasize that these biologically based propensities for nepotism, or kin selection, are elaborated and modified by both environmental and cultural variations. Yet clearly, a biological

---

[4]van den Berghe, *The Ethnic Phenomenon* (cited in note 2), p. 7. See also Pierre van den Berghe and Joseph Whitmeyer, "Social Class and Reproductive Success," *International Journal of Contemporary Sociology* 27 (1990): pp. 29–48.

[5]van den Berghe, "Bridging the Paradigms," pp. 46–47 and *Human Family Systems*, pp. 19–20 (both cited in note 2).

factor operates in the overwhelming tendency of humans to be nepotistic. One cannot, van den Berghe insists, visualize such nepotism as a purely cultural process.

**Reciprocity.** When individuals exchange assistance, they create a bond of reciprocity. Such reciprocity increases the fitness of genes carried by the organisms (as well as the organization of organisms in sociocultural survivor machines); that is, if organisms help each other or can be relied upon to reciprocate for past assistance, the survival of genetic material is increased for both organisms. Such exchange, or what sociobiologists sometimes term *reciprocal altruism*,[6] greatly extends cooperation beyond nepotism, or *inclusive fitness* and *kin selection* in sociobiological jargon. Thus, reciprocal exchange is not a purely social product; it is a behavioral tendency programmed by genes. Such programming occurred in the distant past as natural selection favored those genes that could create new kinds of survival machines, such as nonkin groups and organizations, beyond an individual's physical body and social groupings of close kin. Those genes that could lodge themselves in nonkin groupings organized around bonds of exchange and reciprocity were more likely to survive; today, the descendants of these genes provide a biological push for creating and sustaining such bonds of reciprocity.

At this point, van den Berghe reveals the affinity of such arguments with utilitarianism by introducing the problem of *free-riding* or, as he terms it, *free-loading*. That is, what guarantee does an individual (and its genotype) have that others will indeed reciprocate for favors and assistance that have been given to these others? Here van den Berghe appears to argue that this problem of free-riding created selection pressures for greater intelligence so that our protohuman ancestors could remember and monitor whether or not others reciprocated past favors. But ironically, intelligence also generated greater capacities for sophisticated deceit, cheating, and free-riding, which in turn escalated selection pressures for the extended intelligence to catch and detect such concealed acts of non-reciprocation.

There is, then, a kind of selection cycle operating: Reciprocity increases fitness, but it also leads to cheating and free-riding. Hence, once reciprocity is a mechanism of cooperation, it can generate its own selection pressures for greater intelligence to monitor free-riding, but ironically, increased intelligence enables individuals to engage in more subtle and sophisticated deceptions to hide their free-riding; to combat this tendency, there is increased pressure for greater intelligence, and so on. At some point, culture and structure supplant this cycle by creating organizational mechanisms and cultural ideas to limit free-riding (see Chapter 23 on rational choice theory for a discussion of what these sociocultural mechanisms might be).

Van den Berghe does not pursue this discussion, however, except to point out that this cycle eventually produces "self-deceit." Van den Berghe believes

---

[6]See earlier discussion of Trivers in Chapter 6 and related references in footnotes.

that the best way to deceive is to believe one's own lies and deceptions, and in this way, one can sincerely make and believe verbal pronouncements that contradict, at least in some ways, one's actual behavior. Religion and ideology, van den Berghe posits, are "the ultimate forms of self-deceit," because religion "denies mortality" and ideology facilitates "the transmission of credible, self-serving lies."[7] This conceptual leap from free-riding to religion and ideology is, to say the least, rather vague, but it does provide a sense of what sociobiology tries to do: connect what might be considered purely cultural processes—i.e., religion and ideology—to a fundamental biological process—in this case, reproductive fitness through reciprocity.

**Coercion.** There are limits to social organization for reciprocal exchanges, van den Berghe argues, because each party has to perceive that it receives benefits in the relationship.[8] Such perceptions of benefit can, of course, be manipulated by ideologies and other forms of deceit that hide the asymmetry of the relationship, but there are probably limits to the manipulation of perceptions. Power is an alternative mechanism to both kin selection and reciprocal exchanges because its mobilization allows some organisms to dominate others in their access to resources that promote fitness. Coercion thus enables some to increase their fitness at a cost to others. Although this mechanism is hardly unique to our species, humans "hold pride of place in their ability to use to good effect conscious, collective, organized, premeditated coercion in order to establish, maintain, and perpetuate systems of intra-species parasitism."[9] Coercion allows the elaboration of the size and scale of human organization (states, classes, armies, courts, and so forth), but it is nonetheless tied to human biology as this was molded by selection. That is, genes that could use coercion to create larger and more elaborate social structures as their survival machines were more likely to survive and reproduce. In sum, then, sociality or cooperation and organization are the result of natural selection because it preserved genes that could produce better survival machines through nepotism (kin selection and inclusive fitness), reciprocity (or reciprocal altruism), and coercion (or territorial and hierarchical patterns of dominance). The linkages between biology, on the one side, and culture and society, on the other, are complex and often indirect, even after we recognize that these linkages occur along the three basic dimensions or axes of nepotism, reciprocity, and coercion. For there have certainly been complex interactions between ecological and genetic factors to produce patterns of human (and many other animal) organization; once initiated, selection processes producing greater intelligence allow culture, as an impressive bag of tricks, to operate as a force of human evolution.

---

[7]van den Berghe, *The Ethnic Phenomenon*, p. 9 and "Bridging the Paradigms," p. 48 (both cited in note 2).

[8]van den Berghe, "Bridging the Paradigms" (cited in note 2).

[9]van den Berghe, *The Ethnic Phenomenon*, p. 10. See in note 4: van den Berghe and Whitmeyer, "Social Class and Reproductive Success," pp. 31–32.

**Conceptualizing Cultural Processes**. From van den Berghe's vantage point, culture is created and transmitted in humans through mechanisms that are fundamentally different from those involved in genetic natural selection. Actually, van den Berghe portrays cultural evolution in Lamarckian rather than Darwinian terms: "Acquired cultural characteristics, unlike . . . genetic evolution, can be transmitted, modified, transformed, or eliminated through social learning." In recent years, van den Berghe has come to see culture in some ways as "an emergent phenomenon" that provides humans with another method of adaptation. For van den Berghe, the issue is not the genes versus culture but their interface, for both are intimately intertwined. Although culture is an outgrowth of biological evolution, it now has an autonomy, he says, that provides humans with the ability to modify their own genotypes, making the intricate feedbacks between nature and nurture more complex than ever.[10] So, culture is not a separate entity; it is yet one more product and process of biological evolution driven by natural selection as it produced genes trying to maximize their fitness by nesting themselves in increasingly better survival machines.

**Explanations of Social Phenomena with Sociobiology**. At various times, van den Berghe has used the concepts of sociobiology to explain such empirical phenomena as kinship systems, incest taboos, ethnicity, skin color, sexual selection, and social classes. Probably, his two most detailed empirical analyses are on (1) kinship systems and (2) ethnicity. Each of these will be briefly summarized.

**1. *Kinship*.** In one of his early sociobiological articles, van den Berghe and David Barash endeavored to explain various features of kinship systems by the behavioral strategies males and females pursue to maximize their fitness (that is, keep their alleles in the gene pool). Because the details of their suggestive arguments can be complex, just one example of the kinds of arguments that they make will be summarized.[11]

The widespread preference in human societies for *polygyny* (males with the option for multiple wives), *hypergamy* (females marrying males of higher-ranking kin groups), and double standards of sexual morality (males being given more latitude than females) can be explained in terms of reproductive fitness strategies. Women have comparatively fewer eggs to offer in their lifetime, have intervals when they are infertile (for example, during lactation), and even in the most liberal or egalitarian societies, have to spend more time than men raising children. Hence, a female will seek a reproductive strategy that will ensure the survival of her less abundant genetical

---

[10]van den Berghe, *The Ethnic Phenomenon*, p. 6 and *Human Family Systems*, p. 220 (both cited in note 2).

[11]Pierre van den Berghe and David Barash, "Inclusive Fitness and Family Structure," *American Anthropologist* 79 (1977): pp. 809–23.

material, and the most maximizing strategy is to marry a male with the resources and capacity to ensure the survival of her offspring (and, thereby, one-half of her genotype). Thus, a woman will seek to marry up (hypergamy) in the sense of securing a man who has more resources than her kinship group.

On the male side, men produce an uninterrupted and large supply of sperm and have fewer child-care responsibilities, and so they can afford to be more promiscuous with little cost (and they will derive some benefit from the fitness that comes with spreading their genes around). Although men have an interest in ensuring that as many women as possible bear children with one-half their genes, a male cannot know that a female is bearing his child if she is promiscuous, and so, men also have an interest in restricting female sexual activity through polygyny to ensure that their genes are indeed contained in the genotype of the children born to a female (creating limits of female sexuality outside marriage). Thus, what are commonly viewed as purely cultural phenomena—the preference for polygyny in human societies (or monogamy with promiscuity), hypergamy (marrying up), and sexual double standards (favoring male promiscuity)—can be explained as the result of varying fitness strategies for males and females that have become programmed into their respective genotypes.

**2. *Ethnicity*.** Turning to another empirical example, van den Berghe has sought to apply sociobiology to what has always been his main area of research—ethnicity.[12] Again, kin selection is his starting point, but he extends this idea beyond family relatives helping one another (to maximize their fitness) to a larger subpopulation. Historically, larger kin groups (composed of lineages) constituted a breeding population of close and distant kin who would sustain trust and solidarity with one another while mistrusting other breeding populations. Van den Berghe coined the term *ethny* for ethnic group and views an ethny as an extended nepotism of these more primordial breeding populations. An ethny is a cluster of kinship circles that is created by endogamy (intermarriage of its members) and territoriality (physical proximity of its members and relative isolation from nonmembers). An ethny represents a reproductive strategy for maximizing fitness beyond the narrower confines of kinship, because by forming an ethny—even a very large one of millions of people—individuals can create extended bonds with those who can help preserve their fitness, whether by actually sharing genes or, more typically, by reciprocal acts of altruism to fellow ethnys. An ethny is, therefore, a manifestation of more basic urges for helping those like oneself. Whereas ethnys become genetically diluted as their size increases and become subject to social and cultural definitions, the very tendency to form and sustain ethnys is the result of natural selection as it produced nepotism. Van den Berghe's argument is, of course, much more complicated and

---

[12]van den Berghe, *The Ethnic Phenomenon* (cited in note 2) and see also van den Berghe, "Heritable Phenotypes and Ethnicity," *Behavioral and Brain Sciences* 12 (1989): pp. 544–45.

sophisticated, but we can get at least a general sense for how a supposedly emergent phenomenon—ethnic groups—is explained by reduction to a theoretical perspective built on the principles of genetic evolution.

In summary, the sociobiology models developed by van den Berghe emphasize the interactive effects among genes, culture, and environment. Individuals are viewed as "selfish maximizers" who seek to maximize their own inclusive fitness. To accomplish this goal, different reproductive strategies are employed with variations in reproductive strategies among human societies mostly the result of different cultural adaptations to particular environmental conditions. In recent years, however, van den Berghe and collaborators have highlighted the power of culture in overriding the reproductive consequences of human actions, thereby subverting the genes' game of reproducing themselves. Van den Berghe now says that this subversion of the genes is especially evident in industrial societies where many individuals "are no longer maximizing fitness" because the contraceptive technology and the comforts and security of material affluence have separated the hedonistic rewards of the "good life" from reproductive efforts.[13] Thus, in modern societies, van den Berghe suggests that a more complex model is necessary to assess the quality versus quantity of offspring and the balance between human needs for luxury goods versus reproductive investment.

## Joseph Lopreato's Approach

In the hard-core days of sociobiology (see Chapter 6), scholars followed the evolutionary logic that, in the past, natural selection favored those behavioral adaptations that increased the fitness of individuals in a given environment. All nonadaptive behaviors are weeded out, whereas adaptive behaviors are preserved and transmitted for the ultimate function of maximizing fitness. The research objective, then, is to discover how particular social behaviors are adaptive and, hence, how they promote fitness.[14] In the words of R. D. Alexander, who underscored the importance of viewing humans as organisms whose behaviors evolved to maximize reproductive fitness, "all organisms should have logically evolved to avoid every instance of beneficence or altruism unlikely to bring returns greater than the expenditure it entails."[15] Hence, through the application of such concepts as kin

---

[13]van den Berghe, "Once More with Feeling: Genes, Mind and Culture," *Behavioral and Brain Sciences* 14 (1991): pp. 317–18. See note 4: van den Berghe and Whitmeyer, "Social Class and Reproductive Success," pp. 41–44.

[14]J. Maynard-Smith, "The Theory of Games and the Evolution of Animal Conflicts," *Journal of Theoretical Biology* 47 (1974): pp. 209–21 and see Alexandra Maryanski, "The Pursuit of Human Nature in Sociobiology and Evolutionary Sociology," *Sociological Perspectives* 37 (Fall 1994): pp. 115–27.

[15]R. D. Alexander, "The Search for a General Theory of Behavior," *Behavior Science* 20 (1975): pp. 77–100.

selection and reciprocal altruism, even acts of cooperation or kindness were viewed as selfish genes.

Joseph Lopreato believes the *maximization principle* is still the fountain-head of sociobiology, but if we want to keep "with the logic of natural selection," its strict application is unwarranted.[16] For this reason, Lopreato has undertaken the task of overhauling the maximization principle.

In revamping the maximization principle, Lopreato begins by rejecting the assumption that all adaptations are either related to reproduction or organized around the ultimate goal of reproductive success. Instead, he proposes that for all organisms there is only a tendency for individuals to behave in a way that maximizes their reproductive success.[17] This "could hardly be otherwise" he maintains, because many individual behaviors are clearly neutral or outright maladaptive, and there are good evolutionary reasons for this variability. As he points out, genotypic variation in every generation must exist for selection to act on. This pool of variability must include both neutral traits and maladaptive traits to provide a deviation of fitness from the maximization principle. This variability is retained when genes are recombined into new genotypes, virtually guaranteeing a differential in the adaptive quality of organisms. Over time, this differential will, in turn, produce "a more or less adaptive fit between variations and environmental pressures."[18]

The second step taken by Lopreato is acknowledging that cultural evolution has placed heavy constraints on the maximization principle. In particular, the trappings of human culture have greatly augmented the basic mammalian pleasure principle, which is now skewed in humans toward creature comforts, rather than the maximization of reproductive success. This requires a readjustment of the maximization principle: "Organisms are predisposed to behave so as to maximize their inclusive fitness, but this predisposition is conditioned by the quest for creature comforts."[19]

The third step taken by Lopreato is suggesting that complex causal agents in both evolutionary and cultural phenomena have generated a widespread predisposition for *self-deception*, or the ability to engage in one form of behavior in the belief that it is actually another form of behavior.[20] Once self-deceptive behaviors evolved, Lopreato says, the necessary conditions were created for true ascetic altruism to evolve where individuals in varying degrees evidence a type of "Mother Teresa complex" or self-sacrifice that can, in some instances, redirect the sex drive away from physical satisfaction

---

[16]Joseph Lopreato, "The Maximization Principle: A Cause in Search of Conditions," in *Sociobiology and the Social Sciences*, eds. Robert and Nancy Bell (Lubbock: Texas Tech University Press, 1989), pp. 119–30.

[17]Ibid., p. 121.

[18]Ibid., p. 120–21.

[19]Ibid., p. 125.

[20]Ibid., p. 126.

to spiritual satisfaction through altruistic good works. Lopreato submits that, ironically, self-deceptive behaviors must have evolved through natural selection making it possible to have "true altruism in the absence of altruistic genes."[21] For this reason he recommends a third modification of the maximization principle: "Organisms are predisposed to behave so as to maximize their inclusive fitness, but this predisposition is conditioned by the quest for creature comforts and by self-deception."[22]

A fourth constraint on the maximization principle is sociopolitical revolution, which Lopreato defines as "forcible action in a dominance order by individuals who desire to replace those who have organizational . . . control of their group's resources."[23] Lopreato suggests that the "ultimate cause of revolution is the quest for fitness maximization," because in traditional societies, highly ranked individuals with resources are more likely to have access to multiple females through polygyny, thereby increasing their reproductive success. However, to the degree that resource accumulation becomes an end in itself in modern industrial societies, resource acquisition and maximization of fitness become detached. Here, culture once again disrupts the maximization as behaviors directed at resource acquisition become separated from considerations of genetic fitness. For this reason, Lopreato adds a final variable in his restatement of the maximization principle: "Organicisms are predisposed to behave so as to maximize their inclusive fitness, but this predisposition is conditioned by the quest for creature comforts, by self-deception, and by autonomization of phenotype from genotype."[24]

Lopreato has used his theoretical model to enhance traditional sociological explanations of social phenomena. In a paper with Arlen Carey,[25] for example, Lopreato examines the relationship between fertility and mortality in human societies. Essentially, Carey and Lopreato argue that variations in human fertility have typically been explained by such fertility-reducing mechanisms as abortion, use of contraceptives, sterility, age at marriage, economic value of children, social status of women, and the like. Yet, despite these obvious and important influences on fertility, these explanations cannot provide by themselves an adequate account of one fact: Until recently, rates of reproduction have changed very little in humans' evolutionary history, with human females on average producing only two viable adult offspring. Why should this have historically been the case?

In considering this demographic puzzle, Carey and Lopreato submit that population dynamics do not fluctuate randomly, but fertility rates roughly

---

[21]Ibid., p. 127.

[22]Ibid., p. 127.

[23]Ibid., p. 127.

[24]Ibid., p. 129.

[25]Arlen Carey and Joseph Lopreato, "The Evolutionary Demography of the Fertility-Mortality Quasi-Equilibrium," *Population and Development Review* 21 (1995): pp. 613–30.

correspond with mortality rates, with these two rates tending to behave like systems in equilibrium. In traditional societies, there is a quasi-equilibrium between high mortality rates and high fertility rates. In addition, as Charles Darwin first realized (drawing his inspiration from Thomas Malthus), it is characteristic of most species, notwithstanding the tendency of populations to outpace their resources, to evidence a countertendency toward population stability, suggesting that "the fertility of individuals displays a vigorous tendency to track mortality—a tendency . . . toward a coupled-replacement reproductive strategy."[26] Carey and Lopreato ask this: In humans, what factors might be responsible for maintaining this "fertility/mortality quasi-equilibrium"?

Carey and Lopreato submit that, although all humans are motivated in principle to maximize their reproductive success, they are constrained first by limited resources and the human need for creature comforts. Instead, what the "demographic quasi-equilibrium" pattern suggests is a stabilizing reproductive strategy with natural selection tending to favor fertilities that meet and only slightly exceed corresponding mortalities.[27]

A second mechanism used to regulate the fertility/mortality relationship in human populations, they maintain, is collectively called "life history characteristics."[28] Basically, life history theory holds that natural selection guides the life characteristic of a species to optimize and regulate fertility.[29] Evolutionary ecologists have documented life history characteristics in other species, which include distinct reproductive periods, interbirth intervals, litter size, parental investment, age-specific probabilities of survival, and size and maturity of newborns. Hence, animal populations with low rates of mortality will also have lower fertility rates that are conditioned by smaller litters, delayed births, and bigger offspring because they represent a great investment of parental resources. Carey and Lopreato argue that the fertility/mortality relationship in humans also corresponds to life history characteristics. Members of the human species have a relatively high probability of survival through the reproductive period that is matched historically by a low fertility rate. To regulate this process, puberty begins late in humankind, conception is relatively difficult, fetuses take nine months to develop, single births are the norm, newborns are large, and births are difficult. Carey and Lopreato suggest that "these life history characteristics contribute to a relatively low level of fertility that is associated with a relatively low probability of mortality."[30] Although these facts are well known to demographers, they are rarely viewed as phenomenon forged by natural selection.

------

[26]Ibid., p. 616.

[27]Ibid., p. 617.

[28]Ibid., p. 617–19.

[29]Ibid., p. 619.

[30]Ibid., p. 620.

Still, Carey and Lopreato do not consider these factors sufficient to explain the relationship between fertility and mortality. Instead, they seek a third explanation for the regulation of human fertility, suggesting that psychological attributes "most closely associated with survival and reproduction may be expected to be especially prone to fitness maximization tendencies."[31] In short, there are perhaps psychologically regulated reproductive behaviors toward an optimal level of reproductive behavior that is activated by environmental cues. These cues are used to gauge the relative probabilities of survival of the young.[32] Thus, in a society where infant and child mortality are high, a higher fertility rate would prevail.

Identifying some psychological mechanisms that help regulate human fertility rates is now possible: Belsky, Steinberg, and Draper suggest, for example, that reproductive strategies for individuals in a given population are largely decided during the first five to seven years of life.[33] The crucial determining factor here is resource availability. The amount of resources then influences family life and childrearing, and these shape both the psychological and behavioral development of a child.[34] In turn, these affect the age of puberty and the lifelong reproductive strategy. For instance, Chisholm maintains that this developmental process offers the proximate mechanisms by which individuals internalize the mortality characteristics of their population.[35]

In concluding, they offer these propositions: (1) The greater the perceived probability of offspring survival is within a population, the more intense the two-child psychology is, and (2) the greater the tendency toward creature comforts is among members of a society, the more widespread is the two-child psychology. Thus, Carey and Lopreato believe that human neurobiology has reproductively based predispositions, which are activated by the environment, charting the best reproductive strategy. As they note, "the evolution of the relationship between human fertility and human mortality has forged a tendency toward a reproductive psychology that revolves closely around a near-average two-child family."[36] This can be called the "two-child psychology" tendency. It charts that, in human history, an average of two offspring (or a little more) is typically the best strategy given the

---

[31]Ibid.

[32]Ibid.

[33]Jay Belsky, Laurence Steinberg, and Patricia Draper, "Childhood Experience, Interpersonal Development, and Reproductive Strategy: An Evolutionary Theory of Socialization," *Child Development* 62 (1991): pp. 647–70.

[34]Ibid.

[35]James Chisholm, "Death, Hope, and Life: Life History Theory and the Development of Reproductive Strategies," *Current Anthropology* 34 (1993): pp. 1–12.

[36]Carey and Lopreato, "The Evolutionary Demography of the Fertility-Mortality Quasi-Equilibrium," p. 621; Joseph Lopreato and Mei-Yu Yu, "Human Fertility and Fitness Optimization," *Ethnology and Sociobiology* 9 (1988): pp. 269–89.

costs of motherhood in comfort, health, and overall quality of life. In supporting their thesis, they use historical data that suggest population growth was minimal—at least, until recently.

# Evolutionary Psychology

Sociobiology was the beachhead to an invasion of the social sciences by biology, but over recent decades, evolutionary psychology has gained considerably more influence in the social sciences than sociobiology, especially in sociology. Evolutionary psychology accepts most of the tenets of sociobiology, such as behaviors evolved to maximize the fitness of humans, but inserts the operation of the human brain explicitly into the theory. Natural selection, as it worked on hominin and human phenotypes and the underlying genotypes, has rewired the brain by creating a series of specialized brain modules during the Pleistocene—the more immediate period of evolution of late hominins and early humans. These modules are responsible for many key behaviors that, in the past, solved recurrent problems in human's ancestral environments.

Evolutionary psychology operates under a number of key assumptions:

1. The brain is an information-processing device that has evolved like any other trait in organism.

2. The brain and the adaptive mechanisms that it reveals evolved by natural selection.

3. The various neural mechanisms of the brain are specialized for solving problems generated by selection pressures in human's and hominins' evolutionary past.

4. The human mind, then, is a stone-age mind because its specialized mechanisms for processing information, perception, and universal behaviors evolved during the Pleistocene.

5. Most contents and processes of the brain are unconscious, and mental problems that appear easy to solve are actually difficult problems that are solved unconsciously by complicated set and modules of neurons that have evolved to solve adaptive problems during the course of the evolution of late hominins and early humans.

6. The psychology of humans, then, consists of many specialized mechanisms wired into distinctive modules of neurons that are sensitive to different classes of information and external inputs and that combine to produce human behavior, and by implication, patterns of interaction and even social structures and their cultures.

For example, an evolutionary psychologist might argue that human speech is a psychological mechanism that evolved by selecting on the association cortices, such as the inferior parietal lobe, that enable humans and higher primates the capacity for language facility, followed by selection on relatively discrete areas of the brain (Broca's area) and surrounding tissues for speech production and Wernicke's area for speech comprehension and uploading of meanings into the brain's way of processing information. Moreover, there are modules along the fissure separating the parietal lobe regulating tongue muscle movements and the frontal cortex that give humans (but not the great apes) the ability to produce articulated words in speech. Such speech capacities evolved to solve problems of communication and social bonding among humans, and this line of argument might not be controversial because the modules can be found in the brain. Similarly, the evolution of human emotional capacities is lodged in modules in subcortical areas of the brain. Some subcortical areas like those generating *anger* and *fear*, which date back to the evolution of reptiles, are generated in a discrete module labeled the *amydala*, but other emotions are not so easily isolated in discrete modules; however, evolutionary psychologists still predict that the modules will be found with more research.

Other topics are potentially more controversial. Evolutionary psychologists suggest that, for instance, there are incest avoidance mechanisms (which is probably true, but where is the module for this?), as well as mechanisms for cheater detection, sex-specific preferences, reciprocity, kin selection, altruism, reciprocal altruism, inclusive fitness, alliance tracking, and other universal human behaviors. For evolutionary psychologists, the more universal is a behavior, the more likely is this behavior regulated by neurological mechanisms situated in modules of the human brain. These modules evolved because they enhanced fitness of hominins and then humans during the Pleistocene.

These basic features of evolutionary psychology have been adopted by a small but growing number of sociologists and used to explain human behaviors, often reported in the sociological literature as rates of particular kinds of behaviors. For example, there is a universal behavioral propensity for crime, and especially violent crimes, to be committed by males, increasing during puberty and, then with age, declining dramatically. Sociobiologists[37] sought to explain this universal pattern, and evolutionary psychologists[38] have added characterizations of the mechanisms by which this behavior is produced. Such explanations become "just-so" stories outlining what occurred in the distant past to generate brain modules (rarely specified) that produce particular patterns of behavior, like rates of crime and violent crime among adolescent males. For example, part of the just-so story begins with men's need and desire to gain access to women (so as to pass on their genes), and young men are particularly driven to do so. They are thus more likely to take risks and incur costs in competition with other

---

[37]Martin Daily and Margo Wilson, *Homocide* (New York: De Gruyter, 1988).

[38]Satoshi Kanazawa and Mary C. Still, "Why Men Commit Crimes (and Why They Desist)," *Sociological Perspectives* 18 (2000): pp. 434–47.

males to gain access to females. To ensure that such would be the case, natural selection created a module (not clearly specified except for mention of those parts of the brain responsible for the production of the hormone testosterone). This module evolved long before individuals had much property and a criminal justice system existed, but men still seek resources and status so as to impress females of their qualities and, thereby, maximize their reproductive success. In modern societies, young males have fewer resources than older males, with the result that they seek resources through crime. The story is much more nuanced than this, and it even adds interesting details. Smaller men, contrary to what we might think, will tend to be more aggressive and violent because they have to compensate for the lack of size and thus must gain status and resources to attract females—hence, they are more likely to commit violent crimes to do so.

Other arguments can be developed along these lines. As outlined in the discussion of Pierre van den Berghe's approach, sociobiologists have argued that males and females develop somewhat different strategies to maximize their reproductive fitness. Whereas women produce relatively few eggs in their lifetimes and must make heavy investments in offspring (since they, rather than men, must bear and breastfeed them), males generate daily millions of sperm. Thus, women have a vested interest in ensuring that they hook up with males who can provide resources to their eggs, whereas males maximize their reproductive fitness by being promiscuous. Thus, males will tend to be more promiscuous than women because of biologically driven strategies for maximizing fitness. Evolutionary psychology adds to this scenario the notion that males possess evolved mechanisms in their brains, which drive them to limit female partner's access to other males. For example, males will generally become more *reflexively jealous* (from an emotional module that is not specified) with infidelity by females and more likely to push for restrictive norms on female sexuality in order to ensure that female offspring carry their genes rather than those of another male. These norms can change, however, when women have resources independently of their male sexual partners because, now, they do not need the resources provided by males and thus are likely to resist male control and demand more permissive sexual norms.[39] They are, again, more nuanced versions of this story, but the plotline of the just-so story is clear.

One problematic issue of these explanations by just-so stories is that they are almost always ad hoc. One could construct a just-so story for empirical regularities in behavior that are just the opposite of those illustrated above. The assumptions of evolutionary psychology, as it has incorporated the arguments of sociobiologists, are so general that it is easy to develop a story—or a somewhat pseudo explanation—of almost any behavior regularity. All that is necessary is to hypothesize a module in the brain that evolved to produce a behavior that enhances fitness. The just-so story thus

---

[39]Christine Horne, "Values and Evolutionary Psychology," *Sociological Perspectives* 22 (2004): pp. 477–93.

becomes a series of assertions: a particular behavior is asserted to enhance fitness; therefore, there must be a module producing this behavior, and we know there must be a module because something must produce they fitness-enhancing behavior. But these stories are not only ad hoc; they are generally post hoc, although some have sought to be more predictive.[40] Yet, evolutionary psychologists seem undaunted by these criticisms and, in fact, are highly confident that their approach can explain more than standard social science practices, which tend to assume that biology has very little influence on human behavior, interaction, and patterns of social organization.[41] In fact, Rosemary Hopcroft has produced an introduction to sociology book, demonstrating what she sees as the power of evolutionary psychology to explain standard sociological literatures. This book is well worth reading because it examines many typical sociological topics from the perspective of evolutionary psychology.[42]

# Cross-Species Comparisons

Other sociologists have developed theoretical approaches that compare humans with other species. Here, the goal is to highlight particular questions in the social sciences and to seek answers by comparing humans and their patterns of social organization with other species. These cross-species comparisons may, or may not, also include ideas from sociobiology or evolutionary psychology, but these are not emphasized. The basic idea is to provide answers to questions by comparing human behavior propensities and patterns of social organization to those of other species, sometimes species that are closely related to humans biologically and, at other times, to species that are very distant to humans.

## Richard Machalek's Approach

Richard Machalek has applied modern evolutionary theory to traditional sociological problems.[43] Machalek would like to see a truly comparative sociology or one that crosses species lines. His approach is to search for the foundations and development of *sociality* wherever it is found, in both human and nonhuman species. By identifying the elementary forms of

---

[40]Rosemary Hopcroft, "Status Characteristics among Older Individuals: The Diminished Significance of Gender," *Sociological Quarterly* 47 (2006).

[41]For example, see essays in J. Barkow, Leda Cosmides, and John Tooby, eds., *The Adapted Mind: Evolutionary Psychology and the Generation of Culture* (New York: Oxford University Press, 1992).

[42]Rosemary L. Hopcroft, *Sociology: A Biosocial Introduction* (Boulder, CO: Paradigm Press, 2010).

[43]Richard Machalek, "Why Are Large Societies Rare?" *Advances in Human Ecology* 1 (1992): pp. 33–64.

social life among human and nonhuman organisms, information can be gleaned about how the organizational features among species are assembled. In this effort to create a comparative sociology, Machalek outlines a four-step protocol for conducting a sociological analysis of generic social forms "with a priority on sociality, not the organism."[44]

1. Identify and describe a social form that is distributed across two or more species lines.

2. Identify the "design problems" that might constrain the evolution of this social form. In other words, what prerequisites are necessary for a particular social form to come into existence?

3. Identify the processes that generate a social form.

4. Identify those benefits and beneficiaries of a social form that will help explain the persistence and proliferation of certain social forms over other forms.

In applying this protocol, Machalek focused on the evolution of macro societies, a social form that first appeared in human social evolution about 5,000 years ago. He asked this: What makes human macro societies possible? Machalek suggests that we cannot just look at agrarian and industrial societies to answer this question, but rather, we must subordinate the study of human macro-level societies to the study of macro societies as a general social form. If we take a cross-species comparative approach, it is evident that macro sociality is rare and exists in only two taxonomic orders: insects and human primates.

Machalek describes a macro society as a society with hundreds of millions of members with distinct social classes and a complex division of labor. Among social insects, this social form is very old, but in humans, it is very recent, beginning about 5,000 years ago with the emergence of agrarian societies. Obviously, humans and insects are remote species, separated by at least 600 million years of divergent evolution; hence, they cannot be compared by individual biological characteristics. Indeed, humans and insects are separated by major anatomical differences that include "six orders of magnitude in brain size," and so, intelligence did not play a role in the evolution of insect macro societies. Instead, insect and human macro-societal social forms must be compared strictly for their "social structural design" features in what appears to be a case of convergent evolution.

In considering the fundamental similarities between the organization of human and insect macro societies, Machalek maintains that "whatever the species, all social organisms confront the same basic problems of organizational design and regulation if they are to succeed in evolving a macro

---

[44]Richard Machalek, "Crossing Species Boundaries: Comparing Basic Properties of Human and Nonhuman Societies." (Unpublished manuscript.)

society."[45] When looked at this way, the existence of this social form in two such distinctive and biologically remote taxa allows us to address such questions as this: What constraints must be surmounted before a species can evolve a macro society?

Machalek suggests that macro societies are rare because the evolution of this social form requires successful solutions to a series of difficult and complex problems. He suggests that only insects and humans have managed to push aside or overcome (1) organismic constraints, (2) ecological constraints, (3) cost-benefit constraints, and (4) sociological constraints. Each of these will be briefly examined.

**Organismic Constraints.** In detailing the organismic constraints that must be overcome before complex cooperative behavior can evolve, Machalek highlights the morphology of a species as an important factor that can either promote or inhibit the ability of a species to evolve a macro society. For example, aquatic social species such as whales, who are extremely intelligent and who clearly enjoy a "social life," are hopelessly constrained by their enormous "body plans," a constraint that makes it difficult for them to engage in "diverse forms of productive behavior."[46] And, when a body plan constrains the variety of cooperative behaviors possible, it "also constrains the evolution of a complex and extensive division of labor."[47]

**Ecological Constraints.** In addition to organismic constraints, the ecological niche of a species sets limits on both the population size and complexity of a society. An ecosystem's physical properties can vary in the number of predators, competition for resources like food and shelter, diversity of other species, and mortality rates because of disease. All these can become factors in limiting population size for a given species. Social insects are more likely to find a habitat with ample resources to support their macro societies because they are very small creatures.

**Cost-Benefit Constraints.** In addition to organismic and ecological constraints, the evolution of a macro society will depend on economic factors or various "costs and benefits" that accompany any macro society. Although the evolution of a macro society would seem to be beneficial to any social species, a society with complex and extensive cooperation has both costs and benefits. Using the logic of cost-benefit analysis, a particular evolved trait can be analyzed for the ratio of its costs to benefits. Among social insects like ants, costs (which include such problems as social parasitism where alien species expropriate labor or food from unsuspecting ants) do not exceed benefits. This is because social insects greatly benefit from a

---

[45]Machalek, "Why Are Large Societies Rare?" (cited in note 43), p. 35.

[46]Ibid., p. 42.

[47]Ibid.

complex division of labor that allows them to compensate for the small size of each individual "and thus increase their ergonomic efficiency and effectiveness."[48]

**Sociological Constraints**. Of all the constraints, this is the most important one. Even if all other constraints are overcome, the evolution of a macro society requires a unique form of social interaction that is rare in nature and beyond the capacity of most organisms. Essentially, an organism must overcome three large sociological problems to evolve a macro society:[49]

1. The individuals must be able to engage in impersonal cooperation.

2. The labor of members must be divided among distinct social categories.

3. The division of labor among members must be integrated and coordinated.

In considering these critical design problems that must be surmounted before a macro society can evolve, we should ask why it is that only the social insects and humans have been able to generate a rare and complex form of sociality. If we turn to other social species for clues, we find that the fundamental mechanism underlying social organization in most animals is kinship or genetic relatedness. Machalek argues that kinship bonds effectively restrict the number of individuals within a particular cooperative group, making it very difficult for most species to evolve a macro society. Machalek notes that the general principle that links kinship to social behavior among animals can be stated as follows: "The greater the degree of genetic relatedness among individuals, the higher the probability that they will interact cooperatively."[50] In other words, natural selection has seemingly favored social species with the basic capacity to distinguish individual kin from nonkin, thereby making kinship networks possible. Thus, kinship connections based on individual recognition of relatives are the basis for social cooperation for most social species.

In social insects, however, kin are distinguished from nonkin largely through remote chemical communication, for there is no evidence that "blood relatives" recognize each other as individuals. Thus, in ant societies, members interact with five or six types of ants—not millions of individual ants. Ants treat each other as members of distinct categories or castes. In turn, social categories or castes are occupationally specialized, allowing task specialization (that is, foraging, brood tending, nest repair, defense, and so on) and leading to a complex division of labor. Caste types are recognized by olfactory cues, the dominant mechanism behind the organization of

---

[48]Ibid., p. 44.

[49]Ibid., p. 45.

[50]Ibid., p. 46.

ants. Machalek notes that humans often link a complex division of labor to human intelligence, culture, and technological development, but this social form among insects clearly exists outside the range of human intelligence.

In contrast, despite selection for language and culture, human societies were small and based on face-to-face individualized kinship relations for most of human evolutionary history. Yet, in agrarian times, full-blown hierarchical stratification evolved, leading to the question: How were humans able to escape the constraining influences of personalized kinship relations and their highly evolved capacity for individual recognition? Following Machalek:

> Humans have evolved macro societies because they are empowered by culture to form highly cooperative patterns of behavior with "anonymous others." Thus, for the social insects, a state of permanent personal anonymity enables them to form large, complex societies comprising purely impersonal cooperation among members of different castes. Humans, on the other hand, are capable of forming cooperative social systems based either upon personal relationship or impersonal status-role attributes. [51]

Thus, chemical communication allows insects to convert individuals into social types, whereas humans employ *cognitive culture* and socially constructed typifications. This capacity allows humans to interact cooperatively, not as individuals but as personal strangers, dividing individuals into types of social categories. Machalek believes "it is impersonal cooperation that lies at the very foundation of macrosociality."[52] Social insects and humans have thus "used different but functionally analogous strategies to achieve the capacity for close cooperation among anonymous others, thereby facilitating the evolution of macrosociety."[53] In addition, this impersonality specifies and limits the rights and obligations between (or among) parties to an interaction, for as Machalek notes, status-role constructs "are the evolutionary convergent human analogue to the chemical and tactile typification processes among social insects upon which caste systems are built."[54] Essentially, status-role constructs allow humans to ignore the unique and distinctive qualities of persons, thereby increasing the economy of a cooperative interaction. Unlike social insects, however, humans can also move between personal and impersonal attributes in organizing their social lives.

In sum then, only insects and humans have been able to evolve a system of macro sociality, primarily because of the design problems in creating

---

[51]Ibid., p. 47.

[52]Ibid., p. 48.

[53]Ibid., p. 50.

[54]Ibid.

macro societies. Machalek emphasizes that sociologists have long struggled to understand the elementary forms of social behavior, but this quest has been limited because of a general reluctance by sociologists to expand their perspective to include inquiry into nonhuman social species. It is important, Machalek argues, to see how particular social traits are spread across species. The ability to research questions such as the emergence of a complex division of labor and why it is found in only a few societies can help us discover how it evolved in human societies. In addition, if we compare sociality forms across species by consequences, "we can enhance our understanding of the adaptive value of sociality as a response to ecological challenges."[55] Finally, beginning with the social form and then selecting for observation those species in which that form appears would also allow us to better understand the emergent properties of social systems, the adaptive value and processes that generate particular social forms, and the essential design features that might represent a solution to common problems facing diverse species.

## Alexandra Maryanski's Approach

In recent years, Alexandra Maryanski, in conjunction with sometime collaborator Jonathan Turner, has approached the question of human nature by examining the social network ties of humans' closest living relatives, the apes.[56] As is well known, humans share well over 98 percent of their genetic material with chimpanzees (*Pan*); indeed, chimpanzees are genetically closer to humans than they are to gorillas (*Gorilla*). And both chimpanzees and gorillas who are African apes are certainly closer to humans than they are to orangutans (*Pongo*) or gibbons (*Hylobates*), the other two genera who are Asian apes. In fact, humans and chimpanzees came from the same ancestral primate that lived only about five million years ago, according to the fossil and molecular data.[57]

---

[55]Ibid., p. 61.

[56]Alexandra Maryanski, "The Last Ancestor: An Ecological Network Model on the Origins of Human Sociality," *Advances in Human Ecology*, ed. L. Freese, vol. 1 (1992), pp. 1–32; Alexandra Maryanski and Jonathan Turner, *The Social Cage* (Stanford, CA: Stanford University Press, 1992); and Alexandra Maryanski, "African Ape Social Structure: Is There Strength in Weak Ties?" *Social Networks* 9 (1987): pp. 191–215. For the most recent statement of this argument, see Jonathan H. Turner and Alexandra Maryanski, *On the Origins of Societies by Natural Selection* (Boulder, CO: Paradigm Press, 2008).

[57]See Charles G. Sibley, John A. Comstock, and Jon E. Ahlquist, "DNA Hybridization Evidence of Hominoid Phylogeny: A Reanalysis of the Data," *Journal of Molecular Evolution* 30 (1990): pp. 202–36; M. Goodman, D. A. Tagle, D. H. A. Fitch, W. Bailey, J. Czelusnak, B. F. Koop, P. Benson, and J. L. Slightom, "Primate Evolution at the DNA Level and a Classification of Hominids," *Journal of Molecular Evolution* 30 (1990): pp. 260–66. See also Jonathan H. Turner and Alexandra Maryanski, *Incest: Origins of the Taboo* (Boulder, CO: Paradigm Press, 2005) and *On The Origins of Societies by Natural Selection* (Boulder, CO: Paradigm Press, 2008).

Long-term field studies have documented that primates are highly intelligent, slow to mature, undergo a long period of socialization, and live a long time. The majority of primates are organized into year-round societies that require the integration of a wide variety of age and sex classes, not just adult males and females. In addition, primates have clear-cut social bonding patterns that vary widely among the 187 species of primates.

Using a historical-comparative technique, which is termed *cladistic analysis* in biology, Maryanski began by examining the social relational data on present-day great-ape genera—that is, chimpanzees, gorillas, gibbons, and orangutans.[58] Following this procedure, Maryanski first identified a limited group of entities—in this case, the strength of social bonds between and among age and sex classes in all ape genera—to see if there were structural regularities in the patterning of relations. If phyletically close species living in different environments reveal characteristic traits in common, then it can be assumed that their Last Common Ancestor (LCA) also had similar relational features. For this exercise, Maryanski undertook a comprehensive review of bonding propensities for apes living under natural field conditions in an effort to profile their social network structures, with the goal of uncovering a blueprint of the LCA population to present-day apes and humans.

To assess the validity of these relational patterns, she followed the normal procedures of cladistic analysis by including an *outgroup lineage*—a sample of Old World monkey social networks—for comparison to the networks of apes. She also subjected her data set to two fundamental assumptions associated with this comparative technique: (1) the *Relatedness Hypothesis*, which indirectly assesses whether or not the shared patterns of social relations are caused by chance, and (2) the *Regularity Hypothesis*, which indirectly assesses whether the modifications from the ancestral to descendant forms evidence a systematic bias and are not randomly acquired. Both hypotheses provided strong empirical support for her reconstruction of the ancestral patterns of organization among hominoid (that is, apes and humans).[59]

Her analysis led to a striking conclusion: Like the contemporary apes that are phyletically closest to humans, the LCA population evidenced a fluid organizational structure, consisting of a relatively low level of sociality and a lack of intergenerational continuity in groups over time.

---

[58]This technique is a standard tool for reconstruction in such fields as comparative biology, historical linguistics, and textual criticism. Essentially, the basic procedure is to identify a set of characters believed to be the end points or descendants of an evolutionary or developmental process, with the idea that an "original" or common ancestor can be reconstructed through the detection of shared diagnostic characters.

[59]For discussions of this methodology, see R. Jeffers and I. Lehiste, *Principles and Methods for Historical Linguistics* (Cambridge, MA: MIT Press, 1979); M. Hass, "Historical Linguistics and the Genetic Relationship of Languages," *Current Trends in Linguistics* 3 (1966): pp. 113–53; and N. Platnick and H. D. Cameron, "Cladistic Methods in Textual, Linguistic, and Phylogenetic Analysis," *Systematic Zoology* 26 (1977): pp. 380–85.

The proximal reasons for this structure are a combination of several forces that are still found in all living ape social networks: (a) a systematic bias toward female (and usually male) transfer from the natal unit at puberty, which is the opposite trend from monkeys where only males transfer and females stay to form intergenerational matrilines; (b) and a promiscuous mating pattern that makes paternity difficult to know (the gibbon being the exception); and (c) an abundance of weak social ties and few strong ties among most adults. In addition, the modifications from the LCA social structure suggested that after descendants separated from the ancestral population, the future trend in hominoid evolution involved selection pressures for heightened sociality, seemingly to increase hominoid survival and reproductive success. Indeed, it is an established fact in the fossil record that about 18 million years ago, a huge number of the many species of apes underwent a dramatic decline and extinction, just when species of monkeys suddenly proliferated and, according to the fossil record, moved into the former ape niches, perhaps because monkeys developed a competitive, dietary edge over apes. Whatever the explanation, the fossil record confirms that, when ape niches were being usurped by monkeys, apes began to undergo anatomical modifications in order to fill marginal niches in the arboreal habitat. These adaptations revolved around a peculiar locomotion pattern that involves hand-over-hand movement in the trees through space along with other novel skeletal features that characterize the anatomy of both apes and humans today.[60] Currently, monkeys remain the dominant primates, and apes are a distinct tiny minority; moreover, with the exception of humans, the few remaining nonhuman hominoids—that is, chimpanzee, gorilla, orangutan, and gibbon are now considered "evolutionary failures" and "evolutionary leftovers" because of their small numbers and specialized and restricted niches.

The significance of this finding is important for thinking about human nature. If humans' closest relatives reveal a tendency for relatively weak social ties, then humans are also likely to have this social tendency as part of their genetic coding. What, however, is meant by weak and fluid ties?[61]

---

[60]For discussions, see P. Andrews, "Species Diversity and Diet in Monkeys and Apes during the Miocene," in *Aspects of Human Evolution*, ed. C. B. Stringer (London: Taylor and Francis, 1981), pp. 25–61; J. Temerin and J. Cant, "The Evolutionary Divergence of Old World Monkeys and Apes," *American Naturalist* 122 (1983): pp. 335–51; and R. Ciochon and R. Corruccini, eds., *New Interpretations of Ape and Human Ancestry* (New York: Plenum Press, 1983).

[61]To array social tie patterns, affective ties were assessed on the basis of mutually reinforcing and friendly interactions. Degrees of attachment were described along a simple scale of tie strength: null ties, weak ties, moderate ties, strong ties. Individuals without ties (for example, father-daughter where paternity cannot be known) or who rarely, if ever, interact have null ties; those who interact in a positive manner on an occasional basis have weak ties; those who affiliate closely for a time but without endurance over time (at least for adults) have moderate ties; and those who exhibit extensive nonsexual physical contact with much observable affect (for example, reciprocal grooming) have very high interactional rates and show mutual support with stable and long-term relations over time have strong ties. Scaling

Maryanski confirmed in her review of the data that monkeys have many strong ties, especially among females who live in high-density matrifocal networks. In monkey societies, males disperse at puberty to other groups, whereas females remain behind, forming as many as four generations of strongly tied matrilines (composed of grandmothers, mothers, sisters, aunts, cousins, and daughters). These extended female bonds provide inter-generational continuity and are the backbone of most monkey societies. In contrast, females in ape societies evidence the rare pattern of dispersal where, at puberty, females leave their natal community forever. In addition, males in ape societies (with the exception of the chimpanzee) also depart their natal communities, migrating to a new community. Thus, with both sexes dispersing at puberty, most kinship ties are broken, intergenerational continuity is lost, and the result is a relatively fluid social structure with adult individuals moving about as a shifting collection of individuals within a larger regional population.

In Asia, adult orangutans are nearly solitary, rarely interacting with others. A mother with her dependent young is the only stable social unit. In Africa, chimpanzees and gorillas are more socially inclined, with gorillas living together peacefully in small groups, but individuals are so self-contained that it is uncommon to observe any overt social interactions between adults. Among our closest relatives, the common chimpanzee, adult females are also self-contained, spending most of their days traveling about alone with their dependent offspring. Adult chimpanzee males, in contrast, are relatively more social and are likely to have a few individual friendships with other males because, unlike females in the regional population, they have grown up in this larger regional community. A mother and son also form strong ties. But, except for mother and her young offspring, there are no stable groupings in chimpanzee societies. Thus, chimpanzee males are still highly individualistic and self-reliant, preferring to move about independently in space within a large and fluid regional population.

Thus, if humans' closest African ape relatives evidence behavioral propensities for individualism, autonomy, mobility, and weak social ties, Maryanski argues that these genetically coded propensities are probably part of human nature as well. Indeed, if we examine the societal type within which humans as a species evolved—that is, hunting and gathering—it is clear that it approximates the pattern among the great apes, especially African apes: There is considerable mobility within a larger home range of bands; there is a high degree of individualism and personal autonomy; and except for married couples, relatively loose and fluid social ties are evident. At a biological level, then, Maryanski argues that humans might not have the powerful biological urges for great sociality and collectivist-style social

---

tie strength for primates is a straightforward procedure because age and sex classes have clear-cut social tendencies that have been documented by field researchers during the last fifty years. Also see Maryanski, "The Last Ancestor" (note 56), and Maryanski and Turner, *The Social Cage*, for detailed discussions about how the network analysis of primate social ties was conducted. For general references on network analysis, see Chapter 29.

bonding that sociologists, and indeed social philosophy in general, frequently impute to our nature.[62]

In collaborative work with Jonathan Turner, Maryanski has described the implications in a review of the stages of societal development. Hunting and gathering is the stage of evolution in which basic human biological coding evolved. In these small societies composed of wandering bands within a territory evidence rather loose and fluid social ties among their members, high individual autonomy, self-reliance, and mobility from band to band.[63] Yet, as human populations grew in size and were forced to adopt first horticulture and then agriculture to sustain themselves, they settled down to cultivate land, and in the process, they caged themselves in sociocultural forms that violated basic needs for freedom, some degree of individual autonomy, and fluid ties within a larger community of local groups.

Thus, sociocultural evolution began to override the basic nature of humans. As Maryanski and Turner conclude, market-driven systems of the present industrial and post-industrial era are, despite their many obvious problems, closer than horticulture and agrarianism to the original societal type in which humans evolved biologically, at least in this sense: They offer more choices; they allow and indeed encourage individualism; they are structured in ways that make most social ties fluid and transitory; and they limit strong ties beyond family for many. Maryanski and Turner note that, for many sociologists of the past and today, the very features of human behavior required by market-driven societies are viewed as pathologies that violate humans' basic nature. For Maryanski and Turner, societal evolution has, since the hunting and gathering era, just begun once again to create conditions more compatible with humans' basic hominoid nature as an evolved ape.

Although many of these conclusions are obviously somewhat speculative, the point of Maryanski's analysis is clear: If we use evolutionary approaches from biology, such as cladistic analysis and cross-species comparison with humans' close biological relatives, we can make informed inferences about human nature. Then, we can use these inferences to determine whether sociocultural evolution has been compatible or incompatible with humans' primate legacy. From this analysis, it is possible to examine basic institutional systems, such as kinship, polity, religion, and economy to determine how and why they evolved in the first societal type—that is, hunting and gathering—and how they have interacted with humans' basic nature as an evolved ape during the various stages of societal development.

---

[62]See for example M. G. Bicchieri, *Hunters and Gatherers Today* (New York: Holt, Rinehart & Winston, 1972) for a study of eleven food collecting societies. Also see Margaret Power, *The Egalitarians—Human and Chimpanzee: An Anthropological View of Social Organization* (Cambridge: Cambridge University Press, 1991), pp. xviii, 290; Robert C. Bailey and Robert Aunger, "Humans as Primates: The Social Relationships of Efe Pygmy Men in Comparative Perspective," *International Journal of Primatology*, vol. 11, no. 2 (1990): pp. 127–45, which details some of the similarities between chimpanzee and human hunter-gatherer societies.

[63]Maryanski and Turner, *The Social Cage* (cited in note 56), Chap. 4, pp. 69–90.

# Conclusion

As is evident, Darwinian-inspired theoretical approaches are highly diverse. Sociobiology and evolutionary psychology are closely linked, but outside this theoretical line, Darwinian approaches are diverse. Perhaps the most promising are those approaches that are comparative, examining humans and their societies with an eye to where they converge with, and diverge from, societies organizing other life forms. As Herbert Spencer argued over one-hundred years ago, sociology is the study of the *superorganic* realm—that is, the organization of organisms—and humans are not the only animal that organizes itself into complex social formations. Mahaleck's comparative approach looks for the design problems that natural selection had to overcome to produce macro societies; in isolating these design problems, he hits upon key some of the key forces that facilitate or hinder social organization on a large-scale. In many ways, his analysis confirms the insights of the fist functional sociologists who all recognized that evolution generates macro societies through differentiation and new modes of integration—whether this society be composed of insects or humans. Indeed, Herbert Spencer's emphasis on *superorganic systems* as the subject matter argues for a sociology that studies all animals and life forms that form societies composed of organisms.

Maryanski's approach takes theorizing back to an issue that has always been prominent in theorizing: human nature. But, her approach liberates analysis from speculation about the needs and drives of humans because it uses cladistic analysis to look back in time to the features of the last common ancestor to apes and humans. In so doing, inferences about human nature are tied to data from the networks of primates to reconstruct the nature of sociality among those species of hominins from which all humans have descended. The picture that emerges of humans' distant ancestors—individualistic, mobile, promiscuous, and weak-tie animals that do not form permanent groupings—is very different than the popular image among both sociologists and the lay public of humans as group oriented and collectivistic. No doubt, evolution has made humans more social than the last common ancestor to apes and humans, and to present-day apes as well. But, natural selection does not typically wipe away older traits; rather, it adds new traits onto existing ones, with the result that humans are individualistic and weak-tie animals on whom natural selection has laid down a patina of sociality. There is, in many ways, a conflict in human neuroanatomy between individualism and collectivism that has large consequences for how humans behave, interact, and organize.

The fact that these Darwinian-inspired approaches address traditional sociological questions argues for their persistence in sociology, even as they come under criticisms by those who do not think biological dynamics are necessary in developing sociological theories. Still, even in the face of persistent criticisms, this line of evolutionary sociology is not likely to go away. It is not, as some have claimed, a fad, but a pervasive effort to develop a more interdisciplinary sociology—one that recognizes that humans are animals and, hence, have evolved like all other animals, thereby making biological forces relevant in sociological theorizing.

# PART III

# Conflict Theorizing

## CHAPTER 10

# The Rise of Conflict Theorizing

Along with functionalism, conflict theory is one of sociology's first theoretical orientations. Even some early functional theorists, such as Herbert Spencer,[1] developed conceptualizations of conflict; yet, over the years, these functional approaches increasingly came under attack for underemphasizing conflict and change. In seeking "the function" of sociocultural forces for meeting needs for integration and other system needs and requisites, functionalists tended to underemphasize the effects of inequality in systematically generating conflict, disintegration, and change in social systems.[2]

Conflict theory in sociology began with Karl Marx (1818–1883), but the development of the approach owes a debt to two other early German sociologists, Max Weber (1864–1920) and Georg Simmel (1858–1918). Weber and Simmel also articulated conflict theories, but they were suspicious of Marx's polemics and, as a result, added necessary qualifications and refinements to Marx's ideologically driven ideas. Taken together, Marx, Weber, and Simmel provided the core ideas that still inspire contemporary conflict approaches. Yet, despite the genius of these early masters, conflict theory remained recessive during the first half of the twentieth century, although

---

[1]Herbert Spencer, *The Principles of Sociology* (New York: D. Appleton, 1898; originally published in serial between 1874 and 1896). Spencer argued that war between populations had been an important evolutionary force, because the better organized society usually won and selected out the weaker one or, at least, brought it to the level of organization of the victor. This kind of geopolitical analysis became, in the latter half of the twentieth century, an ever more prominent form of conflict theorizing.

[2]See, for example, David Lockwood, "Some Remarks on 'The Social System,'" *British Journal of Sociology* 7 (1956): pp. 134–46; Ralf Dahrendorf, "Out of Utopia: Toward a Reorientation of Sociological Analysis," *American Journal of Sociology* 744 (1958): pp. 115–27.

considerable research and limited theorizing were performed on particular instances of conflict, such as ethnic tensions or colonialism.

The ideas of Marx, Weber, and Simmel on conflict began to resurface and assume a central place in sociological theory during the 1950s in the works of two German-born sociologists, Ralf Dahrendorf and Lewis Coser. While others were also involved in the development of the new conflict approach, Dahrendorf and Coser set the tone for this revival. In this chapter, I will first explore the key insights of Marx, Weber, and Simmel, and then in Chapter 11, I will review Dahrendorf's and Coser's ideas. From this conceptual base, conflict theory has gone in many interesting directions over the last fifty years, as we will see in Chapters 12–14 on conflict theories and then in Chapters 30–33 on critical theories that borrow heavily from Marx and Weber.

# Karl Marx and Conflict Theory

We will encounter Marx's work in analyzing several theoretical perspectives in present-day sociology; therefore, it is not necessary to outline his entire theoretical corpus here. For now, my goal is to describe the more general, abstracted model of conflict that is packaged between the polemics of the Marxian scheme. For Marx, conflict inevitably arises out of inequalities generated by the means of production within a given historical epoch. Those who own and control the means of production are driven to exploit those who have few resources, with the result that the latter feel deprived and alienated because they have little control over their lives and what they produce. Inherent in any pattern of inequality, then, is a conflict of interests that causes the subordinates in a society to mobilize for conflict with super-ordinates. Mobilization increases, Marx argued, as subordinates become aware of their collective interests and, then, begin to mobilize for conflict as their emotions rise, as ideologies of change are articulated by leaders, and as their sense of deprivation and alienation increases.

Marx's assumptions and implicit laws about the social world and the key forces behind conflict and change in societies are summarized in Table 10.1.[3] As shown in Proposition 1, Marx argued that the degree of inequality in the distribution of resources generates inherent conflicts of interest between those who have and those who do not have valued resources. Proposition 2 then emphasizes that when members of subordinate segments of the society become aware of their true interests in redistributing resources and, thereby,

---

[3]In Karl Marx and Friedrich Engel's *The Communist Manifesto* (New York: International, 1971; originally published in 1847) are the key ideas in these propositions. Further amplification of these ideas came with Marx's *Capital: A Critical Analysis of Capitalist Production*, vol. 1 (New York: International, 1967; originally published in 1867). The critical and polemical substance of these and other works will be explored in Chapter 30 on the emergence of critical theory.

**Table 10.1**   Marx's Abstracted Propositions on Conflict Processes

1. The more unequal the distribution of scarce resources in a society, the greater is the basic conflict of interest between its dominant and subordinate segments.

2. The more subordinate segments become aware of their true collective interests, the more likely they are to question the legitimacy of the existing pattern of distribution of scarce resources.

3. Subordinates are more likely to become aware of their true collective interests when

   A. Changes wrought by dominant segments disrupt existing relations among subordinates

   B. Practices of dominant segments create alienative dispositions

   C. Members of subordinate segments can communicate their grievances to one another, which, in turn, is facilitated by

      1. The ecological concentration among members of subordinate groups

      2. The expansion of educational opportunities for members of subordinate groups

   D. Subordinate segments can develop unifying ideologies, which, in turn, is facilitated by

      1. The capacity to recruit or generate ideological spokespeople

      2. The inability of dominant groups to regulate socialization processes and communication networks among subordinates

4. The more subordinate segments of a system become aware of their collective interests and question the legitimacy of the distribution of scarce resources, the more likely they are to join in overt conflict against dominant segments of a system, especially when

   A. Dominant groups cannot clearly articulate, nor act in terms of, their collective interests

   B. Deprivations of subordinates move from an absolute to relative basis, or escalate rapidly

   C. Subordinate groups can develop a political leadership structure

5. The greater the ideological unification of members of subordinate segments of a system and the more developed their political leadership structure, the more likely are the interests and relations between dominant and subjugated segments of a society to become polarized and irreconcilable.

6. The more polarized the dominant and subjugated, the more violent will be conflict.

7. The more violent is the conflict, the greater is the amount of the structural change within a society and the greater is the redistribution of scarce resources.

reducing inequality, they will begin to question the legitimacy of the system. Next, Proposition 3 specifies the conditions that facilitate subordinates' awareness of their true conflict of interest. Propositions 3-A, 3-B, 3-C, and 3-D deal, respectively, with the disruption in the social situation of deprived populations, the amount of alienation people feel as a result of their situation, the capacity of members of deprived segments to communicate with one another, and their ability to develop a unifying ideology that codifies their true interests. Marx saw these conditions as factors that increase and heighten awareness of subordinates' collective interests and, hence, decrease their willingness to accept as legitimate the right of superordinates to command a disproportionate share of resources.

In turn, some of these forces heightening awareness are influenced by such structural conditions as ecological concentration (3-C-1), educational opportunities (3-C-2), the availability of ideological spokespeople (3-D-1), and the control of socialization processes and communication networks by superordinates (3-D-2). Marx hypothesized (shown in Proposition 4), that the increasing awareness by deprived classes of their true interests and the resulting questioning of the legitimacy of the distribution of resources increases the likelihood that the disadvantaged strata in a society will begin to organize collectively their opposition against the dominant segments of a system. This organization is seen as especially likely under several conditions: disorganization among the dominant segments with respect to organizing to protect their true interests (4-A), sudden escalation of subordinates' sense of deprivation as they begin to compare their situation with that of the privileged (4-B), and mobilization of political leadership to carry out the organizational tasks of pursuing conflict (4-C). Marx emphasized (shown in Proposition 5) that, once deprived groups possess a unifying ideology and political leadership, their true interests begin to take on clear focus and their opposition to superordinates begins to increase—polarizing the interests and goals of superordinates and subordinates. As polarization increases, the possibilities for reconciliation, compromise, or mild conflict decrease, because the deprived are sufficiently alienated, organized, and unified to press for a complete change in the pattern of resource distribution. As Proposition 6 underscores, subordinates begin to see violent confrontation as the only way to overcome the inevitable resistance of superordinates. Finally, Marx noted (shown in Proposition 7) that violent conflict will cause great changes in patterns of social organization, especially its distribution of scarce resources. The propositions in Table 10.1 are stated much more abstractly than Marx would have considered appropriate,[4] but his ideas began to filter back into contemporary sociology in this form. As theorists sought explanations for the forces generating conflict and change, they implicitly drew from Marx this image of society as filled with conflicts of

---

[4]For criticism of efforts of such abstract renderings of Marx, see Richard P. Appelbaum, "Marx's Theory of the Falling Rate of Profit: Towards a Dialectical Analysis of Structural Social Change," *American Sociological Review* 43 (February 1978): pp. 64–73.

interests in the distribution of scarce resources, with inequality in the distribution of valued resources setting into motion the mobilization of the subordinates to pursue conflict against superordinates. Yet, few borrowed only from Marx; as conflict theories came to the forefront in sociology during the 1960s, both Max Weber's and Georg Simmel's works on conflict were also consulted because they correct for some of the mistakes in Marx's theory, while making the emerging general theory of conflict more robust.

# Max Weber and Conflict Theory

Max Weber was highly critical of Marx's theory of conflict, arguing that the unfolding of history is contingent on specific empirical conditions. Conflicts of interests do not, Weber believed, inevitably cause the revolutionary crescendo described by Marx. Yet, like Marx, Weber developed a theory of conflict, and despite a convergence in their theories, Weber saw conflict as highly contingent on the emergence of "charismatic leaders" who could mobilize subordinates. Unlike Marx, Weber saw the emergence of such leaders as far from inevitable, and hence, revolutionary conflict would not always be produced in systems of inequality. Nonetheless, when Weber's implicit propositions shown in Table 10.2 are compared with those of Marx in Table 10.1, considerable overlap is evident.

Most of the principles in Table 10.2 can be found in Weber's discussion of the transition from societies based on traditional authority to those organized around rational-legal authority.[5] In societies where the sanctity of tradition legitimates political and social activity, the withdrawal of legitimacy from these traditions is a crucial condition of conflict, as is emphasized in Proposition 1 of Table 10.2. What, then, causes subordinates to withdraw legitimacy? As indicated in Proposition 2-A, one cause is a high degree of correlation among power, wealth, and prestige or, in Weber's terms, among positions of political power (party), occupancy in advantaged economic positions (class), and membership in high-ranking social circles (status groups). When economic elites, for example, are also social and political elites, and vice versa, then those who are excluded from power, wealth, and prestige become resentful and receptive to conflict alternatives. Another condition (Proposition 2-B) is dramatic discontinuity in the distribution of rewards, or the existence of large gaps in social hierarchies that give great privilege to some and very little to others. When only a few hold power, wealth, and prestige and the rest are denied these rewards, tensions and resentments will inevitably arise. Such resentments become a further inducement for those without power, prestige, and wealth to withdraw legitimacy from those who hoard these resources. A final condition

---

[5]For a fuller discussion, see Jonathan H. Turner, Leonard Beeghley, and Charles Powers, *The Emergence of Sociological Theory*, 7th ed. (Thousand Oaks, CA: Sage, 2012). For original sources, see Max Weber, *Economy and Society* (New York: Bedminster, 1968).

**Table 10.2** Weber's Abstracted Propositions on Conflict Processes

1. Subordinates are more likely to pursue conflict with superordinates when they withdraw legitimacy from political authority.

2. Subordinates are more likely to withdraw legitimacy from political authority when

   A. The correlation among memberships in class, status group, and political hierarchies is high

   B. The discontinuity or degrees of inequality in the resource distributions within social hierarchies is high

   C. Rates of social mobility up social hierarchies of power, prestige, and wealth are low

3. Conflict between superordinates and subordinates becomes more likely when charismatic leaders can emerge to mobilize resentments of subordinates.

4. When charismatic leaders are successful in conflict, pressures to routinize authority through new systems of rules and administration will increase and, with routinization, conflict potential can begin to increase for the new regime.

5. As a system of rules and administrative authority is imposed, the more likely are conditions 2-A, 2-B, and 2-C to be met, and hence, the more likely are new subordinates to withdraw legitimacy from political authority and to pursue conflict with the new superordinates, especially when new traditional and ascriptive forms of political domination are imposed by elites.

(Proposition 2-C) emphasizes low rates of social mobility. When those of low rank have little chance to move up social hierarchies or to enter a new class, party, or status group, resentments will accumulate. Those denied opportunities to increase their access to resources become restive and unwilling to accept the system of traditional authority.

As stressed in Proposition 3 in 10.2, the critical force that galvanizes the resentments inhering in these three conditions is charisma. Weber felt that whether or not charismatic leaders emerge is, to a great extent, a matter of historical chance, but if such leaders do emerge to challenge traditional authority and to mobilize resentments caused by the hoarding of resources by elites and the lack of opportunities among subordinates to gain access to wealth, power, or prestige, then conflict and structural change can occur.

When successful, however, such leaders confront organizational problems of consolidating their gains. As stated in Proposition 4, one result is that charisma becomes routinized as leaders create formal rules, procedures, and structures for organizing followers after their successful mobilization to pursue conflict. And as is emphasized in Proposition 5, if routinization creates new patterns of ascription-based inequalities, thus erecting a new system of traditional authority, renewed conflict can be expected as membership in class, status, and party becomes highly correlated, as the new elites hoard resources, and as social mobility up hierarchies is blocked. Yet, if rational-legal routinization occurs, authority is based on equally applied laws and rules, and performance and ability become the basis for recruitment and promotion in bureaucratic structures. Under these conditions, conflict potential will be mitigated.

Unlike Marx, who tended to overemphasize the economic basis of inequality and to argue for a simple polarization of societies into propertied and nonpropertied (exploited) classes, Weber's Propositions 1 and 2 show more theoretical options. Weber believed that variations in the distribution of power, wealth, and prestige and the extent to which holders of one resource control the other resources become critical. Unlike Marx, who saw this correlation as inevitable, Weber saw more diverse relations among class, status, and party. Moreover, the degree of discontinuity in the distribution of these resources—in other words, the extent to which there are clear gaps and lines demarking privilege and nonprivilege—can also vary. Unlike Marx, Weber did not see the complete polarization of super- and subordinates as inexorable. Finally, the degree of mobility—the chance to gain access to power, wealth, and prestige—becomes a crucial variable in generating the resentments and tensions that make people prone to conflict; unlike Marx, Weber did not see a drop in mobility rates as always accompanying inequality.

In addition to the propositions in Table 10.2, which pertain primarily to intra-societal conflict processes, Weber developed theoretical ideas on inter-societal processes.[6] Because conflict between societies is, as Herbert Spencer recognized early in his work, a basic condition of human societies that have settled in territories and developed political leadership, it is not surprising that Weber also analyzed inter-societal conflict, or the geopolitics between societies. This emphasis has been a prominent theme in the dramatic revival of historical sociology in both its neo-Marxian[7] and neo-Weberian[8] forms and will be explored in later chapters. Weber believed that the degree of legitimacy given by a population to political authority depends upon its capacity to generate prestige in the wider geopolitical system, or what today

---

[6]Max Weber, *Economy and Society* (Berkeley, CA: University of California Press, 1968), pp. 901–1372, especially pp. 901–20.

[7]For example, see Immanuel Wallerstein, *The Modern World System*, 3 volumes (New York: Academic, 1974–1989).

[8]For example, see Randall Collins, *Weberian Sociological Theory* (Cambridge, England: Cambridge University Press, 1986); Michael Mann, *The Sources of Social Power*, vol. 1 (New York: Cambridge University Press, 1986); Theda Skocpol, *States and Social Revolutions* (New York: Cambridge University Press, 1979). The last work combines the analysis of internal revolution and geopolitics, describing the former as a potential consequence of failed policies in the latter. See also Chapter 14.

we might term *world system.* Thus, withdrawal of legitimacy is not just the result of conditions 2-A, 2-B, and 2-C in Table 10.2; legitimacy also depends on the success and prestige of a state in relation to other states.[9]

Political legitimacy is often precarious because it relies on the capacity of political authority to meet the needs among system members for defense and attack against external enemies, even during periods of relative peace. Without this sense of threat and a corresponding success in dealing with this threat, legitimacy lessens. Weber did not argue that legitimacy is always necessary for superordinates to dominate; indeed, there are periods of apathy among members of a population, supported by tradition and routine. And there can also be periods of coercive force by superordinates to quell potential rebellion. Nor did Weber argue that "external enemies" must always be present to keep legitimacy revved up; rather, internal conflicts that pose threats can also give legitimacy to political authority. Thus, the very processes that might lead some to withdraw legitimacy and initiate conflict under charismatic leadership can sometimes bolster the legitimacy of political authority, if enough other groupings in a society feel threatened. Indeed, Weber argued, political authorities often stir up internal or external enemies as a ploy for increasing their legitimacy and power to control the distribution of resources.

But the attention of those with political authority to the external system is not always political. Prestige per se can motivate some groupings to encourage military and other forms of contact with other societies. More important, however, are economic interests. Those economic interests— colonial and booty capitalists, privileged traders, financial dealers, arms exporters, and the like—who rely on the state to sustain their viability encourage foreign military expansion, whereas those economic interests that rely on market dynamics and free trade will usually resist military expansionism because it can hurt domestic productivity, or profits in external markets. Instead, these interests will encourage co-optive efforts through trade relations and market dependencies of external populations on commodities and services provided by these interests.

Table 10.3 presents Weber's argument in more abstract terms; these propositions supplement those in Table 10.2 where the loss of legitimacy is seen by Weber as increasing the likelihood of conflict. The essential point is not so much that Weber developed a mature theory but, rather, that he stimulated a conflict approach that examined the relationship between internal and external conflict processes.

## Georg Simmel and Conflict Theory

Georg Simmel was committed to developing theoretical statements that captured the form of basic social processes, an approach he labeled *formal sociology.* Primarily on the basis of his own observations, Simmel sought to

---

[9]All references in note 8.

**Table 10.3**   Weber's Abstracted Propositions on Geopolitics and Conflict

1. The capacity of political authority to dominate a society is dependent upon its legitimacy.

2. The more those with power can sustain a sense of prestige and success in relations with external societies, the greater will be the capacity of leaders to be viewed as legitimate.

3. When productive sectors of a society depend upon political authority for their viability, they encourage political authority to engage in military expansion to augment their interests; when successful, such expansion increases the prestige and, hence, the legitimacy of political authority.

4. When productive sectors do not depend upon the state for their viability, they encourage political authority to rely upon co-optation rather than military expansion; when successful, such co-optation increases prestige and, hence, the legitimacy of political authority.

5. The more those with power can create a sense of threat from external forces, the greater is their capacity to be viewed as legitimate.

6. The more those with power can create a sense of threat among the majority by internal conflict with a minority, the greater is their capacity to be viewed as legitimate.

7. When political authority cannot sustain a sense of legitimacy, outbreaks of internal conflict are more likely, and when political authority loses prestige in the external system, it loses legitimacy and becomes more vulnerable to internal conflict.

extract the essential properties from processes and events in a wide variety of empirical contexts. In turn, abstract statements about these essential properties could be articulated.

Much like Marx, Simmel viewed conflict as ubiquitous and, hence, subject to analysis in formal terms.[10] In his most famous essay on conflict, Simmel devoted considerable effort to analyzing the positive consequences of conflict for the maintenance of social wholes and their subunits. Simmel recognized, of course, that an overly cooperative, consensual, and integrated society would show "no life process," but his analysis of conflict is still loaded in the direction of how conflict promotes solidarity and unification. Thus unlike Marx, who saw conflict as ultimately becoming violent and revolutionary and leading to the structural change of the system, Simmel

---

[10]All subsequent references to this work are taken from Georg Simmel, *Conflict and the Web of Group Affiliation*, trans. K. H. Wolff (Glencoe, IL: Free Press, 1956).

often analyzed the opposite phenomena—less intense and violent conflicts that promote the solidarity, integration, and orderly change.[11]

Simmel's key ideas on conflict are summarized in Table 10.4. Proposition 1-A overlaps somewhat with those developed by Marx. Like Marx, Simmel emphasized that violent conflict is the result of emotional

---

**Table 10.4**   Simmel's Abstracted Propositions on Conflict Processes

1. The level of violence in conflict is increased when
   A. The parties to the conflict have a high degree of emotional involvement, which, in turn, is related to the respective levels of solidarity among parties to the conflict
   B. The membership of each conflict party perceives the conflict to transcend their individual self-interests, which, in turn, is related to the extent to which the conflict is over value-infused issues

2. The level of violence in conflict is reduced when the conflict is instrumental and perceived by the conflict parties be a means to clear-cut and delimited goals.

3. Conflict will generate the following among the parties to a conflict:
   A. Clear group boundaries
   B. Centralization of authority and power
   C. Decreased tolerance of deviance and dissent
   D. Increased internal solidarity among memberships of each party, but particularly for members of minority parties and for groups engaged in self-defense

4. Conflict will have integrative consequences for the social whole when
   A. Conflict is frequent, low in intensity, and low in violence, which, in turn, allows disputants to release hostilities
   B. Conflict occurs in a system whose members and subunits reveal high levels of functional interdependence, which, in turn, encourages the creation of normative agreements to regulate the conflict so that the exchange of resources is not disrupted
   C. Conflict produces coalitions among various conflicting parties

---

[11]Pierre van den Berghe has argued that a dialectical model of conflict is ultimately one in which unification, albeit temporary, emerges out of conflict. Yet, the differences between Marx and Simmel have inspired vastly different theoretical perspectives in contemporary sociology. See Pierre van den Berghe, "Dialectic and Functionalism: Toward a Theoretical Synthesis," *American Sociological Review* 28 (1963): pp. 695–705.

arousal. Such arousal is particularly likely when conflict groups possess a great deal of internal solidarity. As shown in Proposition 1-B, Simmel indicated that, coupled with emotional arousal, the extent to which members see the conflict as transcending their personal aims and self-interests increases the likelihood of violent conflict. Proposition 2 is Simmel's most important because it contradicts Marx's hypothesis that objective consciousness of interests will lead to organization for violent conflict. Simmel argued that the more clearly articulated are the interests of conflict parties and the more clear-cut and focused are their goals, the more likely are less combative means, such as bargaining and compromise, to be used to meet the specific objectives of the group. Thus, for Simmel, consciousness of common interests can, under unspecified conditions, lead to highly instrumental and nonviolent conflict. In the context of labor-management relations, for example, Simmel's proposition is more accurate than Marx's prediction because violence has more often accompanied labor-management disputes in the initial formation of unions, when interests and goals are not well articulated. As interests become clarified, violent conflict has been increasingly replaced by less violent forms of social negotiation.[12]

The consequences of conflict for (1) the conflict parties and (2) the systemic whole in which the conflict occurs are summarized in Propositions 3 and 4. Propositions 3-A, 3-B, 3-C, and 3-D summarize Simmel's ideas about the functions of conflict for the respective parties to the conflict. Conflict increases the formation of clear-cut group boundaries, the centralization of authority, the control of deviance and dissent, and the enhancement of social solidarity within conflict parties.

Proposition 4, on the consequences of conflict for the social whole, provides an important qualification to Marx's analysis. Marx visualized initially mild conflicts as intensifying as the combatants become increasingly polarized, ultimately resulting in violent conflict that would lead to radical social change in the system. In contrast, Simmel argued that conflicts of low intensity and high frequency in systems of high degrees of interdependence do not necessarily intensify or lead to radical social change. On the contrary, these conflicts release tensions and become normatively regulated, thereby promoting stability in social systems. Further, with the increasing organization of the conflicting groups, and the formation of coalitions among conflict groups, violence will decrease as their goals become better articulated. The consequence of such organization and articulation of interests will be a greater disposition to initiate milder forms of conflict, involving competition, bargaining, and compromise.

---

[12]Admittedly, Marx's late awareness of the union movement in the United States forced him to begin pondering this possibility, but he did not incorporate this insight into his theoretical scheme.

## Conclusions

The propositions summarized in Tables 10.1 through 10.4 document that, by the turn into the twentieth century, sociology had a powerful set of explanatory tools for understanding social conflict. Only Simmel would have approved of my converting discursive texts into more abstract and formal propositional formats, but the enduring significance of Marx, Weber, and Simmel's ideas resides, I believe, in the scientific explanations that they provide—even if Marx and Weber would be somewhat skeptical that there are universal and timeless laws of social conflict. As we will see, both Marx and Weber's analyses of societies have been used for more critical theories that not only eschew science but see it as part of the problem. Yet, as conflict sociology began to remerge, especially in the United States, it was analytical theorists committed to the epistemology of science that brought the legacy of the masters forward into the second half of the twentieth century, as we will see in Chapter 11.

# Early Analytical Conflict Theories

For the first half of the twentieth century, conflict theorizing remained somewhat dormant. There were, of course, analyses of conflict for specific empirical phenomena, such as ethnic strife, class tensions, intersocietal war, colonialism, and other dissociative processes. But, the conflict ideas contained in the works of German masters had not been explicitly incorporated into the mainstream of sociological theory, especially in America. Marxist scholarship was particularly recessive, being repressed in America by the anti-communism of the Cold War era.

With the 1960s, however, came a broad social and intellectual movement that confronted then current institutional practices in Western societies; in this new environment, conflict sociology was reborn, soon becoming an important part of the theoretical canon.

The emerging conflict theories were generally critical of functionalism, seeing this kind of theorizing as being conservative and implicitly legitimating the status quo. Structures were too easily seen as functional for the needs of society, with the result that these structures must exist if a society is to remain viable. For the new conflict theorists, these assumptions in functional theory simply ignored the fact that the social world is filled with conflict, thus requiring a fundamental shift in sociological theorizing. The early critics of conflict theory were, however, committed to the epistemology of science compared to the early critical theorists (see Part VII where critical theories are examined). In Germany, Ralf Dahrendorf was one of the earliest critics of functional theorizing, especially that produced by Talcott Parsons, and he sought to do more than critique functionalism; he proposed a dialectical conflict theory that blended the ideas of the three great German masters—Karl Marx, Max Weber, and Georg Simmel—into an analytical conflict theory. I will examine his theory first. Next I will explore—as contradictory as it sounds—Lewis A. Coser's *functional conflict theory.*

Coser was a German immigrant, fleeing Nazi Germany, and his theory argues that Marx and Marxists are too one-sided, seeing conflict everywhere, while functionalists are opposite, viewing society as too well integrated. By placing a pox on both of their houses, Coser argued that it is important to see the functions of conflict not for integrating societies as much as tearing them apart; furthermore, he found the necessary theoretical leads in his German compatriot of another generation, Geog Simmel. Finally, I will summarize one of my early theories that seeks to integrate Dahrendorf's and Coser's theory without getting caught up in the often overblown critiques of functionalism.

These three theories are *analytical* because they are committed to the goals of science and thus seek to develop concepts and propositions that are highly abstract and, it is hoped, relevant for all times and places. Conflict is seen as a fundamental process in the social universe, with the goal of theorizing to specify the conditions that generate conflict of varying degrees of intensity and violence within social structures. Let me now turn to Dahrendorf's theory.

# Ralf Dahrendorf's Dialectical Theory

## Making Marx's Theory More Abstract

Ralf Dahrendorf linked functional theories to a utopia.[1] Since theory had been so one-sided in studying the functions of structures, an equally one-sided conflict approach might be needed, at least for a time, to generate a more balanced theory of human social organization.[2] The model that emerged from this theoretical calling is a dialectical conflict perspective, which still represents one of the best efforts to incorporate the insights of Marx and (to a lesser extent) Weber and Simmel into a coherent set of theoretical propositions. Dahrendorf believed that the process of institutionalization involves the creation of *imperatively coordinated associations* (ICAs) that, in terms of criteria not specified, represent a distinguishable organization of roles. This organization is characterized by power relationships, with some clusters of roles having power to extract conformity from

---

[1]Ralf Dahrendorf, "Out of Utopia: Toward a Reorientation of Sociological Analysis," *American Journal of Sociology* 64 (1958): p. 127.

[2]As Dahrendorf emphasizes, "I do not intend to fall victim to the mistake of many structural-functional theorists and advance for the conflict model a claim to comprehensive and exclusive applicability . . . it may well be that in a philosophical sense, society has two faces of equal reality; one of stability, harmony, and consensus and one of change, conflict and constraint" (ibid.). Such disclaimers are, in reality, justifications for arguing for the primacy of conflict in society. By claiming that functionalists are one-sided, it becomes fair game to be equally one-sided to balance past one-sidedness.

others. Dahrendorf was somewhat vague on this point, but it appears that any social unit—from a small group or formal organization to a community or an entire society—could be considered an ICA for analytical purposes if an organization of roles displaying power differentials exists. Furthermore, although power denotes the coercion of some by others, these power relations in ICAs tend to become legitimated and can therefore be viewed as authority relations in which some positions have the "accepted" or "normative right" to dominate others. Dahrendorf thus conceived of the social order as maintained by processes creating authority relations in the various types of ICAs existing throughout all layers of social systems.[3]

At the same time, however, power and authority are the scarce resources over which subgroups within a designated ICA compete and fight. They are thus the major sources of conflict and change in these institutionalized patterns. This conflict is ultimately a reflection of where clusters of roles in an ICA stand in relation to authority, because the *objective interests* inherent in any role are a direct function of whether or not a role possesses authority and power over other roles. However, even though roles in ICAs possess varying degrees of authority, any particular ICA can be typified as just two basic types of roles—ruling and ruled. The ruling cluster of roles has an interest in preserving the status quo, and the ruled cluster has an interest in redistributing power, or authority. Under certain specified conditions, awareness of these contradictory interests increases, with the result that ICAs polarize into two conflict groups, each now aware of its objective interests, which then engage in a contest for authority. The resolution of this contest or conflict involves the redistribution of authority in the ICA, thus making conflict the source of change in social systems. In turn, the redistribution of authority represents the institutionalization of a new cluster of ruling and ruled roles that, under certain conditions, polarize into two interest groups that initiate another contest for authority. Social reality is thus typified by this unending cycle of conflict over authority within the various types of ICAs that constitute the social world.

Much like Marx, this image of institutionalization as a cyclical or dialectic process led Dahrendorf into the analysis of only certain key causal relations: (1) Conflict is assumed to be an inexorable process arising from opposing forces within social and structural arrangements; (2) such conflict is accelerated or retarded by a series of intervening structural conditions or variables; and (3) conflict resolution at one point in time creates a structural situation that, under specifiable conditions, inevitably leads to further conflict among opposed forces. Moreover, Dahrendorf's and Marx's models reveal similar causal chains of events leading to conflict and the reorganization of social structure: Relations of domination and

---

[3]Ralf Dahrendorf, "Toward a Theory of Social Conflict," *Journal of Conflict Resolution* 2 (1958): pp. 170–83; Class and Class Conflict in Industrial Society (Stanford, CA: Stanford University Press, 1959), pp. 168–69; Gesellschaft un Freiheit (Munich: R. Piper, 1961); *Essays in the Theory of Society* (Stanford, CA: Stanford University Press, 1967).

subjugation create an "objective" opposition of interests; awareness or consciousness by the subjugated of this inherent opposition of interests occurs under certain specifiable conditions; under other conditions this newfound awareness leads to the political organization and, then, to polarization of subjugated groups, which join in conflict with the dominant group; the outcome of the conflict will usher in a new pattern of social organization; this new pattern of social organization will have relations of domination and subjugation that set off another sequence of events leading to conflict and then change in patterns of social organization.

The intervening conditions affecting these processes are outlined by both Marx and Dahrendorf only with respect to the formation of awareness of opposed interests by the subjugated, the politicization and polarization of the subjugated into a conflict group, and the initiation of conflict. The intervening conditions under which institutionalized patterns generate dominant and subjugated groups and the conditions under which these can be typified as having opposed interests remain unspecified by Dahrendorf, whereas for Marx the conditions of opposition were inherent in the dynamics of capitalism.

## The Causal Imagery in Marx and Dahrendorf

Figure 11.1 outlines the causal imagery of Marx and Dahrendorf. The top row of the figure contains Marx's analytical categories, stated in their most abstract form. The other two rows specify the empirical categories of Marx and Dahrendorf, respectively. Separate analytical categories for the Dahrendorf model are not enumerated because they are the same as those in the Marxian model. The empirical categories of the Dahrendorf scheme differ greatly from those of Marx, but the form of analysis is much the same. For both Marx and Dahrendorf, power differences are automatically transformed into relations of domination and subjugation that, in turn, create opposed interests between superordinates and subordinates. The causal analysis for both begins with an elaboration of the conditions leading to growing class consciousness (Marx) or awareness among quasi groups (Dahrendorf) of their objective interests; then analysis shifts to the creation of a politicized class "for itself" (Marx) or a true "conflict group" (Dahrendorf); finally, emphasis focuses on the emergence of conflict between polarized and politicized classes (Marx) or conflict groups (Dahrendorf).

## Developing Explanatory Propositions

More formally, Dahrendorf outlined three types of intervening empirical conditions: conditions of organization that affect the transformation of latent quasi groups into manifest conflict groups; conditions of conflict that determine the form and intensity of conflict; and conditions of structural change that influence the kind, speed, and depth of the changes in social structure. Thus, the variables in the theoretical scheme are (1) the degree of

**Figure 11.1** The Dialectical Causal Imagery

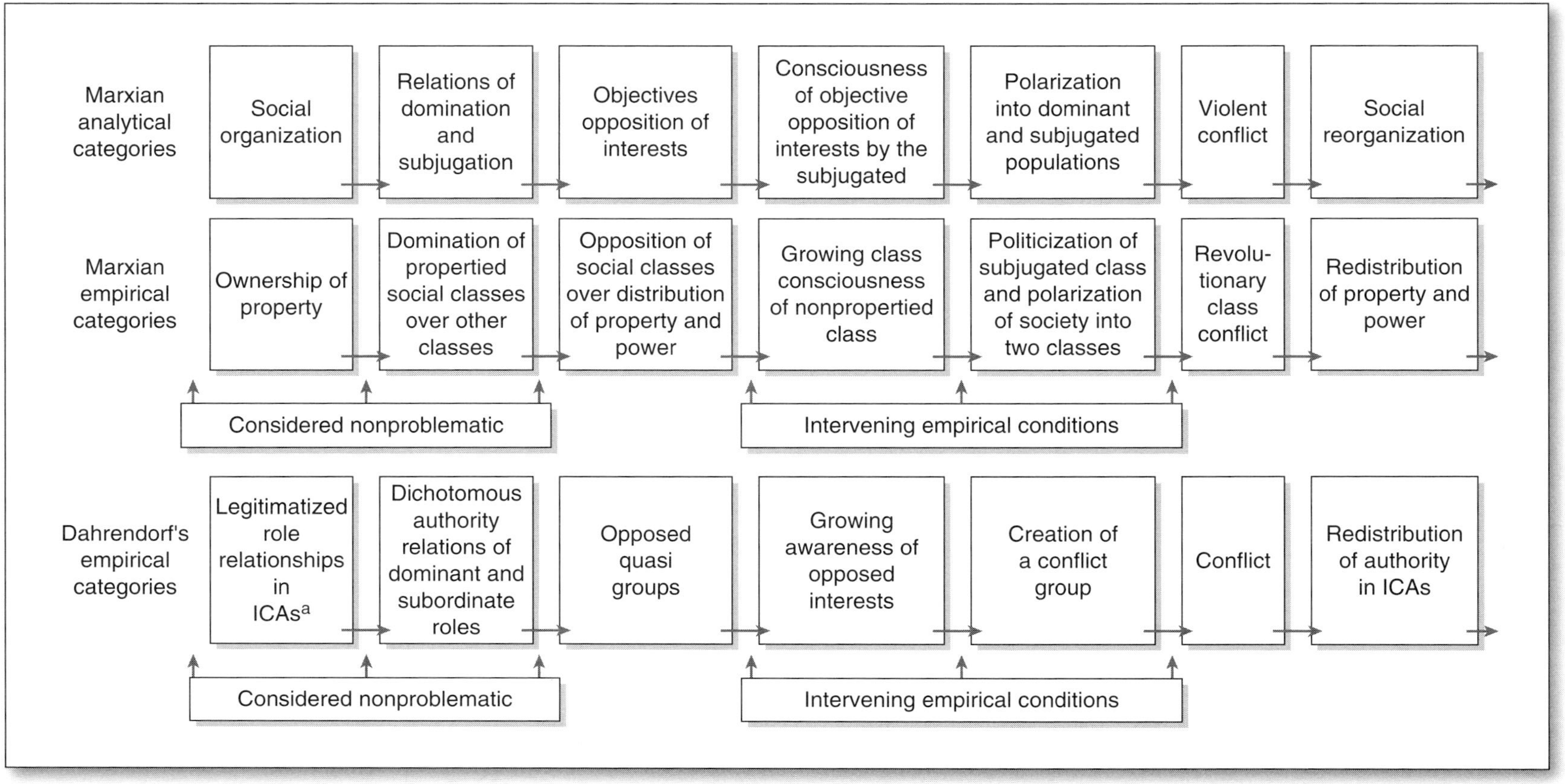

a. ICAs = imperatively coordinated associations.

conflict-group formation, (2) the degree of intensity of the conflict, (3) the degree of violence of the conflict, (4) the degree of change of social structure, and (5) the rate of such change. As is evident in Table 11.1,[4] Dahrendorf's propositions appear to be an elaboration of those developed by Marx (compare Table 11.1 with Table 10.1 in the last chapter).

**Table 11.1**  Dahrendorf's Abstract Propositions

1. Conflict is likely to occur as members of quasi groups in ICAs can become aware of their objective interests and form a conflict group, which, in turn, increase with

   A. The "technical" conditions of organization, which, in turn, depend on

      1. The formation of a leadership cadre among quasi groups

      2. The codification of an idea system, or charter

   B. The "political" conditions of organization, which are dependent on dominant groups permitting organization of opposed interests

   C. The "social" conditions of organization, which, in turn, are related to

      1. Opportunities for members of quasi groups to communicate

      2. Opportunities for recruiting members

2. The less the technical, political, and social conditions of organization are met, the more intense the conflict will be.

3. The more the distribution of authority and other rewards are associated with each other (superimposed), the more intense the conflict will be.

4. The less the mobility between super- and subordinate groups, the more intense the conflict will be.

5. The less the technical, political, and social conditions of organization are met, the more violent the conflict will be.

6. The more the deprivation of the subjugated in the distribution of rewards shifts from an absolute to a relative basis, the more violent the conflict will be.

7. The less is the ability of conflict groups to develop regulatory agreements, the more violent the conflict will be.

8. The more intense is the conflict, the more will be the degree of structural change and reorganization.

9. The more violent is the conflict, the greater will be the rate of structural change.

---

[4]The propositions listed in the table differ from those in a list provided by Dahrendorf in *Class and Class Conflict*, pp. 239–40 in two respects: (1) They are phrased consistently as statements of covariance and (2) they are phrased somewhat more abstractly without reference to class, which in this particular work was Dahrendorf's primary concern.

Like Marx, Dahrendorf saw conflict as related to subordinates' growing awareness of their interests and formation into conflict groups (Proposition 1). Such awareness and group formation are a positive function of the degree to which (a) the technical conditions (leadership and unifying ideology), (b) the political conditions (capacity to organize), and (c) the social conditions (ability to communicate) are met. These ideas clearly come from Marx's discussion (see Table 10.1 on page 207). However, as shown in Proposition 2, Dahrendorf borrows from Simmel and contradicts Marx, emphasizing that if groups are not well organized—that is, if the technical, political, and social conditions are not met—then conflict is likely to be emotionally involving or "intense". Dahrendorf borrowed from Weber (Proposition 3) by stressing that the superimposition of rewards—that is, the degree of correlation among those who enjoy privilege (power, wealth, and prestige)—also increases the emotional involvement of subordinates. Proposition 4 shows that Dahrendorf also takes as much from Weber as from Marx: Dahrendorf believed that the lack of mobility into positions of authority escalates the emotional involvement of subordinates. Proposition 5 is clearly from Simmel and contradicts Marx, in that the violence of conflict is related to the lack of organization and clear articulation of interests. But in Proposition 6, Dahrendorf returns to Marx's emphasis that sudden escalation in people's perception of deprivation—that is, relative deprivation—increases the likelihood of violent conflict. In Proposition 7, however, Dahrendorf returns to Simmel and argues that violence is very much related to the capacity of a system to develop regulatory procedures for dealing with grievances and releasing tensions. And in Propositions 8 and 9, Dahrendorf moves again to Marx's emphasis on how conflict produces varying rates and degrees of structural change in a social system.

## Lewis Coser's Conflict Functionalism

Lewis Coser was one of the first modern conflict theorists, and he published a major work on conflict before Ralf Dahrendorf. Yet, because this work had a functional flavor and was borrowed from Simmel more than Marx, it was not initially seen as a devastating critique of functionalism in quite the same way as Dahrendorf's early polemic. Still, in his more functional version of conflict theory, Coser launched what became the standard polemic against functionalism: Conflict is not given sufficient attention, and related phenomena such as deviance and dissent are too easily viewed as "pathological" for the equilibrium of the social system.[5] Yet, although Coser consistently maintained that functional theorizing "has too often neglected the dimensions of power and interest," he did not follow either Marx's or Dahrendorf's emphasis on the disruptive consequences of violent conflict. Rather, Coser sought to correct Dahrendorf's analytical excesses by emphasizing the

---

[5]Lewis A. Coser, *The Functions of Social Conflict* (London: Free Press, 1956).

integrative and "adaptability" functions of conflict for social systems.[6] Thus, Coser justified his efforts by criticizing functionalism for ignoring conflict and by criticizing conflict theory for underemphasizing the functions of conflict.[7] In so doing, he turned to Georg Simmel's view of conflict as promoting social integration of the social systems, or at least of some of its critical parts.

Coser's analysis then proceeded as follows: (1) Imbalances in the integration of system parts lead to (2) the outbreak of varying types of conflict among these parts, which in turn causes (3) temporary reintegration of the system, which leads to (4) increased flexibility in the system's structure, increased capability to resolve future imbalances through conflict, and increased capacity to adapt to changing conditions. Coser executed this approach by developing, at least implicitly in his discursive argument, a variety of propositions that I have extracted and formalized in the tables below.

## The Causes of Conflict

Much like Weber, Coser emphasized that the withdrawal of legitimacy from an existing system of inequality is a critical precondition for conflict.[7] In contrast, dialectical theorists such as Dahrendorf tended to view the causes of conflict as residing in "contradictions" or "conflicts of interest." In such dialectical theories, as subordinates become aware of their interests, they pursue conflict; hence the major theoretical task is to specify the conditions raising levels of awareness. But Coser argued that conflicts of interest are likely to be exposed only after the deprived withdraw legitimacy. Coser emphasized that the social order is maintained by some degree of consensus over existing sociocultural arrangements and that disorder through conflict occurs only when conditions decrease this consensus.

Two such conditions are specified in Propositions 1-A and 1-B of Table 11.2, both of which owe their inspiration more to Weber than to Marx. When channels for expressing grievances do not exist and when the deprived's

[6]A listing of some of Coser's prominent works, to be used in subsequent analysis, reveals the functional flavor of his conflict perspective: *The Functions of Social Conflict* (cited in note 5); "Some Social Functions of Violence" *Annals of the American Academy of Political and Social Science* 364 (1960); "Some Functions of Deviant Behavior and Normative Flexibility," *American Journal of Sociology* 68 (1962): pp. 172–81; and "The Functions of Dissent," in *The Dynamics of Dissent* (New York: Grune & Stratton, 1968), pp. 158–70. Other prominent works with less revealing titles but critical substance include "Social Conflict and the Theory of Social Change," *British Journal of Sociology* 8 (1957): pp. 197–207; "Violence and the Social Structure," in *Science and Psychoanalysis*, ed. J. Masserman, vol. 7 (New York: Grune & Stratton, 1963), pp. 30–42. These and other essays are collected in Coser's *Continuities in the Study of Social Conflict* (New York, Free Press, 1967). One should also consult his *Masters of Sociological Thought* (New York: Harcourt Brace Jovanovich, 1977, reprinted by Waveland Press in 2003).

[7]Lewis Coser, "Durkheim's Conservatism and Its Implications for His Sociological Theory," in *Émile Durkheim, 1858–1917: A Collection of Essays*, ed. K. H. Wolff (Columbus: Ohio State University Press, 1960); also reprinted in Coser's *Continuities in the Study of Social Conflict.*

**Table 11.2** Coser's Propositions on the Causes of Conflict

1. Subordinate members in a system of inequality are more likely to initiate conflict as they question the legitimacy of the existing distribution of scarce resources, which, in turn, is caused by

   A. Few channels for redressing grievances

   B. Low rates of mobility to more privileged positions

2. Subordinates are most likely to initiate conflict with superordinates as their sense of relative deprivation and, hence, injustice increases, which, in turn, is related to

   A. The extent to which socialization experiences of subordinates do not generate internal ego constraints

   B. The failure of superordinates to apply external constraints on subordinates

desire for membership in higher ranks is thwarted, the withdrawal of legitimacy becomes more likely.

As Proposition 2 in Table 11.2 indicates, the withdrawal of legitimacy, in itself, is not likely to result in conflict. People must first become emotionally aroused. The theoretical task then becomes one of specifying the conditions that translate the withdrawal of legitimacy into emotional arousal, instead of some other emotional state such as apathy and resignation. Here Coser drew inspiration from Marx's notion of relative deprivation. For, as Marx observed and as a number of empirical studies has documented, absolute deprivation does not always foster revolt.[8] When people's expectations for a better future suddenly begin to exceed perceived avenues for realizing these expectations, only then do they become sufficiently aroused to pursue conflict. The level of arousal will, in turn, be influenced by their commitments to the existing system, by the degree to which they have developed strong internal constraints, and by the nature and amount of social control in a system. Such propositions, for example, lead to predictions that, in systems with absolute dictators who ruthlessly repress the masses, revolt by the masses is less likely than in systems where some freedoms have been granted and where the deprived have been led to believe that things will be getting better. Under these conditions, the withdrawal of legitimacy can be accompanied by released passions and emotions.

---

[8]The propositions in Table 11.2 are extracted from *The Functions of Social Conflict* (cited in note 5), pp. 8–385; "Social Conflict and the Theory of Social Change" (cited in note 5), pp. 197–207; and "Violence and Social Structure" (cited in note 6). James Davies, "Toward a Theory of Revolution," *American Journal of Sociology* 27 (1962): pp. 5–19; Ted Robert Gurr, *Why Men Rebel* (Princeton, NJ: Princeton University Press, 1970); and "Sources of Rebellion in Western Societies: Some Quantitative Evidence," *Annals* 38 (1973): pp. 495–501.

## The Violence of Conflict

Coser's most important propositions on the level of violence in a conflict are presented in Table 11.3.[9] As most functional theorists emphasized, Coser's Proposition 1 in Table 11.3 is directed at specifying the conditions under which conflict will be less violent. In contrast, dialectical theorists, such as Marx, often pursued just the opposite: specifying the conditions under which conflict will be more violent. Yet the inverse of Coser's first proposition can indicate a condition under which conflict will be violent. The key concept in this proposition is *realistic issues*. Coser reasoned that realistic conflict involves the pursuit of specific aims against real sources of hostility, with some estimation of the costs to be incurred in such pursuit.

As noted in Chapter 10, Simmel recognized that, when clear goals are sought, compromise and conciliation are likely alternatives to violence. Coser restated this proposition (shown in Proposition 2 in Table 11.3) on conflict over "nonrealistic issues," such as ultimate values, beliefs, ideology, and vaguely defined class interests. When nonrealistic, the conflict will be violent. Such nonrealism is particularly likely when conflict is about core values, which emotionally mobilize participants and make them unwilling to compromise (Proposition 2-A). Moreover, if conflict endures for a long period of time, it becomes increasingly nonrealistic as parties become emotionally involved, as ideologies become codified, and as the enemy is portrayed in increasingly negative terms (Proposition 2-B). Proposition 3 shows a more structural variable to the analysis of conflict violence. In

---

**Table 11.3**   Coser's Propositions on the Violence of Conflict

1. When groups engage in conflict over realistic issues (obtainable goals), they are more likely to seek compromises over the means to realize their interests, and hence, the less violent the conflict will be.

2. When groups engage in conflict over nonrealistic issues, the greater is the level of emotional arousal and involvement in the conflict, and hence, the more violent the conflict will be, especially when

   A. Conflict occurs over core values

   B. Conflict endures over time

3. When functional interdependence among social units is low, the less available are the institutional means for absorbing conflicts and tensions, and hence, the more violent the conflict will be.

---

[9]These propositions are taken from Coser's *Functions of Social Conflict* (cited in note 5), pp. 45–50. Again, they have been made more formal than Coser's more discursive text.

systems in which there are high degrees of functional interdependence among actors—that is, where there are mutual exchanges and cooperation—conflict is less likely to be violent.

## The Duration of Conflict

As shown in the propositions of Table 11.4, Coser underscored that conflicts with a broad range of goals or with vague ones will be prolonged.[10] When goals are limited and articulated, it is possible to know when they have been attained. With perception of attainment, the conflict can be terminated. Conversely, with a wide variety or long list of goals, a sense of attainment is less likely to occur—thus prolonging the conflict. Coser also emphasized that knowledge of what would symbolically constitute victory and defeat will influence the length of conflict. If the parties do not have the ability to recognize defeat or victory, conflict is likely to be prolonged to a point where one party destroys the other. Leadership has important effects on conflict processes; the more leaders can perceive that complete attainment of goals is not possible and the greater their ability is to convince followers to terminate conflict, the less prolonged the conflict will be.

**Table 11.4**   Coser's Propositions on the Duration of Conflict

1. Conflict will be prolonged when
    A. The goals of the opposing parties to a conflict are expansive
    B. The degree of consensus over the goals of conflict is low
    C. The parties in a conflict cannot easily interpret their adversary's symbolic points of victory and defeat

2. Conflict will be shortened when
    A. Leaders of conflicting parties perceive that complete attainment of goals is possible only at very high costs, which, in turn, is related to
        1. The equality of the power between conflicting groups
        2. The clarity of indexes of defeat or victory in a conflict
    B. Leaders' capacity to persuade followers to terminate conflict, which, in turn, is related to
        1. Centralization of power in conflict parties
        2. Integration within conflict parties

---

[10]These propositions come from Coser, "The Termination of Conflict," in *Continuities,* pp. 37–52 and *The Functions of Social Conflict* (cited note 5), pp. 20, 48–55, 59, 128–33.

## The Functions of Conflict

For Coser, conflict is functional when it promotes integration based on solidarity, clear authority, functional interdependence, and normative control. In Coser's terms, it is more adaptive. Other conflict theorists might argue that conflict in such a system is dysfunctional because integration and adaptability in this specific context may be highly exploitive. Nonetheless, Coser divided his analysis of the functions of conflict along lines similar to those by Simmel: the functions of conflict for (1) the respective parties to the conflict and (2) the systemic whole in which the conflict occurs.

In the propositions listed in Table 11.5, the intensity of conflict—that is, people's involvement in and commitment to pursue the conflict—and its level of violence increase the demarcation of boundaries (Proposition 1-A), centralization of authority (Proposition1-B), structural and ideological solidarity (Proposition1-C), and suppression of dissent and deviance (Proposition 1-D) within each of the conflict parties.[11] Conflict intensity is presumably functional because it increases integration, although centralization of power as well as the suppression of deviance and dissent create malintegrative pressures in the long run (see Proposition 2). Thus, there

**Table 11.5**  Coser's Propositions on the Functions of Conflict for the Respective Parties

1. The more violent or intense is the conflict, the more the conflict will generate
   A. Clear-cut boundaries for each conflict party
   B. Centralized decision-making structures for each conflict party, especially when these parties are structurally differentiated
   C. Structural and ideological solidarity among members of each conflict party, especially when the conflict is perceived to affect the welfare of all segments of the conflict parties
   D. Suppression of dissent and deviance within each conflict party as well as forced conformity to norms and values
2. The more conflict between parties leads centers of power to force conformity within conflict groups, the greater is the accumulation of hostilities and the more likely is internal group conflict to surface in the long run.

[11]These propositions are taken from Coser, *Functions of Social Conflict* (cited in note 5), pp. 37–38, 45, 69–72, 92–95.

appears to be an inherent dialectic in conflict-group unification—one that creates pressures toward dis-unification. Unfortunately, Coser did not specify the conditions under which these malintegrative pressures are likely to surface. In focusing on positive functions—that is, forces promoting integration—the analysis ignored a promising area of inquiry. This bias becomes even more evident when Coser shifts attention to the functions of conflict for the systemic whole within which the conflict occurs. These propositions are listed in Table 11.6.[12]

Coser's propositions are not presented in their full complexity in Table 11.6, but the essentials of his analysis are clear. In Proposition 1, complex systems that have a large number of interdependencies and exchanges are more likely to have frequent conflicts that are less emotionally involving and violent than conflicts in those systems that are less complex and in which tensions accumulate. The nature of interdependence, Coser argued, causes conflicts to erupt frequently, but because they emerge periodically, emotions do not build to the point that violence is inevitable. Conversely, systems in which there are low degrees of functional interdependence will often polarize into hostile camps; when conflict does erupt, it will be intense and violent. In Proposition 2, frequent conflicts of low intensity and violence are seen to have certain positive functions. First, such

---

**Table 11.6**   Coser's Propositions on the Functions of Conflict for the Social Whole

1. The more differentiated and functionally interdependent are the units in a system, the more likely is conflict to be frequent but of low degrees of intensity and violence.

2. The lower are the intensity and violence of conflicts, the more likely are conflicts to
   A. Increase the level of innovation and creativity of system units
   B. Release hostilities before they polarize system units
   C. Promote normative regulation of conflict relations
   D. Increase awareness of realistic issues
   E. Increase the number of associative coalitions among social units

3. The more conflict promotes 2-A through 2-E, the greater will be the level of internal social integration of the system whole and the greater will be its capacity to adapt to its external environment.

---

[12]Ibid., pp. 45–48. See the following works cited: "Social Conflict and the Theory of Social Change"; "Some Social Functions of Violence"; and "The Functions of Dissent."

frequent and low-intensity conflicts will force those in conflict to reassess and reorganize their actions (Proposition 2-A). Second, these conflicts will release tensions and hostilities before they build to a point where adversaries become polarized around nonrealistic issues (Proposition 2-B). Third, frequent conflicts of low intensity and violence encourage the development of normative procedures—laws, courts, mediating agencies, and the like—to regulate tensions (Proposition 2-C). Fourth, these kinds of conflicts also increase a sense of realism over what the conflict is about. That is, frequent conflicts in which intensity and violence are kept under control allow conflict parties to articulate their interests and goals, thereby allowing them to bargain and compromise (Proposition 2-D). Fifth, conflicts promote coalitions among units that are threatened by the action of one party or another. If conflicts are frequent and of low intensity and violence, such coalitions come and go, thereby promoting flexible alliances (Proposition 2-E). If conflicts are infrequent and emotions accumulate, however, coalitions often polarize threatened parties into ever more hostile camps, with the result that, when conflict does occur, it is violent. And Proposition 3 simply states Coser's functional conclusion that, when conflicts are frequent and when violence and intensity are reduced, conflict will promote flexible coordination within the system and increased capacity to adjust and adapt to environmental circumstances. This increase in flexibility and adaptation is possible because of the processes listed in Proposition 2-A through 2-E.

## Jonathan Turner's Synthesis of Coser and Dahrendorf

By the mid-1970s, Dahrendorf's and Coser's theories had been the subject of considerable analysis. The problems of each theory had been frequently discussed, and most importantly, an entirely new generation of conflict theories was beginning to emerge. In one last-gasp effort to resolve the points of dispute among conflict theorists, I sought to synthesize the arguments of both Dahrendorf's and Coser's theories into one general approach that could articulate the conditions under which conflict will erupt in systems of inequality.[13] I have expanded this model considerably over the last four decades,[14] but the essence of theory presented here remains much the same because the dynamics of conflict arising out of inequalities are rather well understood now, and indeed, the early masters and early analytical theorists of the contemporary era of sociological theorizing had the dynamics well conceptualized.

---

[13]Jonathan H. Turner, "A Strategy for Reformulating the Dialectical and Functional Theories of Conflict," *Social Forces* 53 (1975): pp. 433–44.

[14]Jonathan H. Turner, *Theoretical Principles of Sociology*, volume 1 (New York: Springer, 2010).

## An Anaytical Model of Conflict Dynamics

I began synthesis by developing what I termed in Chapter 1 an *analytical modeling* of Dahrendorf's and Coser's theories. In Figure 11.2, the numbers above each box in the diagram emphasize the steps in the processes leading to overt conflict. The arrows connecting each box mark the direction of this sequence. The arrows pointing upward between numbered statements represent propositions that each theorist develops for specifying the conditions under which the state of affairs described will be realized. As can be seen, however, neither Dahrendorf nor Coser presented propositions to explain why social systems reveal interdependence or why an unequal distribution of scarce resources should exist. These propositions are simply boundary conditions of their theories. That is, in social systems that reveal the unequal distribution of scarce resources among interdependent units, Stages 3, 4, 5, 6, 7, 8, and 9 will be activated if certain conditions are met at each stage. The theory is thus devoted to outlining the conditions under which sequences of events will occur, ultimately resulting in overt conflict. In more recent work, I have sought to fill out this analytical model by developing propositions explaining the forces in Statements 1 and 2 by examining the institutional forces that increase inequality and lead to the formation of stratification systems.[15]

The reverse causal arrows of the diagram in Figure 11.2 connecting various statements emphasize that the causal model is more complex than just indicated. Events at various stages feed back and influence the weights of variables at earlier stages, making the conflict process a sequence with many built-in cycles. For example, efforts at "organization of conflict groups" will feed back and influence "awareness of objective interests". If the reverse causal loop is positive—that is, organization is successful and thus increases awareness—then the weights of variables in Steps 5, 6, and 7 are altered. In turn, other stages, such as the increased emotional arousal, the occurrence of collective outbursts (Box 6), and the escalation of emotional involvement will shape subsequent stages, such as the degree of organization of conflict groups. Similar feedback or, more accurately, reverse causal cycles for other stages within the overall causal sequence were also postulated by Coser and Dahrendorf. To synthesize the theories, I began at Statement 3, where Coser's and Dahrendorf's theories began.

## Stage 3: Withdrawal of Legitimacy

Coser and Dahrendorf differed in their conceptualizations of how inequalities initiate the conflict process. Dahrendorf emphasized awareness and Coser the withdrawal of legitimacy. In Figure 11.2, the combined model hypothesized that an initial withdrawal of legitimacy with respect to

---

[15]Jonathan H. Turner, *Theoretical Principles of Sociology*, volume 3 (New York: Springer 2011).

**Figure 11.2**  Propositions on the Conflict Process

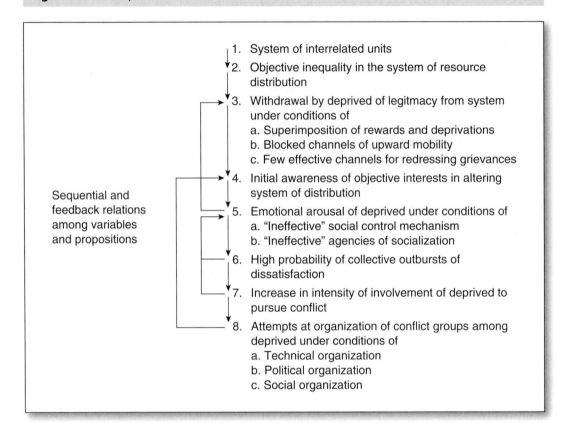

inequality is the first step in the conflict process. Such withdrawal is likely when channels of upward mobility are insufficient to accommodate people's aspirations, thus creating a sense of blockage among deprived segments of the population; channels for redressing grievances against the system of inequality are insufficient relative to the demand for expressing grievances; and   rewards and deprivations are superimposed on each other—that is, having (or not having) access to one resource is highly correlated with access (or lack of access) to other scarce resources. Hence, those with money also enjoy power, prestige, health, and other rewards, whereas the reverse is true for the deprived. These propositions are borrowed from Coser's analysis. In placing these propositions first in the causal sequence, I presumed that people must begin to question the system before they will begin to perceive their objective interests in altering the system of resource distribution.

## Stage 4: Initial Awareness of Objective Interests

In Dahrendorf's theory, a group's awareness is influenced by the technical (leaders, ideology, and so forth), political (creation of opposition organizations), and social (opportunities to communicate, to recruit members) conditions. The more these technical, political, and social conditions can be met, the more likely are the deprived to be aware of their objective interests in altering the present system of resource distribution. However, Coser's theory emphasized the inadequacy of this formulation. As people withdraw legitimacy from a system, they do not suddenly become aware of their interests. Only an initial awareness is likely. Thus, Dahrendorf's technical, political, and social conditions are premature in that they do not exert their full impact until later in the causal sequence, when actors have become disillusioned, initially aware, and emotionally aroused. Only then do people begin to seek leaders, organization, unifying beliefs, and means for communication.

## Stage 5: Emotional Arousal of the Deprived

The major failing of Dahrendorf's scheme was that it is too mechanical. Actors do not seem to have emotion, and actually, Dahrendorf stayed clear of the psychology of the deprived. Coser's emphasis on emotional arousal of the deprived was thus an important supplement to Dahrendorf's analysis. Coser appeared to recognize that withdrawal of legitimacy and initial awareness of interests lead to emotional arousal, which, under other conditions, drives actors to pursue conflict. Coser postulated two conditions influencing arousal: the degree to which socialization practices among the deprived, and socialization agents in the broader system, create internal psychological controls in actors and the extent to which social control mechanisms can suppress, channel, or deflect emotional arousal. Thus, the greater are the internal psychological constraints and the more effective is the external social control, the less likely is overt emotional arousal among the deprived. The reverse is true under conditions of weak social and psychological control.

## Stage 6: Periodic Collective Outbursts

The conflict process is often marked by individual and collective outbursts of emotion and frustration. These often result in conflict as the agencies of social control in a system seek to suppress these outbursts. Such outbursts are, of course, a form of conflict in themselves, but they are also a stage in a process leading to other forms of conflict, such as a society-wide revolution or serious collective bargaining relations among conflict parties. Collective outbursts occur, as Simmel initially emphasized, when the technical, political, and social conditions postulated by Dahrendorf have not been realized. The impact of critical feedback loops outlined in Figure 11.2 must be recognized in this process. Aroused emotions feed back on questions about legitimacy. Aroused emotions will decrease commitments to the system and foster a sense of increased awareness of interests. In turn, increased withdrawal of legitimacy and awareness escalates emotions to a point where collective outbursts are more likely.

Another critical feedback loop comes from Stages 6, 7, and 8 in the conflict process. When outbursts occur, they release frustrations, but if social control is harsh and highly repressive, outbursts also increase the level of emotional arousal (hence, the feedback loop between Statements 6 and 5). Moreover, as actors become more motivated to channel emotions into conflict activities (Statement 7), this too increases emotional arousal. And, finally, if highly motivated actors can become organized—in accordance with technical, political, and social conditions—then this will influence awareness of objective interests), which in turn will arouse emotions, but as Simmel understood more than Marx did, this arousal is now focused and less likely to lead to collective outbursts. Rather, deprived actors will become motivated to increase their organization and bargain with superordinates over resource redistribution.

## Stage 7: Increased Intensity

Intensity is the degree to which actors are motivated to pursue their interests and engage in conflict. Intensity involves emotional arousal, but it denotes the channeling of emotional energies and the willingness to sustain these energies in the pursuit of objective interests and to incur the costs in doing so. One condition increasing intensity is the failure of collective outbursts. In the wake of an outburst—a ghetto riot or a wildcat strike, for example—some people become more committed to pursue conflict once they recognize that others would be prepared to join them. Moreover, the use of social control agents—police and troops, for instance—to suppress outbursts often helps solidify emotional commitments and bring into sharper perspective the targets of conflict-oriented activity.

## Stage 8: Efforts at Organization

Once the deprived have withdrawn legitimacy, become somewhat aware of their interests, been emotionally aroused, participated in, or observed, outbursts of their fellows, and become committed to realizing their interests, then people are likely to become receptive to organization. Their ability to organize, as Dahrendorf emphasized, is a function of the following: the availability of leaders and unifying beliefs (technical conditions); the tolerance of political organization and the resources to organize (political conditions); and the capacity to communicate grievances and to recruit members into organizations (social conditions). With this increased recruitment into organizations, articulation of objective interests becomes more explicit (thus, feeding back to Statement 4), and hence, the emotional arousal of actors (5) will be less likely to result in spontaneous outbursts (6), but instead, in a growing commitment (or intensity) to use organizations to pursue objective interests (7).

Stages 3 to 8 have thus set the stage for open conflict. Although conflict in the form of collective or individual outbursts might have preceded Stage 9, these outbursts can also be viewed as steps in a more inclusive conflict process. Moreover, several feedback cycles in the overall process will influence not only the probability of outbursts but also subsequent forms of conflict. Before presenting Coser's and Dahrendorf's propositions influencing the nature of conflict at Stage 9, however, it is wise to summarize and assess those presented thus far. Propositions identifying the conditions under which awareness of objective interests follows the withdrawal of legitimacy still need to be specified (Stage 4). Perhaps some incipient level of technical, political, and social conditions must exist, as Dahrendorf's theory emphasized. Another propositional gap can be seen for Step 6. The conditions under which emotional arousal leads to collective outbursts have not been specified. The literature on collective behavior emphasizes such variables as (a) a precipitating incident that symbolizes the situation of the deprived and suddenly escalates their emotions to a point where internal psychological inhibitions and external agents of social control are temporarily ineffective in preventing an outburst; (b) a high degree of propinquity among the deprived who witness the precipitating event, thus increasing mutual communication of hostilities and frustrations; and (c) the availability of objects—persons, organizations, or symbols—that can serve as targets of frustrations.

## Stage 9: The Degree of Violence in the Conflict

Coser's and Dahrendorf's propositional inventories offered three propositions on the conditions influencing the degree of violence of a conflict: (a) The extent to which the technical, political, and social conditions are met is negatively related to violence; that is, the less the conditions are met, the more likely is conflict to be violent. (b) The failure to define true interests, independently of core values, is negatively related to the violence of conflict. Thus, if conflict parties cannot distinguish between their core values and specific goals for realizing their interests, then the conflict is likely to be *moral* rather than *instrumental*, with the result that compromises over moral issues become difficult to make. In contrast, compromises over specific goals are easier to make because they do not involve a moral issue that evokes great emotion. (c) A system that does not have a means for regularizing conflict interaction through legal norms and agencies of mediation is likely to reveal high rates of violent conflict. If a system cannot regulate conflicts between parties with laws, courts, mediating agencies, and other structures, it is difficult for conflict parties to bargain, compromise, and trust each other, because no mechanism exists for mediating conflicts of interest and for enforcing agreed-on compromises.

These three propositions have important interrelationships. A conflict group that realizes the technical, political, and social conditions of organization is likely to be able to articulate its interests, independently of values and beliefs. A system revealing well-organized conflict groups is also likely to have developed regulatory mechanisms, and if it has not, the potential for conflict might force the emergence of such regulatory mechanisms. Or, the existence of regulating mechanisms may actually facilitate the organization of conflict groups (constituting another political condition of conflict group organization). Of course, it is indeed possible for well-organized groups to mix values and goals, or to view them as inseparable. And it is possible for well-organized conflict groups to confront one another in the absence of any regulation. Under these conditions, then, conflict violence is likely to increase. These propositions and their interrelations are summarized in Figure 11.3

**Figure 11.3**  Propositions on the Degree of Conflict Violence

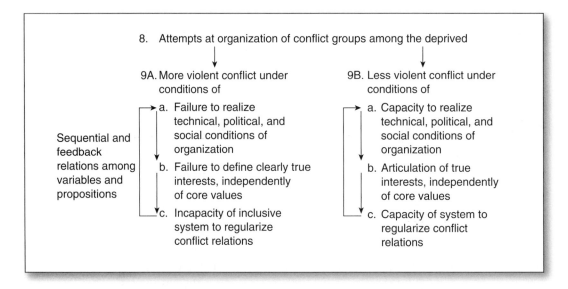

## Conclusions

As is evident from these early analytical theories, conflict dynamics arising from systems of inequality were rather well understood by the mid-1970s. Of course, not all conflict arises from inequalities. For example, conflict can emerge when actors have interests and goals that collide, or war between nation states may arise not so much over inequality as over goals such as conquering territory. Still, inequality fuels much conflict in its many manifestations. As we will see in the next chapters, conflict theories have emerged within many different research traditions, but all embody a good many of the elements outlined in these early analytical theories. At the same time, they have significantly expanded the understanding of conflict from where it stood in these early years of the contemporary period in sociological theorizing.

## CHAPTER 12

# Randall Collins' Analytical Conflict Theory

During the last thirty years, Randall Collins has consistently employed a conflict approach, emphasizing that inequalities inevitably set into motion conflict processes, some of which are relatively mild and routinized, but many of which can become more violent. As with any theorist committed to science, Collins sees the goal of a sociological theory of conflict as using a few key ideas to generate explanations of the full range of social processes in human interaction and organization. At the core of all of Collins' theorizing is an emphasis on micro-level social processes from which all other meso- and macro-level sociocultural formations are built, sustained, and changed. Micro-social processes are conceptualized in a number of ways, but through all of his work runs the notion of *interaction rituals*; thus, we should begin with this topic.

## Interaction Rituals

In his *Conflict Sociology: Toward an Explanatory Science*,[1] Randall Collins has been one of the most forceful advocates of a sociology grounded in conceptualizations of face-to-face interaction. Collins' early analytical theorizing draws upon a variety of theories. One source of theoretical inspirations is Max Weber's analysis; other elements of his theory come from Émile Durkheim's analysis of rituals; still additional elements come from Erving Goffman's dramaturgical theory of ritual performances (Chapter 19). And, over time, the theory has come to emphasize the effects of emotions, as they are aroused in interaction rituals, on conflict processes. As noted

---

[1]Randall Collins, *Conflict Sociology: Toward an Explanatory Science* (New York: Academic, 1975).

above, Collins' argument is that macro-level phenomena are, ultimately, created and sustained by micro encounters among individuals.[2] In essence, large and long-term social structures are built from interaction rituals that have been strung together over time. If true understanding of social reality is to be achieved by sociological theorizing, then the dynamics of face-to-face interaction must be theorized and examined emprically, even if this examination only involves sampling of interaction rituals within a macrostructure.[3]

## The Early Conceptualization of Interaction Rituals

Interaction rituals occur when individuals are physically co-present, when these individuals reveal a common focus of attention, when they develop a common emotional mood, when they represent their common focus and mood with symbols (words, objects, phrases, speech styles, and the like), and when they develop a sense of moral righteousness about these symbols. The dynamics of these rituals revolve around several elements. First, individuals bring to a face-to-face encounter *cultural capital,* or resources that they command in the broader society (for example, power and authority, knowledge, education, network ties and alliances, experiences) or that they accumulated in past interactions of a particular type (for example, memories, information, knowledge, other resources that they can use again when an interaction is reconstituted). Second, individuals bring a level of *emotional energy* to the interaction, which, in turn, is related to (a) the level of cultural capital they possess, (b) the power and prestige or status that they enjoy in the interaction situation, and (c) their memories about the levels of positive emotions or enhanced cultural capital received from the previous time the interaction occurred. Third, individuals *monitor situations* along several lines: (a) the respective resources of other actors relative to self; (b) the number of others present in a situation; (c) the number of alternative options to the present interaction that are available to self and others; (d) the amount of work-practical, ceremonial, and social content of the interaction; and most important, (e) the payoff in the amount of positive emotional energy and augmentation of cultural capital likely to be gained from a person's assessment of the inequalities in resources, the alternatives that might be pursued, the number of others presently monitoring the situation, the nature of the situation (as social, work-practical, or ceremonial), and the experiences (emotional energy and cultural capital received) in previous interactions of this nature.

---

[2]Randall Collins, "On the Micro-Foundation of Macro-Sociology," *American Journal of Sociology* 86 (1981): pp. 984–1014.

[3]Randall Collins, "Micro-Translation as a Theory of Building Strategy," in *Advances in Social Theory and Methodology: Toward an Integration of Micro- and Macro-Sociology,* eds. K. Knorr-Cetina and A. V. Cicourel (London: Routledge, 1981), pp. 84–96.

These properties of interaction rituals were first outlined in the mid-1970s in Collins' *Conflict Sociology*,[4] which was Weberian in several senses. First, interaction rituals are Collins' more robust portrayal of what Weber had viewed as action, and like Weber, Collins moves rapidly from the analysis of micro social processes to meso-level social forces, such as stratification and organizations, and then to truly macro-level processes operating at the societal and inter-societal levels. Yet, in developing this early view of interaction rituals, there is a heavy dose of Émile Durkheim's theory of rituals developed in his *The Elementary Forms of the Religious Life*[5] and, closer to the present, Erving Goffman's[6] theorizing on encounters of face-to-face interaction. Indeed, as we see in Chapter 19 on Goffman's work, Collins initial conceptualization of interaction rituals is virtually identical to Goffman's definition of *the encounter*, but with a large difference: Collins theorizes the meso and macro levels of social organization, something that Goffman never did. Second, and this is what made Collins' early conflict theory Weberian, the dynamics of interaction rituals become ever more recessive as analysis became more macro—just as notions of individual action were soon abandoned as Weber theorized about meso and macro social processes.

In *Conflict Sociology,* Collins proposed the following steps for building social theory. First, examine typical real-life situations in which people encounter one another. Second, focus on the material arrangements that affect interaction—the physical layout of situations, the means and modes of communication, the available tools, weapons, and goods. Third, assess the relative resources that people bring to, use in, or extract from encounters. Fourth, entertain the general hypotheses that those with resources press their advantage, that those without resources seek the best deal they can get under the circumstances, and that stability and change are to be explained through the lineups and shifts in the distribution of resources. Fifth, assume that cultural symbols—ideas, beliefs, norms, values, and the like—are used to represent the interests of those parties who have the resources to make their views prevail. Sixth, look for the general and generic features of particular cases so that more abstract propositions can be extracted from the empirical particulars of a situation.

Collins is particularly concerned with the distribution of individuals in physical space, with their respective capital or resources to use in exchanges, and with inequalities in resources. The respective resources of individuals—especially power, material, and symbolic resources—are critical to understanding what

---

[4]See Collins, *Conflict Sociology*, p. 153, where the elements of what later became known as *interaction rituals* are listed (cited in note 1).

[5]Émile Durkheim, *The Elementary Forms of the Religious Life* (New York: Free Press, 1947; originally published in 1912).

[6]Erving Goffman, *Encounters* (Indianapolis, IN: Bobbs-Merrill, 1961) and *Interaction Ritual* (Garden City, NY: Anchor Books, 1967).

transpires in interaction rituals. *Power resources* enable individuals to coerce or to have others do so on one's behalf; *material resources* are wealth and the control of money as well as property or the capacity to control the physical setting and people's place in it; and *symbolic resources* are the respective levels of linguistic and conversational resources as well as the capacity to use cultural ideas, such as ideologies, values, and beliefs, for one's purposes.

A central consideration in all Collins' propositions in his early work is *social density*, or the number of people co-present in a situation where an encounter takes place. Social density is, of course, often part of the macro-structural environment as it has been built up in past chains of interaction. But it can also be a material resource that some individuals can use to their advantage. Thus the interaction in an encounter will be most affected by the participants' relative resources and the density or number of individuals co-present. These variables influence the two underlying micro-level processes emphasized in Collins' scheme: talk and ritual.

## Talk and Ritual

Collins sees talk as the emission of verbal and nonverbal gestures that carry meaning and that are used to communicate with others and to sustain (or create) a common sense of reality.[7] Talk is one of the key symbolic resources of individuals in encounters, and much of what transpires among interacting individuals is talk and the use of this cultural capital to develop their respective lines of conduct. As can be seen in Proposition 1 in Table 12.1, the likelihood that people will talk is related to their sheer co-presence: If others are near, a person is likely to strike up a conversation.

More important sociologically are conversations that are part of a chain of previous encounters. If people felt good about a past conversation, they will usually make efforts to have another; if they perceive each other's resources, especially symbolic or cultural but also material ones, as desirable, then they will seek to talk again. And if they have developed ritualized interaction that affirms their common group membership, they will be likely to enact those rituals again. As Proposition 2 indicates, conversations among equals who share common levels of resources will be more personal, flexible, and long-term because people feel comfortable with such conversations.

As a result, the encounter raises their levels of emotional energy and increases their cultural capital. That is, people are eager to talk again and to pick up where they left off. However, the nature of talk in an encounter changes dramatically when there is inequality in the resources of the participants. As shown in Proposition 3, subordinates will try to avoid wasting or losing emotional energy and spending their cultural capital by keeping the interaction brief, formal, and highly ritualized with trite and inexpensive words. Yet, as Proposition 4 indicates, even under conditions of inequality and

---

[7]Collins, *Conflict Sociology*, pp. 156–57 (cited in note 1).

**Table 12.1** Key Propositions on the Conditions Producing Talk and Conversation

1. The likelihood of talk and conversational exchanges among individuals is a positive and additive function of (a) the degree of their physical co-presence, (b) the emotional gratifications retained from their previous conversational exchanges, (c) the perceived attractiveness of their respective resources, and (d) their level of previous ritual activity.

2. The greater the degree of equality and similarity that exists in the resources of individuals, the more likely conversational exchanges are to be (a) personal, (b) flexible, and (c) long-term.

3. The greater the level of inequality that exists in the resources of individuals, the more likely conversational exchanges are to be (a) impersonal, (b) highly routinized, and (c) short-term.

4. The greater the amount of talk among individuals, especially among equals, the more likely are (a) strong, positive emotions; (b) sentiments of liking; (c) common agreements, moods, outlooks, and beliefs; and (d) strong social attachments sustained by rituals.

even more when equality exists, people who interact and talk in repeated encounters will tend, over time, to develop positive sentiments and will have positive emotional feelings. Moreover, they will also converge in their definitions of situations and develop common moods, outlooks, beliefs, and ideas. And, finally, they will be more likely to develop strong attachments and a sense of group solidarity, which is sustained through rituals.

Thus, the essence of interaction is talk and ritual as mediated by an exchange dynamic; as chains of encounters are linked together over time, conversations take on a more personal and also a ritualized character that results from and, at the same time, reinforces the growing sense of group solidarity among individuals. Such is the case because the individuals have invested their cultural capital (conversational resources) and have derived positive feelings from being defined as group members. Collins' intent is thus clear: to view social structure as the linking of encounters together through talk in rituals that arouse emotions. This basic view of the micro reality of social life pervades all Collins' sociological theory to this day, although he has further developed the conception of interaction rituals.

## Deference and Demeanor

Inequality and stratification are structures only in the sense of being temporal chains of interaction rituals and exchanges among varying numbers of people with different levels of resources. Thus, to understand these structures, we must examine what people actually do across time and in space. One thing that people do in interaction is exhibit *deference* and *demeanor*. Collins and coauthor Joan Annett define deference as the process of manipulating gestures to show respect to others, or if one is in a position to command respect, the process of gesture manipulation is to elicit respect from others.[8] The actual manipulation of gestures is termed demeanor. Deference and demeanor are, therefore, intimately connected to each other. They are also tied to talk and rituals, because talk involves the use of gestures and because deference and demeanor tend to become routinized. Hence, deference and demeanor can be visualized as one form of talk and ritual activity—a form that is most evident in those interactions that create and sustain inequalities among people.

As would be expected from the above summary, Collins visualizes in *Conflict Sociology* several variables as central to understanding deference and demeanor:

1. Inequality in resources, particularly wealth and power

2. Social density variables revolving around the degree to which behaviors are under the surveillance of others in a situation

3. Social diversity variables revolving around the degree to which communications networks are cosmopolitan (that is, not restricted to only those who are co-present in a situation)

In Table 12.2, these variables are incorporated into a few abstract propositions that capture the essence of Collins' and Annett's numerous propositions and descriptions of the history of deference and demeanor.[9] In these propositions, Collins and Annett argue that rituals and talk revealing deference and demeanor are most pronounced between people of unequal status, especially when their actions are observable and when communication outside the situation is restricted. Such density and surveillance are, of course, properties of the meso- and macrostructure as they distribute varying numbers of people in space. As surveillance decreases, however, unequals avoid contact or perform deference and demeanor rituals in a perfunctory manner. For example, military protocol will be much more pronounced between an officer and enlisted personnel in public on a military base than in situations where surveillance is lacking (for example, off the base). Moreover, Collins and Annett stress that inequalities and low mobility between unequal groups create pressures for intra-group deference and demeanor rituals, especially when communications outside the group are low (for example, between new army recruits and their officers or

---

[8]Randall Collins and Joan Annett, "A Short History of Deference and Demeanor," in *Conflict Sociology*, pp. 161–224 (cited in note 1).

[9]Ibid., pp. 216–19.

**Table 12.2**   Key Propositions on Deference and Demeanor

1. The visibility, explicitness, and predictability of deference and demeanor rituals and talk among individuals increase with

   A. Inequality in resources among individuals, especially with respect to

      1. Material wealth

      2. Power

   B. Surveillance by others of behaviors, and surveillance increases with

      1. Co-presence of others

      2. Homogeneity in outlook of others

   C. Restrictiveness of communication networks (low cosmopolitanism), and restrictiveness decreases with

      1. Complexity in communications technologies

      2. Mobility of individuals

2. The greater is the degree of inequality among individuals and the lower is the level of surveillance, the more likely behaviors are to be directed toward

   A. Avoidance of contact and emission of deference and demeanor by individuals

   B. Perfunctory performance of deference and demeanor by individuals when avoidance is not possible

3. The greater the degree of inequality among individuals and the lower the level of cosmopolitanism among individuals, the more likely behaviors are to be directed toward simplified but highly visible deference and demeanor.

4. The greater is the degree of inequality among individuals, and the less is the degree of mobility among groups with varying levels of resources, the more visible, explicit, and predictable are deference and demeanor rituals and talk within these groups.

5. The greater is the equality among individuals, and the greater is the degree of cosmopolitanism and/or the less is the level of surveillance, the less compelling are deference and demeanor talk and rituals.

between prison inmates and guards). But as communication outside the group increases or as surveillance by group members decreases, deference and demeanor will decrease.

## Class Cultures

These exchange processes revolving around talk, ritual, deference, and demeanor explain what are often seen as more macro processes in societies.

One such process is variation in the class cultures, a point of emphasis that also reveals the Weberian thrust of Collins' early theory of conflict. That is, people in different social classes tend to exhibit diverging behaviors, outlooks, and interpersonal styles. These differences can be seen in two main variables:

1. The degree to which one possesses and uses the capacity to coerce, to materially bestow, and to symbolically manipulate others so that one can give orders in an encounter and have these orders followed

2. The degree to which communication is confined to others who are physically co-present in a situation or, conversely, the degree to which communication is diverse, involving the use of multiple modes of contact with many others in different situations

Using these two variables, as well as several less central variables such as wealth and physical exertion on the job, Collins describes the class cultures of American society. More significantly for theory building, he also offers several abstract propositions that stipulate certain important relationships among power, order giving, communication networks, and behavioral tendencies among individuals. These relationships are restated in somewhat altered form in Table 12.3.[10] With these principles, Collins explains variations in the behaviors, outlooks, and interpersonal styles of individuals in different occupations and status groups. For example, those occupations that require order giving, that reveal high co-presence of others, and that involve little physical exertion will generate behaviors that are distinctive and that circumscribe other activities, such as whom one marries, where one lives, what one values, and what activities one pursues in various spheres of life. Different weights to these variables would cause varying behavioral tendencies in individuals. Thus, from the processes delineated in the propositions of Table 12.3, understanding of such variables as class culture, ethnic cultures, lifestyles, and other concerns of investigators of stratification is achieved. But such understanding is anchored in the recognition that these class cultures are built and sustained by interaction chains in which deference and demeanor rituals have figured prominently. Thus, a class culture is not mere internalization of values and beliefs or simple socialization (although this is no doubt involved); rather, a class culture is the result of repeated encounters among unequals under varying conditions imposed by the meso- and macrostructures as they have been built from past chains of interaction.

## Organizational Processes

Like Weber before him, Collins also uses an extensive analysis of organizations and develops a rather long inventory of propositions on organizations'

---

[10]Collins, *Conflict Sociology*, pp. 49–88.

**Table 12.3**   Key Propositions on Class Cultures

1. Giving orders to others in a situation increases with the capacity to mobilize and use coercive, material, and symbolic resources.

2. The behavioral attributes of self-assuredness, the initiation of talk, positive self-feelings, and identification with the goals of a situation are positively related to the capacity to give orders to others in that situation.

3. The behavioral attributes of toughness and courage increase as the degree of physical exertion and danger in that situation escalates.

4. The degree of behavioral conformity exhibited in a situation is positively related to the degree to which people can communicate only with others who are physically co-present in that situation and is negatively related to the degree to which people can communicate with a diversity of others who are not physically co-present.

5. The outlook and behavioral tendencies of an individual are an additive function of those spheres of life—work, politics, home, recreation, community—where varying degrees of giving or receiving orders, physical exertion, danger, and communication occur.

properties and dynamics.[11] These propositions overlap, to some degree, with those on stratification, because an organization is typically internally stratified with a comparatively clear hierarchy of authority. Table 12.4 lists three groups of propositions from Collins' analysis. These revolve around processes of organizational control, the administration of control, and the general organizational structure.

In the propositions shown in Table 12.4, control within an organization increases with the concentration of coercive, material, and symbolic resources. The pattern of control varies, however, with the particular type of resource—whether coercive, material, or symbolic—that is controlled and with the configuration among these resources, as is summarized in Propositions 3, 4, and 5. Control within an organization must be administered, and the pattern of such administrative control varies with the nature of the resources used to gain control. Collins extends Weber's analysis of organizations, and Propositions 6 through 9 summarize various patterns in the administration of control. In the end, Collins sees the profile of an organization's structure as reflecting the nature and concentration of resources, as well as how these are used to administer control. Propositions 10 and 11 review Collins' basic argument.

---

[11]Ibid., pp. 286–347.

**Table 12.4**   Key Propositions on Organizations

---

**Processes of Organizational Control**

1. Control in patterns of organizations is a positive and additive function of the concentration among individuals of (a) coercive resources, (b) material resources, and (c) symbolic resources.

2. The form of control in organizations depends on the configuration of resources held by those individuals seeking to control others.

3. The more control is sought through the use of coercive resources, the more likely those subject to the application of these resources are to (a) seek escape; (b) fight back, if escape is impossible; (c) comply if (a) and (b) are impossible and if material incentives exist; and (d) sluggishly comply if (a), (b), and (c) do not apply.

4. The more control is sought through the use of material resources, the more likely those subject to the manipulation of material incentives are to (a) develop acquisitive orientations and (b) develop a strategy of self-interested manipulation.

5. The more control is sought through the use of symbolic resources, the more likely those subject to the application of such resources are to (a) experience indoctrination into values and beliefs; (b) be members of homogeneous cohorts of recruits; (c) be subject to efforts to encourage intra-organizational contact; (d) be subject to efforts to discourage extra-organizational contact; (e) participate in ritual activities, especially those involving rites of passage; and (f) be rewarded for conformity with upward mobility.

**Administration of Control**

6. The more those in authority employ coercive and material incentives to control others, the greater is the reliance on surveillance as an administrative device to control.

7. The more those in authority use surveillance to control, the greater are (a) the level of alienation by those subject to surveillance, (b) the level of conformity in only higher visible behaviors, and (c) the ratio of supervisory to nonsupervisory individuals.

8. The more those in authority employ symbolic resources to control others, the greater is their reliance on systems of standardized rules to achieve control.

9. The greater is the reliance on systems of standardized rules, the greater are (a) the impersonality of interactions, (b) the standardization of behaviors, and (c) the dispersion of authority.

**Organizational Structure**

10. Centralization of authority is a positive and additive function of (a) the concentration of resources; (b) the capacity to mobilize the administration

of control through surveillance, material incentives, and systems of rules; (c) the capacity to control the flow of information; (d) the capacity to control contingencies of the environment; and (e) the degree to which the tasks are to be routinized.

11. The bureaucratization of authority and social relations is a positive and additive function of (a) record-keeping technologies, (b) nonkinship agents of socialization of potential incumbents, (c) money markets, (d) transportation facilities, (e) nonpersonal centers of power, and (f) diverse centers of power and authority.

## The State and Economy

As did Max Weber, Collins eventually moves to the analysis of the state that, though a type of complex organization, still controls and regulates the entire society. As the propositions in Table 12.5 summarize,[12] the size and scale of the state depend on the productive capacity of the economy; in the

**Table 12.5**   Key Propositions on the State, Economy, and Ideology

1. The size and scale of political organization are a positive function of the productive capacity of the economy.    *under determined*

2. The productive capacity of the economy is a positive and additive function of (a) level of technology, (b) level of natural resources, (c) population size, and (d) efficiency in the organization of labor.

3. The form of political organization is related to the levels of and interactive effects among (a) size of territories to be governed; (b) the absolute numbers of people to be governed; (c) the distribution and diversity of people in a territory; (d) the organization of coercive force (armies); (e) the distribution (dispersion or concentration) of power and other resources among a population; and (f) the degree of symbolic unification within and among social units.

4. The stability of the state is a negative and additive function of

   A. The capacity for political mobilization by other groups, which is a positive function of

      1. The level of wealth

      2. The capacity for organization as a status group

   B. The incapacity of the state to resolve periodic crises

---

[12]Ibid., pp. 348–413.

end, the state can only be supported by a large economic surplus. In turn, as is summarized in Proposition 2, the productive capacity of the economy is related to technologies, natural resources, the number of people who must be supported, and the efficiency with which the division of labor is organized. The particular form of state power varies enormously, but these forms vary under the impact of basic forces summarized in Proposition 3. The stability of the state is also a crucial variable, especially for a conflict theory. As Proposition 4 summarizes, the state must be able to prevent mobilization by groups pursuing counter-power, and it must be able to resolve periodic crises. When it cannot, the state becomes unstable.

Like Weber before him, Collins recognizes that much of the state's viability depends on the relation of the state to surrounding societies. No society exists in isolation. A state almost always finds itself in competition with other societies. And, the ability of the state to prevail in this world of geopolitics often determines its form, viability, and stability.

## Geopolitics

Borrowing from Weber but adding his own ideas, Collins argues that there are sociological reasons for the historical facts that only certain societies can form stable empires and that societies can extend their empires only to a maximal size of about 3 to 4 million square miles.[13] When a society has a resource (money, technology, population base) and marchland advantage (no enemies on most of its borders), it can win wars, but eventually, it will (a) extend itself beyond its logistical capacities, (b) bump up against another empire, (c) lose its marchland advantage as it extends its borders and becomes ever more surrounded by enemies, and (d) lose its technological advantages as enemies adopt them.

The result of these forces is that empires begin to stall at a certain size as each of these points of resistance is activated. These processes indicate that internal nation-states will not build long-term or extensive empires because they are surrounded by enemies, increasingly so as they extend territory. Rather, marchland states, with oceans, mountains, or unthreatening neighbors at their back, can move out and conquer others, because they have to fight a war on only one front. But eventually, they overextend, confront another marchland empire, lose their technological advantage, and acquire enemies on a greater proportion of their borders (thereby losing the marchland advantage and, in effect, becoming an internal state that must now fight on several borders). Sea and air powers can provide a kind of marchland advantage, but the logistical loads of distance from home bases and maintenance of sophisticated technologies make such empires vulnerable. Only when it encounters little resistance can an empire be maintained

---

[13]See Randall Collins, *Weberian Sociological Theory* (Cambridge, England: Cambridge University Press, 1986), pp. 167–212 and "Long-Term Social Change and the Territorial Power of States" in his *Sociology Since Midcentury: Essays in Theory Cumulation* (New York: Academic, 1981).

across oceans and at great distances by air; as resistance mounts, the empire collapses quickly as its supply lines are disrupted. Table 12.6 summarizes these ideas more formally.

**Table 12.6**  Key Propositions on Geopolitics

1. The possibility of winning a war between nation-states is a positive and additive function of

    A. The level of resource advantage of one nation-state over another, which is a positive function of

        1. The level of technology

        2. The level of productivity

        3. The size of the population

        4. The level of wealth formation

    B. The degree of marchland advantage of one nation-state over another, which is a positive and additive function of

        1. The extent to which the borders of a nation-state are peripheral to those of other nation-states

        2. The extent to which a nation-state has enemies on only one border

        3. The extent to which a nation-state has natural buffers (mountains, oceans, large lakes, and so on) on most of its borders

2. The likelihood of an empire is a positive function to the extent to which a marchland state has resource advantages over neighbors and uses these advantages to wage war.

3. The size of an empire is a positive and additive function of the dominant nation-states' capacity to

    A. Avoid showdown war with the empire of other marchland states

    B. Sustain a marchland advantage

    C. Maintain territories with standing armies

    D. Maintain logistical capacity for communications and transportation, which is a positive function of levels of communication, transportation, and military technologies and a negative and additive function of

        1. The size of a territory

        2. The distances of borders from the home base

    E. Diffusion of technologies to potential enemies

4. The collapse of an empire is a positive and additive function of

    A. The initiation of war between two empires

    B. The overextension of an empire beyond its logistical capacity

    C. The adoption of its superior technologies by enemy nation-states

From these propositions listed in Tables 12.1 to 12.6, it is easy to see Collins' approach to conflict processes as neo-Weberian. Like Weber, Collins begins with a conceptualization of micro processes—in Weber's case, types of meaningful action, and in Collins' theory, interaction rituals. Then, their analysis shifts to the meso level, examining patterns of stratification and forms of complex organizations. Finally, both Weber and Collins move to the analysis of the state and geopolitics. In all these levels of analysis, their concern is with inequalities of resources and how these inequalities generate tension and potential conflict. Collins' *Conflict Sociology* is now in its fourth decade in print, and so, it should not be surprising that Collins has expanded on this propositional scheme. As he has done so, stating arguments formally has declined, but it is still clear that he is generating explanatory ideas, now in a more discursive format, or what I termed *discursive scheme* in Chapter 1.

# Ritual and Emotions

Over the last decade, Collins has refined and extended his original conception of interaction rituals and, as I will summarize in the next section, used this newer view of interaction rituals to develop an explanation of interpersonal violence. In Figure 12.1, I have taken the liberty of revising Collins' analytical scheme into a more robust analytical model, where causal relations among the forces driving interaction rituals are delineated in ways that are consistent with his discursive scheme outlined in his *Interaction Ritual Chains*.[14] Let me review the elements in this analytical model, moving from left to right as the interaction ritual unfolds and builds up emotional energy, which Collins sees as the driving force of interaction. The theory emphasizes longer-term emotional energy that builds up and is sustained across chains of interaction rituals or episodes of interaction. When positive emotional energy is built up across chains of interaction rituals, social solidarity increases leading the production or reproduction of social structures, whereas when negative emotional energy is aroused, conflict becomes more likely, and solidarity declines.

The variables on the left of Figure 12.1 indicate some of the conditions that increase the likelihood that interaction rituals will take place. The more separated are persons by *ecological barriers* from others, the more individuals will feel *co-present*; furthermore, the more individuals are engaged in *common actions* or tasks, the more likely are these individuals to have a *mutual focus of attention* and the more likely are they to emit *stereotypical greeting rituals* to each other. These rituals—often as simple as asking "How are you?" or some such formality—generate mildly positive *transient positive emotions* that begin to shape a *shared mood*, which, in turn, increases the common or mutual focus of attention. As the interaction proceeds, it tends

---

[14]Randall Collins, *Interaction Ritual Chains* (Princeton, NJ: Princeton University Press, 2004).

**Figure 12.1** Collins' Elaborated Model of Interaction Rituals

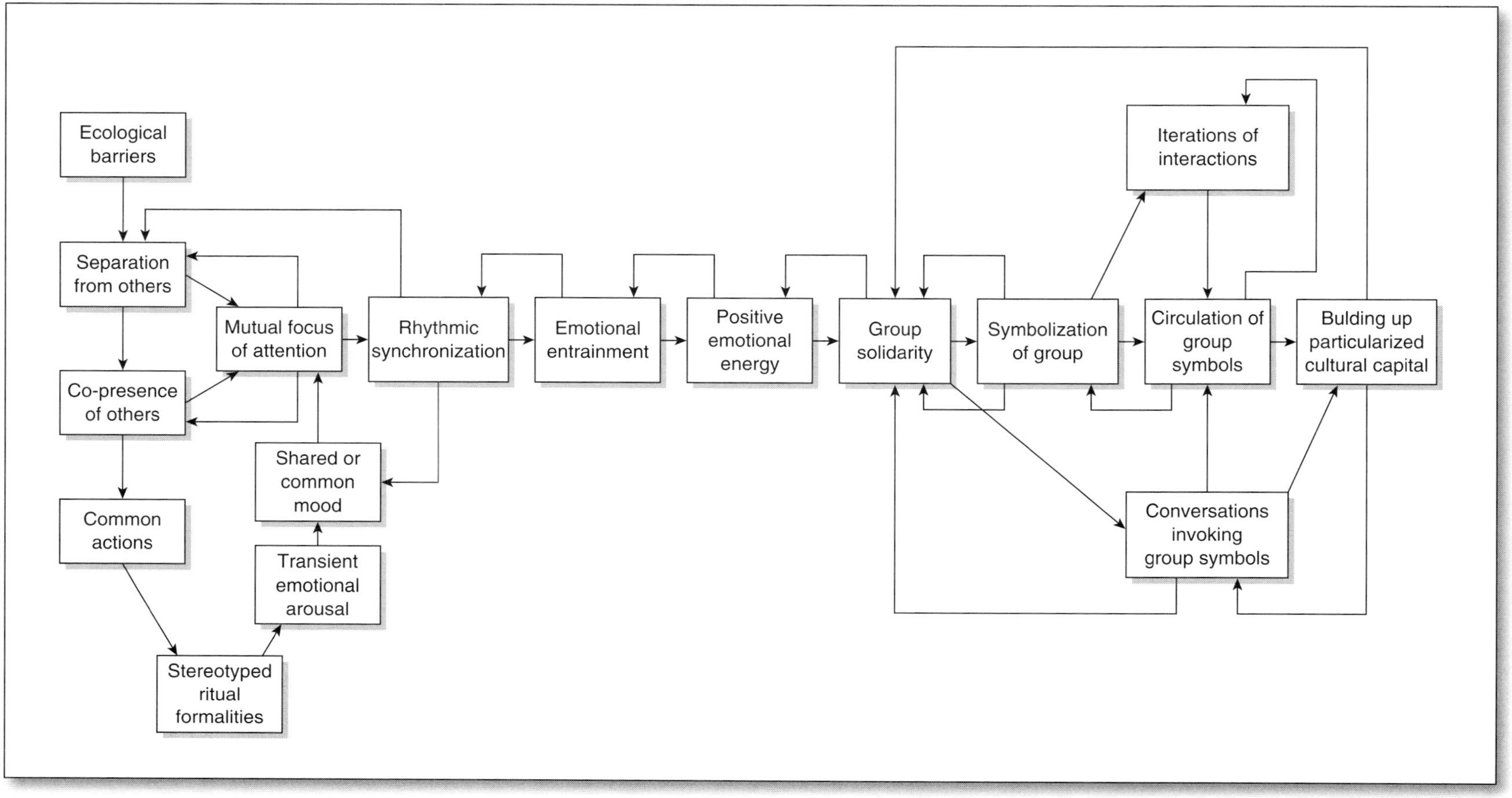

251

to fall into *rhythmic synchronization* of talk and body language. Individuals establish a rhythm to their verbal exchanges, as well as the movements of their bodies.

The more rhythmically in sync individuals become, the more likely are they to become emotionally entrained, with the result that the mere transient emotions initiated with stereotyped formalities are transformed into *collective effervescence*—an idea that comes from Émile Durkheim's analysis. This effervescence is evident by continued synchronization of talk and bodies by individuals, and the more effervescence occurs, the greater will be individuals' sense of emotional entrainment, which, in turn, increases their level of positive emotional energy.

As positive emotions are aroused, the level of *group solidarity* among those co-present increases; the greater this sense of solidarity and the more it is evoked in subsequent interaction rituals among the same individuals, the more likely are they to have needs to *symbolize the group* in some way—whether through words, physical objects, particular behaviors. This process of symbolization—again, an idea borrowed from Émile Durkheim—emphasizes that solidarity and the positive emotions around it lead individuals to have needs to mark the group, much like a totem pole symbolized a community of preliterate peoples. Indeed, sometimes individuals erect physical objects to symbolize their solidarity, but they can also use phrases, songs, symbols on hats or uniforms, forms of dress, jokes, phrases, shared memories, and almost anything that marks a group can be used. With symbols, and continued interaction over times among individuals, the more these symbols are evoked, and the more likely are they to sustain conversations at any give encounter. And, the more likely are these symbols to motivate individuals to repeat the encounter over time—thus setting up chains of interaction rituals. As these chains of interaction continue, members develop *particularistic capital*, or experiences only shared among group members, and this capital can be used in subsequent interactions to reinforce group symbols and the sense of solidarity.

The reverse causal arrows flowing from right to left emphasize that interaction rituals are recursive in the sense that symbolization increases solidarity as does particularized cultural capital; solidarity feeds back to increase positive emotional arousal; emotional arousal feeds back and increases the very sense of effervescence that generated the emotional arousal; effervescence feeds back on rhythmic synchronization, making people more animated and in sync; synchronization increases the shared mood and mutual focus of attention; and a heightened mutual focus of attention makes people feel a stronger sense of co-presence and separation from others. And, then, these processes begin to feed forward, activating the cycle of the ritual outlined in the figure once again.

As these cycles are iterated over time, they build up solidarity and group symbols; in so doing, they build up social structures and their cultures or, if the structure already exists, they reproduce it or, potentially, change it. Collins has emphasized the relationship between emotions and interaction rituals, but he has generally emphasized only positive emotional energy. There is, of course, the converse process of arousing negative emotional energy. Such is likely to be the case when the ritual process breaks down or never really gets started. Or, it is also possible when individuals are stuck in interactions where they gain no rewarding particularistic capital and consistently experience negative emotions at the hands of others. Under these conditions, people will leave an encounter or never repeat it again, but often, people are stuck or perceive that they are stuck in a chain of interaction rituals that are painful—as an abusive marriage must be for the subordinate family member(s).[15]

# The Theory of Micro Violence

In his book, *Violence: A Micro-Sociological Theory*,[16] Collins employs his interaction ritual theory as a kind of interpretive framework in a more discursive manner to explain many manifestations of violence. He employs the theory of interaction rituals to draw attention to the sociology of violence, emphasizing that situations more than individuals are the appropriate units of analysis. With this emphasis on situations, he sets out to explain many diverse kinds of situation violence. I will focus only on the theoretical argument, which is relatively brief, rather than on the many interesting empirical variations of situational violence.

## Emotional Fields

Potentially violent situations are shaped by what Collins terms *an emotional field*, which consists of fears and tension. *Fear* is almost always the dominant emotion of parties in a violent situation, with such fear being a physiological reaction. Tension comes from the fact that most interactions most of the time generate some level of positive emotional arousal through the interaction ritual dynamics enumerated in Figure 12.1 earlier, with the result that a violent situation arousing fear stands in tension with what Collins considers a neurologically hardwired propensity of humans to experience positive emotional energy in interaction rituals. Since this propensity stands in juxtaposition with fear about the possibility of violence, the emotional field will always evidence tension. For violence to occur, one side or potentially both sides must turn this tension into aggressive action and, in so doing, overcome fear.

---

[15]See works by Erika Summers-Effler on negative emotional energy that seeks to theorize this bias in Collins' theory. For example, see her "The Micro Potential for Social Change," *Sociological Theory* 20 (2002): pp. 41–60 and "Defensive Strategies: The Formation and Social Implications of Self-Destructive Behavior," *Advances in Group Processes* 21 (2004): pp. 309–25.

[16]Randall Collins, *Violence: A Micro-Sociological Theory* (Princeton, NJ: Princeton University Press).

## The Power of Confrontational Tension and Fear

This *confrontation tension*, as Collins terms it, signals that violence is not easy for people because the arousal of intense fear goes against the natural propensity of humans to fall into the phases of interaction rituals that arouse positive emotions. Even when people are highly motivated to engage in violent conflict, they experience this confrontational tension, which makes it difficult to pull the trigger on violence. Indeed, most violent situations fail to become violent, or often protagonists dance around violence with posturing and threats but never actually engage in violent acts. And, even if violent acts occur, they rarely are extended or even reciprocated by the other party. Collins documents that even in collective violence such as crowds and warfare, relatively few members of the groups supposedly engaged in violence actually commit violence. For example, only a relatively small proportion of soldiers actually aim their guns on the enemy, or in the cases of riots, most people dance around or stand in the background rather than take part in actual violence against a target.

What, then, allows individuals to overcome the confrontational tension that holds them back from actual violence? Collins offers a number of conditions that can turn a violent situation into real, collective violence. One, and perhaps the most important, is that interaction rituals are used to mobilize actors to commit violence. That is, the stages of the ritual are unleashed so that individuals gain positive emotional entrainment, effervescence, positive emotional energy, solidarity, group symbols, and particularized culture by engaging in concerted violence against another group. It also helps if this group is geographically separated so that their cues cannot be observed, as would be the case with two groups of soldiers fighting each other from a distance. The military learned the power of interaction rituals redirected toward collective violence against enemies a long time ago. Soldiers are separated, and then required to engage in stereotyped formalities, to have a mutual focus of attention, to become rhythmically synchronized in their interactions during training, to become emotionally entrained and aroused, to develop group solidarity that is symbolized by not only uniforms and badges/patches on these uniforms but also by symbols unique to a particular military group, such as flags and banners, which are reinforced by particularized cultural capital. Terrorist organizations also reveal these same qualities, using interaction rituals generating positive emotion for engaging in conflict to overcome the fear and confrontation tension of violent situations.

With this relatively simple conceptual framework, Collins is able to explore many facets of violence because situations all evidence fear by parties in a situation, plus the pull of interaction rituals, creating confrontational tension. The networks of the parties to a conflict and the solidarities that they have built up have large effects on whether or not individuals in a violent situation can overcome confrontational tension. Thus, when violence is examined with a micro-level theory focusing on situations rather than individuals or larger-scale meso and macro social structures, the dynamics of violence that emerge are very different than images of violent individuals or organizations coordinating the violent acts of individuals—whether armies, terrorists, rioters, gang members, and so on. Violence is not easy; it is often very short-lived and not even very violent; furthermore, when collectively organized, most participants do not really participate in the actual violence.

# Conclusions

For more than forty years, Collins has been a dominant theoretical sociologist. While he has theorized about many topics, the underlying core of his theorizing has focused on conflict in its many manifestations. His insistence that all general theory be built around what individuals do in micro situations has many followers in other theoretical traditions, but in his earlier work and even in much of his recent work, the focus on interaction rituals often gives way to more emergent properties of the meso and macro realm. Yet, as his theory on violence documents, Collins is committed to employing a micro-level theory to understand meso- and macro-level phenomena because social structures and culture are ultimately built up, reproduced, or changed by what individuals are doing at the micro level of interaction rituals. Interestingly, his early work was—despite the formulation of the model of interaction rituals—often lost sight of micro-level ritual activities of individuals, but his recent theorizing seeks to bring micro-level processes to explanations of all social phenomena.

## CHAPTER 13

# Marxian Conflict Theories

The review of Karl Marx's theory of conflict in Chapter 10 removed much of the more emancipatory substance of Marx's ideas about the dynamics of capitalist societies. I abstracted Marx's substantive categories to produce a general theory of conflict in systems of inequality, which is how Marx's ideas began to filter back into the sociological cannon during the middle decades of the twentieth century. Yet, Marx considered himself to be a revolutionary,[1] and his life's work was to develop a theoretical system that could explain the self-destructive dynamics of capitalism and the emergence of communism.[2] This more substantive and emancipatory thrust of Marx's work was never lost in sociological theorizing, but the theory had to be revised because the revolution by the proletariat did not occur and because the communist systems of the twentieth century were hardly emancipatory. As we will see in Chapters 30 and 31, this failure of Marxian predictions led to the emergence of critical theory in a rather pessimistic guise. In this chapter, however, I will review some theories that sustain both the substantive thrust of Marx's ideas and the view that the contradictions of capitalism will, perhaps, open the doors for new, more democratic and less exploitive forms of social organization.

## A Brief Review of Marx's Substantive Argument

To appreciate the creative directions that Marx's ideas have taken over the last two decades, it is wise to review some substantive points of emphasis in Marx's analytical scheme. Marx believed his theoretical goal was to explain

---

[1]Karl Marx and Friedrich Engels, *The Communist Manifesto* (New York: International, 1978; originally published in 1848).

[2]Karl Marx, *Capital*, 3 volumes (New York: International, 1967; originally published in 1867, 1885, and 1894).

the contradictions in capitalist modes of economic production and how these would lead to the conflict processes that would eventually usher in communism. His predictions were wrong, perhaps because of some fatal errors in his logic, but his analysis is still useful.

For Marx, capitalism is an economic system where those who own and control the means of production seek to make profits from the goods that they sell in competitive markets. In such a system, labor must sell itself as a commodity to capitalists and must do so under unfavorable circumstances where the supply of workers is high, relative to demand, thereby driving the wages of labor down (and, hence, reducing the costs of labor for capitalists). The key to profits for capitalists is to make labor work beyond the actual labor time needed to make the goods that pay their wages; the difference is *surplus value* or profit for capitalists. The greater this surplus value is, the more workers are *exploited* by capitalists who, in essence, appropriate the surplus value of the goods produced by workers for their own gain. So, in Marx's view, labor power is the ultimate source of value of products as well as the source of profits for capitalists. Capitalism is thus sustained by exploitation.

But capitalists face a dilemma: They must compete with each other in markets, and hence, the price that they can get for products is driven down to the point where it becomes difficult to make a profit. As businesses fail, laborers are thrown out of work, which in turn means that they do not have wages to buy goods in markets. As a result, demand for goods declines; with this decline in demand, profits of capitalists also decline. Capitalists seek to get around this *declining rate of profit* by using more productive technologies and machinery in place of labor, thereby putting more laborers out of work and lessening demand for the goods produced by capitalists. Although such efforts can give capitalists a short-term advantage over their competitors and increase their profits for a time, technologies and machinery are soon copied by competitors. As a consequence, a new round of competition over price occurs. This new round of competition, however, must confront the lessened capacity of unemployed labor to purchase goods in markets where prices are coming down.

In this process of declining profits, many capitalists go under, and indeed, their competitors might buy them out, creating oligopolies and monopolies that can better manipulate prices when they do not have to compete. But they must do so in conditions of lessening demand in markets where labor does not have wages to buy goods. Moreover, the many capitalists who have lost out in the competition are without money to buy goods and services, and indeed, many are driven into the proletariat. Eventually, even as monopolies gain control of key productive sectors, they have trouble making a profit; goods can go unsold because there is not enough money in the hands of workers and displaced bourgeoisie to buy them. As goods remain unsold, capitalists reduce production, but as workers are laid off, cutting back production only decreases the buying power of workers in markets.

Thus, Marx felt that capitalism would, in the end, move toward a situation where profits and production were declining while unemployment and monopoly control of production were increasing.

From this situation would come the mobilization by the proletariat for revolution. Such revolutionary efforts had to confront, however, the power of capitalists to control the state and ideological system. But, as crises of unemployment deepen, mobilization by the proletariat can overcome the power of the state to control coercively and the capacity of ideology to impart false consciousness. Such mobilization is facilitated by the very acts of capitalists in (a) concentrating workers so that they can communicate their grievances, (b) making them appendages to machines and thereby increasing their sense of alienation, and (c) subjecting them to a decline in, or uncertainty about, their living standards. All these acts of capitalists lead workers to question the legitimacy of political authority and the appropriateness of dominant ideologies. Under these conditions, leaders emerge and articulate counter-ideologies that mobilize the proletariat to incur the risks and costs of conflict with the bourgeoisie. They are helped by the bourgeoisie who "sow the seeds of their own destruction" by forcing on workers the conditions listed under (a), (b), and (c) above.

This brief summary does not, of course, capture the depth, texture, or subtlety of Marx's analysis of capitalism, but it gives us the tools to place into context the two basic directions of theorizing that Marx's work continues to inspire. One prominent direction is revising Marx's conception of exploitation and its effects on class processes in modern societies. The other direction has been to move beyond the nation-state as a unit of analysis to a world system level where, it is argued, the contradictions of capitalism will ultimately emerge. A third direction is toward critical theories that we will examine in Part VII at the end of the book. For the present, let us focus on the first two directions where authors use Marx's substantive ideas to build scientific theories of class and world system dynamics, saving the third critical direction for Part VII.

# Neo-Marxian Class Analysis

In the late twentieth century, Marxist theory has confronted several problems. First, the predicted collapse of capitalism had not occurred, despite the Great Depression and periodic recessions throughout the century, continuing into the twenty-first century. Second, the projected polarization of capitalist societies into bourgeoisie and proletarians was countered by the growth of a large and varied middle classes of managers, experts, small business operators, skilled manual workers, and others who do not seem highly disadvantaged and who do not see themselves as exploited. Third, capitalism had appeared to emerge as the clear victor in the contest between capitalism and communism, although state-managed societies operating under the ideological banner of communism were hardly what Marx had in mind. Nonetheless, the historical predictions of Marx and the trajectory of capitalism into socialism and communism had not occurred, and into the second decade of the new twenty-first century, still have not occurred.

Yet, despite these troubling issues, Marxism has remained a viable intellectual tradition, driven perhaps by an emancipatory zeal emphasizing the elimination of exploitation of the disadvantaged by the advantaged. Still, Marxist intellectual circles have been in crisis for more than a decade, as many former Marxists have moved to other forms of radical thinking or have become critical theorists and postmodernists—perspectives that are explored in the chapters of Part VII. Although some still cling to the orthodox picture of Marx, briefly summarized earlier, most Marxists have changed Marx's core ideas to fit current historical realities.

Among these Marxists are several important scholars,[3] but in an effort to summarize the issues with which they have had to deal, I will focus on the work of Erik Olin Wright who has, in his words, sought to do more than merely draw from the Marxian tradition, but, instead, contribute to "the reconstruction of Marxism." Wright has termed his and fellow travelers' approach *analytical Marxism.* But before discussing the basic concepts in Wright's scheme, let us set the stage with his more meta-theoretical assertions.

## The Analytical Marxism of Erik Olin Wright

The goal of analytical Marxism is to shed some of the baggage of orthodox Marxist analysis while retaining the core ideas that make Marx's theory unique.[4] Analytical Marxism retains the emancipatory thrust of Marx, stressing that the goal is to reduce, if not eliminate, inequalities and exploitation. Indeed, emphasis is on constructing scientific theory about how socialism can emerge from the dynamics inhering in capitalist exploitation. But this emancipatory thrust does not abandon a commitment to the conventional norms of science in which theoretical ideas are assessed against empirical observations. Moreover, the goal is to produce abstract

---

[3]For example, Perry Anderson, *Considerations on Western Marxism* (London: New Left Review, 1976); Michael Buraway, *The Politics of Production* (London: Verso, 1985); Sam Bowles and Herbert Gintis, *Democracy and Capitalism* (New York: Basic Books, 1986); G. A. Cohen, *History of Labor and Freedom: Themes from Marx* (Oxford: Clarendon, 1988) and *Karl Marx's Theory of History: A Defense* (Princeton, NJ: Princeton University Press, 1978); John Elster, *Making Sense of Marx* (Cambridge: Cambridge University Press, 1978); Barry Hindess and Paul Q. Hirst, *Capital and Capitalism Today* (London: Routledge, 1977); Claus Offe, *Disorganized Capitalism: Contemporary Transformations of Work and Politics* (Cambridge: Cambridge University Press, 1985); Adam Przeworski, *Capitalism and Social Democracy* (Cambridge: Cambridge University Press, 1985); John A. Roemer, *A General Theory of Exploitation and Class* (Cambridge, MA: Harvard University Press, 1982) and *Analytical Foundations of Marxian Economic Theory* (Cambridge: Cambridge University Press, 1981); and Michael Burawoy and Erik Olin Wright, "Sociological Marxism," in *Handbook of Sociological Theory,* ed. J. H. Turner (Kluwer Academic/Plenum, 2001), pp. 459–86.

[4]Erik Olin Wright, "What Is Analytical Marxism?" *Socialist Review* 19 (1989): pp. 35–56.

formulations that specify the mechanisms generating empirical regularities in the world, and for the analytical Marxist, particular concern is with the mechanisms flowing from social class structures. As I will summarize later, Wright's most recent work has sought to outline in more detail these paths to emancipation.[5]

**Social Class, Emancipation, and History.** Marxist theory posits an historical trajectory: feudalism to capitalism, then capitalism to communism. In this historical trajectory, class inequalities will be eliminated, and communism will usher in a classless society. In this trajectory and outcome, class is the pivotal dynamic, mobilizing individuals to seek alternative social relations in which exploitation is eliminated. Wright believes that these three basic orienting assumptions—that is, historical trajectory, class emancipation, and class as the driving force of history—need to be mitigated somewhat.[6] Emphasis should be on how the dynamics of capitalism present possibilities for new, less exploitive social arrangements rather than on the inevitability of the forces driving human society toward communism. In this vein, emphasis on class emancipation should not blindly pursue the goal of a classless society but, rather, present a critique of existing social relations to reduce class inequalities and exploitation. Moreover, emphasis on class as the driving force of history must be tempered by a recognition that class is one of many forces shaping the organization of a society, both in the present and future.

Wright's theoretical work stresses this last consideration: What mechanisms revolving around social class generate what outcomes? As a Marxist, Wright views the class structure of a society as limiting the nature of class formation (the organization of individuals) and class struggle (the use of organization to transform class structures). He posits a simple model, as delineated in Figure 13.1.[7] In this model, class struggle transforms the nature of class formations and class structure, whereas class formations select or channel class struggle in certain directions depending on the nature of organization of class members. The key dynamic in Wright's program, however, is class structure; as the model outlines, class structure limits the nature of class formation and class struggle. The goal of a reconstituted Marxian analysis must, therefore, examine the properties of class structure in capitalist societies if class formations and emancipatory class struggles are to be understood.

**Micro-Level versus Macro-Level Class Analysis.** In Wright's view, Marxian class analysis must confront two impulses. One is to retain Marx's vision of

---

[5]Erik Olin Wright, *Envisioning Real Utopias* (London: Verso, 2010).

[6]Erik Olin Wright, "Class Analysis, History and Emancipation," *New Left Review* 202 (1993): pp. 15–35.

[7]Ibid., p. 28.

**Figure 13.1**   Wright's General Model of Class Analysis

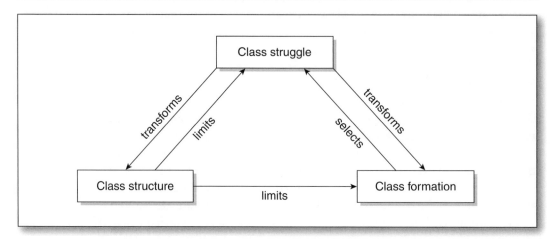

the class structure in society as ultimately polarizing into two conflictual classes. In the capitalist historical epoch, these are the bourgeoisie who own the means of production versus the proletariat who are exploited. The other impulse is to explore "the complexity of the class structural concept itself in the hope that such complexity will more powerfully capture the explanatory mechanisms embedded in class relations."[8] Wright argues that this complexity is not as evident when analysis stays at the macro level, focusing on the global characteristics of capitalism as composed ultimately of owners and workers. However, when research moves to the micro level of the individual and seeks to understand the locations of individuals in the class system, a much more varied, complex, and contradictory picture emerges. If the causal effects of class relations are to be understood, it is necessary to explore class processes at the micro level.

Wright's basic strategy has been to examine the jobs that people hold, because in their jobs, individuals connect to the system of production and the class relations that inhere in this system. For most of his work in the 1970s and 1980s,[9] Wright sought to construct a "relational map of locations of individuals" in the class system, but by the 1990s, he had recognized that "the simple linkage of individuals-in-jobs to classes" must be modified in several important ways: Individuals can occupy more than one job; they can have indirect and mediated relations to a job (as is the case with children

---

[8]Erik Olin Wright, "Rethinking, Once Again, the Concept of Class Structure," in *The Debate on Classes*, ed. E. O. Wright (London: Verso, 1989), p. 269.

[9]See, in particular, Erik Olin Wright, *Class, Crisis and the State* (London: Verso, 1978), *Class Structure and Income Distribution* (New York: Academic, 1979), and *Classes* (London: Verso, 1985); Erik Olin Wright and Luca Perrone, "Marxist Class Categories and Income Inequality," *American Sociological Review* 42 (1977): pp. 32–55.

and others who do not directly participate in the system of formal employ-ment); they can move about jobs and cross class locations during the course of a career; and they can have contradictory locations in the class system.[10] In essence, as we will see shortly, Wright's conceptual scheme has tried to deal with these kinds of complexities that a micro-level analysis exposes; indeed, his conceptualizations have changed during the course of the last twenty years as he has confronted both data[11] and conceptual criticisms.[12]

When class analysis turns micro, the vagueness of much macro-level Marxian theory is revealed. Wright argues that, in a reconstructed Marxian analysis, it is important to be specific about the mechanisms involved in gen-erating class formation and class struggle effects. He illustrates the differences between a macro-level and micro-level view of class mechanisms by summa-rizing the three ways in traditional Marxism that class structure is seen to exert effects on class formation and struggle:[13] (1) material interests, (2) lived experiences, and (3) collective capacities. Below, I examine each of these.

(1)  *Material interests.* The first mechanism by which class structure exerts causal effects on class formation and struggle is through individuals' material interests. There are two basic types of material interests: (a) eco-nomic welfare or "the total package of toil-leisure-incomes available to a person,"[14] with people having an interest in reducing their toil and in increasing their leisure and consumption and (b) economic power or the capacity to control how surplus products are distributed, with surplus product being defined as "that part of the total social product that is left over after all the inputs into production (both labor power and physical capital) have been reproduced."[15] Thus, the material interests of individuals are determined by their economic welfare and economic power.

The concept of exploitation ties these two types of material interests together. Those with economic power can use this power to appropriate productive surplus from those without power. In so doing, they increase their economic welfare at the expense of those whose surplus product they take. In Marxian class analysis, the material interests of classes are not just different; they are opposed in a kind of zero-sum game.

---

[10]Wright, "Rethinking, Once Again, the Concept of Class Structure" (cited in note 8).

[11]See, for examples, Wright's own comparative survey research on class structures, which can be found in "The Comparative Project on Class Structures and Class Consciousness: An Overview," *Acta Sociologica* 32 (1989): pp. 3–22; *Class Structure and Income Distribution* (cited in note 9); *Classes*; and Wright and Perrone, "Marxist Class Categories and Income Inequality" (cited in note 9).

[12]See the chapters in Wright, *The Debate on Classes* (cited in note 8).

[13]Wright, "Rethinking, Once Again, the Concept of Class Structure" (cited in note 8).

[14]Ibid., p. 281.

[15]Ibid., p. 282.

The material interests of individuals circumscribe their options. Depending on their respective material interests, people make different choices, employ diverse strategies, and make varying trade-offs. When individuals share material interests, their choices, strategies, and trade-offs should converge because they face similar dilemmas as they pursue economic welfare and economic power. In Marx's macro-level approach, social systems polarize around two classes with different material interests, fueled by exploitation. In a more micro-level approach to material interests, a more complex and, at times, contradictory picture emerges of individuals with diverse perceptions about what they should do in pursuing their economic welfare and in seeking economic power. Moreover, the lived experiences of individuals as they make choices and pursue strategies can also diverge, or at a minimum, individuals do not perceive that they have common material interests (a problem that Marx dismissed, perhaps too quickly, as "false consciousness").

(2)   *Lived experiences.* In Marxian theory, common material interests as dictated by class location lead to common experiences. Those who do not own capital are seen to have similar subjective understandings of the world because they are forced to sell their labor, because they are dominated and bossed around, and because they are unable to control the surplus products of their labor. When individuals are exploited this way, they are also alienated,[16] and together, these forces give alienated individuals a common experience that, Marx felt, would lead to their collective mobilization.[17] Yet, a more micro-level approach reveals that individuals might not have similar experiences, or at the very least, they do not see their lived experiences as similar because they occupy somewhat different jobs that locate them at different points in the class system.

(3)   *Collective capacities.* The third class force in traditional Marxian analysis flows from the first two: People with common material interests and lived experiences possess a capacity for collective action. Moreover, as Marx emphasized, capitalists are forced by their own material interests to create many of the conditions that facilitate collective mobilization, such as concentrating workers in factories and urban areas, making them appendages to machine technologies, disrupting their life routines through layoffs, providing literacy and media access, and encouraging other forces that shape class formation and struggle. This kind of scenario has a certain plausibility when examined at the macro level, but on the individual level, the contradictory locations of individuals in jobs and their differentiation across an array of middle-class locations make collective mobilization more problematic. Individuals do not see that they have common material interests or that they share common lived experiences; thus, they do not naturally organize collectively. Even alliances and coalitions among individuals who

---

[16]Marx conceived of alienation as the result of workers' inability to determine what they produce, how they produce, and to whom the products of their labor are sold.

[17]See propositions in Table 10.1 on p. 207 for a list of these conditions.

see that they share some interests become problematic, although once formed, these alliances have strength (because the costs of compromises have already been incurred).[18]

Thus, in Wright's micro approach, the three class forces in Marxian analysis do not reveal the same degree of coherence as when they are examined from a more macro level. Moreover, micro analysis shows that, in contrast with traditional Marxism, these forces are not necessarily correlated with each other. When analysis moves to the micro level, "there is no longer necessarily a simple coincidence of material interests lived experience, and collective capacity."[19] People who might seem to have common material interests do not perceive this to be the case, nor do they reveal a driving need to mobilize collectively. In a micro approach to understanding class mechanisms, then, the complexity of the class system makes traditional macro-level Marxian causal forces too global and crude to account for the specifics of class formation and struggle.

**The Problem of the Middle Class.** Wright's entry into Marxist analysis began with the question of how to account for the emergence and proliferation of jobs in the middle classes,[20] and although he has sought to move in different directions, this question is still at the core of his theoretical formulations. In his effort to build a "map of the class structure," Wright recognizes that the array of middle-class positions posed the biggest challenge to traditional Marxian class analysis. If class structures are to be seen as relevant to the class formation and to the struggle by classes for social emancipation, then a more fine-grained analysis of this structure is necessary. Wright's analytical project has thus involved an effort to isolate the mechanisms being generated by this more complex class system. Through his empirical and theoretical work during the last three decades, he has proposed several ways to conceptualize class structures and the mechanism for class formation and struggle that inhere in these structures. Some of these have been rejected, others retained, and most modified and integrated in new ways by Wright. In contrast with orthodox Marxism, Wright has been willing to change his mind and to develop, elaborate, and qualify ideas in his effort to isolate the causal mechanisms of class structures in advanced capitalist societies. He has, in essence, proposed several models of class structures, the basic elements of which are briefly summarized here.

**Contradictory Class Locations**. Wright's first attempt at conceptualizing the middle classes in Marxian terms led him to develop the idea of *contradictory*

---

[18]Wright, "Class Analysis, History and Emancipation" (cited in note 6).

[19]Wright, "Rethinking, Once Again, the Concept of Class Structure" (cited in note 8), p. 296.

[20]Wright and Perrone, "Marxist Class Categories"; Wright, *Classes* and *Class, Crisis and the State* (cited in note 9).

*class locations.*[21] Individuals can occupy a class location that is contradictory because it puts people into different classes, presumably giving them contradictory material interests and diverse lived experiences and collective capacities. These locations are contradictory because, for example, many managers, semi-autonomous wage earners, professionals and experts, and small-scale employers can reveal varying amounts and combinations of (a) owning the means of their production, (b) purchasing the labor of others, (c) controlling and managing the labor of others, and (d) selling their labor. To illustrate, a manager sells labor to an owner of a business, but at the same time this manager will be involved in hiring and controlling the labor of others. Similarly, a skilled consultant sells labor, but might own the facilities by which this labor is organized. Such variations can put individuals in contradictory class locations in the sense that they are neither owners of the means of production nor helpless sellers of their labor; they have an element of both, and hence, they have contradictory material interests and, no doubt, lived experiences and collective capacities. They might not see themselves as exploiters or as exploited; indeed, they can be both in varying proportions.

This approach made Wright a prominent Marxist theorist, but it also brought criticism that, in turn, led Wright to pursue an alternative conceptualization. One problem was that domination (telling others what to do) and exploitation (extracting surplus product) were somewhat decoupled. For example, managers could give orders, but they did not directly enjoy the economic welfare of appropriated surplus (this went to owners of the means of production). Another problem revolved around employment in the state or government. Are those employed by the state workers in the means of economic production? If not, then their status is unclear: They are paid labor, but their products are not directly appropriated by capitalists. They are managers and hence can direct not only each other but perhaps workers and even owners in the economy. These conceptual problems, coupled with the difficulties that Wright encountered in measuring contradictory locations of individuals, led him to propose a new conceptualization of the middle classes.[22]

**Multiple Exploitation.** Adopting ideas from John Roemer,[23] Wright's second solution to the problem of the middle classes was to posit an exploitation nexus that varies by the kinds of assets that individuals possess and their degree of ownership or control of these assets. The four assets are (a) labor power assets, (b) capital assets, (c) organization assets, and (d) skill or credential assets. Each of these leads to a particular type of exploitation: Individuals who only have labor assets are likely to be exploited because they depend on those who have the economic power to extract the surplus

---

[21]Wright, *Class, Crisis and the State* and *Class Structure and Income Distribution* (cited in note 9).

[22]Wright, *Classes* (cited in note 9).

[23]Roemer, *A General Theory of Exploitation and Class* (cited in note 3).

value of their labor; capital assets can be used to invest in equipment and labor as a means of extracting the surplus product generated by technology and labor; organization assets can be used to manage and control others in ways that extract surplus products; and skills or educational credentials can be employed to extract extra resources beyond the resources it took to acquire and maintain these skills and credentials.

This approach allowed Wright to address the issue of the middle class by re-coupling the concepts of exploitation (of surplus) and domination (through control or order giving). In essence, what had been domination was translated into a new type of exploitation by those with organization assets, highly valued skills, and educational credentials. At the same time, the exploitation envisioned by Marx—extraction by capitalists of surplus value from workers—could remain close to Marx's original formulation. A particular society could then be typified by the combinations and configurations of these various types of exploitation.

Wright preferred this conceptualization of the middle classes to the contradictory class location formulation because it allowed him to put exploitation back as the central mechanism by which economic welfare and economic power are connected, thereby making his scheme more consistent with Marx's original formulation.[24] Moreover, it allowed him to conceptualize managers in the state, professionals, and other skilled workers with some degree of autonomy through Marxian-inspired class dynamics: they too are exploiters, just like capitalists, but they use different assets to extract surplus value and product from others.

This approach also came under heavy criticism, leading Wright to back down from some of the assertions in this model.[25] First, those with skills and credentials are not so much exploiters of the less skilled as advantaged workers who can prevent capitalists from exploiting them as much as their less-skilled counterparts are exploited (because capitalists value and need their skills and credentials). Second, managers inside government as well as in the private capitalist sector can move up the organizational hierarchy and use their higher salaries to buy into the capitalist sector (via purchase of stocks, bonds, and so on), thereby confusing just what their material interests would be. Third, the location of individuals in the state bureaucracy would determine the mix of assets; for example, those higher in the state might possess more capital assets or at least a mix of organization and capital assets, whereas those lower in the hierarchy would possess only organization assets, and those lower still would possess only labor assets to be exploited. Coupled with the problems of measuring these various types of assets and documenting empirically how they led to different forms of exploitation caused Wright to shift his scheme yet again.[26]

---

[24]Wright, "Rethinking, Once Again, the Concept of Class Structure" (cited in note 8).

[25]Wright, "Class Analysis, History and Emancipation" (cited in note 6).

[26]Erik Olin Wright, *Class Counts* (Cambridge, UK: Cambridge University Press, 1997).

**The Emerging Scheme.** As Wright has dealt with the conceptual and empirical problems of measuring class locations at the micro level, he has responded to criticisms by elaborating new concepts or, perhaps more accurately, reformulating older ideas in a new guise. These new conceptualizations still revolve primarily around the problem of the middle classes, but they reveal a more eclectic character.[27]

One idea is the notion of multiple locations. Like most traditional Marxists, Wright had originally assumed that individuals had one class location, even if this location was contradictory and placed a person into classes with different material interests. But, people often have more than one job, and hence, can actually have several class locations. For example, a person can have a salaried day job and then operate a small business at night or on weekends, thus being both a proletarian and capitalist.

Another idea deals with mediated locations. Individuals are often connected to a class via networks of others who hold a job or own capital. Children, wives, and husbands can all have a mediated relation to a class location of a parent or spouse, and these mediated relations can become complicated. For example, if a female manager is married to a carpenter, each has a mediated relation to the other's class location, and their children, if they have any, will bear mediated relations to both classes. Wright proposes the notion of an overall class interest in these situations, which is a "weighted combination of these direct and mediated locations," that may or may not be contradictory.

Still another idea in Wright's evolving scheme is a concern with temporal locations. Careers might not significantly change a person's class location, but often, careers do involve movement across class locations, as when individuals move up government and corporate hierarchies, when a small business gets large, when workers begin to form companies, and when students move from school to job and then into a career track. People's class locations can thus change over time, giving them different material interests, lived experiences, and collective capacities.

Yet another idea is a conceptualization of distinct strata within classes. The argument is that, within basic classes such as owners and workers, there are distinctive strata whose members might have somewhat different material interests and most likely have very different lived experiences and collective capacities. These strata can take a number of forms. For example, professionals and experts with skills and credentials can be seen as able to collect rents on their skills and credentials, which make them a distinct stratum within the working class (they are still part of the working class because they must sell their labor power). Temporal mobility in a career can often increase these rents; if the rents are sufficiently high, they can be

---

[27]For brief reviews of the ideas presented here, see Wright, "Rethinking, Once Again, the Concept of Class" (cited in note 8) and "Class Analysis, History and Emancipation" (cited in note 6).

invested as capital, thereby giving a person a position within a stratum of the capitalist class as well as the working class. Similarly, managers or manual workers can translate their skills and career mobility into rents that can then become capital. All these workers are in contradictory locations because they are, on the one hand, workers who are paid a salary and, on the other hand, investors in businesses that hire workers. Thus, the basic classes envisioned by Marx—workers and owners of the means of production—can be reconceptualized by distinct strata within these broad classes, with the incumbents in various strata potentially having a contradictory class location as both workers and capitalists.

The issue of state employment can be translated into a state mode of production. Rather than view high-level state workers as organization exploiters, it is better to visualize the state as producing goods and services of a particular kind and, hence, as revealing distinct classes (and perhaps strata within these classes). The dominant class would be those who direct the appropriation and allocation of surplus productivity that the state acquires to support itself (in forms such as taxes, fees, tariffs, and the like). The subordinate class would be those who actually perform the services and produce the goods provided by the state. Within the state mode of production could be various combinations of contradictory positions. For example, a state manager can control the actions of other workers but be controlled by elite decision makers in the dominant class of the state; a state manager who can command a high salary can invest this rent in the private sector, which places this individual in both the economic and state modes of production. Relations in the state mode of production can also be mediated, as when high-level members of the dominant class have relations with corporations doing business with government or being regulated by government. Moreover, the career path of many incumbents in both the economic and government modes of production can involve movement back and forth between these modes, thereby shifting the class location of individuals.

A further set of ideas developed in Wright's evolving project moves beyond the problem of the middle classes. The existence of an unemployable and often welfare-dependent segment of a population has led Wright to introduce a distinction between *nonexploitive economic oppression* and *exploitive economic oppression*. In exploitive economic oppression, one group's economic welfare is increased by virtue of the exploitation of another group whose welfare declines because the latter's surplus products are appropriated by the former. This situation is oppressive not just because of exploitation per se but because the exploiting group often uses morally sanctioned and legitimated coercion to get its way. Yet, even under these oppressive conditions of exploitation, the exploited have some power because their exploiters depend on them, so the exploitation often involves implicit negotiation and consent. In nonexploitive economic oppression, there is no transfer of surplus productivity to an exploiter. Instead, the economic welfare of exploiters depends on the exclusion of the oppressed from access to valued resources being consumed by oppressors. Under these conditions, Wright argues, genocide can occur because the goal of exploiters is to get rid of those who might seek access to resources that they have, or covet. Yet, even here, the nonexploited oppressed have a resource: the capacity to disrupt efforts at consumption by exploiters. Thus, the nonexploited oppressed can often force exploiters to provide some resources (as happens with those who pay for the welfare of those who are kept out of the economy).

## Sustaining the Emancipatory Dream: Envisioning Real Utopias

Any theoretical approach that engages the substance of Marx's vision and seeks to explain why the predicted revolutions did not occur must, in the end, come back to this question. Much of Wright's theorizing has sought to explain why conditions in advanced capitalism made revolution in a Marxian sense difficult. At the same time, Wright uses Marx's basic ideas to show that advanced capitalism still creates contradictions that, it is hoped, will lead to fundamental social change toward socialism. In his recent book, *Envisioning Real Utopias*,[28] Wright again outlines what is wrong with capitalism and explores alternatives guided by the socialist compass toward social empowerment of the people and the construction of a new kind of state and economy.

Theoretically, perhaps the most interesting part of this effort comes in the book's last section on transformation. Here Wright seeks to lay out various potential trajectories of change. In so doing, he specifies the conditions and circumstances under which such change is possible.

*The Overall Model.* In Figure 13.2, I have taken some liberties to lay out Wright's scenarios for how transformative change from capitalism to socialism can come about. Capitalism systematically generates harms, and "[s]ocial structures and institutions that systematically impose harms on people require vigorous mechanisms of active social reproduction in order to be sustained over time."[29] These harms come through oppression and exploitation; as Figure 13.2 denotes under "mechanisms of social reproduction" (of harmful social relations), there are four basic mechanisms.

One is *coercion* that involves "imposing various kinds of punishments for making . . . challenges"[30] to the system of oppression and exploitation. Coercion can come from state and non-state actors that use actual coercion or the threat of coercion to keep people from mobilizing to change the system generating social harms. Another mechanism inheres in *institutional rules*, or rules of the game, that make courses of action that challenge the system difficult to pursue. A third mechanism is built into *ideology* and, more broadly, culture that are very much responsible for reproduction. The

---

[28]Wright, *Envisioning Real Utopias* (cited in note 5).

[29]Ibid., p. 276.

[30]Ibid., p. 279.

**Figure 13.2**   Wright's Envisioning of the Path to the Transformative Change

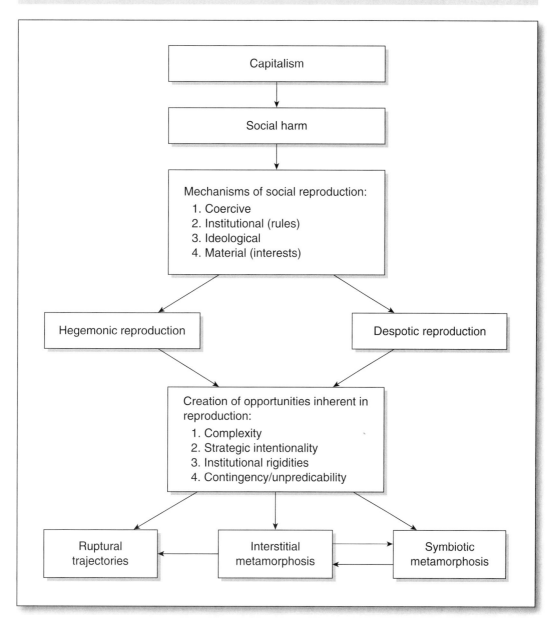

means of cultural production is dominated by those with power who, through control of media and other domains where culture is produced, instill in individuals both consciously and unconsciously commitments to norms, beliefs, and ideologies that keep them from mounting challenges to the system. And the fourth mechanism is *material interests* that people perceive they have in the capitalist system, with any proposal for transformation often being perceived to threaten these interests. This dependence on the system, even an exploitive system, will often make people fearful of change; moreover, capitalism has a tendency to pull people into the very relations that exploit them and; yet, people still sustain fears that another system will challenge their interests in this exploitive system.

The operation of various configurations of these four mechanisms generates two kinds of social reproduction: (1) despotic and (2) hegemonic. *Despotic reproduction* relies upon coercion and the institutional rules by which coercion is meted out, whereas *hegemonic reproduction* is less obvious and draws people into the system willingly because they see their material interests as inhering in the system. Coupled with indoctrination into beliefs, ideologies, and normative rules, people abide by the rules because they often believe in them and also because their interests are tied to the system that they legitimate.

Yet, no system of exploitation and domination is so powerful that it does not reveal limits, gap, and contradictions that are, in essence, inherent weaknesses of the system. These weaknesses generate not only recognition by at least some that the system is flawed and harmful but also potential *opportunities for transformative change.* There are four principle sources of these opportunities. One is *complexity* of the system. Complex systems have many gaps, cleavages, conflicts of interest, contradictions, needs for trade-offs, power use, and other forces that make people more aware of the broader system and, potentially, motivated to change it. A second source of opportunity is *strategic intentionality,* which becomes available as actors in a society seek to develop practices that reproduce the system. For example, struggles over designs of programs, inadequate or biased knowledge to deal with problems, arrogant and often stupid decisions by powerful actors, and unintended consequences of actions in complex systems are inevitable in efforts to build up and reproduce institutional systems. A third source of opportunity resides in *institutional rigidities* and path dependency in which a social order is reproduced even as it generates tensions. Once institutional systems are in place and supported by powerful ideologies, they are difficult to change, even if they are creating discontent among sectors of a society that might increasingly see the system for what it is and be ready to engage in actions to change it. The last source of opportunity for transformations is the fact of *contingency and unpredictability.* Economic and political processes are not always predicable, even with powerful reproductive forces in play. One change can suddenly cascade across a system in an unpredictable manner, thereby opening people's eyes to problems and potentially motivating them to protest against the system.

Up to this point, Wright summarizes in more abstract ways the basic thrust of Marx's argument that there are contradictions in systems of inequality and use of exploitive power; coupled with actions of the powerful who are locked into the system, they end up creating conditions that make the system vulnerable. It is at this point in his vision of realistic utopias that Wright cautions about the difficulty in making exact predictions about change trajectories, as the lesson of Marx's failed prophecy underscores. Yet, Wright quickly adds that "[m]any of the predictions of historical materialism have in fact been borne out by the actual history of capitalism."[31] For example, the globalization

---

[31]Ibid., p. 301.

of capitalism, the growth and domination of corporations, the process of commodification of just about everything, including human relations, and other processes have come to pass. Yet, there is always the problem of predicting which of many potential trajectories will emerge at any given time. Wright's solution is to delineate a number of different trajectories, which he groups under three general labels: (1) ruptural, (2) interstitial metamorphosis, and (3) symbiotic metamorphosis. His analysis is complex and nuanced, and so, I can only outline these in general terms.

*Alternative Trajectories of Transformation.* For each of these three potential trajectories, there is an associated logic of transformation, set of key actors for the transformation, strategic logic for dealing with the state, strategic logic for dealing with the capitalist class, and metaphors of what would constitute a success. Wright anticipates his more detailed discussion with a table somewhat like the one presented in Table 13.1.

(1) Ruptural transformations. Wright recognizes that political democracy and capitalism co-evolve; while the harms of capitalism and the imperfections in democracy in capitalist systems generate grievances, the chances of ruptural changes are less likely in capitalist systems where some degree of democracy exists. Receptiveness of the population to socialist goals depends upon the degree to which material interests of the population

**Table 13.1**  Wright "Models" of Transformative Trajectories

|  | **Ruptural** | **Interstitial Metamorphosis** | **Symbiotic Metamorphosis** |
|---|---|---|---|
| Politics and logic of transformation: | Revolution toward Socialism/ communism | Anarchists/anarchism | Social democratic |
| Key actor in transformation: | Classes organized as political parties/ actors | Social movements | Coalitions of social forces with labor |
| Strategic logic in dealing with state: | Attack the state | Propose and build alternative formations outside of state | Use the state by bringing the struggle to terrain of state |
| Strategic logic in dealing with capitalist class: | Confront the bourgeoisie | Ignore the bourgeoisie | Collaborate with bourgeoisie |
| Metaphors of success: | War, conflict, and victories and defeats | Ecological competition among alternative social formations | Evolutionary aspirations for transformations |

*Source:* Erik Olin Wright, *Envisioning Realistic Utopias*, p. 304

can be tied to socialism, while at the same time diminishing the "push back" of capitalists and their control of the means of ideological production. Moreover, there would need to be coalitions among middle- and working-class members of a society, an occurrence that appears unlikely in current capitalist societies. Wright thus appears to imply that this route to socialism is indeed a less realistic utopia.

(2)    Interstitial Transformation or Metamorphosis. These are transformations that begin in the holes, spaces, and cracks in the institutional structure of a capitalist society. Such *interstitial activities* are evident in almost all capitalist societies, with many having the goal of building "alternative institutions and emancipatory ideals and that are created primarily through direct action of one sort or another rather than through the state."[32] For Wright, these interstitial strategies have two routes to socialism—one by altering conditions that make a ruptural strategy feasible and the other by expanding the scope of interstitial action to the point that capitalism no longer imposes so many restraints. Wright ponders a number of trajectories but, in the end, concludes that "it is difficult to see how they could ever by themselves erode the basic structural power of capital sufficiently to dissolve the capitalist limits on emancipatory social change."[33] Thus, neither the expansion of interstitial activities and structural formations nor the ruptural strategy appears to offer feasible strategies for transformations. What, then, of the third transformative trajectory, symbiotic metamorphosis?

(3)    Symbiotic Metamorphosis. In this approach, the bottom-up forces of change seek to empower people while resolving problems that capitalist have faced. Change is evolutionary and involves a class compromise that balances the interests of labor and the general citizenry with goals of capitalists. Several key spheres of activity are critical for this class compromise. First is the sphere of exchange and the dynamics of markets where the population meets capitalists. There must be real compromises in this sphere between the interests of non-elite and non-capitalist classes and capitalists. Second is the sphere of production in which the relations between labor in firms and capital must be more balanced, with conflicts between the two involving negotiations among actors who are more equal. And third is the sphere of politics, where class compromises in the formation and implementation of state policies increasingly meet the interests of both the state and members of non-elite classes. Wright conducts a thought experiment in which *the relative power* of capital to realize its interests and classes to develop associational power is assessed. When capital's power is high, the associational interests of labor are high, and vice versa. At either extreme, Wright argues, are zones of "unattainability," and thus, it is the middle ground where both parties can realize some of their interests that are most viable. The United States is, Wright argues, on one side of this zone, favoring

---

[32]Ibid., p. 324.

[33]Ibid., p. 355.

capital or class associational interests, while a society like Sweden is on the other side of this zone. Thus, the implication is that the United States needs to move toward the Swedish side where the interests of capital and non-elite classes are more equally balanced so that each side is able to meet many of its goals.

**Assessing Wright's Neo-Marxist Approach.** Wright appears to have moved from trying to explain why predictions by Marx about class formation and revolution were never realized in a capitalist system to developing scenarios whereby many of the emancipatory goals of Marx can be realized in capitalist societies. Such societies will be democratic and will reveal non-elite classes whose interests are more equally weighted against the interests of capitalists. In this way, the constraints of modern capitalism imposed on class associational power are reduced, and the capacity of non-elite actors to realize their interests is increased. Rather than envisioning *real utopias*—plural—Wright appears to come down to one: a version of democratic socialism that currently exists in parts of the capitalist world. The other trajectories to socialism are, in essence, considered unrealistic by Wright, whereas, in contrast, the symbiotic metamorphosis is considered the most realistic. Along the way to this conclusion, Wright appears to argue that the globalization of capitalism has set up conditions whereby those capitalists societies, such as the United States, that favor capital over class associational power can be transformed. Thus, in the end, Wright has done what many Marxist scholars have done over the last few decades: considered the dynamics of the world system and its effects on class relations in capitalist societies.

# Neo-Marxian World-Systems Analysis

In the 1970s, Marxian-inspired theory began to shift the unit of analysis from nation-states to relations among societies. Capitalism was viewed as a dynamic engine of transformation that would create a world-level economy. This world-capitalist economy, in turn, would reveal many of the same contradictions that Marx had predicted for capitalism within a particular society. The study of empires and imperialism had, of course, long been a major topic in a variety of disciplines—history, political science, economics, and sociology. Some of the flavor of what world-systems analysts would argue was captured early by the British economist J. A. Hobson in his view that capitalist nations need to conquer and exploit other nations to stave off many of the problems predicted by Marx.[34] But, Immanuel Wallerstein codified Marxist ideas into a coherent conceptual scheme for the analysis of

---

[34]John Atkinson Hobson, *Capitalism and Imperialism in South Africa* (London: Contemporary Review, 1900); *The Conditions of Industrial Peace* (New York: Macmillan, 1927); *Confessions of an Economic Heretic* (London: G. Allen and Unwin, 1938); *The Economics of Distribution* (London: Macmillan, 1900).

the world system.[35] His work, in turn, has stimulated much further theoretical and empirical effort.

## Immanuel Wallerstein's Analysis of the "World System"

**World Empires and World Economy**. Immanuel Wallerstein begins his historical analysis on the emergence of a capitalist world system by distinguishing between two basic forms of inter-connection among societies: (1) world empires and (2) world economy. A world empire is created by military conquest or threats of such conquest, and then extraction of resources, usually in the form of tribute, from those populations that have been defeated or threatened. Often these conquered societies can retain considerable autonomy as long as they pay the tribute demanded by their conquerors. Whether through direct appropriation, taxation, or tribute, dominant nations can accumulate wealth and use their wealth to finance the privilege of elites and the military activities of the polity. Military empires are thus built around a strong state that administers the flow of taxes, franchises, and tributary wealth, while financing and coordinating the military for war making and conquest. Wallerstein argues that this was, historically, the dominant form of societal inter-connection among societies before the 1400s when the capitalist revolution had begun, although many debate this point and emphasize that trade-based and empire-based systems of domination existed long before modern European capitalism.[36] Moreover, many argue that imperial and trade forms of world-system domination had come and gone in various cycles many times in history,[37] long before the modern world system began to develop in the 1400s. Nonetheless, the important point is that one form of connection among nations is through state-based imperialism. Indeed, this form has persisted

---

[35]Immanuel Wallerstein, *The Modern World System*, 3 volumes (New York: Academic, 1974, 1980, 1989). Earlier work by scholars such as Andre Gunder Frank on dependency theory anticipated much of what Wallerstein was to argue: Underdeveloped societies, especially those in Latin America, could not go through the stages to modernization because they were economically dependent on advanced economies, and this dependency and the corresponding exploitation by advanced industrial powers kept them from becoming fully industrialized and modern. See, for example, Frank's *Capitalism and Underdevelopment in Latin America* (New York: Monthly Review Press, 1967). See also his later work, *Dependent Accumulation* (New York: Monthly Review Press, 1979). Also, historians such as Fernand Braudel had conducted analyses of world-systems processes. For his overview, see *Civilization and Capitalism*, 3 volumes (New York: Harper & Row, 1964).

[36]For a review, see Christopher Chase-Dunn and Peter Grimes, "World-Systems Analysis," *Annual Review of Sociology* 21 (1995): pp. 387–417. See also Albert J. Bergesen, ed., *Studies of the Modern World System* (New York: Academic Press, 1980).

[37]See Christopher Chase-Dunn and T. D. Hall's edited collection of essays on *Core/Periphery Relations in Precapitalist Worlds* (Boulder, CO: Westview, 1991) as well as their coauthored *Rise and Demise: Comparing World Systems* (Boulder, CO: Westview Press, 1997). See also Andre Gunder Frank and B. K. Gills, eds., *The World System: Five Hundred Years or Five Thousand?* (London: Routledge, 1993).

for most of the twentieth century, as the Soviet Union before its breakup can attest.

Wallerstein, as well as other historical sociologists, emphasize that the structural dilemma for imperial forms of governance is sustaining the resource levels necessary to support privilege of elites as well as a large military and administrative bureaucracy needed to control resentful peasants or other non-elites, especially those in conquered populations. Corruption and graft only aggravate these problems, but in the end, the state leaders face fiscal crises and must confront a variety of enemies within and outside their homeland borders. Eventually, the empire collapses, often because two imperial empires come to a showdown conflict, as Collins emphasized in his analysis of geopolitics (see Table 12.6 on page 249).

In contrast with an empire, a world economy reveals a different structure composed of (a) multiple states at its core, some of which have approximately equal military power; (b) competition among these core states in both the military and economic arena, with the latter being dominated by markets; and (c) peripheral states whose cheap labor and raw resources are extracted through trade, but trade that is vastly unequal because of the military power and economic advantages of the core states in market transactions.

**Core, Periphery, and Semiperiphery**. Wallerstein's distinction among the core and periphery at the world-system level parallels in a rough way Marx's notion of capitalists and proletarians at the societal level. *Core* nations correspond to capitalist class at the societal level and, like the capitalist class, extract surplus value through exploitation. The core areas of the world systems are the great military powers of their time. Since military power ultimately rests on the economy's ability to support the use of coercive force, these military powers are also leading economic powers. There are external areas to the core, and these become the *periphery* when a core state decides to colonize them or engage in exploitive trade. The periphery consists of less developed countries whose resources are needed and, with threats of potential or actual military intervention, are taken in exploitive market transactions. Wallerstein also distinguishes what is termed the *semiperiphery*, which comprises (a) minor nations in the core area and (b) leading states in the periphery. These semiperipheral states have a higher degree of economic development and military strength than the periphery but not as much as the core states; they are often used as intermediaries in trade between core and periphery.[38]

The semiperiphery can also be the origin of mobility among states and, at times, areas of the periphery can become semiperipheral and, perhaps,

---

[38]For a somewhat different analyses, see Christopher Chase-Dunn, *Global Formation* (Cambridge: Blackwell, 1989) and "World Systems Theorizing" in *Handbook of Sociological Theory* (cited in note 3). See also Volker Bornschier and Christopher Chase-Dunn, *Transnational Corporations and Underdevelopment* (New York: Praeger, 1985).

even part of the core area (as with the history of the United States and Japan). Similarly, much of Southeast Asia is moving today from either semi-peripheral (China, for example) or even peripheral (India, for instance) to the core. Japan is clearly at the core in the current world system, whereas India and other parts of Asia are still somewhat semiperipheral but clearly capable of moving to a new core over the next few decades.

The basic connection that drives the world economy, however, is the relationship between the core and periphery. The core has a large consumer market for both basic and luxury goods, a well-paid labor force (at least relative to the labor force in the periphery), a comparatively low rate of taxation enabling the accumulation of private wealth, a high level of technology (both economic and military) coupled with market-driven needs to sustain technological innovation, and a set of large-scale firms that engage in trade with peripheral states. The periphery has resources that consumers in the core states desire, and because states in the periphery are at a trading disadvantage (because of their lack of military strength and their lack of technology and capital to develop their own resources), each exchange between core and periphery in a market transfers wealth to the core. This exploitation by the core perpetuates the problems of development in the periphery, because peripheral states do not receive sufficient money from the core to finance infrastructural development (roads, transportation, and communication) or to afford educational and other welfare-state needs.[39] Moreover, because of the lack of economic development and the high degree of economic uncertainty in peripheral nations, individual citizens view children as their only potential source of economic security in the future, thereby having more babies and causing population growth that places even greater burdens on the state. As a consequence, peripheral states not only remain poor and underdeveloped but they are typically becoming overpopulated and politically unstable—a situation that only sustains their problems of development and their dependence on core states for trade.

**The Dynamics of the World Economy.** A world economy reveals its own dynamics, some of which are much the same as in empires, but others of which are unique to capitalism. What the core states have all had in common with older forms of empire building are their constant wars with each other, especially over conquest and control of the periphery. Moreover, they encounter many of the same fiscal problems of empires in trying to sustain wealth, profits, and well-being at home along with a large military and administrative system to wage war and to control their own citizens and dissidents in their conquered or dominated territories. Indeed, core states are often just ahead of problems, as they colonize ever-more territory to

---

[39]This was the essential point of dependency theorists (cited in note 35). See also Chase-Dunn and Grimes, "World Systems Theorizing" for a brief overview of wave analysis (cited in note 38). For a short, but very clear, summary of Wallerstein's argument, see Randall Collins, *Theoretical Sociology* (New York: Harcourt Brace Jovanovich, 1988), pp. 96–97.

sustain the costs of their prosperity while financing the administrative and coercive basis of control at home and abroad. When these competing powers begin to fight closer to home, they often ruin their respective economies through the costs of financing war and then maintaining control. Such wars make core states vulnerable enough that new powers can move into the core and supplant them (as has occurred with, for example, Spain and Portugal).

Another dynamic, Wallerstein argues, is the cyclical tendencies of the world economy. Wallerstein emphasizes what are termed *Kondratieff waves*, which are long-term oscillations in the world system, running approximately every 150 years.[40] At the beginning of a Kondratieff wave, the demand within core states for goods is high, which increases production and the need for ever-more raw materials. This need for raw materials leads to the expansion of the core states into external areas, making the latter peripheral suppliers of resources to the core. The next step in the Kondratieff wave occurs when the supplies of raw materials and the production of goods exceed demands for them, leading core states to reduce geographical expansion but, equally important, for businesses to reduce production and, thereby, set off the down cycle emphasized by Marx: lowered domestic demand, decreased production, intense competition for market share driving profits down, increased unemployment as production declines, and consequently, even less demand for goods, further reductions in production, business failures, and growth of monopolies and oligopolies.

This concentration of capital, however, sets the stage for the next point in the wave: High unemployment generates class conflict as workers demand better working conditions and wages; such demands eventually lead to higher wages for workers as the state responds to political pressures and large corporations give in; concentrated capital meantime seeks new technologies and ever-more efficient means of production to lower costs; with more wages, economic demand increases, and with new technologies and capital investment, a new period of higher profits and relative prosperity ensues, leading to increased demand for raw materials from peripheral states. But eventually, this new round of prosperity falls victim to the forces predicted by Marx: Market saturation through over-production of goods relative to demand, intense competition over price, increased unemployment, decreased demand, further decreases in production, increases in business failures, and crisis bring to a close this long 150 year wave.

**Other Cyclical Dynamics in the World Economy**. Within these long waves are shorter cycles that have been extensively studied by not only conventional economists but world-systems analysts as well.[41] These all operate much as Marx had predicted but without the great revolution at their end.

---

[40]See Chase-Dunn and Grimes, "World Systems Theorizing" (cited in note 38) for a brief review of empirical and conceptual work on these cycles.

[41]Ibid., p. 404.

The classic business cycle, sometimes termed *Juglar cycle*, appears to last from five to seven years. Production expands to increased market demand, unemployment declines, demand in markets increases further because workers have income, production expands more, and then, oversupply of goods in relation to demand starts a recession. Some have argued that part of this cycle reflects the replacement costs of new machinery, which tends to wear out about every eight years, forcing new capital investments that can drive market demand, but once this demand is met, it can also set into motion the decline demand for capital goods. Such capital demand is especially important in high-technology core nations where much employment revolves around making equipment and providing services for other businesses. Capital demand can become as significant, or more so, as household consumer demand for goods and services.[42]

Another cycle is what is termed the *Kuznet cycle*; these operate over a twenty-five-year period in core and semiperipheral states.[43] Just why these cycles occur is unknown, although there are several hypotheses. One is related to generational turnover in which, about every twenty years, demand for basic household purchases such as houses and other buildings declines—and, hence, production and employment decrease—until the next generation has sufficient money to drive up demand for these goods, thereby setting off another wave of prosperity.

**Hegemonic Sequences.** As Wallerstein argued,[44] but as others have developed further, there are oscillations in the degree of centralization among the core nations of the world system. Before capitalism,[45] these oscillations revolved around the rise and fall of empires through war, conquest, tribute, and collapse. With capitalism, however, the nature of the oscillation changes. Hegemonic core states seek to control trade, particularly trade across oceans, and thereby connect core and periphery in an exploitive trade arrangement. The dominant state or states can prevent military empires from encroaching on this trade and can force empires to act as capitalists in the system of world trade (as with the former Soviet Union and as is occurring in China today).

Thus, the cycle of centralization revolves around the rise and fall of hegemonic core states that have been able to dictate the terms of trade in the world system. Shifts in this domination by a core state can come with wars,

---

[42]Ibid., pp. 404–5.

[43]Wallerstein, *The Modern World System* (cited in note 35).

[44]See Chase-Dunn and Grimes, "World Systems Theorizing" (cited in note 38), pp. 411–14, for a useful review.

[45]For an example of a test of the world system model, see Ronan Van Rossem, "The World System Paradigm as General Theory of Development: A Cross-National Test," *American Sociological Review* 61 (1996): pp. 508–27.

but unlike precapitalist empire building, the domination that ensues is oriented toward dictating the terms of trade as much as toward outright conquest of territory or extraction of tribute in response to military threats. The rise of a new hegemonic state gives the state greater access to the resources of other peripheral and semiperipheral states, while enabling it to dominate other core states (as has been the case, for example, with the United States in the post-World War II period, at least to this point).

In addition to war, hegemonic states often rise because of new economic or military technology that gives them advantages. Under these conditions, states can charge rents for their innovations or use them to control trade and, in the case of military technology, to make threats that improve the terms of trade. As these innovations are copied, however, the advantages can be lost or neutralized, setting the stage for another potential hegemonic state to emerge because of new technologies and other productive or military advantages.

## The End of Capitalism?

Wallerstein and many other world-systems analysts still accept Marx's vision that capitalism will collapse, but for world-systems theory, capitalism must first penetrate the entire world for its contradictions to emerge. As long as peripheral states exist to be exploited by the core, capitalism can sustain itself by relying on the resources and the cheap labor of less developed countries. But once capitalism exists everywhere, there is no longer an escape from the processes outlined by Marx. The problems endemic to capitalism—saturation of markets, decreased demand, lowered production, and further decreases in demand—will lead to the collapse of capitalist modes of production, a period of conflict between old-line capitalists (along with their allies in the state) and the broader population that seeks a better way to distribute resources fairly. In the wake of these crises will come world-level socialism, and perhaps, even world government. Although the details of this ultimate scenario vary among analysts, the emancipatory thrust of Marx's predictions remains. Whether these predictions are any more accurate than Marx's remains to be seen, but regardless of their accuracy, world-systems theory has provided important insights into basic dynamics of human organization.

# Conclusion

Varieties of analytical class analysis along with diverse approaches to world-systems analysis attest to the continued viability of Marxian-inspired sociological theory. For unlike the more abstracted approaches of Dahrendorf and Turner, which took Marx's ideas and made them more abstract to fit changing empirical conditions, class and world-systems analyses retain much of the substantive flavor of Marx's theory and extend these substantive arguments in useful and creative ways. The key dynamic remains exploitation, whether by those who control capital within a society or by those nations who dominate other nations militarily and economically.

Moreover, although a certain caution and moderation are evident, the emancipatory thrust of Marx is retained: In the long run, it is supposed, the contradictions of capitalism will indeed lead to a revolution or more moderated transformations in which there is less inequality in the distribution of resources among people within societies and between societies.

What makes these neo-Marxian approaches appealing is their willingness to confront data and to use empirical studies to modify, qualify, and change theoretical statements. This is not to say, however, that these theorists' emancipatory ideology does not make them reluctant to accept findings that might contradict the emphasis on exploitation as the central mechanism within and between societies but that, at least, there is a willingness to move outside the narrow confines of Marx's original formulation. In this way, they keep Marx alive as a viable source of theoretical development.

## CHAPTER 14

# Conflict Theories in Historical-Comparative Sociology

Both Karl Marx and Max Weber saw societal revolutions as emerging from conditions of high inequality that, in turn, produce mass mobilization of subordinates to pursue conflict against superordinates. Although Marx's and Weber's abstract theories converged, important differences can be found in their respective formulations. One difference is that Marx saw revolution by the proletariat as inevitably arising from the contradictions of capitalism and the exploitation that capitalism systematically generates, whereas Weber saw revolutions as historically contingent and far from inevitable. Another difference is that Weber saw internal societal conflict as related to external geopolitical processes, as these influence the legitimacy of political regimes (see the propositions in Table 10.2 on page 210). A related difference is that Weber saw power and its manifestation in the state as a distinct actor and, indeed, as a separate basis for stratification, whereas Marx tended to view the state as simply a tool of the dominant social class and as a *superstructure* of the underlying economic relations. Yet, despite their differences, both theorists sought to develop historical interpretations about when revolutions are likely to occur, and although Weber was certainly the more devoted historian, their efforts to analyze revolutionary conflict by marshaling historical data stimulated a distinctive branch of conflict theory in the modern era.

This branch of theorizing involves historical descriptions of conflicts in agrarian societies making the transition to modernity. Moreover, key figures in this branch of theorizing tend to use comparative analyses of case histories

---

*This chapter is coauthored with Rebecca S. K. Li.

to make more analytical, abstract, and generalizable statements about the generic conditions producing social conflict. In this sense, these approaches are Weberian because they systematically seek comparisons among societies and develop generalizations from historical cases, but there is almost always a Marxian strain in these works, emphasizing how the exploitive actions of dominant classes create the conditions that lead to mass mobilizations of subordinates. Indeed, the first efforts to develop a comparative-historical theory of conflict began with Marxian assumptions about inequality and class conflict, but over time, as comparative-historical sociology developed, it has taken on a more Weberian tone, seeking to document how certain conditions, when converging at a point or points in history, increase the likelihood of societal revolutions.

In discussing several prominent theories in this tradition, we will emphasize the more abstract theoretical statements that emerge from the comparative analyses of specific historical cases. In a sense, such an exercise violates the empirical intent of these Weber-inspired works, but this exercise is also true to Weber's goal of developing more analytical models and statements. Weber himself evidenced considerable ambivalence about the generalizability of models from one historical case to others; most comparative-historical analyses of conflict reveal a similar ambiguity about the appropriateness of more abstract generalizations. In this chapter, we will ignore this uncertainty and extract the theoretical statements of researchers and convert them into more abstract theoretical arguments.

# Mass Mobilization and State Breakdown

Theories of social conflict emerging from comparative-historical sociology tend to emphasize two related factors. One factor is the conditions that lead the masses to mobilize ideologically, politically, and organizationally to pursue conflict against those who dominate them. The other factor is the processes leading to the breakdown of the state and its capacity to control the population. Obviously, these two factors are interrelated, but the theories tend to give more emphasis to one or the other. Some emphasize the forces leading to mobilization, whereas others recognize that the power of the state must also erode before mobilizations can be successful. Indeed, the historical record reveals that revolts and other forms of civil disruption are fairly common in human societies, but true society-wide revolutions where the distribution of power and other resources are dramatically changed are rather rare. Because of their rarity, revolutions have fascinated historical sociologists. To explain why they occur, or do not occur, the various theories revolve around specifying the forces (1) leading to mobilization of the masses to pursue conflict with the dominant sectors of the society and (2) causing the state to lose legitimacy as well as the capacity to regulate and control members of the population. Figure 14.1 summarizes the two basic factors in various theories.

**Figure 14.1**   The Two Lines of Emphasis in Historical-Comparative Theories of Revolutions

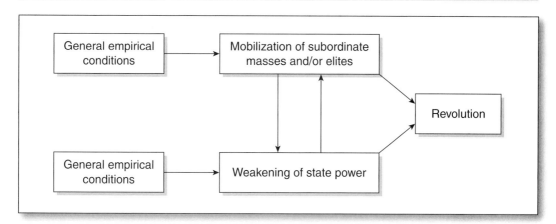

# Barrington Moore on the Origins of Dictatorship and Democracy

One of the earliest analyses of conflict in societies undergoing the transition from an agrarian to an industrial base of social organization was Barrington Moore's comparative study of the conditions producing dictatorships or democracies.[1] In his analysis of these conditions, which can be considered the maturing tradition building on Marx and Weber, the theoretical leads to be developed by more contemporary historical sociologists were first exposed. Moore argued that there are three routes to modernization. One is where feudal landowners become capitalists, replacing with hired labor the peasants who once lived on and worked the land in tenancy agreements, and then selling the products of this hired labor in markets for profits. This route converts the old landed aristocracy into capitalists and, in the end, leads them to become reluctant allies with the bourgeoisie. This route is the most likely to produce democracy, and it is the path that both Britain and the United States (after the elimination of slavery) pursued.

A second route to modernization is where the landowners enter capitalist markets to sell their products but where they keep the peasants on the land, forcing them to increase productivity through the traditional controls of tenancy and patronage that inhere in feudalism. Under these conditions, the landowners must ally themselves with the bureaucrats in the state to keep control of peasants who are increasingly exploited as

[1]Barrington Moore, *Social Origins of Dictatorship and Democracy: Lord and Peasant in the Making of the Modern World* (Boston: Beacon, 1966).

capitalist landowners seek to extract ever-more profit from the peasants' labor. In Moore's view, this path leads to a fascist state, and this was the route that Japan and Germany/Prussia took during their initial transition to modernity.

The third and final route to modernization is where the landowners become absentee owners, collecting rents from the peasants who produce directly for markets in which prices can vary enormously but who must typically pay constant or even escalating rents to landlords. Decreases in the prices of goods sold in markets, coupled with constant or escalating rents, make peasants aware of their exploitation and the larger political-economy in which they must operate. This awareness and the emotion that it arouses result in peasant revolts, which can lead to mass mobilizations and societal revolutions. In the wake of revolution, whether successful or not, state power is increased to consolidate the power of the victorious faction in the revolution and to control potential dissidents. The exact form of the state can vary, as is evident with the difference between France after its major revolution and Russia or China in the wake of their respective revolutions. In either case, a strong state emerges.

In this descriptive scenario are more general propositions about the conditions increasing or decreasing mass mobilization of peasants for conflict. These more abstract propositions are summarized in Table 14.1, and we will discuss the implications of each. For mobilization of the subordinate masses to occur, they must remain a coherent whole performing similar tasks and having similar life experiences (Proposition 1-A). In the historical cases studied by Moore, the absentee landlord extracting rents from peasants who remained on their land and produced for the market was most likely to meet this condition because the traditional residence patterns and productive work routines of the feudal peasantry were retained, but under conditions of exploitation by landowners and fluctuation in market prices for the goods produced by peasants.[2]

Proposition 1-B in Table 14.1 stresses that subordinates must experience collective solidarity if they are to become mobilized to pursue conflict. Yet, other conditions in agrarian societies undergoing the transition to modernity will increase solidarity. For instance, solidarity increases with subordinates' sense of threat, and as Moore stressed, this sense of threat can come from many sources. One source is those who dominate them and engage in practices that threaten subordinates' livelihood and well-being. Another source of threat can reside in the state's efforts to repress peasants. Still another source of threat can come from outside the society when armies invade and threaten the lives and livelihood of subordinates.[3] A final source

---

[2]According to Moore, this was the case with China before the Communist Revolution—many landlords moved to the city and lived on rent collected from peasants and interests of the debt peasants borrowed from them (see *Social Origins of Dictatorship and Democracy*, pp. 218–21, cited in note 1).

[3]The Japanese army served as an external enemy that pulled the peasants together in China during the Japanese occupation in World War II.

**Table 14.1** Abstracted Propositions from Barrington Moore's Analysis

1. The potential for mass mobilization of the subordinates to pursue conflict with superordinates in a system of inequality will increase when

   A. The subordinates constitute a coherent whole in their physical location, their daily routines, and their lived experiences

   B. The subordinates experience collective solidarity. This sense of solidarity will increase when

      1. Subordinates experience a sense of threat from either those who dominate them or those from outside the society who might dominate them through conquest

      2. Subordinates can avoid divisive competition with each other over

         a. Land and tenancy rights to farmland

         b. Markets buying their labor

         c. Commodity markets selling their goods

      3. Subordinates experience the conditions listed under 1-C and 1-D below

   C. The traditional inter-connections between the communities of subordinates and superordinates are weakened. This weakening will increase when

      1. Subordinates and superordinates are placed in more direct competition with each other for resources or, at least, are perceived by subordinates to be so

      2. Superordinates are no longer perceived as providing indispensable and otherwise unavailable resources to subordinates

      3. Subordinates' relations to superordinates have moved from a paternalistic to market-driven form, but this effect of market forces operates only if subordinates do not compete directly with each other for resources in a market controlled by external sources of power

      4. Superordinates become increasingly removed and absent from the daily routines of subordinates

   D. The subordinates perceive that superordinates are exploiting them. This sense of exploitation will increase when

      1. Subordinates are forced to provide ever more of their resources to external powers, whether to the state or to those who own the means of their production

      2. Subordinates experience the conditions listed in 1-C, delineating the forces that weaken the connection between communities of subordinates and superordinates

of threat comes from the conditions leading to a breakdown of the traditional inter-connections between superordinates and subordinates. Solidarity is not, however, inevitable. For example, as Moore emphasizes, commercialization of agriculture where estate labor is hired under highly competitive labor market conditions (that is, there is a surplus of labor relative to demand) will reduce the potential for mass mobilization—a proposition that goes against Marx's prediction about the effects of labor markets on workers.

This last source of threat is particularly important; the degree of connectedness and contact between the subordinate masses and those above them in the stratification system is critical to the mobilization of the masses. When there is a strong inter-connection between the communities of superordinates and subordinates, or at least a sense of a strong connection by subordinates, the potential for mass mobilization is lessened, as was historically the case with traditional feudalism where the lord, his squire or overseer, and peasantry all lived on the manorial estate in nonmarket relations guided by paternalism and traditional tenancy understandings. Conversely, forces that weaken this inter-connection will increase the likelihood of mass mobilization, as occurs when the landlord becomes absent and extracts rents regardless of the prices that peasants directly marketing their goods can secure. More generally, the connection between subordinates' and superordinates' respective communities is also weakened when they must compete with each other for resources, or think that they must, when superordinates are no longer perceived to provide indispensable and vital resources, when subordinates' relations with superordinates become market driven, and when superordinates become absent and removed from daily work routines of subordinates. Again, the route to modernity most likely to meet these conditions is the absentee landlord extracting rents from peasants who work the land but who must also be subject to the vicissitudes of price fluctuations in markets.

Like Marx, Moore sees the rate and degree of exploitation experienced by the subordinate masses as crucial. Exploitation or at least the sense of being exploited increases as subordinates must give up more resources to superordinates, especially when the traditional inter-connections between the communities of dominated and dominant are weakened. When this sense of exploitation is at its maximum—as is the case where peasants are forced to pay constant or escalating rents to absentee landlords but must endure price fluctuations in the markets where they sell their products—exploitation is laid bare, and hence, mass mobilization potential increases. The state can also play an important role in this sense of exploitation because the more peasants are restive, the more landlords depend on the state's coercive powers, which, in turn, means that the state must extract ever more resources from the lords and, ultimately, their peasants to finance repression. If the state taxes lords too severely, the lords become a potential source of revolt, but in the end, the increased taxes are taken from the peasants who must increase their output or suffer a diminished standard of living as landowners extract ever more of the peasants' surplus product to pay for the coercive activities of the state. Again, when this additional extraction comes from increased rents by absentee landlords trying to repress their restive peasants who must endure market fluctuations, the sense of exploitation is likely to be maximal.

In sum, Moore's approach is Marxian in its assumptions—conflict emerges from high levels of exploitation—but it adds Weberian qualifications. The most obvious is that revolution is most likely in systems that have not gone completely capitalist; instead, the landed aristocracy has perhaps become more capitalistic but in a way that exposes their exploitation of peasants. Indeed, revolution is the least likely in the very industrial systems that Marx thought would experience a revolution where labor, even agrarian labor, had been pushed into exploitive labor markets. Moore's work thus marked an important beginning for a new form of conflict theory. Along with others working in the historical-comparative arena, Moore's efforts inspired not only his own students but also others to examine the forces producing mass mobilization of peasants and revolutionary conflict in agrarian societies.

# Jeffrey Paige's Theory of Agrarian Revolution

Jeffrey Paige's book on agrarian revolution[4] was one of the first works in the more contemporary era to take Marx's basic ideas and adapt them to the analysis of revolutions and other forms of mass mobilization among peasants in agrarian societies. Paige argues that Marx's ideas about the conditions producing revolution and mass mobilization are, in essence, correct but that these conditions are not met in industrial societies.[5] Rather, they are much more likely to exist in agrarian economies engaged in exporting their agricultural products. The peasants who work the agricultural estates represent a more volatile pool of exploited labor than Marx's proletarian workforce in factories. Thus, Paige believes the conditions producing mobilization and conflict are more likely in agrarian than industrial societies. Moreover, the nature of the relation between the cultivators (actual workers in the fields) and the noncultivators (who own the land and control the activities of cultivators) is crucial in determining the nature of the mobilization by cultivators and the intensity of the conflict between these subordinates and their superordinate masters.

Like Marx, Paige sees the conflict between owners and workers as flowing from their respective relations to the means of production in agrarian societies, but unlike Marx, he argues that revolution is unlikely when the conflict is about purely economic matters, such as wages. Rather, revolutionary conflict will occur only when the economic conflict moves into the political arena and attacks the system of control and authority in a society. Moreover, the likelihood that conflict will enter this broader arena depends more on

---

[4]Jeffrey Paige, *Agrarian Revolution: Social Movements and Export Agriculture in the Underdeveloped World* (New York: Free Press, 1975).

[5]Ibid., pp. 33–34.

the actions of the dominant than of the subordinate classes. Hence, the actions of the dominant class determine just how mobilized the subordinate class will be and just how far their mobilization will proceed.

Some of Paige's key propositions have been extracted and presented in abstract terms in Table 14.2. These propositions lay out the conditions

---

**Table 14.2**    Key Propositions in Paige's Model of Agrarian Revolutions

1. Conflicts of interest between cultivators and noncultivators lead to the mass mobilization of cultivators when

    A. Cultivators are receptive to radical ideologies

    1. This receptiveness to radical ideologies will increase when cultivators' ties to the land are tenuous and unstable.

    2. This receptiveness to radical ideologies is decreased, however, when

        a. Cultivators' survival margins are so thin and precarious that they fear the risks of accepting the tenets of a radical ideology

        b. Cultivators have so few alternative means for making a living that the potential costs of accepting a radical ideology become too high

        c. Cultivators live in traditional communities in which paternalistic traditions and tight social control make radical ideologies either unappealing or too risky

    B. Cultivators can experience collective solidarity

    1. This sense of solidarity will increase when agricultural production encourages high levels of interdependence among cultivators.

    2. This sense of solidarity will decrease, however, when cultivators are highly dependent on noncultivators for crucial resources and services.

    C. Cultivators have been able to engage in successful collective actions

    1. This capacity to engage in collective actions is increased when

        a. Noncultivators' direct control of the cultivators' actions is weak

        b. Cultivators constitute a homogenous population

        c. Cultivators are required by the process of production to cooperate

        d. Cultivators have access to organizational resources provided by outside political actors

        e. Cultivators perceive that they can gain real economic benefits from collective action

    2. This capacity to engage in collective actions is, however, decreased when

        a. Cultivators have opportunities for upward mobility

        b. Cultivators see themselves as engaged in competition among themselves for resources, especially opportunities for upward mobility

2. The likelihood that mobilization of cultivators will lead to revolutionary movements is related to the actions of noncultivators. The reactions of noncultivators to mobilization by cultivators increase the potential for violence when

 A. The conditions increasing the mass mobilization of cultivators listed under 1 are met

 B. Noncultivators do not possess great economic advantages over cultivators and, consequently, are more likely to resort to repression using the state's coercive power rather than pursuing economic manipulation of, and bargaining with, cultivators. Such repression will increase when

  1. Noncultivators have little capital beyond the export crops produced on their land, giving them relatively little economic advantage over cultivators

  2. Noncultivators do not engage in capital-intensive processing of the crops produced on their land, thereby making them dependent on exports of unfinished crops and, hence, giving them relatively little economic advantage over cultivators

  3. Noncultivators cannot afford to hire free labor, thereby making them unresponsive to the economic demands of cultivators and increasing their use of forced labor while employing tight and rigid control of labor

   a. The ability of noncultivators to afford to yield to cultivators' economic demands is reduced when production is inefficient and less profitable.

   b. The ability of noncultivators to afford to yield to cultivators' demands is improved, however, when production can be increased through mechanization that expands production at lower costs per worker.

  4. Noncultivators' repressive control is less likely, however, when production necessitates a constant supply of disciplined labor, leading noncultivators to perceive the benefits of labor organizations and the need to make compromises in managing cultivators.

under which, first, the conflicts of interest between cultivators (peasants, farm labor) and noncultivators (owners and managers of the land) move from conflicts over narrow economic issues, escalate into violence, and thereby move into the political arena. The propositions listed under 1 in Table 14.2 apply Marx's essential argument to agrarian economies engaged in exporting agricultural products. Paige sees cultivators' receptiveness to radical, change-oriented political ideologies as crucial. When cultivators' ties and connections to the land on which they work are tenuous and unstable, they are more likely to be receptive to radical ideologies. But, when cultivators can barely survive by their work on the land, when they have few alternative means for making a living, and when they are part of traditional agrarian communities, they become less receptive to radical ideologies. Only when the production processes encourage high levels of interdependence among workers can solidarity be generated, and this solidarity-producing effect can be undermined when cultivators reveal very high degrees of dependence on noncultivators for crucial resources and services.

Receptiveness to radical ideologies and solidarity among cultivators is not, however, sufficient for mass mobilization of violence and movement into the political arena. Cultivators must also be capable of engaging in effective collective actions; without the ability to engage in such actions, revolutionary movements and changes in the politics of a society are not possible. This capacity to engage in collective actions is increased when noncultivators cannot directly control the actions of cultivators. The ability to pursue collective actions is further enhanced when cultivators constitute a homogenous population, when they cooperate in the production processes and hence have an organizational base for collective action built into the work setting, and when they perceive that it is possible to gain real benefits over potential losses from collective actions. Yet, the ability to engage in collective actions is undermined when cultivators have opportunities for individual upward mobility and when they perceive themselves in competition with each other for resources, particularly those revolving around chances for mobility.

Paige emphasizes, however, that these conditions facilitating mass mobilization—that is, ideology, solidarity, and collective action—are influenced by the options and reactions of noncultivators. The form of conflict will, Paige argues, ultimately reflect the way in which the dominant sectors of the society respond to the conflicts of interests as well as the conflicts over narrow economic issues between cultivators and noncultivators. Proposition 2 in Table 14.2 lists some conditions that increase the level of violence and extension of conflict beyond the economic to the political arena.

One condition is, of course, those forces listed under Proposition 1 increasing mass mobilization potential among cultivators, but this potential is more likely to be realized when noncultivators are forced to act in certain ways. When noncultivators depend on the state and military to maintain control of their land and the labor working the land, they are more likely to engage in rigid and repressive actions to control cultivators—a tactic that will increase the anger and dispositions of cultivators to engage in mass mobilization, if they can. Noncultivators engaged primarily in exporting raw agricultural products, especially products in which additional production processes are not performed before export, are particularly likely to depend on the external state and military to ensure the viability of their operations. Repressive and rigid control is also likely when noncultivators cannot afford, or at least perceive that they cannot afford, free labor that makes them disposed to employ forced labor under rigid external control. Such perceptions by noncultivators are increased when production is inefficient and yields only low to modest profits. However, if noncultivators can increase production through capital investments, especially investments in equipment that reduce reliance on labor and that increase each cultivator's productivity, then noncultivators are more likely to perceive that they can yield to cultivators' economic demands and resolve the conflict as an economic rather than political matter. Furthermore, the need to repress labor is lessened even more when noncultivators depend on a constant supply of disciplined and skilled labor, leading noncultivators to perceive the benefits of labor organizations and compromises with them in exchange for maintaining a constant supply of labor.

# Charles Tilly's Theory of Resource Mobilization

In *From Mobilization to Revolution*,[6] Charles Tilly described the basic ideas that became important in all subsequent theorizing on social revolutions. Tilly distinguished in this early work between a revolutionary situation and a revolutionary outcome. A revolutionary situation exists when some kind of collective action against centers of power is evident—whether these actions be demonstrations, riots, social movements, revolts, civil wars, or other manifestations of antagonism toward the state. A revolutionary outcome is when there is an actual transfer of power. Ultimately, Tilly argues, revolutionary situations emerge when contenders to power can mobilize financial, organizational, and coercive resources, and a revolutionary outcome is likely when this mobilization is greater than the capacity of the state to mobilize its coercive, material, and administrative resources.

Table 14.3 delineates some general conditions of a revolutionary situation.[7] The first condition is multiple contenders to power; two of the most likely contenders are those segments of the population who are consistently denied access to power or the political arena and those segments of the older power elite that are left out, or feel that they are excluded, from their traditional access to centers of power in the state. Another general condition increasing the potential for a revolutionary situation is that a significant part of the population is prepared to follow or support one of the competing contenders to the state's power. Such support becomes more likely as the state fails to meet obligations to the population and as it makes efforts to extract rapidly more resources from the population. This latter condition is most likely when the state is engaged in war and, as a result, runs short of money. The third basic condition leading to a revolutionary situation is that the state cannot, or is unwilling to, repress with coercive force the activities of those who challenge its power. This inability to use its own power against competing sources of power is likely when the state has few resources; when it has made ineffective and inefficient use of its resources through support of privilege, patronage, military adventurism, corruption, and archaic system of

---

[6]Charles Tilly, *From Mobilization to Revolution* (Reading, MA: Addison-Wesley, 1978). At the same time, John McCarthy and Meyer Zald were formulating another, more formal resource mobilization model; see their "Resource Mobilization in Social Movements: A Partial Theory," *American Journal of Sociology* 82 (1977): pp. 1212–39.

[7]Tilly, *From Mobilization to Revolution* (cited in note 6), pp. 200–211.

**Table 14.3** Tilly's Core Theory of Resource Mobilization

1. The more evident are multiple contenders to the state's power, the more likely is a revolutionary situation to exist. The likelihood of multiple contenders increases when

   A. Segments of the population have been kept out of the political arena or denied access to power

   B. Older power elites feel that they are being excluded from centers of power and, hence, are losing some of the traditional access to power

2. The more that significant segments of the population are willing to support or follow one of the competing contenders to the state's power, the more likely is a revolutionary situation to exist. The likelihood of an important segment following contenders to state power increases when

   A. The state is perceived to have failed in its responsibilities to the population, and the more rapidly escalating is the perception of failure to meet its responsibilities, the greater is the willingness of some segments to follow contenders to the state's power

   B. The state escalates resource extraction from members of a population, with such rapid escalation typically occurring when the state needs resources to finance war

3. The less willing, or able, is the state to suppress coercively competing contenders to its power, the more likely is a revolutionary situation to exist. The likelihood of such reluctance to use its power increases when

   A. The state is in fiscal crises and does not have the resources to engage in repression

   B. The state has ineffective mechanisms for resource (tax) collection and inefficient ways of using the resources that it does collect

   C. The state is inhibited from using its powers for repression because its military, or a segment of its coercive arm, is associated or allied with one of the contenders to its power

tax collection, and when it is inhibited from using power because portions of its military have close associations with at least one of the contenders to its power.

Tilly's argument in this first important work was highly theoretical, but in his more empirical analyses of the history of societies in Europe, he has tended to stay closer to the details of particular cases. Nonetheless, the basic elements of the theory summarized in Table 14.3 remain, and in his work *European Revolution, 1492–1992*[8] Tilly blends these theoretical ideas into his historical descriptions; in so doing, he adds considerable detail to the core theoretical ideas presented in Table 14.3.

---

[8]Charles Tilly, *European Revolutions, 1492–1992* (Oxford, UK and Cambridge, MA: Blackwell, 1993).

Table 14.4 summarizes some of these refinements in more detail; later, we present only the most important lessons to be derived from the propositions in Table 14.4. One very important condition affecting the capacity of the state to mobilize its resources and, thereby, resist potential contenders to its power is its involvement in international military competition. The more the state engages in such competition with other state powers, the more resources it drains away from the domestic arena, and hence, the more vulnerable it becomes, particularly so when it loses a war. The loss of a war not only drains material resources from a society but also erodes the symbolic resources that the state uses to legitimate itself. The likelihood that a state will engage in war, and eventually lose a war, is related to the military strength of its neighbors; the stronger the neighbors are and the more frequent conflict is with them, the more likely is the state to lose a war at some point in time.

Mobilization for military conflict has two contradictory effects on state power. On the one hand, the stronger the military power of the state, the greater is its coercive power to suppress mobilization by contenders to its power. This coercive strength increases to the extent that the military is organized professionally and maintains at the ready a standing army that can be efficiently and rapidly used to repress contenders to state power. On the other hand, if the military is engaged in external military competition, its coercive capacity is not available domestically, and if military activity outside a society's core borders is expensive, then the capacity to finance alternative domestic sources of coercion is correspondingly reduced.

Whether inside or outside the state's borders, another dilemma of having a strong military is its loyalty to leaders in the state. If the military is not loyal to rulers, or exists as a separate entity somewhat detached from the administrative guidance of the leaders in the state, it can then become a source of contending power. Moreover, this type of military is more likely to ally itself with other sources of contending power.[9] Thus, if the military allies itself with a contender to the state's power, or itself seeks to take state power, then a revolutionary situation very likely will be transformed into a revolutionary outcome in which there is a transfer of power.

Thus, the state's ability to maintain high degrees of coercive power relative to potential contenders is a crucial condition in avoiding a revolutionary situation leading to a revolutionary outcome. This capacity is not only related to absolute military power but also to the capacity of the state to (a) deflect grievances away from itself and (b) co-opt into its structure potential contenders to power. The more the state can do either or both, the more likely is it to avoid both a revolutionary situation and outcome. Thus, if the state can make relatively inexpensive concessions to contenders to power, without hurting either its financial or coercive basis of power, the state might stave off a revolutionary situation, and if it can avoid becoming

---

[9]Tilly points out that military seizure was a common kind of revolutionary situation in Iberia (see pp. 86, 101 in Tilly, *European Revolutions*).

**Table 14.4** Refinements to Tilly's Theory

1. The capacity of a state to avoid a revolutionary situation or outcome is positively related to its ability to mobilize coercive resources and to suppress potential contenders to power.

   A. This capacity to mobilize coercive resources is reduced when the state is engaged in international military competition that, in turn, causes

      1. Financial resources to flow away from the state

      2. Coercive resources to be deployed away from geographical centers of power

   B. This capacity to mobilize coercive resources is also reduced when the military is well organized but somewhat independent of the administrative centers of power, thereby making it more likely that

      1. The military will be less loyal to the key decision makers in the state

      2. The military itself will become a contender for state power

      3. The military will ally itself with at least one of the contenders for state power

   C. This capacity to mobilize coercive resources increases, however, when the military meets all of the following conditions:

      1. The military is professional and well organized

      2. The military maintains a standing army and does not need to recruit an army before it can act

      3. The military is not engaged in extensive geopolitical conflict

2. The capacity of the state to avoid a revolutionary situation or outcome is positively related to its ability to make strategic concessions to potential contenders to power. This capacity increases when

   A. The concessions to be made are not expensive

   B. The concessions to be made do not erode the state's coercive basis of power

   C. The concessions increase the strength of the state's symbolic basis of power or its legitimacy in the eyes of key segments of the population

3. The capacity of the state to avoid a revolutionary situation or outcome is positively related to the state's fiscal situation. The ability to remain fiscally sound is reduced when

   A. The state is engaged in expensive military activity against other states

   B. The state must engage in excessive patronage of elites

   C. The state does not have efficient or effective means for tax collection and other forms of resource extraction

the target for grievances by either elites or the masses, the state will be in a better position to hold onto its power and avoid a revolutionary situation.

The state is always in a precarious situation, however. Concessions to one segment of a population often arouse the hostility of others. Frequently, it is not possible to deflect hostility away from the state. This inability to deflect hostility becomes particularly likely when the state is engaged in expensive forms of patronage to satisfy demands of elite segments of the population and when it incurs the costs of military activity with other societies. Under these conditions, the state must often increase its demands (taxes) on the population for extra resources, and when it does so, resentments against the state increase because old agreements are now seen as violated and new indignities are being imposed. When mass discontent is coupled with resentments from portions of the nobility, a revolutionary situation exists and, moreover, a revolutionary outcome becomes more possible. These events are particularly likely when the state's mechanisms for collecting and distributing material resources are inefficient and ineffective and when the state's political institutions are geographically concentrated, thereby making them an easier target for seizure by contenders to state power.

# Theda Skocpol's Analysis of States and Social Revolutions

Theda Skocpol's comparative analysis of social revolutions in various agrarian societies builds on Moore's and Tilly's approaches but adds some additional refinements.[10] Like most historical analysts of revolutions, she sees the process of mass mobilization of peasants as crucial, and she adopts a key idea from Weber and Tilly: Internal revolutionary processes are related to the state's activities in the international arena. Skocpol's basic argument is that "revolutionary situations have developed due to the emergence of politico-military crises of the state and class domination."[11] Thus, although class inequalities provide much of the drive for the mass mobilization of peasants, such mobilization is not likely to be successful unless the state is experiencing a crisis of legitimacy stemming from military defeats in the international arena.

Skocpol's main examples of successful revolutions are the French Revolution of 1789, the Russian Revolution of 1917, and the Communist Chinese Revolution of 1949, which are compared with the relative stability in societies such as Japan, Germany/Prussia, and England where full-scale

---

[10]Theda Skocpol, *States and Social Revolutions: A Comparative Analysis of France, Russia, and China* (New York: Cambridge University Press, 1979).

[11]Ibid., p. 17.

social revolutions did not occur during the agrarian era nor in the transition to commercial capitalism. All of the societies in Skocpol's pool of case studies possessed certain common characteristics: (1) They all evidenced administrative and military control under a monarch. (2) The monarch could not, however, directly control agrarian socioeconomic relations. (3) The major surplus-extracting class was the landed aristocracy who passed some of their wealth to the monarch. (4) All of the aristocracy depended on the work of a large peasant population. (5) Market relations, commercial classes, and even early industrial classes (in later periods) could exist within these societies, but these classes were subordinate to the monarchial state and landed aristocracy. (6) The aristocracy in all these societies had become dependent on the state to provide positions of patronage in the court and administrative bureaucracy. (7) Yet, although the aristocracy and state were generally aligned, their interests diverged over the aristocracy's desire, on the one side, to create personal wealth and privilege through peasant labor or commercial activities and the monarch's desire, on the other side, to finance military adventures and state-sponsored economic development.

The scenario for a full-scale social revolution begins to unfold when the state is defeated in military activities with other states, thereby unleashing the mass mobilization potential of the peasants and arousing the hostility of the aristocracy. Such hostility from elites is particularly likely when the state seeks reforms in the aftermath of a military defeat and, in the process, threatens the old landed aristocracy. As a result, the state becomes vulnerable to a revolution from below by the masses or above by the upper classes that often pursue their own narrow interests (for patronage and privilege) and weaken the state's capacity to respond to revolutionary mass mobilization by peasants.

But peasants do not automatically mobilize, despite their grievances. Peasants can successfully revolt only under certain conditions: First, they must be capable of developing solidarity with each other. Second, they must have some autonomy from direct day-to-day supervision and control by landlords and their agents. Third, the state must be so weakened by its military defeats that it cannot exert effective coercive control over periodic peasant revolts (which are quite common in all agrarian societies).

The scholarly detail of Skocpol's analysis is, of course, typical of historical-comparative work in sociology, but for our purposes, we need to lay out the underlying theory. Table 14.5 reviews the key propositions. Proposition 1 in Table 14.5 examines the conditions that facilitate mass mobilization, and Proposition 2 reviews the causes of state breakdown that, in turn, allow mass mobilization to flower into a full-scale revolution.

As Proposition 1 underscores, mass mobilization of subordinates requires solidarity among them, and such solidarity increases when subordinates perceive that they have a common enemy,[12] but solidarity is reduced to the extent that subordinates must compete with each other in commercialized

---

[12]Skocpol illustrates this point in her analysis of anti-seigniorial movement among the French peasants who welded together in the resistance against the seigneurs (see *States and Social Revolutions,* pp. 123–25).

**Table 14.5**   Skocpol's Propositions on the State and Social Revolution

1. The mass mobilization of subordinates in a system of inequality increases when

   A. Subordinates can develop a sense of solidarity

      1. Solidarity is increased when subordinates can perceive that they have a common enemy

      2. Solidarity is reduced, however, when subordinates must compete with each other in a commercialized economy

   B. Subordinates have autonomy from direct supervision by superordinates

      1. Autonomy from direct supervision increases when

         a. Subordinates have control of the process of production

         b. Subordinates have organizational forms that shield them from direct supervision and control

         c. Subordinates can retain local communities insulating them from direct sanctioning, which is more likely when sanctioning systems centralized in state structures are removed from the communities of subordinates

      2. Autonomy from direct supervision decreases, however, when subordinates are structurally tied to, and hence dependent on, those who dominate them. This is related to the converse of the conditions listed under 1-B-1(a, b, c) above.

   C. Subordinates perform economic activities crucial to the well being of superordinates, thereby giving subordinates the capacity to disrupt the power of superordinates through collective actions

   D. Subordinates have organizational resources with which to pursue conflict with superordinates

2. The likelihood that the mass mobilization of subordinates will escalate into a full-scale and successful social revolution increases when

   A. The central coercive apparatus of a society is weak and cannot, therefore, suppress revolts by subordinates or power-plays by elites

      1. The weakness of the central coercive apparatus increases when the state is defeated in a war. Defeat becomes ever more likely when

         a. The military structure of the state is disintegrated and poorly organized

         b. The military has not been able to sustain its autonomy from domestic conflict and domestic intrusion

         c. The ratio of career and professional officers to noncareer and nonprofessional in the military is low

         d. The productive capacity of the economy supporting military activities is low relative to the productive capacity of enemies

*(Continued)*

(Continued)

B. The state experiences fiscal crises and cannot, therefore, finance reforms or suppress revolts by subordinates and power plays by elites

  1. The state's fiscal crises will tend to worsen when it loses a war, or remains overextended in external military activities

  2. The state's fiscal crises will deepen when the economy's productivity remains low relative to the population size to be supported

  3. The state's fiscal crises will be aggravated when the mechanisms for extracting revenues (taxes) from the members of the society are indirect and inefficient

C. The state's power relative to the dominant segments of the society decreases

  1. The state's relative power declines when the networks among elites are dense and strong

  2. The state's relative power declines when its control over the military is weakened

  3. The state's relative power declines if elite segments of the population have both short-term interests and sufficient organizational strength to prevent the state from instituting reforms that would lessen the fiscal crisis or appease subordinate segments of the population

  4. The state's relative power declines when the elite segments of the population are threatened by the state's activities, that is, when the elites fear erosion of their privileges and wealth. This sense of threat by elites increases as

     a. Elites remain dependent on the central state for their wealth, prestige, and power

     b. Elites feel that their opportunities for mobility are restricted by the state and the economic system supported by the state

     c. Elites see efforts at social reform by the state as undermining their traditional sources of power, prestige, and wealth

labor markets and other competitive mechanisms for allocating resources. Mass mobilization also requires that subordinates have some degree of autonomy from those who are supposed to regulate their activities, and this autonomy is enhanced when subordinates exert control over the processes of production, when subordinates evidence organizational structures that insulate them somewhat from direct monitoring,[13] and when subordinates can retain community structures providing additional insulation from the central sanctioning system in a society. But, this autonomy will be reduced

---

[13]According to Skocpol's analysis, this was the case with French and Russian peasants.

to the extent that subordinates are structurally interdependent with, and even more so if they are dependent on, those who dominate them. Conversely, mass mobilization is also facilitated when subordinates perform productive activities crucial to the well-being of superordinates, and this dependence of superordinates can give subordinates a sense of their own power and capacity to mobilize. Finally, following Tilly's theory of resource mobilization (see Table 14.3), the organizational resources of subordinates will influence just how extensive mass mobilization can be. When there are existing organizational forms, or the capacity to use the organizational systems of superordinates, mass mobilization becomes more likely.

Mass mobilization cannot occur, or be effective, without a weakening state power, for without a weak state, mass mobilization cannot be transformed into full-scale social revolution. One critical force is a decline in the state's coercive capacities to repress revolts by the masses and power plays by elites. This weakening of the state's coercive power follows from a defeat in an external war. Factors influencing the likelihood of defeat include the level of disintegration of the military's organizational structure,[14] the degree of the military's autonomy from resource-draining domestic conflict, the ratio of professional to nonprofessional military personnel, and most important, lower productive capacity in the economy than a state's military adversaries (ultimately the economy supports the military, so if this capacity is less than an adversary has, a war is likely to be lost).

Another force weakening the state is fiscal crisis. When the state experiences a fiscal crisis, its legitimacy is undermined and its capacity to mobilize coercive and administrative control is diminished. These financial problems will escalate when a state loses a war or remains overextended in military commitments, draining resources away from the state and its ability to control the domestic population. Fiscal crises are also aggravated when the productivity of the economy is low relative to the size of the population to be employed and supported; thus, if a population grows without a corresponding increase in productivity, a fiscal crisis will eventually ensue. Fiscal crises are further aggravated when the state's tax collection systems are indirect (such as when the monarch extracts peasants' surplus labor through elites or delegates tax collection to local governments or elites) or when the tax collection system is inefficient (when accurate records are not kept or adequate monitoring of tax collection does not occur). Thus, if the state cannot efficiently and effectively appropriate wealth, it will soon experience a fiscal crisis.

Yet another critical force weakening the state is the relative power of dominant segments of the population, especially elites. As the power of elites increases, there is a corresponding decline in the power of the state. This balance of power works against the state to the extent that elites have dense and strong network ties independent of the central authority of the

---

[14]Skocpol argues that the military disintegration in Russia during World War I was the main reason for state breakdown in Russia and the success of the 1917 Revolution that followed.

state, to the degree that the state's control over its military becomes weakened, to the extent that elites' short-term interests in maintaining their privilege prevent the state from making reforms that might quell the masses, and to the degree that elites feel threatened by the activities of the state.

In sum, then, the propositions in Table 14.5 might have broader applicability than the particular historical cases examined by Skocpol. These propositions might also help explain why revolutions are so rare, especially once the agrarian phase of a society has passed and most societies have moved into more commercial, market-driven, and industrial forms of organization. When subordinates cannot easily mobilize (because the converse of the conditions listed in Proposition I prevail) and when the state is strong, periodic revolts and riots do not as easily become transformed into full-scale social revolutions.

# Jack Goldstone's Theory of State Breakdown

Unlike other theorists examined in this chapter, Jack Goldstone did not begin with Marxian assumptions about social class relations and their inherent potential for revolutionary conflict. In his *Revolution and Rebellion in the Early Modern World*, Goldstone argued that revolutions in modernizing agrarian societies between 1640 and 1840 were caused, ultimately, by the effects of population growth.[15] As populations grow, pressures are exerted on (1) the economy to increase productivity and (2) the polity to stimulate production, expand administrative control of the population, and maintain order through coercive force. When these key institutional systems cannot make the necessary adaptations to population growth, the potential for mass mobilization of peasants and revolt by elites against the state escalates, eventually causing state breakdown. Population growth does not, however, immediately throw a society into chaos and state breakdown; rather, it can take many decades for the pressures exerted by population growth to become evident and for the masses and elites to become sufficiently disenchanted to initiate conflict.

The fundamental problem with all agrarian societies is that they typically reveal rigid institutional structures. A hereditary monarchy is usually incapable of making the reforms that are necessary to accommodate a growing population's need for economic opportunities, and the land-based aristocracy generally resists changes in the economic system that would undermine its power and privilege. This rigidity can, in the end, lead to a situation where three forces converge: (1) a fiscal crisis in which the state simply does not have enough income to sustain its activities, to initiate economic reforms, or to control the restive population; (2) severe divisions and anger among elites, many of whom cannot secure the traditional spoils of state patronage and are, as a result, downwardly mobile; and (3) mass

---

[15]Jack Goldstone, *Revolution and Rebellion in the Early Modern World* (Berkeley: University of California Press, 1991)

mobilization of peasants who cannot secure work or income. Goldstone's analysis of various empirical cases is detailed and complex, but the general model can be summarized in more abstract terms, as is done in the following discussion and in Table 14.6.

**Table 14.6**   Goldstone's Theory of State Breakdown

1. The long-term potential for state breakdown through mass mobilization of non-elites increases when

   A. Population growth generates demands among non-elites for goods and income that exceed the productive capacity of the economy

   B. Population growth exceeding the productive capacity of the economy causes rapid price inflation

   C. Population growth increases the proportion of the population in younger age cohorts whose members are potentially more violent and more easily mobilized to pursue conflict than those in older age cohorts

   D. Population growth, as it causes price inflation and overburdens the productive capacities of the economy, escalates rural misery and forces many to migrate to urban areas in search of limited or nonexistent economic opportunities

2. The long-term potential for state breakdown through mobilization of elites increases when

   A. Population growth creates a larger pool of elites who seek the state's patronage for privilege and positions

   B. Population growth, as it causes price inflation, leads to a situation where

      1. Some traditional landed elites become financially strapped and, hence, desirous of state patronage and positions to prevent their downward mobility

      2. Some upwardly mobile elites, often gaining wealth through commercial activity, seek state patronage and positions as a confirmation of their new-found station in life

   C. Population growth, because it causes price inflation coupled with other fiscal pressures on the state, makes it impossible for the state to accommodate all of the demand for elite patronage and positions

3. The long-term potential for state breakdown through fiscal crises increases when

   A. Population growth exceeds the economy's capacity to absorb and provide goods for the population, thereby creating a shortage of resources and causing price inflation

*(Continued)*

(Continued)

B. The state's mechanisms for revenue collection are inflexible and inefficient

C. The state's efforts to seek new formulas for revenue collection arouse the hostility of elites as well as that of non-elites

D. The state's expenditures on military activities exceed its ability to finance wars, especially when

   1. The state expands military activities during periods of rapid price inflation

   2. The state engages in military activities in an effort to secure more resources to overcome the effects of price inflation, thereby incurring expenses for which it cannot afford to pay

E. The state is forced to borrow funds to sustain its military and administrative activities

4. The likelihood of state breakdown increases when

   A. Mass mobilization of non-elites to pursue conflict is increasing

   B. Mobilization of segments of elites is increasing

   C. Fiscal crises within the state are escalating to the point where the state's administrative and coercive control of the masses and elites is dramatically weakened

The driving force behind state breakdown through mass mobilization of peasants and revolt by at least some segments of traditional elites is population growth. As the rate of population growth increases, several demands are placed on economic institutions. First, the economy must expand to provide a living for the growing population; this expansion is often very difficult because of the nature of feudal agrarian systems where only so many tenants can be accommodated. Second, if the economy does not expand and keep pace with population growth, then resources become scarce. As goods become scarce, price inflation ensues in accordance with the laws of supply and demand. Third, as price inflation escalates, real incomes for all workers decline, increasing the level of misery in rural areas. Fourth, as conditions in rural areas deteriorate, many peasants leave the land and migrate to urban areas in search of opportunities that, if the economy is not expanding, cannot be fully realized, thereby creating a pool of disgruntled and unemployed urban workers. Fifth, population growth also ensures that the proportion of younger age cohorts relative to cohorts of middle-aged and elderly will increase, and as their proportion increases, the young are more disposed to revolt and commit acts of violence than are older members of the society.

Sixth, population growth also affects the life chances of elites in several important ways: (a) the number of aspirants for elite positions increases; (b) price inflation dramatically affects mobility of elites, some of whom become downwardly mobile whereas others (who take advantage of commercial opportunities when demand for goods is high) become upwardly mobile; (c) the net effect of such mobility is to increase the pool of aspirants for state patronage as upwardly mobile elites aspire to new positions of privilege and influence, and downwardly mobile elites see patronage as their only hope against a worsening of their economic situation; (d) these demands for patronage increase the level of competition among elites for patronage positions, often at precisely the time the state itself is experiencing fiscal crises (ultimately caused by price inflation), thereby limiting the state's ability to meet the demand for elite patronage and, as a result, creating dissatisfaction among some segments of the elite population.

Seventh, the state's fiscal crisis will continue to mount for a number of inter-related reasons: (a) price inflation increases the costs to the state for administrators, goods and services, military personnel, and virtually all activities of the state; (b) the state might have engaged in military warfare in an effort to increase its resources because of inflation and growing demands of elites, or simply because of leaders' competition with other societies, but such military adventurism is expensive and can aggravate the fiscal crisis of the state; (c) the state often begins to borrow from elites, especially those upwardly mobile elites who have resources garnered from commercial activity, though this debt only increases the fiscal problems of the state; and (d) the state often increases tax revenues to stave off crisis, but increased taxation will antagonize some elites who are already downwardly mobile as well as many wage-earning workers who have little disposable income. If new tax revenues can be secured, this flow of money reduces the fiscal crisis even as it increases the potential for elite and mass mobilization against the state. Moreover, if the state can secure resources in the international arena via conquest or trade, it can similarly reduce the fiscal crisis and, thereby, avoid internal conflict.

The picture that Goldstone paints, then, is a series of converging forces that have been initiated by population growth. When they all come together, state breakdown becomes likely. That is, (1) if the fiscal crisis of the state is acute, (2) if elites are in intense competition with each other for position and patronage, (3) if some elites are mobilized against the state because of their downward mobility, failure to receive patronage, and increased tax burden, and (4) if the younger masses in rural estates and migrants to urban areas cannot secure sufficient income and, hence, are restive and potentially mobilized for conflict, then the convergence of these four forces leads to state breakdown as the masses and segments of the elite population mobilize to overthrow the government and as the fiscal problems of the state make it incapable of responding with sufficient administrative or coercive power to resist this two-pronged revolt by elites and masses. Table 14.6 states Goldstone's argument more abstractly so that its potential for explaining revolt in a broader range of societies can be appreciated.

# Conclusion

Historical-comparative sociology has, during the last four decades, produced some of the most scholarly and important works in sociology. Most of this work has had a theoretical bent, though always tempered by the particulars of specific empirical cases. Of particular interest to many historical-comparative sociologists has been the dynamics of power, especially as these dynamics are set into motion by conflict-producing inequalities and external conflicts with other societies. Historical-comparative sociology has, of course, examined many other substantive topics, but the most theoretical wing of this approach to sociology has tended to be most interested in conflict processes, particularly those generating social revolutions that redistribute power.

Reading the propositions in Tables 14.1 through 14.6, it is clear that the theories overlap, although each adds something new or provides a refinement to the others. The conditions producing a social revolution—the kind Marx thought to be inevitable and Weber saw as only probable—rarely converge. Some of these conditions always exist in agrarian societies, but the necessary mix of conditions producing a true revolution does not seem to have happened very often in human history. Moreover, the very conditions that generate high revolutionary potential in agrarian societies appear, on net balance, to be mitigated or eliminated in capitalist-industrial societies. Paige makes this point explicit, but it is one of the inescapable conclusions from this line of work in historical-comparative sociology. Thus, even though a good many historical-comparative sociologists have started with Marxian assumptions, they have tended to come to Weberian conclusions: Revolutions take a unique convergence of forces, even in agrarian societies where there is so much potential for conflict stemming from the high degrees of inequality. This convergence appears to be less likely in mature capitalist systems, but as we will see in the next chapter, neo-Marxist theorists continue to adapt and adjust the basic Marxian model to the present.

# PART IV

# Interactionist Theorizing

## CHAPTER 15

# The Rise of Interactionist and Phenomenological Theorizing

The first sociological theorists in Europe were concerned primarily with macro-level phenomena, but with the beginning of the twentieth century, theorists in Europe and America turned to the analysis of micro-level processes. They began to understand that the structure of society is, in some ultimate sense, created and maintained by the actions and interaction of individuals. Thus, increasingly, they sought to discover the fundamental processes of interaction among people. This burst of creative activity generated a wide range of micro-level theories that will, for the sake of simplicity, be labeled *interactionism*. The rise of interactionism also marks the beginning of American theory as an active contributor to the theoretical canon of sociology. Hence, it is appropriate that we begin with the American contribution to interactionism, turning later to the European micro-oriented tradition that emerged in the early decades of the last century.

## Early American Insights into Interaction

A philosopher at the University of Chicago, George Herbert Mead, made the great breakthrough in understanding the basic properties of human social interaction. His was not a blazing new insight but rather a synthesis of ideas that had been developed by others. Yet, without his synthesis, the study of interaction would have been greatly retarded. To appreciate Mead's genius, let me first review those from whom he drew inspiration and then explore how he pieced their ideas into a model of interaction that still serves as the basic framework for most interactionist theories.

## William James' Analysis of "Self"

The Harvard psychologist William James (1842–1910) was perhaps the first social scientist to develop a clear concept of self. James recognized that humans have the capacity to view themselves as objects and to develop self-feelings and attitudes toward themselves. Just as humans can (a) denote symbolically other people and aspects of the world around them, (b) develop attitudes and feelings toward these objects, and (c) construct typical responses toward objects, so they can denote themselves, develop self-feelings and attitudes, and construct responses toward themselves. James called these capacities *self* and recognized their importance in shaping the way people respond in the world.

James developed a typology of selves: the *material self*, which includes those physical objects that humans view as part of their being and as crucial to their identity; the *social self*, which involves the self-feelings that individuals derive from associations with other people; and the *spiritual self*, which embraces the general cognitive style and capacities typifying an individual.[1] This typology was never adopted by subsequent interactionists, but James' notion of the social self became a part of all interactionists' formulations. Moreover, within one interactionist tradition, the notion of identity has replaced the concept of self; here, just as William James sought to do, efforts to conceptualize the various types of identities that people possess have become very much a part of recent theorizing and research. So, in a different way, James' original idea—that people have multiple selves and identities—has been rediscovered, as we will see in the next chapter on identity theories in symbolic interactionism.

James' concept of the social self recognized that people's feelings about themselves arise from interaction with others. As he noted, "a man [*sic*] has as many social selves as there are individuals who recognize him."[2] Yet James did not carry this initial insight very far. He was, after all, a psychologist who was more concerned with internal psychological functioning of individuals than with the social processes from which the capacities of individuals arise.

## Charles Horton Cooley's Analysis of "Self"

Charles Horton Cooley (1864–1929) offered two significant extensions in the analysis of self.[3] First, he refined the concept of viewing self as the process in which individuals see themselves as objects, along with other objects, in their social environment. Second, he recognized that self emerges from communication with others. As individuals interact with each other, they interpret each

---

[1] William James, *The Principles of Psychology* (New York: Henry Holt, 1890), vol. 1, pp. 292–99.

[2] Ibid., p. 294.

[3] Charles Horton Cooley, *Human Nature and the Social Order* (New York: Scribner's, 1902) and *Social Organization: A Study of the Larger Mind* (New York: Scribner's, 1916).

other's gestures and thereby see themselves from the viewpoint of others. They imagine how others evaluate them, and they derive images of themselves as well as self-feelings and attitudes. Cooley termed this process *the looking glass self*: the gestures of others serve as mirrors or *looking glasses* (in nineteenth-century terminology) in which people see and evaluate themselves, just as they see and evaluate other objects in their social environment.

Cooley also recognized that self arises from interaction in-group contexts. He developed the concept of *primary group* to emphasize that participation in front of the looking glass in some groups is more important in the genesis and maintenance of self than participation in other groups. Those small groups in which personal and intimate ties exist are the most important in shaping people's self-feelings and attitudes.

Cooley thus refined and narrowed James' notion of self and forced the recognition that it arises from symbolic communication with others in-group contexts. He made the concept of self more sociological, and in so doing, his insights were to profoundly influence George Herbert Mead.

## John Dewey's Pragmatism

John Dewey (1859–1952) was, for a brief period, a colleague of Cooley's at the University of Michigan. But more important was Dewey's enduring association with George Herbert Mead, whom he brought to the University of Chicago. As the chief exponent of a school of thought known as *pragmatism*, Dewey stressed the process of human adjustment to the world in which humans constantly seek to master the conditions of their environment. Thus, the unique characteristics of humans arise from the process of adjusting and adapting to their life conditions.

What is unique to humans, Dewey argued, is their capacity for thinking, or *mind*. Mind is not a structure but *a process* that emerges from humans' efforts to adjust to their environment. Mind for Dewey is the process of (a) denoting objects in the environment, (b) ascertaining potential lines of conduct, (b) imagining the consequences of pursuing each line, (c) inhibiting inappropriate responses, and then, (d) selecting a line of conduct that will facilitate adjustment. Mind is thus the process of thinking, which involves deliberation:

> Deliberation is a dramatic rehearsal (in imagination) of various competing possible lines of action. . . . Deliberation is an experiment in finding out what the various lines of possible action are really like. It is an experiment in making various combinations of selected elements . . . to see what the resultant action would be like if it were entered upon.[4]

---

[4]John Dewey, *Human Nature and Human Conduct* (New York: Henry Holt, 1922), p. 190. For an earlier statement of these ideas, see John Dewey, *Psychology* (New York: Harper & Row, 1886).

Dewey's conception of mind as a process of adjustment rather than as a thing or entity was critical in shaping Mead's thoughts. Much as Cooley had done for the concept of self, Dewey demonstrated that mind emerges and is sustained through interactions in the social world.

## Pragmatism, Darwinism, and Behaviorism in Mead's Thought

At the time that Mead began to formulate his synthesis, the convergence of several broad intellectual traditions was crucial because it appears to have influenced the direction of his thought. Mead considered himself a *behaviorist*, but not the mechanical stimulus/response type where conceptions of the black box of human cognition were excluded in favor of only observable stimuli and observable responses to such stimuli. For extreme behaviorists, only what is observable could be theorized. Many of Mead's ideas actually were intended as a refutation of such prominent behaviorists as John B. Watson. Mead accepted the basic premise of behaviorism—that is, the view that reinforcement guides and directs action (see Chapter 21 on the rise of exchange theory for more detail on behaviorist arguments). However, he used this principle in a novel way. Moreover, he rejected as untenable the methodological presumption of early behaviorism that it was inappropriate to study the internal dynamics of the human mind. James', Cooley's, and Dewey's influence ensured that Mead would rework the principle of reinforcement in ways that allowed for the consideration of mind and self.

Another strain of thought that shaped Mead's synthesis is *pragmatism*, as it was acquired through exposure with Dewey. Pragmatism sees organisms as practical creatures that come to terms with the actual conditions of the world. Coupled with behaviorism, pragmatism offered a new way of viewing human life: Human beings seek to cope with their actual conditions, and they learn those behavioral patterns that provide gratification. The most important type of gratification is adjustment or adaptation to social contexts.

This argument was buttressed in Mead's synthesis by yet another related intellectual tradition, *Darwinism*. Mead recognized that humans are organisms seeking a niche in which they can adapt. Historically, this was true of humans as an evolving species; more importantly, it is true of humans as they discover a niche in the social world and seek to adjust and adapt to the conditions of this social niche. Mead's commitment to behaviorism and pragmatism thus allowed him to apply the basic principle of Darwinian theory to each human: That which facilitates survival or adaptation of the organism to its environment will be retained in its behavioral repertoire.

In this way, behaviorist, pragmatist, and Darwinian principles blended into an image of humans as attempting to adjust to the world around them and as retaining those behavioral capacities—particularly for mind and self—that enable them to adapt to their surroundings. Mind, self, and other unique features of humans evolve from efforts to survive in the social environment. They are thus capacities that arise from the processes of coping, adjusting, adapting, and achieving the ultimate gratification or reinforcement: survival. For this reason, Mead's analysis emphasizes the processes by which the infant organism acquires mind and self as an adaptation to society. But Mead did much more; he showed how society is viable only from the capacities for mind and self among individuals. From Mead's perspective, the capacities for mind, self, and society are intimately connected.

## George Herbert Mead's Synthesis

The names of James, Cooley, and Dewey figure prominently in the development of interactionism, but Mead brought their related concepts together into a coherent theoretical perspective that linked the emergence of the human mind, the social self, and the structure of society to the process of social interaction.[5] Mead appears to have begun his synthesis with two basic assumptions: (1) the biological frailty of human organisms forces their cooperation with one another in group contexts in order to survive, and (2) those actions within and among human organisms that facilitate their cooperation, and hence, their survival or adjustment will be retained as part of the behavioral repertoire of the organism. Starting from these assumptions, Mead drew from the ideas of other scholars to explain how mind, the social self, and society arise and are sustained through interaction.

**Mind**. Following Dewey's lead, Mead recognized that the unique feature of the human mind is its capacity to (1) use symbols to designate objects in the environment, (2) rehearse covertly alternative lines of action toward these objects, and (3) inhibit inappropriate lines of action and select a proper course of overt action. Again, borrowing from Dewy, Mead termed this process of using symbols or language covertly a process of *imaginative rehearsal*, revealing his conception of mind as a process rather than as a structure. Further, the existence and persistence of society, or cooperation in organized groups, were viewed by Mead as dependent on this capacity of

---

[5]Mead's most important sociological ideas can be found in the published lecture notes of his students. His most important exposition of interactionism is found in his *Mind, Self, and Society*, ed. C. W. Morris (Chicago: University of Chicago Press, 1934). Other useful sources include *George Herbert Mead, Selected Writings* (Indianapolis: Bobbs-Merrill, 1964) and Anselm Strauss, ed., *George Herbert Mead on Social Psychology* (Chicago: University of Chicago Press, 1964). For excellent secondary sources on the thought of Mead, see Tamotsu Shibutani, *Society and Personality: An Interactionist Approach* (Englewood Cliffs, NJ: Prentice Hall, 1962); Anselm Strauss, *Mirrors and Masks: The Search for Identity* (Glencoe, IL: Free Press, 1959); Bernard N. Meltzer, "Mead's Social Psychology," in *The Social Psychology of George Herbert Mead* (Ann Arbor, MI: Center for Sociological Research, 1964), pp. 10–31; Jonathan H. Turner, "Returning to Social Physics: Illustrations from George Herbert Mead," *Perspectives in Social Theory* 2 (1981) and *A Theory of Social Interaction* and *Face-to-Face* (Stanford, CA: Stanford University Press, 1988 and 2002, respectively). For a more global overview of Mead's ideas, see John D. Baldwin, *George Herbert Mead: A Unifying Theory for Sociology* (Beverly Hills, CA: Sage, 1986).

humans to imaginatively rehearse lines of action toward one another and thereby select those behaviors that facilitate cooperation.

Much of Mead's analysis focused not so much on the mind of mature organisms as on how this capacity first develops in individuals. Unless mind emerges in infants, neither society nor self can exist. In accordance with principles of behaviorism, Darwinism, and pragmatism, Mead stressed that mind arises from a selective process in which an infant's initially wide repertoire of random gestures is narrowed, as some gestures bring favorable reactions from those on whom the infant depends for survival. This selection of gestures facilitating adjustment can occur either through trial and error or through conscious coaching by those with whom the infant must cooperate. Eventually, through either of these processes, gestures come to have common meanings for both the infant and those in its environment. With this development, gestures now denote the same objects and carry similar disposition for all the parties to an interaction. Gestures that have such common meanings are termed *conventional gestures* by Mead. These conventional gestures have increased efficiency for interaction among individuals because they allow more precise communication of desires and wants as well as intended courses of action—thereby increasing the capacity of organisms to adjust to one another.

The ability to use and to interpret conventional gestures with common meanings represents a significant step in the development of mind, self, and society. By perceiving and interpreting gestures, humans can now assume the perspective (dispositions, needs, wants, and propensities to act) of those with whom they must cooperate for survival. By reading and then interpreting covertly conventional gestures, individuals can imaginatively rehearse alternative lines of action that will facilitate adjustment to others. Thus, by being able to put oneself in another's place, or in Mead's phrasing, to "take the role of the other" or *role-take*, the covert rehearsal of action reaches a new level of efficiency, because actors can better gauge the consequences of their actions for others and thereby increase the probability of cooperative interaction.

Thus, when an organism develops the capacity (1) to understand conventional gestures, (2) to employ these gestures to take the role of others, and (3) to imaginatively rehearse alternative lines of action, Mead believed that such an organism possesses the behavioral capacity for *mind*.

**Self**. Drawing from James and Cooley, Mead stressed that, just as humans can designate symbolically other actors in the environment, so they can symbolically represent themselves as objects. The interpretation of conventional gestures during the normal process of interaction not only facilitates human cooperation but it also serves as the basis for self-assessment and evaluation. This capacity to derive images of oneself as an object of evaluation in interaction depends on the behavioral capacities of mind to use conventional gestures, to role-take with others, and to covertly assess alternative lines of conduct.

Following Cooley's lead, Mead emphasized that as humans mature, the transitory *self-images* derived from specific others in each interactive situation eventually become crystallized into a more or less stabilized *self-conception* of oneself as a certain type of object. With these self-conceptions, individuals' actions take on consistency, because they are now mediated through a coherent and stable set of attitudes, dispositions, or meanings *about oneself* as a certain type of person.

Mead chose to highlight three stages in the development of self, each stage marking not only a change in the kinds of transitory self-images an individual can derive from role taking but also an increasing crystallization of a more stabilized self-conception. The initial stage of role taking in which self-images can be derived is termed *play*. In play, infant organisms are capable of assuming the perspective of only a limited number of others, at first only one or two others. Later, by virtue of biological maturation and practice at role taking, the maturing organism becomes capable of taking the role of several others engaged in organized activity. Mead termed this stage the *game* because it designates the capacity to derive multiple self-images from, and to cooperate with, a group of individuals engaged in some coordinated activity. (Mead typically illustrated this stage by giving the example of a baseball game in which all individuals must symbolically assume the role of all others on the team to participate effectively.) The final stage in the development of self occurs when an individual can *take the role of the generalized other* or "community of attitudes" evident in a society. At this stage, individuals are seen as capable of assuming the overall perspective of a community, or general beliefs, values, and norms. This means that humans can both (1) increase the appropriateness of their responses to other with whom they must interact and (2) expand their evaluative self-images from the expectations of specific others to the standards and perspective of the broader community. Thus, it is this ever-increasing capacity to take roles with an ever-expanding body of others that marks the stages in the development of self.

**Society**. Mead believed society or institutions represent the organized and patterned interactions among diverse individuals.[6] The organization of interactions depends on the behavioral abilities of mind. Without the capacities of mind to take roles and imaginatively rehearse alternative lines of activity, individuals could not coordinate their activities. The immediate effect of such role taking lies in the *control* that the individuals are able to exercise over their responses. Social control of actions of the individuals can take place in the behavioral capacities of individuals through role taking. Thus, the most effective social control is

---

[6]For a more detailed analysis, see Jonathan H. Turner, "A Note on G. H. Mead's Behavioristic Theory of Social Structure," *Journal for the Theory of Social Behavior* 12 (July 1982): pp. 213–22 as well as *Face-to-Face* (cited in note 5) and *Theoretical Principles in Sociology, Volume 2 on Microdynamics* (New York: Springer, 2010).

self-control as individuals role-take with others in organized social contexts as well as with generalized others, using the information gleaned to engage in both self-control and self-evaluation.[7]

This process of self-control underscores the fact society, as Mead's label patterns of social organization, depends on the capacities of self, especially the process of evaluating oneself from the perspective of the generalized other. Without the ability to see and evaluate oneself as an object from this community of attitudes, social control would rest solely on self-evaluations derived from role taking with specific and immediately present others—thus making coordination of diverse activities among larger groups extremely difficult.[8]

Although Mead was vitally concerned with how society and its institutions are maintained and perpetuated by the capacities of mind and self, these concepts also allowed him to view society as constantly in flux and rife with potential change. Role taking and imaginative rehearsal are ongoing processes among the participants in any interaction situation and give individuals opportunities for adjusting and readjusting their responses. Furthermore, the insertion of self as an object into the interactive process underscores that the outcome of interaction will be affected by the ways in which self-conceptions alter the initial reading of gestures and the subsequent rehearsal of alternative lines of behavior. Such a perspective thus emphasizes that social organization is both perpetuated by and altered through the adaptive capacities of mind and the mediating impact of self:

> Thus the institutions of society are organized forms of group or social activity—forms so organized that the individual members of society can act adequately and socially by taking the attitudes of others toward these activities. . . . [But] there is no necessary or inevitable reason why social institutions should be oppressive or rigidly conservative, or why they should not rather be, as many are, flexible and progressive, fostering individuality rather than discouraging it.[9]

This passage contains a clue to Mead's abiding distaste for rigid and oppressive patterns of social organization. He viewed society as a constructed phenomenon that arises from the cooperative interactions among individuals. As such, society can be altered or reconstructed through the processes denoted by the concepts of mind and self. However, Mead went one step further and stressed that change is frequently unpredictable, even by those emitting the change-inducing behavior. To account for this

---

[7]Mead, *Mind, Self, and Society* (cited in note 5), p. 254.

[8]Ibid., pp. 256–57.

[9]Ibid., pp. 261–62.

indeterminacy of action, Mead used two concepts first developed by James: the *I* and the *me*.[10] For Mead, the *I* points to the impulsive tendencies of individuals, and the *Me* represents the self-image of behavior after it has been emitted. With these concepts Mead emphasized that the *I*, or impulsive behavior, cannot be completely predicted because the individual can only "know in experience" (the *Me*) what has actually transpired and what the consequences of the *I* have been. As a result, interaction is also a constant process of *I-Me interchanges*; individuals behave (*I*), then derive feedback about what they have done (*Me*), make behavioral adjustments (*I*) on the basis of this feedback through their capacities for self and mind, derive more feedback on the effects of these adjustments (*Me*), only to make further behavioral adjustments, and so on in a cycle of I-Me interaction that endures during the course of interaction and often in the thoughts of persons after the interaction has been terminated. Humans are, then, locked into these I-Me cycles; they are part of the processes inherent in mind, self, and society.

In sum, Mead believes society represents those constructed patterns of coordinated activity that are maintained by, and changed through, symbolic interaction among and within actors. Both the maintenance and the change of society, therefore, occur through the processes of mind and self. Although many of the interactions causing both stability and change in groups are viewed by Mead as predictable, the possibility for spontaneous and unpredictable actions that alter existing patterns of interaction is also likely.

This conceptual legacy had a profound impact on a generation of American sociologists before the posthumous publication of Mead's lectures in 1934 in a book titled *Mind, Self, and Society*. Yet, despite the suggestiveness of Mead's concepts, they failed to address some important theoretical issues. The most important of these issues concerns the vagueness of his concepts in denoting the nature of social organization or society and the precise points of articulation between society and the individual. Mead viewed society as organized activity, regulated by the generalized other, in which individuals make adjustments and cooperate with one another. Such adjustments and the cooperation are seen as possible by virtue of the capacities of mind and self. Whereas mind and self emerged from existent patterns of social organization, the maintenance or change of such organization was viewed by Mead as a reflection of the processes of mind and self. Yet, Mead did not have a well-developed conception of what structure is, nor do his ideas fully capture the properties of social structures, even at the micro level of face-to-face interaction, to say anything of more macro sociocultural formations. Thus, it is not surprising that other American scholars sought to conceptualize structure with somewhat more precision than provided by Mead's great synthesis.

---

[10]See James, *The Principles of Psychology* (cited in note 1), pp. 135–76.

## Conceptualizing Structure

Though Mead's synthesis provided the initial conceptual breakthrough, it did not satisfactorily resolve the problem of how participation in the structure of society shaped individual conduct, and vice versa. In an effort to resolve this vagueness, sociological inquiry began to focus on the concept of *role*. Individuals were seen as playing roles associated with positions in larger networks of positions. With this vision, efforts to understand more about social structures and how individuals are implicated in them intensified during the 1920s and 1930s. This line of inquiry became known as *role theory*, which I will examine in Chapter 17.

**Robert Park's Role Theory**. Robert Park, who came to the University of Chicago near the end of Mead's career, was one of the first to extend Mead's ideas through an emphasis on roles. As Park observed, "everybody is always and everywhere, more or less consciously, playing a role."[11] But Park stressed that roles are linked to structural positions in society and that self is intimately linked to playing roles within the confines of the positions of social structure:

> The conceptions which men form of themselves seem to depend upon their vocations, and in general upon the role they seek to play in communities and social groups in which they live, as well as upon the recognition and status which society accords them in these roles. It is status, i.e., recognition by the community, that confers upon the individual the character of a person, since a person is an individual who has status, not necessarily legal, but social.[12]

Park's analysis stressed that self emerges from the multiple roles that people play.[13] In turn, roles are connected to positions in social structures. This kind of analysis shifts attention to the nature of society and how its structure influences the processes outlined in Mead's synthesis.

**Jacob Moreno's Role Theory**. Inspired in part by Mead's concept of role taking and by his own earlier studies in Europe, Jacob Moreno who immigrated to the United States, was one of the first to develop the concept of

---

[11]Robert E. Park, "Behind Our Masks," *Survey Graphic* 56 (May 1926): p. 135. For a convenient summary of the thrust of early research efforts in role theory, see Ralph H. Turner, "Social Roles: Sociological Aspects," *International Encyclopedia of the Social Sciences* (New York: Macmillan, 1968) as well as his "Role Theory" in *Handbook of Sociological Theory*, ed. J. H. Turner (Kluwer Academic/Plenum, 2001), pp. 223–54.

[12]Robert E. Park, *Society* (New York: Free Press, 1955), pp. 285–86.

[13]Indeed, Park studied briefly with Simmel in Berlin and apparently acquired insight into Simmel's study of the individual and the web of group affiliations (see later discussion). Coupled with his exposure to William James at Harvard, who also stressed the multiple sources of self, it is clear that Mead's legacy was supplemented by Simmel and James through the work of Robert Park.

*role playing.* In *Who Shall Survive?* and in many publications in the journals that he founded in America, Moreno began to view social organization as a network of roles that constrain and channel behavior.[14] In his early works, Moreno distinguished different types of roles: (a) *psychosomatic roles*, in which behavior is related to basic biological needs, as conditioned by culture, and in which role enactment is typically unconscious; (b) *psychodramatic roles*, in which individuals behave in accordance with the specific expectations of a particular social context; and (c) *social roles*, in which individuals conform to the more general expectations of various conventional social categories (for example, worker, Christian, mother, and father).

Despite the suggestiveness of these distinctions, their importance comes not so much from their substantive content as from their intent: to conceptualize social structures as organized networks of expectations that require varying types of role enactments by individuals. In this way, analysis can move beyond the vague Meadian conceptualization of society as coordinated activity regulated by the generalized other to a conceptualization of social organization as various types of interrelated role enactments regulated by varying types of expectations.

**Ralph Linton's Role Theory.** Shortly after Moreno's publication of *Who Shall Survive?*, the anthropologist Ralph Linton further conceptualized the nature of social organization, and the individual's embeddedness in it, by distinguishing among the concepts of *role*, *status*, and *individuals*:

> A status, as distinct from the individual who may occupy it, is simply a collection of rights and duties. . . . A role represents the dynamic aspect of status. The individual is socially assigned to a status and occupies it with relation to other statuses. When he puts the rights and duties which constitute the status into effect, he is performing a role.[15]

This passage contains several important conceptual distinctions. Social structure reveals several distinct elements: (a) a network of status positions, (b) a corresponding system of expectations attached to these positions, and (c) a set of individual behaviors that are enacted to meet the expectations of particular networks of interrelated positions. In retrospect, these distinctions might appear self-evident and trivial, but they made possible the subsequent elaboration of many interactionist concepts:

1. Linton's distinctions allow us to conceptualize society as a clear-cut variable: the nature and kinds of interrelations among positions and the types of expectations attending these positions.

---

[14]Jacob Moreno, *Who Shall Survive?* (Washington, DC: 1934); rev. ed. (New York: Beacon House, 1953).

[15]Ralph Linton, *The Study of Man* (New York: Appleton-Century-Crofts, 1936), p. 28.

2. The variables Mead denoted by the concepts of mind and self can be analytically distinguished from both social structure (status positions and expectations) and behavior (role enactment).

3. By conceptually separating the processes of role taking and imaginative rehearsal from both social structure and behavior, the points of articulation between society and the individual can be more clearly marked, because role taking denotes the process of interpreting the expectations attached to networks of statuses and role denotes the enactment of these expectations as mediated by self.

Thus, by offering more conceptual insight into the nature of social organization, Park, Moreno, and Linton provided a needed supplement to Mead's suggestive concepts. Now, it would be possible to understand more precisely the interrelations among mind, self, and society.

# Early European Insights

## Georg Simmel's Analysis of Interaction

Georg Simmel was perhaps the first European sociologist to begin a serious exploration of interaction, or *sociability* as he called it. In so doing, he elevated the study of interaction from the taken-for-granted.[16] For Simmel, as for the first generation of American sociologists in Chicago, the macrostructures and processes studied by functional and some conflict theories—class, the state, family, religion, evolution—are ultimately reflections of the specific interactions among people. These interactions result in emergent social phenomena, but considerable insight into these emergent phenomena can be attained by understanding the basic interactive processes that first give them, and then sustain, their existence.

In Chapter 10, Simmel's analysis of the forms of conflict (and, in Chapter 21, his exchange theory) are summarized. But Simmel's study of interaction extends beyond just the analysis of conflict and exchange; he was also concerned with understanding the forms and consequences of many diverse types of interactions. Some of his most important insights, which influenced American interactionists, concern the relationship between the individual and society. In his famous essay on the web of group affiliations, for example, Simmel emphasized that human personality emerges from, and is shaped by, the particular configuration of a person's group affiliations.[17] What people are—that is, how they think of themselves and are prepared to act—is circumscribed by their group memberships. As he emphasized, "the genesis of the personality [is] the

[16]Georg Simmel, "Sociability," in *The Sociology of Georg Simmel*, ed. K. H. Wolff (New York: Free Press, 1950), pp. 40–57.

[17]Georg Simmel, *Conflict and the Web of Group Affiliations*, trans. R. Bendix (Glencoe, IL: Free Press, 1955; originally published in 1922).

point of intersection for innumerable social influences, as the end-product of heritages derived from the most diverse groups and periods of adjustment."[18]

Although Simmel did not analyze the emergence of human personality in great detail, his formal sociology did break away from the macro concerns of early German, French, and British sociologists. He began in Europe a mode of analysis that became the prime concern of the first generation of American sociologists. Simmel thus could be considered one of the first European interactionists.

## Émile Durkheim's Metamorphosis

In *Division of Labor in Society*, Émile Durkheim portrayed social reality as an emergent phenomenon sui generis and as not reducible to the psychic states of individuals. Yet, in his later works, such as *The Elementary Forms of the Religious Life*, Durkheim began to ask: How does society rule the individual? How is it that society "gets inside" individuals and guides them from within? Why do people share common orientations and perspectives?[19] Durkheim never answered these questions effectively because his earlier emphasis on social structures prevented him from seeing the micro reality of interactions among individuals implicated in macro social structures. But it is significant that the most forceful advocate of the sociologistic position—that is, the subject matter of sociology cannot be reduced to the psychology of individuals—became intrigued with the relationship between the individual and society. Two critical lines of interactionist thought emerged from *Elementary Forms*: (1) the analysis of ritual and (2) the concern with categories of thought. Each of these is outlined below.

1. As Durkheim became interested in the ultimate basis of social solidarity, he turned to the analysis of religion in simple societies. From his reading of secondary accounts on aborigines in Australia, he concluded in *Elementary Forms* that religious worship is, actually, the worship of society, a worship that is sustained by imputing a sacredness to the force of society as it constrains its members and that is emotionally charged by the enactment of rituals. Thus, the basic behavioral mechanism by which solidarity is created and sustained, Durkheim argued, is the enactment of rituals that focus people's attention, arouse emotions, and create a common sense of solidarity. Durkheim never pursued the implications of this insight for the study of interaction, but later theorists began to recognize that interpersonal rituals are a key mechanism for creating and sustaining patterns of interaction. And some even asserted that the ultimate bases of macrostructures are

---

[18]Ibid., p. 141.

[19]Émile Durkheim, *The Elementary Forms of the Religious Life* (New York: Free Press, 1954; originally published in 1912).

chains of interaction rituals—a line of argument that was later pursued by modern American theorists.[20]

2. The concern with the categories of the human can be found throughout *Elementary Forms* also influenced social theory in the contemporary era. Durkheim emphasized that "the collective conscience" is not "entirely outside us" and that people's definitions of, and orientations to, situations are related to the organization of subjective consciousness. The categories of this consciousness, however, reflect the structural arrangements of society. Hence, varying macrostructures generate different forms of thought and perception of the world. Such forms feed back and reinforce social structures.

The first line of thought exerted considerable influence in interactionist thinking, whereas the second formed the core idea behind much *structuralist* social theory (see Chapters in Part VI on structuralism). Although Durkheim's ideas on ritual and categories of thought were never as rigorously or systematically developed as his earlier work on macro processes (see Chapter 2 on the rise of functionalism), these were perhaps his most original ideas.

## Max Weber's Analysis of "Social Action"

Max Weber was also becoming increasingly concerned with the micro social world later in his career, although his most important insights were in macro and historical sociology. Yet Weber's definition of sociology was highly compatible with the flourishing American school of interactionism. For Weber, sociology is "that science which aims at the interpretative understanding of social behavior in order to gain an explanation of its causes, its course, and its effects."[21] Moreover, the behavior to be studied by sociology is seen by Weber as social action that includes:

All human behavior when and insofar as the acting individual attaches a subjective meaning to it. Action in this sense may be overt, purely inward, or subjective; it may consist of positive intervention in a situation, of deliberately refraining from such intervention, or passively acquiescing in the situation. Action is social insofar as by virtue of the subjective meaning attached to it by the acting individual (or individuals), it takes account of the behavior of others and is thereby oriented in its course.[22]

---

[20]Randall Collins develops this idea in *Conflict Sociology* (New York: Academic, 1975) and Interaction Ritual Chains (Princeton, NJ: Princeton University Press, 2004). But perhaps the most significant adoption of Durkheim's emphasis on ritual was by the late Erving Goffman, the subject of Chapter 19.

[21]Max Weber, *Basic Concepts in Sociology* (New York: Citadel, 1964), p. 29.

[22]Max Weber, *The Theory of Social and Economic Organization* (New York: Free Press, 1947; originally published after Weber's death), p. 88.

Thus, Weber recognized that the reality behind the macrostructures of society—classes, the state, institutions, and nations—are built from, reproduced through, and changed by the micro-level interactions among people. Moreover, Weber's methodology stresses the need for understanding macrostructures and processes "at the level of meaning." In the real world, actors interpret and give meaning to the reality around them and act on the basis of these meanings. Yet, despite this key insight, Weber's actual analysis of social structures—class, status, party, change, religion, bureaucracy, and the like—rarely follows his own methodological prescriptions. As with other European thinkers, he tended to focus on social and cultural structures and the impact of these structures on one another. The interacting and interpreting person is often lost amid Weber's elaborate taxonomies of structures and analyses of historical events. This failing attracted the attention of Alfred Schutz who, more than any other European thinker, translated phenomenology into a perspective that could be incorporated into interactionist theory.

## European Phenomenology

Phenomenology began as the project of the German philosopher Edmund Husserl (1859–1938).[23] In his hands, this project showed few signs of being anything more than an orgy of subjectivism.[24] The German social thinker Alfred Schutz, however, took Husserl's concepts and transformed them into an interactionist analysis that has exerted considerable influence on modern-day interactionism. Schutz's migration to the United States in 1939 facilitated this translation, especially as he came into contact with American interactionism, but his most important ideas were formulated before he immigrated. His subsequent work in America involved an elaboration of basic ideas originally developed in Europe.

**Edmund Husserl's Project**. Husserl's ideas have been selectively borrowed and used in ways that he would not have condoned to develop modern phenomenology and various forms of interactionist thought. In reviewing

---

[23]For some readable, general references on phenomenology, see George Psathas, ed., *Phenomenological Sociology* (New York: Wiley, 1973); Richard M. Zaner, *The Way of Phenomenology: Criticism as a Philosophical Discipline* (New York: Pegasus, 1970); Peter L. Berger and Thomas Luckman, *The Social Construction of Reality* (Garden City, NY: Doubleday, 1966); Herbert Spiegelberg, *The Phenomenological Movement*, vols. 1 and 2, 2nd ed. (The Hague: Martinus Nijhoff, 1969); Hans P. Neisser, "The Phenomenological Approach in Social Science," *Philosophy and Phenomenological Research* 20 (1959): pp. 198–212; Stephen Strasser, *Phenomenology and the Human Sciences* (Pittsburgh: Duquesne University Press, 1963); Maurice Natanson, ed., *Phenomenology and the Social Sciences* (Evanston, IL: Northwestern University Press, 1973); and Quentin Lauer, *Phenomenology: Its Genesis and Prospect* (New York: Harper Torchbooks, 1965).

[24]Zygmunt Bauman, "On the Philosophical Status of Ethnomethodology," *Sociological Review* 21 (February 1973), p. 6.

Husserl's contribution, therefore, it is best to focus more on what was borrowed than on the details of his complete philosophical scheme. With this goal in mind, several features of his work can be highlighted: (1) the basic philosophical dilemma, (2) the properties of consciousness, (3) the critique of naturalistic empiricism, and (4) the philosophical alternative to social science.[25] These are briefly reviewed below.

1. Basic questions confronting all inquiry are: What is real? What actually exists in the world? How is it possible to know what exists? For the philosopher Husserl, these are central questions that required attention. Husserl reasoned that humans know about the world only through experience. All notions of an external world, "out there," are mediated through the senses and can be known only through mental consciousness. The existence of other people, values, norms, and physical objects is always mediated by experiences as these register on people's conscious awareness. One does not directly have contact with reality; contact is always indirect and mediated through the processes of the human mind.

Because the process of consciousness is so important and central to knowledge, philosophic inquiry must first attempt to understand how this process operates and how it influences human affairs. This concern with the process of consciousness—or how experience creates a sense of external reality—became the central concern of phenomenology.

2. Husserl initially made reference to the "world of the natural attitude." Later he used the phrase *lifeworld*. In either case, with these concepts he emphasized that humans operate in a taken-for-granted world that permeates their mental life. It is the world that humans sense to exist. It is composed of the objects, people, places, ideas, and other things that people see and perceive as setting the parameters for their existence, for their activities, and for their pursuits.

This lifeworld or world of the natural attitude is reality for humans. Two features of Husserl's conception of natural attitude influenced modern interactionist thought: (a) The lifeworld is taken for granted. It is rarely the topic of reflective thought, and yet, it structures and shapes the way people act and think. (b) Humans operate on the presumption that they experience

---

[25]Husserl's basic ideas are contained in the following: *Phenomenology and the Crisis of Western Philosophy* (New York: Harper & Row, 1965; originally published in 1936); *Ideas: General Introduction to Pure Phenomenology* (London: Collier-Macmillan, 1969; originally published in 1913); and "Phenomenology," in *The Encyclopedia Britannica*, 14th ed., vol. 17, col. 699–702, 1929. For excellent secondary analyses, see Helmut R. Wagner, "The Scope of Phenomenological Sociology," in *Phenomenological Sociology*, ed. G. Psathas, pp. 61–86 and "Husserl and Historicism," Social Research 39 (Winter 1972): pp. 696–719; Aron Gurwitsch, "The Common-Sense World as Social Reality," *Social Research* 29 (Spring 1962): pp. 50–72; Robert J. Antonio, "Phenomenological Sociology," in *Sociology: A Multiple Paradigm Science*, ed. G. Ritzer (Boston: Allyn & Bacon, 1975), pp. 109–12; Robert Welsh Jordan, "Husserl's Phenomenology as an 'Historical Science,'" *Social Research* 35 (Summer 1968): pp. 245–59.

the same world. Because people experience only their own consciousness, they have little capacity to directly determine if this presumption is correct. Yet people act as if they experienced a common world.

Human activity, then, is conducted in a lifeworld that is taken for granted and that is presumed to be experienced collectively. This brought Husserl back to his original problem: How do humans break out of their lifeworld and ascertain what is real? If people's lifeworld structures their consciousness and their actions, how is an objective science of human behavior and organization possible? These questions led Husserl to criticize what he termed naturalistic science.

3. Science assumes that a factual world exists, independent of, and external to, human senses and consciousness. Through the scientific method, this factual world can be directly known. With successive efforts at its measurement, increasing understanding of its properties can be ascertained. But Husserl challenged this vision of science: if one can know only through consciousness and if consciousness is structured by an implicit lifeworld, then how can objective measurement of some external and real world be possible? How can science measure objectively an external world when the only world that individuals experience is the lifeworld of their consciousness?

4. Husserl's solution to this problem is a philosophical one. He advocated what he termed the search for the *essence of consciousness*. To understand social events, the basic process through which these events are mediated— that is, consciousness—must be comprehended. The substantive content of consciousness, or the lifeworld, is not what is important; rather, the abstract properties of consciousness per se are to be the topics of philosophic inquiry.

Husserl advocated what he termed the radical abstraction of the individual from interpersonal experience. Investigators must suspend their natural attitude and seek to understand the fundamental processes of consciousness per se. One must discover, in Husserl's words, "Pure Mind." To do this, it is necessary to perform "epoch"—that is, to see if the substance of one's lifeworld can be suspended. Only when divorced from the substance of the lifeworld can the fundamental and abstract properties of consciousness be exposed and understood. With understanding of these properties, real insight into the nature of reality would be possible. If all that humans know is presented through consciousness, it is necessary to understand the nature of consciousness in abstraction from the specific substance or content of the lifeworld.

Husserl was not advocating Weber's method of *verstehen*, or sympathetic introspection into an investigator's own mind. Nor was Husserl suggesting the unstructured and intuitive search for people's definitions of situations. These methods would, he argued, only produce data on the substance of the lifeworld and would be no different than the structured measuring instruments of positivism. Rather, Husserl's goal was to create an abstract theory of consciousness that bracketed out, or suspended, any presumption of "an external social world out there." Not surprisingly, Husserl's philosophical doctrine failed. He never succeeded in developing an abstract theory of consciousness, radically abstracted from the lifeworld. But his ideas set into motion a new line of thought that became the basis for modern phenomenology and for its elaboration into ethnomethodology and other forms of theory.

**Alfred Schutz's Phenomenological Interactionism.** Alfred Schutz (1899–1959) migrated to the United States in 1939 from Austria, after spending a year in Paris. With his interaction in American intellectual circles and the translation of his early works into English, Schutz's contribution to sociological theorizing has become increasingly recognized.[26] This contribution resided in his ability to blend Husserl's radical phenomenology with Weber's action theory and American interactionism (Chapter 16). This blend, in turn, stimulated the further development of phenomenology, the emergence of ethnomethodology (Chapter 20), and the refinement of other interactionist theoretical perspectives.

Schutz's work began with a critique of his compatriot Weber, who employed the concept of social action in his many and varied inquiries.[27] Social action occurs when actors are consciously aware of each other and attribute meanings to their common situation. For Weber, then, a science of society must seek to understand social reality "at the level of meaning." Sociological inquiry must penetrate people's consciousness and discover how they view, define, and see the world. Weber advocated the method of *verstehen*, or sympathetic introspection. Investigators must become sufficiently involved in situations to be able to get inside the subjective world of actors. Causal and statistical analysis of complex social structures would be incomplete and inaccurate without such *verstehen* analysis.

Schutz's first major work addressed Weber's conception of action. Schutz's analysis is critical and detailed, and need not be summarized here, except to note that the basic critique turns on Weber's failure to use his *verstehen* method and to explore why, and *through what processes*, actors come to share common meanings. In Schutz's eye, Weber simply assumed that actors share subjective meanings, leading Schutz to ask: Why and how do actors come to acquire common subjective states in a situation? How do they create a common view of the world? This is the problem of *intersubjectivity*, and it is central to Schutz's intellectual scheme.

---

[26]For the basic ideas of Alfred Schutz, see his *The Phenomenology of the Social World* (Evanston, IL: Northwestern University Press, 1967; originally published in 1932); *Collected Papers*, vols. 1, 2, 3 (The Hague: Martinus Nijhoff, 1964, 1970, and 1971, respectively). For excellent secondary analyses, see Maurice Natanson, "Alfred Schutz on Social Reality and Social Science," *Social Research* 35 (Summer 1968): pp. 217–44.

[27]Schutz, *The Phenomenology of the Social World* (cited in note 26).

Schutz departed immediately from Husserl's strategy of holding the individual in radical abstraction and of searching for "Pure Mind" or the abstract laws of consciousness. He accepted Husserl's notion that humans hold a natural attitude and lifeworld that is taken for granted and that shapes who they are and what they will do. He also accepted Husserl's notion that people perceive that they share the same lifeworld and act *as if* they lived in a common world of experiences and sensations. Moreover, Schutz acknowledged the power of Husserl's argument that social scientists cannot know about an external social world out there independently of their own lifeworld.[28]

Having accepted these lines of thought from Husserl, however, Schutz advocated Weber's strategy of sympathetic introspection into people's consciousness. Only by observing people in interaction, rather than in radical abstraction, can the processes whereby actors come to share the same world be discovered. Social science cannot understand how and why actors create a common subjective world independently of watching them do so. This abandonment of Husserl's phenomenological project liberated phenomenology from philosophy and allowed sociologists to study empirically what Schutz considered the most important social reality: the creation and maintenance of *intersubjectivity*—that is, a sense among people in interaction of a common subjective world.[29] Unfortunately, Schutz died just as he was beginning a systematic synthesis of his ideas; as a result, only a somewhat fragmented but suggestive framework is evident in his collective work. But his early analysis of Weber, Husserl, and interactionism led to a concern with some key issues: (1) How do actors create a common subjective world? (2) What implications does this creation have for how social order is maintained?

All humans, Schutz asserted, carry in their minds rules, social recipes, conceptions of appropriate conduct, and other information that allows them to act in their social world. Extending Husserl's concept of lifeworld, Schutz views the sum of these rules, recipes, conceptions, and information as the individual's "stocks knowledge at hand." These stocks of knowledge give people a frame of reference or orientation with which they can interpret events as they pragmatically act on the world around them. Several features of these stocks of knowledge at hand are given particular emphasis by Schutz:

1. People's reality *is* their stocks of knowledge. For the members of a society, stock knowledge constitutes a "paramount reality"—a sense of an absolute reality that shapes and guides all social events. Actors use this stock knowledge and sense of reality as they pragmatically seek to deal with others in their environment.

---

[28]Richard M. Zaner, "Theory of Intersubjectivity: Alfred Schutz," *Social Research* 28 (Spring 1961): p. 76.

[29]For references to interactionists, see Schutz, *Collected Papers* (cited in note 26).

2. The existence of stocks of knowledge bestows a sense of reality on events and gives the social world, as Schutz agreed with Husserl, a *taken-for-granted* character. The stock knowledge is rarely the object of conscious reflection but, rather, an implicit set of assumptions and procedures that are silently used by individuals as they interact.

3. Stocks of knowledge are learned. They are acquired through socialization within a common social and cultural world, but it becomes the reality for actors in this world.

4. People operate under a number of assumptions that allow them to create a sense of "reciprocity of perspectives." That is, others with whom an actor must deal are considered to share an actor's stock of knowledge at hand. And, although these others might have unique components in their stocks of knowledge because of their particular biographies, these can be ignored by actors.

5. The existence of stocks of knowledge, their acquisition through socialization, and their capacity to promote reciprocity of perspectives all give actors in a situation a sense or presumption that the world is the same for all and that it reveals identical properties for all. What often holds society together is this presumption of a common world.

6. The presumption of a common world allows actors to engage in the *process of typification.* Action in most situations, except the most personal and intimate, can proceed through mutual typification as actors use their stock knowledge to categorize one another and to adjust their responses to these typifications.[30] With typification, actors can effectively deal with their world; every nuance and characteristic of their situations does not have to be examined. Moreover, typification facilitates entrance into the social world; it simplifies adjustment because humans can treat each other as categories, or as "typical" objects of a particular kind.

These points of emphasis in Schutz's thought represented a blending of ideas from European phenomenology and American interactionism. The emphasis on stocks of knowledge is clearly borrowed from Husserl, but it is highly compatible with Mead's notion of the generalized other. The concern with the taken-for-granted character of the world as it is shaped by stocks of knowledge is also borrowed from Husserl but is similar to early interactionists' discussions of habit and routine behaviors. The emphasis on the acquired nature of stocks of knowledge coincides with early interactionists' discussions of the socialization process. The concern with the reciprocity of perspectives and with the process of typification owes much to Husserl and Weber but is compatible with Mead's notion of role taking, by which actors read one another's role and perspective.

---

[30]Ralph H. Turner's emphasis on role differentiation and accretion is an example of how these ideas have been extended by role theorists. See Chapter 17.

Still, the major departure from much interactionist theory should also be emphasized: Actors operate on an unverified presumption that they share a common world, and this sense of a common world and the practices that produce this sense are crucial in maintaining social order. In other words, social organization might be possible not so much by the substance and content of stocks of knowledge, by the reciprocity of perspectives, or by successful typification as by the often fragile and unverifiable *presumption* that actors share intersubjective states. Schutz did not carry this line of inquiry far, but he inspired new avenues of phenomenological inquiry that did.

# Building on Early Interactionist Insights

Given its diverse sources, interactionist theorizing, by the twentieth century's end, diverged in many directions. At first, however, those who extended Mead's synthesis and those who expanded on the idea of role stayed within the broad parameters of Mead's views, but by the 1960s, new lines of interactionist thinking began to emerge, inspired more by the European masters than by Mead and those who had followed Mead in America. Thus, as interactionism matured at the midcentury, it might have exhausted the Meadian legacy, and to a degree, purely Meadian micro sociology began to stagnate. Indeed, actual theorizing began to take a back seat to debates on the methodology of inquiry, particularly about whether or not a science of interaction was possible or appropriate. At the same time, however, interesting empirical work was conducted by those following the Meadian tradition. Nonetheless, new theory within the strictly Meadian framework became increasingly hard to find in the literature.

As Mead-inspired interactionism stagnated, however, new alternatives emerged and reinvigorated the study of interaction. Today, it would be hard to visualize a coherent interactionist orientation. New micro-level ideas and interesting extensions and elaborations of old ones are still emerging, as we will see, but the midcentury coherence in the study of interaction has been lost. Yet, in the second decade of the twenty-first century, it is not unreasonable to conclude that the process of interaction is probably the *best understood* dimension of the social universe. So what had seemed like stagnation was, in fact, a convergence of ideas on the fundamental properties and processes of human interaction. What is not fully resolved, however, is the connection between these microdynamics and the larger-scale sociocultural formations in which they transpire.

## CHAPTER 16

# Symbolic Interactionist Theories of Identity

George Herbert Mead's foundational work was termed *symbolic interactionism* by Herbert Blumer, who took over Mead's famous social psychology course after Mead's death and who became a persistent advocate of symbolic interactionism for half a century. I am not sure if Mead would have approved this label, but more importantly, symbolic interactionism, as it has evolved over the last sixty years, has tended to focus on the dynamics of *self* more than either symbols or interaction—as Blumer had advocated. People's behaviors in interaction with others in social settings are governed by their conception of themselves. Self serves as a kind of gyroscope for keeping behaviors consistent and in line; moreover, as has increasingly been emphasized in symbolic interactionist theory, individuals are motivated to verify their sense of self in the eyes of others.

The notion of *identity* became one prominent way to reconceptualize self over the last few decades.[1] In general terms, self is now viewed as a set or series of identities that can be invoked individually or simultaneously in

---

[1] Aside from these figures, others seeking a theory of self and identity include Eugene Weinstein, Mary Glenn Wiley, and William DeVaughn, "Role and Interpersonal Style as Components of Interaction," *Social Forces* 45 (1966): pp. 210–16; Peter J. Burke and Judy C. Tully, "The Measurement of Role/Identity," *Social Forces* 55 (1977): pp. 881–97; Nelson N. Foote, "Identification as the Basis for a Theory of Motivation," *American Sociological Review* 16 (1951): pp. 14–21; Tamotsu Shibutani, *Society and Personality* (Englewood Cliffs, NJ: Prentice Hall, 1961); Anselm Strauss, *Mirrors and Masks* (Glencoe, IL: Free Press, 1959); Gregory P. Stone, "Appearance and the Self" in *Behavior and Social Processes*, ed. Arnold M. Rose (Boston: Houghton Mifflin, 1962). For a review of the history of identity and self theories, see Viktor Gecas and Peter J. Burke, "Self and Identity," in *Sociological Perspectives on Social Psychology*, eds. Karen S. Cook, Gary Alan Fine, and James S. House (Boston: Allyn & Bacon, 1995), pp. 41–67. For a very recent review of identity theories, see Peter J. Burke and Jan E. Stets, *Identity Theory* (New York: Oxford University Press, 2009).

situations, but once evoked, individuals' actions are directed at having others verify an identity or identities. At the same time, identities can act as filters of selective perception and interpretation as individuals mutually role-take with one another.

Thus, the effort to develop a more refined theory of self has been the major thrust of much interactionist theorizing. In this chapter, I will review several of these new theories of identity dynamics. Moreover, the most recent work on identity processes has converged with more recent theorizing on the sociology of emotions for the obvious reason that people put their identities on the line during interaction; thus, depending upon whether individuals succeed in verifying or fail in getting others to verify an identity or identities, the emotions that are aroused will shape the subsequent flow of the interaction and, over time, the structure of a person's identity system.

# Sheldon Stryker's Identity Theory

## Designations and Definitions

In Sheldon Stryker's view, human social behavior is organized by symbolic designations of all aspects of the environment, both physical and social.[2] Among the most important of these designations are the symbols and associated meanings of the positions that people occupy in social structures. These positions carry with them shared expectations about how people are to enact roles and, in general, to comport themselves in relation to others. As individuals designate their own positions, they call forth in themselves expectations about how they are to behave, and as they designate the positions of others, they become cognizant of the expectations guiding the role behaviors of these others. They also become aware of broader frames of reference and definitions of the situation as these positional designations are made. And most importantly, individuals designate themselves as objects in relation to their location in structural positions and their perceptions of broader definitions of the situation.

---

[2]Sheldon Stryker, *Symbolic Interactionism: A Structural Version* (Menlo Park, CA: Benjamin/Cummings, 1980); "Identity Salience and Role Performance: The Relevance of Symbolic Interaction Theory for Family Research," *Journal of Marriage and the Family* (1968): pp. 558–64; "Fundamental Principles of Social Interaction," in *Sociology*, ed. Neil J. Smelser, 2nd ed. (New York: Wiley, 1973), pp. 495–547. For a more recent version of the theory, see Sheldon Stryker and Richard T. Serpe, "Commitment, Identity Salience, and Role Behavior," in *Personality, Roles, and Social Behavior*, eds. William Ickes and Eric Knowles (New York: Springer-Verlag, 1982), pp. 199–218; Richard T. Serpe and Sheldon Stryker, "The Construction of Self and the Reconstruction of Social Relationships," *Advances in Group Processes* 4 (1987): pp. 41–66; and Sheldon Stryker, "Exploring the Relevance of Social Cognition for the Relationship of Self and Society," in *The Self-Society Dynamic: Cognition, Emotion, and Action*, eds. Judith Howard and Peter L. Callero (Cambridge: Cambridge University Press, 1991): pp. 19–41.

Behavior is, however, not wholly determined or dictated by these designations and definitions. It is true that people are almost always aware of expectations associated with positions, but as they present themselves to others, the form and content of the interaction can change. The amount of such change will vary with the type of larger social structure within which the interaction occurs; some structures are open and flexible, whereas others are more closed and rigid. Still, all structures impose limits and constraints on what individuals do when engaged in face-to-face interaction.

## Identities and the Salience Hierarchy

Stryker reasoned that identities are parts of larger sense of self, and as such, they are internalized self-designations associated with positions that individuals occupy within various social contexts. Identity is thus a critical link between the individual and social structure because identities are designations that people make about themselves in relation to their location in social structures and the roles that they play by virtue of this location. Identities are organized into a *salience hierarchy*, and those identities high in the hierarchy are more likely to be evoked than those lower in this hierarchy. Not all situations will invoke multiple identities, but many do. The salience hierarchy determines those identities that are invoked by people as they orchestrate their roles and interpret the role behaviors of others. As a general rule, Stryker proposes that when an interaction situation is isolated from structural constraints, or these structural constraints are ambiguous, individuals will have more options in their choice of an identity, and hence, they will be more likely to evoke more than one identity. But as a situation becomes embedded within social structures, the salience hierarchy becomes a good predictor of what identities will be used in interaction with others.

## Commitment and Self

Stryker introduced the idea of *commitment* as a means for conceptualizing the link between social structure and self. *Commitment* designates the degree to which a person's relationship to others depends on being a certain kind of individual with a particular identity. The greater this dependence is, the more a person will be committed to a particular identity and the higher this identity will be in the person's salience hierarchy. Having an identity that is based on the views of others, as well as on broader social definitions, will tend to produce behaviors that conform to these views and definitions.

When people reveal such commitment to an identity in a situation, their sense of self-esteem becomes dependent on the successful execution of their identity. Moreover, when an identity is established by reference to the norms, values, and other symbols of the broader society, esteem is even more dependent on successful implementation of an identity. In this way, cultural definitions and expectations, social structural location, identity, and esteem associated with that identity all become interwoven. And in this process, social structure constrains behavior and people's perceptions of themselves and others.

## The Key Propositions

In the early version of the theory, Stryker developed a series of "hypotheses" about the conditions producing the salience of an identity, the effects of identities high in the salience hierarchy on role behaviors, the influence of commitment on esteem, and the nature of changes in identity. These are rephrased somewhat and summarized in Table 16.1. To state Stryker's argument more discursively, here is what he proposed: The more individuals reveal commitment to an identity, the higher this identity will be in the salience hierarchy. If this identity is positively evaluated in terms of the reactions of others and broader value standards, then this identity will move up a person's hierarchy. When the expectations of others are congruent and consistent, revealing few conflicts and disagreements, individuals will be even more committed to the identity presented to these others because they speak with the same voice. And finally, when the network of these others on whom one depends for identity is large and extended, encompassing many others rather than just a few, the higher in the salience hierarchy will this identity become.

Once an identity is high in the salience hierarchy of an individual, role performances will become ever-more consistent with the expectations attached to this identity. Moreover, when identities are high in the salience hierarchy, individuals will tend to perceive situations as opportunities to play out this identity in roles, and they will actively seek out situations where they can use this identity. In this way, the congruence between those identities high in people's hierarchies and the expectations of situations increases.

This congruence increases commitment because individuals come to see their identities as depending on the continued willingness of others to confirm their identities. As commitment increases, and as individuals become dependent on confirmation of their identities from others, their role performances have ever-more consequences for their level of self-esteem. Moreover, as people become committed to identities and these identities move up in their salience hierarchy, they come to evaluate their role performances through broader cultural definitions and normative expectations; as people make such evaluations, they become even more committed to their identities.

External events can, however, erode commitments to an identity. When this occurs, people are more likely to adopt new identities, even novel identities. As individuals begin to seek new identities, change is likely to move in the direction of those identities that reflect their values. In this way, cultural values pull the formation of new identities in directions that will increase

**Table 16.1**  A Revised Formulation of Stryker's Hypotheses on the Salience of Identity

1. The more individuals are committed to an identity, the higher will this identity be in their salience hierarchy.

2. The degree of commitment to an identity is a positive and additive function of

   A. The extent to which this identity is positively valued by others and broader cultural definitions

   B. The more congruent the expectations of others on whom one depends for an identity

   C. The more extensive the network of individuals on whom one depends

   D. The larger the number of persons in a network on whom one depends for an identity

**The Consequences of High Salience**

3. The higher in a person's salience hierarchy is an identity, the more likely will that individual

   A. Emit role performances that are consistent with the role expectations associated with that identity

   B. Perceive a given situation as an opportunity to perform in that identity

   C. Seek out situations that provide opportunities to perform in that identity

**The Consequences of Commitment to Identity**

4. The greater the commitment to an identity, the greater will be

   A. The effect of role performances on self-esteem

   B. The likelihood that role performances will reflect institutionalized values and norms

**Changing Commitments to Identity**

5. The more external events alter the structure of a situation, the more likely are individuals to adopt new identities.

6. The more changes in identity reinforce and reflect the value-commitments of the individual, the less the individual resists change in adopting a new identity.

the congruence between cultural definitions and role performance as individuals develop new identity commitments and as their self-esteem becomes dependent on successful role performance of these identity commitments.

## Identity and Emotions

Emotions are implicated in these processes in several ways.[3] First, those role enactments that generate positive affect and reinforcement from others in a situation strengthen a person's commitment to an identity, moving it higher in the salience hierarchy. As individuals receive this positive feedback from others, their self-esteem is enhanced, which further increases commitment to the identity, raising it in the salience hierarchy and increasing the chances that this identity will shape subsequent role performances.

Second, when role performances of a person and others are judged inadequate in light of normative expectations, cultural values, definitions of the situation, or identities being asserted, negative emotional reactions mark this inadequacy. Conversely, when role performances are adequate or even more than adequate and exemplary, positive emotions signal this fact. Thus, emotions are *markers of adequacy* in role performances, telling individuals that their performances are acceptable or unacceptable. This marking function of emotions works in several ways. The individual reads the gestures of others to see if a role performance has been accepted, and if it has, then the person experiences positive emotions and will become further committed to the identity presented in the role performance. If, on the other hand, the reaction is less than positive, then the individual will experience negative emotions—such as *anger* at self, *shame*, and *guilt*—and mobilize to improve the role performance, or if this is not possible, to lower the commitment to this identity being asserted in the role, moving it lower in the salience hierarchy and, thereby, causing selection of a different identity that can be more adequately played out in a role. Not only do individuals get emotional about their own performances as they role-take with others and assess themselves in light of the responses of others, but they also inform others about the latter's role performances. Because role performances must be coordinated and meshed together to be effective, inadequacy by others will disrupt one's own role performance, and if this occurs, a person will manifest some form of *anger* and negatively sanction others. Thus, emotions become ways for individuals to mutually signal and mark the adequacy of their respective role performances in ways that facilitate the coordination and integration of roles.

Finally, emotions are also a sign of *which* identities are high in a person's salience hierarchy. If emotional reactions are intense when a role performance fails or when it is successful, this intensity indicates that a person is committed to the identity being played in a role and that the identity is high in the salience hierarchy. Conversely, if the emotional reaction of the

---

[3]Sheldon Stryker, "The Interplay of Affect and Identity: Exploring the Relationship of Social Structure, Social Interaction, Self and Emotions." Paper presented at the American Sociological Association meetings, Chicago, 1987; Sheldon Stryker and Richard Serpe, "Commitment, Identity Salience and Role Behavior: Theory and a Research Example," in *Personality, Roles and Social Behavior*, eds. W. Ickes and E. Knowles (New York: Springer-Verlag, 1982), pp. 199–218.

individual is of low intensity, then this might signal that the identity is lower in the salience hierarchy and relatively unimportant to the individual.

In identity theory, then, emotions motivate individuals to play roles in which they receive positive reinforcement, and emotions also inform individuals about the adequacy of their performances and their commitments to identities in the salience hierarchy. Emotions thus drive individuals to play roles in ways that are consistent with normative expectations, definitions of the situation, cultural values, and highly salient feelings about self.

# George J. McCall and J. L. Simmons' Theory of Identity

## Role Identity and Role Support

In contrast with Stryker's more structural theory, where culture and social structure designate many of the identities held by individuals, George J. McCall and J. L. Simmons emphasized that roles are typically improvised as individuals seek to realize their various plans and goals.[4] A role identity is, therefore, "the character and the role that an individual devises for himself (herself as well) as an occupant of a particular social position."[5] Role identity constitutes an imaginative view of oneself in a position, often a rather idealized view of oneself. Each role identity thus has a conventional portion linked to positions in social structure as well as an idiosyncratic portion constructed in people's imaginations.

Role identities become part of individuals' plans and goals because legitimating one's identity in the eyes of others is always a driving force of human behavior. Moreover, people evaluate themselves through the role performances intended to confirm a role identity. But, as McCall and Simmons emphasized, the most important audiences for a role performance are individuals themselves who assess their performances with respect to their own idealized view of their role identity. Still, people must also seek role support from relevant audiences outside their own minds for their role identities. This support involves more than audiences granting a person the right to occupy a position, and it includes more than approval from others for conduct by those in a position. For an individual to feel legitimated in a role, audiences must also approve of the more expressive content—the style, emotion, manner, and tone—of role performances designed to legitimate a role identity.

Because much of a role identity is rather idealized in the individual's mind and because a person must seek legitimization along several fronts, there is always discrepancy and disjuncture between the role identity and

---

[4]George J. McCall and J. L. Simmons, *Identities and Interactions* (New York: Basic Books, 1960). A second edition of this book was published in 1978, although the theory remained virtually unchanged.

[5]Ibid., p. 67.

the role support received for that identity. People idealize too much, and they must seek support for performances that can be misinterpreted. As a result, there is almost always some *dissatisfaction* by individuals about how much their role identity has been legitimated by audiences. These points of disjuncture between identity and legitimating support motivate and drive individual behavior. Indeed, for McCall and Simmons, the most distinctive emotion among humans is the "drive to acquire support for (their) idealized conceptions of (themselves)."

## The Mechanisms for Maintaining Role Support

To overcome the discrepancy between what people desire and get in role support for an identity, several mechanisms are employed. One is the accumulation of *short-term credit* from interactions where discrepancies have been minimal; these emotional credits can then carry individuals through episodes where the responses from others provide less than whole-hearted role support. A second mechanism is *selective perception of cues* from others where individuals only see those responses confirming an identity. A third mechanism is *selective interpretation* of cues whereby the individual sees the cues accurately but puts a spin or interpretation on them that supports a role identity. A fourth mechanism is *withdrawing from interactions* that do not support an identity and seeking alternative situations where more support can be garnered. A fifth mechanism is *switching to a new role identity* whose performance will bring more support from others. A sixth mechanism is *scapegoating* audiences, blaming them for causing the discrepancy between performance and support. A seventh mechanism is *disavowing unsuccessful performances* that individuals had hoped to legitimate. And a final defensive mechanism is deprecating and *rejecting the audience* that withholds support for a role identity. When these mechanisms fail, individuals experience misery and anguish, and through such experiences, people learn to be cautious in committing themselves so openly and fully to particular role performances in front of certain audiences.[6]

## The Hierarchy of Prominence

The cohesiveness role identities of individuals vary, McCall and Simmons argued, in how the elements of an identity fit together and in the compatibility among various role identities. There is also a hierarchy of prominence among role identities; although this hierarchy can shift and change as circumstances dictate, it tends to exist at any given point in an interaction. This prominence reflects the idealized view of individuals, the extent to which these ideals have been supported by audiences, the degree to which individuals have committed themselves to these identities, the extrinsic and intrinsic rewards (to be discussed shortly) associated with an identity, and

---

[6]Ibid., p. 75.

the amount of previous investment in time and energy that has been devoted to an identity.

From this perspective, interaction revolves around each individual asserting through role performances identities that are high in their prominence hierarchy and that they seek to legitimate in their own eyes as well as in the eyes of others. At the same time, each individual is interpreting the gestures of others to determine just what identity is high in the prominence hierarchy of others and whether or not the role performances of others are worthy of role support and other rewards. To some degree, the external structure of the situation provides the necessary information about what positions people occupy and what expectations are placed on them by virtue of incumbency in these positions. Yet, for McCall and Simmons, most interactions are to some degree ambiguous and unstructured, allowing alternative role performances and varying interpretations of these performances.

Much of the ambiguity in interaction is eliminated through simple role taking in a person's inner forum or cognitive repertoire of vocabularies, gestures, motives, and other information that marks various identities and role performances. Humans have, therefore, the capacity to construct interpretations in light of the vast amounts of information that they accumulate in their inner forum or what Alfred Schutz called "stocks of knowledge at hand." This information might have to be assembled in somewhat different proportions and balances, but humans' capacity for mind and thought enables them to do so with amazing speed and accuracy.

Individuals will often improvise a role, adjusting their identities and role performances in light of how they interpret the roles of others. As such improvisation occurs, various expressive strategies are employed; these strategies revolve around orchestrating gestures to present a certain image of self and to claim a particular identity that is high in the prominence hierarchy. Conversely, individuals read the dramaturgical presentations of others to *altercast* and determine the self that is being claimed by these others. In essence, then, interaction is the negotiation of identities, whereby people make expressive and dramaturgical presentations over identities that are high in their respective prominence hierarchies and that can be supported, or that can go unsupported, on the basis of role performances.

## The Underlying Exchange Dynamic

This process of negotiation among individuals is complex and subtle, involving an initial but very tentative agreement to accept each other's claims. In this way, people avoid interrupting the expressive strategies that are being used to impart their respective identities. As this process unfolds, however, it moves into a real exchange-negotiation whereby individuals seek the rewards that come with legitimization of their role performances. At this point McCall and Simmons merge their interactionist theory with exchange theory (see chapters in Part V).

They begin by classifying three basic types of rewards: First, there are *extrinsic rewards*, such as money or other reinforcers, that are visible to all. Second, there are *intrinsic rewards* that provide less visible means of reinforcement for the individual—rewards such as satisfaction, pride, and comfort. And third, and most important, there is *support for an identity*, which McCall and Simmons believe is the most valuable of all rewards. Individuals are motivated to seek a profit—rewards less the costs in securing them—in all their interactions. Moreover, there are separate types of calculi for each of these three categories of reward, and there are rules of the marketplace: Rewards received by each party to an exchange should be roughly comparable in their type (whether extrinsic, intrinsic, or identity support), and rewards should be received in proportion to the investments individuals incur in receiving them (a principle of *distributive justice*).

These negotiations are affected by what McCall and Simmons term the salience of identities, which are those identities that, for the immediate interaction at hand, are the most relevant in an individual's hierarchy of prominence. This salience of identities constitutes, in McCall and Simmons' words, a situated self that is most pertinent to the present interaction. This situational self determines a person's preferences about which role identities he or she will enact in a given situation, but the preferences of the situational self are fluid and changeable. In contrast, the ideal self is more stable than the situated self, while being the highest-order identity in the prominence hierarchy. A person's ideal self will thus influence which identities should be salient in an interaction and how they will be invoked to constitute a situated self. Besides the prominence hierarchy, other factors also influence the formation of a situated identity. The needs that an individual feels for support of an identity, the extrinsic and intrinsic rewards to be received by claiming a situated self, and the opportunity for profitable enactment of a role in relation to a situated self all shape identity formation.

All these factors are, in McCall and Simmons' view, potential reinforcers or payoffs for roles emitted in claiming an identity. These payoffs vary in value, however. Support of the *ideal self* brings greater rewards than either extrinsic or intrinsic rewards. The patterns of payoffs for rewards can also vary. For extrinsic and intrinsic types of rewards, when payoffs match expectations and desires, needs for them decline somewhat (in accordance with satiation or the principle of marginal utility). If people receive either more or less than they expected or desired of these two types of rewards, then their immediate need for these rewards suddenly escalates. In contrast, the payoff schedule for role support for an identity reveals a more complicated pattern. Role support for what was desired or expected does not increase the desire for further role support of an identity. A moderate discrepancy between the support sought and received increases the desire for support of an identity. But, extreme discrepancies operate differently, depending on the sign of the discrepancy: If people receive support that greatly exceeds their expectations, they immediately desire more role support, whereas if they dramatically receive less role support than expected, their desire for this role support drops rapidly.

Because payoffs will almost always, or at least eventually, be less than expected, discrepancies will be chronic, even after individuals have employed all the defense mechanisms to reduce discrepancies that were discussed earlier. Hence, people are constantly driven to overcome this discrepancy, but this search to reduce discrepancy is complicated by the payoff schedule for role support. Moderate discrepancies drive people to seek more role support, whereas large ones reduce efforts to secure role support for an identity. And when people have received more support than they expected for an identity, they want even more of this reward, raising this identity in salience and, over time, increasing its prominence in the hierarchy.

# Peter J. Burke's Identity Control Theory

Working squarely within the symbolic interactionist tradition, Peter J. Burke and various colleagues, particularly Jan E. Stets, have developed yet another variant of identity theory.[7] For Burke, individuals carry general views of themselves to all situations, or an *idealized self*, but it is the *working self* or *self-image* that guides moment-to-moment interaction.[8] The idealized self may, of course, influence just how individuals see themselves in a situation, but the key dynamics of self revolve around trying to verify this working self or self-image in situations as individuals play roles. At other times, Burke has also conceptualized self as a rough hierarchy.[9] At the more abstract level is a *principle self* in which cultural standards contained in broader values and beliefs become part of how individuals see themselves, but this principle-level self influences behavior in situations through *a program-level identity* consisting of the goals that individuals seek to realize in a concrete situation. In general, the more a program-level identity is guided by a principle-level self and the more the goals of the program-level self are realized in a situation, the greater are persons' sense of efficacy and

---

[7]Peter J. Burke, "The Self: Measurement Implications from a Symbolic Interactionist Perspective," *Social Psychology Quarterly* 43 (1980): pp. 18–20; "An Identity Model for Network Exchange," *American Sociological Review* 62 (1997): pp. 134–50; "Attitudes, Behavior, and the Self," in *The Self-Society Dynamic,* eds. Judith Howard and Peter L. Callero (cited in note 2), pp. 189–208, "Identity Processes and Social Stress," *American Sociological Review* 56 (1991): pp. 836–49; P. J. Burke and D. C. Reitzes, "An Identity Theory Approach to Commitment," *Social Psychology Quarterly* 54 (1991): pp. 239–51; P. J. Burke and Jan E. Stets, "Trust and Commitment through Self-Verification," *Social Psychology Quarterly* 62 (1999): pp. 347–66; and Peter J. Burke and Jan E. Stets, *Identity Theory* (New York: Oxford University Press).

[8]Burke, "The Self: Measurement Implications from a Symbolic Interactionist Perspective" (cited in note 7).

[9]T. Tsushima and P. J. Burke, "Levels, Agency, and Control in Parent Identity," *Social Psychology Quarterly* 62 (1999): pp. 173–89.

the more positive are their sentiments toward themselves and the situation.[10] Yet, unlike other identity theories, Burke's approach does not place great emphasis on a salience or prominence hierarchy. Instead, the theory seeks to explain the internal dynamics of self as individuals play a role in an effort to verify the identity associated with this role.

## Role Identities

For Burke, self is an occupant of a role in a situation. This situation is, in turn, typically embedded in a larger social structure and associated cultural meanings, Roles are thus the link between self, on the one side, and social structure and culture, on the other. By virtue of playing a role, individuals incorporate meanings and expectations associated with this role into their identity in the situation. Individuals have diverse experiences and any role has multiple meanings; thus, the identities associated with a role will vary from person to person. Burke's identity theory, however, is less concerned with the actual content of a role identity than with the dynamics of how this identity is sustained in interaction with others in a situation. This emphasis leads Burke to see identity as a cybernetic control system in which individuals seek to regulate their behaviors so that feedback from others signals that these others have verified the identities presented by individuals.

## Identity as a Cybernetic Control System

In conceptualizing identity as a cybernetic control system, Burke sees the dynamics of this system as revolving around following elements:[11]

1. An *identity standard* operating as a *comparator* or criterion for assessing whether or not an identity is verified and for directing initial behavior in a role

2. A set of inputs from others who are responding to the behaviors of a person playing a role and asserting an identity

3. A comparison of inputs with the comparator to determine if the responses of others are congruent with the identity standard guiding role behaviors

4. A set of behavioral outputs on the environment guided by the degree to which inputs match the identity standard contained in the comparator

These elements are delineated in Figure 16.1. Individuals have a set of meanings about their identity in a situation. This identity is translated into a standard that, in turn, becomes a comparator or basis for matching inputs

---

[10]Ibid. See also Peter J. Burke, "Identity Processes and Social Stress" (cited in note 7).

[11]Peter J. Burke, "Identity Processes and Social Stress" (cited in note 7).

**Figure 16.1** The Cybernetic Control System in Burke's Theory

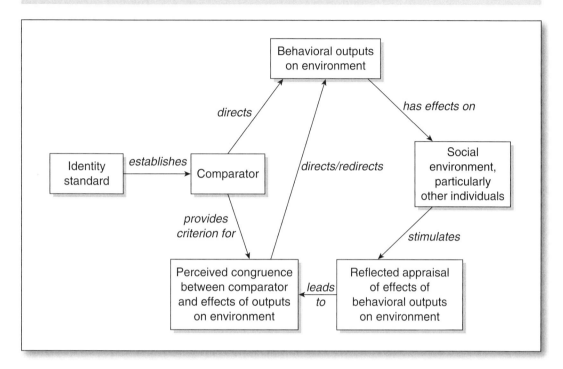

to the standard to see if, indeed, the standard has been realized. As individuals play a role in a situation, they emit outputs of meaningful behavior on the environment, particularly to other individuals in the situation who, in turn, respond to these behavioral outputs. As individuals emitting outputs role-take with others in a situation, they experience *reflected appraisals* that become inputs of self-meanings that are compared to the identity standard. Depending on whether or not the identity standard is met, the next round of behavioral outputs will vary. When the identity standard is realized, individuals will experience more positive emotions, and their subsequent behavioral outputs will revolve around commitments to others in the situation. When inputs from others signal that the identity standard is not realized, people will experience negative emotions, and the next round of behavioral outputs will seek to change the responses of others so that a role identity can be confirmed.

Thus, in Burke's theory, humans are motivated to have inputs match up with identity standards. Behavior is goal directed in the sense that individuals try to elicit from others in a situation responses that match their identity standard. To achieve this result, individuals orchestrate their gestures and use other signs in behavioral performances that, they hope, will allow them to receive inputs that match the identity standard.[12]

---

[12]Lee Freese and Peter J. Burke, "Persons, Identities, and Social Interaction," in *Advances in Group Processes*, eds. Barry Markovsky, K. Heimer, and Jody O'Brien (Greenwich, CT: JAI, 1994).

In Burke's model, a separate control system is operative for each identity.[13] That is, if multiple identities are presented in a situation, each is guided by the dynamics outlined in Figure 16.1. For example, if a professor seeks to present an identity as both an intellect and a sexually attractive person, then two role identities—intellect and sexy—are revealed in behavioral outputs, and two cybernetic control systems revolving around two comparators (dictated by the two identities), two sets of inputs, two comparisons, and two outputs are operative. However, higher-level identities—or what Burke sometimes terms *principle-level identities*—often provide more general frames of reference for lower-level or program identities, thereby simplifying the control process. For instance, if a college professor is in the classroom, the higher-level identity revolving around beliefs in the importance of intellectual activity per se may provide guidance for how the lower-level program identity of being sexually attractive is to be orchestrated in role behaviors. In this way, the two identities are not contradictory, and the control systems guiding efforts at confirmation will not work at cross-purposes.

## Multiple Identities

In recent years, Burke along with Jan Stets has identified three types of identities: person identity or an individual self-conception (or what some call core-identity); role identity tied to particular roles; and social identity tied to a social group.[14] Individuals can have all three of these identities in play during an interaction, but the dynamics of identity control operate in the manner described above. Also, people have different levels of identity, such as a principle identity or a moral identity. These too, as well as other identities that a person may have, operate in the same cybernetic manner outlined in Figure 16.1.

Since many potential identities can be in play at any given moment for a person, identity-control dynamics can become complicated. Still, there is probably some limit on how many identities can be salient since humans have limited cognitive capacities to store the relevant information and bring it to bear in a particular situation.

## Identity and Emotions

In a number of research projects, Burke and Jan Stets have explored the effects of verification, or the failure to verify an identity, on people's emotional arousal.[15] When role identities are verified by the responses of others, people will experience positive emotions, and moreover, they will generally

---

[13]Peter J. Burke, "Relationships Among Multiple Identities" (Conference in Bloomington, IN: The Future of Identity Theory and Research, 2001).

[14]Burke and Stets, *Identity Theory* (cited in note 7); see Table on p. 129.

[15]P. J. Burke and Jan E. Stets, "Trust and Commitment through Self-Verification" (cited in note 7).

have enhanced self-esteem, which can insulate them from the negative efforts of periodic failures to confirm the identity. When a role identity is not verified, people will experience distress, anxiety, and other negative emotions, including lowered self-esteem.

**Identity Verification.** If a role identity is consistently confirmed in interaction with others, individuals will increasingly come to trust these others; they will develop commitments to these others; they will reveal emotional attachments to these others; and they will become more oriented to the group and social structure in which a role identity is confirmed. For example, a person whose identity standard demands that he or she be considered a good student will feel positive emotions toward others, such as professors and follow students, when this identity is confirmed; if this verification consistently occurs in school situations, this person will trust others, develop attachments to them, and become oriented to the intellectual culture of the university community.

As a role identity is verified across repeated encounters with others in a situation, individuals develop trust in others, commitments to the situation, and positive emotions toward those who have verified their identity. As these reactions to identity verification play out, the salience to the person of the role identity being presented and verified increases. And the more salient an identity—that is, the more important it is to the individual and the more it guides behavioral outputs—the greater the motivation of the individual to ensure that inputs from the environment do indeed confirm this identity. Thus, a student who has enjoyed success in confirming the role identity of good student will be increasingly motivated to verify this identity as it takes on greater salience.

**Failure to Verify Identity.** More interesting, perhaps, are situations where inputs from others' responses do not match the identity standard. Several conditions produce this outcome. One is where a person's outputs cannot change the situation, no matter how hard he or she tries; under these conditions, a person experiences a loss of efficacy and a greater sense of alienation, disaffection, and estrangement. For instance, a person who cannot match performance with a work identity and, yet, who cannot leave his or her job will experience this range of negative emotions. Another condition is interference from other identities possessed by a person where confirmation of one role identity does not allow another to be confirmed. For instance, a person who has an identity as a good student and a great athlete will often discover in college that only one of these two identities can be consistently confirmed. Still another condition is an over-controlled identity in which the elements of a role identity are so rigidly woven together that a person sees a perceived slight to one of these elements as an attack on all elements. Such identities will be difficult to verify, even if most of the elements are accepted by others in the situation, because the individual is simply too rigid in his or her expectations for how others should respond. A final condition increasing the likelihood of failure to verify an identity is where an identity is only episodically played out in a role or only occasionally becomes salient, with the result that the individual is simply out of practice in emitting the behavioral outputs that allow others to verify the identity.[16]

Whatever the source of incongruence between (1) the expectations dictated by an identity standard and (2) the responses of others, discrepancies between (1) and (2) will inevitably cause individuals to experience distress and potentially other negative emotions. Several conditions increase the level of distress experienced. One is the importance to a person of others who have failed to verify a role identity. The more significant to an individual are others whose responses fail to match identity standards, the more intense is the sense of distress and the more motivated is the individual to adjust behavioral outputs to secure the appropriate responses from these significant others. Another condition is the salience of the role identity itself. The more important to a person the verification of a role identity in a situation, the more distressed that person will become when this identity is not verified. Still another condition is the more that a role identity reflects a commitment to others and the group, the more intense is the sense of distress when others do not verify the identity, especially if this identity is built around principle-level elements or the cultural values and beliefs of the group. Another condition influencing the level of stress is the direction and degree of incongruity between expectations set by a role identity and the non-confirming responses of others. When the responses of others fall below expectations, individuals will experience distress and be motivated to adjust behavioral outputs to secure verifying responses from others. More complicated is when expectations established by an identity standard are exceeded. Preliminary research indicates that the degree to which expectations are exceeded determines the responses of individuals.[17] The more expectations are exceeded, the more individuals are forced to adjust their identity standards and, as a result, the more they will experience distress, whereas if expectations are exceeded to a more moderate degree, the identity standards do not have to be radically adjusted, and hence, the person will experience positive emotions.

Failure to verify an identity repeatedly will, over time, cause less intense negative emotions because people begin to adjust their identity standards

---

[16]Burke, "Identity and Social Stress" (cited in note 7) and "Social Identities and Psychosocial Stress," in *Perspectives on Structure, Theory, Life-Course, and Methods*, ed. H. Kaplan (San Diego, CA: Academic Press, 1996); Burke and Stets, *Identity Theory* (cited in note 7), pp. 77–79.

[17]Jan E. Stets, "Justice, Emotion, and Identity Theory," (Conference in Bloomington, IN: The Future of Identity Theory and Research, 2001); Jan E. Stets and T. M. Tsushima, "Negative Emotion and Coping Responses within Identity Control Theory," *Social Psychology Quarterly* 64 (2001), pp. 283–295.

downward, lowering their expectations for how others will respond.[18] But when an identity standard is not initially verified, individuals will adjust their outputs in an effort to get the identity verified. Thus, for example, a student who has the identity of good student will study much harder if he or she does not meet expectations on an examination, although if this individual consistently fails to do well, the role identity and expectations associated with this identity will be adjusted downward, and the student's motivation to study harder will likely decline. Another option when an identity standard is not verified is for the individual to leave the situation, if possible, and thereby avoid the negative emotions that come from incongruities between expectations and responses of others.

In sum, Burke's identity theory generates a number of testable propositions, some of which are summarized in Table 16.2. These and other propositions are implied by the theory, but equally important, they also come from efforts to test the theory. Although some research has been performed on the other identity theories summarized in this chapter, Burke's theory is subject to ongoing research. The generalizations offered in this chapter have, to varying degrees, been confirmed by research. Moreover, in recent years, efforts have been made to reconcile Burke's identity theory with that offered by Stryker as well as McCall and Simmons.[19] Thus, it is likely that various theories of self will become more unified in the future.

## Jonathan H. Turner's Theory on Transactional Needs

As part of my general theory of microdynamic processes, I see *transactional needs* as a critical force in human interaction.[20] Humans have certain

---

[18]All cited in note 17.

[19]Jan E. Stets and Peter J. Burke, "A Sociological Approach to Self and Identity Theory" (cited in note 1); Sheldon Stryker and Peter J. Burke, "The Past, Present, and Future of Identity Theory," *Social Psychology Quarterly* 63 (2000): pp. 284–97.

[20]See, for examples, *A Theory of Social Interaction* (Stanford, CA: Stanford University Press, 1988); *Face-to-Face: Toward a Sociological Theory of Interpersonal Behavior* (Stanford, CA: Stanford University Press, 2002); *Theoretical Principles of Sociology, Volume 2 on Microdynamics* (New York: Springer, 2010); *Human Emotions: A Sociological Theory* (London: Routledge, 2008); "Toward a Theory of Embedded Encounters," *Advances in Group Processes* 17 (2000): pp. 285–322; Jonathan H. Turner and Jan E. Stets, "The Moral Emotions," in *Handbook of The Sociology of Emotions*, eds. Jan E. Stets and Jonathan H. Turner (New York: Springer, 2006), pp. 544–68; Jonathan H. Turner, "Emotions and Social Structure: Toward a General Theory," in *Emotions and Social Structure*, eds. D. Robinson and J. Clay-Warner (New York: Elsevier, 2008), pp. 319–42; Jonathan Turner, "Self, Emotions, and Extreme Violence: Extending Symbolic Interactionist Theorizing," *Symbolic Interaction* 30 (2008): pp. 290–301; "Toward A Theory of Interpersonal Processes," in *Sociological Social Psychology*, eds. J. Chin and J. Cardell (Boston, MA: Allyn and Bacon, 2008), pp. 65–95; Jonathan Turner, "Identities, Emotions, and Interaction Processes," *Symbolic Interaction* 34 (2011): pp. 330–39.

**Table 16.2** Key Proposition of Burke's Identity Theory

1. The more salient an identity in a role, the more motivated are individuals to achieve a sense of congruence between the expectations established by the identity standard and the responses of others in a situation.

2. The more the responses of others match the expectations dictated by an identity standard, the more positive are the emotions experienced by individuals and the greater their self-esteem, and the more enhanced are positive emotions toward self, the more likely are individuals to

   A. Develop a sense of trust with others who have verified their identity

   B. Develop emotional attachments to these others

   C. Develop commitments to these others

   D. Become oriented to the standards of the group in which the situation is embedded

3. The less the responses of others match an identity standard, the more likely are the emotions experienced by individuals to be negative, with the incongruence between expectations set by an identity standard and the responses of others increasing with

   A. Multiple and incompatible identity standards from two or more role identities

   B. An over-controlled self in which the elements of the identity are tightly woven and create inflexible identity standards

   C. A lack of practice in displaying an identity in a role

   D. Efforts to change and/or leave the situation that have consistently failed

4. The intensity of negative emotions from a failure to verify an identity increases with

   A. The salience of an identity in the situation

   B. The significance of the others who have not verified an identity

   C. The degree of incongruity, whether above or below expectations associated with an identity standard

5. The intensity of negative emotions from the failure to verify an identity will decrease over time as the identity standard is readjusted downward so as to lower expectations.

fundamental need-states that, to varying degrees, are always activated when individuals interact. These are transactional needs in two senses: First, some of these needs, and typically all of them, are activated during interaction; second, success or failure in meeting these needs dramatically affects the flow of interaction. These needs are listed in Table 16.3, but I will only focus on the most important need in this hierarchy of need-states: the need to verify self and the identities making up self. I have come to visualize self as composed of four fundamental *identities*, although people can probably have an identity about almost anything. For example, recently, there has been great interest in people's moral identities or the extent to which, and the arenas into which, people see themselves as moral.[21] Still, the most central identities are (1) *core identity*, or the fundamental cognitions and feelings that people have about themselves that are generally salient in almost all situations (some have termed this *person identity*); (2) *social identities*, or the cognitions and feelings that people have of themselves as members of social categories (for example, gender, sexual preference, ethnicity, class, or any social category) that define people as distinctive and that generally lead to differential evaluation of memberships in social categories; (3) *group identities*, or cognitions and feelings about self that stem from membership in, or identification with, corporate units revealing divisions of labor (groups, communities, and organizations being the most likely sources of a group identity); and (4) *role identities,* or the roles that people play in any social context, but particularly the roles associated with membership in the divisions of labor in corporate units and, at times, memberships in social categories or what I term *categoric units.*[22]

I am skeptical that there is a neat linear hierarchy of prominence or salience among identities, as is posited by most identity theories, but I would argue that some are more general than others; the more general is the identity and the more likely it is relevant and salient in a wide variety of situations, the more individuals seek to have it verified by others. Figure 16.2 summarizes the relations among the four identities that I am emphasizing. The core identity is the most general, followed successively by the social identity, group identity, and role identity. I also emphasize several properties of this hierarchy of identities. First, the lower an identity is in generality, the more likely are individuals to be aware and able to articulate their identity. For example, most people can probably tick off the cognitions and feelings that they have of themselves in role and group identities, whereas social identities and core identities are not only more complex but they also have elements that are unconscious even as they affect the behaviors of persons

Second, the higher is an identity in the hierarchy portrayed in Figure 16.2, the more intense are the emotions associated with this identity. Moreover, many of the emotions, particularly negative ones, may be repressed, but this

---

[21]See, for example, Steven Hitlin, ed., *Handbook of The Sociology of Morality* (New York: Springer, 2010); Steven Hintlin, *Moral Selves, Evil Selves: The Social Psychology of Conscience* (London, UK: Palgrave/Macmillan, 2008).

[22]This label comes from *Amos Hawley, Human Ecology: A Theoretical Essay* (Chicago, IL: University of Chicago Press, 1986). I now use this term to denote a category of persons, seeing this category as constituting a social unit that defines individuals as distinctive, while carrying a level of evaluation of moral worth and set of expectations for the behavior of persons who are members of such categoric units.

**Table 16.3**   Transactional Needs

1. ***Verification of identities***: Needs to verify one or more of the four basic identities that individuals present in all encounters

   (a) ***Core identity***: The conceptions and emotions that individuals have about themselves as persons that they carry to most encounters

   (b) ***Social identity***: The conception that individuals have of themselves by virtue of their membership in categoric units that, depending upon the situation, will vary in salience to self and others; when salient, individuals seek to have others verify this identity.

   (c) ***Group identity***: The conception that individuals have about their incumbency in corporate units (groups, organizations, and communities) and/or their identification with the members, structure, and culture of a corporate unit; when individuals have a strong sense of identification with a corporate unit, they seek to have others verify this identity.

   (d) ***Role identity***: The conception that individuals have about themselves as role players, particularly roles embedded in corporate units nested in institutional domains; the more a role identity is lodged in a domain, the more likely will individuals seek to have others verify this identity.

2. ***Making a profit in the exchange of resources***: Needs to feel that the receipt of resources by persons in encounters exceeds their costs and investments in securing these resources and that their shares of resources are just and fair compared to (a) the shares that others receive in the situation and (b) reference points that are used to establish what is a just share.

3. ***Group inclusion***: Needs to feel that one is a part of the ongoing flow of interaction in an encounter; the more focused is the encounter, the more powerful is this need.

4. ***Trust***: Needs to feel that others' are predictable, sincere, respective of self, and capable of sustaining rhythmic synchronization through talk and body language

5. ***Facticity***: Needs to feel that, for the purposes of the present interaction, individuals share a common intersubjectivity that the situation is indeed as it seems and that the situation has an obdurate character

does not prevent these repressed emotions from affecting behavior or individuals' emotional reactions when these identities are not verified by others.

Third, because they are more general, social and core identities are carried to virtually all social situations, whereas role identities and group identities are more likely to be salient when actually in a role or responding to a group. Yet, I should not over-generalize because some roles can be highly salient—say, the role of mother—and invoked outside the family in a wide variety of situations, while group identities can often be carried about to many situations, as is the case with a rapid fan of a sports team.

**Figure 16.2**   Types and Levels of Identity Formation

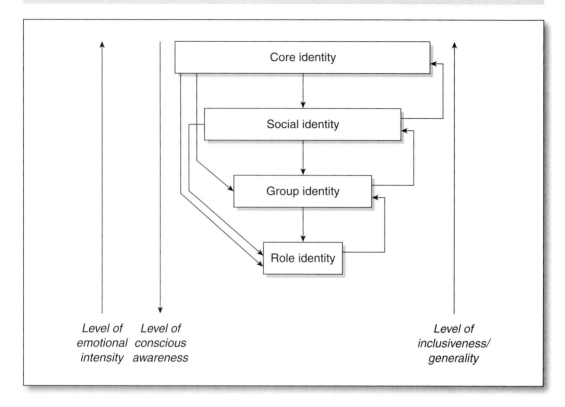

Fourth, identities are often embedded in each other, with lower-level or narrower identities being successively embedded in more general identities. Consequently, failure to verify a role identity can arouse intense emotions because it is also part of a group, social, and core identity. For example, a person's role identity as mother may be a larger component of her core identity, with the result that a great deal is at stake when this mother seeks to have her mother-identity verified through various roles. In fact, it may also be involved in social identity (as a female) and even group identity (family), thus making its verification critical because, if the role of mother is not verified, this mother's entire identity structure will be perceived as under attack and potentially collapsing.

The dynamics of identities reveal many of the cybernetic processes outlined in Burke's theory. People orchestrate their behaviors in an effort to verify any or all of the four identities in a situation; if others signal their acceptance of an identity or identities, a person will experience positive emotions from *satisfaction* at the lower-intensity end to *joy* and *pride* at the higher-intensity end of positive emotions. In contrast, if an identity is not verified, individuals will experience negative emotions such as *anger, fear, embarrassment, shame, guilt,* and many other negative emotions. When people are aware of their emotions, these emotions signal to them that, a la Stryker's argument, something has gone wrong in the presentation of self and that, following Burke's theory, motivates individuals to re-appraise their behavior and modify their actions so as to secure verification of an identity. But, these dynamics only unfold if a person is aware that an identity has not been verified.

As McCall and Simons suggest, people often invoke a variety of defensive strategies to protect self from this fate. People often engage in selective perception and/or interpretation of the responses of others; they often disavow the audience that has rejected their claims to verification; and they often leave situations where they cannot have identities confirmed by others. Yet, I do not think that McCall and Simons go far enough; people often repress the negative emotions that have come from failure to verify an identity; they simply push these feelings below the level of consciousness and do not feel them consciously, although the emotions may still be evident to others or become transmuted to a new, often more volatile, emotion that others must endure. Thus, true defense mechanisms break the cybernetic cycle from behavior at time$_1$, followed response of others, assessment of others and, then, behavior at time$_2$ that takes into account these responses from others and, thereby, seeks to ensure that the identity on the line is verified.

In Table 16.4, I enumerate various types of *defense mechanisms*, seeing *repression* as the master mechanism that removes emotions from consciousness; then, additional types of defense mechanism may be subsequently activated: *displacement* (venting emotions directed at self on others); *projection* [imputing the repressed emotion(s) to other(s)]; *sublimation* (converting negative emotions into positive emotional energy); *reaction formation* (converting intense negative emotions into positive emotions directed at others who caused the negative emotion); and *attribution* (imputing the cause of emotional reactions). The first five defense mechanisms are those often posited by the psychoanalytic tradition, while the last—attribution—comes from cognitive psychology (earlier from Gestalt psychology). Attribution is generally not considered a defense mechanism, but I think that it may be the most sociologically important mechanism. People make attributions for their experiences, and they generally make self-attributions (that is, see themselves as responsible) when experiencing positive emotions, whereas with negative emotions, they may blame others, categories of others, and social structures in an effort to protect self from having negative self-feelings.

This *proximal bias* for positive emotions to be attributed to self or others in the immediate situation and this *distal bias* for negative emotions to target more remote objects as responsible for these negative feelings have large effects on interaction and people's commitment to others and social structures. People feel positive emotions about themselves and perhaps immediate others when experiencing the positive emotions that come with identity verification. They feel that they have been positively sanctioned and have

**Table 16.4**  Repression, Defense, Transmutation, and Targeting Emotions

| Repressed Emotions | Defense Mechanism | Transmutation to | Target |
|---|---|---|---|
| anger, sadness, fear, shame, guilt, and alienation | displacement | anger | others, corporate units, and categoric units |
| anger, sadness, fear, shame, guilt, and alienation | projection | little but some anger | imputation of anger, sadness, fear, shame, or guilt to dispositional states of others |
| anger, sadness, fear, shame, guilt, and alienation | reaction formation | positive emotions | others, corporate units, and categoric units |
| anger, sadness, fear, shame, guilt, and alienation | sublimation | positive emotions | tasks in corporate units |
| anger, sadness, fear, shame, guilt, and alienation | attribution | anger | others, corporate units, and categoric units |

met situational expectations, and in so doing, they feel good about themselves because their identity or identities have been verified. In contrast, when people have not met expectations, have been negatively sanctioned, and hence, have failed to confirm an identity in a situation, the negative emotions aroused, such as *shame*, are too painful and are repressed. Then more remote others, such as members of a social category or social structures, are blamed for their feelings. In this way, despite feeling negative emotions, a person can protect self by seeing objects outside of self as causally responsible for negative emotions. These negative emotions generate prejudices against members of social categories (by gender, ethnicity, religious affiliation, for example) and alienation and/or loss of commitment to social structures seen as causing negative emotions. In contrast, positive emotions increase commitments to others and situations.

If emotions have these proximal and distal biases, how are more remote objects, such as social structures, ever to generate commitments for individuals when self-verification, meeting expectations, and receiving positive sanctions from others remain local, tied to encounters at the micro level of social organizations? What would allow for positive emotions to break the centripetal force of the proximal bias built into attribution processes? My answer is that when people *consistently experience* positive emotions in par-ticular types of situations, they begin to make attributions to the larger social structures in which these situations are embedded. As they do so, they develop positive feelings about, and commitments to, these structures because they see these structures as causally responsible for the verification of self and the positive feelings that arise from identity verification. In this manner, consistent self-verification will ultimately lead to commitments to those social structures in which encounters have aroused the positive emo-tions than come with self-verification. And, the more identities that are verified, the greater will these commitments ultimately be. Indeed, if a group-identity with particular types of corporate units or even a whole society did not already exist, it is likely to form when individuals validate other identities within a particular type of social structure. And to the extent that other identities are tied to roles in divisions of labor and are verified in encounters within this division of labor, identity dynamics become the underlying force behind commitments to this social structure and perhaps the larger institutional domain in which this structure is lodged. For example, a good student who has consistently been rewarded and had the role identity of student verified will, over time, develop com-mitments to successive schools and eventually the entire institutional domain of education.

In this way, forces like transactional needs for verification of self can have large effects on more macro-level social structures, and vice versa. Macrostructures that set people up for success in verifying role identities and any other identities tied to these roles in groups and organizations will reap what they sow: commitments from individuals. And these commit-ments may eventually move to the institutional domains or whole society in which these groups and organizations are embedded.[23]

# Conclusions

Over the last forty-five years, Mead's seminal ideas about the dynamics of self have been significantly extended and refined theoretically and assessed by careful empirical research. Theories now emphasize that individuals carry multiple identities, although there is some disagreement as to whether or not, or perhaps the degree to which, they constitute a linear hierarchy of prominence or salience. What is clear is that there are cybernetic/Gestalt dynamics operating for self. Persons seek to have their identities verified by others by assessing others' reactions to their behavioral outputs to see if these outputs are consistent with an identity and are acceptable to others. Yet, some would argue that this cybernetic process can be distorted by the

---

[23]I have developed many formal propositions on these identity dynamics and their effects on macrostructures. See, for examples, my *Face-to-Face* and *Theoretical Principles of Sociology* (both cited in note 20).

repression of the negative emotions that are aroused when such an important dimension of human behavior—verification of identities—becomes problematic. But, all identity theories agree that the failure to verify an identity generates negative emotions that motivate individuals to bring perceptions of self in line with others' responses to self. Such is the case even if the responses of others and the emotions felt by a person to these responses must be repressed to gain congruence. For most identity theories, there is a clear cognitive bias emphasizing that people generally bring their behavioral outputs, identities, and reactions of others to presentations of identities into congruence; only the more psychoanalytically oriented identity theories would also suggest that congruence can be achieved by the activation of defense mechanisms. Needs for verification of identities for all symbolic interactionists are the driving force of interaction, and the flow of interaction revolves around the extent to which people's identities are mutually verified. And when they are, individuals feel positive emotions and may, if these emotions persist, begin to make commitments to the larger social structures in which interactions occur.

Identity verification dynamics are one key to understanding the connection between micro interactions and macro social structures. Emotions are the key link, and the most powerful emotions come from identity dynamics. So, larger scale social structures depend upon the consistent arousal of the positive emotions that come with identity verification in face-to-face interactions. Thus, identity theories go a long way to closing what is often considered a gap between the micro level of interaction among people and the macro level of social structure of a society.

## CHAPTER 17

# Role Theories

By the midpoint of the twentieth century, the idea that individuals are connected to larger social structures by virtue of incumbency in status positions and roles pervaded sociological theory. *Role* was the key concept that linked individuals and social structure, and as a result of this emphasis, role theorizing became prominent. Yet, much of this role theorizing was, in reality, descriptions of expectations and behaviors in various empirical settings, or at best, more theoretical conceptualizations of a narrow range of role processes. Still, there were several efforts to build a theory of roles, particularly by Ralph H. Turner. Then, in the last two decades of the twentieth century, theorizing about roles seems to disappear at about the same time as theorizing on status processes increased, as is explored in the next chapter. It may be that understanding of roles had become so complete that theorizing on this fundamental property of the social universe was felt to be no longer necessary. Still, some more modest efforts to add to the existing body of theorizing have emerged in recent years; thus, theorizing on roles continues on a more modest scale, while theorizing on status processes remains the more dominant approach. Let me begin with Ralph H. Turner's approach.[1]

## Ralph H. Turner's Role Theorizing

Over the course of several decades, Ralph H. Turner mounted a consistent line of criticism against what he characterized as *structural role theory*.[2] This

---

[1]I should emphasize that, despite our similar names, Ralph H. Turner is not related to Jonathan H. Turner.

[2]See, for example, Ralph H. Turner, "Role-Taking: Processes versus Conformity," in *Human Behavior and Social Processes*, ed. A. Rose (Boston: Houghton Mifflin, 1962): pp. 20–40; Jonathan H. Turner, "Role," *Blackwell Encyclopedia of 20th Century Social Thought* (Oxford: Blackwell, 1996).

criticism incorporated several lines of attack: (1) Earlier role theory had presented an overly structured vision of the social world, with its emphasis on norms, status positions, and the enactment of normative expectations. (2) Role theory had tended to concentrate an inordinate amount of research and theory-building effort on "abnormal" social processes, such as role conflict and role strain, thereby ignoring the normal processes of human interaction. (3) Role theory was not a theory but rather a series of disjointed and unconnected propositions and empirical generalizations. (4) Role theory did not recognize Mead's concept of role taking as its central dynamic. As a corrective to these problems, in the decades around the midcentury, Turner offered a conceptualization of roles that emphasized the process of interaction over the dictates of social structures and cultural scripts.[3]

## The Process of Role Making

Turner used Mead's concept of role taking to describe the nature of social action. Turner assumed that "it is the tendency to shape the phenomenal world into roles which is the key to the role-taking as the core process in interaction."[4] Turner stressed that actors read the gestures or cues—words, bodily countenance, voice inflections, dress, facial expressions, and other gestures—as they interact to put themselves in the other's role and, thereby, to adjust their lines of conduct in ways that can facilitate cooperation. In emphasizing this point, Turner was simply following Mead's definition of taking the role of the other, or role taking.

Turner then extended Mead's concept. He first argued that cultural definitions of roles are often vague and even contradictory. At best, they provide a general framework within which actors must construct a line of conduct. Thus actors make their roles and communicate to others what role they are playing. Turner then argued that humans act *as if* all others in their environment are playing identifiable roles.[5] Humans assume others to be playing a role, and this assumption is what gives interaction a common basis. Operating with this folk assumption, people then read gestures and cues in an effort to determine what role others are playing.[6] This effort is facilitated

---

[3]Ralph H. Turner, "Unanswered Questions in the Convergence between Structuralist and Interactionist Role Theories," in *Perspectives on Sociological Theory*, eds. S. N. Eisenstadt and H. J. Helle (London: Sage, 1985). In particular, this article addresses Warren Handel, "Normative Expectations and the Emergence of Meaning as Solutions to Problems: Convergence of Structural and Interactionist Views," *American Journal of Sociology* 84 (1979): pp. 855–81.

[4]Turner, "Role-Taking: Processes versus Conformity" (cited in note 2).

[5]Ibid.; "Social Roles: Sociological Aspects," *International Encyclopedia of the Social Sciences* (New York: Macmillan, 1968).

[6]Ralph H. Turner, "The Normative Coherence of Folk Concepts," *Research Studies of the State College of Washington* 25 (1957).

by others creating and asserting their roles, with the result that they actively emit cues about what roles they are attempting to play.

For Turner, then, role taking was also role making. Humans make roles in three senses: (1) People are often faced with only a loose cultural framework in which they must make a role to play. (2) They assume others are playing a role and thus make an effort to discover the underlying role behind a person's acts. (3) They seek to make a role for themselves in all social situations by emitting cues to others that give them claim on a particular role. Interaction is, therefore, a joint and reciprocal process of *role taking* and *role making*.

## The Folk Norm of Consistency

As people interact with one another, Turner argued, they assess behavior less for its conformity to imputed norms or positions in a social structure and more for the consistency of behavior. Humans seek to group one another's behavior into coherent wholes or *gestalts*; by doing so, they can make sense of one another's actions, anticipate one another's behavior, and adjust to one another's responses. If another's responses are inconsistent and not seen as part of an underlying role, then interaction will prove difficult. Thus, there is an implicit *norm of consistency* in people's interactions with one another. Humans attempt to assess the consistency of others' actions to discern the underlying role that is being played.

## The Tentative Nature of Interaction

Turner echoed Herbert Blumer's position when he stated that "interaction is always a tentative process, a process of continuously testing the conception one has of the role of the other."[7] Humans are constantly interpreting additional cues emitted by others and using these new cues to see if they are consistent with those previously emitted and with the imputed roles of others. If they are consistent, then the actor will continue to adjust responses in accordance with the imputed role of the other. But as soon as inconsistent cues are emitted, the identification of the other's role will undergo revision. Thus, the imputation of a particular role to another person will persist only as long as it provides a stable framework for interaction. The tentative nature of the role-making process points to another facet of roles: the process of role verification.

## Role Verification

Actors seek to verify that behaviors and other cues emitted by people in a situation do indeed constitute a role. Turner argued that such efforts at verification or validation are achieved by applying external and internal criteria. The most often used internal criterion is the degree to which an

---

[7]Turner, "Role-Taking: Processes versus Conformity" (cited in note 2), p. 23.

actor perceives a role to facilitate interaction. External criteria can vary, but in general they involve assessment of a role by important others, relevant groups, or commonly agreed-on standards. When an imputed role is validated or verified in this way, then it can serve as a stable basis for continued interaction among actors.

## Self-Conceptions and Roles

All humans reveal self-conceptions of themselves as certain kinds of objects. Humans develop self-attitudes and feelings from their interactions with others, but as Turner and all role theorists emphasized, actors attempt to present themselves in ways that will reinforce their self-conceptions.[8] Because others will always seek to determine an individual's role, it becomes necessary for the individual to inform others, through cues and gestures, about the degree to which self is anchored in a role. Thus, actors will signal one another about their self-identity and the extent to which their role is consistent with their self-conception. For example, roles not consistent with a person's self-conception will likely be played with considerable distance and disdain, whereas those that an individual considers central to self-definitions will be played much differently.[9]

In sum, Turner's approach maintains many of the same concerns of early role theory (see Chapter 15), but with an emphasis on the behavioral aspect of roles, because actors impute roles to one another through behavioral cues. The notion in early analysis that roles are conceptions of expected behaviors is preserved, for assigning of a role to a person invokes an expectation that a certain type and range of responses will ensue. The view that roles are the norms attendant on status positions is given less emphasis than in early theories but not ignored, because norms and positions can be the basis for assigning and verifying roles.[10] And, emphasis is placed on socialization of individuals into a common role repertoire that enables them, when on the social stage, to denote each other's roles and play the appropriate reciprocal role.

---

[8]Ralph H. Turner, "The Role and the Person," cited in *American Journal of Sociology* 84 (1978): pp. 1–23.

[9]Turner, "Social Roles: Sociological Aspects" (cited in note 5). Turner has extensively analyzed this process of self-anchorage in roles. See, for example, Ralph H. Turner, "The Real Self: From Institution to Impulse," *American Journal of Sociology* 81 (1970): pp. 989–1016; Ralph H. Turner and Victoria Billings, "Social Context of Self-Feeling," in *The Self-Society Interface: Cognition, Emotion, and Action*, eds. J. Howard and P. Callero (Cambridge: Cambridge University Press, 1990); Ralph H. Turner and Steven Gordon, "The Boundaries of the Self: The Relationship of Authenticity to Inauthenticity in the Self-Conception," in *Self-Concept: Advances in Theory and Research*, eds. M. D. Lynch, A. A. Norem-Hebeisen, and Kenneth Gergen (Cambridge, MA: Ballinger, 1981).

[10]Ralph H. Turner, "Rule Learning as Role Learning," *International Journal of Critical Sociology* 1 (1974): pp. 10–28.

## Building a Role Theory

Although Turner accepted a process orientation, he was committed to developing interactionism into "something akin to axiomatic theory."[11] He had recognized that role theory was segmented into a series of narrow propositions and hypotheses and that role theorists had been reluctant "to find unifying themes to link various role processes."

Turner's strategy was to use propositions from the numerous research studies to build more formal and abstract theoretical statements. His goal was to maintain a productive dialogue between specific empirical propositions and more abstract theoretical statements. Turner advocated the use of what he termed *main tendency propositions* to link concepts to empirical regularities and to consolidate the thrust of these regularities.[12] What Turner sought was a series of statements that highlight what tends to occur in the normal operation of systems of interaction. To this end, Turner provided a long list of main tendency propositions on (a) roles as they emerge, (b) roles as an interactive framework, (c) roles in relation to actors, (d) roles in organizational settings, (e) roles in societal settings, and (f) roles and the person. The most important of these propositions will be examined.[13]

**Emergence and Character of Roles.** Turner begins by outlining certain empirical tendencies on the initial emergence and then the properties of roles once they have emerged. Five of these generalizations about the emergence and character of roles are summarized below:

1. In any interactive situation, behavior, sentiments, and motives tend to be differentiated into units that can be termed roles; once differentiated, elements of behavior, sentiment, and motives that appear in the same situation tend to be assigned to existing roles. (Tendencies for *role differentiation and accretion*)

2. In any interactive situation, the meaning of individual actions for ego (the actor) and for any alter (others) is assigned on the basis of the imputed role. (Tendencies for *meaningfulness*)

3. In connection with every role, there is a tendency for certain attributes of actors, aspects of behavior, and features of situations to become salient cues for the identification of roles. (Tendencies for *role cues*)

4. Every role tends to acquire an evaluation for rank and social desirability. (Tendencies for *evaluation*)

---

[11]Ralph H. Turner, "Strategy for Developing an Integrated Role Theory," *Humboldt Journal of Social Relations* 7 (1980): pp. 123–39 and "Role Theory as Theory," unpublished manuscript.

[12]Turner, "Strategy" (cited in note 11), pp. 123–24.

[13]Turner, "Social Roles: Sociological Aspects" (cited in note 5).

5. The character of a role—that is, its definition—will tend to change if there are persistent changes in either the behaviors of those presumed to be playing the role or the contexts in which the role is played. (Tendencies for *behavioral correspondence*)

In these five propositions, individuals are seen as viewing the world in terms of roles, as employing a "folk norm" to discover the consistency of behaviors and to assign behavioral elements to an imputed role (role differentiation and accretion), as using roles to interpret and define situations (meaningfulness tendency), as searching roles for signals about the attributes of actors as well as the nature of the situation (role cues), and as evaluating roles for their power, prestige, and esteem, while assessing them for their degree of social desirability and worth (tendency for evaluation). When role behaviors or situations are permanently altered, the definition of role will also undergo change (behavioral correspondence).

**Role as an Interactive Framework**. Next, Turner argues the interactions are only viable when individuals can identify each other's roles. Moreover, roles tend to be complements of others—as is the case with wife/husband, parent/child, boss/employee roles—and thus operate to regularize interaction among complementary roles. Finally, roles that prove useful and that allow stable and fruitful interaction are translated into expectations that future transactions will and should occur as in the past. Below are additional generalizations on these dynamics.

6. The establishment and persistence of interaction tend to depend on the emergence and identification of ego and alter roles. (Tendency for *interaction in roles*)

7. Each role tends to form as a comprehensive way of coping with one or more relevant alter roles. (Tendency for *role complementarity*)

8. There is a tendency for stabilized roles to be assigned the character of legitimate expectations and to be seen as the appropriate way to behave in a situation. (Tendency for *legitimate expectations*)

**Role in Relation to Actor**. Once actors identify and assign one another to roles, Turner argues that the roles persist; moreover, new actors will tend to be assigned to those roles that already exist in a situation. Humans also tend to adopt roles for the duration of an interaction, while having knowledge of the roles that others are playing. In addition, individuals carry with them general conceptions of what a role entails and what constitutes adequate performance. Finally, the adequacy of a person's role performance greatly influences the extent to which the role, along with the rights, privileges, and complementary behaviors that it deserves, will be acknowledged. These processes are summarized in the following generalizations:

9. Once stabilized, the role structure tends to persist, regardless of changes in actors. (Tendency for *role persistence*)

10. There is a tendency to identify a given individual with a given role and a complementary tendency for an individual to adopt a given role for the duration of the interaction. (Tendency for *role allocation*)

11. To the extent that ego's role is an adaptation to alter's role, it incorporates some conception of alter's role. (Tendency for *role taking*)

12. Role behavior tends to be judged as adequate or inadequate by comparison with a conception of the role in question. (Tendency to *assess role adequacy*)

13. The degree of adequacy in role performance of an actor determines the extent to which others will respond and reciprocate an actor's role performance. (Tendency for *role reciprocity*)

**Role in Organizational Settings**. Roles are often played out in organizations revealing divisions of labor organized to achieve particular goals. By emphasizing that roles are often embedded in organizations, Turner incorporated Ralph Linton's and other early theorists' insight that status and role can be highly related. When so coupled, the goals and authority systems of the organization constrain all role dynamics, although Turner also emphasizes that not all roles are part of networks of status positions in social structures. Turner never abandoned Mead's emphasis that much interaction occurs in contexts where roles are not immersed within networks of clearly defined status positions. The following generalizations summarize Turner's views on the relation of roles to organizational settings.

14. To the extent that roles are incorporated into an organizational setting, organizational goals tend to become crucial criteria for role differentiation, evaluation, complementarity, legitimacy or expectation, consensus, allocation, and judgments of adequacy. (Tendency for *organization goal dominance*)

15. To the extent that roles are incorporated into an organizational setting, the right to define the legitimate character of roles, to set the evaluations on roles, to allocate roles, and to judge role adequacy tends to be lodged in particular roles. (Tendency for *legitimate role definers*)

16. To the extent that roles are incorporated into an organizational setting, differentiation tends to link roles to statuses in the organization. (Tendency for *status*)

17. To the extent that roles are incorporated into an organizational setting, each role tends to develop as a pattern of adaptation to multiple alter roles. (Tendency for *role-sets*)

18. To the extent that roles are incorporated into an organizational setting, the persistence of roles is intensified through tradition and formalization. (Tendency for *formalization*)

**Role in Societal Setting.** Many roles are identified, assumed, and imputed in relation to a broader societal context. In the tendencies listed previously, Turner first argued that people tend to group behaviors in different social contexts into as few unifying roles as is possible or practical. Thus, people will identify a role as a way of making sense of disparate behaviors in different contexts. At the societal level, values are the equivalent of goals in organizational settings for identifying, differentiating, allocating, evaluating, and legitimating roles. As people assume multiple roles in societal settings, however, they tend to assume roles that are consistent with one another. These dynamics are summarized in the following propositions in Turner's scheme.

19. Similar roles in different contexts tend to become merged, so they are identified as a single role recurring in different relationships. (Tendency for *economy of roles*)

20. To the extent that roles refer to more general social contexts and situations, differentiation tends to link roles to social values. (Tendency for *value anchorage*)

21. The individual in society tends to be assigned and to assume roles consistent with one another. (Tendency for *allocation consistency*)

**Role and the Person.** The *person* is a concept employed by Turner to denote *the distinctive repertoire of roles* that an individual enacts, an idea borrowed from Georg Simmel who argued that individuals are the sum total of their configurations of roles played in societies. Individuals always seek to resolve tensions among roles and to avoid contradictions between their self-conceptions and roles, because to have contradictions decreases that chances that self will be verified.

22. Actors tend to act to alleviate role strain arising from role contradiction, role conflict, and role inadequacy and to heighten the gratifications of high role adequacy. (Tendency to resolve *role strain*)

23. Individuals in society tend to adopt a repertoire of role relationships as a framework for their own behavior and as a perspective for interpretation of the behavior of others. (Tendency to be *socialized into common culture*)

24. Individuals tend to form self-conceptions by selectively identifying certain roles from their repertoires as more characteristically "themselves" than other roles. (Tendency to *anchor self-conception*)

25. The self-conception tends to stress those roles that supply the basis for effective adaptation to relevant alters. (*Adaptation of self-conception* tendency)

26. To the extent that roles must be played in situations that contradict the self-conception, those roles will be assigned role distance, and mechanisms for demonstrating lack of personal involvement will be employed. (Tendency for *role distance*)

In developing these *tendency propositions* summarizing what occurs empirically when roles are played, Turner recognizes that these and other tendency propositions do not specify the conditions under which the tendency actually would occur. The propositions are thus only descriptive; they do not say why such tendencies should occur. Yet, Turner believed that to be true theory, role analysis must specify some of these basic conditions causing these tendencies in roles to occur. Without this extra step, there is no theory because the propositions outlined above are in need of a theoretical explanation about why these are the prevailing tendencies in role behaviors. And so, Turner has sought to add more explanatory content—that is, to indicate when and why the tendencies exist.

## Generating Explanatory Laws

Turner initiates his more explanatory efforts by specifying conditions under which particular tendencies become evident. For example, the tendencies for individuals to identify with a role and for others around the individual to make such an identification are likely to emerge when (a) allocation of roles is less flexible, (b) roles are highly differentiated, (c) roles are implicated in conflictual relationships, (d) performance of roles is judged as competent, (e) roles are considered difficult, (f) roles are either of high or low rank, (g) power is vested in a role, and so on.[14,15] These kinds of propositions were very suggestive, but Turner began to feel that they were somewhat ad hoc. Hence, he was led to ask the following: Are there some underlying processes that can explain the tendencies and the conditions under which they become manifest? This question inspired him, along with various collaborators, to develop what he felt were true *explanatory propositions* that would stand at the top of a deductive system explaining the tendencies and the conditions under which they are activated.

These explanatory propositions bring Turner's work from the midcentury into the more contemporary theoretical time frame. But for ease of exposition, it is best to deal with these explanatory "laws" here. In their most recent reworking, Turner and Paul Colomy posit three underlying processes

---

[14]Turner, "Role and the Person" (cited in note 8).

[15]In his most recent effort, "Strategy for Developing an Integrated Role Theory," Turner focused on *role allocation* and *role differentiation* because he views these as the two most critical tendencies. The example of the person and role results in the same explanatory principles. Thus, this illustration provides additional examples of Turner's strategy.

that can explain the other propositions in Turner's developing theory: (1) functionality, (2) tenability, and (3) representation.[16] We will briefly examine each of these. I should emphasize that Turner later narrows the explanatory focus of functionality, representation, and tenability to account primarily for role differentiation.[17]

**Functionality.** When activities are organized to meet explicit goals in an efficient and effective manner, then considerations of functionality are dominant. Such considerations are most likely when the organization of individuals (into a division of labor composed of status positions) to achieve goals can potentially involve conflicts of interest among the participants and when these participants must be recruited from diverse pools of individuals who differ in their abilities. Under these conditions, the differentiation and accretion of roles are organized in highly instrumental ways so that goals can be achieved within a minimum of conflict and friction.

**Tenability.** When roles form and differentiate in ways that allow individuals to gain personal rewards and gratifications, considerations of tenability are evident. Thus, as individuals calculate their costs and rewards, and indeed are encouraged by the organization of roles to do so, tenability dominates functionality.

**Representation**. When the accretion and differentiation of roles involve the embodiment of cultural values, considerations of representation are evident. Moreover, the salience of representation of roles increases, however, when roles are implicated in group conflict and when incumbents in roles are recruited from homogeneous pools of individuals. When representation dominates the organization of roles, tenability will become more important than functionality.

The propositions developed for functionality, tenability, and representation are more complex than this brief discussion, but the general intent is clear. These propositions serve as the higher-order laws in propositional scheme that is explanatory because they explain the tendency propositions by specifying the conditions under which they hold true. Although this strategy is suggestive, Turner has never fully implemented it by subsuming all the tendency propositions under these three laws in an explanatory proposition scheme. Yet, unlike much role theorizing from the midcentury, Turner's approach recognized that generalizations about roles from empirical observations need to be organized in ways facilitating their explanation

[16]Ralph H. Turner and Paul Colomy, "Role Differentiation: Orienting Principles," *Advances in Group Processes* 5 (1987): pp. 1–47.

[17]Ralph H. Turner, "Role Theory," in *Handbook of Sociological Theory*, ed. J. H. Turner (Kluwer Academic/Plenum, 2001), pp. 233–54.

by more abstract principles.[18] For Turner, the relative amounts of functionality, tenability, and representation would provide the needed explanatory push. This strategy has not, I believe, been entirely successful; this may be because the explanatory propositions do not adequately take account of the close connection between status and role. Moreover, the failure of role theory to be fully explanatory may also explain why theorizing turned increasingly to status dynamics in the latter decades in the twentieth century and up to the present. Thus, a theory of roles may require first a theory of status dynamics, as is explored in the next chapter.

# Jonathan Turner's Supplemental Conception of Role Dynamics

## The Centrality of Roles

For some years, I have been trying to extend Ralph Turner's views on the dynamics of roles within the context of micro-level interaction processes more generally. Increasingly, as the behavioral component of microdynamics, roles are at the center of what occurs as people interact face-to-face. In a very real sense, role behaviors are the vehicle by which all other micro processes operate. For example, status dynamics (see next chapter) revolving around one's location in a social structure are partially determined by how one plays a role; the same is true for what aspects of culture are made relevant to a situation. Thus, it is from roles that we asses such critical matters as the following: What stocks of knowledge are important in a situation? What motives are driving people in an interaction? What does the use of situational ecology and physical props mean in a situation to a person and others? What identity is salient and how is it to be verified? What does the emotional dispositions of others and virtually all other micro social processes are? It is true that we often know much about a situation and others in this situation by familiarity with social structures, but humans will need to fine-tune this knowledge of social structures through the visible

---

[18]For representative examples of the variety of empirical research conducted by Turner, see "The Navy Disbursing Officer as a Bureaucrat," *American Sociological Review* 12 (1947): pp. 342–48; "Moral Judgment: A Study in Roles," *American Sociological Review* 17 (1952): pp. 70–77; "Occupational Patterns of Inequality," *American Journal of Sociology* 50 (1954): pp. 437–47; "Zoot-Suiters and Mexicans: Symbols in Crowd Behavior" (with S. J. Surace), *American Journal of Sociology* 62 (1956): pp. 14–20; "The Changing Ideology of Success: A Study of Aspirations of High School Men in Los Angeles," *Transactions of the Third World Congress of Sociology* 5 (1956): pp. 35–44; "An Experiment in Modification of the Role Conceptions," *Yearbook of the American Philosophical Society* (1959), pp. 329–32; "Some Family Determinants of Ambition," *Sociology and Social Research* 46 (1962): pp. 397–411; *The Social Context of Ambition* (San Francisco: Chandler & Sharp, 1964); "Ambiguity and Interchangeability in Role Attribution" (with Norma Shosid), *American Sociological Review* 41 (1976); and "The True Self Method for Studying Self-Conception," *Symbolic Interaction* 4 (1981): pp. 1–20.

role behaviors of each person in a situation. Thus, Mead was certainly correct that role taking or reading the gestures of others is critical in being able to cooperate with others, and R. Turner has provided an important reciprocal of role taking in his concept of role making. Role taking is possible only through the role-making efforts of others. These role-making processes can be consciously orchestrated and manipulated, or unconsciously presented to others as they role-take.

## Expanding the Notions of Role Taking and Role Making

In my general theory of microdynamic processes,[19] I have emphasized that certain forces drive interaction processes, including the following: (a) roles, (b) emotions, (c) status, (d) motives and need-states, (e) culture, (f) situational ecology, and (g) situational demography. In Table 17.1, I define each of these fundamental microdynamic forces. Mead and R. Turner's dual ideas of role taking and role making have led me recently to recoceptualize the processes by which people execute these microdynamic processes delineated in Table 17.1.[20] Just as people role-make and role-take, so they *emotion-take* and *emotion-make*, *status-take* and *status-make*, *motive-take* and *motive-make*, *culture-take* and *culture-make*, *ecology-take* and *ecology-make*, and *demography-take* and *demography-make*. Much of this "taking and making" on dynamics other than roles occurs through role taking and role making. By observing the role behaviors of others in order to determine the emotions, status, motive states, relevant culture, meanings of ecology and demography that apply to an interaction, people engage in much more than role taking. The also gain information on all of the basic interpersonal forces driving interaction. Reciprocally, by orchestrating both consciously and unconsciously behaviors that signal to others a person's emotional state, status claims, need-states and motives, cultural preferences, and interpretations of situational ecology and demography, individuals can greatly facilitate the role taking of others as they seek to cooperate with this person. Let me now elaborate briefly on these dual dynamics of *making* and *taking* operate not only for roles but also for other micro-level processes.

## Activating Microdynamic Forces in Interaction

**Stocks of Knowledge at Hand.** R. Turner's conception of roles implicitly includes the idea that individuals have a certain amount of knowledgeability

---

[19]Jonathan H. Turner, *Theoretical Principles of Sociology, vol. 2, Microdynamics* (New York: Springer, 2010).

[20]Ibid. See also Jonathan H. Turner, *Face-to-Face: Toward a Theory of Interpersonal Behavior* (Stanford, CA: Stanford University Press, 2002) and "Identities, Emotions, and Interaction Processes," *Symbolic Interaction* 34, no.3, pp. 330–39 as well as "Neurology and Interpersonal Behavior: The Basic Challenge for Neurosociology," in *Neurosociology*, eds. D. Franks and J. Turner (New York: Springer, 2012).

| **Table 17.1**   Broad Definitions of Microdynamic Forces |
| --- |

**Ecological forces**: Boundaries, configurations of the physical space, and the props in space as these constrain the behaviors of individuals in focused and unfocused encounters

**Demographic forces**: Numbers of individuals co-present, their density, their movements, and their characteristics as these constrain the behaviors of individuals in focused and unfocused encounters

**Status forces**: Positional locations and their organization within corporate units revealing divisions of labor and memberships in categoric units defined by parameters as they constrain behaviors of individuals in focused and unfocused encounters

**Roles forces**: Moment-by-moment configurations of gestures mutually emitted and interpreted by persons to communicate their respective dispositions and likely courses of action as these constrain behaviors in focused and unfocused encounters

**Cultural forces**: Systems of symbols organized into texts, values, beliefs and ideologies, and norms as they generate expectations and thereby constrain the behaviors of individuals in focused and unfocused encounters

**Motivational forces**: Universal need-states as these constrain behaviors of individuals in focused and unfocused encounters. The most important need-states are (a) verifying identities, (b) realizing profits in exchanges of resources with others, and (c) achieving a sense of inclusion in the ongoing flow of interaction.

**Emotional forces**: Types and valences of affect aroused, experienced, and expressed that constrain the behaviors of individuals in focused and unfocused encounters

about roles. If they did not, they probably could not role-take effectively. For R. Turner, this stock of knowledge at hand about what elements of behaviors go together to make up a coherent role is governed by a "folk norm of consistency." In contrast, I do not see these dynamics as normative but as hardwired cognitive capacities and propensities to order perceptions into coherent and understandable patterns. As people role-take and thus read the gestures of others, they scan their stocks of knowledge to discern the role being played by others; and then, on the basis of this scanning, they will try to play a role that is complementary, unless they deliberately wish to initiate conflict (which people often do). This search for patterns is directed by a hardwired bias in humans for consistency and congruence among cognitions, not only for those coming from observations but also for those cognitions stored in the human frontal cortex.

As part of the structure and operation of the human brain, then, humans always seek consistency and patterns among elements of cognitions, whether these be about roles, status, culture, motive states, or situational ecology or demography. Gestalt psychology made this point many decades ago and, once again, I do not think that there is a norm of consistency but that this is simply way the brain works. Human brains seek to understand meanings of the outside world, and one way to establish meanings is to understand what elements of situations fit into a pattern of gestures marking roles that can then be interpreted. During interaction, people wait for the consistency in patterns to emerge, but if a situation remains chaotic to a person, then it will be highly stressful and force this person to continue scanning stocks of knowledge for a consistent pattern of information. If no observed pattern is found in stocks of knowledge, individuals will generally leave such situations and avoid them in the future.

What is true of roles is also the case for other microdynamic processes. Humans store in their stocks of knowledge vast inventories of information about emotions, status, motive states, culture, ecology, and demography that they draw upon to understand the dispositions and behaviors of others. People are naturally scanning their stocks of knowledge for the salient expectations for cultural norms, for status cues, for beliefs, and values, for motives of others, for the attributions others are making, for the meanings of situational ecology and use of spaces and props in situations, and for meanings of the various categories of others and their movements and distribution in space. As individuals role-take, they access their stocks of knowledge not only for information about roles but also for information about emotions, status, culture, motives, situational ecology, situational demography, and attributions people are making. At the same time, in their role-making efforts, persons are also signaling their intentions and preferences to others about their emotions, their status, their motives, and their interpretations of the relevant culture, their meanings of situation ecology, and their views on the significance, if any, of situational demography.

**Drawing Upon Stocks of Knowledge.** Often people already know much of this information by virtue of previous experiences or general knowledge about particular types of situations. For example, before you enter a classroom, you already know about roles, status, emotions, culture, motives, ecology, and demography of such a situation, with the result that it is not necessary to actively role-take with specific others in the situation. If we wanted to extend Mead's notion of the generalized other, we could view this as role taking with a generalized other or set of prescriptions and proscriptions about classrooms, but I prefer Schutz's terms about stocks of knowledgeability that we have acquired over our lifetimes about emotions, status, roles, culture, motives, ecology, and demography of interpersonal situations. We scan this knowledge and then go on automatic pilot when, for example, entering a classroom.

Still, despite generalized knowledge about classrooms, we may have to actively role-take and role-make, emotion-take and emotion-make, status-take and status-make, culture-take and culture-make, motive-take and motive-make, ecology-take and ecology-make, or demography-take and demography-make. For example, if the classroom is much smaller than expected, if the teacher is older or younger, if others are of diverse social categories (say, ethnicity and gender) or of the same category (all female and young), if there are no chairs lined in row but chairs are around a large table, if the class is important to your sense of identity as a student, if you recognize the rules of a seminar class are different than those of a lecture class, and so on, then you will have to re-scan your stocks of knowledge and begin to more actively reading the gestures of others to recalibrate your sense of the situation and the actions of others. So, even when situations are familiar and relatively structured, people often must actively role-take and scan their stocks of knowledge for additional information about appropriate roles but also about culture, emotions, status, and meanings of situational ecology and demography

As a general rule, the more embedded is a situation within a group, organization, or community, the more likely are people to understand the relevant roles, appropriate emotions, distribution of status, salient elements of culture, and meanings of situational ecology and demography. As a result, they will have an easy time scanning the relevant stocks of knowledge and will not have to be so active in role taking when interacting with others, *unless* something is new or different about the situation that goes against the stocks of knowledge that have been accessed during initial scans. If something is new and unexpected, then a person will need to reinterpret the gestures of others and the situation in general with respect to roles, status, motives, culture, ecology, and demography. This person will have to work harder at finding the relevant stocks of knowledge in order to cooperate with others.

# Conclusion

My point in presenting some of my own work with the pioneering work of Ralph Turner is to demonstrate that, despite the decline of theorizing about roles, there is still very much theorizing to be done. Roles are central to, and intertwined with, all other microdynamic processes; thus, the key to a more general theory of not only roles dynamics but all other forces driving interpersonal behavior is to unpack the notions of role taking and making and to see them as the essential dynamic revolving around all other micro forces driving interaction (my views about these forces are the forces delineated in Table 17.1).

There are, then, many potential leads to expanding the theory of roles, once we link roles to everything else that occurs when humans interact. Thus, Ralph H. Turner's theorizing takes us much of the way in developing a more robust theory of role processes; my approach, I hope, opens upon further avenues for building on R. Turner's theory.

## CHAPTER 18

# Status Theories

Early twentieth-century sociology and anthropology developed the concept of *status* to denote the location of persons in social structures and cultural fields. Each status position was seen as part of a structure composed of interrelated positions regulated by cultural norms, ideologies, and beliefs. Yet, there still remains considerable ambiguity over just what status denotes. One view is that, as it was mentioned above, status is a location in a network of positions within varying types of social units. Another view is that status is the prestige that persons are able to garner in a situation. Still another is that status is the power and authority that individuals can have vis-à-vis other status locations. Yet another conception is that status is the location of expectations attached to positions that govern how individuals should behave in a particular position and vis-à-vis other status positions. A related view is that status and the expectations associated with status direct role behaviors of individuals. Another view is that status—conceptualized as *diffuse status characteristics*—is a marker of membership of persons in social categories (e.g., gender, ethnicity, class, religious affiliation). In turn, there are expectation states for, and evaluations of, members in such categories.

All of these visions of status are not contradictory; each highlights a particular property of status. In recent decades, as theorizing about roles has declined, theorizing about status has increased. Most of this theorizing comes from those emphasizing the *differential expectation states* that emerge when (a) individuals occupy different positions in divisions of labor of collectively organized social units or what can be termed *corporate units*, (b) individuals behave in ways that allow them to claim prestige and power/authority over others in a situation, and (c) individuals are members of differentially evaluated social categories. Our review of status theories will emphasize these dimensions of status.

---

*This chapter is coauthored with David G. Wagner.

# The Phenomenology of Status

As emphasized in the last chapter, individuals engage in a process of *status making* and *status taking*.[1] They seek to assert and claim, if they can, status relative to others (status making) and, reciprocally, interpret the gestures of others and situational cues to determine the status of others. Often social structures determine people's respective status locations, but even under this condition, people seek to present status cues to others about matters that they can control, such as their competence, which, in turn, entitles them to prestige and deference from others. Status can also be constrained by the social categories in which people are placed—categories such as gender, race, ethnicity, class, or any social difference that marks individuals as distinctive and as subject to a certain level of evaluation. As noted earlier, these have been termed *diffuse status characteristics* by those theorizing within the expectation states tradition (to be discussed shortly); these diffuse status characteristics establish expectations for how people should behave and, at the same time, may impose standards of evaluation for social and moral worth of persons. These evaluative standards, or what are sometimes termed *referential structures* in expectation states theorizing, are beliefs about qualities and characteristics of members of social categories.

Much like roles, individuals acquire a considerable amount of knowledgeability about the various dimensions of status. When interacting with others in a situation, people scan these stocks of knowledge in order to determine the expectations for, and evaluations of, individuals' locations in divisions of labor, their performances relative to the performances of others, and their membership in differentially evaluated social categories. People thus carry in their brains inventories of conceptions about status as locations in a social structure, behavioral performances marking competence or its converse, or memberships in a social category. Co-presence will typically activate a scanning for status of self and others in a situation, and with interaction comes even more pressure on individuals to determine each other's status so as to know the expectations for, and evaluations of, self and others.

Moreover, individuals carry in their stocks of knowledge information about the roles that can be played by virtue of status locations and diffuse status characteristics, what identities can be presented to others, what

---

[1]Jonathan H. Turner, *Face-to-Face: Toward a Sociological Theory of Interpersonal Behavior*, (Stanford, CA: Stanford University Press, 2002); *Theoretical Principles of Sociology*, vol. 2, *Microdynamics* (New York: Springer 2010); "Identities, Emotions, and Interaction Processes," *Symbolic Interaction* 34 (2010): pp. 330–39; "Toward A Theory of Interpersonal Processes," in *Sociological Social Psychology*, eds. J. Chin and J. Cardell (Boston, MA: Allyn and Bacon, 2008), pp. 65–95; "Emotions and Social Structure: Toward a General Theory," in *Emotions and Social Structure*, eds. D. Robinson and J. Clay-Warner (New York: Elsevier, 2008), pp. 319–42.

emotions can and should be displayed, what resources can be used and secured in exchanges with others, what elements of culture (norms, beliefs, ideologies, values) can be invoked to regulate and evaluate each other, what situational props can be used and by whom with what status, and many other features that drive encounters.

Thus, people carry a great deal of information about status, and they actively pull from their stocks of knowledge the relevant information in status taking and status making with others. And as they play roles, people continue to status-take and status-make to verify that self and others are living up to the expectations attached to their respective status.

# Clarity of Status in Situations

Individuals are selectively attentive to status cues when they interact with others and especially so when status is ambiguous.[2] A key variable in status taking and making, then, is the clarity of status. The more status of self and others is easily understood, the more likely is interaction to proceed smoothly because all persons understand the expectations for, and the respective evaluations of, self and all other persons in the situation. If, for example, we know that a person is a professor and others are students, expectations are relatively clear and unambiguous; as a result, the interaction can proceed. If, in contrast, students encounter professors, and vice versa, in a store in a shopping mall, there is some ambiguity as to which dimensions of status apply. Are professors fellow shoppers, or do the respective status locations at the college or university trump all status considerations? The answer to such questions might well depend on more fine-grained status distinctions, such as the students are graduate students and the professor is an assistant professor. Here, a diffuse status characteristic—respective age—intersects with status as a location in the division of labor of the university and, in all likelihood, reduces status distance and activates expectation states for individuals behaving in the status of shoppers.

In general, the more embedded a status is in a social structure and the more a status is embedded in what Jonathan Turner calls a *categoric unit* (conceived as diffuse status characteristics by expectation state theorizing), the greater will be the clarity of status and the less individuals will need to status-take in the situation. And, status taking will be made even easier if diffuse status characteristics are highly visible, such as is the case with gender and ethnicity when accompanied by distinctive phenotypical traits like skin color or an eye fold. This clarity increases when there is correlation or consolidation of differentially evaluated diffuse status characteristics with inequality in the power and prestige of locations in the division of labor of corporate units. That is, high-, middle-, and low-ranking status positions

---

[2]Turner, *Face-to-Face* (cited in note 1), pp. 192–205.

are filled by individuals with diffuse status characteristics that match the hierarchy of positional locations in social structure. If, on the other hand, the two types of status intersect in that high- and low- evaluation individuals (by virtue of their diffuse status characteristics) are distributed across high and low positions in the division of labor, then status taking and status making as well as role taking and role making become more complicated for all because clarity has been reduced. The consequence is that individuals will need to exert more effort at status taking and status making.

Thus, clarity will increase when positions in divisions of labor are more hierarchical, when memberships in categoric units are more discrete (one is either a member or not, as would be the case with gender), and when differential evaluations of diffuse status characteristics are correlated with location in a hierarchy of positions. Much of this clarity in status also makes what J. Turner termed *culture taking* and *culture making* easier as well. Individuals know *which* norms, beliefs, and ideologies to invoke in setting up expectations for how individuals should behave; the greater the differential evaluation in what are sometimes termed *status beliefs* and the greater is the clarity of these beliefs, the easier will status taking and making become. And, if these beliefs are tied to societal-level values and institutional-level ideologies (about good/bad, right/wrong, appropriate/inappropriate), the clarity and degree of differential evaluation in status beliefs will be that much more evident to individuals.

# Expectation States and Status

One of the most carefully and explicitly developed theoretical research programs in sociology to emerge in the second half of the twentieth century is a related set of theories known as *expectation states theory*. Although this program was originally the pursuit of Joseph Berger and his colleagues, students, and associates, expectation states theory has in recent years attracted the attention of many other investigators as well.[3]

---

[3]Many others have been integral to the development of theories in the expectation states program, particularly Morris Zelditch, Jr. and Bernard P. Cohen. Nevertheless, Berger has been the intellectual force at the center of the program since its inception. Many of those who have since made separate contributions to the program first made contributions in collaboration with Berger. For examples of overviews of the progress, see Joseph Berger, Thomas L. Conner, and M. Hamit Fisek, eds., *Expectation States Theory: A Theoretical Research Program* (Cambridge, MA: Winthrop, 1974; reprinted by University Press of America in 1982); Joseph Berger, David G. Wagner, and Morris Zelditch, Jr., "Theory Growth, Social Processes, and Metatheory," in *Theory Building in Sociology*, ed. J. H. Turner (Newbury Park, CA: Sage, 1989), pp. 19–43; Joseph Berger and Morris Zelditch, Jr., eds., *Status Rewards and Influence* (San Francisco: Jossey-Bass, 1985); Joseph Berger, Bernard P. Cohen, and Morris Zelditch, Jr., "Status Characteristics and Expectation States," in *Sociological Theories in Progress*, eds. J. Berger, M. Zelditch, Jr., and B. Anderson (Boston: Houghton Mifflin, 1966), pp. 29–46; David G. Wagner and Joseph Berger, "Status Characteristics Theory: The Growth of a Program," in *Theoretical Research Programs: Studies*

Expectation states approaches are interactionist theories in several senses. First, behavior is assumed to be situationally constrained, with actors learning how to behave from social and cultural frames of reference available in the situation. Second, these frames of reference exert their influence through the perceptions of individuals, and what people believe or expect to be true about the situation can dictate perceptions of reality; indeed, expectations are reality for persons in most situations. Finally, these beliefs and expectations emerge and are maintained by the process of interaction itself.

## The Core Ideas of Expectation States Theorizing

The most central concept to the theory is, perhaps obviously, the notion of an *expectation state*. Expectation states represent stabilized anticipations for future behavior of one actor relative to that of another. Thus, a person is expected to perform more capably or less capably relative to another individual or other individuals. Furthermore, expectations are always both task specific and person specific in the sense that person *A* may be expected to perform more capably than person *B* with respect to one task (say, repairing an automobile engine) and less capably than person *B* on a second task (say, playing a Beethoven quartet). Similarly, person *A* may be expected to perform more capably than person *B* but less capably than person *C* on the same task.

Because the self constitutes a social object, actors can also have expectations for themselves relative to specific others, although what actors are able to report about self-expectations is just as prone to error and misinterpretation as what they can report about expectations for others. Nevertheless, individuals behave as if they have adopted a specific set of expectations.

Expectation states are generated from a variety of different sources, such as evaluation of task performances during the course of an interaction, locations in divisions of labor, memberships in social categories, reflection on the appraisals of significant others, allocation of material or symbolic rewards, activation of differences in people's power and prestige, and assessment of justice and equity. These and other sources provide information from the broader social environment, and when individuals interact on a task, this information becomes salient in the immediate, local situation. Expectation states then emerge and organize information into a coherent

*in the Growth of Theory*, eds. J. Berger and M. Zelditch, Jr. (Palo Alto, CA: Stanford University Press, 1993), pp. 23–63; David G. Wagner and Joseph Berger, "Expectation States Theory: An Evolving Research Program," in *New Directions in Contemporary Sociological Theory*, eds. J. Berger and M. Zelditch, Jr. (New York: Rowman & Littlefield, 2002), pp. 41–76; Shelley J. Correll and Cecilia L. Ridgeway, "Expectation States Theory," in *The Handbook of Social Psychology*, ed. John Delamater (New York: Kluwer-Plenum, 2003), pp. 29–51; Joseph Berger and Murray Webster, Jr., "Expectations, Status, and Behavior," in *Contemporary Social Psychological Theories*, ed. Peter J. Burke (Palo Alto, CA: Stanford University Press, 2006), pp. 268–300.

picture, or definition, of the situation. This picture enables individuals to select behaviors that are appropriate to the situation and to avoid those that are not. Because these behaviors are generally consistent with definitions of the situation, they tend to reinforce established expectations, and typically, it requires the introduction of new information or a change in the local situation to break this self-perpetuating cycle. These core ideas can be summarized as follows:

1. Given certain conditions, individuals organize salient information from the social environment into expectations for behavior in the immediate situation of interaction. (*The salience of social information for expectation formation*)

2. Individuals behave in accordance with their expectations regarding the immediate situation of interaction. (*The behavioral implications of expectations*)

3. Individuals' behavior in the immediate situation of interaction tends to reinforce established expectations. (*The reinforcement of expectations*)

Conditions sufficient to activate the information-organizing process are not always present, however. Consequently, behavior can be relatively stable over extended periods of time, changing only when the new conditions arise. Indeed, from the perspective of expectation states theory, individuals do not continuously reorganize or renegotiate their definitions of the situation; rather, they generally behave in accordance with their existing definitions, reorganizing or renegotiating only when necessary.

## Application of Core Ideas in Expectation States Theorizing

**Power and Prestige.** The expectation states program began with Joseph Berger's interest in accounting for the behaviors of individuals in undifferentiated groups. In particular, he sought to understand the emergence and maintenance of power and prestige differences in the behavior of two actors in these initially undifferentiated groups. Berger's *behavior-expectation theory* was initially designed to explain why inequalities in power and prestige evolve so very quickly in groups, even when members are initially similar in status. These inequalities include differences in opportunities to contribute to consideration of the group's task or problem (such as asking a question), actual attempts to provide solutions to these tasks and problems (such as answering a question), evaluations of the contributions (such as criticism of a proposed answer), and acceptance or rejection of influence (such as deferring to another actor with whom one has disagreed). Moreover, these inequalities were highly correlated, forming a single hierarchy of observable power and prestige differences among members of the group. Once such a hierarchy emerged, it tended to be stable—even over different group discussions on different days.

Behavior-expectation theories were developed initially to explain these phenomena as a consequence of an underlying structure of expectations for future task performance that seemed to emerge from the interactions among group members. Once these expectations exist, they determine the course of future interaction in the group, thereby reinforcing the existing structure of expectations. Thus, the inequalities are highly correlated because they are generated by the same underlying expectations. Further, unless other structural factors intervene (for example, new group members and new information are introduced or the task focus of the group changes), the structure of expectations and the observable power and prestige hierarchy will remain stable. Adopting the principles described earlier, this process can be summarized as follows:

1. Actors behave toward others in a manner consistent with their expectations. An actor who is considered more capable than others is offered more opportunities to interact, makes more contributions to the interaction, more often has those contributions evaluated positively, and has more influence when disagreements occur. (*The behavioral consequences of expectations*)

2. Expectations tend to remain the same as long as the actors involved in the situation and the tasks that they are performing remain the same. (*The persistence of expectations*)

Although these expectation states processes occur under a wide variety of conditions, they are most evident in situations where actors who are initially similar in status work together collectively on a task that they value. Thus, we might observe expectation processes in jury deliberations, business conferences, family vacation planning, or a group of teenagers planning a trip to the movies. They might also be evident in the interaction among members of a basketball team but might be less likely to occur in the interaction between members of opposing teams because they are not working toward a common goal.[4]

Other work in behavior-expectation theory has focused on the process by which expectations emerge from interaction.[5] This work suggests that

---

[4]Berger first developed this argument in his doctoral dissertation: Joseph Berger, "Relations Between Performance, Rewards, and Action-Opportunities in Small Groups" (unpublished doctoral dissertation, Harvard University, 1958). See also Joseph Berger and Thomas L. Conner, "Performance Expectations and Behavior in Small Groups," *Acta Sociologica* 12 (1969): pp. 186–98.

[5]See, for example, Joseph Berger, Thomas L. Conner, and W. McKeown, "Evaluations and the Formation and Maintenance of Performance Expectations," *Human Relations* 22 (1969): pp. 481–502; Thomas J. Fararo, "An Expectation States Process Model," in *Mathematical Sociology* (New York: Wiley, 1973), pp. 229–37.

resolving disagreements forces actors to evaluate their own and others' performances and to accept or reject influence from others on the basis of these evaluations. Any time a decision must be made, there is some likelihood that the individuals will develop an expectation state for each other that is, in a very real sense, an anticipation for the quality of an actor's future contribution. This expectation state will be consistent with the preponderance of evaluations for the contributions of each individual in the group. More generally, we can summarize the process in these terms:

> 3. The more consistent the evaluations of an actor's past interaction are, the more likely the actor and others are to expect a level of capability from the actor in the future that realizes past evaluations. (*The emergence of expectations*)

Later work has developed and extended these arguments. For example, inequalities with respect to any aspect of the group's interaction, not just the evaluation of an individual's performance, might generate expectations and spread to other aspects of the interaction.[6] Power and prestige hierarchies can emerge from interaction involving any number of actors as well as from different types of actors.[7] Finally, objective evaluations from external sources of information that contradict established expectations can help overcome existing expectations. Such changes depend on the number and extremity of the contradicting evaluations.[8]

**Status Characteristics.** As noted earlier, actors are similar or different with respect to status distinctions such as ethnicity, age, race, or gender that might be significant in society at large. Status characteristics theory describes how actors organize information about initial status differences that they use to generate expectations for performance. As with behavior-expectation theory, these expectations then govern the interaction, ensuring that power and prestige are distributed in accord with expectations.

Research has shown that external status distinctions become the basis for internal ones; status inequalities significant in the larger society become important in the task situation of a small group. These distinctions, present even as the group is being formed, govern the distribution of power and

---

[6]Joseph Berger and Thomas L. Conner, "Performance Expectations and Behavior in Small Groups: A Revised Formulation," in *Expectation States Theory: A Theoretical Research Program*, eds. Berger, Conner, and Fisek, pp. 85–109; see also M. Hamit Fisek, "A Model for the Evolution of Status Structures," pp. 55–83, in the same volume.

[7]Thomas J. Fararo and John Skvoretz, "E-State Structuralism: A Theoretical Method," *American Sociological Review* 51 (1986): pp. 591–602.

[8]See, for example, Martha Foschi and R. Foschi, "A Bayesian Model for Performance Expectations: Extension and Simulation," *Social Psychology Quarterly* 42 (1979): pp. 232–41.

prestige; furthermore, these effects occur whether or not the status distinction is associated with the group's task.[9]

Status distinctions are, as emphasized earlier, characterized as diffuse status characteristics, with a characteristic being diffuse for a particular individual in the situation if (1) the characteristic has two or more states that the individual evaluates differently, (2) the individual associates a general expectation with each status state, and (3) the individual associates a distinct set of expectations for specific abilities or traits with each state.[10] Gender, race, ethnicity, educational attainment, occupation, and physical attractiveness are each examples of these kinds of diffuse status characteristic, because they generally meet the three features listed above. The properties that define a characteristic are based on attributions made by the individual. These attributions invoke those beliefs in cultural systems to which the individual has been exposed. Thus,

1. If actors have differentiated diffuse status or if a status they share is culturally associated with a task that the actors perform, then the actors will attribute generalized expectations and specific abilities to themselves and each other consistent with their status. (*The salience of status information*)

A second principle concerns establishing the relevance of salient status; hence, the "burden of proof" principle emphasizes that status information will be assumed to be task relevant *unless* there is specific information to the contrary.

2. Actors assume that salient status information applies to every new task and every new situation unless they have a specific knowledge or belief that demonstrates its inapplicability. (*The relevance of status information*)

3. An actor with a status advantage is expected to perform more capably than the actor with a status disadvantage. (*The assignment of expectations*)

Finally, in line with this basic expectation assumption, people behave in accordance with their expectations. Opportunities to initiate action, actual performance outputs, communicated evaluations of performance, and influence will all reflect the difference in self-expectations and expectations for others. Thus, the presence of a single diffuse status characteristic that discriminates between actors is sufficient to generate differentiated power and prestige behavior, provided that the status differences are not dissociated from the task.

---

[9]For a summary of some of this research, see Bernard P. Cohen, Joseph Berger, and Morris Zelditch, Jr., "Status Conceptions and Interaction: A Case Study of the Problem of Developing Cumulative Knowledge," in *Experimental Social Psychology*, ed. C. G. McClintock (New York: Holt, Rinehart, and Winston, 1972), pp. 449–83.

[10]See Joseph Berger, Bernard P. Cohen, and Morris Zelditch, Jr., "Status Characteristics and Expectation States," in *Sociological Theories in Progress*, pp. 29–46; the paper was updated, with a report on empirical results in *American Sociological Review* 37 (1972): pp. 241–55.

**Multiple Characteristic Status Situations.** One important dilemma for individuals in interaction, and hence for a theory of expectation states, is where multiple status characteristics are present.[11] In essence, theorists and researchers asked: What are the implications for expectations and behavior when individuals can be distinguished by more than one status characteristic, especially when the implications of these statuses are inconsistent?[12]

What appears to occur is that individuals add up two subsets of information. One combines all of the positive information relevant to a person in a situation; another is all of the negative information. Then, the positive and negative subsets are subtracted from each other, leaving a net evaluation and expectations that is either positive or negative depending upon which subset was greater. Once this composite of information is established, additional information will have less impact on the already established evaluation and expectation states derived from this evaluation. The following principles summarize this process:

1. Actors combine information from multiple salient status differences to form aggregated expectations for self and others. (*The combining principle*)

2. Actors combine positive status information into one (positively valued) set and negative information into a second (negatively valued) set. Expectations are aggregated by summing the values of these two sets. (*The principle of organized subsets*)

3. Each additional piece of status information added to a set increases the value of that set as a whole, but each new piece of status information affects the whole set at a decreasing rate or to a lesser degree than earlier pieces of status information. (*The attenuation principle*)

Finally, the basic expectation assumption is modified to accommodate the multiple bases for the formation of expectations.

4. Once expectation states form from multiple bases, these combined expectation states determine each actor's relative power and prestige relative to other actors. (*The behavioral implications of combined expectations*)

**The Evolution of Expectation States.** While expectation states may be established by clearly defined positions in social structures and by pervasive

---

[11]See Joseph Berger and M. Hamit Fisek, "A Generalization of the Theory of Status Characteristics and Expectation States," in *Expectation States Theory*, pp. 163–205; and Joseph Berger, M. Hamit Fisek, Robert Z. Norman, and Morris Zelditch, Jr., *Status Characteristics and Social Interaction* (New York: Elsevier, 1977).

[12]The effects of another kind of status difference, referred to as a specific status characteristic, are also considered. Specific status differences apply only to a specific task or kind of task (for example, involving mathematical or artistic ability).

status beliefs, status may not be clear or specified. The result is that expectations will evolve in situations because individuals are disposed to look for status information and to use this information to establish expectations for self and others.[13] Once expectation states form, they will exert a disproportionate influence on the expectations for individuals during subsequent interactions, as long as no new status information is introduced into the situation. The result of these processes are the following:

1. The expectations and behavior of actors will tend to become stable across consecutive interaction situations as long as no new information is introduced into the situation. (*Stability of status positions*)

2. Given external evaluations of an actor's performance in a previous situation, (a) differential evaluations that are consistent with the actors' power and prestige positions in the group increase the inequality; (b) differential evaluations that are inconsistent with the actors' power and prestige positions in the group decrease the inequality (and can even invert it); and (c) if the evaluations of both actors are similar, then any expectation advantage held by one of the actors will be reduced. (*Assignment of success or failure*)

3. If actors have diffuse status characteristics from outside the group and specific status positions within the local situation that are inconsistent with each other, then their expectations and behavior will stabilize across consecutive interaction situations at a value between what would result from either the diffuse or specific statuses alone, again as long as no new information is introduced into the situation. (*The effects of interventions*)

**Status Cues, Expectations, and Behavior.** Individuals use a variety of social cues (such as patterns of speech, posture, direct references to background or experience, styles of dress) to help form expectations. And, when status is ambiguous, unspecified, or unknown, individuals will rely even more on these cues, typically associated with role-making and status-making behaviors of individuals.

In expectation states theory, indicative cues are distinguished from expressive cues, and task cues are separated from categorical cues. Indicative cues (for example, "I'm a doctor.") directly label the actor's status state whereas expressive cues (a man's style of dress, for example) provide information from which status states can be inferred. The task/categorical distinction is independent of the indicative/expressive distinction. Task cues

---

[13]Joseph Berger, M. Hamit Fisek, and Robert Z. Norman, "The Evolution of Status Expectations: A Theoretical Extension," in *Sociological Theories in Progress: New Formulations,* eds. J. Berger, M. Zelditch, Jr., and B. Anderson (Newbury Park, CA: Sage, 1989), pp. 100–130.

(for example, fluency of speech) provide information about the actor's capacities on an immediate task, whereas categorical cues (for example, language syntax) provide information about states of status characteristics that actors possess. Using these distinctions, status cues theory yields the following propositions:[14]

1. If no prior status differences exist in the situation, then differences in task cues will help generate expectation states, which in turn determine the distribution of power and prestige behavior in the situation. (*Task cues in the absence of status differences*)

2. If status differences exist from the outset in a situation, then the differentiation in task cues will produce congruent differences in expectations, which, in turn, determine congruent differences in the rates of task cue behaviors. Consequently, rates of task cue behaviors will be consistent with the initial status differences. (*Status governance of task cues*)

3. If for some reason, the differentiation in task cues is inconsistent with differentiation in categorical cues, then information from both sets combines to determine the actors' expectations and behavior. (*Combining inconsistent task and categorical cues*)

Task cues provide information about capacities on an immediate task, whereas categorical cues provide information about diffuse status characteristics that might become relevant to the task. Hence, the strength of relevance of task cues is greater than that of categorical cues, signaling that, when inconsistent, the effect of task cues will be greater than the effect of categorical cues. We should add, however, that the experimental studies of most expectation states theory are oriented to completions of tasks in artificial and temporary groups; when groups are more stable, these dynamics, especially those outlined in Proposition 3 above, may change. In longer term interactions, the effect of initially salient diffuse status characteristics may become diluted as individuals get to know each other and much additional status information becomes salient. However, this effect will be minimized if diffuse status characteristics are correlated with inequalities in positional status in divisions of labor (e.g., all bosses are men and all secretaries are women; under these conditions, both expectations for, and evaluations of, positional and diffuse status characteristics will be reinforced). In contrast, if diffuse status characteristics and inequalities in status and prestige are not correlated, then the expectations for tasks in differentiated positional status will remain, while the salience of diffuse status characteristics may be diluted. Thus, it could be hypothesized that[15]

---

[14]Joseph Berger, Murray A. Webster, Jr., Cecilia Ridgeway, and Susan J. Rosenholtz, "Status Cues, Expectations, and Behavior," in *Advances in Group Processes* 3 (1986): pp. 1–22.

[15]Unlike most generalizations, these propositions are not documented with research findings; they are hypotheses derived from theories outside of the experimental tradition of

4. The relative salience and power of expectations states for positional status and diffuse status characteristics increase for both to the extent that they are correlated with each other (e.g., high rank positions are held by individuals possessing highly evaluated diffuse status characteristics, and vice versa).

5. The relative salience and power of expectations states for positional status and diffuse status characteristics will be diluted for diffuse characteristics over time with high rates of interaction and more dramatically so and more rapidly when there is no correlation between incumbency in ranked positions and differentially evaluated members possessing diffuse status characteristics; as a result, task expectations and evaluations associated with status will be more salient than diffuse status characteristics.

**Legitimation of Power and Prestige Hierarchies.** Another theory in the expectation states a program is concerned with the process of the legitimization of power and prestige orders, and inequalities in status more generally. Legitimization processes are especially important for leaders with traditionally low diffuse status characteristics (for example, women or minorities)as they seek to engage successfully in the directive behaviors ordinarily expected of a leader. Legitimization is also likely to influence effectiveness of controlling behaviors such as dominating and propitiating behaviors. For without being seen as having the right to engage in leadership activities, the power and prestige order will be disrupted.

Part of any person's social framework is consensual beliefs, operating as referential structures to connect status positions with the diffuse statuses, task capacities, and task achievements.[16] This information becomes activated in the local situation and helps generate expectations regarding status in the group. As actors behave in accordance with these expectations, they validate the expectations and establish their legitimacy.

1. When referential beliefs from the larger society are activated in the immediate interaction situation, actors create expectations about who will occupy high- and low-valued status positions in the situation. (*Referential beliefs and valued status positions*)

---

expectation states research and theory. See Turner, *Face-to-Face* and *Theoretical Principles of Sociology* (both cited in note 1).

[16]See Cecilia L. Ridgeway and Joseph Berger, "Expectations, Legitimacy, and Dominance in Task Groups," *American Sociological Review* 51 (1986): pp. 603–17; Cecilia L. Ridgeway and Joseph Berger, "The Legitimation of Power and Prestige Orders in Task Groups," in *Status Generalization: New Theory and Research*, eds. M. A. Webster and M. Foschi (Stanford, CA: Stanford University Press, 1988), pp. 207–31; Cecilia L. Ridgeway, "Gender Differences in Task Groups: A Status and Legitimacy Account," also in Webster and Foschi (1988), pp. 188–206.

2. Given expectations regarding the possession of high- and low-valued status positions in a situation, actors are likely to display differences in respect, esteem, and generalized deference behavior to others that are consistent with these expectations. (*Valued status positions and behavior*)

3. When behaviors consistent with expected status positions are validated by others and when they coincide with actual differences in power and prestige behaviors, the power and prestige hierarchy is likely to become legitimated. (*Behavioral validation and legitimacy*)

An actor's behavior is validated by another if this other engages in supportive behavior or if this other's behavior does not contradict the behavior of the actor seeking validation and, hence, legitimacy. Legitimization requires actors to make assumptions about what ought to be in the immediate situation. Expectations become normative, with the presumption that there will be collective support for these norms. A high-status person has a right to expect a higher degree of esteem, respect, and generalized deference than does a low-status individual. At the same time, others have the right to expect more valued contributions from this high-status person than from low-status actors. In addition, high-status actors develop rights to exercise, if necessary, controlling behaviors—dominating and propitiating behaviors—over the actions of others.

**Formation of Reward Expectations.** Referential structures can be activated in a particular task situation, and when activated, each provides a standard for the formation of individuals' expectations for reward in a situation.[17] Several propositions have been derived from expectation states theories on the operation of standards as determined by activation of referential structures. The first of these concerns how information from multiple standards is treated in generating reward expectations.

1. If multiple referential structures establishing standards for allocation of rewards are activated in the immediate situation of interaction, actors combine the information from all activated structures in generating expectations for reward. (*Combining referential structures*)

The second and third theorems consider how increases in the consistency or inconsistency of status characteristics affect the degree of inequality in reward expectations.

2. Increases in the amount of consistent status information salient for an actor in the immediate interaction situation increase the inequality in reward expectations. (*Status consistency and inequality in reward expectations*)

---

[17]Joseph Berger, M. Hamit Fisek, Robert Z. Norman, and David G. Wagner, "The Formation of Reward Expectations in Status Situations," in *Status, Rewards, and Influence*, pp. 215–61.

3. Increases in the amount of inconsistent status information salient for an actor in the immediate interaction situation, however, decrease the inequality in reward expectations. (*Status inconsistency and equality in reward expectations*)

The fourth proposition focuses on the interdependence of task and reward expectations.

4. Changes in an actor's task expectations (accomplished by adding or eliminating relevant status distinctions) produce correlated changes in the actor's reward expectations; in turn, changes in an actor's reward expectations (accomplished by adding or deleting standards of allocation) produce correlated changes in task expectations. (*The interdependence of expectations*)

One consequence of the interdependence of task and reward expectations is that referential standards can produce differences in the *significance* of status characteristics. Differences in the relative importance of status characteristics often depend on whether or not these characteristics are the basis on which rewards and privileges are expected to be distributed. Statuses that differ in this respect should also differ in their significance or importance (or "weight") in the interaction. The fifth theorem establishes the differential significance of status characteristics.

5. Status characteristics have a greater effect on the actor's task expectations if they are the basis for referential standards of allocation than if they are not. (*The social significance of status differences*)

**Distributive Justice.** Individuals may make assessment about whether or not their rewards, however calculated and expected, are fair and just. Expectation states theorizing offers an alternative to exchange theories on how justice is determined by individuals.[18] How do they respond when they perceive an injustice in the distribution of rewards? The status value theory of distributive justice considers these questions. Exchange theories develop what is, in essence, an equity theory emphasizing that evaluations of justice and injustice are based on comparisons of one actor's ratio of the rewards received to actual investments made to receive these rewards, compared with the ratio of at least one other actor in the immediate situation.[19] If rewards are seen as exceeding the costs and investments of persons and, at

---

[18]See Joseph Berger, Morris Zelditch, Jr., Bo Anderson, and Bernard P. Cohen, "Structural Aspects of Distributive Justice: A Status Value Formulation," in *Sociological Theories in Progress*, vol. 2, eds. J. Berger, M. Zelditch, Jr., and B. Anderson (Boston: Houghton Mifflin, 1972), pp. 119–46.

[19]See J. S. Adams, "Inequity in Social Exchange," in *Advances in Experimental Social Psychology* 2 (1965): pp. 267–99.

the same time, in the same ratio of cost/investments relative to rewards as those who are also engaged in similar exchanges, then the payoff for activities will be considered fair and just.

In contrast, the status value theory of distributive justice argues that theories emphasizing comparisons of rewards to investments are inadequate. As an alternative explanation, the value of objects to individuals is based on the status that they represent and signify status rather than being considered only for their consummatory value (less costs and investments), as is the case in equity theories. For example, the value of a key to the executive washroom is viewed by the status, honor, esteem, and importance that it conveys to the person who possesses the valued good (rather than by the consummatory value that comes with convenience and privacy).

Justice issues, therefore, involve questions of status consistency and inconsistency between expectations and allocations of rewards. As long as actors receive the status value that they expect, the situation is seen as just. If actors receive a status value different from what they expect, however, then the situation is seen as unjust. Thus, one's sense of justice is not so much a matter of the ratio of rewards received to investments made, compared with the ratio for others in a situation as an assessment of rewards in relation to what was expected.

These expectations for reward depend on referential structures, and the activation of referential structures enables actors to relate their general cultural framework to their immediate situation. When a particular referential structure is activated, individuals expect to receive rewards commensurate with their relevant status. Basically, *what is* in general cultural definitions becomes *what is expected to be* in the immediate situation. Thus, a man who believes that men are generally better paid than women will expect a higher level of reward when he is interacting with a woman—provided, of course, that gender is a relevant and salient status characteristic to the actors and that a relevant referential structure has been activated. To summarize more formally

1. If an actor activates referential structures, and thereby culturally associates different levels of reward with different status positions, then he or she is likely to develop expectations for the allocation of rewards in the immediate interaction situation that are consistent with this cultural association. (*The activation of referential structures*)

2. If an actor receives the level of reward that is consistent with expectations created by the cultural association of referential structures to status characteristics, then the actor will regard the situation as just. (*The effect of expectations on assessments of justice*)

3. If an actor receives a level of reward inconsistent with expectations, generated by the cultural association of referential structures with status characteristics, the actor will regard the situation as unjust. (*The effect of expectations on assessments of injustice*)

A reverse process can also operate in the sense that an allocation of differentially evaluated rewards can generate performance expectations consistent with this allocation. This process is most likely to occur when a referential structure is activated and when the relevant status distinction is based primarily on performance. To state this more formally,

4. If an actor is allocated a differentiated level of reward, differentiated performance expectations consistent with the allocated level of reward are likely to develop. (*The effect of differential rewards on expectations*)

**Sources of Self-Evaluation.** Source theory considers how expectations can emerge through the reflected appraisals of significant others. Source theory uses ideas regarding unit evaluations and expectations developed in behavior-expectation theory, as well as ideas from status characteristics theory. As with status characteristics theory in general, the original version of source theory dealt only with the simplest situation, involving a single evaluator. How do the appraisals of those with the right to evaluate affect the expectations and behavior among others in a situation? Under some circumstances, an evaluator can become a source of evaluations for the actor—that is, an evaluator whose assessments matter to the actor or, in other words, a "significant other." The likelihood of a particular evaluator becoming a source is directly related to an individual's expectations for this evaluator:

1. The higher are an actor's expectations for an evaluator, the greater is the likelihood that this evaluator will become a source of evaluations for the actor. (*The effect of external evaluations on expectations*)

When this occurs, the actor's expectations and behavior are determined by the evaluations of the source:

2. Given a source as an evaluator, an actor's evaluations, expectations, and behavior will be shaped and directed by this source's evaluations. (*The effects of sources of evaluation*)

An actor's expectations for an evaluator are likely to be affected by any status characteristics that the evaluator possesses. An extension of the original source theory by Murray Webster showed that status is directly related to the likelihood of becoming a source:[20]

3. A high-status evaluator is more likely to become a source for an actor than is a low-status evaluator. (*The effect of evaluator status on evaluation importance*)

---

[20]Murray A. Webster, Jr., "Sources of Evaluations and Expectations for Performance," *Sociometry* 32 (1969): pp. 243–58.

If there are multiple evaluators and their evaluations conflict, actors apparently use source information in much the same way that they use status information. They process and combine all the salient cues to form composite expectations.[21]

4. Actors combine the unit evaluations of multiple conflicting sources to form self-expectations. (*Combining source evaluations*)

**Stability and Change in Status Beliefs.** Expectations states for status will tend to endure, unless new information is added that forces people to revise expectations. Indeed, as we will see later, negative emotions are aroused when individuals go against expectations, leading to sanctions by others on those who would violate the status order.[22] Once expectations states have emerged, they are difficult to change; this stability in expectations states is particularly problematic for members of less-valued social categories by virtue of the expectations on, and evaluations of, their diffuse status characteristics. The reason for this difficulty is that status beliefs are more than situational; rather, they tend to be part of the more general beliefs that people in a society carry. For example, prejudices against particular categories of persons are universal in societies, and these become backup for local status beliefs that are used to establish expectations for individuals in encounters and groupings that carry a heavy evaluative element. When there is general consensus over status beliefs about members possessing diffuse status characteristics, they are very difficult to eliminate, but there are certain conditions when this is possible.[23] The key is persistent and consistent challenges to status beliefs. These challenges can come from broader social movements—e.g., the civil rights movement, women's movement—that mount a persistent attack on prejudicial beliefs and the attendant status beliefs about members of particular social categories. In conjunction with

---

[21]See especially Murray A. Webster, Jr. and B. Sobieszek, *Sources of Self Evaluation* (New York: Wiley, 1974). For further extensions of this idea, see J. C. Moore, "Role Enactment and Self-Identity: An Expectation States Approach," in *Status, Rewards, and Influence: How Expectations Organize Interaction*, eds. J. Berger and M. Zelditch, Jr. (San Francisco: Jossey-Bass, 1985), pp. 262–316.

[22]Cecilia L. Ridgeway, "Affect," in *Group Processes: Sociological Analyses*, eds. M. Foschi and E. J. Lawler, (Chicago, IL: Nelson-Hall), pp. 205–30; "Status and Emotions from an Expectation States Theory," in *Handbook of The Sociology of Emotion*, eds. J. E. Stets and J. H. Turner (New York: Springer, 2006).

[23]Cecilia L. Ridgeway, "Conformity, Group-Oriented Motivation, and Status Attainment in Small Groups," *Social Psychology Quarterly* 41 (1978): pp.175–88; "Status in Groups: The Importance of Motivation," *American Sociological Review* 47 (1982): pp. 76–88. See also: C. L. Ridgeway, K. Backor, Y. E. Li, J. E. Tinkler, and K. G. Erickson, "How Easily Does a Social Difference Become a Status Distinction: Gender Matters," *American Sociological Review* 74 (2009): pp. 44–62; Ridgeway, and J. Berger, "Expectations, legitimacy, and Dominance in Task Groups," *American Sociological Review* 51 (1986): pp. 603–17; Ridgeway, "The Legitimation of Power and Prestige Orders in Task Groups," in *Status Generalization: New Theory and Research*, (Stanford, CA: Stanford University Press, 1988).

such movements, but potentially as a separate force, individuals can persistently challenge status beliefs in face-to-face situations. Such challenges are particularly effective if members of more valued social categories lead the way. Over time, and with persistent questioning of implicit status beliefs, change in general status beliefs in a society can occur. For example, in the United States, these dynamics have dramatically altered status beliefs about formerly devalued categories of persons: minorities (African Americans, Latinos, Asians), women, and gay/lesbians. Thus,

1. The more local status beliefs are drawn from broader status beliefs in a society, and the greater is the consensus over these beliefs, the more resistant to change are beliefs about members of social categories possessing devalued diffuse status characteristics

2. The more persistent and widespread are challenges to these beliefs at the local level, especially by higher status members of groups and the more these efforts are backed up by a social movement and counter-ideology against these beliefs, the more likely will status beliefs about diffuse status characteristics change toward a more favorable evaluation

3. The more these status beliefs change, the less salient will older status beliefs be, and hence, the more likely are members of formerly devalued social categories to hold higher status in groupings and in the division of labor in larger social units

Status beliefs about individuals in positions carrying different amounts of power and prestige are also subject to these dynamics, but there are additional processes whereby status beliefs about particular individuals in specific situations can be altered.[24] Whether status beliefs evolve from individuals' performances or are imposed by an existing structure, those in lower status positions will generally have a difficult time breaking expectations attached to their status location, as earlier propositions summarizing research have documented. And, as we will see below in the analysis of

---

[24]Cecilia L. Ridgeway, "Where Do Status Beliefs Come From?" in *Status, Network, and Structure*, eds. J Szmatka and J. Berger (Stanford, CA: Stanford University Press, 1998); "The Formation of Status Beliefs: Improving Status Construction Theory," *Advances in Group Processes* 17 (2000): pp 77–102; "Inequality, Status, and the Construction of Status Beliefs," in *Handbook of Sociological Theory*, ed. J. Turner, (New York: Kluwer/Plenum, 2001), pp. 323–42; C. L. Ridgeway, E. Boyle, K. Kulpers, and D. Robinson, "How Do Status Beliefs Develop? The Role of Resources and Interaction," *American Sociological Review* 63 (1998): pp. 331–50; C. L. Ridgeway and S. J. Correll, "Unpacking the Gender System: A Theoretical Perspective on Cultural Beliefs and Social Relations," *Gender and Society* 18 (2004): pp. 510–31; C. L. Ridgeway and K. G. Erickson, "Creating and Spreading Status Beliefs," *American Journal of Sociology* 106 (2000): pp. 579–615; C. L. Ridgeway and C. Johnson, "What is the Relationship Between Socioemotional Behavior and Status in Task Groups?" *American Journal of Sociology* 95 (1990): pp.1189–212; C. L. Ridgeway, C. L. Walker, and H. A. Walker, "Status Structure," in *Sociological Perspectives on Social Psychology*, eds. K. S. Cook, G. A. Fine, and J. S. House (Boston: Allyn & Bacon, 1995), pp. 282–310.

emotions, efforts of lower-status people to change their status and/or challenge high-status individuals will generally invite negative sanctions from the higher-status persons who are challenged but also negative sanctions from their fellow lower-status individuals. Disruption of the status order represents a failure per se to abide by expectations, which, in turn, arouses negative emotions. People generally seek to avoid negative emotions, and thus they will sanction negatively those who violate the status order and the expectation states on which it is based. How, then, in local situations where expectations are established are lower-status persons to display their competence without threatening the status order and inviting negative sanctions? The key appears to be to consistently demonstrate competence in activities without directly challenging the legitimated status order. Strategically, this often means rather indirect means—asking polite questions, offering tentative suggestions, and other non-confrontational techniques—that still evidence the trappings of subordination, while demonstrating competence. Over time, under these conditions, an individual's status and associated expectations states can rise through a more evolutionary than revolutionary process. Thus,

4. Direct challenges by lower-status individuals to the legitimated status order will invite negative emotional reactions of both higher- and lower-status members of a group. Both sets of individuals do so because of the power of legitimated expectations attached to lower and higher status.

5. The status order can change when lower-status individuals use indirect and soft interpersonal techniques to demonstrate their higher levels of competence without making direct challenges to higher-status persons. For example, a person might ask useful questions or phrase ideas as potential suggestions for approval by higher-status persons; this type of indirection can be very effective because it demonstrates non-threatening competence. Over time, this non-threatening competence can lead to the revaluation of their general level of competence, thereby causing the expectation states attached to these competent persons and their rights to claim greater prestige and, potentially, power.

## Status and Emotions

When expectations are realized in a situation, individuals will generally experience positive emotions, whereas when they are not, individuals will feel negative emotions. There are several general theories[25] outside the status theorizing tradition that make this fundamental point about any set of

---

[25]Jonathan H. Turner, *Human Emotions: A Sociological Theory* (London, UK: Routledge, 2008).

expectations, but here we focus on theories that are within status-tradition. Many of these come from the expectation states theory program, and so, we will begin with these.

## Expectation States Theories of Affect

As is evident from the above review of theory-research traditio... expectation states theorizing, the central idea in these theories is that members of groups are assigned a status by virtue of their performances and/or an existing status structure within some unit organization. Incumbency in status or possession of diffuse status characteristics establishes expectations for people's competence and for their role behaviors. Such assignment to a status and its corresponding expectations can thus be based on diffuse characteristics, such as age, ethnicity, education, gender, wealth, and other traits that individuals bring to the group from the outside, as well as be based on internal organizational forces establishing lines of authority, rank, and division of labor. In more recent years, one of the many creative branches in this general theoretical program has been the analysis of emotions. Let us review them but without the formalizations since most of these theories have not been formalized.

**Cecilia Ridgeway's Theory**. Like most research and theory within the expectation states tradition, Ridgeway's[26] and Johnson's[27] work focuses mostly on task-oriented groups, where individuals are temporarily assembled to realize a clearly stated goal or purpose. As Ridgeway and Johnson argue, even the most transitory task-oriented group develops an affect structure as members agree and disagree on how to best accomplish the group's goals. Moreover, disagreements can also involve status challenges as lower-status members seek to raise their position and refuse to defer to the arguments of higher-status members.

In all groups, Ridgeway has argued, broader societal culture penetrates group structures as a set of norms or blueprint rules that indicate how people are supposed to behave in particular types of groups, whether task-oriented work groups or more informal and intimate groups. Following Hochschild's point of emphasis, these blueprint rules include (a) "feeling rules" about what kinds of emotions are to be experienced in a situation and (b) "display rules" about what emotions can be expressed publicly and how they are to be expressed. An affect-arousing event will, therefore, activate

[26]Cecilia L. Ridgeway, "Status in Groups: The Importance of Emotion," *American Sociological Review* 47 (1982): pp. 76–88; "Affect," in *Group Processes: Sociological Analysis* (cited in note 22).

[27]Cecilia L. Ridgeway and Cathryn Johnson, "What is the Relationship Between Socioemotional Behavior and Status in Task Groups?" (cited in note 23).

these feeling and display rules; yet, status expectation processes are still important in organizing the way affect is mobilized and managed.

Disagreements represent one class of affect-arousing events, and when such disagreements among group members occur, status in the group determines whether individuals will blame themselves or others for the disagreement. If a person holds an equal or higher status compared with the other(s) with whom a disagreement exists, then this person will be likely to attribute the disagreement to other(s), and this person will feel and express *annoyance* (a mild form of anger). On the other hand, if an individual is of lower status than the person(s) with whom there is a disagreement, then this individual will tend to blame self and experience *depression*. For this reason, Ridgeway and Johnson note that superiors are far more likely to express anger and annoyance with subordinates than the reverse: The superior is expected to be more competent and, when authority is challenged, anger ensues because expectation states are being violated by inferiors, whereas when subordinates disagree with superordinates, expectation states force them to attribute the blame to themselves (because they are presumed to be less knowledgeable and competent). And, because no reward is to be gained from continuing to blame oneself, individuals tend not to pursue the disagreement. Instead, the lower-status person withdraws, often to the point of experiencing depression.

These disagreement-anger episodes can disrupt the solidarity of the group, however, even as the status order is reconfirmed. Anger and annoyance do not promote positive sentiments of liking and mutual trust. Depression by subordinates leads them to withdraw commitment from the group, thereby eroding solidarity further. In contrast, agreement among people of different status has the opposite effect: It promotes solidarity. If those who agree are of lower status, then the higher-status persons feel satisfaction (a moderate form of *happiness*) about the fact that subordinates agree with them. If those who agree are of equal or higher status, then individuals are likely to feel a more intense form of happiness, such as *gratitude*, that comes when superordinates agree with them. When people experience these positive emotions, Ridgeway and Johnson argue, they become motivated to reward those who agree with them; as they do so, all parties develop positive sentiments and become more likely to agree in the future. From this cycle of positive reinforcement comes enhanced group solidarity.

These status processes also help explain why groups typically reveal more positive than negative affect. As noted earlier, disagreements emanating from lower-status persons are sanctioned because they violate the expectations associated with lower- and higher-status group members, and hence, lower-status individuals soon stop punishing themselves and keep quiet. If disagreement can be avoided and agreement can be reached, then the positive emotions of *satisfaction, happiness,* and *gratitude* initiate cycles of positive reinforcement that evolve into solidarity that further orients group members to express agreement and to reward each other with positive sentiments.

As noted earlier, an interesting dynamic is initiated when a lower-status person is highly assertive and refuses to back down. Expectation states lead others to sanction the lower-status person negatively as being too pushy and self-interested—what is termed the *backlash effect* against those who violate the status order. Thus, lower-status individuals will almost always have difficulty in groups where they seek to raise their status by displaying competence in an assertive manner; assertions of such competence will be defined as violating the status order and the expectations associated with this order. One strategy for overcoming this backlash effect is to couch assertions of competence in friendly and unthreatening ways, perhaps as suggestions rather than as challenges. In this manner, lower-status group members can, over time, slowly raise their status and change the expectations associated with them.

Another interesting facet of this theory is the argument that the degree of congruence between the status structure and the distribution of affect shapes rates of participation in making decisions. When high-status members are liked more than low-status members, their power to influence decisions is enhanced. Lower-status members not only see higher-status members as more competent, but they also like them. Because of this congruence in status and sentiment, lower-status individuals are more likely to accept decisions of higher-status members. Congruence of affect and status thus amplifies the influence of status in task groups, and research by Janet R. Johnston demonstrates that such is also the case in more long-term and intimate groups as well. Johnston's findings have, in turn, stimulated Joseph Berger's long-standing research program exploring expectation processes in more intimate and longer-term groups.

**Joseph Berger's Affect-Expectations Theory**. Joseph Berger argues that as emotional reactions emerge and are repeated over time within groups, these reactions generate affect expectation states that shape and guide the flow of interaction.[28] Such affect expectation states unfold in a series of stages: (a) Affect is aroused during the interaction; (b) an exchange of affect occurs and begins to set up expectation for what will happen in the current interaction; (c) these affect states also begin to generate an emotional orientation toward others in the situation that involves more stable sentiments—whether positive or negative—that will shape the course of subsequent interactions; and eventually, (d) assignment of personality characteristics consistent with the affect that is exchanged and the emotional orientations of individuals will occur, further circumscribing current and future interactions.

Through this approximate sequence, the affect structure of a group stabilizes the interaction, giving it consistency over time. Moreover, people

---

[28]Joseph Berger, "Directions in Expectation States Research," in *Status Generalization: New Theory and Research*, eds. M. Webster and M. Foschi (Stanford, CA: Stanford University Press, 1988), pp. 450–74.

develop situational identities as they exchange affect and impute personalities to each other. Once these identities are formed, they become expectations for what will occur in the situation, thereby further stabilizing the interaction. Individuals thus become driven and constrained to act in certain ways through the exchange of affect and the development of affect expectations. Yet, this kind of affective structure does not completely determine or circumscribe what occurs in the group. For, if expressive exchanges consistently do not confirm the affect expectations that have developed, then the affective orientations of individuals, the imputation of personality traits, and perhaps, the situational identities of individuals will all change, and new affect expectations will begin to emerge.

**Robert Shelly's Theory of Status and Sentiments**. Robert Shelly argues that emotions and sentiments can be seen as different.[29] Sentiments are milder, low-intensity emotions that vary along a continuum of liking and disliking others in a situation. In Shelly's theory, sentiments arise from people's reactions to performances and behaviors, and they set up expectation states for future interactions in a situation. These sentiment-based expectation states exert, he believes, an independent effect on behaviors distinct from that exerted by expectations associated with status. However, if status is highly salient in a situation because performances among individuals have already created a status order or because it is built into the social structure of a larger social unit, then status will trump expectation states arising from sentiments. Thus, the effect of sentiments will exert less influence on expectation states than will status, as long as status considerations—and expectations that come with differential levels of power and prestige that accompanies status—influence on people's behaviors, their evaluations of these behaviors, and the formation of expectation states for future interaction.

Shelly posits two potential models of these processes. One is the constituent model, outlined in Figure 18.1 (A) in which status and sentiments each exerts an independent influence on the formation of expectation states. The other is the translation model, delineated in Figure 18.1 (B), where sentiments are part of the expectations that form around status. That is, as individuals interact, they come to reveal positive or negative sentiments about individuals that arise as they interact, and these sentiments affect how persons will interact with others in varying status positions. Not only this; they become incorporated into the expectation states as a separate

---

[29]Robert K. Shelly, "How Sentiments Organize Interaction," *Advances in Group Processes* 16 (1993): pp. 113–32; "How Performance Expectations Arise from Sentiments," *Social Psychology Quarterly* 64 (2001): pp. 72–87; "Emotions, Sentiments, and Performance Expectations," *Advances in Group Processes* 21 (2004): pp. 146–65. See also R. K. Shelly, I. M. Handley, J. Baer, and S. Watson, "Group and Affect: Sentiments, Emotions, and Performance Expectations," Current Research in *Social Psychology* 6 (2001): pp. 1–12; R. K. Shelly and M. Webster, Jr., "Compatible Social Processes: Some New Theoretical Principles and a Test," *Sociological Perspectives* 40 (1997): pp. 1317–34.

**Figure 18.1** Shelly's Two Models on the Relationship among Sentiment, Status, and Behavior

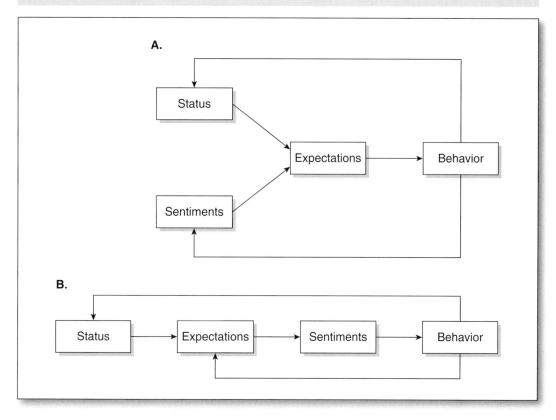

expectation for how much they will like or dislike others. These affect expectation states operate alongside more general expectations states for performances generated by individuals' relative locations in the status order. This status order emerges via a number of potential routes, including: a status order that have may have evolved on the basis of individuals' performances, a division of labor that is imposed by a larger social unit, or a status that comes with memberships in categoric units, or diffuse status characteristics. Whatever the origins of this status order, a series of affect expectations will also evolve, and these will interact with expectations associated with status per se.

It is possible that both processes operate simultaneously or intersect in ways that influence expectations states attached to status locations. When, for instance, status becomes salient, the expectations states from sentiments get blended with those for status. For example, a person may come to possess mild negative sentiments toward a boss in high-status (authority) position, and these are blended with expectation states for this high-status person as, say, "a competent but irritating jerk whose directive I must follow." If this same person's status is not salient, then the negative sentiments would dominate in the absence of status cues.

**Lovaglia and Houser's Status-Compatible Theory.** Michael Lovaglia, at times in collaboration with Jeffrey Houser, developed a theory that examines the degree to which the emotions that arise among lower- and higher-status persons in groups increase or decrease the social distance between these persons.[30] Expectation state theories all argue that higher-status individuals will be given more opportunities to perform, will receive higher evaluations, and will have more influence over decisions than lower-status individuals. The result is that higher-status persons will experience more positive emotions like *pleasure* and *happiness*, while lower-status persons will experience more negative emotions such as *anger* and *frustration*. The more the emotions of individuals' emotions are compatible with their status—positive emotions for higher-status individuals and negative emotions for lower-status persons—the more likely is the degree of the social distance between higher- and lower-status members to *decrease*.

We will not develop the complete description of the dynamics involved, but basically, the processes works as follows: When high-status persons feel positive emotions, they are likely to treat lower-status individuals better, giving them more chances to contribute, praising them positively, and in general evaluating their performances more positively. The result is that social distance between the two ranks decreases. Compared to higher-status individuals, lower-status persons experience more negative emotions in general, and more specifically, they often hold negative feelings about higher-status persons; as a result of these negative emotions, the social distance between the two ranks will increase because these individuals may give higher-status persons fewer opportunities to talk, evaluate them negatively, and not easily defer to higher-status person's wishes and directions.

Thus, one generalization is that when individuals feel emotions appropriate for their status—positive for higher-status persons, negative for lower-status individuals—and act on these feelings, social status differences are, ironically, reduced. In being pleasant to lower-status persons, the higher status person reduces social distance, whereas in their negativity and failure to honor the status order, lower-status members can reduce status distance with higher-status persons.

There are more complicated dynamics in this process that revolve around *attributions*. For example, higher-status persons who feel that they do not deserve their rank (they were just lucky) will experience status-incompatible emotions

---

[30]Michael J. Lovaglia and Jeffrey A. Houser, "Emotional Reactions and Status in Groups," *American Sociological Review* 61 (1996): pp. 867–83; Michael J. Lovaglia, "Status, Emotion and Structural Power," in *Status, Network, and Structure*, eds. J. Szmatka and J. Skvoretz (Stanford, CA: Stanford University Press, 1997), pp.159–78. See also J. H. Houser and M. J. Lovaglia, "Status, Emotion, and the Development of Solidarity in Stratified Task Groups," *Advances in Group Processes* 19 (2002): pp. 109–37.

such as *anxiety*, *fear*, and perhaps even *guilt*. These emotions reduce the distance between this higher- and lower-ranking person. If a lower-ranking person makes a negative self-attribution that he or she did not have the ability to be anything else, that person will see the lower rank as proper, will accept status differences, and will thereby increase the social distance with higher-ranking individuals. There is a number of other potential scenarios that lead to increased and decreased solidarity in group by virtue of the level of status differences and people's emotional reactions to their particular status.

## Theodore Kemper's Status-Power Theory

Theodore Kemper was one of the pioneers in the sociology of emotions. Originally, he termed his approach *a social interactional theory of emotions*,[31] and more recently, he has teamed with Randall Collins to develop the theory further.[32] The basic idea of the theory is quite simple: Individuals' relative power and status in social relationships and changes in their power and status have important effects on their emotional states. Power is the ability to compel others to follow one's wishes and dictates, whereas status is the giving and receiving of unforced deference, compliance, respect, and honor. All social relationships reveal power and status dimensions. According to Kemper and Collins, these dimensions are fundamental to understanding interaction and emotions. From Kemper's review of the literature on emotions, he concluded that there are four basic and primary emotions: *fear*, *anger*, *happiness/satisfaction*, and *sadness/depression*.[33] These primary emotions can, however, be elaborated into more complex combinations and variants, creating such complex and important emotions as *guilt*, *shame*, *pride*, *jealousy*, *love*, and other variants and combinations of the four primary emotions. Indeed, Kemper has argued that these primary emotions have a neurophysiological basis, having been selected in humans' evolutionary history because they promoted survival. Kemper thus attempts to explain how power and status generate the four basic emotions and important variants.

The theory distinguishes among (1) *structural emotions*, which are those affective states aroused by the relative power and status of individuals within social structures; (2) *situational emotions*, which arise by virtue of changes in power and status during the process of interaction; and

---

[31]Theodore D. Kemper, *A Social Interactional Theory of Emotions* (New York: Wiley, 1979); "Predicting Emotions from Social Relations," *Social Psychology Quarterly* 54 (1991): pp. 330–42. See also Kemper's recently published *Status, Power, and Ritual: A Relational Reading of Durkheim, Goffman, and Collins* (Surrey, UK: Ashgate, 2011).

[32]Theodore D. Kemper and Randall Collins, "Dimensions of Microinteractionism," *American Journal of Sociology* 96 (1990): pp. 32–68.

[33]Theodore D. Kemper, "How Many Emotions are There? Wedding the Social and the Autonomic Component," *American Journal of Sociology* 93 (1987): pp. 263–89.

(3) *anticipatory emotions*, which revolve around individuals' expectations for power and status in social relations. The dynamics of emotion thus inhere in the status and power that individuals actually hold, the status and power that is gained or lost during interaction, and the power and status that was expected in an interaction. The basic propositions of the theory are extracted and summarized in Table 18.1. What follows is a more discursive review of the argument made.

When people have power and increase their power within social relationships, they experience a sense of satisfaction, security, and confidence. If individuals do not have power and, more importantly, lose power, they will experience *anxiety* and *fear*, leading them to lose confidence. Thus, to have power or to gain it gives people the confidence to secure and use more power, whereas to not possess power or to lose it does just the opposite and takes away the confidence so necessary to garnering and sustaining power.

Just what people expect before they interact, and what they actually get, is very important in the production of emotions. When individuals expect or anticipate a gain in power but do not receive this gain, their *anxiety* and fear will escalate, and they begin to lose confidence in themselves. Conversely, when individuals have anticipated a loss of power but do not lose power, they experience satisfaction, and they might begin to gain confidence.

For status, a more extensive set of arguments is presented. Much like power, when people experience a gain in status, they will also experience satisfaction. Moreover, they will come to like those who have given them status, and if the relationship persists, they will form stronger bonds with these supportive others. If individuals experience a loss of status in social relations, they will experience *shame* and *embarrassment*, especially if they believe that this loss of status is the result of their own actions and, hence, their own fault. If this loss is sufficiently great, they will experience not only shame but also *depression*. However, if they perceive that this loss of status is caused by the unfair and inappropriate actions of others, they will experience *anger* and become aggressive toward these others. As their anger rises, they move into a power mode of interaction—seeking to compel others to acknowledge their status.

The attribution of status loss to oneself or to others is, however, complicated by what people have anticipated before the interaction. If they have anticipated no gain or loss in status, and experience neither, then they feel *satisfied* (a mild version of happiness). If they have anticipated an increase in status but did not get it, and if they perceive that this failure to receive status has been the result of their own actions, then they will experience *shame* and, perhaps, *depression*. If the failure to receive expected status is seen as the result of others' inappropriate actions, then individuals will mobilize *anger* and become aggressive. And if individuals get more status than they anticipated, they will become satisfied.

The giving of status to others also generates emotions. When a person freely bestows status on another, the giver of status experiences *satisfaction*,

**Table 18.1**   Kemper's Status-Power Theory of Emotions

**Power and Emotions**

1. The more a person experiences an increase in power in social relations, the greater will be this person's sense of security and confidence; conversely, the more a person experiences a loss of power in social relations, the greater will be this person's sense of anxiety and fear, leading to a loss of confidence.

2. The more a person anticipates a gain in power in social relations but does not receive this gain, the greater will be this person's sense of anxiety and, potentially, sense of fear; conversely, the more a person anticipates a loss of power in social relations but does not receive this loss, the greater will be this person's sense of satisfaction and, potentially, sense of confidence.

**Status and Emotions**

3. The more a person experiences an increase in status in social relations, the greater will be this person's sense of satisfaction and well-being, the greater will be this person's sense of liking for those who gave status, and the more likely will the givers and receivers of status form bonds of solidarity.

4. The more a person experiences a loss of status in social relations as a result of his or her own actions, the greater will be this person's sense of shame and embarrassment and, if the loss is sufficiently great, sense of depression as well.

5. The more a person experiences a loss of status in social relations as a result of another's actions, the greater will be the person's sense of anger and the more likely will this person be ready to fight, transforming this person's conduct to a power mode of behavior.

6. A person's reaction to no change in status in social relations will

   A. Lead to satisfaction if this person anticipated no change

   B. Lead to shame, and perhaps depression, if this person anticipated an increase in status and perceives that the failure to realize this anticipated increase was caused by his or her own actions

   C. Lead to anger and aggression if this person anticipated an increase in status and perceives that the failure to realize this anticipated increase was caused by the actions of others

   D. Lead to satisfaction and well-being if this person receives more status than anticipated

7. The more a person gives status, the greater will be the sense of satisfaction, if this status is given freely, and the more the receiver of status will express appreciation and gratitude, which, in turn, will increase the sense of satisfaction for the giver of status.

8. The more a person withholds status, when the giving of status is due, the greater will be the sense of guilt and shame.

and the recipient of the status will express *appreciation* and *gratitude*, which will feed back and increase the giver's sense of satisfaction. When a person withholds status that another deserves, this individual will feel guilt and *shame* for not doing what is appropriate, and persons who did not receive what they deserved (and expected) will experience *anger* if they correctly perceive that the other has wronged them.

In sum, then, for Kemper—and for Collins as well, in their collaborative work—emotion is ultimately tied to the relative power and status of individuals in social relationships, to shifts in status and power, and to both anticipation and attribution of who is responsible for these shifts. In the end, emotion is driven by those conditions (1) that give people the power to tell others what to do, or that take this power away, and (2) that bestow prestige, deference, and voluntary compliance, or that take this status away.

# Conclusion

As is evident, status dynamics have been theorized considerably more than role dynamics. Fifty years ago, the reverse would have been true. This theorizing on status has been dominated by expectation states research and theorizing, which is one of the most enduring and successful theoretical research traditions in sociology. We have emphasized this tradition but also sought to introduce other theoretical programs that have also examined status dynamics. What is currently lacking is complete integration of the work on status within other interactionist traditions, particularly role theories and identity theories. For example, much behavior in situations is directed at seeking to verify self and identity as much as expectations associated with status; thus, there needs to be integration between interactionist and expectation states theories. One route might be to view efforts of identity-verification as another kind of expectations state that interacts in complex ways with expectations attached to the status order.

Still, despite the failure to integrate interactionist theories and, at times, to theorize only within a narrow range of scope conditions, the dynamics of status are rather well understood. Moreover, the existing expectation states tradition continues to expand and develop, thus indicating that, despite an enormous accumulation of knowledge over the last fifty years, new knowledge on status dynamics per se is still being generated. Still, it would be useful if more integration of expectation states work with other interactionist traditions would also move forward.

## CHAPTER 19

# Dramaturgical Theories

## Erving Goffman on "The Interaction Order"

Erving Goffman was perhaps the most creative theorist of interaction processes in the second half of the twentieth century. In one of his last statements before his death in 1982, he defined the analysis of face-to-face interaction as the *interaction order*,[1] but unlike many micro-level theorists and researchers, Goffman did not proclaim that the interaction order is all that is real. Rather, he simply argued that this interaction order constitutes a distinctive realm of reality that reveals its own unique dynamics. For "to speak of the relative autonomous forms of life in the interaction order . . . is not to put forward these forms as somehow prior, fundamental, or constitutive of the shape of macroscopic phenomena."[2] Goffman recognized that, at best, there is a "loose coupling" of the micro and macro realms. Macro phenomena, such as commodities markets, urban land-use values, economic growth, and society-wide stratification, cannot be explained by micro-level analysis.[3] Of course, one can supplement macro-level explanations by recording how individuals interact in various types of settings and encounters, but these analyses will not supplant macro-level explanations. Conversely, what transpires in the interaction order cannot be explained solely by macro processes. Rather, micro-level processes are always transformed in ways unique to the individuals involved in interaction.

---

[1] Erving Goffman, "The Interaction Order," *American Sociological Review* (February 1983): pp. 1–17. See also Anne W. Rawls, "The Interaction Order Sui Generis. Goffman's Contribution to Social Theory," *Sociological Theory* 5, no. 2 (1987): pp. 136–49; Stephan Fuchs, "The Constitution of Emergent Interaction Orders, A Comment on Rawls," *Sociological Theory* 5, no. 1 (1988): pp. 122–24.

[2] Goffman, "The Interaction Order," (cited in note 1) p. 9.

[3] Ibid.

To be sure, macro phenomena constrain and circumscribe interaction and, at times, guide the general form of the interaction, but the inherent dynamics of the interaction itself preclude a one-to-one relation to these structural parameters. Indeed, the form of interaction can often be at odds with macrostructures, operating smoothly in ways that contradict these structures without dramatically changing them. Thus, the crude notion that interaction is constrained by macrostructures in ways that "reproduce" social structure does not recognize the autonomy of the interaction order. For interaction "is not an expression of structural arrangements in any simple sense; at best it is an expression advanced in regard to these arrangements. Social structures don't 'determine' culturally standard displays (of interaction rituals), they merely help select from the available repertoire of them."[4] Thus, there is a "loose coupling" of "interactional practices and social structures, a collapsing of strata and structures into broader categories, the categories themselves not corresponding one-to-one to anything in the structural world."[5] There is, then, "a set of transformation rules, or a membrane selecting how various externally relevant social distinctions will be managed within the interaction."[6]

These transformations are, however, far from insignificant phenomena. Much of what gives the social world a sense of *being real* arises from the practices of individuals as they deal with one another in various situations. "We owe our unshaking sense of realities,"[7] to the rules of interpersonal contact. Moreover, although a single gathering and episode of interaction might not have great social significance, "through these comings together much of our social life is organized."[8] The interaction order is thus a central topic of sociological theory.

Goffman's approach to this domain is unique.[9] Although we must "keep faith with the spirit of natural science, and lurch along, seriously kidding ourselves that our rut has a forward direction,"[10] we must not become over-enamored with the mature sciences. Social life is "ours to study naturalistically," but our study should not be rigid.[11] Instead, ad hoc observation,

---

[4]Ibid., p. 11. Italics in original.

[5]Ibid.

[6]Ibid.

[7]Erving Goffman, *Encounters: Two Studies in the Sociology of Interaction* (Indianapolis: Bobbs-Merrill, 1961), p. 81.

[8]Erving Goffman, *Behavior in Public Places: Notes on the Social Organization of Gatherings* (New York: Free Press, 1963), p. 234.

[9]For a useful set of essays on Goffman's analysis, see Paul Drew and Anthony Wootton, eds., *Erving Goffman: Exploring the Interaction Order* (Cambridge, England: Polity, 1988); see also a recent symposium on Goffman in *Sociological Perspectives*, 39, no. 3 (1996) and Thomas Scheff et al. *Goffman Unbound* (Boulder CO: Paradigm Press, 2006).

[10]Goffman, "The Interaction Order" (cited in note 1), p. 2.

[11]Ibid., p. 17.

cultivation of anecdotes, creative thinking, illustrations from literature, examination of books of etiquette, personal experiences, and many other sources of unsystematic data should guide inquiry into the micro order. Indeed, "human life is only a small irregular scab on the face of nature, not particularly amenable to deep systematic analysis."[12] Yet human life can be studied in the spirit of scientific inquiry.

# The Dramaturgical Metaphor

In both his first and last major works—*The Presentation of Self in Everyday Life* and *Frame Analysis*, respectively—Goffman analogized to the stage and theater. Hence the designation of his work as *dramaturgical* has become commonplace.[13] This designation is, however, somewhat misleading because it creates the impression that there is a script, a stage, an audience, props, and actors playing roles. Such imagery is in tune with role theory (discussed in Chapter 17). While Goffman did not reject this analogy, and indeed he frequently used it, the interaction order is dramatic in another sense: Individuals are actors who put on a performance, often cynical and deceptive, for one another, and people actively manipulate the script, stage, props, and roles for their own purposes and self-interest. This more cynical view of Goffman's dramaturgy is perhaps closer to the mark, but it too is somewhat misleading.[14] Commentators have often portrayed Goffman as presenting a kind of "con man"[15] view of human social interaction—a metaphor that captures some of the examples and topics of his approach but obscures the more fundamental processes found in Goffman's theorizing.

We can use the metaphor of dramaturgy in a less extreme sense. In Goffman's work, there is concern with a cultural script, or a set of normative rules; there is a heavy emphasis on how individuals manage their impressions and play roles; there is a concern with stages and props (physical space and objects); there is an emphasis on staging, on the manipulation of gestures, on the meanings attached to spacing, and on the use of props and other physical aspects of a setting. Moreover, in contrast to symbolic interactionist approaches where self and identities are the anchors for interaction, Goffman views self as situational, determined more by the cultural

---

[12]Ibid.

[13]Erving Goffman, *The Presentation of Self in Everyday Life* (Garden City, NY: Anchor, 1959) and *Frame Analysis: An Essay on the Organization of Experience* (Boston: Northeastern University Press, 1986; originally published in 1974 by Harper & Row).

[14]See, for example, Randall Collins, *Theoretical Sociology* (San Diego: Harcourt Brace Jovanovich, 1988), pp. 203–7, 291–98, and *Four Sociological Traditions* (New York: Oxford University Press, 1998).

[15]For example, see R. P. Cuzzort and E. W. King, *Twentieth-Century Social Thought*, 4th ed. (Fort Worth, TX: Holt, Rinehart & Winston, 1989), Chapter 12.

script, stage, and audience than by enduring and transituational configurations of self-attitudes, self-feelings, or identities. And finally, there is a particular emphasis on how performances create a theatrical ambiance—a mood, definition, and sense of reality.

This version of the dramatic metaphor provides only a broad orientation to Goffman's approach. We need to fill in this orientation with more details. To do so, I will review Goffman's most important works and try to pull the diverse vocabularies and concepts together into a more unified theoretical perspective—dramaturgical in its general contours but more than just a clever metaphor.[16]

# The Presentation of Self

The *Presentation of Self in Everyday Life* was Goffman's first major work and was largely responsible for the designation of Goffman as a dramaturgical theorist.[17] The basic argument is that individuals deliberately and inadvertently give off signs that provide others with information about how to respond. From such mutual use of "sign-vehicles," individuals develop a "definition of the situation," which is a "plan for cooperative activity," but which, at the same time, is "not so much a real agreement as to what exists but rather a real agreement as to whose claims concerning what issues will be temporarily honored."[18] In constructing this overall definition of a situation, individuals engage in performances in which each orchestrates gestures to *present oneself* in a particular manner as a person having identifiable characteristics and deserving of treatment in a certain fashion. These performances revolve around several interrelated dynamics:

(1) A performance involves the creation of a *front*. A front includes the physical "setting" and the use of the physical layout, its fixed equipment like furniture and other "stage props" to create a certain impression. A front also involves (a) "items of expressive equipment" (emotions, energy, and other capacities for expression); (b) "appearance," or those signs that tell others of an individual's social position and status as well as the "ritual state" of the individual with respect to social, work, or recreational activity;[19] and (c) "manner," or those signs that inform others about the role that an

---

[16]See Stephan Fuchs, "Second Thoughts on Emergent Interaction Orders," *Sociological Theory* 7, no. 1 (1989), pp. 121–23.

[17]Goffman, *The Presentation of Self in Everyday Life* (cited in note 13).

[18]Ibid., pp. 9–10.

[19]From this discussion, Randall Collins (see Chapter 12 in this work) took his idea of situations as either work-practical, ceremonial, or social. Also, Collins' notion of interaction rituals is much the same as Goffman's definition of encounters. See Collins' recent *Interaction Ritual Chains* (Princeton, NJ: Princeton University Press, 2004).

individual expects to play.[20] As a general rule, people expect consistency in these elements of their fronts—use of setting and its props, mobilization of expressive equipment, social status, expression of ritual readiness for various types of activity, and efforts to assume certain roles.[21] There are a relatively small number of fronts, and people know them all. Moreover, fronts tend to be established, institutionalized, and stereotypical for various kinds of settings, with the result that "when an actor takes an established role, usually he (she) finds that a particular front has already been established for it."[22]

(2) In addition to presenting a front, individuals use gestures in what Goffman termed *dramatic realization*, or the infusion into activity of signs that highlight commitment to a given definition of a situation. The more a situation creates problems in presenting a front, Goffman argued, the greater will be efforts at dramatic realization.[23]

(3) Performances also involve *idealizations* or efforts to present oneself in ways that "incorporate and exemplify the officially accredited values of society."[24] When individuals are mobile, moving into a new setting, dramatic efforts at idealization will be most pronounced. Idealization creates a problem for individuals, however: If the idealization is to be effective, individuals must suppress, conceal, and underplay those elements of themselves that might contradict more general values.

(4) Such efforts at concealment are part of a more general process of *maintaining expressive control*. Because minor cues and signs are read by others and contribute to a definition of a situation, actors must regulate their muscular activity, their signals of involvement, their orchestration of front, and their ability to be fit for interaction. The most picayune discrepancy between behavior and the definition of a situation can unsettle the interaction, because "the impression of reality fostered by a performance is a delicate, fragile thing that can be shattered by very minor mishaps."[25]

(5) Individuals can also engage in *misrepresentation*. The eagerness of one's audience to read gestures and determine one's front makes that audience vulnerable to manipulation and duping.[26]

---

[20]Note the similarity of this idea to Ralph H. Turner's discussion (see Chapter 17) on role making.

[21]Goffman, *The Presentation of Self* (cited in note 13), pp. 24–25.

[22]Ibid., p. 27.

[23]Ibid., p. 32.

[24]Ibid., p. 35. Note how this idea parallels the notion of representational aspect of roles developed by Ralph H. Turner and Paul Colomy (see Chapter 17).

[25]Ibid., p. 56.

[26]This is a consistent theme in Goffman's work that, perhaps, he overemphasized. See, for example, Erving Goffman, *Strategic Interaction* (Philadelphia: University of Pennsylvania Press, 1969).

(6) Individuals often attempt to engage in *mystification*, or the maintenance of distance from others, as a way to keep them in awe and in conformity to a definition of a situation. Such mystification is, however, limited primarily to those of higher rank and status.

(7) Individuals seek to make their performances seem real and to avoid communicating a sense of contrivance. Thus individuals must communicate or, at least, appear to others as sincere, natural, and spontaneous.

These procedures for bringing off a successful performance and thereby creating an overall definition of a situation are the core of Goffmanian sociology. They become elaborated and extended in subsequent works, but Goffman never abandoned the idea that fundamental to the interaction order are the efforts of individuals to orchestrate their performances, even in deceptive and manipulative ways, so as to maintain a particular definition of the situation. These ideas are presented propositionally in Table 19.1.

Although the propositions in Table 19.1 constitute only an opening chapter in *The Presentation of Self*, they are by far the most enduring portions of this first major work. The rest of the book is concerned with

**Table 19.1**  Goffman's Propositions on Interaction and Performance

1. As individuals make visual and verbal contact, the more likely they are to use gestures to orchestrate a performance, with the success of this performance depending on

   A. Presentation of a coherent front that, in turn, is a positive and additive function of

      1. Control of physical space, props, and equipment in a setting

      2. Control of expressive equipment in a setting

      3. Control of signals marking propensity for types of ritual activity

      4. Control of signals marking status outside and inside the interaction

      5. Control of signals pertaining to identifiable roles

   B. Incorporation and exemplification of general cultural values

   C. Imbuing a situation with a personal mystique

   D. Signaling sincerity

2. As individuals in a setting orchestrate their performances and, at the same time, accept one another's performances, they are likely to develop a common definition of the situation.

3. As a common definition of the situation emerges, the ease of the interaction increases.

performances sustained by more than one individual. Goffman introduced the concept of *team* to denote performances that are presented by individuals who must cooperate to effect a particular definition of the situation. Often two teams must present performances to each other, but more typically, one team constitutes a performer and the other an audience. Team performers generally move between a front region, or *frontstage*, where they coordinate their performances before an audience, and a back region, or *backstage*, where team members can relax. Goffman also introduced the notion of *outside*, or the residual region beyond the frontstage and backstage. Frontstage behavior is polite, maintaining a decorum appropriate to a team performance (for example, selling cars, serving food, meeting students, and so on), whereas backstage behavior is more informal and is geared toward maintaining the solidarity and morale of team performers. When outsiders or members of the audience intrude on performers in the backstage, a tension is created because team members are caught in their nonperforming roles.[27]

A basic problem of all team performances is maintaining a particular definition of the situation in front of the audience. This problem is accentuated when there are large rank or status differences among team members,[28] when the team has many members,[29] when the frontstage and backstage are not clearly partitioned, and when the team must hide information contrary to its image of itself. To counteract these kinds of problems, social control among the team's members is essential. When members are backstage, such control is achieved through morale-boosting activities, such as denigrating the audience, kidding one another, shifting to informal address, and engaging in stage talk (talk about performances on frontstage). When they are onstage, control is sustained by realigning actions revolving around subtle communications among team members that, hopefully, the audience will not understand.

*Breaches* of the performances occur when a team member acts in ways that challenge the definition of the situation created by the team's performances. Attempts to prevent such incidents involve further efforts at social control, especially a backstage emphasis on (a) playing one's part and not emitting unmeant gestures, (b) showing loyalty to the team and not the audience, and (c) exercising foresight and anticipating potential problems with the team or the audience. Team members are assisted in social control by members of the audience who (a) tend to stay away from the backstage, (b) act disinterested when exposed to backstage behavior, and (c) employ elaborate etiquette (exhibiting proper attention and interest, inhibiting their own potential performances, avoiding faux pas) to avoid a scene with the team.

---

[27]Goffman, *The Presentation of Self* (cited in note 13), pp. 137–38.

[28]Ibid., p. 92.

[29]Ibid., p. 141.

What is true of teams and audiences is, Goffman implied, also true of individuals. Interaction involves a performance for others who constitute an audience. One seeks to sustain a performance when moving to the front-stage and relax a front when moving to a backstage region. People try very hard to avoid mistakes and faux pas that could breach the definition of the situation, and they are assisted in this effort by others in their audience who exercise tact and etiquette to avoid a scene. Such are the themes of *The Presentation of Self,* and most of Goffman's work represented a conceptual elaboration of them. The notion of teams recedes, but general model elaborating these themes into a theory of interaction among individuals emerges.

# Focused Interaction

Goffman generally employed the terms *unfocused* and *focused* to denote two basic types of interaction. *Unfocused interaction* "consists of interpersonal communications that result solely by virtue of persons being in one another's presence, as when two strangers across the room from each other check up on each other's clothing, posture, and general manner, while each modifies his (her) own demeanor because he himself is under observation."[30] As will be explored later, such unfocused interaction is, Goffman argued, an important part of the interaction order, for much of what people do is exchange glances and monitor each other in public places. *Focused interaction,* in contrast, "occurs when people effectively agree to sustain for a time a single focus of cognitive and visual attention, as in a conversation, a board game, or a joint task sustained by a close face-to-face circle of contributors."[31]

## Encounters

Focused interaction occurs within what Goffman termed *encounters,* which constitute one of the core structural units of the interaction order. Goffman mentioned encounters in his first work, *The Presentation of Self in Everyday Life,* but their full dimensions are explored in his next book, *Encounters.*[32] There, an encounter is defined as focused interaction revealing the following characteristics:[33]

1. A single visual and cognitive focus of attention

2. A mutual and preferential openness to verbal communication

---

[30]Goffman, *Encounters,* p. 7 (cited in note 7).

[31]Ibid.

[32]Ibid.

[33]Ibid., p. 18. Note the similarity of this definition to Randall Collins' portrayal of interaction rituals (see Chapter 12).

3. A heightened mutual relevance of acts

4. An eye-to-eye ecological huddle, maximizing mutual perception and monitoring

5. An emergent "we" feeling of solidarity and flow of feeling

6. A ritual and ceremonial punctuation of openings, closings, entrances, and exits

7. A set of procedures for corrective compensation for deviant acts

To sustain itself, an encounter develops a *membrane*, or penetrable barrier to the larger social world in which the interaction is located. Goffman typically conceptualized the immediate setting of an encounter as a gathering, or the assembling in space of co-present individuals; in turn, gatherings are lodged within a more inclusive unit, the social occasion, or the larger undertaking sustained by fixed equipment, distinctive ethos and emotional structure, program an agenda, rules of proper and improper conduct, and preestablished sequencing of activities (beginning, phases, high point, and ending). Thus, encounters emerge from episodes of focused interaction within gatherings that are lodged in social occasions.[34]

The membrane of an encounter, as well as its distinctive characteristics previously listed, are sustained by a set of rules. In *Encounters*, Goffman lists several; later, in what is probably his most significant work, *Interaction Ritual*, he lists several more.[35] Let us combine both discussions by listing the rules that guide focused interaction in encounters:

1. *Rules of irrelevance*, which "frame" a situation as excluding certain materials (attributes of participants, psychological states, cultural values and norms, etc.)[36]

2. *Rules of transformation*, which specify how materials moving through the membrane created by rules of irrelevance are to be altered to fit into the interaction

3. *Rules of realized resources*, which provide a general schemata and framework for expression and interpretation for activities among participants

4. *Rules of talk*, which are the procedures, conventions, and practices guiding the flow of verbalizations with respect to[37]

---

[34]Goffman, *Behavior in Public Places* (cited in note 8), pp. 18–20.

[35]Goffman, *Encounters* (cited in note 7), pp. 20–33; Erving Goffman, *Interaction Ritual: Essays on Face-to-Face Behavior* (Garden City, NY: Anchor, 1967), p. 33.

[36]The concept of frame, which Goffman said that he took from Gregory Bateson, became central in Goffman's later work. See the closing section in this chapter.

[37]These rules come from Goffman, *Interaction Ritual* (cited in note 35), p. 33.

    a.  Maintaining a single focus of attention

    b.  Establishing "clearance cues" for determining when one speaker is done and another can begin

    c.  Determining how long and how frequently any one person can hold the floor

    d.  Regulating interruptions and lulls in the conversation

    e.  Sanctioning participants whose attention wanders to matters outside the conversation

    f.  Ensuring that nearby people do not interfere with the conversation

    g.  Guiding the use of politeness and tact, even in the face of disagreements

5.  *Rules of self-respect*, which encourage participants to honor with tact and etiquette their respective efforts to present themselves in a certain light

Interaction is thus guided by complex configurations of rules that individuals learn how to use and apply in different types of encounters, logged in varying types of gatherings and social occasions. The reality of the world is, to a very great extent, sustained by people's ability to invoke and use these rules.[38] When these rules are operating effectively, individuals develop a *state of euphoria*, or what Randall Collins has termed enhanced *emotional energy*. However, encounters are vulnerable to *dysphoria* or tension when these rules do not exclude troublesome external materials or fail to regulate the flow of interaction. Such failures are seen by Goffman as incidents or breaches; when they can be effectively handled by tact and corrective procedures, they are then viewed as integrations because they are blended into the ongoing encounter. The key mechanism for avoiding dysphoria and maintaining the integration of the encounter is the use of ritual.

## Ritual

In *Interaction Ritual*, Goffman's great contribution is the recognition that minor, seemingly trivial, and everyday rituals—such as "Hello, how are you?" "Good morning," "Please, after you," and so on—are crucial to the maintenance of social order.[39] In his words, he "reformulated Émile Durkheim's social psychology in a modern dress"[40] by recognizing that, when individuals gather and begin to interact, their behaviors are highly ritualized. That is, actors punctuate each phase of interpersonal contact with stereotypical sequences of behavior that invoke the rules of the

---

[38]Here Goffman anticipates much of ethnomethodology, which is examined in Chapter 20.

[39]Goffman, *Interaction Ritual* (cited in note 35).

[40]Particularly Durkheim's later work, as it culminated *in Elementary Forms of the Religious Life* (New York: Free Press, 1947; originally published in 1912).

encounter and, at the same time, become the medium or vehicle by which the rules are followed. Rituals are thus essential for (a) mobilizing individuals to participate in interaction; (b) making them cognizant of the relevant rules of irrelevance, transformation, resource use, and talk; (c) guiding them during the course of the interaction; and (d) helping them correct for breaches and incidents.

Among the most significant are those rituals revolving around deference and demeanor. *Deference* pertains to interpersonal rituals that express individuals' respect for others, their willingness to interact, their affection and other emotions, and their engagement in the encounter. In Goffman's words, deference establishes "marks of devotion" by which an actor "celebrates and confirms his (her) relationship to a recipient."[41] As a result, deference contains a "kind of promise, expressing in truncated form the actor's avowal and pledge to treat the recipient in a particular way in the on-coming activity."[42] Thus, seemingly innocuous gestures—"It's nice to see you again," "How are things?" "What are you doing?" "Good-bye," "See you later," and many other stereotypical phrases as well as bodily movements—are rituals that present a demeanor invoking relevant rules and guiding the opening, sequencing, and closing of the interaction.

Deference rituals, Goffman argued, can be of two types: (1) *avoidance rituals* and (2) *presentational rituals*. Avoidance rituals are those that an individual uses to keep distance from another and to avoid violating the "ideal sphere" that lies around the other. Such rituals are most typical among unequals. Presentational rituals "encompass acts through which the individual makes specific attestations to recipients concerning how he regards them and how he will treat them in the on-coming interaction."[43] Goffman saw interaction as constantly involving a dialectic between avoidance and presentational rituals as individuals respect each other and maintain distance while trying to make contact and get things done.[44]

In contrast, *demeanor* is "that element of the individual's ceremonial behavior conveyed through deportment, dress, and bearing which serves to (inform) those in his immediate presence that he is a person of certain desirable or undesirable qualities."[45] Through demeanor rituals, individuals present images of themselves to others and, at the same time, communicate that they are reliable, trustworthy, and tactful.

Thus, through deference and demeanor rituals, individuals plug themselves into an encounter by invoking relevant rules and demonstrating their capacity to follow them, while indicating their respect for others and presenting themselves as certain kinds of individuals. The enactment of such

---

[41]Goffman, *Interaction Ritual* (cited in note 35), pp. 56–67.

[42]Ibid., p. 60.

[43]Ibid.

[44]Ibid., pp. 75–76.

[45]Ibid., p. 77.

deference and demeanor rituals in concrete gatherings, especially encounters but also including unfocused situations, provides a basis for the integration of society. For "throughout . . . ceremonial obligations and expectations, a constant flow of indulgences is spread through society, with others who are present constantly reminding the individual that he must keep himself together as a well demeaned person and affirm the sacred quality of these others."[46]

## Roles

In presenting themselves to others, individuals also seek to play a particular role. Thus, as people present a front, invoke relevant rules, and emit rituals, they also try to orchestrate a role for themselves. For Goffman, then, a role is "a bundle of activities visibly performed before a set of others and visibly meshed into the activities these others perform."[47] In the terms of Ralph Turner's analysis (see Chapter 17), individuals attempt to "make a role" for themselves; if successful, this effort contributes to the overall definition of the situation.

In trying to establish a role, the individual "must see to it that the impressions of him that are conveyed in the situation are compatible with role-appropriate personal qualities effectively imputed to him."[48] Thus, individuals in a situation are expected to try to make roles for themselves that are consistent with their demeanor, their self as performed before others, and their front (stage props, expressive equipment, appearance). If the inconsistency between the attempted role and these additional aspects of a performance becomes evident, then others in the situation are likely to sanction the individual through subtle cues and gestures. These others are driven to do so because discrepancy between another's role and other performance cues disrupts the definition of the situation and the underlying sense of reality that this definition promotes. Thus, role is contingent on the responses and reactions of others, and because their sense of reality partially depends on successful and appropriate role assumption, an individual will have difficulty changing a role in a situation once it is established.

Often, however, people perceive a role to be incompatible with their image of themselves in a situation. Under these conditions, they will display what Goffman termed _role distance_, whereby a separation of the person from a role is communicated. Such distancing, Goffman argued, allows the individual to (a) release the tension associated with a role considered to be "beneath his (her) dignity," (b) present additional aspects of self that extend beyond the role, and (c) remove the burden of "complete compliance to the

[46]Ibid., p. 91.

[47]Goffman, _Encounters_ (cited in note 7), p. 96.

[48]Ibid., p. 87.

role," thereby making minor transgressions less dramatic and troublesome for others.[49]

Role distance is but an extreme response to the more general process of role embracement. For any role, individuals will reveal varying degrees of attachment and involvement in the role. One extreme is role distance, whereas the other extreme is what Goffman termed *engrossment*, or complete involvement in a role. In general, Goffman argued, those roles in which individuals can direct what is going on are likely to involve high degrees of embracement, whereas those roles in which the individual is subordinate will be played with considerable role distance.[50]

As is evident, then, the assumption of a role is connected to the self-image that actors project in their performance. Although the self that one reveals in a situation depends on the responses of others who can confirm or disconfirm that person's self in a situation, the organization of a performance onstage before others is still greatly circumscribed by self.

## Self

Goffman's view of self is highly situational and contingent on the responses of others. Although one of the main activities of actors in a situation is to present themselves to others, Goffman was highly skeptical about a *core* or *transituational* self-conception that is part of an individual's personality. In almost all his works, he took care to emphasize that individuals do not have an underlying personality or identity that is carried from situation to situation, as most symbolic interactionists would emphasize. For example, in his last major book, *Frame Analysis*,[51] he argued that people in interaction often presume that the presented self provides a glimpse at a more coherent and core self, but in reality, this is simply a folk presumption because there is "no reason to think that all these gleanings about himself that an individual makes available, all these pointings from his current situation to the way he is in his other occasions, have anything very much in common."[52]

Yet, even though there is no transituational or core self, people's efforts to present images of themselves in a particular situation and others' reactions to this presentation are central dynamics in all encounters. Individuals constantly emit demeanor cues that project images of themselves as certain kinds of persons, or in the vocabulary of *The Presentation of Self*, they engage in *performances*. In *Interaction Ritual*, Goffman rephrased this argument somewhat, and in so doing, he refined his views on self. In encounters, an individual *acts out a line*, which is "a pattern of verbal and nonverbal acts by which he expresses his view of the situation and, through this, his evaluation

---

[49]Ibid., p. 113.

[50]Ibid., p. 107.

[51]Goffman, *Frame Analysis* (cited in note 13).

[52]Ibid., p. 299.

of the participants, especially himself."[53] In developing a line, an individual presents a face, which is "the positive social value a person effectively claims for himself by the line others assume he has during a particular contact."[54] Individuals seek to *stay in face* or to maintain face by presenting an image of themselves through their line that is supported by the responses of others and, if possible, sustained by impersonal agencies in a situation. Conversely, a person is in wrong face or out of face when the line emitted is inappropriate and unaccepted by others. Thus, although a person's social face "can be his most personal possession and the center of his security and pleasure, it is only on loan to him from society; it will be withdrawn unless he conducts himself in a way that is worthy of it."[55]

As noted earlier, Goffman argued that a key norm in any encounter is "the rule of self-respect," which requires individuals to maintain face and, through tact and etiquette, the face of others. Thus, by virtue of tact or the "language of hint . . . , innuendo, ambiguities, well-placed phrases, carefully worked jokes, and so on,"[56] individuals sustain each other's face; in so doing, they confirm the definition of the situation and promote a sense of a common reality. For this reason, a given line and face in an encounter are difficult to change once established, because to alter face (and the line by which it is presented) would require redefining the situation and recreating a sense of reality. And, because face is "on loan" to a person from the responses of others, the individual must incur high costs—such as embarrassment or a breach of the situation—to alter a line and face.

Face engagements are usually initiated with eye contact, and once initiated, they involve ritual openings appropriate to the situation (as determined by length of last engagement, amount of time since previous engagement, level of inequality, and so forth). During the course of the face engagement, each individual uses tack to maintain, if possible, each other's face and to sanction, if necessary, each other into their appropriate line. In particular, participants seek to avoid a scene or breach in the situation, so they use tact and etiquette to save their own face and that of others. Moreover, as deemed appropriate for the type of encounter (as well as for the larger gathering and more inclusive social occasion), individuals will attempt to maintain what Goffman sometimes termed *the territories of self*, revolving around such matters as physical props, ecological space, personal preserve (territory around one's body), and conversational rights (to talk and be heard), which are necessary for people to execute their line and maintain face.[57] In general, the higher the rank of individuals, the greater

---

[53]Goffman, *Interaction Ritual* (cited in note 35), p. 5.

[54]Ibid.

[55]Ibid., p. 10.

[56]Ibid., p. 30.

[57]Erving Goffman, *Relations in Public: Micro Studies of the Public Order* (New York: Harper Colophon, 1972; originally published in 1971 by Basic Books), pp. 38–41.

their territories of self in an encounter.[58] To violate such territories disrupts or breaches the situation, forcing remedial action by participants to restore their respective lines, face, definitions of the situation, and sense of reality.

## Talk

Throughout his work, but especially in later books such as *Frame Analysis*[59] and in numerous essays (see those collected in *Forms of Talk*[60]), Goffman emphasized the significance of verbalizations for focusing people's attention. When *talk* is viewed interactionally, "it is an example of that arrangement by which individuals come together and sustain matters having a ratified, joint, current, and running claim upon attention, a claim which lodges them together in some sort of intersubjective, mental world."[61] Thus, in Goffman's view, "no resource is more effective as a basis for joint involvement than speaking" because it fetches "speaker and hearer into the same interpretation schema that applies to what is thus attended."[62]

Talk is thus a crucial mechanism for drawing individuals together, focusing their attention, and adjudicating an overall definition of the situation. Because talk is so central to focusing interaction, it is normatively regulated and ritualized. One significant norm is the prohibition against self-talk, because, when people talk to themselves, it "warns others that they might be wrong in assuming a jointly maintained base of ready mutual intelligibility."[63] Moreover, other kinds of quasi talk are also regulated and ritualized. For example, response cues or "exclamatory interjections which are not full-fledged words"—"Oops," "Wow," "Oh," and "Yikes"—are regulated as to when they can be used and the way they are uttered.[64] Verbal fillers—"ah," "uh," "um," and the like—are also ritualized and are used to facilitate "conversational tracking." In essence, they indicate that "the speaker does not have, as of yet, the proper word but is working on the matter" and that he or she is still engaged in the conversation. Even seemingly emotional cues and tabooed expressions, such as all the "four-letter words," are not so much an expression of emotion as "self-other alignment" and assert that "our inner concerns should be theirs." Such outbursts are normative and ritualized because this "invitation into our interiors tends to be made only when it will be easy to other persons present to see where the voyage takes them."[65]

---

[58]Ibid., pp. 40–41.

[59]Goffman, *Frame Analysis* (cited in note 13).

[60]Erving Goffman, *Forms of Talk* (Philadelphia: University of Pennsylvania Press, 1981).

[61]Ibid., pp. 70–71.

[62]Ibid., p. 71.

[63]Ibid., p. 85. Although, with a bluetooth and other devices, people today often engage in what seems like "self talk."

[64]Ibid., p. 120.

[65]Ibid., p. 121.

In creating a definition of the situation, Goffman argued, talk operates in extremely complex ways. When individuals talk, they create what Goffman termed *a footing*, or assumed foundation for the conversation and the interaction. Because verbal symbols are easily manipulated, people can readily change the footing or basic premises underlying the conversation.[66] Such shifts in footing are, however, highly ritualized and usually reveal clear markers. For example, when a person says something like "Let's not talk about that," the footing of the conversation is shifted, but in a ritualized way; similarly, when someone utters a phrase like "That's great, but what about . . . ?" this person is also changing the footing through ritual.

Shifts in footing raise a question that increasingly dominated Goffman's later works: the issue of embedding. Goffman came to recognize that conversations are layered and, hence, embedded in different footings. There are often multiple footings for talk, as when someone says one thing but means another or when a person hints or implies something else. These layerings of conversations, which embed them in different contexts, are possible because speech is capable of generating subtle and complex meanings. For example, irony, sarcasm, puns, wit, double-entendres, inflections, shadings, and other manipulations of speech demonstrate the capacity of individuals to shift footings and contextual embeddings of a conversation (for example, think of a conversation in a work setting involving romantic flirtations; it will involve constant movement in footing and context). Yet, for encounters to proceed smoothly, these alterations in footing are, to some extent, normatively regulated and ritualized, enabling individuals to sustain a sense of common reality—an idea that ethnomethodology was to pursue (see next chapter).

Talk is thus a critical dimension of focused interaction. Without it, the gestures and cues that people can emit are limited and lack the subtlety and complexity of language. And, as Goffman began to explore this complexity in later works, earlier notions about definitions of situations seemed too crude because people could construct multiple, as well as subtly layered, definitions of any situation—an issue that we will explore near the end of this chapter. For our purposes here, the critical point is that talk focuses attention and pulls actors together, forcing their interaction on a face-to-face basis. But, despite the complexity of how this focusing can be done, talk is still normatively and ritually regulated in ways that produce a sense of shared reality for individuals.[67]

Table 19.2 summarizes Goffman's analysis of focused encounters. Focused encounters occur when social occasions put people in face-to-face contact, and the viability of the encounter depends on rules, rituals, and the

---

[66]Goffman termed this *reframing* (see later section) when it involved a shift in frame. However, footing and re-footing can occur within an existing frame, so a person can change the footing of a conversation without breaking or changing a frame.

[67]Again, this line of emphasis is what gives Goffman's work an ethnomethodological flair. See next chapter.

**Table 19.2** Goffman's General Proposition on Focused Interaction

1. Encounters are created when
   A. Social occasions put individuals in physical proximity
   B. Gatherings allow face-to-face contact revolving around talk
2. The viability of an encounter is a positive and multiplicative function of
   A. The availability of relevant normative rules to guide participants with respect to such issues as
      1. Irrelevance, or excluded matters
      2. Transformation, or how external matters are to be incorporated
      3. Resource use, or what local resources are to be drawn from
      4. Talk, or how verbalizations are to be ordered
      5. Self-respect, or the maintenance of lines and face
   B. The availability of ritual practices that can be used to
      1. Regulate talk and conversation
      2. Express appropriate deference and demeanor
      3. Invoke and punctuate normative rules
      4. Repair breaches to the interaction
   C. The capacity of individuals to present acceptable performances with respect to
      1. Lines, or directions of conduct
      2. Roles, or specific clusters of rights and duties
      3. Faces, or specific presentations of personal characteristics
      4. Self, or particular images of oneself

capacity of individuals to present acceptable performances. The statements under 1 and 2 reveal the basic argument in Goffman's approach.

## Disruption and Repair in Focused Interaction

Goffman stressed that disruption in encounters is never a trivial matter:

Social encounters differ a great deal in the importance that participants give to them but, whether crucial or picayune, all encounters represent occasions when the individual can become spontaneously involved in the proceedings and derive from this a firm sense of reality. And this feeling is not a trivial thing, regardless of the package in which it comes. When an incident occurs . . . then the reality is threatened. Unless the disturbance is checked, unless the interactants regain their proper involvement, the illusion of reality will be shattered.[68]

When a person emits gestures that contradict normative roles, present a contradictory front, fail to enact appropriate rituals, seek an inappropriate role, attempt a normatively or ritually incorrect line, or present a wrong face, there is potential for a scene. From the person's point of view, there is a possibility of embarrassment, to use Goffman's favorite phrase; once embarrassed, an individual's responses can further degenerate in an escalating cycle of ever greater levels of embarrassment. From the perspective of others, a scene disrupts the definition of the situation and threatens the sense of reality necessary for them to feel comfortable. Individuals implicitly assume that people are reliable and trustworthy, that they are what they appear to be, that they are competent, and that they can be relied on; thus, when a scene occurs, these implicit assumptions are challenged and threaten the organization of the encounter (and, potentially, the larger gathering and social occasion).

For this reason an individual will seek to repair a scene caused by the use of inappropriate gestures, and others will use tact to assist the individual in such repair efforts. The sense of order of a situation is thus sustained by a variety of corrective responses by individuals and by the willingness of others to use tact and to ignore minor mistakes to employ tact to facilitate an offending individual's corrective efforts. People "disattend" much potentially discrepant behavior, and when this is no longer an option, they are prepared to accept apologies, accounts, new information, excuses and other ritually and normatively appropriate efforts at repair. Of course, this willingness to accept people as they are, to assume their competence, and to overlook minor interpersonal mistakes makes them vulnerable to manipulation and deceit.

## Unfocused Interaction

Goffman was one of the few sociologists to recognize that behavior and interaction in public places, or in unfocused settings, are important features of the interaction order and, by extension, of social organization in general. Such simple acts as walking down the street, standing in line, sitting in a waiting room or on a park bench, standing in an elevator, going to and from a public restroom, and many other activities represent a significant realm of social organization. These unfocused situations in which people are co-present but not involved in prolonged talk and face encounters represent a crucial topic of sociological inquiry—a topic that is often seen as trivial but

---

[68]Goffman, *Interaction Ritual* (cited in note 35), p. 135.

that embraces much of people's time and attention. In two works, *Relations in Public* and *Behavior in Public Places*, Goffman explored the dynamics of unfocused gatherings.[69]

Unfocused gatherings are like focused interactions in their general contours: They are normatively regulated; they call for performances by individuals; they include the presentation of a self; they involve the use of rituals; they have normatively and ritually appropriate procedures for repair; and they depend on a considerable amount of etiquette, tact, and inattention. Let us explore each of these features in somewhat greater detail.

Much like a focused interaction, unfocused gatherings involve normative rules concerning spacing, movement, positioning, listening, talking, and self-presentation. But, unlike focused interaction, norms do not have to sustain a well-defined membrane. There is no closure, intense focus of attention, or face-to-face obligations in unfocused encounters. Rather, rules pertain to how individuals are to comport themselves *without* becoming the focus of attention and involved in a face encounter. Rules are thus about how to move, talk, sit, stand, present self, apologize, and perform other actions necessary to sustain public order without creating a situation requiring the additional interpersonal work of focused interaction.

When in public, individuals still engage in performances, but because the audience is not involved in a face engagement or prolonged tracks of talk, the presentation can be more muted and less animated. Goffman used a variety of terms to describe these presentations, two of the most frequent being *body idiom*[70] and *body gloss*.[71] Both terms denote the overall configuration of gestures, or demeanor, that an individual makes available and gleanable to others. (Conversely, others are constantly scanning to determine the content of others' body idiom and body gloss.) Such demeanor denotes a person's direction, speed, resoluteness, purpose, and other aspects of a course of action. In *Relations in Public*, Goffman enumerated three types of body gloss:[72] (1) *orientation gloss*, or gestures giving evidence to others confirming that a person is engaged in a recognizable and appropriate activity in the present time and place; (2) *circumspection gloss*, or gestures indicating to others that a person is not going to encroach on or threaten the activity of others; and (3) *overplay gloss*, or gestures signaling that a person is not constrained or under duress and is, therefore, fully in charge and control of his or her other movements and actions. Thus the public performance of an individual in unfocused interaction revolves around providing information that one is of "sound character and reasonable competency."[73]

---

[69]Cited in notes 57 and 8, respectively: Goffman, *Relations in Public* and *Behavior in Public Places*.

[70]Goffman, *Behavior in Public Places* (cited in note 57), p. 35.

[71]Goffman, *Relations in Public* (cited in note 8), p. 8.

[72]Ibid., pp. 129–38.

[73]Ibid., p. 162.

In public and during unfocused interactions, the territories of self become an important consideration. Goffman listed various kinds of territorial considerations that can become salient during unfocused interaction, including (a) *fixed geographical spaces* attached to a particular person, (b) *egocentric preserves* of non-encroachment that surround individuals as they move in space, (c) *personal spaces* that others are not to violate under any circumstances, (d) *stalls* or bounded places that an individual can temporarily claim, (e) *use spaces* that can be claimed as an individual engages in some instrumental activity, (f) *turns* or the claimed order of doing or receiving something relative to others in a situation, (g) *possessional territory* or objects identified with self and arrayed around an individual's body, (h) *informational preserve* or the body of facts about a person that is controlled and regulated, and (i) *conversational preserve* or the right to control who can summon and talk to an individual.[74] Depending on the type of unfocused interaction, as well as on the number, age, sex, rank, position, and other characteristics of the participants, the territories of self will vary, but in all societies, there are clearly understood norms about which configuration of these territories is relevant and to what degree it can be invoked.

These territories of self are made visible through what Goffman termed *markers*. Markers are signals and objects that denote the type of territorial claim, its extent and boundary, and its duration. Violation of these markers involves an encroachment on a person's self and invites sanctioning, perhaps creating a breach or scene in the public order. Indeed, seemingly innocent acts—such as inadvertently taking someone's place, butting in line, cutting someone off, and the like—can become a violation or befoulment of another's self and, as a result, invite an extreme reaction. Thus, social organization in general depends on the capacity of individuals to read those markers that establish their territories of self in public situations.

Violations of norms and territories create breaches and potential scenes, even when individuals are not engaged in focused interaction. These are usually repaired through ritual activity, such as the following: (a) *accounts* explaining why a transgression has occurred (ignorance, unusual circumstances, temporary incompetence, unmindfulness, and so on); (b) *apologies* (some combination of expressed embarrassment or chagrin, clarification that the proper conduct is known and understood, disavowal and rejection of one's behavior, penance, volunteering of restitution, and so forth); and (c) *requests*, or a preemptive asking for license to do something that might otherwise be considered a violation of a norm or a person's self.[75] The use of these ritualized forms of repair sustains the positioning, movement, and smooth flow of activity among people in unfocused situations; without these repair rituals, tempers would flair and other disruptive acts would overwhelm the public order.

---

[74]Ibid., Chap. 2.

[75]Ibid., pp. 109–20.

**Table 19.3**   Goffman's General Propositions on Unfocused Interaction

1. Order in unfocused interaction is a positive and multiplicative function of

   A. The clarity of normative rules regulating behavior in ways that limit face encounters and talk

   B. The capacity of individuals to provide demeanor cues with respect to

      1. Orientation, or the appropriateness of activities at the present time and place

      2. Circumspection, or the willingness to avoid encroachment on, and threat to, others

      3. Overplays, or the capacity to signal that one can control and regulate conduct without duress and constraint

   C. The capacity of individuals to signal with clear markers those configurations of normatively appropriate territories of self with respect to

      1. Fixed geographical spaces that can be claimed

      2. Egocentric preserves of non-encroachment that can be claimed during movement in space

      3. Personal spaces that can be claimed

      4. Stalls of territory that can be temporarily used

      5. Use spaces that can be occupied for instrumental purposes

      6. Turns of performing or receiving goods that can be claimed

      7. Possessional territory and objects identified with, and arrayed around, self

      8. Informational preserves that can be used to regulate facts about individuals

      9. Conversational preserves that can be invoked to control talk

   D. The availability of configurations of normatively appropriate repair rituals revolving around

      1. Accounts, or explanations for transgressions

      2. Apologies, or expressions of embarrassment, regret, and penance for mistakes

      3. Requests, or redemptive inquiries about making a potential transgression

   E. The availability and clarity of rituals to reinforce norms and to order conduct by restricting face engagements among individuals

   F. The availability of ritualized procedures for ignoring minor transgressions of norms and territories of self (tact and etiquette)

The significance of ritualized responses for repair only highlights the importance of ritual in general for unfocused interaction. As individuals move about, stand, sit, and engage in other acts in public, these activities are punctuated with rituals, especially as people come close to contact with each other. Nods, smiles, hand gestures, bodily movements, and if necessary, brief episodes of talk (especially during repairs) are all highly ritualized, involving stereotyped sequences of behavior that reinforce norms and signal individuals' willingness to get along with and accommodate each other.

In addition to ritual, much unfocused interaction involves tact and inattention. By simply ignoring or quietly tolerating small breaches of norms, self, and ritual practices, people can gather and move about without undue tension and acrimony. In this way, unfocused interactions are made to seem uneventful, enabling individuals to cultivate a sense of obdurate reality in the subtle glances, nods, momentary eye contact, shifting of direction, and other acts of public life.

In Table 19.3, the key propositions implied in Goffman's discussion are enumerated. The relationships among the variables listed in the propositions are multiplicative in that each one accelerates the effects of the other in maintaining order in public situations of unfocused gatherings. This interactive effect allows public order to be sustained without reliance on focused talk and conversation.

# Frames and the Organization of Experience

Goffman's last major work, *Frame Analysis: An Essay on the Organization of Experience*,[76] is hardly an "essay" but rather an 800-page treatise on phenomenology, or the subjective organization of experience in social situations. It is a dense and rambling work, but it nonetheless returns to a feature of interaction that guided Goffman's work from the very beginning: the construction of *definitions of situations*. That is, how is it that people define the reality of situations?

## What Is a Frame?

The concept of frame appeared in Goffman's first major work, *The Presentation of Self*, and periodically thereafter. Surprisingly, he never offered a precise definition of this term, but the basic idea is that people "interpret" events or "strips of activity" in situations with a "schemata" that cognitively encircles or frames what is occurring.[77] The frame is much like a picture frame in that it marks off the boundary of the pictured events, encapsulating and distinguishing them from the surrounding environment. Goffman's early

---

[76]Goffman, *Frame Analysis* (cited in note 13).

[77]See Goffman, *Frame Analysis* (cited in note 13), p. 10, for the vagueness of his portrayal.

discussion of the "rules of irrelevance" in encounters—that is, considerations, characteristics, aspects, and events in the external world to be excluded during a focused interaction—represented an earlier way of communicating the dynamics of framing. Thus, as people look at the world, they impose a frame that defines what is to be pictured on the inside and what is to be excluded by what Goffman termed the *rim of the frame* on the outside. Human experience is organized by frames, which provide an interpretive "framework" or "frame of reference" for designating events or "strips of activity."

## Primary Frames

Goffman argued that, ultimately, interpretations of events are anchored in a primary framework, which is a frame that does not depend on some prior interpretation of events.[78] Primary frameworks are thus anchored in the real world, at least from the point of view of the individual's organization of experience. People tend to distinguish, Goffman emphasized, between natural and social frameworks.[79] A *natural frame* is anchored in purely physical means for interpreting the world—body, ecology, terrain, objects, natural events, and the like. A *social frame* is lodged in the world created by acts of intelligence and social life. These two kinds of primary frameworks can vary enormously in their organization; some are clearly organized as "entities, postulates, and roles," whereas most others "provide" only a lore of understanding, an approach, a perspective.[80] All social frameworks involve rules about what is to be excluded beyond the rim of the frame, what is to be pictured inside the frame, and what is to be done when acting within the frame. Yet, as humans perceive and act, they are likely to apply several frameworks, giving the organization of experience a complexity that Goffman only alluded to in his earlier works.

Although Goffman stressed that he was not analyzing social structure with the concept of frames, he was clearly developing a neo-Durkheimian argument, recasting Durkheim's social psychology—especially the notion of how the "collective conscience rules people from within"—into more complex and dynamic terms.[81] For, as he argued, taken all together, the primary frameworks of a particular social group constitute a central element of its culture, especially insofar as understandings emerge concerning principal classes of schemata, the relations of these classes to one another, and the sum total of forces and agents that these interpretive designs acknowledge to be loose in the world.[82]

---

[78]Ibid., p. 21.

[79]Ibid., pp. 21–24.

[80]Ibid., p. 21.

[81]See Durkheim, *Elementary Forms of the Religious Life* (cited in note 40).

[82]Goffman, *Frame Analysis* (cited in note 13), p. 27.

Yet, for the most part, Goffman concentrated on the dynamics of framing within the realms of personal experiences and the interaction order, leaving Durkheim's concerns about macrocultural processes to others. Indeed, as was so often the case with Goffman, he became so intrigued with the interpersonal manipulation of frames for deceitful purposes and with the fluidity and complexity of framing in contingent situations that it is often difficult to discern whether or not the analysis is still sociological.

## Keys and Keying

What makes framing a complex process, Goffman argued, is that frames can be transformed. One basic way to transform a primary frame is to engage in *keying*, which is "a set of conventions by which a given activity, one already meaningful in terms of some primary framework, is transformed into something patterned on this activity but seen by the participants to be something quite else."[83] For example, a theatrical production of a family setting is a keying of real families; a hobby, such as woodworking, is a keying of a more primary set of occupational activities; a daydream about a love affair is a keying of real love; a sporting event is a keying of some more primary activity (running, fleeing, fighting, and so on); practicing and rehearsing are keyings of real performances; joking about someone's love life is a keying of love affairs; and so on. Primary frameworks are seen by people as real, whereas keyings are seen as less real; the more one rekeys a primary framework—say, performing a keying of a keying of a keying (and so on)—the less real is the frame. The rim of the frame is still ultimately a primary framework, anchored in some natural or social reality, but humans have the capacity to continually rekey and layer or *laminate* their experiences. Thus terms like *definition of the situation* do not adequately capture this layering of experience through keying, nor do such terms adequately denote the multiplicity of frameworks that people can invoke because of their capacities for shifting primary frameworks and rekeying existing ones.

## Fabrications

The second type of frame transformation—in addition to keying—is *fabrication*, which is "the intentional effort of one or more individuals to manage activity so that a party of one or more others will be induced to have a false belief about what it is that is going on."[84] Unlike a key, a fabrication is not a copy (or a copy of a copy) of some primary framework, but an effort to make others think that something else is going on. Hoaxes, con games, and strategic manipulations all involve fabrications—getting others to frame a situation in one way while others manipulate them as another, hidden, framework.

---

[83]Ibid., pp. 43–44.

[84]Ibid., p. 83.

## The Complexity of Experience

Thus, as people interact, they frame situations as primary frameworks, but they can also key these primary frames and fabricate new ones for purposes of deception and manipulation. From Goffman's viewpoint, an interaction can involve many keyings and rekeyings (that is, layers and laminations of interpretation) as well as fabrications. Once keying or fabrication occurs, further keying and fabrication actually are facilitated because they initiate an escalating movement away from a primary framework. Goffman never stated how much fabrication (and fabrication on fabrications) and keying (or keying on keyings) can occur in interaction, but he did see novels, dramatic theater, and cinema as providing the vehicles for the deepest layering of interaction (because each is an initial keying of some primary frame in the real world, which then opens the almost infinite possibilities for rekeying and fabrication).

Yet there are procedures in interaction—typically ritualized and normatively regulated—for bringing participants' experiences back to the original primary frame—that is, for wiping away layers of keyings and fabrications. For example, when people have become caught up in benign ridicule and joking about something, a person saying "seriously now . . ." is trying to wipe the slate clean of keyings (and rekeyings) and come back to the primary frame on which the mocking and joking were based. Such rituals (with the normative obligation to try to be serious for a moment) seek to re-anchor the interaction in the real world.

In addition to keyings and deliberate fabrications, individuals can *misframe* events—whether from ignorance, ambiguity, error, or initial disputes over framing among participants. Such misframing can persist for a time, but eventually, individuals seek to clear the frame by getting a correct reading of information so they can reframe the situation correctly. Such efforts to clear the frame become particularly difficult and problematic, however, when fabrication has been at least part of the reason for the misframing.[85]

Thus, framing is a very complex process—one that, Goffman contended, sociologists are not willing to address seriously. The world that people experience is not unitary, and it is subject to considerable manipulation, whether for benign or deceptive purposes. And, because of humans' capacity for symbol use (especially talk), the processes of reframing, keying, and fabrication can create highly layered and complex experiences. Yet, during interaction, people seek to maintain a common frame (a need that, Goffman was all too willing to assert, makes them vulnerable to manipulation through fabrication). For without a common frame—even one that has been keyed or fabricated—the interaction cannot proceed smoothly. Unfortunately, Goffman concentrated on framing as "organizing experience" per se rather than on framing as it organizes experience during focused and unfocused

---

[85]See ibid., p. 449, for a list of the conditions that make individuals inadvertently vulnerable to misframing. Also, see p. 463 for how misframing can be the result of deception and manipulation.

interaction. Hence the analysis of framing is provocative and suggestive, but too often it wanders away from the sociologically relevant topic—*the interaction order.*

In sum, Erving Goffman's works represent a truly seminal breakthrough in the analysis of social interaction. The emphasis on self-presentations, norms, rituals, and frames presented sociological theory at the midcentury with many important conceptual leads that have been adopted by diverse theoretical traditions. There are, however, some questionable points of emphasis that should be mentioned in closing. First, Goffman's somewhat cynical and manipulative view of humans and interaction—which have been consistently downplayed in this chapter—often takes analysis in directions that are not as fundamental to human organization as he implied. Second, Goffman's rather extreme situational view of self as only a projected image, and perhaps a mirage, in each and every situation is probably overdrawn. The denial of a core self or permanent identity certainly runs against the mainstream of interactionist theorizing and perhaps reality itself. And third, Goffman's work tended, at times, to wander into a rather extreme subjectivism and interpersonal nihilism where experience is too layered and fickle and where interaction is too fluid and changeable by the slightest shift in frame and ritual. Yet, even with these points of criticism, Goffman's sociology represents a monumental achievement—certainly equal to that of George Herbert Mead, Alfred Schutz, and Émile Durkheim. Indeed, Erving Goffman can be considered the premier micro-level theorist of the last six decades.

## Extensions of Goffmanian Dramaturgy

Goffman was, rather surprisingly, one of the first contemporary sociologists to conceptualize emotions. Indeed, sociology in general tended to ignore the topic of emotions between Charles Horton Cooley's analysis of pride and shame in the first decade of the twentieth century to the late 1960s and 1970s—a rather surprising gap given the significance of emotions in human affairs.[86] Yet, Goffman never developed a robust theory of emotions but instead frequently mentioned the importance of *embarrassment,* or what we might see as a mild form of *shame.* When an individual cannot successfully present a self, and when he or she fails to abide by the script by talking inappropriately, incorrectly using rituals, failing to stay within the frame, inappropriately categorizing a situation, misusing stage props, or expressing inappropriate emotions, the negative emotions aroused in the audience will lead to negative sanctioning of the person who will, in turn, experience embarrassment. Often, the audience will not actually need to sanction those

---

[86]See for reviews, Jonathan H. Turner and Jan E. Stets, *The Sociology of Emotions* (Cambridge, UK: Cambridge University Press, 2005); Jan E. Stets and Jonathan H. Turner, eds., *Handbook of the Sociology of Emotions* (New York: Springer, 2006).

who have breached an encounter because individuals will typically recognize the breach and feel embarrassed. Under these conditions, a sequence of repair rituals ensues, revolving around sanctions, apologies, and re-presentation of a more appropriate face and line. People are motivated to do so because they implicitly recognize that the social fabric and moral order are at stake. Encounters depend upon the smooth flow of interaction that sustains the moral order. People in encounters are thus highly attuned to the cultural script and the mutual presentations of self in accordance with the script.

Even though Goffman himself did not develop a very robust conception of emotions, many of those who followed him did. The sociology of emotions did not exist in sociology during most of Goffman's career, but by the time he died in the 1980s, the study of emotions, and hence, theorizing about emotional dynamics, had become more prevalent. Today, it is one of the leading edges of micro theorizing in sociology. Let me follow up on this observation by reviewing a sample of the sociologists who used the dramaturgical perspective pioneered by Goffman to develop new theories of emotional processes.

## Arlie Hochschild on Emotional Labor

Arlie Russell Hochschild was one of the first sociologists to develop a view of emotions as managed performances by individuals within the constraints of situational norms and broader cultural ideas about what emotions can be felt and presented in front of others.[87] For Hochschild, the *emotion culture* consists of a series of ideas about how and what people are supposed to experience in various types of situations, and this culture is filled with emotional ideologies about the appropriate attitudes and feelings for specific spheres and activities.[88] Emotional markers are events in the biographies of individuals that personify and symbolize more general emotional ideologies.

In any context, Hochschild emphasizes, there are norms of two basic types: (1) *feeling rules* that indicate (a) the amount of appropriate emotion that can be felt in a situation, (b) the direction, whether positive or negative,

---

[87]Arlie R. Hochschild, "Emotion Work, Feeling Rules, and Social Structure," *American Journal of Sociology* 85 (1979): pp. 551–75; *The Managed Heart: The Commercialization of Human Feeling* (Berkeley: University of California Press, 1983).

[88]Steven L. Gordon has provided a useful analysis of emotion culture, one that has been highly influential in not only Hochschild's work but by other theorists and researchers as well. See "The Sociology of Emotion," *in Social Psychology: Sociological Perspectives*, eds. M. Rosenberg and R. H. Turner (New York: Basic Books, 1981), pp. 562–92; "Institutional and Impulsive Orientations in Selectively Appropriating Emotions to the Self," in *The Sociology of Emotions: Original Essays and Research Papers*, eds. D. D. Franks and E. D. McCarthy (Greenwich, CT: JAI, 1989), pp. 115–26; and "Social Structural Effects on Emotions," in *Research Agendas in the Sociology of Emotions*, ed. T. D. Kemper (Albany, NY: State University of New York Press, 1990), pp. 145–79.

of the emotion, and (c) the duration of the emotion and (2) *display rules* that indicate the nature, intensity, and style of expressive behavior to be emitted. Thus, for any interaction, feeling and display, rules circumscribe what can be done. These rules reflect ideologies of the broader emotion culture, the goals and purposes of groups in which interactions are lodged, and the distribution of power and other organizational features of the situation.

The existence of cultural ideologies and normative constraints on the selection and emission of emotions forces individuals to manage the feelings that they experience and present to others. At this point, Hochschild's analysis becomes dramaturgic, for much like Goffman before her, she sees actors as having to manage a presentation of self in situations guided by a cultural script of norms and broader ideologies. There are various types of what Hochschild terms *emotion work* or mechanisms for managing emotions and making the appropriate self presentation: (1) *body work* whereby individuals actually seek to change their bodily sensations in an effort to evoke the appropriate emotion (for example, deep breathing to create calm); (2) *surface acting* where individuals alter their external expressive gestures in ways that they hope will make them actually feel the appropriate emotion (for instance, emitting gestures expressing joy and sociality at a party in the attempt to feel happy); (3) *deep acting* where individuals attempt to change their internal feelings, or at least some of these feelings, in the hope that the rest of the appropriate emotions will be activated and fall into place (for example, evoking feelings of *sadness* in an effort to feel sad at a funeral); and (4) *cognitive work* where the thoughts and ideas associated with particular emotions are evoked in an attempt to activate the corresponding feelings.

As Hochschild stresses, individuals are often put in situations where a considerable amount of emotion work must be performed. For example, in her pioneering study of airline attendants, the requirement that attendants always be friendly, pleasant, and helpful even as passengers were rude and unpleasant placed an enormous emotional burden on the attendants.[89] They had to manage their emotions through emotion work and present themselves in ways consistent with highly restrictive feeling and display rules. Virtually all encounters require emotion work, although some, such as the one faced by airline attendants, are particularly taxing and require a considerable amount of emotion management in self-presentations.

In emphasizing emotion work, Hochschild not only incorporates elements of Erving Goffman's but also adds a critical edge that is more reminiscent of Karl Marx's views on alienation. For Hochschild, individuals often engage in strategic performances that are not gratifying. Cultural scripts thus impose requirements on how they feel. As a general rule then, emotion work will be most evident when people confront emotion ideologies, emotion rules, and display rules that go against their actual feelings,

---

[89]Hochschild, *The Managed Heart* (cited in note 87).

and especially when they are required by these rules to express and display emotions that they do not feel. Complex social systems with hierarchies of authority, or market systems forcing sellers of goods and providers of services to act in certain ways to customers who have more latitude in expression of emotions, are likely to generate situations where individuals must engage in emotion work. Since these types of systems are more typical of industrial and post-industrial societies, Hochschild sees modernity as dramatically increasing the amount of emotion work that people must perform. Such work is always costly because people must, to some degree, repress their true emotions as they try to present themselves in ways demanded by the cultural script.

Another extension of this line of reasoning is more in tune with Erving Goffman's repeated fascination with how individuals "con" one another. If the feeling and display rules are known by all participants in an encounter, an individual is in a position to manipulate gestures in order to convince others that he or she also feels the same emotions and has the same goals when, in fact, he or she may have a devious purpose. A good "con man," for instance, can appear to be helpful to people experiencing difficulty by displaying gestures indicating that he feels their pain and that he is doing his best to help them out of a difficult situation when, in reality, he is trying to cheat them. Yet, most of the time in most situations, individuals make a good faith effort to feel and express the appropriate emotions because the rules of culture have a moral quality that invites negative feelings and sanctions for their violation, even in seemingly trivial interactions. Thus, people implicitly understand that to violate feeling and display rules is to disrupt the encounter and, potentially, the larger social occasion.

## Morris Rosenberg's Emphasis on Reflexivity and Dramatic Presentations

Morris Rosenberg's basic argument emphasizes that reflexivity, or thinking about the effects of one's actions, will change the physiological nature of human emotions.[90] Through the reflexive process, a person's emotions are transformed into something different. The reflexive process operates through at least three different paths: (1) emotional identification, (2) emotional displays, and (3) emotional experiences. In *emotional identification*, reflexivity is cognitive with individuals making interpretations, inferences, or attributions to understand their inner feelings. In *emotional displays*, reflexivity is reflected in individuals' regulation of emotional gestures to produce a certain effect on the audience, a point that has an affinity with Hochschild's surface acting. In *emotional experiences*, reflexivity appears in

---

[90]Morris Rosenberg, "Reflexivity and Emotions," *Social Psychology Quarterly* 53 (1990): pp. 3–12; "Self processes and emotional experiences," in *The Self-Society Interface: Cognition, Emotion and Action*, eds. J. A. Howard and P. L. Callero (New York: Cambridge University Press, 1991).

internal states of arousal, an idea similar to Hochschild's deep acting. Each of these is examined below.

(1) **Emotional identification**. People's internal states of arousal are ambiguous, with the result that people turn to information in the environment to help them make sense of what they are feeling. Alternatively, they may be feeling multiple emotions in a situation as, for example, when one feels mournful and relieved at the death of a loved one. This ambiguity over emotional experience forces people to *think about* their feelings and, hence, become reflexive.

There are, Rosenberg argues, three cognitive factors influencing emotional identification: (1) causal assumptions, (2) social consensus, and (3) cultural scenarios. *Causal assumptions* emerge from the socialization process. Adults and peers teach culturally specified connections among stimuli/ events and the outcomes generated. As these assumptions are learned and stored in memory, individuals develop what Rosenberg calls an *emotional logic*. People learn, for example, that when someone offers an insult, the sensation of heart pounding is to be labeled anger (rather than some other emotion like happiness). Thus, when actors are faced with ambiguous internal feelings, they turn to the emotional logic that they have learned in order to make sense out of the ambiguity. *Social consensus* helps inform actors as to what they are inwardly feeling. By observing how others respond, and in particular if others are responding in the same way, individuals are given guidance about how to label their inner feelings. Finally, inner experiences become more identifiable by calling up in one's mind *cultural criteria* against which they can compare their current experiences. For example, if a person is trying to identify whether a feeling is love for another, this person may think about whether the current situation reflects love as presented in cultural ideologies and lore.

(2) **Emotional displays.** Reflexivity also operates at the behavioral level in which individuals either reveal or hide their emotions. The goal is to convince an audience that they are experiencing certain emotions. There are three devices or mechanisms that people use to manage emotional displays: (1) *verbal devices* such as words, metaphors, or poetic imagery that convey emotionality; (2) *facial expressions* and other *physical expressions* such as voice pitch, volume, and speed of speech (for example, when one is upset, pitch and volume is higher and speech is faster); and (3) *physical objects* such as props or costumes (for example, wearing black conveys sorrow) to signal one's emotions.

Persons engage in three types of emotional display: (1) emotions signaling conformity to norms, thereby giving actions a moral character and affirming that there is commitment to the cultural script; (2) emotions as a means toward obtaining a goal, thus communicating that actions are instrumental; and (3) emotions designed to reveal the experience of pleasure, thereby revealing a concern with positive emotional outcomes for both self and others.

**(3) Emotional experiences**. As Hochschild emphasized, individuals often manipulate inner emotional experiences in order to feel differently. Through *body work*, such as running, controlled breathing, relaxation techniques, and biochemical strategies (for instance, alcohol, drugs, or hypnosis), individuals attempt to change their feelings. Through *cognitive work*, individuals attempt to think differently in order to feel differently. These efforts to change emotional experiences can only work, however, if individuals can succeed in achieving *selective attention*, *perspectual selectivity*, and *selective interpretation*. In *selective attention*, individuals actively try to control what they think, either directly or indirectly. In direct selective attention, people seek to push particular emotions out of their minds and substitute new emotions in their place, whereas in indirect cognitive work individuals will try to avoid situations activating emotions that they do not wish to experience. In *perspectival selectivity*, people seek to manage emotions by altering their perspective or frame of reference. For example, a person who is feeling impatient may alter the time perspective ("Everything will work out in time." "Time heals all wounds."), or an individual who is feeling depressed may think about others who are worse off, thereby making the current problem seem less significant. In *selective interpretation*, people seek to assign meanings to events that will generate positive emotional outcomes. One strategy is selective attribution or the assignment of causality in a manner that benefits the self. For example, people have a tendency to take responsibility for successes, while denying responsibility for failures. Another strategy of attribution is to attribute failure to a lack of effort rather than a lack of ability.

## Peggy Thoits' Theory of Emotional Deviance

Peggy Thoits uses the dramaturgical perspective to develop a theory of emotional deviance.[91] In so doing, she adds to Hochschild's theory. Thoits' theory revolves around three basic issues: (1) the *sources* for which a discrepancy between one's feeling state and feeling rules is likely to emerge, (2) the various *emotion management strategies* or *coping styles* to resolve the discrepancy, and (3) the conditions under which *emotion management fails* and thereby causes motivational deviance. Each of these is discussed below.

(1) **The sources of discrepancy**. Discrepancy between what is felt and what is expected by feeling rules causes individuals to feel *stress*. Stress increases under certain conditions: (a) multiple role occupancy, (b) subcultural marginality, (c) normative and nonnormative role transitions, and (d) rigid rules governing

[91]Peggy A. Thoits, "Self-Labelling Processes in Mental Illness: The Role of Emotional Deviance," *American Journal of Sociolology* 91(1985): pp. 317–42; "Emotional Deviance: Research Agendas," in *Research Agendas in the Sociology of Emotions*, ed. T. A. Kemper (Albany, NY: State University of New York Press, 1990), pp.180–203.

roles and rituals. Both *multiple role occupancy* and *subcultural marginality* involve instances where a person may be subjected to conflicting feeling rules because of participation in different roles or groups. In either case, persons must cope with potentially contradictory expectations (whether in multiple roles or in subcultural differences among subpopulations): the greater is the contradiction, the greater will be the level of stress experienced by individuals. Movement to a new role or *nonnormative role transitions* often generates ambiguity over appropriate behavior and feelings in the new roles. Finally, *strict feeling rules* associated with roles and rituals in a situation ensure that even minor departures from feeling rules will be stressful.

(2) **Emotion management strategies.** When feelings depart from the feeling rules, individuals seek to manage their emotions by bringing subjective emotional experiences into line with the normative requirements of the situation. Thoits identifies two primary modes that persons use to change their emotional experience: behavioral and cognitive. In *behavioral manipulations*, individuals alter their behaviors in the hopes that their feelings will fall into line with the cultural script. In *cognitive manipulations*, individuals try to change the *meaning* of the situation (to them) in order to bring feelings into line with normative expectations for how one should feel in the situation.

(3) **Emotional deviance.** No matter how hard they try, behavioral and cognitive strategies to reduce the discrepancy between actual feelings and feeling rules simply do not work for some individuals. The result is, of course, stress. This stress may be seen by others as a sign of psychological problems (in its mild form) or mental illness (in its more severe form). The level of stress experienced by individuals is related to (a) the degree of discrepancy in the situation and (b) the level of social support individuals feeling stressed can draw upon. If the negative feelings revolving around stress continue, however, others may withdraw their social support, thereby making the situation even more stressful. And if these others begin to label a person as deviant, they may push the stressed individual further into a state of emotional deviance. And, ironically, when people cannot get support from others, they may turn to mental health professionals who, ironically, will also implicitly label them as emotionally deviant.

## Candace Clark's Theory on the Dramaturgy and Strategy of Sympathy

Candace Clark has extended the dramaturgical perspective with the detailed analysis of sympathy as both a dramatic and strategic process[92]—two points

---

[92]Candace Clark, *Misery and Company: Sympathy in Everyday Life* (Chicago, IL: University of Chicago Press, 1997); "Sympathy Biography and Sympathy Margin," *American Journal of Sociology* 93 (1987): pp. 290–321; and "Emotions and Micropolitics in Everyday Life: Some patterns and Paradoxes," in *Research Agendas in The Sociology of Emotions*, ed. T. D. Kemper (Albany, NY: State University of New York Press, 1990).

of emphasis in Goffman's theory. Like all dramaturgical theories, Clark visualizes a *feeling culture* consisting of beliefs, values, rules, logics, vocabularies, and other symbolic elements that frame and direct the process of sympathizing. Individuals are implicitly aware of these cultural elements, drawing upon them to make dramaturgical presentations and displays on a stage in front of an audience of others. Although there are cultural rules guiding behavior, many dimensions of culture do not constitute a clear script but, instead, operate more like the rules of grammar that allow actors to organize feeling elements, such as feeling ideologies, feeling rules, feeling logics, and feeling vocabularies, into a framework for emitting and responding to sympathy.

Each individual feels the weight of expectations from culture about how sympathizing is to occur, and each must engage in a performance using whatever techniques are appropriate to feeling and displaying the appropriate emotions. In particular, surface acting, deep acting, and use of rituals to arouse and track emotions are often employed by actors who are seeking to present a self in accordance with a script assembled from relevant cultural elements.

**Strategic Dimensions of Sympathy Giving**. There is also a strategic dimension to sympathizing, a point of emphasis that follows Goffman's view of encounters as highly strategic. Individuals do not passively play roles directed by a cultural script; rather, they also engage in games of *microeconomics* and *micropolitics*. With respect to *microeconomics*, Clark argues that emotions are often exchanged in the sympathy giving and taking, and even sympathy as an act of kindness and altruism is subject to these exchange dynamics. Feeling rules often require that recipients of sympathy must give back to their sympathizers emotions like *gratitude, pleasure,* and *relief.* In regard to *micropolitics*, which is discussed in more detail later, individuals always seek to enhance their place or standing vis-à-vis others, even when they remain unaware of their efforts to gain standing at the expense of others. Such contests over *place* vis-à-vis others introduce inequalities into encounters and, hence, the tensions that always arise from inequality. Sympathy, like any set of emotions, can be an important tool for individuals to enhance their place or standing in an encounter. By giving sympathy to someone, a person established that they are in a higher place since the person receiving sympathy needs help. There is a kind of strategic dramaturgy involved, and Clark outlines several strategies for gaining a favorable place: display mock sympathy that draws attention to another's negative qualities; bestow an emotional gift in a way that underscores another's weakness, vulnerability, problems; bestow sympathy on superordinates to reduce distance between places marked by inequalities; remind others of an emotional debt by pointing out problems for which sympathy is given, thereby not only lowering the other's place but also establishing an obligation for the recipient of sympathy to reciprocate; use sympathy in ways that make the others feel negative emotions such as *worry, humiliation, shame,* or *anger,* thereby lowering their place.

**Integrative Effects of Sympathy**. Even though there is a darker side to sympathy processes in games of microeconomics and micropolitics, sympathy at the level of the encounter has integrative effects on the larger social order. First, positive emotions are exchanged—that is, sympathy for other positive emotions like *gratitude*, thereby making both parties to the exchange feel better. Second, the plight of those in need of sympathy is acknowledged by those giving sympathy, thus reinforcing social bonds per se above and beyond whatever exchange will eventually occur. Third, sympathy operates as a safety valve in allowing those in difficulty a temporary release from normal cultural proscriptions and prescriptions while remobilizing their energies to meeting cultural expectations in the future. Fourth, sympathizing is also the enactment of a moral drama because it always involves invoking cultural guidelines about justice, fairness, and worthiness for those who receive the emotions marking sympathy. Fifth, even though games of micropolitics can make one party superior and another inferior (the receiver of sympathy), they do establish hierarchies that order social relations, although they also create the potential for negative emotional arousal and conflict.

**Societal Changes and the Extension of Sympathy**. Clark argues that the range of plights for which sympathy can be claimed is expanding. Part of the reason for this change is that high levels of structural differentiation, especially in market-driven systems emphasizing individualism, have isolated the person from traditional patterns of embeddedness in social structures; as a result, culture highlights the importance of the individual and the problems that individuals confront. Sympathy is now to be extended to emotional problems that individuals have, such as stress, identity crises, divorce, loneliness, criminal victimization, difficult relationships, dissatisfaction at work, home, school, and many other plights of individuals in complex societies. This same differentiation has created new professions that operate as sympathy entrepreneurs who highlight certain plights and advocate their inclusion in the list of conditions invoking sympathetic responses. The expansion of medicine and psychotherapy has added a host of new ills, both physical and mental, that are to be objects of sympathy. The social sciences have added even more, including the plight of people subject to racism, sexism, patriarchy, discrimination, urban blight, lower class position, poor job skills, difficult family life, and the like. Thus, modern societies, at least those in the West, have greatly expanded the list of conditions calling for sympathetic responses.

Given the wide array of plights that can be defined as deserving of sympathetic responses, there are implicit sorting mechanisms or cultural logics that enable actors to assemble from cultural elements definitions of who is worthy of sympathy. One cultural logic revolves around establishing responsibility for a person's plight. Americans, for example, implicitly array a person's plight, Clark argues, on a continuum ranging from blameless at one pole to blameworthy at the other. Those who are blameless are deserving of sympathy, whereas those who are blameworthy deserve less sympathy. "Bad luck" is one way in which blame is established; those who have had bad luck deserve sympathy, while those who have brought problems on themselves are not deserving of sympathy.

Clark adds a list of competing rules for "determining what plights were unlucky for members of a category" and, hence, deserving of sympathy. One rule is "the special deprivation principle" that highlights deprivations experienced by individuals that are out of the ordinary. Another is "the special burden principle" emphasizing that those who have particularly difficult tasks to perform are entitled to sympathy. Still another is "the balance of fortune principle" that those who lead fortunate and pampered lives (celebrities, rich people, and the powerful) deserve less sympathy than the ordinary person or the unfortunate individual. Still another rule is "the vulnerability principle" stressing that some categories of persons (e.g., children, the aged, women) are more vulnerable to misfortune than others and are thereby deserving of sympathy. Another rule is "the potential principle" arguing that those whose futures have been cut short or delayed (e.g., children) are more deserving of those who have already had a chance to realize their potential (e.g., elderly). Yet another rule is "the special responsibility principle" arguing that those who have special abilities and knowledge, but who do not use them well or wisely, are less deserving of sympathy. And a final rule that is particularly important in establishing whether or not people are deserving of sympathy is "the social worth principle" emphasizing that people who are worthy by virtue of possessing status, power, wealth, cultural capital, and other resources are entitled to sympathy. There is, then, a cultural script for deciding who is deserving of how much sympathy in a society.

Clark notes that there are off-the-shelf ways in contemporary societies for expressing sympathy that involve a considerable reduction of the emotion work that a person giving sympathy must endure. These include: greeting cards, offerings (like flowers), prayers, tolerance of behaviors, time off from obligations, easing the pressure, listening, visitations, stereotyped rituals of touching and talk, composure work giving people time to put on a face, offers of help, and the like. But the use of standardized ways to offer sympathy still require some emotion work as the sympathizer tries to decide upon the right combination of these off-the-shelf actions.

One of the most interesting concepts in Clark's conceptualization is the notion of *lines of sympathy credit* given to individuals. Each individual has, in essence, a *sympathy margin*, which is a line of emotional credit indicating how much sympathy is available to a person. These sympathy margins are, like all credit, subject to negotiation; and just how much of a margin an individual can claim depends upon the individual's moral worth, his or her past history of being a good individual who has been sympathetic to others, and the nature of his or her plight. Cultural rules dictate that family members get the largest sympathy margins, that people who have social value (in terms of wealth, education, authority, beauty, fame, and other forms of social capital) receive large margins, that those who have demonstrated kindness and goodness in their other roles be given large margins, and that the deserving poor (and others in plight) who are trying to help themselves receive large sympathy margins.

There is, however, a limit to sympathy margins. If a person has used all of his or her sympathy credits, no more credit will be offered. And in fact, others will often feel and express negative emotions to those who have sought to overextend their line of credit. Moreover, if individuals who have been given sympathy credits do not attempt to pay others back with the appropriate emotions, those who extended the sympathy credits will withdraw further credit and experience negative emotional arousal.

**Sympathy Etiquette.** The processes of claiming, accepting, and repaying credit are guided, Clark argues, by *sympathy etiquette*—an idea that pervades Goffman's analysis of encounters. Indeed, if the rules of sympathy etiquette have been breached in the past actions of a person, this individual will have his or her line of credit reduced. Thus, individuals calculate whether a person has a flawed biography or problem credit rating when deciding how much sympathy to offer. There are several basic cultural rules, Clark's data indicate, that guide efforts by individuals to claim sympathy. These are phrased as prohibitions about claiming sympathy: Do not make false claims; do not claim too much sympathy; do not take sympathy too readily; do not take it for granted; be sure to secure some sympathy to keep your emotional accounts open and emotional credit rating high; and reciprocate with gratitude and appreciation to those who have given sympathy.

To these rules are corresponding rules for sympathizers: Do not give sympathy that is not due; do not give too much sympathy out of proportion to the plight; and do not give sympathy that goes unacknowledged or underappreciated. People can under-invest or over-invest in sympathy. Over-investors do not follow the rules above, whereas under-investors do not keep their sympathy accounts open so that they can, if needed, make claims to sympathy in future.

## Randall Collins on Interaction Rituals

Randall Collins' conflict theory was examined in Chapter 12. At the core of this theory is the notion of interaction rituals,[93] the elements of which roughly correspond to Goffman's analysis of the encounter. For Collins, interaction rituals contain the following elements: (1) a physical assembly of co-present individuals; (2) mutual awareness of each other; (3) a common focus of attention; (4) a common emotional mood among co-present individuals; (5) a rhythmic coordination and synchronization of conversation

---

[93]Randall Collins, *Conflict Sociology: Toward an Explanatory Science* (New York: Academic Press, 1975) and *Interaction Ritual Chains* (Princeton, NJ: Princeton University Press, 2004).

and nonverbal gestures; (6) emotional entrainment of participants; (7) a symbolic representation of this group focus and mood with objects, persons, gestures, words, and ideas among interacting individuals; (8) circulation of particularized cultural capital; and (9) a sense of moral righteousness about these symbols marking group membership. Figure 12.1 on page 251 portrays the dynamics of such rituals.

In Collins' view, there is a kind of market for interaction rituals, which increases people's strategic actions in interaction rituals. Individuals weigh the costs in time, energy, cultural capital, and other resources that they must spend to participate in the various rituals available to them; then, they select those rituals that maximize emotional profits. In this sense, Collins proclaimed emotional energy to be the common denominator of rational choice.[94] Thus, rather than representing an irrational force in human inter-action, Collins sees the pursuit of emotions as highly rational: People seek out those interaction rituals in a marketplace of rituals that maximize prof-its (costs less the positive emotional energy produced by the ritual). The search for emotional energy is, therefore, the criterion by which various alternative encounters are assessed for how much emotional profit they can generate.

Humans are, in a sense, emotional junkies, but they are implicitly rational about it. They must constantly balance those encounters where interaction rituals produce high levels of positive emotional energy (such as lovemaking, family activities, religious participation, and gatherings of friends) with those more practical, work activities that give them the mate-rial resources to participate in more emotionally arousing encounters. Indeed, those who opt out of these work-practical activities and seek only high-emotion encounters (such as dropouts in a drug culture) soon lose the material resources to enjoy emotion-arousing encounters. Moreover, within the context of work-practical activity, individuals typically seek out or cre-ate encounters that provide increases in emotional energy. For example, workers might create an informal subculture in which social encounters produce emotional energy that makes work more bearable, or as is often the case with professionals, they seek the rituals involved in acquiring power, authority, and status on the job as highly rewarding and as giving them an emotional charge (such is almost always the case, for instance, with worka-holics who use the work setting as a place to charge up their levels of emo-tional energy).

Not only are there material costs as well as expenditures of cultural capi-tal in interaction rituals, but emotional energy is itself a cost. People spend their emotional energy in interaction rituals, and they are willing to do so as long as they realize an emotional profit—that is, the emotional energy spent is repaid with even more positive emotions flowing from the common focus of attention, mood, arousal, rhythmic synchronization, and symbolization. When

---

[94]Randall Collins, "Emotional Energy as the Common Denominator of Rational Action," *Rationality and Society* 5 (1993): pp. 203–30.

interaction rituals require too much emotional energy without sufficient emotional payoff, then individuals gravitate to other interaction rituals where their profits are higher.

What kinds of rituals provide the most positive emotional energy for the costs involved? For Collins, those encounters where individuals can have power (the capacity to tell others what to do) and status (the capacity to receive deference and honor) are the most likely to generate high emotional payoffs. Hence, those who possess the cultural capital to command respect and obedience are likely to receive the most positive emotional energy from interaction rituals.

Meso- and macro-level social orders are built up, sustained, and changed by interaction rituals, depending upon the degree to which they generate positive and negative emotional energy. When the elements in Collins' model portrayed on page 250 are working successfully, people develop positive emotions, experience increases in their cultural capital, and develop commitments to groups. When these processes do not flow smoothly or are breached, then the converse ensues—a line of argument consistent with Goffman's analysis of when encounters are breached.

Finally, interaction rituals impose barriers to violent conflict at the micro level because individuals in a conflict situation have a legacy of the gravitational pull of interaction rituals, which are the opposite of violent conflict, and because potential conflict activates fear.[95] This combination keeps individuals from participating in conflict and generally limits the duration and intensity of interpersonal violence. Yet, if interaction rituals can be chained together toward the pursuit of conflict, then violence is more likely to occur, but even then, fear and the pull of successful interaction rituals reduce the involvements of many who are organized for conflict.

If Goffman were developing the theory, he would make much the same argument, indicating that people derive positive emotions from encounters and are highly motivated to repair them when they are breached. Encounters thus sustain the social and moral orders of more meso and macro social organization, and they pull people away from interpersonal violence. Only when encounters are organized for violence that is perceived to sustain a moral order can they effectively be used for longer-term violence.

# Conclusion

As is clear, then, Goffman's dramaturgical theory has been extended in interesting directions, especially in the sociology of emotions. In these theories of emotions, emphasis is on discrepancy between the cultural script in situations and individuals' feelings and emotions. In complex, differentiated

---

[95]Randall Collins, *Violence: A Micro-Sociological Theory* (Princeton, NJ: Princeton University Press, 2008).

societies driven by market forces, many situations require people to express emotions that they do not feel. Or, as is the case with Clark's theory, the occasions and situations for expressing sympathy have expanded in modern societies. In both cases, there are both dramatic and strategic processes involved, as Goffman emphasized.

People seek to present self in ways that conforms to the culture, particularly the feeling and display rules, and if they cannot feel what they are supposed to feel, they seek to alter their feelings and, failing this, at least express overtly the appropriate emotions. They must, therefore, engage in stress drama to sustain encounters. At the same time, actors always behave strategically; their dramatic presentations are often instrumental and revolve around securing resources in situations through strategic actions and dramatic presentations of self.

Until Goffman, sociological theorizing did not emphasize these dynamics, which is particularly surprising in light of the fact that humans in their daily lives talk about these matters all of the time. Indeed, gossip is often about the dramatic, manipulative, and strategic actions of others. And so, it was appropriate for Goffman to build a micro sociology about dynamics that occur in virtually all encounters, and since people respond emotionally in encounters and, once again, gossip about people's emotional state, it was equally appropriate to take dramaturgy into the sociology of emotions.

CHAPTER 20

# Ethnomethodological Theories

I n the 1960s, a new kind of interactionist theorizing emerged. This approach drew more from the phenomenological tradition of Alfred Schutz than from the pragmatist tradition of George Herbert Mead, and it proposed an alternative approach to analyzing interaction: explore the methods used by people to construct *a sense of ongoing reality*. This emphasis became known as *ethnomethodology*. As this label underscores, ethnomethodology is the study of (*ology*) the interpersonal "methods" that people (*ethno*) use.[1] Like Edmund Husserl and Schutz, ethnomethodologists ask how people create and sustain for each other the *presumption* that the social world has a real character.

---

[1] For some readable summaries of ethnomethodology, see Hugh Mehan and Houston Wood, *The Reality of Ethnomethodology* (New York: Wiley, 1975); John Heritage, *Garfinkel and Ethnomethodology* (Cambridge, England: Polity, 1984) and "Ethnomethodology," in *Social Theory Today*, eds. Anthony Giddens and Jonathan Turner (Cambridge, England: Polity Press, 1987); Melvin Pollner, *Mundane Reasoning: Reality in Everyday Sociological Discourse* (Cambridge: Cambridge University Press, 1987) and Wes Sharrock, "Fundamentals." See, in particular, Alfred Schutz, *Collected Papers I: The Problem of Social Reality*, ed. Maurice Natanson (The Hague: Martinus Nijhoff, 1962); *Collected Papers II: Studies in Social Theory*, ed. Arvid Broderson (The Hague: Martinus Nijhoff, 1964); and *Collected Papers III: Studies in Phenomenological Philosophy* (The Hague: Martinus Nijhoff, 1966). For adaptations of these ideas to interactionism and ethnomethodology, see Alfred Schutz and Thomas Luckmann, *The Structure of the Lifeworld* (Evanston, IL: Northwestern University Press, 1973), as well as Thomas Luckmann, ed., *Phenomenology and Sociology* (New York: Penguin, 1978). See also Robert C. Freeman, "Phenomenological Sociology and Ethnomethodology," in *Introduction to the Sociologies of Everyday Life*, eds. J. Douglas and Patricia Adler (Boston: Allyn & Bacon, 1980).

# The Reflexive and Indexical Nature of Interaction

Schutz postulated one basic reality—*the paramount*—in which people's conduct of their everyday affairs occurs.[2] Most early ethnomethodologists, however, were less interested in whether or not there is one lifeword or multiple "realities." Far more important in ethnomethodological analysis was the development of concepts and principles that could help explain how people construct, maintain, and change their lines of conduct as they seek to *sustain the presumption* that they share the same reality. At the core of ethnomethodological analysis are two basic assumptions about (1) the reflexive and (2) the indexical nature of all interaction.

## Reflexive Action and Interaction

Much interaction sustains a particular vision of reality. For example, ritual activity directed toward the gods sustains the belief that gods influence everyday affairs. Such ritual activity is an example of reflexive action; it maintains a certain vision of reality. Even when intense prayer and ritual activity do not bring forth the desired intervention from the gods, the devout, rather than reject beliefs, proclaim that they did not pray hard enough, that their cause was not just, or that the gods in their wisdom have a greater plan. Such behavior is *reflexive*. It upholds or reinforces a belief, even in the face of evidence that the belief might be incorrect.

Much human interaction is reflexive. Humans interpret cues, gestures, words, and other information from one another in a way that sustains a particular vision of reality. Even contradictory evidence is reflexively interpreted to maintain a body of belief and knowledge. The concept of reflexivity thus focuses attention on how people in interaction go about maintaining the presumption that they are guided by a particular reality. Much of ethnomethodological inquiry has addressed this question of how reflexive interaction occurs. That is, what concepts and principles can be developed to explain the conditions under which different reflexive actions among interacting parties are likely to occur?

## The Indexicality of Meaning

The gestures, cues, words, and other information sent and received by interacting parties have meaning in a *particular context*. Without some knowledge of the context—the biographies of the interacting parties, their avowed purpose, their past interactive experiences, and so forth—it would

---

[2]See, in particular, Schutz, *Collected Papers I, II,* and *III.* For adaptations of these ideas to interactionism and ethnomethodology, see Schutz and Luckmann, *The Structure of the Lifeworld,* as well as Luckmann, *Phenomenology and Sociology.* See also Freeman, "Phenomenological Sociology and Ethnomethodology." (All cited in note 1.)

be easy to misinterpret the symbolic communication among interacting individuals. To say that an expression is *indexical* then is to emphasize that the meaning of that expression is tied to a particular context.

This notion of indexicality drew attention to the problem of how actors in a context construct a vision of reality in that context. They develop expressions that invoke their common vision about what is real in their situation. The concept of *indexicality* thus directs investigators to actual interactive contexts to see how actors go about creating indexical expressions—words, facial and body gestures, and other cues—to sustain the presumption that a particular reality governs their affairs.

With these two key concepts, reflexivity and indexicality, the interactionists' concern with the process of symbolic communication was retained by ethnomethodology, and much of the phenomenological legacy of Schutz was rejuvenated. Concern was with how actors use gestures to construct a lifeworld, body of knowledge, or natural attitude about what is real. The emphasis was not on the content of the lifeworld but on the methods or techniques that actors use to create, maintain, or even alter a vision of reality. As Hugh Mehan and Houston Wood noted, "the ethnomethodological theory of reality constructor is about the *procedures* that accomplish reality. It is not about any specific reality."[3]

# Harold Garfinkel's Early Studies

Harold Garfinkel's *Studies in Ethnomethodology* firmly established ethnomethodology as a distinctive theoretical perspective.[4] Although the book was not a formal theoretical statement, the studies and the commentary in it established the domain of ethnomethodological inquiry: Subsequent ethnomethodological research and theory began with Garfinkel's insights and took them in a variety of directions.

Garfinkel's work saw ethnomethodology as a field of inquiry that sought to understand the methods people employ to make sense of their world. He placed considerable emphasis on language as the vehicle by which this reality construction is done. Indeed, for Garfinkel, interacting individuals' efforts to account for their actions—that is, to represent them verbally to others—are the primary method by which a sense of the world is constructed. In Garfinkel's terms, *to do* interaction is *to tell* interaction, or in other words, the primary folk technique used by actors is verbal description. In this way, people use their accounts to construct a sense of reality.

Garfinkel placed enormous emphasis on indexicality—that is, members' accounts are tied to particular contexts and situations. An utterance,

---

[3]Hugh Mehan and Houston Wood, *The Reality of Ethnomethodology* (New York: Wiley, 1975).

[4]Harold Garfinkel, *Studies in Ethnomethodology* (Englewood Cliffs, NJ: Prentice Hall, 1967).

Garfinkel noted, indexes much more than it actually says; it also evokes connotations that can be understood only in the context of a situation. Garfinkel's work was thus the first to stress the indexical nature of interpersonal cues and to emphasize that individuals seek accounts to create a sense of reality.

In addition to laying much of the groundwork for ethnomethodology, Garfinkel and his associates conducted several interesting empirical studies to validate their assumptions about what is real. One line of empirical inquiry became known as the *breaching experiment*, in which the normal course of interaction was deliberately interrupted. For example, Garfinkel reported a series of conversations in which student experimenters challenged every statement of selected subjects. The end result was a series of conversations revealing the following pattern:

*Subject*:       I had a flat tire.

*Experimenter*: What do you mean, you had a flat tire?

*Subject*:       (*appears momentarily stunned and then replies in a hostile manner*): What do you mean, "What do you mean?" A flat tire is a flat tire. That is what I meant. Nothing special. What a crazy question![5]

In this situation, the experimenter was apparently violating an implicit rule for this type of interaction (such as accepting statements at face value) and thereby aroused not only the hostility of the subject but also a negative sanction, "What a crazy question!" Seemingly, in any interaction, there are certain background features that everyone should understand and that should not be questioned so that all parties can "conduct their common conversational affairs without interference."[6] Such implicit methods appear to guide a considerable number of everyday affairs and are critical for the construction of at least the perception among interacting humans that an external social order exists. Through breaching, Garfinkel hoped to discover the implicit ethnomethods being used by forcing actors to engage *actively* in the process of reality reconstruction after the situation had been disrupted.

Other research strategies also yielded insights into the methods parties use in an interaction for constructing a sense of reality. For example, Garfinkel and his associates summarized the decision rules jurors employed in reaching a verdict.[7] By examining a group such as a jury, which must by the nature of its task develop an interpretation of what really happened, the ethnomethodologists sought to achieve some insight into the generic properties of the processes of constructing a *sense of social reality*. From the

---

[5]Ibid., p. 42.

[6]Ibid.

[7]Ibid., pp. 104–115.

investigators' observations of jurors, it appeared that "a person is 95 percent juror before [coming] near the court," indicating that, through their participation in other social settings and through instructions from the court, they had accepted the "official" rules for reaching a verdict. However, these rules were altered somewhat as participants came together in an actual jury setting and began the "work of assembling the 'corpus' which serves as grounds for inferring the correctness of a verdict."[8] Because the inevitable ambiguities of the cases before them made it difficult for strict conformity to the official rules of jury deliberation, new decision rules were invoked to allow jurors to achieve a "correct" view of "what actually happened." But, in their retrospective reporting to interviewers of how they reached the verdicts, jurors typically invoked the "official line" to justify the correctness of their decisions. When interviewers drew attention to discrepancies between the jurors' ideal accounts and their actual practices, jurors became anxious—indication that somewhat different rules had been used to construct the corpus of what really happened.

In sum, these two examples of Garfinkel's research strategy illustrate the general intent of much early ethnomethodological inquiry: to penetrate natural social settings or to create social settings in which the investigator could observe humans attempting to assert, create, maintain, or change the rules for constructing the appearance of consensus over the structure of the real world. By focusing on the process or methods for constructing a reality rather than on the substance or content of the reality itself, research from the ethnomethodological point of view could potentially provide a more interesting and relevant answer to the question of how and why society is possible. Garfinkel's studies stimulated a variety of research and theoretical strategies.

## Aaron V. Cicourel's Critique

Aaron V. Cicourel has been one of the most persistent critics of sociological research methodologies, particularly the notion that more quantitative methods somehow reduce bias. But he also created a more substantive approach that had much in common with ethnomethodology. Cicourel even questions Garfinkel's assertion that interaction and verbal accounts are the same process.[9] Cicourel notes that humans see, sense, and feel much that they cannot communicate with words. Humans use *multiple modalities* for communicating in situations. Verbal accounts represent crude and incomplete translations of what is actually communicated in interaction. This recognition has led Cicourel to rename his brand of ethnomethodology *cognitive sociology*.

---

[8]Ibid., p. 110.

[9]Aaron V. Cicourel, *Method and Measurement in Sociology* (New York: Free Press, 1964); "Cross Modal Communication," in *Linguistics and Language Science*, Monograph 25, ed. R. Shuy (Washington, DC: Georgetown University Press, 1973).

The details of his analysis are less important than the general intent of his effort to transform sociological research and theory. Basically, he sought to uncover the universal *interpretive procedures* by which humans organize their cognitions and give meaning to situations.[10] Through these interpretive procedures, people develop a sense of social structure and can organize their actions. These interpretive procedures are universal and invariant in humans, and their discovery would allow understanding of how humans create a sense of social structure in the world around them.

When analysis is one of the methods that people use to construct a sense of reality, the task of the theorist is to isolate the general types of interpersonal techniques that people employ in interaction. Cicourel, for example, summarized several such techniques or methods isolated by ethnomethodologists: (1) searching for the normal form, (2) doing reciprocity of perspectives, and (3) using the et cetera principle.[11]

1. **Searching for the Normal Form.** If interacting parties sense that ambiguity exists about what is real and that their interaction is strained, they will emit gestures to tell each other to return to what is normal in their contextual situation. Actors are presumed to hold a vision of a normal form for situations or to be motivated to create one; hence, much of their action is designed to reach this form.

2. **Doing a Reciprocity of Perspectives.** Borrowing from Schutz's formulation, ethnomethodologists emphasized that actors operate under the presumption that they would have the same experiences were they to switch places. Furthermore, until they are so informed by specific gestures, actors can ignore differences in perspectives that might arise from their unique biographies. Thus, much interaction will be punctuated by gestures that seek to assure others that a reciprocity of perspectives does indeed exist.

3. **Using the Et Cetera Principle.** In examining an actual interaction, much is left unsaid. Actors must constantly fill in or wait for information necessary to make sense of another's words or deeds. When actors do so, they are using the *et cetera principle*. They are agreeing not to disrupt the interaction by asking for the needed information; they are willing to wait or to fill in. For example, in the conversation reported by Garfinkel about the flat tire, the experimenter who asked, "What do you mean, you had a flat tire?" was not observing the et cetera principle, and as a result, the subject became angry in an effort to sanction the experimenter to abide by the folk rules. Or, to take another example, the common phrase *you know* which often appears after an utterance, is typically an assertion by one actor to

---

[10]Aaron V. Cicourel, *Cognitive Sociology* (London: Macmillan, 1973) and "Basic Normative Rules in the Negotiation of Status and Role," in *Recent Sociology No. 2*, ed. H. P. Dreitzel (New York: Macmillan, 1970).

[11] Aaron V. Cicourel, *Cognitive Sociology* (cited in note 10), pp. 85–88. It should be noted that these principles were implicit in Garfinkel's *Studies in Ethnomethodology* (cited in note 4).

another invoking the et cetera principle. The other is thus informed not to disrupt the interaction or the sense of reality in the situation with a counter-utterance, such as "no, I do not know."

These three general types of folk methods were examples of what ethnomethodologists sought to discover, although most researchers appear reluctant to make these explicit or to theorize beyond their empirical observations of how particular folk methods are used. For some ethno-methodologists, the ultimate goal of theory is to determine the conditions under which of these and other interpersonal techniques would be used to construct, maintain, or change a sense of reality. Yet, few such propositions are to be found in the ethnomethodological literature.

# Harvey Sacks' Analysis of Conversational Turn Taking

Until his early death in 1976, Harvey Sacks exerted considerable influence within ethnomethodology.[12] Although his work was not well known outside ethnomethodological circles, it represented an attempt to extend Garfinkel's concern with verbal accounts, while eliminating some of the problems posed by indexicality.

Sacks was one of the first ethnomethodologists to articulate the phenom-enological critique of sociology and to use this critique to build what he thought was an alternative form of theorizing. The basic thrust of Sacks' critique can be stated as follows: Sociologists assume that language is a resource used in generating concepts and theories of the social world. However, sociologists are confusing resource and topic. In using language, sociologist are creating a reality; their words are not a neutral vehicle but *the topic of inquiry* for true sociological analysis—a point of emphasis that is today the core topic of ethnomethodological inquiry.

If the pure properties of language can be understood, then it would be possible to have an objective social science without confusing resource with subject matter. Sacks' research tended to concentrate on the formal proper-ties of language-in-use. Typically, Sacks took verbatim transcripts of actors

---

[12] Harvey Sacks, "Sociological Description," *Berkeley Journal of Sociology* 8 (1963): pp. 1–17; Harvey Sacks, "An Initial Investigation of the Usability of Conversational Data for Doing Sociology," in *Studies in Interaction*, ed. David Sudnow (New York: Free Press, 1972); see also Harvey Sacks, *Lectures on Conversation, 2 volumes* (New York: Blackwell, 1992). Sack's best-known study, for example, is the coauthored article with Emanuel Schegloff and Gail Jefferson, "A Simplest Systematics for the Analysis of Turn Taking in Conversation," *Language* 50 (1974): pp. 696–97. For a review of the current techniques of conversational analysis, see Alain Coulon, *Ethnomethodology* (London, UK: Sage, 1995); Douglas W. Maynard and Marilyn R. Whalen, "Language, Action, and Social Interaction," in *Sociological Perspectives on Social Psychology*, eds. K. S. Cook, G. A. Fine, and J. S. House (Boston, MA: Allyn & Bacon, 1995).

in interaction and sought to understand the formal properties of the conversation while ignoring its substance. Such a tactic resolved the problem of indexicality because Sacks simply ignored the substance and context of conversation and focused on its form. For example, sequences of talk among actors might occupy his attention.

In analyzing conversational talk, Sacks and various collaborators would emphasize the fact that conversations involve turn taking. One party in a conversation talks, and then another does. The ways in which turns are taken become a key dynamic in the conversation as, for instance, when individuals pause and offer clearance cues that the other can now talk, when they interrupt each other, when they talk over each other, when they pause but keep the conversational floor, and other methods that people use to structure the flow of everyday conversations. For Sacks, the formal properties of turn taking offered a new way to examine action and interaction.

Sacks thus began to take ethnomethodology into formal linguistics, a trend that has continued and now seems to dominate current ethnomethodology in an approach that has been labeled *conversational analysis.* More importantly, Sacks sought to discover universal forms of interaction—that is, abstracted terms of talk—that might apply to all conversations. In this way, he began to search for the laws of reality construction among interacting individuals.

## Zimmerman, Pollner, and Wieder's Situational Approach

Sacks and Cicourel focused on the universal properties, respectively, of language use and cognitive perception/representation. This concern with invariance, or universal folk methods, became increasingly prominent in ethnomethodological inquiry. In several essays for example, Don Zimmerman, D. Lawrence Wieder, and Melvin Pollner developed an approach that sought the universal procedures people employ to construct a sense of reality.[13] Their position was perhaps the most clearly stated of all ethnomethodologies, drawing inspiration from Garfinkel but extending his ideas. Their basic tenet can be summarized along the following lines:

1. In all interaction situations, humans attempt to construct the appearance of consensus over relevant features of the interaction setting.

2. These setting features can include attitudes, opinions, beliefs, and other cognitions about the nature of the social setting in which they interact.

---

[13]Don H. Zimmerman and Melvin Pollner, "The Everyday World as a Phenomenon," in *Understanding Everyday Life*, ed. J. D. Douglas (Chicago, IL: Aldine, 1970); Lawrence Wieder, *Language and Social Reality* (The Hague: Mouton, 1973).

3. Humans engage in a variety of explicit and implicit interpersonal practices and methods to construct, maintain, and perhaps alter *the appearance* of consensus over these setting features.

4. Such interpersonal practices and methods result in the assembling and disassembling of what can be termed an *occasional corpus*—that is, the *perception* by interacting humans that the current setting has an orderly and understandable structure.

5. This appearance of consensus is not only the result of agreement on the substance and content of the occasioned corpus but also a reflection of each participant's compliance with the rules and procedures for assemblage and disassemblage of this consensus. In communicating, in however subtle a manner, that parties accept the implicit rules for constructing an occasioned corpus, they go a long way in establishing consensus about what is in the interaction setting.

6. In each interaction situation, the rules for constructing the occasioned corpus will be unique in some respects and hence not completely generalizable to other settings, thus requiring that humans in each and every interaction situation use interpersonal methods in searching for agreement on the implicit rules for the assembly of an occasioned corpus.

7. Thus, by constructing, reaffirming, or altering the rules for constructing an occasioned corpus, members in a setting can offer one another the appearance of an orderly and connected world, which compels certain perceptions and actions on their part.

From these kinds of assumptions about human interaction, Zimmerman, Pollner, and Wieder's ethnomethodology took its subject matter. Rather than focusing on the actual content and substance of the occasioned corpus and on the ways members believe it to force certain perceptions and actions, attention was drawn primarily to the *methods humans use* to construct, maintain, and change the *appearance* of an orderly and connected social world. These methods are directly observable and constitute a major portion of people's actions in everyday life. In contrast, the actual substance and content of the occasioned corpus are not directly observable and can only be inferred. Furthermore, in concentration on the *process* of creating, sustaining, and changing the occasioned corpus, we can ask a number of questions: Is not the process of creating the appearance of a stable social order for one another more critical to understanding how society is possible that the actual substance and content of the occasioned corpus? Is there anything more to society than members' presumptions that society is "out there" forcing them to do and see certain things? Hence, order is not the result of the particular structure of the corpus; rather, order resides in the human capacity *to continually assemble and disassemble the corpus* in each and every interaction situation. This perspective suggested to ethnomethodologists that theoretical attention should therefore be placed on the ongoing process of assembling and disassembling the appearance of social order and on the particular methods people employ in doing so.

# Emanuel Schegloff's Conversational Analysis

Over the last several decades, Emanuel Schegloff has been one of the most important figures working within the conversation approach suggested by Garfinkel and firmly established by Sacks. Indeed, some of Sacks' most important early works were coauthored with Schegloff.[14] Like Garfinkel before him, Schegloff has mounted a critique of how sociologists conceptualize action and how actions generate intersubjectivity. Most sociologists visualize action without really looking at what individuals do in face-to-face interaction, while seeing intersubjectivity as achieved by socialization into a common culture. By analyzing the dynamics revolving around conversations as they unfold, it is possible to get a much more fine-grained view of action; equally significant, it is possible to understand the problem of order—of how society is held together—from the elementary and more fundamental processes by which it is constructed: talk and conversation among people in situations.

Conversation analysis is now a highly technical way of analyzing strips of conversations, typically recorded and then converted into a transcript. There is a system of notation for indicating pauses, points of emphasis, overlaps, and other features of conversations. What has typified Schegloff's work is detailed analysis of conversations using this notation system, but for our purposes, the details of how the data are arrayed are less important than the actual methods employed by individuals in conversations. These patterns can contribute to a theory of action at its most fundamental level. Of the various discoveries in Schegloff's ongoing research, several sets of findings can be used to illustrate the potential of conversational analysis.

1. **Confirming Allusions.**[15] In conversations, individuals often allude to something. At times, these allusions are explicit; at other times, the allusion implies more than the explicit reference. Schegloff notes that, in some conversations, another party in the conversation repeats the phrasing of words,

---

[14]For example, Harvey Sacks, Emanuel Schegloff, and Gail Jefferson, "A Simplest Systematics" (cited in note 12) and Emanuel A. Schegloff, "Opening Up Closings," *Semiotic* 7 (1973): pp. 280–327.

[15]Emanuel A. Schegloff, "Confirming Allusions: Toward an Empirical Account of Action," *American Journal of Sociology* 102 (1996): 161–216.

indicating an allusion. For example, a phone conversation (made up for illustration) may proceed something like this:

*Janice:*  How are you John?

*John:*  Fine. How are you?

*Janice:*  Doing OK, I guess.

*John:*  Oh . . .

*Janice:*  Went drinking.

*John:*  Went drinking, eh?

The last two turns of the conversation involve Janice making an allusion to drinking (and to the fact that she is only "OK I guess"), and then John repeats the phrase "went drinking." He could have said "I see," or some other phrase, but rather, he repeats the phrase. This pattern is noticeable in many conversations, and Schegloff asks, Is something special going on here? What are these repeats doing? Schegloff's analysis and answer are complex, but the basic generalization is that when people confirm allusions, they indicate that indeed they understand what is being indicated explicitly, but moreover, they understand less explicit allusions accompanying those that are explicit. For instance, if Janice is depressed as a result of drinking, John's repetition of "went drinking" confirms the sense of what drinking does to Janice above and beyond making her tired. Confirmation of allusions thus becomes a mechanism for achieving intersubjectivity, and as such, this particular pattern in conversations can be seen as an ethnomethod used by individuals to create a sense of a shared reality.

**2. Repair after Next Turn.**[16] In conversations, minor and major misunderstandings occur all the time. When these occur, people's sense of intersubjectivity—that is, of sharing a common sense for what is occurring—breaks down, and if such misunderstandings cannot be repaired in the flow of the conversation, the interaction will remain breached. Schegloff initially observed in many conversations that there is what he termed *a third position repair* revealing the following basic structure: Person *A* makes a statement that he or she feels adequate (first position); Person *B* hears this statement and emits a response appropriate to his or her understanding of what Person *A* has said (the second position); but sensing that his or her original statement has not communicated the intended meaning, Person *A* (in the third position) now seeks to make the repair and communicate the intended meaning; and then, Person *B* typically begins the response to the repair with the phrase "oh" indicating that the repair has been understood. For example,

[16]Emanuel A. Schegloff, "Repair After Next Turn: The Last Structurally Provided Defense of Intersubjectivity in Conversation," *American Journal of Sociology* 97 (1992): pp. 1295–345.

below is a simplified version of a more detailed and coded conversation reported by Schegloff:

*Annie:*     Which ones are closed, and which ones are open?

*Zebrach:*   Most of them. This, this, this. (*pointing*)

*Annie:*     I don't mean the shelters. I mean the roads.

*Zebrach:*   Oh! (*and after a pause, he tells Annie about roads*)

This form of conversation can be found often, and it allows parties to effortlessly make repairs to conversations that are off track. The process can be more complicated in that several more sequences of conversation can occur before the party in the third position of the sequence realizes the misunderstanding, but it is still possible when the third position is taken to make the necessary corrections.

A *fourth position repair* allows the person who has misunderstood to acknowledge the repair effort, and thereafter put the conversation back on an intersubjective footing. For example, (1) Person *A* makes a statement, (2) Person *B* responds, (3) Person *A* makes the repair after sensing that Person *B* did not get the intended meaning, and then (4) Person *B* (now in the fourth position) acknowledges the repair effort, perhaps initially by the phrase "oh," followed by more talk that moves the conversation further along in the proper direction.

**3. Overlaps in Conversations.**[17] People often begin talk at the same time, and this can be problematic because it is in the nature of conversations for people to turn-take, with one speaking, then another speaking, and so on. Some overlaps are nonproblematic because they do not deny the speaker holding the floor the right to talk. For example, another person might begin talking just as another is winding down; another speaker might add "continuers" such as "uh huh" to let the speaker know that his or her talk is understood; another may add a word that the speaker is searching for without grabbing the conversational floor; and others may add speech and other vocalizations in a kind of chorus to support the line of talk by a speaker. Moreover, overlaps are generally over very quickly, although they can persist at times.

Schegloff visualizes a number of procedures for dealing with overlaps, and their use constitutes a set of mechanisms or folk methods for managing overlaps in ways that allow the parties to sustain the conversation. One set of mechanisms revolves around shifts in the way talk is produced: getting

---

[17]Emanuel A. Schegloff, "Overlapping Talk and The Organization of Turn-Taking for Conversation," *Language in Society* 29 (2000): pp. 1–63; see also his "Accounts of Conduct in Interaction Interruption, Overlap, and Turn-Taking," in *Handbook of Sociological Theory*, ed. J. H. Turner (New York: Kluwer Academic/Plenum, 2001).

louder, variations of pitch, talking faster, suddenly cutting off talk in progress with special markers (such as bringing teeth and lips together in a
dramatic fashion). Another set of mechanisms revolves around the rhythm
of the conversation that can be conceptualized as successive *beats* of talk
production. Overlaps proceed in such beats, with people often all stopping
after the first beat of overlap or with one person continuing after a beat or
two. Yet another is what Schegloff calls *pre-onset* strategies to keep others
from starting to talk, such as speeding up the talk, and there are *post-onset*
strategies, such as slowing down and deliberately overpronouncing words.

Those working within the broad confines of ethnomethodology have
studied these and other aspects of conversations. Such work is highly suggestive, but at present, there is virtually no theoretical integration of the
many observations of researchers. Thus, there is relatively little theorizing in
conversational analysis; most work is highly descriptive, and yet, many
scholars like Schegloff clearly have theoretical pretensions.

# Conclusion

Ethnomethodology has uncovered a series of interpersonal processes that
traditional symbolic interactionists, who tend to follow Mead more than
Schutz, have failed to recognize. The implicit methods that people use to
communicate a sense of social order are a very crucial dimension of social
interaction and organization, and the theoretical goal of ethnomethodology
is to specify the generic conditions under which various folk methods are
used by individuals. But, despite many interesting findings, this goal still
seems far away—even after forty years of research.

In the end, ethnomethodology has become a rather isolated theoretical
research program. Its practitioners increasingly focused on conversational
analysis—a mode of inquiry initiated by Sacks and carried forward by a
number of creative scholars. But their work has not had a great impact on
mainstream sociological theory, inside or outside the interactionist tradition, although scholars as diverse as Jürgen Habermas (Chapter 31), Pierre
Bourdieu (Chapter 27), Anthony Giddens (Chapter 28), and Randall
Collins (Chapter 12) have all acknowledged a debt to ethnomethodology.
There is, then, something important and fundamental about the assertions
of ethnomethodologists.

# PART V

# Exchange Theorizing

## CHAPTER 21

# The Rise of Exchange Theorizing

From its very beginnings, sociological theory focused on market forces that were transforming the modern social world. Adam Smith[1] was, of course, the first to formulate the laws of supply and demand, but what is often forgotten is that Smith also posed the key questions that guided all nineteenth-century sociological theory: What force or forces are to hold modern societies together as they differentiate and as actors pursue their narrow and specialized interests? His answer was a combination of moral and symbolic forces along with the "invisible hand of order" that comes when rational actors pursue their self-interests in open and free markets. For early sociologists, as well as many today, this invisible hand was indeed just that, invisible; moreover, for most early sociologists, it was not the answer to the question posed by Smith. The result was for exchange theorizing to remain dormant for many decades, well into the twentieth century. Indeed, much early theorizing in sociology represented an effort to formulate an alternative answer to Smith's question. Yet, Smith's emphasis on culture as an integrating force was retained by early sociologists, even as sociologists rejected notions of invisible hands of order inhering in free markets. Still, while arriving rather late in sociology, exchange theorizing is now one of its dominant theoretical perspectives.

## Exchange Theory in Classical Economics

Given Adam Smith's influence on sociology and the impact of other British Isle thinkers on nineteenth-century social thought, it is perhaps best to begin

---

[1]Adam Smith, *An Inquiry into the Nature and Causes of the Wealth of Nations* (London: Davis, 1805; originally published in 1776).

with the ideas that come from this tradition. All of these early British Isle classical economists considered themselves "moralists" and hence were concerned with broad ethical issues like justice, freedom, and fairness.[2] The label *utilitarianism* was meant to capture the broader moral concerns of these early moralists, but the term now tends to be associated with a narrow vision of their work, as is evident today in neoclassical economic theory. Economic theorists of the present era portray humans as rational persons who seek to maximize their material benefits, or *utility*, from transactions or exchanges with others in a free and competitive marketplace. Free in the marketplace, people have access to necessary information; they can consider all available alternatives, and on the basis of this consideration, rationally select the course of activity that will maximize material benefits. Entering into these rational considerations are calculations of the *costs* involved in pursuing various alternatives, with such costs being weighed against material benefits in an effort to determine which alternative will yield the maximum payoff or profit (benefits less costs). This view of the early utilitarians is generally considered too narrow to offer an adequate explanation for how differentiated societies become integrated, although some exchange theorists argue that this narrow view can explain all of the dynamics of interest to sociologists.

With the emergence of sociology as a self-conscious discipline, there was considerable revision to this utilitarian conception of humans as rational. In the end, many sociologists muted extreme utilitarian assumptions in the ways enumerated below:

1. Humans do not seek to maximize profits, as utilitarians argued, but they nonetheless attempt to make some profit in their social transactions with others.

2. Humans are not perfectly rational, but they do engage in calculations of costs and benefits in social transactions.

3. Humans do not have perfect information on all available alternatives, but they are usually aware of at least some alternatives, which form the basis for assessments of costs and benefits.

4. Humans always act under social structural and cultural constraints, but they still compete with one another in seeking to make a profit in their exchanges of resources.

5. Although humans always seek to make a profit in their transactions, they are limited by the resources that they have when entering an exchange relation.

In addition to these alterations of utilitarian assumptions, exchange theory removes human interaction from the limitations of material

---

[2]Charles Camic, "The Utilitarians Revisited," *American Journal of Sociology* 85 (1979): pp. 516–50.

transactions in an economic marketplace, requiring two more additions to the previous list:

6. Humans do engage in economic transactions in clearly defined marketplaces in all societies, but these transactions are only special cases of more general exchange relations occurring among individuals in virtually all social contexts.

7. Humans do pursue material goals in exchanges, but they also mobilize and exchange nonmaterial resources, such as sentiments, services, and symbols.

# Exchange Theory in Anthropology

## Sir James Frazer

In 1919, Sir James Frazer's (1854–1941) second volume of *Folklore in the Old Testament* conducted what was probably the first explicit exchange-theoretic analysis of social institutions.[3] In examining a wide variety of kinship and marriage practices among "primitive" (pre-literate) societies, Frazer was struck by the clear preference of Australian aborigines for cross-cousin over parallel-cousin marriages: "Why is the marriage of cross-cousins so often favored? Why is the marriage of ortho-cousins [that is, parallel cousins] so uniformly prohibited?"[4]

Although the substantive details of Frazer's descriptions of the aborigines' practices are fascinating in themselves (if only for their inaccuracy), the form of explanation marks his theoretical contribution. In a manner clearly indebted to utilitarian economics, Frazer launched an economic interpretation of the predominance of cross-cousin marriage patterns. In this explanation Frazer invoked the "law of economic motives": By having "no equivalent in property to give for a wife, an Australian aborigine is generally obliged to get her in exchange for a female relative, usually a sister or daughter."[5] Thus, the material or economic motives of individuals in society (lack of property and desire for a wife) explain various social patterns (cross-cousin marriages). Frazer went on to postulate that, once a particular pattern emanating from economic motives becomes established in a culture, it constrains other social patterns that can potentially emerge.

---

[3]Sir James George Frazer, *Folklore in the Old Testament*, vol. 2 (New York: Macmillan, 1919); see also his *Totemism and Exogamy: A Treatise on Certain Early Forms of Superstition and Society* (London: Dawsons of Pall Mall, 1968; originally published in 1910) and his Preface to Bronislaw Malinowski's *Argonauts of the Western Pacific* (London: Routledge & Kegan Paul, 1922), pp. vii–xiv.

[4]Frazer, *Folklore* (cited in note 3), p. 199.

[5]Ibid., p. 198.

Frazer believed that the social and structural patterns that typify a particular culture reflect economic motives in humans, who attempt to satisfy their basic economic needs in exchanges. Although Frazer's specific explanation was found to be sadly wanting by subsequent generations of anthropologists, especially Bronislaw Malinowski and Claude Lévi-Strauss, modern exchange theory in sociology invokes a similar conception of social organization:

1. Exchange processes are the result of efforts by people to realize basic needs.

2. When yielding payoffs for those involved, exchange processes lead to the patterning of interaction.

3. Such patterns of interaction not only serve the needs of individuals but also constrain the kinds of social structures that can subsequently emerge.

In addition to anticipating the general profile of modern explanations about how elementary exchange processes create more complex patterns in a society, Frazer's analysis also foreshadowed another concern of contemporary exchange theory: social systems' differentiation of privilege and power. Much as Karl Marx had done a generation earlier, Frazer noted that those who possess resources of high economic value can exploit those who have few such resources, thereby enabling the former to possess high privilege and presumably power. Hence the exchange of women among the aborigines was observed by Frazer to lead to the differentiation of power and privilege in at least two separate ways. First, "since among the Australian aboriginals women had a high economic and commercial value, a man who had many sisters or daughters was rich and a man who had none was poor and might be unable to procure a wife at all." Second, "the old men availed themselves of the system of exchange in order to procure a number of wives for themselves from among the young women, while the young men, having no women to give in exchange, were often obliged to remain single or to put up with the cast-off wives of their elders."[6] Thus, at least implicitly, Frazer supplemented the conflict theory contribution with a fourth exchange principle:

4. Exchange processes differentiate groups by their relative access to valued commodities, resulting in differences in power, prestige, and privilege.

As provocative and seemingly seminal as Frazer's analysis appears, it had little direct impact on modern exchange theory. Rather, contemporary theory remains indebted to those in anthropology who reacted against Frazer's utilitarianism.

---

[6]Ibid., pp. 200–201 for this and immediately preceding quote.

## Bronislaw Malinowski and Nonmaterial Exchange

Despite Malinowski's close ties with Frazer, Malinowski developed an exchange perspective that radically altered the utilitarian slant of Frazer's analysis of cross-cousin marriage. Indeed, Frazer himself, in his preface to Malinowski's *Argonauts of the Western Pacific*, recognized the importance of Malinowski's contribution to the analysis of exchange relations.[7] In his now-famous ethnography of the Trobriand Islanders—a group of South Seas Island cultures—Malinowski observed an exchange system termed *the Kula Ring*, a closed circle of exchange relations among tribal peoples inhabiting a wide ring of islands. What was distinctive in this closed circle, Malinowski observed, is the predominance of exchange of two articles—armlets and necklaces—which the inhabitants constantly exchanged in opposite directions around the ring of islands. Armlets traveling in one direction around the Kula Ring were exchanged for necklaces moving in the opposite direction around the ring. In any particular exchange between individuals, an armlet would always be exchanged for a necklace.

In interpreting this unique exchange network, Malinowski distinguished material or economic from nonmaterial or symbolic exchanges. In contrast with the utilitarians and Frazer, who did not conceptualize nonmaterial exchange relations, Malinowski recognized that the Kula was not only an economic or material exchange network but also a symbolic exchange, cementing a web of social relationships: "One transaction does not finish the Kula relationship, the rule being 'once in the Kula, always in the Kula,' and a partnership between two men is a permanent and lifelong affair."[8] Although purely economic transactions did occur within the rules of the Kula, the ceremonial exchange of armlets and necklaces was observed by Malinowski to be the Kula's principal function.

The natives themselves, Malinowski emphasized, recognized the distinction between purely economic commodities and the symbolic significance of armlets and necklaces. However, to distinguish economic from symbolic commodities does not mean that the Trobriand Islanders failed to assign graded values to the symbolic commodities; indeed, they made gradations and used them to express and confirm the nature of the relationships among exchange partners as equals, superordinates, or subordinates. But, as Malinowski noted, "in all forms of [Kula] exchange in the Trobriands, there is not even a trace of gain, nor is there any reason for looking at it from the purely utilitarian and economic standpoint, since there is no enhancement of mutual utility through the exchange."[9] Rather, the motives behind the Kula were social-psychological, for the exchanges in the ring were viewed by Malinowski to have implications for the needs of both individuals and

---

[7]Bronislaw Malinowski, *Argonauts of the Western Pacific* (London: Routledge & Kegan Paul, 1922), p. 81.

[8]Ibid., pp. 82–83.

[9]Ibid., p. 175.

society (recall from Chapter 2 that Malinowski was also a founder of functional theory). From his functionalist framework, he interpreted the Kula to mean "the fundamental impulse to display, to share, to bestow [and] the deep tendency to create social ties."[10] Malinowski, then, considered an enduring social pattern such as the Kula Ring to have positively functional consequences for satisfying individual psychological needs and societal needs for social integration and solidarity.

This form of functional analysis presents many logical difficulties. Nevertheless, Malinowski's analysis made several enduring contributions to modern exchange theory:

1. In Malinowski's words, "the meaning of the Kula will consist in being instrumental to dispel [the] conception of a rational being who wants nothing but to satisfy his simplest needs and does it according to the economic principle of least effort."[11]

2. Psychological rather than economic needs are the forces that initiate and sustain exchange relations and are therefore critical in the explanation of social behavior.

3. Exchange relations can also have implications beyond two parties, for as the Kula demonstrates, complex patterns of indirect exchange can maintain extended and protracted social networks.

4. Symbolic exchange relations are the basic social process underlying both differentiation of ranks in a society and the integration of society into a cohesive whole.

With this emphasis, Malinowski helped free exchange theory from the limiting confines of utilitarianism. By stressing the importance of symbolic exchanges for both individual psychological processes and patterns of social integration, he anticipated the conceptual base for two basic types of exchange perspectives, one emphasizing the importance of psychological processes and the other stressing the significance of emergent cultural and structural forces on exchange relations.

## Marcel Mauss and the Emergence of Exchange Structuralism

Reacting to what he perceived as Malinowski's tendency to overemphasize psychological instead of social needs, Marcel Mauss reinterpreted Malinowski's analysis of the Kula.[12] In this effort, he formulated

[10]Ibid.

[11]Ibid., p. 516.

[12]Marcel Mauss, *The Gift*, trans. I. Cunnison (New York: Free Press, 1954; originally published as *Essai sur le don en sociologie et anthropologie* [Paris: Presses universitaires de France,

the broad outlines of a *collectivistic*, or *structural-exchange*, perspective.[13] Mauss believed the critical question in examining an exchange network as complex as that of the Kula was, "In primitive or archaic types of societies, what is the principle whereby the gift received has to be repaid? What force is there in the thing which compels the recipient to make a return?"[14] The force compelling reciprocity was, Mauss believed, society or the group. As he noted, "It is groups, and not individuals, which carry on exchange, make contracts, and are bound by obligations."[15] The individuals actually engaged in an exchange represent the moral codes of the group. Exchange transactions among individuals are conducted in accordance with the rules of the group, thereby reinforcing these rules and codes. Thus, for Mauss, the over concern with individuals' self-interests by utilitarians and the overemphasis on psychological needs by Malinowski are replaced by a conception of individuals as representatives of social groups. In the end, exchange relations create, reinforce, and serve a group morality that is an entity sui generis, to borrow a famous phrase from Mauss' mentor, Émile Durkheim. Furthermore, in a vein similar to that of Frazer, once such a morality emerges and is reinforced by exchange activities, it regulates other activities in the social life of a group, beyond particular exchange transactions.

Mauss' work has received scant attention from sociologists, but he was the first to forge a reconciliation between the exchange principles of utilitarianism and the structural, or collectivistic, thought of Émile Durkheim. In recognizing that exchange transactions give rise to and, at the same time, reinforce the normative structure of society, Mauss anticipated the structural position of some contemporary exchange theories. Mauss' influence on modern theory has been indirect, however. It is through Lévi-Strauss' structuralism that the French collectivist tradition of Durkheim and Mauss has influenced the exchange perspectives of contemporary sociological theory.

---

1925]). It should be noted that Mauss rather consistently misinterpreted Malinowski's ethnography, but through such misinterpretation, he came to visualize a "structural" alternative to "psychological" exchange theories.

[13]In Peter Ekeh's old but still excellent discussion of Mauss and Lévi-Strauss, *Social Exchange Theory and the Two Sociological Traditions* (Cambridge, MA: Harvard University Press, 1975), pp. 55–122, the term *collectivist* is used in preference to *structural* and is posited as the alternative to individualistic or psychological exchange perspectives. I prefer the terms *structural* and *psychological*; thus, although I am indebted to Ekeh's discussion, these terms will be used to make essentially the same distinction. My preference for these terms will become more evident in subsequent chapters, since, in contrast with Ekeh's analysis, I consider Peter M. Blau and George C. Homans to have developed, respectively, structural and psychological theories. Ekeh considers the theories of both Blau and Homans to be individualistic, or psychological.

[14]Mauss, *The Gift* (cited in note 12), p. 1.

[15]Ibid., p. 3.

## Claude Lévi-Strauss and Structuralism

In 1949, Lévi-Strauss launched an analysis of cross-cousin marriage in his classic work, *The Elementary Structures of Kinship*.[16] In restating Durkheim's objections to utilitarians, Lévi-Strauss took exception to Frazer's utilitarian interpretation of cross-cousin marriage patterns. And, similar to Mauss' opposition to Malinowski's emphasis on psychological needs, Lévi-Strauss developed a sophisticated structural-exchange perspective.

In rejecting Frazer's interpretation of cross-cousin marriage, Lévi-Strauss first questioned the substance of Frazer's utilitarian conceptualization. Frazer, he noted, "depicts the poor Australian aborigine wondering how he is going to obtain a wife since he has no material goods with which to purchase her, and discovering exchange as the solution to this apparently insoluble problem: 'men exchange their sisters in marriage because that was the cheapest way of getting a wife.'" In contrast, Lévi-Strauss emphasized that "it is the exchange which counts and not the things exchanged." For Lévi-Strauss, exchange must be viewed by its functions for integrating the larger social structure. Lévi-Strauss then attacked Frazer's and the utilitarians' assumption that the first principles of social behavior are economic. Such an assumption contradicts the view that social structure is an emergent phenomenon that operates according to its own irreducible laws and principles.

Lévi-Strauss also rejected psychological interpretations of exchange processes, especially the position advocated by behaviorists (see later section). In contrast with psychological behaviorists, who see little real difference in the laws of behavior between animals and humans, Lévi-Strauss emphasized that humans possess a cultural heritage of norms and values that separates their behavior and societal organization from that of animal species. Human action is thus qualitatively different from animal behavior, especially in social exchange. Animals are not guided by values and rules that specify when, where, and how they are to carry out social transactions. Humans, however, carry with them into any exchange situation learned definitions of how they are to behave—thus ensuring that the principles of human exchange will be distinctive.

Furthermore, exchange is more than the result of psychological needs, even those that have been acquired through socialization. Exchange cannot be understood solely through individual motives, because exchange relations are a reflection of patterns of social organization that exist as an entity *sui generis*. Exchange behavior is thus regulated from without by norms and values, resulting in processes that can be analyzed only by their consequences, or functions, for these norms and values.

In arguing this view, Lévi-Strauss posited several fundamental exchange principles. First, all exchange relations involve costs for individuals, but in

---

[16]Claude Lévi-Strauss, *The Elementary Structures of Kinship* (Boston: Beacon, 1969). This is a translation of Lévi-Strauss' 1967 revision of the original *Les structures élémentaires de la parenté* (Paris: Presses universitaires de France, 1949).

contrast with economic or psychological explanations of exchange, such costs are attributed to society—to those customs, rules, laws, and values that require behaviors incurring costs. Yet individuals do not assign the costs to themselves, but to the social order. Second, for all those scarce and valued resources in society—whether material objects, such as wives, or symbolic resources, like esteem and prestige—their distribution is regulated by norms and values. As long as resources are in abundant supply or are not highly valued in a society, their distribution goes unregulated, but once they become scarce and highly valued, their distribution is soon regulated. Third, all exchange relations are governed by a norm of reciprocity, requiring those receiving valued resources to bestow on their benefactors other valued resources. In Lévi-Strauss' conception of reciprocity are various patterns of reciprocation specified by norms and values. In some situations, norms dictate *mutual* and direct rewarding of one's benefactor, whereas in other situations the reciprocity can be *univocal*, involving diverse patterns of indirect exchange in which actors do not reciprocate directly but only through various third (fourth, fifth, and so forth) parties. Within these two general types of exchange reciprocity—mutual and univocal—numerous subtypes of exchange networks can be normatively regulated.

Lévi-Strauss believed that these three exchange principles offer a more useful set of concepts to describe cross-cousin marriage patterns, because these patterns can now be viewed by their functions for the larger social structure. Particular marriage patterns and other features of kinship organization no longer need be interpreted merely as direct exchanges among individuals but can be conceptualized as exchanges between individuals and society. In freeing exchange from the analysis of only direct and mutual exchanges, Lévi-Strauss offered a tentative theory of societal integration and solidarity. His explanation extended Durkheim's provocative analysis and indicated how various subtypes of direct and univocal exchange both reflect and reinforce different patterns of societal integration and organization.

This theory of integration is, in itself, of theoretical importance, but it is more significant for our present purposes to stress Lévi-Strauss' impact on current sociological exchange perspectives. Two points of emphasis strongly influenced modern sociological theory.

1. Various forms of social structure, rather than individual motives, are the critical variables in the analysis of exchange relations.

2. Exchange relations in social systems are frequently not restricted to direct interaction among individuals but are protracted into complex networks of indirect exchange. On the one hand, these exchange processes are caused by patterns of social integration and organization; on the other hand, they promote diverse forms of such organization.

Lévi-Strauss's work represents the culmination of a reaction to economic utilitarianism as it was originally incorporated into anthropology by Frazer. Malinowski recognized the limitations of Frazer's analysis of only material or economic motives in direct exchange transactions. As the Kula Ring demonstrates, exchange can be generalized into protracted networks involving noneconomic motives that have implications for societal integration. Mauss drew explicit attention to the significance of social structure in regulating exchange processes and to the consequences of such processes for maintaining social structure. Finally, in this intellectual chain of events in anthropology, Lévi-Strauss began to indicate how different types of direct and indirect exchange are linked to different patterns of social organization. This intellectual heritage has influenced both the substance and the strategy of exchange theory in sociology, but it has done so only after considerable modification of assumptions and concepts by a particular strain of psychology: *behaviorism.*

## Psychological Behaviorism and Exchange Theory

As a psychological perspective, behaviorism began from insights derived from observations of an accident. The Russian physiologist Ivan Petrovich Pavlov (1849–1936) discovered that experimental dogs associated food with the person bringing it.[17] He observed, for instance, that dogs on which he was performing secretory experiments would salivate not only when presented with food but also when they heard their feeder's footsteps approaching. After considerable delay and personal agonizing, Pavlov undertook a series of experiments on animals to understand such "conditioned responses."[18] From these experiments, he developed several principles that were later incorporated into behaviorism. These include the following:

(1) A stimulus consistently associated with another stimulus producing a given physiological response will, by itself, elicit that response.

(2) Such conditioned responses can be extinguished when gratifications associated with stimuli are no longer forthcoming.

(3) Stimuli that are similar to those producing a conditioned response can also elicit the same response as the original stimulus.

(4) Stimuli that increasingly differ from those used to condition a particular response will decreasingly be able to elicit this response.

Thus, Pavlov's experiments exposed the principles of conditioned responses, extinction, response generalization, and response discrimination. Although Pavlov clearly recognized the significance of these findings for human behavior, his insights came to fruition in America under the tutelage of Edward Lee Thorndike and John B. Watson—the founders of behaviorism.

---

[17]See, for relevant articles, lectures, and references, I. P. Pavlov, *Selected Works*, ed. K. S. Kostoyants, trans. S. Belsky (Moscow: Foreign Languages Publishing House, 1955) and *Lectures on Conditioned Reflexes*, 3rd ed., trans. W. H. Grant (New York: International, 1928).

[18]I. P. Pavlov, "Autobiography," in *Selected Works* (cited in note 17), pp. 41–44.

Edward Lee Thorndike conducted the first laboratory experiments on animals in America. During these experiments, he observed that animals would retain response patterns for which they were rewarded.[19] For example, in experiments on kittens placed in a puzzle box, Thorndike found that the kittens would engage in trial-and-error behavior until emitting the response that allowed them to escape. And, with each placement in the box, the kittens would engage in less trial-and-error behavior, indicating that the gratifications associated with a response allowing the kittens to escape caused them to learn and retain this response. From these and other studies, which were conducted at the same time as Pavlov's, Thorndike formulated three principles or laws: (1) the *law of effect*, which holds that acts in a situation producing gratification will be more likely to occur in the future when that situation recurs; (2) the *law of use*, which states that the situation-response connection is strengthened with repetitions and practice; and (3) the *law of disuse*, which argues that the connection will weaken when practice is discontinued.[20]

These laws converge with those presented by Pavlov, but there is one important difference. Thorndike's experiments involved animals engaged in free trial-and-error behavior, whereas Pavlov's work was on the conditioning of physiological—typically glandular—responses in a tightly controlled laboratory situation. Thorndike's work could thus be seen as more directly relevant to human behavior in natural settings.

John B. Watson was only one of several thinkers to recognize the significance of Pavlov's and Thorndike's work, but he soon became the dominant advocate of what was becoming explicitly known as behaviorism.[21] Watson's opening shot for the new science of behavior was fired in an article entitled "Psychology as the Behaviorist Views It":

> Psychology as the behaviorist views it is a purely objective experimental branch of natural science. Its theoretical goal is the prediction and control of behavior. Introspection forms no essential part of its methods, nor is the scientific value of its data dependent upon the readiness with which they lend themselves to interpretation in terms of consciousness. The behaviorist, in efforts to get a unitary scheme of animal response, recognizes no dividing line between man and brute.[22]

---

[19]Edward L. Thorndike, "Animal Intelligence: An Experimental Study of the Associative Processes in Animals," *Psychological Review Monograph*, Supplement 2 (1989).

[20]See Edward L. Thorndike, *The Elements of Psychology* (New York: Seiler, 1905), *The Fundamentals of Learning* (New York: Teachers College Press, 1932) and *The Psychology of Wants, Interests, and Attitudes* (New York: D. Appleton, 1935).

[21]Others who recognized their importance include Max F. Meyer, *Psychology of the Other-One* (Columbus, OH: Missouri Book, 1921) and Albert P. Weiss, A *Theoretical Basis of Human Behavior* (Columbus, OH: Adams, 1925).

[22]J. B. Watson, "Psychology as the Behaviorist Views It," *Psychological Review* 20 (1913): pp. 158–77. For other basic works by Watson, see *Psychology from the Standpoint of a Behaviorist*, 3rd ed. (Philadelphia: Lippincott, 1929); *Behavior: An Introduction to Comparative Psychology* (New York: Henry Holt, 1914).

Watson thus became the advocate of the extreme behaviorism against which many vehemently reacted.[23] For Watson, psychology is the study of stimulus-response relations, and the only admissible evidence is overt behavior. Psychologists are to stay out of the Pandora's box of human consciousness and to study only observable behaviors as they are connected to observable stimuli.[24]

In many ways, behaviorism is similar to utilitarianism because it operates on the principle that humans are reward-seeking organisms pursuing alternatives that will yield the most reward and the least punishment. Rewards are simply another way of phrasing the economist's concept of *utility*, and *punishment* is somewhat equivalent to the notion of *cost*. For the behaviorist, reward is any behavior that reinforces or meets the needs of the organism, whereas punishment denies rewards or forces the expenditure of energy to avoid pain (thereby incurring costs).

Modern exchange theories have borrowed the notion of reward from behaviorists and used it to reinterpret the utilitarian exchange heritage. In place of utility, the concept of reward has often been inserted, primarily because it allows exchange theorists to view behavior as motivated by psychological needs. However, the utilitarian concept of cost appears to have been retained in preference to the behaviorist's formulation of punishment, because the notion of cost allows exchange theorists to visualize more completely the alternative rewards that organisms forego in seeking to achieve a particular reward.

Despite these modifications of the basic concepts of behaviorism, its key theoretical generalizations have been incorporated with relatively little change into some forms of sociological exchange theory:

1. In any given situation, organisms will emit those behaviors that will yield the most reward and the least punishment.

2. Organisms will repeat those behaviors that have proved rewarding in the past.

3. Organisms will repeat behaviors in situations that are similar to those in the past in which behaviors were rewarded.

4. Present stimuli that on past occasions have been associated with rewards will evoke behaviors similar to those emitted in the past.

5. Repetition of behaviors will occur only as long as they continue to yield rewards.

---

[23]For example, in *Mind, Self, and Society* (Chicago: University of Chicago Press, 1934), Mead has eighteen references to Watson's work.

[24]For a more detailed discussion of the emergence of behaviorism, see Jonathan H. Turner, Leonard Beeghley, and Charles Powers, *The Emergence of Sociological Theory*, 7th ed. (Newbury Park, CA: Wadsworth, 2012).

6. An organism will display emotion if a behavior that has previously been rewarded in the same or similar situation suddenly goes unrewarded.

7. The more an organism receives rewards from a particular behavior, the less rewarding that behavior becomes (because of satiation) and the more likely the organism is to emit alternative behaviors in search of other rewards.

These principles were discovered in laboratory situations where experimenters typically manipulated the environment of the organism; thus, it is difficult to visualize the experimental situation as interaction. The experimenter's tight control of the situation precludes the possibility that the animal will affect significantly the responses of the experimenter. This has forced modern exchange theories using behaviorist principles to incorporate the utilitarian's concern with transactions, or exchanges. In this way humans can be seen as mutually affecting one another's opportunities for rewards. In contrast with animals in a Skinner box or some similar laboratory situation, humans exchange rewards. Each person represents a potentially rewarding stimulus situation for the other.

As sociological exchange theorists have attempted to apply behaviorist principles to the study of human behavior, they have inevitably confronted the problem of the black box: Humans differ from laboratory animals in their greater ability to engage in a wide variety of complex cognitive processes. Indeed, as the utilitarians were the first to emphasize, what is distinctly human is the capacity to abstract, to calculate, to project outcomes, to weigh alternatives, and to perform a wide number of other cognitive manipulations. Furthermore, in borrowing behaviorists' concepts, contemporary exchange theorists have also had to introduce the concepts of an introspective psychology and structural sociology. Humans not only think in complex ways; their thinking is emotional and circumscribed by many social and cultural forces (first incorporated into the exchange theories of Mauss and Lévi-Strauss). Once it is recognized that behaviorist principles must incorporate concepts denoting both internal psychological processes and constraints of social structure and culture, it is also necessary to visualize exchange as frequently transcending the mutually rewarding activities of individuals in direct interaction. The organization of behavior by social structure and culture, coupled with humans' complex cognitive abilities, allows protracted and indirect exchange networks to exist.

When we review the impact of behaviorism on some forms of contemporary exchange theory, the vocabulary and general principles of behaviorism are clearly evident, but concepts have been redefined and the principles altered to incorporate the insights of the early utilitarians as well as the anthropological reaction to utilitarianism. The end result has been for proponents of an exchange perspective employing behaviorist concepts and principles to abandon much of what made behaviorism a unique perspective as they have dealt with the complexities introduced by human cognitive capacities and their organization into sociocultural groupings.

# The Sociological Tradition and Exchange Theory

The vocabulary of exchange theory clearly comes from utilitarianism and behaviorism. Anthropological work forced the recognition that cultural and social dynamics need to be incorporated into exchange theory. When we look at early sociological work, however, the impact of early sociological theorists on modern exchange theory is difficult to assess for several reasons. First, much sociological theory represented a reaction *against* utilitarianism and extreme behaviorism and, therefore, has been reluctant to incorporate concepts from these fields. Second, the most developed of the early exchange theories—that provided by Georg Simmel in his *The Philosophy of Money*—were not translated into English until the 1970s.[25] (German-reading theorists, such as Peter Blau and Talcott Parsons, were to some degree influenced by Simmel's ideas.) Third, the topics of most interest to many sociological exchange theorists—differentiations of power and conflict in exchanges—have more typically been conceptualized as conflict theory rather than as exchange theory. But, as will become evident, sociological theories of exchange converge with those on conflict processes, and Marx's and Weber's ideas exerted considerable influence on sociologically oriented exchange theories.

## Marx's Theory of Exchange and Conflict

Most contemporary theories of exchange examine situations where actors have unequal levels of resources with which to bargain. Those with valued resources are in a position to strike a better bargain, especially if others who value their resources do not possess equally valued resources to offer in exchange. This fact of social life is the situation described in Marx's conflict theory.[26] Capitalists have the power to control the distribution of material rewards, whereas all that workers have is their labor to offer in exchange. Although labor is valued by the capitalist, it is in plentiful supply, and thus no one worker is in a position to bargain effectively with an employer. As a consequence, capitalists can get labor at a low cost and can force workers to do what they want. As capitalists press their advantage, they create the very conditions that allow workers to develop

---

[25]Georg Simmel, *The Philosophy of Money*, trans. T. Bottomore and D. Frisby (Boston: Routledge & Kegan Paul, 1978; originally published in 1907).

[26]Karl Marx and Frederick Engels, *The Communist Manifesto* (New York: International, 1971; originally published 1848); Karl Marx, *Capital: A Critical Analysis of Capitalist Production*, vol. 1 (New York: International, 1967; originally published in 1867).

resources—political, organizational, ideological—that workers can then use to strike a better bargain with capitalists and, in the end, to overthrow them.

Granted, this is simplifying Marx's implicit exchange theory, but the point is clear: Dialectical conflict theory is a variety of exchange theory. Let us list some of these exchange dynamics more explicitly:

1. Those who need scarce and valued resources that others possess but who do not have equally valued and scarce resources to offer in return will be dependent on those who control these resources.

2. Those who control valued resources have power over those who do not. That is, the power of one actor over another is directly related to (a) the capacity of one actor to monopolize the valued resources needed by other actors and (b) the inability of those actors who need these resources to offer equally valued and scarce resources in return.

3. Those with power will press their advantage and will try to extract more resources from those dependent on them in exchange for fewer (or the same level) of the resources that they control.

4. Those who press their advantage in this way will create conditions that encourage those who are dependent on them to (a) organize in ways that increase the value of their resources and, failing this, to (b) organize in ways that enable them to coerce those on whom they are dependent.

If the words capitalist and proletarian are inserted at the appropriate places in the previous list, Marx's exchange model becomes readily apparent. Dialectical conflict theory is thus a series of propositions about exchange dynamics in systems in which the distribution of resources is unequal. And, as will become evident in the next chapters, sociological exchange theories have emphasized these dynamics that inhere in the unequal distribution of resources. Such is Marx's major contribution to exchange theory.

## Georg Simmel's Exchange Theory

In Simmel's *The Philosophy of Money*[27] is a critique of Marx's "value theory of labor"[28] and, in its place, a clear exposition of exchange theory. *The Philosophy of Money* is, as its title indicates, about the impact of money on

---

[27]See note 25.

[28]Marx, *Capital* (cited in note 26).

social relations and social structure. For Simmel, social exchange involves the following elements:[29]

1. The desire for a valued object that one does not have

2. The possession of the valued object by an identifiable other

3. The offer of an object of value to secure the desired object from another

4. The acceptance of this offer by the possessor of the valued object

Contained in this portrayal of social exchange are several additional points that Simmel emphasized. First, value is idiosyncratic and is, ultimately, tied to an individual's impulses and needs. Of course, what is defined as valuable is typically circumscribed by cultural and social patterns, but how valuable an object is will be a positive function of (a) the intensity of a person's needs and (b) the scarcity of the object. Second, much exchange involves efforts to manipulate situations so that the intensity of needs for an object is concealed and the availability of an object is made to seem less than what it actually is. Inherent in exchange, therefore, is a basic tension that can often erupt into other social forms, such as conflict. Third, to possess an object is to lessen its value and to increase the value of objects that one does not possess. Fourth, exchanges will occur only if both parties perceive that the object given is less valuable than the one received. Fifth, collective units as well as individuals participate in exchange relations and hence are subject to the four processes listed. Sixth, the more liquid the resources of an actor are in an exchange—that is, the more that resources can be used in many types of exchanges—the greater that actor's options and power will be. For if an actor is not bound to exchange with any other and can readily withdraw resources and exchange them with another, then that actor has considerable power to manipulate any exchange.

Economic exchange involving money is only one case of this more general social form, but it is a very special case. When money becomes the predominant means for establishing value in relationships, the properties and dynamics of social relations are transformed. This process of displacing other criteria of value, such as logic, ethics, and aesthetics, with a monetary criterion is precisely the long-term evolutionary trend in societies. This trend is both a cause and effect of money as the medium of exchange. Money emerged to facilitate exchanges and to realize even more completely humans' basic needs. But, once established, money has the power to transform the structure of social relations in society.

Thus, the key insight in *The Philosophy of Money* is that the use of different criteria for assessing value has an enormous impact on the form of social relations. As money replaces barter and other criteria for determining values, social relations are fundamentally changed. Yet, they are transformed

---

[29]Simmel, *The Philosophy of Money* (cited in note 25), pp. 85–88.

in accordance with some basic principles of social exchange, which are never codified by Simmel but are very clear. In Table 21.1, these ideas are summarized as abstract exchange principles.

**Table 21.1** Georg Simmel's Exchange Principles

1. **Attraction Principle**: The more actors perceive as valuable one another's respective resources, the more likely an exchange relationship is to develop among these actors.

2. **Value Principle**: The greater is the intensity of an actor's needs for a resource of a given type, and the less available is that resource, the greater is the value of that resource to the actor.

3. **Power Principles**
   A. The more an actor perceives as valuable the resources of another actor, the greater is the power of the latter over the former.
   B. The more liquid are an actor's resources, the greater will be the exchange options and alternatives and, hence, the greater will be the power of that actor in social exchanges.

4. **Tension Principle**: The more actors in a social exchange manipulate the situation in an effort to misrepresent their needs for a resource or conceal the availability of resources, the greater is the level of tension in that exchange and the greater is the potential for conflict.

# Conclusion: Exchange Theory in the Contemporary Era

Curiously, despite Adam Smith's influence on sociological theory in the nineteenth century and behaviorists' impact on early social psychology, a clear sociological approach to exchange theory did not emerge until the 1960s. When it finally arrived, this approach has remained prominent within the sociological canon since the midcentury, and today, it is one of the most important perspectives within sociological theorizing. In the next three chapters on the maturing tradition during the 1960s and 1970s, we will explore how economic and behaviorist ideas were brought back into sociological theory and blended with the discipline's concern with social structure, power, and inequality. Then, we can explore the two surviving variants of this midcentury burst of creative activity, primarily rational choice theories and the exchange network approaches.

## CHAPTER 22

# Early Exchange Theories

In the early 1960s, exchange theory emerged as a distinctive perspective in sociology. Suddenly, some of America's most prominent theorists were exploring the social universe using ideas borrowed from utilitarian economics and psychological behaviorism. For all these thinkers, a fundamental property of the social universe is the exchange of resources among actors, driven by needs to secure rewards or utilities. In this first chapter on the maturing exchange tradition, I examined the works of George C. Homans, Peter M. Blau, and Richard Emerson, all of whom forced sociological theory to become attuned to the process of exchange. These were the first sociologists in the modern era to adopt exchange ideas in sociology and develop coherent theories, thus breaking what had clearly been an informal taboo against either behaviorist or utilitarian ideas. But in their hands, exchange theory became acceptable and is now an important theoretical perspective in sociology.

## George C. Homans' Early Behaviorist Approach

George C. Homans made a theoretical conversion to exchange theory in the late 1950s, borrowing ideas from his behaviorist colleague at Harvard, B. F. Skinner, who was the most prominent behaviorist in the world at the time. Yet, Homans recognized that he would have to enter the black box of human cognition, perhaps through the back door, but nonetheless, he would have to conceptualize what people feel and think. In so doing, he drew concepts from utilitarian tradition in economics and dressed them up in behaviorist conceptual clothing. In developing his behavioristic exchange theory, Homans also developed a view of theorizing using the vocabulary of axiomatic theory without its logical rigor or substance. But, the basic idea was that the axioms from which all sociological laws can ultimately be deduced are psychological in nature, not only psychology but behaviorist laws at that (with elements of utilitarian economics slipping in). To say the least, this advocacy created a rather heated debate because, as I emphasized in chapters on evolutionary (biological) sociology, sociologists are highly defensive when it comes to reductionism or reducing sociology to some other field, and psychology and economics no less. In making this argument for theoretical deduction and reduction, Homans also insisted that sociology must begin with behavior and interaction, seeing theories of macrostructures as ultimately explained by the actions of people seeking rewards and weighing their rewards against cost. This too threatened many sociologists.

## Borrowing from B. F. Skinner

Given Homans' commitment to axiomatic theorizing and his concern with face-to-face interaction among individuals, it was perhaps inevitable that Homans would look toward Skinner and, indirectly, to the early founders of behaviorism—I. P. Pavlov, Edward Lee Thorndike, and J. B. Watson. But Homans borrowed directly from Skinner's reformulations of early behaviorist principles.[1] Stripped of its subtlety, Skinnerian behaviorism states as its basic principle that, if an animal has a need, it will perform activities that in the past have satisfied this need. A first corollary to this principle is that organisms will attempt to avoid unpleasant experiences but will endure limited amounts of such experiences as a cost in emitting the behaviors that satisfy an overriding need. A second corollary is that organisms will continue emitting certain behaviors only as long as they continue to produce desired and expected effects. A third corollary of Skinnerian psychology emphasizes that, as needs are satisfied by a particular behavior, animals are less likely to emit the behavior. A fourth corollary states that, if in the recent past a behavior has brought rewards, and if these rewards suddenly stop, the organism will appear angry and gradually cease emitting the behavior that formerly satisfied its needs. A final corollary holds that, if an event has consistently occurred at the same time as a behavior that was rewarded or punished, the event becomes a stimulus and is likely to produce the behavior or its avoidance.

These principles were derived from behavioral psychologists' highly controlled observations of animals, whose needs could be inferred from deprivations imposed by the investigators. Although human needs are much more difficult to ascertain than those of laboratory pigeons and mice, and despite the fact that humans interact in groupings that defy experimental controls, Homans believed that the principles of operant psychology could be applied to the explanation of human behavior in both simple and complex groupings.

One of the most important adjustments of Skinnerian principles to fit the facts of human social organization involved the recognition that needs

---

[1]George C. Homans, *Social Behavior: Its Elementary Forms* (New York: Harcourt Brace Jovanovich, 1961; second edition in 1972).

are satisfied by other people and that people reward and punish one another. In contrast with Skinner's animals, which only indirectly interact with Skinner through the apparatus of the laboratory and which have little ability to reward Skinner (except perhaps to confirm his principles), humans constantly give and take, or exchange, rewards and punishments.

The conceptualization of human behavior as exchange of rewards (and punishments) among interacting individuals led Homans to incorporate, in altered form, the first principle of elementary economics: Humans rationally calculate the long-range consequences of their actions in a marketplace and attempt to maximize their material profits in their transactions. However, this basic economic assumption must be altered in four ways: (1) People do not always attempt to maximize profits; they seek only to make some profit in exchange relations. (2) Humans do not usually make either long-run or rational calculations in exchanges, for in everyday life, "the Theory of Games is good advice for human behavior but a poor description of it." (3) The things exchanged involve not only money but also other commodities, including approval, esteem, compliance, love, affection, and other less materialistic goods. (4) The marketplace is not a separate domain in human exchanges, for all interaction involves individuals exchanging rewards (and punishments) and seeking profits.

## The Basic Exchange Principles

In Table 22.1, Homans' last formulation of principles based on Skinnerian psychology is listed. Those actions that have brought people rewards are likely to be emitted again (Principle 1); the more similar a situation is to one that brought rewards, the more likely are people to emit behaviors to secure these rewards (Principle 2); and people pursue those behaviors that bring them the most valuable rewards (Principle 3).

Principle 4 indicates the condition under which the first three propositions fall into temporary abeyance. In accordance with the reinforcement principle of satiation or the economic law of marginal utility, humans eventually define activities that have been consistently rewarded as less valuable and begin to emit other activities in search of different rewards (again, however, in accordance with the principles enumerated in Propositions 1 through 3).

Principle 5 introduces a more complicated set of conditions that qualify Propositions 1 through 4. From Skinner's observation that pigeons reveal "anger" and "frustration" when they do not receive an expected reward, Homans reasoned that humans will probably reveal the same behavior. This principle is close to Skinner's principle but with the obvious addition of elements from the black box of human cognition—expectations for rewards, emotions like anger and satisfaction, and states of approval. Interestingly, this aggression/approval proposition was a reformulaton in Skinnerian vocabulary (but not substance) of an earlier principle in the first edition of *Social Behavior: Its Elementary Forms*, where Homans postulated a law of distributive justice, which emphasized that individuals calculate the extent to which their rewards less costs and investments (accumulated costs) are seen as fair and just by individuals; in addition, when these justice calculations lead persons to see that their rewards are not proportional to their costs and investments compared to others, they become *angry*; conversely, when they see rewards as fair they experience *satisfaction*. Ironically, it is this first formulation on what Homans' termed *distributive justice* was to have more influence on sociological exchange theories, perhaps because there has been a long tradition within philosophy and jurisprudence about justice. In either case, Homans has entered the black box because his actors now think and feel, whereas observable Skinner would never have entertained such notions in his insistence that only stimuli and overt behavior can be measured, and hence, only stimulus-response can be theorized.

**Table 22.1**  Homans' Exchange Propositions

---

1. **Success Proposition**: For all actions taken by persons, the more often a particular action of a person is rewarded, the more likely the person is to perform that action.

2. **Stimulus Proposition**: If in the past the occurrence of a particular stimulus or set of stimuli has been the occasion on which a person's action has been rewarded, then, the more similar the present stimuli are to the past ones, the more likely the person is to perform the action or some similar action now.

3. **Value Proposition**: The more valuable to a person the result of his or her action is, the more likely he or she is to perform the action.

4. **Deprivation/Satiation Proposition**: The more often in the recent past a person has received a particular reward, the less valuable any further unit of that reward becomes for that person.

5. **Aggression/Approval Propositions**
   A. When a person's action does not receive the reward expected or receives punishment that was not expected, he or she will be angry and become more likely to perform aggressive behavior. The results of such behavior become more valuable to that person.

   B. When a person's action receives the reward expected, especially greater reward than expected, or does not receive punishment expected, he or she will be pleased and become more likely to perform approving behavior. The results of such behavior become more valuable to that person.

6. **Rationality Proposition**: In choosing between alternative actions, a person will choose that one for which, as perceived by him or her at the time, the value of the result, multiplied by the probability of getting that result, is greater.

In addition to Principles 1 through 5, Homans introduces a *rationality proposition*, which summarizes the stimulus, success, and value propositions. I have placed this proposition in Table 22.1 because it is so prominent in Homans' actual construction of illustrative deductive explanations. To translate the somewhat awkward vocabulary of Principle 6 as Homans wrote it: People make calculations about various alternative lines of action. They perceive or calculate the value of the rewards that might be yielded by various actions. But they also temper this calculation through perceptions of how probable the receipt of rewards will be. Low probability of receiving highly valued rewards would lower their reward potential. Conversely, high probability of receiving a lower-valued reward increases their overall reward potential. This relationship can be stated by the following formula:

$$Action = Value \times Probability$$

People are, Homans asserted, rational in the sense that they are likely to emit that behavior, or action, among alternatives in which value on the right side of the equation is largest. For example, if $Action_1$ is highly valued (say, at a level of 10), but the probability of getting it by emitting $Action_1$ is low (.20 or 20%), and if $Action_2$ is less valued (say, 5), but the probability of receiving it is greater (.50) than $Action_1$, then the actor will emit $Action_2$ (because $10 \times .20 = 2$ will yield less reward than $5 \times .50 = 2.5$).

Homans believed that these basic principles or laws explain, in the sense of deductive explanation, patterns of human organization. Indeed, he often saw these principles as *axioms*. As is obvious, they are psychological in nature. Moreover, these psychological axioms constitute from Homans' viewpoint the only general sociological propositions, because "there are no general sociological propositions that hold good of all societies or social groups as such." Yet, Homans did not say that there cannot be sociological laws. On the contrary, these laws are the very propositions that are to be deduced from the psychological axioms. Thus, sociological propositions will be conspicuous in the deductive system emanating from the psychological principles. The basic form of deductive systems[23] that Homans sought, but never really developed, can be illustrated in Figure 22.1.

---

[2]Homans championed this conception of theory in a large number of works; see, for example, Homans, *Social Behavior* (cited in note 1); Homans, *The Nature of Social Science* (New York: Harcourt, Brace & World, 1967); "Fundamental Social Processes," in *Sociology*, ed. N. J. Smelser (New York: Wiley, 1967), pp. 27–78; "Contemporary Theory in Sociology," in *Handbook of Modern Sociology*, ed. R. E. L. Faris (Skokie, IL: Rand McNally, 1964), pp. 251–77; and "Bringing Men Back In," *American Sociological Review* 29 (December 1964): pp. 809–18. For an early statement of his position, see George C. Homans, "Social Behavior as Exchange," *American Journal of Sociology* 63 (August 1958): pp. 597–606; "Discovery and the Discovered in Social Theory," *Humboldt Journal of Social Relations* 7 (Fall-Winter 1979–1980): pp. 89–102.

[3]The previous uses Homans' vocabulary, but as emphasized in Chapter 1, axiomatic theory for sociology is unrealistic, and Homans' deductions were so loose and descriptive as to fall far short any resembling a real axiomatic explanation.

**Figure 22.1**   Forms of Homans' Deductive Explanations

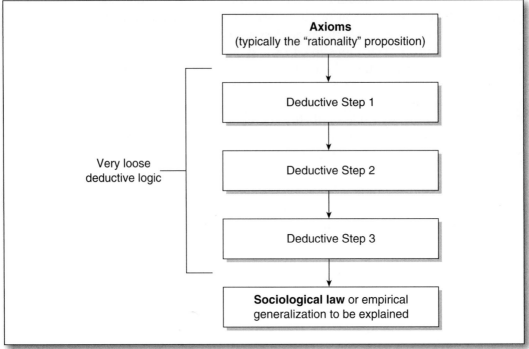

Homans argued that the goal of science is always to be reductive, wherever possible. Thus, if sociological principles can be deduced from psychological ones, this is nothing more than one of the goals of science. Moreover, reduction should not stop there; the principles of psychology or behavior should, to some degree, be deducible from biology, and so on through chemistry and physics. Homans would often deride sociologists for their over-concern with reduction, arguing in essence that if they had some laws, they would worry less about whether or not they are reducible to the principles of behavior. Yet, for all of his bravado on these points, Homans never pursued the most obvious issue: develop principles of sociology. He had, in some ways, the cart before the horse because, if the goal is to use psychological axioms about behavior to explain sociological principles about interaction and social organization, it is necessary to have some sociological principles. Of course, there were laws in sociology, but he never used these in "demonstrations" of his deductive logic, which in the end would argue that people do things because they are rewarding; thus, any law of sociology can be "deduced" from one or more of his axioms presented in Table 22.1. This epistemological argument never went very far, but the substance of Homans' behavioristic exchange theory did.

## From Behavior to Macrostructure

Homans provided many illustrations of how behavioristic principles can explain research findings in social psychology, but there was little rigor in them. They were simply statements stacked on top of each other, typically with the rationality proposition at the top. The logic of deduction was simply words rather that any formal or precise calculus of deduction. Yet, one of the most interesting chapters in *Social Behavior*,[4] comes at the end of the book where Homans offered a view of how exchange processes can explain population-level and societal-level social phenomena. Phrased as a *last orgy* in his explication, Homans addressed the issue of how societies and civilizations are, ultimately, built from the face-to-face exchanges of people in groups. His scenario went something like this:

> At points in history, some people have the capital to reinforce or provide rewards for others, whether it comes from their possessing a surplus of food, money, a moral code, or valued leadership qualities. With such capital, institutional elaboration can occur, because some can invest their capital by trying to induce others (through rewards or threats of punishments) to engage in novel activities.

These new activities can involve an "intermeshing of the behavior of a large number of persons in a more complicated or roundabout way than has hitherto been the custom." Whether this investment involves conquering territory and organizing a kingdom or creating a new form of business organization, those making the investment must have the resources—whether it be an army to threaten punishment, a charismatic personality to morally persuade followers, or the ability to provide for people's subsistence needs—to keep those so organized in a situation where they derive some profit. At some point in this process, such organizations can become more efficient and hence rewarding to all when the rewards are clearly specified as generalized reinforcers, such as money, and when the activities expended to get their rewards are more clearly specified, such as when explicit norms and rules emerge. In turn, this increased efficiency allows greater organization of activities. This new efficiency increases the likelihood that generalized reinforcers and explicit norms will be used to regulate exchange relations and hence increase the profits to those involved. Eventually the exchange networks involving generalized reinforcers and an increasingly complex body of rules require differentiation of subunits—such as a legal and banking system—that can maintain the stability of the generalized reinforcers and the integrity of the norms.

From this kind of exchange process, social organization—whether at a societal, group, organizational, or institutional level—is constructed. The emergence of most patterns of organization is frequently buried in the recesses of history, but such emergence is typified by these accelerating processes: (1) People with capital (reward capacity) invest in creating more complex social relations that increase their rewards and allow those whose activities are organized to realize a profit. (2) With increased rewards, these people can invest in more complex patterns of organization. (3) Increasingly complex patterns of organization require, first of all, the use of generalized reinforcers and then the codification of norms to regulate activity. (4) With

---

[4]Homans, *Social Behavior* (cited note 1), Chap. 16.

**Figure 22.2**   Homan's Image of Social Organization

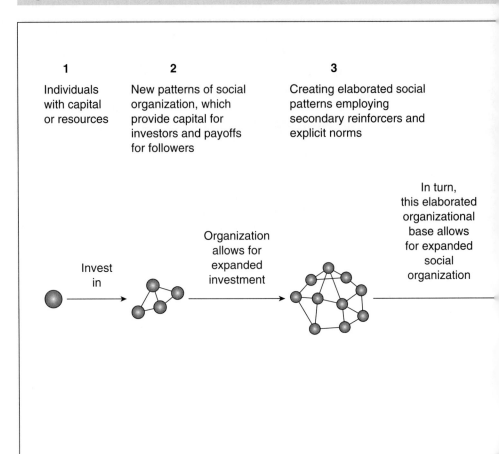

**1**

Individuals
with capital
or resources

**2**

New patterns of social
organization, which
provide capital for
investors and payoffs
for followers

**3**

Creating elaborated social
patterns employing
secondary reinforcers and
explicit norms

In turn,
this elaborated
organizational
base allows
for expanded
social
organization

Organization
allows for
expanded
investment

Invest
in

this organizational base, it then becomes possible to elaborate further the pattern of organization, creating the necessity for differentiation of subunits that ensure the stability of the generalized reinforcers and the integrity of norms. (5) With this differentiation, it is possible to expand even further the networks of interaction, because there are standardized means for rewarding activities and codifying new norms as well as for enforcing old rules.

However, these complex patterns of social organization employing formal rules, and secondary or generalized reinforcers can never cease to meet the more primary needs of individuals. Institutions first emerged to meet these needs, and no matter how complex institutional arrangements become and how many norms and formal rules are elaborated, these extended interaction networks must ultimately reinforce humans' more primary needs. When these arrangements cease meeting the primary needs from which they ultimately sprang, an

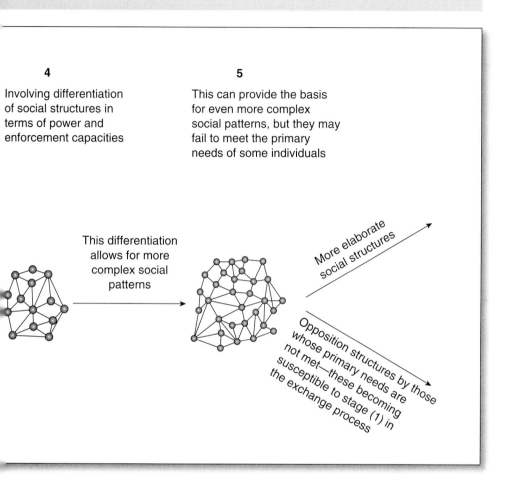

**4**

Involving differentiation of social structures in terms of power and enforcement capacities

**5**

This can provide the basis for even more complex social patterns, but they may fail to meet the primary needs of some individuals

This differentiation allows for more complex social patterns

More elaborate social structures

Opposition structures by those whose primary needs are not met—these becoming susceptible to stage (1) in the exchange process

institution is vulnerable and apt to collapse if alternative actions, which can provide primary rewards, present themselves as a possibility. In this situation, low- or high-status persons—those who have little to lose by nonconformity to existing prescriptions—will break from established ways to present to others a more rewarding alternative. Institutions might continue to extract conformity for a period, but they will cease to do so when they lose the capacity to provide primary rewards.

Thus, complex institutional arrangements must ultimately be satisfying to individuals, not simply because of the weight of culture or norms but because they are constructed to serve people:

> Institutions do not keep going just because they are enshrined in norms, and it seems extraordinary that anyone should ever talk as if

they did. They keep going because they have payoffs, ultimately payoffs for individuals. Nor is society a perpetual-motion machine, supplying its own fuel. It cannot keep itself going by planting in the young a desire for these goods and only those goods that it happens to be able to provide. It must provide goods that men (and presumably women) find rewarding not simply because they are sharers in a particular culture but because they are men.[5]

That institutions of society must also meet primary needs sets the stage for a continual conflict between institutional elaboration and the primary needs of humans. As one form of institutional elaboration meets one set of needs, it can deprive people of other important rewards—opening the way for deviation and innovation by those presenting the alternative rewards that have been suppressed by dominant institutional arrangements. In turn, the new institutional elaborations that can ensue from innovators who have the capital to reward others will suppress other needs, which, through processes similar to its inception, will set off another process of institutional elaboration.

In sum, this sketch of how social organization is linked to elementary processes of exchange represents an interesting perspective for analyzing how patterns of social organization are built, maintained, altered, and broken down. Moreover, the broad contours of this kind of argument were repeated by other exchange theorists as they applied the principles of behaviorism or classical economics to explanations of larger-scale patterns of human organization. Yet, little of Homans' explicit imagery was retained in later theories, although the effort to move from micro principles about behavior of individuals to macro-level patterns of organization remained a critical concern in exchange theories.

# Peter M. Blau's Dialectical Exchange Theory

A few years after George C. Homans' behavioristic approach appeared, another leading sociological theorist—Peter M. Blau—explored exchange theory.[6] Though he accepted the behavioristic underpinnings of exchange

---

[5]Ibid., p. 366

[6]Peter M. Blau's major exchange work is *Exchange and Power in Social Life* (New York: Wiley, 1964). This formal and expanded statement on his exchange perspective was anticipated in earlier works. For example, see Peter M. Blau, "A Theory of Social Integration," *American Journal of Sociology* 65 (May 1960): pp. 545–56; "Interaction: Social Exchange," in *International Encyclopedia of the Social Sciences*, vol. 7 (New York: Macmillan, 1968), pp. 452–58; and Peter M. Blau, *The Dynamics of Bureaucracy*, 1st and 2nd ed. (Chicago: University of Chicago Press, 1955, 1963). It is of interest to note that George C. Homans in *Social Behavior: Its Elementary Forms* (cited in note 1) makes frequent reference to the data summarized in this latter work.

as a basic social process, Blau recognized that sociological theory had to move beyond simplistic behavioristic conceptualizations of human behavior. Similarly, crude views of humans as wholly rational had to be modified to fit the realities of human behavior. In the end, he developed a dialectical approach, emphasizing that within the strains toward integration arising from exchange are forces of opposition and potential conflict. Moreover, his analysis has a Simmelian thrust because, much like Georg Simmel, Blau tried to discover the form of exchange processes at both the micro and macro levels, and in so doing, he sought to highlight what was common to exchanges among individuals as well as among collective units of organization.

## The Basic Exchange Principles

Although Blau never listed his principles in a formal inventory, general principles are nonetheless easy to extract from his discursive discussion. In Table 22.2, the basic principles are summarized. Proposition 1, which can be termed the *rationality principle*, states that the frequency of rewards and the value of these rewards increase the likelihood that actions to secure these rewards will be emitted by persons and collective actors. Propositions 2-A and 2-B on *reciprocity* borrow from Bronislaw Malinowski's and Claude Lévi-Strauss' initial discussion as reinterpreted by Alvin Gouldner.[7] Blau postulated that "the need to reciprocate for benefits received in order to continue receiving them serves as a 'starting mechanism' of social interaction."[8] Equally important, once exchanges have occurred, a "fundamental and ubiquitous norm of reciprocity" emerges to regulate subsequent exchanges. Thus, inherent in the exchange process per se is a principle of reciprocity. Over time, and as the conditions of Principle 1 are met, a social norm of reciprocity, whose violation brings about social disapproval and other negative sanctions, emerges in exchange relations.

Blau recognized that people establish expectations about what level of reward particular exchange relations should yield and that these expectations are normatively regulated. These norms are termed *norms of fair exchange* because they determine what the proportion of rewards to costs should be in a given exchange relation. Blau also asserted that aggression is forthcoming when these norms of fair exchange are violated. These ideas are incorporated into Principles 3-A and 3-B and are termed the *justice principles*.[9] Following economists' analyses of transactions in the

---

[7]Alvin W. Gouldner, "The Norm of Reciprocity," *American Sociological Review* 25 (April 1960): pp. 161–78.

[8]Blau, *Exchange and Power* (cited in note 6), p. 92.

[9]See Peter M. Blau, "Justice in Social Exchange," in *Institutions and Social Exchange: The Sociologies of Talcott Parsons and George C. Homans*, eds. H. Turk and R. L. Simpson (Indianapolis: Bobbs-Merrill, 1971), pp. 56–68. See also Blau, *Exchange and Power* (cited in note 6), pp. 156–57.

**Table 22.2** Blau's Implicit Exchange Principles

1. **Rationality Principle**: The more profit people expect from one another in emitting a particular activity, the more likely they are to emit that activity.

2. **Reciprocity Principles**

    A. The more people have exchanged rewards with one another, the more likely are reciprocal obligations to emerge and guide subsequent exchanges among these people.

    B. The more the reciprocal obligations of an exchange relationship are violated, the more disposed deprived parties are to sanction negatively those violating the norm of reciprocity.

3. **Justice Principles**

    A. The more exchange relations have been established, the more likely they are to be governed by norms of fair exchange.

    B. The less norms of fairness are realized in an exchange, the more disposed deprived parties are to sanction negatively those violating the norms.

4. **Marginal Utility Principle**: The more expected rewards have been forthcoming from the emission of a particular activity, the less valuable the activity is and the less likely its emission is.

5. **Imbalance Principle**: The more stabilized and balanced some exchange relations are among social units, the more likely are other exchange relations to become imbalanced and unstable.

marketplace, Blau introduced a principle on *marginal utility* (Proposition 4). The more a person has received a reward, the more satiated he or she is with that reward and the less valuable are further increments of the reward.[10] Proposition 5 on imbalance completes the listing of Blau's abstract laws. For Blau, as for all exchange theorists, established exchange relations are seen to involve costs or alternative rewards foregone. Most actors must engage in more than one exchange relation, and so the balance and stabilization of one exchange relation is likely to create imbalance and strain in other necessary exchange relations. Blau believed that social life is thus filled with dilemmas in which people must successively trade off stability and balance in one exchange relation for strain in others as they attempt to cope with the variety of relations that they must maintain.

---

[10]Blau, *Exchange and Power* (cited in note 6), p. 90.

## Elementary Systems of Exchange

Blau initiated his discussion of elementary exchange processes with the assumption that people enter into social exchange because they perceive the possibility of deriving rewards (Principle 1). Blau labeled this perception *social attraction* and postulated that, unless relationships involve such attraction, they are not relationships of exchange. In entering an exchange relationship, each actor assumes the perspective of another and thereby derives some perception of the other's needs. Actors then manipulate their presentation of self to convince one another that they have the valued qualities that others should desire. In adjusting role behaviors in an effort to impress others with the resources that they have to offer, people operate under the principle of reciprocity, for by indicating that one possesses valued qualities, each person is attempting to establish a claim on others for the receipt of rewards from them. All exchange operates under the presumption that people who bestow rewards will receive rewards in turn as payment for value received.

Individuals attempt to impress one another through competition in which they reveal the rewards that they have to offer in an effort to force others, in accordance with the norm of reciprocity, to reciprocate with an even more valuable reward. Social life is thus rife with people's competitive efforts to impress one another and thereby extract valuable rewards. But, as interaction proceeds, it inevitably becomes evident to the parties in an exchange that some people have more valued resources to offer than others, which puts those individuals in a unique position to extract rewards from all others who value the resources that they have to offer.

At this point in exchange relations, groups of individuals become differentiated by the resources that their members possess and the kinds of reciprocal demands that they can make on others. Blau then asked an analytical question: What generic types or classes of rewards can those with resources extract in return for bestowing their valued resources on others? Blau conceptualized four general classes of such rewards: *money, social approval, esteem or respect,* and *compliance.*

Blau first ranked these generalized reinforcers by their value in exchange relations among individuals. In most social relations, money is an inappropriate reward and hence is the least valuable. Social approval is an appropriate reward, but for most humans, it is not very valuable, thus forcing those who derive valued services to offer with great frequency more valuable rewards like esteem or respect to those providing valued services. In many situations, the services offered can command no more than respect and esteem from others. At times, however, the services offered are sufficiently valuable to require those receiving them to offer, in accordance with the principles of reciprocity and justice, the most valuable class of rewards—compliance with one's requests.

When people can extract compliance in an exchange relationship, they have *power.* They have the capacity to withhold rewarding services and thereby punish or inflict heavy costs on those who might not comply. To conceptualize the degree of power possessed by individuals, Blau formulated four general propositions that determine the capacity of powerful individuals to extract compliance. These are listed and reformulated in Table 22.3.[11]

These four propositions list the conditions leading to differentiation of members in social groups by their power. To the extent that group members cannot supply some services in return, seek alternative rewards, potentially use physical force, or do without certain valuable services, individuals who provide valuable services will be able to extract esteem and approval from group members; if group members value these resources highly, those who provide them can use power and command compliance. Naturally, as Blau emphasized, most social groups reveal complex patterns of differentiation of power, prestige, and patterns of approval, but of particular interest to him are the dynamics involved in generating power, authority, and opposition. Blau believed that, power differentials in groups create two contradictory forces: (1) strains toward integration and (2) strains toward opposition and conflict.

## Strains Toward Integration

Differences in power inevitably create the potential for conflict. However, such potential is frequently suspended by a series of forces promoting the conversion of power into authority, in which subordinates accept as legitimate the leaders' demands for compliance. Principles 2 and 3 in Table 22.4 denote two processes fostering such group integration: Exchange relations always operate under the presumption of reciprocity and justice, forcing

**Table 22.3** Conditions for Gaining Power in Social Exchange

1. The fewer services people can supply in return for the receipt of particularly valued services, the more those providing these particularly valued services can extract compliance.

2. The fewer alternative sources of rewards people have, the more those proving valuable services can extract compliance.

3. The less those receiving valuable services from particular individuals can employ physical force and coercion, the more those providing the services can extract compliance.

4. The less those receiving the valuable services can do without them, the more those providing the services can extract compliance.

[11]Ibid.

those deriving valued services to provide other rewards in payment. In providing these rewards, subordinates are guided by norms of fair exchange, in which the costs that they incur in offering compliance are to be proportional to the value of the services that they receive from leaders. Thus, to the extent that actors engage in exchanges with leaders and to the degree that the services provided by leaders are highly valued, subordination must be accepted as legitimate in accordance with the norms of reciprocity and fairness that emerge in all exchanges.

Under these conditions, groups elaborate additional norms specifying just how exchanges with leaders are to be conducted to regularize the requirements for reciprocity and to maintain fair rates of exchange. Leaders who conform to these emergent norms can usually assure themselves that their leadership will be considered legitimate. Blau emphasized that, if leaders abide by the norms regulating exchange of their services for compliance, norms carrying negative sanctions typically emerge among subordinates

**Table 22.4** Blau's Propositions on Exchange Conflict

1. The probability of opposition to those with power increases when exchange relations between super- and subordinates become imbalanced, with imbalance increasing when

    A. Norms of reciprocity are violated by the superordinates

    B. Norms of fair exchange are violated by superordinates

2. The probability of opposition increases as the sense of deprivation among subordinates escalates, with this sense of deprivation increasing when subordinates can experience collectively their sense of deprivation. Such collective experience increases when

    A. Subordinates are ecologically and spatially concentrated

    B. Subordinates can communicate with one another

3. The more subordinates can collectively experience deprivations in exchange relations with superordinates, the more likely are they to codify ideologically their deprivations and the more likely are they to oppose those with power.

4. The more deprivations of subordinates are ideologically codified, the greater is their sense of solidarity and the more likely are they to oppose those with power.

5. The greater the sense of solidarity is among subordinates, the more they can define their opposition as a noble and worthy cause and the more likely they are to oppose those with power.

6. The greater is the sense of ideological solidarity, the more likely are subordinates to view opposition as an end in itself and the more likely are they to oppose those with power.

stressing the need for compliance to leaders' requests. Through this process, subordinates exercise considerable social control over one another's actions and thereby promote the integration of super- and subordinate segments of groupings.

Authority, therefore, "rests on the common norms in a collectivity of subordinates that constrain its individual members to conform to the orders of a superior."[12] In many patterns of social organization, these norms simply emerge from the competitive exchanges among collective groups of actors. Frequently, however, for such normative agreements to be struck, participants in an exchange must be socialized into a common set of values that define not only what constitutes fair exchange in a given situation but also the way such exchange should be institutionalized into norms for both leaders and subordinates. Although it is quite possible for actors to arrive at normative consensus in the course of the exchange process itself, an initial set of common values facilitates the legitimization of power. Actors can now enter into exchanges with a common definition of the situation, which can provide a general framework for the normative regulation of emerging power differentials. Without common values, the competition for power is likely to be severe. In the absence of guidelines about reciprocity and fair exchange, considerable strain and tension will persist as definitions of these are worked out. For Blau, legitimization "entails not merely tolerant approval but active confirmation and promotion of social patterns by common values, either preexisting ones or those that emerge in a collectivity in the course of social interaction."[13]

With the legitimization of power through the normative regulation of interaction, as confirmed by common values, the structure of collective organization is altered. One of the most evident changes is the decline in interpersonal competition, for now actors' presentations of self can shift from a concern about impressing others with their valuable qualities to an emphasis on confirming their status as loyal group members. Subordinates accept their status and manipulate their role behaviors to ensure that they receive social approval from their peers as a reward for conformity to group norms. Leaders can typically assume a lower profile because they no longer must demonstrate their superior qualities in each and every encounter with subordinates—especially because norms now define when and how they should extract conformity and esteem for providing their valued services. Thus, with the legitimization of power as authority, the interactive processes (involving the way group members define the situation and present themselves to others) undergo a dramatic change, reducing the degree of competition and thereby fostering group integration.

With these events, the amount of direct interaction between leaders and subordinates usually declines, because power and ranking no longer must be constantly negotiated. This decline in direct interaction marks the

---

[12]Ibid., p. 208.

[13]Ibid., p. 221.

formation of distinct subgroupings as members interact with those of their own social rank, avoiding the costs of interacting with either their inferiors or their superiors. In interacting primarily among themselves, subordinates avoid the high costs of interacting with leaders, and although social approval from their peers is not a particularly valuable reward, it can be extracted with comparatively few costs—thus allowing a sufficient profit. Conversely, leaders can avoid the high costs (of time and energy) of constantly compet-ing and negotiating with inferiors regarding when and how compliance and esteem are to be bestowed on them. Instead, by having relatively limited and well-defined contact with subordinates, they can derive the high rewards that come from compliance and esteem without incurring excessive costs in interacting with subordinates—thereby allowing for a profit.

## Strains Toward Opposition

Thus far, Blau's exchange perspective is decidedly functional. Social exchange processes—attraction, competition, differentiation, and integration—are analyzed by how they contribute to creating a legitimated set of normatively regulated relations. Yet, Blau was keenly aware that social organization is always rife with conflict and opposition, creating an inevi-table dialectic between integration and opposition in social structures.

Blau's exchange principles, summarized in Table 22.4, allow the concep-tualization of these strains for opposition and conflict. As Principle 2-B on reciprocity documents, the failure to receive expected rewards in return for various activities leads actors to attempt to apply negative sanctions that, when ineffective, can drive people to violent retaliation against those who have denied them an expected reward. Such retaliation is intensified by the dynamics summarized in Principle 3-B on justice and fair exchange, because when those in power violate such norms, they inflict excessive costs on sub-ordinates, creating a situation that, at a minimum, leads to attempts to sanc-tion negatively and, at most, to retaliation. Finally, Principle 5 on the inevitable imbalances emerging from multiple exchange relations emphasizes that to balance relations in one exchange context by meeting reciprocal obligations and conforming to norms of fairness is to put other relations into imbal-ance. Thus, the imbalances potentially encourage a cyclical process in which actors seek to balance previously unbalanced relations and thereby throw into imbalance currently balanced exchanges. In turn, exchange relations that are thrown into imbalance violate the norms of reciprocity and fair exchange, thus causing attempts at negative sanctioning and, under some conditions, retaliation.

Blau hypothesizes that the more imbalanced exchange relations are experienced collectively, the greater is the sense of deprivation and the greater is the potential for opposition. Although he did not explicitly state the case, Blau appears to argue that increasing ideological codifica-tion of deprivations, the formation of group solidarity, and the emer-gence of conflict as a way of life—that is, members' emotional involvement in and commitment to opposition to those with power—will increase the intensity of the opposition. These propositions offered a suggestive lead for conceptualizing inherent processes of opposition in exchange relations.[14]

## Macrostructural Exchange Systems

Although the general processes of attraction, competition, differentiation, integration, and opposition are evident in the exchange among units forming macrostructures, Blau saw several fundamental differences between these exchanges and those among microstructures.

1. In complex exchanges among macrostructures, the significance of shared values increases, for through such values indirect exchanges among macrostructures are mediated.

2. Exchange networks among macrostructures are typically institutionalized. Although spontaneous exchange is a ubiquitous feature of social life, there are usually well-established historical arrangements that circumscribe the basic exchange processes of attraction, competition, differentiation, integration, and even opposition among collective units.

3. Macrostructures are themselves the product of more elementary exchange processes, so the analysis of macrostructures requires the analysis of more than one level of social organization.[15]

**Mediating Values.** Blau believed that the interpersonal attraction of elementary exchange among individuals is replaced by shared values at the macro level. These values can be conceptualized as media of social transactions in that they provide a common set of standards for conducting the complex chains of indirect exchanges among social structures and their individual members. Such values are viewed by Blau as providing effective mediation of complex exchanges because the individual members of social structures have usually been socialized into a set of common values, leading them to accept these values as appropriate. Furthermore, when coupled with codification into laws and enforcement procedures by those groups and organizations with power, shared values provide a means for mediating the complex and indirect exchanges among the macrostructures of large-scale systems. In mediating indirect exchanges among groups and

---

[14]Peter M. Blau, "Dialectical Sociology: Comments," *Sociological Inquiry* 42 (Spring 1972): p. 185. This article was written in reply to an attempt to document Blau's shift from a functional to a dialectical perspective; see Michael A. Weinstein and Deena Weinstein, "Blau's Dialectical Sociology," *Sociological Inquiry* 42 (Spring 1972): pp. 173–82.

[15]Blau, "Contrasting Theoretical Perspectives," in *The Micro-Macro Link*, eds. J. C. Alexander, B. Gisen, R. Münch, and N. J. Smelser. (Berkeley: University of California Press, 1987), pp. 253–311.

organizations, shared values provide standards for the calculation of (a) expected rewards, (b) reciprocity, and (c) fair exchange.

Thus, because individuals are not the units of complex exchanges, Blau emphasizes that, for complex patterns of social organization to emerge and persist, a *functional equivalent* of direct interpersonal attraction must exist. Values assume this function and ensure that exchange can proceed in accordance with the principles presented in Table 22.2. And even when complex exchanges do involve people, their interactions are frequently so protracted and indirect that one individual's rewards are contingent on others who are far removed, requiring that common values guide and regulate the exchanges.

**Institutionalization.** Whereas values facilitate processes of indirect exchange among diverse types of social units, institutionalization denotes those processes that regularize and stabilize complex exchange processes.[16] As people and various forms of collective organization become dependent on particular networks of indirect exchange for expected rewards, pressures for formalizing exchange networks through explicit norms increase. This formalization and regularization of complex exchange systems can be effective in three minimal conditions: (1) The formalized exchange networks must have profitable payoffs for most parties to the exchange. (2) Most individuals organized into collective units must have internalized through prior socialization the mediating values used to build exchange networks. And, (3) those units with power in the exchange system must receive a level of rewards that moves them to seek actively the formalization of rules governing exchange relations.

Institutions are historical products whose norms and underlying mediating values are handed down from one generation to another, thereby limiting and circumscribing the kinds of indirect exchange networks that can emerge. Institutions exert a kind of external constraint on individuals and various types of collective units, bending exchange processes to fit their prescriptions and proscriptions. Institutions thus represent sets of relatively stable and general norms regularizing different patterns of indirect and complex exchange relations among diverse social units.

Blau stresses that all institutionalized exchange systems reveal a counter-institutional component "consisting of those basic values and ideals that have not been realized and have not found expression in explicit institutional forms, and which are the ultimate source of social change."[17] To the extent that these values remain unrealized in institutionalized exchange relations, individuals who have internalized them will derive little payoff from existing institutional arrangements and will therefore feel deprived, seeking alternatives to dominant institutions. These unrealized values, even

---

[16]Blau, *Exchange and Power* (cited in note 6), pp. 273–80.

[17]Ibid., p. 279.

when codified into an opposition ideology advocating open revolution, usually contain at least some of the ideals and ultimate objectives legitimated by the prevailing culture. This indicates that institutional arrangements "contain the seeds of their potential destruction" by failing to meet all the expectations of reward raised by institutionalized values.

Blau never enumerated the conditions for mobilization of individuals into conflict groups, but his scheme explicitly denoted the source of conflict and change: counter-institutional values whose failure of realization by dominant institutional arrangements creates deprivations that can lead to conflict and change in social systems. Such tendencies for complex exchange systems to generate opposition can be explained by the basic principles of exchange. When certain mediating values are not institutionalized in a social system, exchange relations will not be viewed as reciprocated by those who have internalized these values.

Thus, in accordance with Blau's principles of reciprocity (see Table 22.2), these segments of a collectivity are more likely to feel deprived and to seek ways of retaliating against the dominant institutional arrangements, which, from the perspective dictated by their values, have failed to reciprocate. For those who have internalized values that are not institutionalized, it is also likely that perceptions of fair exchange have been violated, leading them, in accordance with the principles of justice, to attempt to sanction negatively those arrangements that violate alternative norms of fair exchange. Finally, in institutionalized exchange networks, the balancing of exchange relations with some segments of a collectivity inevitably creates imbalances in relations with other segments (the imbalance principle in Table 22.2), thereby violating norms of reciprocity and fairness and setting into motion forces of opposition.

Unlike direct interpersonal exchanges, however, opposition in complex exchange systems is between large collective units of organization, which, in their internal dynamics, reveal their own propensities for integration and opposition. This requires that the analysis of integration and opposition in complex exchange networks be attuned to various levels of social organization. Such analysis needs to show, in particular, how exchange processes among the units comprising macrostructures, whether for integration or for opposition, are partly influenced by the exchange processes occurring among their constituent substructures.

**Levels of Social Organization.** For Blau, the "dynamics of macrostructures rest on the manifold interdependences between the social forces within and among their substructures."[18] Blau simplifies the complex analytical tasks of examining the dynamics of substructures by positing that organized collectivities, especially formal organizations, are the most important substructures in the analysis of macrostructures. Thus, the theoretical analysis of complex exchange systems among macrostructures requires that primary

---

[18]Ibid., p. 284.

attention be drawn to the relations of attraction, competition, differentiation, integration, and opposition among various types of complex organizations. In emphasizing the pivotal significance of complex organizations, Blau posited a particular image of society that should guide the ultimate construction of sociological theory.

Organizations in a society must typically derive rewards from one another, thus creating a situation in which they are both attracted to, and in competition with, one another. Hierarchical differentiation between successful and less successful organizations operating in the same sphere emerges from this competition. Such differentiation usually creates strains toward specialization in different fields among less successful organizations as they seek new sources of resources. To provide effective means for integration, separate political organizations must also emerge to regulate their exchanges. These political organizations possess power and are viewed as legitimate only as long as they are considered by individuals and organizations to follow the dictates of shared cultural values. Typically, political organizations are charged with several objectives: (1) regulating complex networks of indirect exchange by the enactment of laws; (2) controlling through law competition among dominant organizations, thereby ensuring the latter of scarce resources; and (3) protecting existing exchange networks among organizations, especially those with power, from encroachment on these rewards by organizations opposing the current distribution of resources.

Blau, believed that differentiation and specialization occur among macrostructures because of the competition among organizations in a society. Although mediating values allow differentiation and specialization among organizations to occur, it is also necessary for separate political organizations to exist and regularize, through laws and the use of force, existing patterns of exchange among other organizations. Such political organizations will be viewed as legitimate as long as they normatively regulate exchanges that reflect the tenets of mediating values and protect the payoffs for most organizations, especially the most powerful. The existence of political authority inevitably encourages opposition movements, however, for now opposition groups have a clear target—the political organizations—against which to address their grievances. As long as political authority remains diffuse, opposition organizations can only compete unsuccessfully against various dominant organizations. With the legitimization of clear-cut political organizations charged with preserving current patterns of organization, opposition movements can concentrate their energies against one organization, the political system.

In addition to providing deprived groups with a target for their aggressions, political organizations inevitably must aggravate the deprivations of various segments of a population because political control involves exerting constraints and distributing resources unequally. Those segments of the population that must bear the brunt of such constraint and unequal distribution usually experience great deprivation of the principles of reciprocity and fair exchange, which, under various conditions, creates a movement against the existing political authorities. To the extent that this organized opposition forces redistribution of rewards, other segments of the population are likely to feel constrained and deprived, leading them to organize into an opposition movement. The organization of political authority ensures that, in accordance with the principle of imbalance, attempts to balance one set of exchange relations among organizations throw into imbalance other exchange relations, causing the formation of opposition organizations. Thus, built into the structure of political authority in a society are inherent forces of opposition that give society a dialectical and dynamic character.

### Blau's Image of Social Organization

Figure 22.3 summarizes Blau's view of social organization at the micro level and the macro-organizational level. Clearly, the same processes operate at both levels of exchange: (1) social attraction, (2) exchange of rewards, (3) competition for power, (4) differentiation, (5) strains toward integration, and (6) strains toward opposition. Thus, the Simmelian thrust of Blau's effort is clear because he sees the basic form of exchange as much the same, regardless of whether the units involved in the exchange are individuals or collective units of organization. There are, of course, some differences between exchange among individuals and organizational units, and these are noted across the bottom of the figure.

# Richard Emerson's Power-Dependence Theory of Exchange

In the early 1960s, Richard M. Emerson followed Georg Simmel's lead in seeking a formal sociology of basic exchange processes—much as Blau had sought to do. In essence, Emerson asked this: Could exchange among individual and collective actors be understood by the same basic principles? Emerson provided a creative answer to this question by synthesizing behaviorist psychology and sociological network analysis. The psychology gave him the driving force behind exchanges, whereas the network sociology allowed him to conceptualize *the form of social relations* among both individual and collective actors in the same terms. What emerged was exchange network analysis that, after Emerson's early death, was carried forward by colleagues and students.

Emerson borrowed the basic ideas of behaviorist psychology, but unlike many working in this tradition, he became more concerned with the form of relationships among the actors rather than the properties and characteristics

**Figure 22.3** Blau's Image of Social Organization

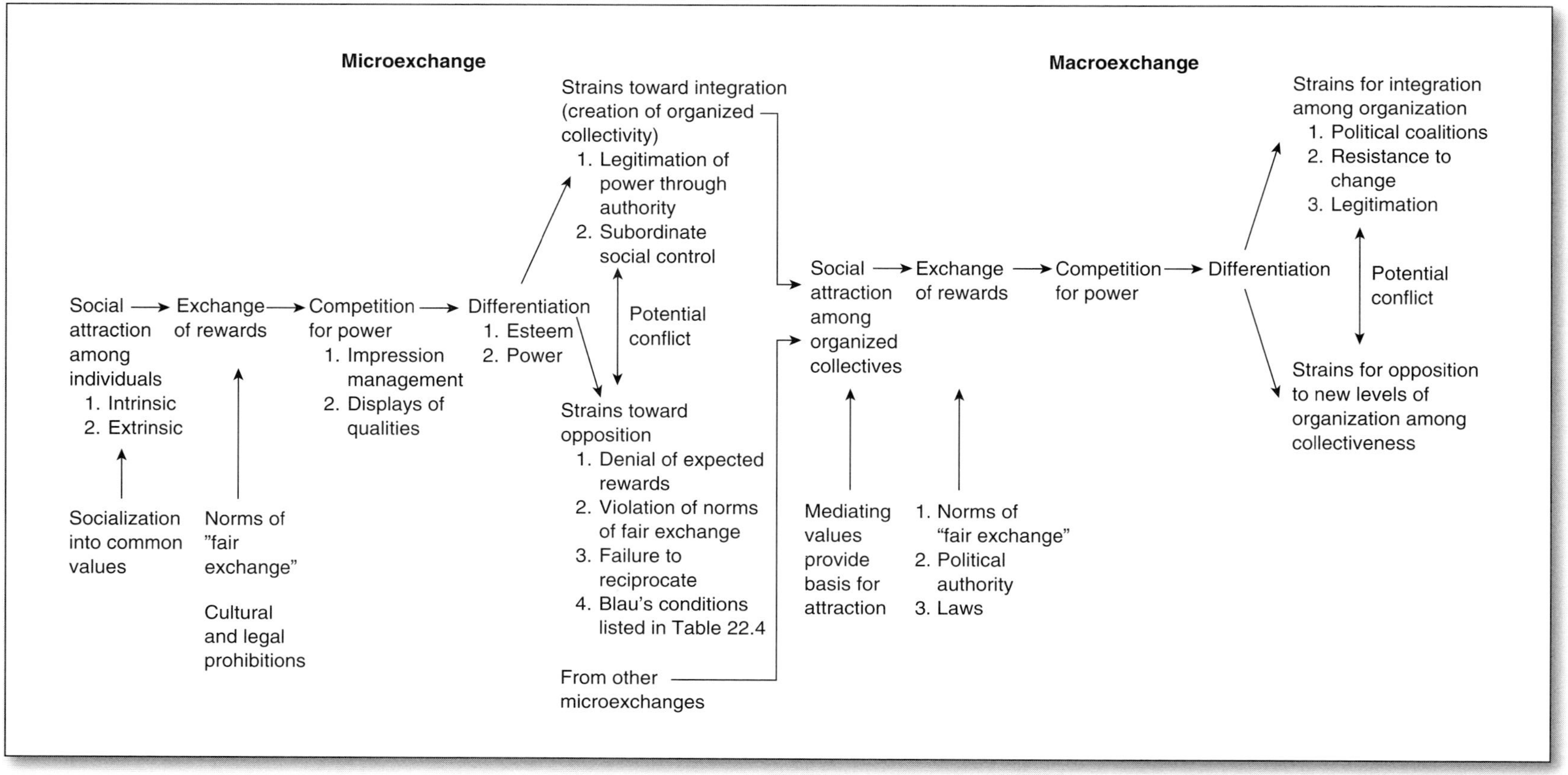

of the actors themselves.[19] This simple shift in emphasis profoundly affected how he built his exchange theory. The most significant departure from earlier exchange theories was that concern with why actors entered an exchange relationship in the first place given their values and preferences[20] was replaced by an emphasis on the existing exchange relationship and what is likely to transpire in this relationship in the future. Emerson believed that if an exchange relationship exists, this means that actors are willing to exchange valued resources, and the goal of theory is not so much to understand how this relationship originally came about but, instead, what will happen to it over time. Thus, the existing exchange relationship between actors becomes the unit of sociological analysis, not the actors themselves. In Emerson's eye, then, social structure is composed of exchanges among actors seeking to enhance the value of their resources. Thus behaviorism, which posited a dynamic but atomized actor, was blended with network sociology, which conceptualized structure without dynamic actors.

## The Core Ideas

The key dynamics in Emerson's theory are (1) *power*, (2) *power use*, and (3) *balancing*.[21] Actors have *power* to the extent that others depend on them for resources; hence, the power of Actor *A* over Actor *B* is determined by the dependence of *B* on *A* for a resource that *B* values, and vice versa. *Dependence*, which is the ultimate source of power in Emerson's scheme, is determined by the degree to which (a) resources sought from other actors are highly valued and (b) alternatives for these resources are few or too costly to pursue. Under these conditions, where *B* values *A*'s resources and

---

[19]Emerson's perspective is best stated in his "Exchange Theory, Part I: A Psychological Basis for Social Exchange" and "Exchange Theory, Part II: Exchange Relations and Network Structures," in *Sociological Theories in Progress*, eds. J. Berger, M. Zelditch, and B. Anderson (New York: Houghton Mifflin, 1972), pp. 38–87. Earlier empirical work that provided the initial impetus to, or the empirical support of, this theoretical perspective includes "Power-Dependence Relations," *American Sociological Review* 17 (February 1962): pp. 31–41; "Power-Dependence Relations: Two Experiments," *Sociometry* 27 (September 1964): pp. 282–98; John F. Stolte and Richard M. Emerson, "Structural Inequality: Position and Power in Network Structures," in *Behavioral Theory in Sociology*, ed. R. Hamblin (New Brunswick, NJ: Transaction Books, 1977). Other more conceptual works include "Operant Psychology and Exchange Theory," in *Behavioral Sociology*, eds. R. Burgess and D. Bushell (New York: Columbia University Press, 1969), and "Social Exchange Theory," in *Annual Review of Sociology*, eds. A. Inkeles and N. Smelser, vol. 2 (1976), pp. 335–62.

[20]Curiously, Emerson returned to this question in his last article. See Richard M. Emerson, "Toward a Theory of Value in Social Exchange," in *Social Exchange Theory*, ed. Karen S. Cook (Newbury Park, CA: Sage, 1987), pp. 11–46. See, in the same volume, Jonathan H. Turner's critique of this shift in Emerson's thought: "Social Exchange Theory: Future Directions," pp. 223–39.

[21]Karen S. Cook, Richard M. Emerson, Mary R. Gilmore, and Toshio Yamagishi, "The Distribution of Power in Exchange Networks," *American Journal of Sociology* 87 (1983): pp. 275–305.

where no attractive alternatives are available, the *B*'s dependence on *A* is high; hence, the power of *A* over *B* is high. Conversely, where *B* has resources that *A* values and where alternatives for *A* are limited, *B* has power over *A*. Thus, both actors can reveal a high degree of mutual dependence, giving each *absolute power* over the other and, thereby, increasing *structural cohesion* because of the high amounts of *total* or *average power* in the exchange relationship.

When one actor has more power than an exchange partner, however, this actor will engage in *power use* and exploit its exchange partner's dependence to secure additional resources or to reduce the costs it must incur in getting resources from this dependent partner. If *A* has power over *B* because of *B*'s dependency on *A*, then *A* has the *power advantage* and will use it.

Such relations are *power imbalanced*, and Emerson felt that imbalance and power use would activate what he termed *balancing* operations. In a situation where *A* has a power advantage over *B*, *B* has four options: (1) *B* can value less the resources provided by *A*; (2) *B* can find alternative sources for the resources provided by *A*; (3) *B* can increase the value of the resources it provides *A*; and (4) *B* can find ways to reduce *A*'s alternatives for the resources that *B* provides. All these balancing mechanisms are designed to reduce dependency on *A*, or alternatively, to increase *A*'s dependency on *B* in ways that balance the exchange relationship and give it a certain equilibrium.

Exchange in networks can be of two general types: (1) those where actors negotiate and bargain over the distribution of resources and (2) those where actors do not negotiate but, instead, sequentially provide resources with the expectation that these rewards will be reciprocated. This distinction between what can be termed *negotiated exchanges* and *reciprocal exchanges* is important because it reflects different types of exchanges in the real world. When actors negotiate, they try to influence each other before the resources are divided, as when labor and management negotiate a contract or when individuals argue about whether to go to the movies or to the beach. The dynamics of negotiated exchange are distinctive because they typically take longer to execute, because they generally involve considerably more explicit awareness and calculation of costs and benefits, and because they are often part of conflicts among parties who seek a compromise acceptable to all. In contrast, reciprocal exchanges involve the giving of resources unilaterally by one party to another with, of course, some expectation that valued resources will be given back, as occurs when a person initiates affection with the intent that the other will respond with the same emotion. Reciprocal exchanges are thus constructed in sequences of contingent rewarding, whereas as negotiated exchanges unfold in a series of offers and counteroffers before resources are distributed.

These seminal ideas form the core of Emerson's theoretical scheme. Before his untimely death, Emerson had been collaborating with Karen Cook and their mutual students to test the implications of these ideas for different types of networks. The basic goal was to determine how the structure of the network—that is, the pattern of connections among actors—influences, and is influenced by, the distribution of power, power use, and balancing.

## Social Structure, Networks, and Exchange

Emerson's portrayal of social networks will be simplified; for our purposes, here the full details of his network terminology need not be addressed. Although Emerson followed the conventions of graph theory and developed a number of definitions, only two definitions are critical:

*Actors*: Points $A$, $B$, $C$, . . . , $n$ in a network of relations. Different letters represent actors with different resources to exchange. The same letters—that is, $A_1$, $A_2$, $A_3$, and so forth—represent different actors exchanging similar resources.

*Exchange relations*: $A$—$B$, $A$—$B$—$C$, $A_1$—$A_2$, and other patterns of ties that can connect different actors to each other, forming a network of relations.

The next conceptual task was to visualize the forms of networks that could be represented with these two definitions. For each basic form, new corollaries and theorems were added as Emerson documented the way in which the basic processes of dependence, power, and balance operate. His discussion was only preliminary, but it illustrated his perspective's potential. Several basic social forms are given special treatment: (a) unilateral monopoly, (b) division of labor, (c) social circles, and (d) stratification.

**Unilateral Monopoly.** In the network illustrated in Figure 22.4, actor $A$ is a source of valuable resources for actors $B_1$, $B_2$, and $B_3$. Actors $B_1$, $B_2$, and $B_3$ provide rewards for $A$, but because $A$ has multiple sources for rewards and the $B$'s have only $A$ as a source for their rewards, the situation is a unilateral monopoly. Such a structure often typifies interpersonal as well as intercorporate units. For example, $A$ could be a female date for three different men, $B_1$, $B_2$, and $B_3$. Or $A$ could be a corporation that is the sole supplier of raw resources for three other manufacturing corporations, $B_1$, $B_2$, and $B_3$. Or $A$ could be a governmental body and the $B$s could be dependent agencies. An important feature of the unilateral monopoly is that, by Emerson's definitions, it is imbalanced, and thus, its structure is subject to change.

Emerson developed additional corollaries and theorems to account for the various ways this unilateral monopoly can change and become balanced. For instance, if no $A_2$, $A_3$, . . . , $A_n$ exist and the $B$s cannot communicate with each other, the following proposition would apply (termed by Emerson *Exploitation Type I*):

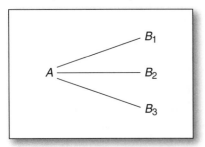

**Figure 22.4**   A Unilateral Monopoly

*The more an exchange relation between A and multiple Bs approximates a unilateral monopoly, the more additional resources each B will introduce into the exchange relation, with A's resource utilization remaining constant or decreasing.*

Emerson saw this adaptation as short-lived, because the network will become even more unbalanced. Assuming that the Bs can survive as an entity without resources from A, then a new proposition applies (termed by Emerson *Exploitation Type II*):

*The more an exchange relation between A and multiple Bs approximates a unilateral monopoly, the less valuable to Bs are the resources provided by A across continuing transactions.*

This proposition thus predicts that balancing Operation 1—a decrease in the value of the reward for those at a power disadvantage—will balance a unilateral monopoly where no alternative sources of rewards exist and where Bs cannot effectively communicate. Other balancing operations are possible, if other conditions exist. If Bs can communicate, they might form a coalition (balancing Operation 4) and require A to balance exchanges with a united coalition of Bs. If one B can provide a resource not possessed by the other Bs, then a division of labor among Bs (Operations 3 and 4) would emerge. Or if another source of resources, that is $A_2$, can be found (Operation 2), then the power advantage of $A_1$ is decreased. Each of these possible changes will occur under varying conditions, but these propositions provide a reason for the initiation of changes—a reason derived from basic principles of operant psychology (the details of these derivations are not discussed here).

**Division of Labor.** The emergence of a division of labor is one of many ways to balance exchange relations in a unilateral monopoly. If each of the Bs can provide different resources for A, then they are likely to use these in the exchange with A and to specialize in providing A with these resources. This decreases the power of A and establishes a new type of network. For example, in Figure 22.5, the unilateral monopoly at the left is transformed to the division of labor form at the right, with $B_1$ becoming a new type of actor (Actor C) with its own resources; with $B_2$ also specializing and becoming a new actor (Actor D); and with $B_3$ doing the same and becoming Actor E.

Emerson developed an additional proposition to describe this kind of change, in which each B has its own unique resources: The more resources are distributed *nonuniformly* across Bs in a unilateral monopoly with A, the more likely is each B to specialize and establish a separate exchange relation with A. Several points should be emphasized. First, the units in this transformation can be individual or collective actors. Second, the change in the structure or form of the network is described as a proposition systematically derived from operant principles, corollaries, and other theorems.

**Figure 22.5**   The Transformation of a Unilateral Monopoly to Division of Labor

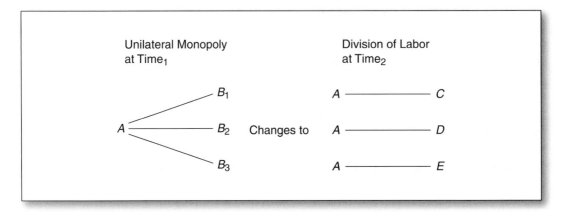

The proposition could thus apply to a wide variety of micro and macro contexts. For example, it could apply to workers in an office who specialize and provide $A$ with resources not available from others. This proposition could also apply to a division in a corporation that seeks to balance its relations with the central authority by reorganizing itself in ways that distinguish it, and the services it can provide, from other divisions. Or this proposition could apply to relations between a colonial power ($A$) and its colonized nations ($B_1$, $B_2$, $B_3$), which specialize (become $C$, $D$, and $E$) in their predominant economic activities to establish a less dependent relationship with $A$.

**Social Circles.** Emerson emphasized that some exchanges are *intercategory* and others *intracategory*. An intercategory exchange is one in which one type of resource is exchanged for another type—money for goods, advice for esteem, tobacco for steel knives, and so on. The networks discussed thus far have involved intercategory exchanges between actors with different resources ($A$, $B$, $C$, $D$, $E$). An intracategory is one in which the same resources are being exchanged—affection for affection, advice for advice, goods for goods, and so on. As indicated earlier, such exchanges are symbolized in Emerson's graph approach by using the same letter—$A_1$, $A_2$, $A_3$, and so forth—to represent actors with similar resources. Emerson then developed another proposition to describe what will occur in these intracategory exchanges:

> *The more an exchange approximates an intracategory exchange, the more likely are exchange relations to become closed.*

Emerson defined *closed* either as a circle of relations, as is diagrammed in Figure 22.6, or as a balanced network in which all actors exchange with one

**Figure 22.6**   Closure of Intracategory Exchanges

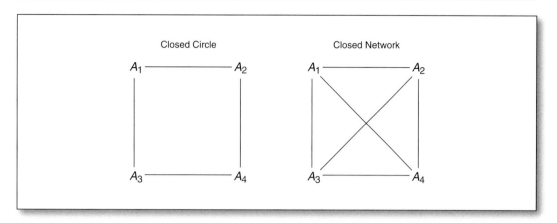

another. Emerson offered the example of tennis networks to illustrate the balancing process. If two tennis players of equal ability, $A_1$ and $A_2$, play together regularly, this is a balanced intracategory exchange—tennis for tennis. However, if $A_3$ enters and plays with $A_2$, then $A_2$ now enjoys a power advantage, as is diagramed in Figure 22.7.

This is now a unilateral monopoly, but unlike those discussed earlier, it is an intracategory monopoly. $A_1$ and $A_3$ are dependent on $A_2$ for tennis. This relation is unbalanced and sets into motion processes of balance. $A_4$ might be recruited, creating either the circle or balanced network diagramed in Figure 22.6. Once this kind of closed and balanced network is achieved, it resists entry by others, $A_5$, $A_6$, $A_7$, ..., $A_n$, because the network becomes unbalanced as each additional actor enters. Such a network, of course, is not confined to individuals; it can apply to nations forming a military alliance or common market, to cartels of corporations, and to other collective units.

**Figure 22.7**   Imbalanced Intracategory Exchanges

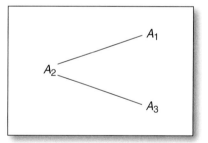

**Stratified Networks.** The discussion about how intracategory exchanges often achieve balance through closure can help us understand processes of stratification. If, for example, tennis players $A_1$, $A_2$, $A_3$, and $A_4$ are unequal in ability, with $A_1$ and $A_2$ having more ability than $A_3$ and $A_4$, an initial circle might form among $A_1$, $A_2$, $A_3$, and $A_4$; but, over time, $A_1$ and $A_2$ will find more gratification in playing each other, and $A_3$ and $A_4$ might have to incur too many costs in initiating invitations to $A_1$ and $A_2$. An $A_1$ and $A_3$ tennis match is unbalanced; $A_3$ will have to provide additional resources—the tennis balls, praise, esteem, self-deprecation. The result will be for two classes to develop:

Upper social class $A_1$—$A_2$

Lower social class $A_3$—$A_4$

Moreover, $A_1$ and $A_2$ might enter into new exchanges with $A_5$ and $A_6$ at their ability level, forming a new social circle or network. Similarly, $A_3$ and $A_4$ might form new tennis relations with $A_7$ and $A_8$, creating social circles and networks with players at their ability level. The result is stratification that reveals the pattern in Figure 22.8. Emerson's discussion of stratification processes was tentative, but he developed a proposition to describe these stratifying tendencies:

> *The more resources are equally valued and the more resources are unequally distributed across a number of actors, the more likely is the network to stratify by resource magnitudes and the more likely are actors with a given level of resources to form closed exchange networks.*

Again, this theorem can apply to corporate units as well as to individuals. Nations become stratified and form social circles, as is the case with the distinctions between the developed and underdeveloped nations and the alliances among countries within these two classes. Or this theorem can apply to traditional sociological definitions of class, because closed networks tend to form among members within, rather than across, social classes.

**Figure 22.8**   Stratification and Closure of Exchanges

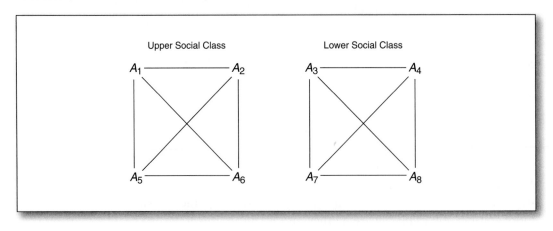

**Centrality in Networks and the Distribution of Power.** In Figure 22.9, Actor $A_1$ is in a position of centrality in relation to actors $A_2$, $A_3$, and $A_4$. Centrality can be measured and conceptualized in several ways, but the basic theoretical idea is relatively straightforward: Some positions in a network mediate the flow of resources by virtue of being in the middle of ties to other points. Thus, in Figure 22.9, Actor $A_1$ mediates the flow of resources among Actors $A_2$, $A_3$, and $A_4$; hence, in this network, $A_1$ is in a position of high centrality. Similarly, further out on the network, Actors $A_2$, $A_3$, and $A_4$ are also central between the peripheral actors at the ends of the network ($A_5$ through $A_{13}$) and the most central actor, $A_1$. For example, $A_2$ is central with respect to $A_1$, on the one side, and $A_5$, $A_6$, and $A_7$, on the other. The same is true for the other peripheral $A$s connected to $A_3$ and $A_4$. Emerson and his coauthors then hypothesize:

> *In networks revealing centrality, power will decentralize toward those actors who possess the highest degree of access to resources.*

In the network in Figure 22.9, resources are flowing from actors $A_5$ through $A_{13}$ to $A_4$, $A_3$, and $A_2$, and then, on to $A_1$. Power-dependence theory predicts that this network will have a tendency to collapse around those actors who can control direct access to resources—in this case, Actors $A_2$, $A_3$, and $A_4$. Why should this be so?

The answer resides in the power advantage $A_2$, $A_3$, and $A_4$ have over the respective $A$s from whom they are getting resources. $A_5$ through $A_{13}$ have no other source for resources than $A_2$, $A_3$, and $A_4$, whereas each of these more central $A$s has alternative sources for resources. Thus, those actors at the edges of the network depend on $A_2$, $A_3$, and $A_4$; indeed, each of these three $A$s enjoys a *unilateral monopoly.* They have, therefore, the most direct access to resources, and they enjoy a power advantage because they can play the dependent $A$s (that is, $A_5$ through $A_{13}$) off against each other. $A_1$ ultimately depends on $A_2$, $A_3$, and $A_4$; hence, if the latter are willing to trade with $A_1$, then $A_1$ must have resources that they value. If not, the network will collapse into its three unilateral monopolies revolving around $A_2$, $A_3$, and $A_4$. For this network to remain stable, therefore, $A_1$ actually has to possess another resource that $A_2$, $A_3$, and $A_4$ value highly and that they cannot get readily elsewhere (hence, in the conventions of network diagrams, $A_1$ actually becomes $B$ or some other letter indicating that it is providing different resources to $A$s).

Let me put some empirical content into these network dynamics. Let me make the most central figure, $A_1$ represent the king in a feudal system, and $A_2$, $A_3$, and $A_4$ are the lords of the king's realm. These lords provide resources to the king through their unilateral monopoly over peasants on their estates, and so, they pass on to the king some portion of the resources ultimately generated by peasants. What, then, does the king give back in exchange for this flow of resources? The answer is almost always problematic for kings, and this is why feudal systems tend to collapse: the lords of the realm are closer to the material resources that sustain the king. Typically, the king provides the coordination of armies and other necessary activities among the lords (who are often feuding amongst themselves) for defense of the realm. This capacity to organize a kingdom is the resource that the king gives back to lords.

Many network structures approximate this one. The important point is that they are inherently unstable because those who enjoy the unilateral monopolies eventually become resentful that they have to pass on resources to a more central actor, and if they begin to perceive that this actor does not provide enough in return, they break off the exchange and thereby change the distribution of power in the network. More recent work in networks, even in networks where actors are less likely to break off exchange, also found that the locus of power shifted toward the sources of supply of resources that were most highly valued.

In sum, Richard Emerson infused exchange theory with a means to analyze social structures by conceptualizing exchange processes as occurring in networks. The same dynamics—power, dependence, and balancing operations— drive the formation of these networks, whether the actors in them be individual people or collective actors like groups, organizations,

**Figure 22.9** Power and Centrality in Exchange Networks

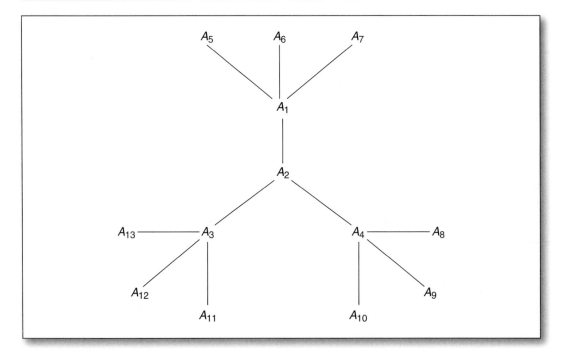

and nation-states. While most of the empirical work in this exchange tradition has been done in experimental laboratories, the fact that the dynamics are the same for individuals or corporate actors means that tests of the theory can be applied to macro-level social processes—just as Georg Simmel argued in his "formal sociology."

# Conclusion

Along with James S. Coleman, whose work is examined in the next chapter on rational choice theories, the works of Homans, Blau, and Emerson set the agenda for more recent exchange theories. Homans and Emerson started with behaviorist assumptions, while Blau and rational choice theories examined in the next chapter began with assumptions of utilitarian economics. The two converge as soon as the extreme behavioristic assumptions of not entering the black box of human cognition and emotion are taken by those working with behaviorist ideas. In the end, individuals are seen as decision-making animals that make calculations—sometimes explicitly and other times more implicitly—about the payoffs to be gained relative to costs and investments in exchanges with others. As might be expected for sociologists, all early theorists incorporated power into the analysis of exchange: those with more valuable resources that others desire and that are not easily attained elsewhere will be able to extract compliance from these others and, moreover, will often seek to exploit others by demanding ever-more resources from these others—a line of thinking reminiscent of Karx Marx.

Today, two distinctive and dominant exchange traditions can be seen in sociological exchange theorizing. One is rational choice theory that seeks to explain emergent phenomena such as the creation of norms, social solidarity, and control systems emerging as a consequence of individuals making rational decisions to impose controls on their actions in order to reduce negative externalities (costs and punishments) and, thereby, increase their profits. The other tradition extends Emerson's network exchange theory in many interesting directions, including the analysis of trust, solidarity, commitment, and punishment in exchange dynamics. In so doing, both of these traditions have strayed from their original behaviorist and neoclassical foundations, which was inevitable in sociology that from its beginnings viewed both behaviorism and utilitarianism suspiciously. Once liberated from its intellectual roots, contemporary exchange theory has become one of the dominant theoretical traditions in sociology—even though this tradition only emerged in the modern era of theorizing beginning around 1950 and extending to the present.

## CHAPTER 23

# Rational Choice Theories

Adam Smith, who formulated the basic laws of supply and demand for free markets, is often viewed as the founder of utilitarian economics, as I emphasized in Chapter 21. In Smith's formulation, actors are conceptualized as rational and as seeking to maximize their utilities, or benefits.[1] Yet, his utilitarian ideas also led Smith to formulate the basic question guiding much sociological theory in the nineteenth century: What forces are to hold society together in a world where market-driven production and consumption lead individuals into ever-more specialized social niches? What, then, was to keep specialization from splitting society apart? As noted in Chapter 21, Adam Smith had two answers: (1) the laws of supply and demand in markets would operate as a kind of "invisible hand of order" in matching people's needs to production[2] and in controlling fraud, abuse, and exploitation, and (2) differentiated societies would develop sentiments (i.e., values, beliefs, ideologies, norms) appropriate to the new social order being created by markets.[3]

Through the midpoint of this century, sociologists were suspicious of the first answer, wondering how social order could emerge from rational actors pursuing their own self-interests in markets operating by profit and greed. The second answer—an emphasis on moral codes—was more appealing but was basically unknown to most sociologists, who had long forgotten that Adam Smith had recognized the importance of cultural codes as an essential force of social organization. As a result, for more than half the twentieth century, sociologists were critical of the utilitarians' views. In essence, they asked this: How could selfish, resource-maximizing actors ever

---

[1]Adam Smith, *An Inquiry into the Nature and Causes of the Wealth of Nations* (Indianapolis: Liberty Fund, 1981; originally published in 1775–1776).

[2]Adam Smith, *The Theory of Moral Sentiments* (Indianapolis: Liberty Fund, 1974; originally published in 1759 and later revised in light of the questions raised in *The Wealth of Nations*).

[3]Ibid.

create the moral codes and modes of cooperation so necessary for an orderly society? Their answer was that such utilitarian theories could not explain the emergent forces holding societies together.

Yet, by midcentury, exchange theories were becoming a prominent part of the sociological canon, as we saw in Chapters 21 and 22. Some were couched in behavioristic psychology and others in the utilitarian terminology of classical economics. In either case, the goal was to demonstrate how reward- or utility-seeking and rational actors could construct sociocultural systems. In effect, these new theorists took the challenge that had been presented by sociology's distrust of utilitarianism: Demonstrate how a model of an individualistic, rational, self-interested, and utility-maximizing actor can create the social and cultural forces that bind the members of society together. In this chapter, I will review two such efforts to meet this challenge through the theoretical approach that is now known as rational choice theorizing.[4]

# Michael Hechter's Theory of Group Solidarity

Michael Hechter's theory of group solidarity seeks to explain how rational, resource-maximizing actors create and remain committed to the normative structure of groups. Table 23.1 summarizes his utilitarian assumptions, but the basic ideas are straightforward: Individuals reveal preferences in hierarchies of utility (value); they seek to maximize these preferences; and under certain conditions, it is rational for them to construct cultural and social systems to maximize utilities. Most theories of culture and social structure, Hechter argues, simply assume the existence of emergent sociocultural phenomena but do not explain *how* and *why* they would ever emerge in the first place. Rational choice theory can, he believes, offer this explanation for why actors construct and then abide by the normative obligations of groups. And, if such a fundamental process as group solidarity can be explained by rational choice assumptions, virtually all emergent social phenomena can be similarly understood.

## The Basic Problem of Order in Rational Choice Theorizing

Individuals depend upon others in a group context for those resources, or goods, that will maximize their utilities, or rewards. These individuals cannot produce the good for themselves and, hence, must rely on others to

---

[4]This approach has different names in other disciplines, but the core ideas come in neoclassical theory in economics and game theory in economics and political science and, to an extent, in sociology and anthropology. Michael Hechter, *Principles of Group Solidarity* (Berkeley: University of California Press, 1987); "Rational Choice Foundations of Social Order," in *Theory Building in Sociology*, ed. J. H. Turner (Newbury Park, CA: Sage, 1988).

**Table 23.1** Assumptions of Rational Choice Theory

1. Humans are purposive and goal oriented.

2. Humans have sets of hierarchically ordered preferences or utilities.

3. In choosing lines of behavior, humans make rational calculations about
   A. The utility of alternative lines of conduct with reference to the preference hierarchy
   B. The costs of each alternative in terms of utilities foregone
   C. The best way to maximize utility

4. Emergent social phenomena—social structures, collective decisions, and collective behavior—are ultimately the result of rational choices made by utility-maximizing individuals.

5. Emergent social phenomena that arise from rational choices constitute a set of parameters for subsequent rational choices of individuals in the sense that they determine
   A. The distribution of resources among individuals
   B. The distribution of opportunities for various lines of behavior
   C. The distribution and nature of norms and obligations in a situation

produce it for them or join others in its joint production. For example, if companionship and affection are high preferences, this "good" can be attained only in interaction with others, usually in groups; if money is a preference, then this good can usually be attained in modern settings through work in an organizational context. Thus the goods that meet individual preferences can often be secured only in a group. Groups are thus conceptualized in rational choice theory as existing to provide or produce goods for their members.

Those goods that are produced by the activities of group members can be viewed as *joint goods*, because they are produced jointly in the coordinated activities of group members. Such joint goods vary along a critical dimension: their degree of *publicness*. A *public good* is available not only to the members of the group but to others outside the group as well. Furthermore, once the good is produced, its use by one person does not diminish its supply for another. For instance, radio waves, navigational aids, and roads are public goods because they can be used by those who did not produce them and because their use by one person does not (at least to a point) preclude use by another. In contrast with public goods are *private goods*, which are produced for consumption by their producers. Moreover, consumption by one person decreases the capacity of others to consume the good. Private goods are thus kept out of the reach of others to ensure that only a person, or persons, in the group producing them can consume them.

The basic problem of order for rational choice theorists revolves around the question of public goods. This problem is described as the *free-rider* dilemma.[5] People are supposed to produce public goods jointly. Yet, it is "rational" to consume public goods without paying the costs of contributing to their production. To avoid the costs of contributing to production is *free-riding*. If everybody free-rides, then the joint good will never be produced. How, then, is this dilemma avoided?

An answer to this question has been controversial in the larger literature in economics, but the basic thrust of the argument is that, if a good is highly public, people can be coerced (through taxes, for example) to contribute to its production (say, national defense), or they can be induced to contribute by being rewarded (salaries, praise) for their contribution. Another way to prevent free-riding is to exclude those who do not contribute to production from consumption, thereby decreasing the degree of publicness of the good. This exclusion can result in a group that throws out noncontributing members or does not allow them to join in the first place. A final way to control free-riders is to impose user fees or prices for goods that are consumed.

Thus, for rational choice theory, the basis of social order revolves around creating group structures to produce goods that are consumed in ways that limit free-riding—that is, consumption without contributing in some way, directly or indirectly, to the production of the good. The sociologically central problem of social solidarity thus becomes one of understanding how rational egoists go about (a) establishing groups that create normative obligations on their members to contribute and, then, (b) enforcing their conformity—thereby diminishing the problem of free-riding. Solidarity is thus seen as a problem of *social control*.

## The Basis of Social Control: Dependence, Monitoring, and Sanctioning

In rational choice theory, groups exist to provide joint goods. The more an individual depends on a group for resources or goods that rank high in his or her preference hierarchy, the greater is the potential power of the group over that individual. When people depend on a group for a valued good, it is rational for them to create rules and obligations that will ensure access to this joint good. Such is particularly likely to be the case when: (1) valued joint goods are not readily available elsewhere, (2) individuals lack information about alternatives, (3) costs of exiting the group are high, (4) moving or transfer costs to new groups are high, and (5) personal ties, as unredeemable sunk investments, are strong.

---

[5]Mancur Olson, *The Logic of Collective Action* (Cambridge, MA: Harvard University Press, 1965).

*Dependence* is thus the incentive behind efforts to create normative obligations in order to ensure that actors will get their share of a joint good. Groups thus have power over individuals who are dependent on the resources generated by the group; as a result of this power, the *extensiveness of normative* obligations in a group is related to the degree of *dependence.* Hence, dependence creates incentives not just for norms but for extensive norms that guide and regulate to a high degree.

Yet Hechter is quick to emphasize that "the extensiveness of a group alone . . . has no necessary implications for group solidarity."[6] What is crucial is that group members will comply with these norms. Compliance is related to a group's *control capacity,* which in turn is a function of (1) monitoring and (2) sanctioning. *Monitoring* is the process of detecting nonconformity to group norms and obligations, whereas *sanctioning* is the use of rewards and punishments to induce conformity. When the monitoring capacity of a group is low, then it becomes difficult to ensure compliance to norms because conformity is a cost that rational individuals will avoid, if they can. And, without monitoring, sanctioning (imposing costs) cannot effectively serve as an inducement to conformity.

Hechter believes, then, that solidarity is the product of dependence, monitoring, and sanctioning. But solidarity is also related to the nature of the group, which led Hechter to distinguish types of groups by the nature of joint goods produced.

## Types of Groups

Hechter views *control capacity*—that is, monitoring and sanctioning—as operating differently in two basic types of groups. If a grouping produces a joint good for a market and does not itself consume the good, then control capacity can be potentially reduced because the profits from the sale of the good can be used to "buy" conformity of those producing the good for consumption by others. Conformity can be bought, for example, because members are compensated for their labor; furthermore, if they are highly dependent on a group for this compensation, then it is rational to conform to norms. But, because the same compensation can be achieved in other groups, it is less likely that dependence on the group will be high, which thereby reduces the extensiveness of norms. The result is that the level of monitoring and the use of sanctions must be high in such groups, for it would be rational for the individual to free-ride and take compensation without a corresponding effort to produce the marketable good. Yet, if monitoring and sanctioning are too intrusive and impose costs on individuals, then it is rational to leave the group and seek compensation elsewhere. Moreover, as we will see, extensive monitoring and sanctioning are costly and cut into profits—hence limiting the social control capacity of the group. The control capacity of these *compensatory groups,* as Hechter calls them, is thus problematic and ensures that solidarity will be considerably lower than in obligatory groups.

---

[6]Hechter, *Principles of Group Solidarity* (cited in note 4), p. 49.

*Obligatory groups* produce a joint good for their members' *own* consumption. Under these conditions, it is rational to create obligations for contributions from members; if dependence on the joint good is high, then there is considerable incentive for conformity because there is no easy alternative to the joint good (unlike the case in groups in which a generalized medium like money is employed as compensation). Moreover, monitoring and sanctioning can usually be more efficient because monitoring typically occurs as a by-product of joint production of a good that the members consume and because the ultimate sanction—expulsion from the group—is very costly to members who value this good. As Hechter notes:

> Due to greater dependence, obligatory groups have lower sanctioning and monitoring costs. Since every group has one relatively costless sanction at its disposal—the threat of expulsion—then the greater the dependence of group members, the more weight this sanctioning causes. [Moreover,] . . . monitoring and sanctioning are to some extent substitutable. If the value of the joint good is relatively large, the threat of expulsion can partly compensate for inadequate monitoring. The more one has to lose by noncompliance, the less likely one is to risk it.[7]

There is an implicit variable in Hechter's analysis: *group size.* In general terms, compensatory groups organize larger numbers of individuals to produce marketable goods, whereas obligatory groups are smaller and provide goods for their members that cannot be obtained (or, only at great cost) in a market. Thus, not only will dependence be higher in obligatory groups but monitoring and sanctioning also will be considerably easier, thereby increasing solidarity, which Hechter defines as the extent to which members' private resources are contributed to a collective end. High contributions of private resources can occur only with extensive norms and high conformity—two conditions unlikely to prevail in compensatory groups. In Hechter's terms, then, high solidarity can be achieved only in obligatory groups in which dependence on a jointly produced and consumed good is high, in which monitoring is comparatively easy because of small size and because members can observe one another's production and consumption of the good, and in which sanctioning is built into the very nature of the good (that is, receiving a good is a positive sanction, whereas expulsion or not receiving the good is a very costly negative sanction). Under these conditions, people will commit their private resources—time, energy, and self—to the production of the joint good and, in the process, promote high solidarity.

For Hechter, then, high degrees of solidarity are possible only in obligatory groups, in which dependence, monitoring, and sanctioning are high. Figure 23.1 represents his argument, modified in several respects. First, group size is added as a crucial variable. As obligatory groups get large, their monitoring and sanctioning capacity decreases. Second, on the far left is

---

[7]Ibid., p. 126.

**Figure 23.1** The Determinants of Group Solidarity

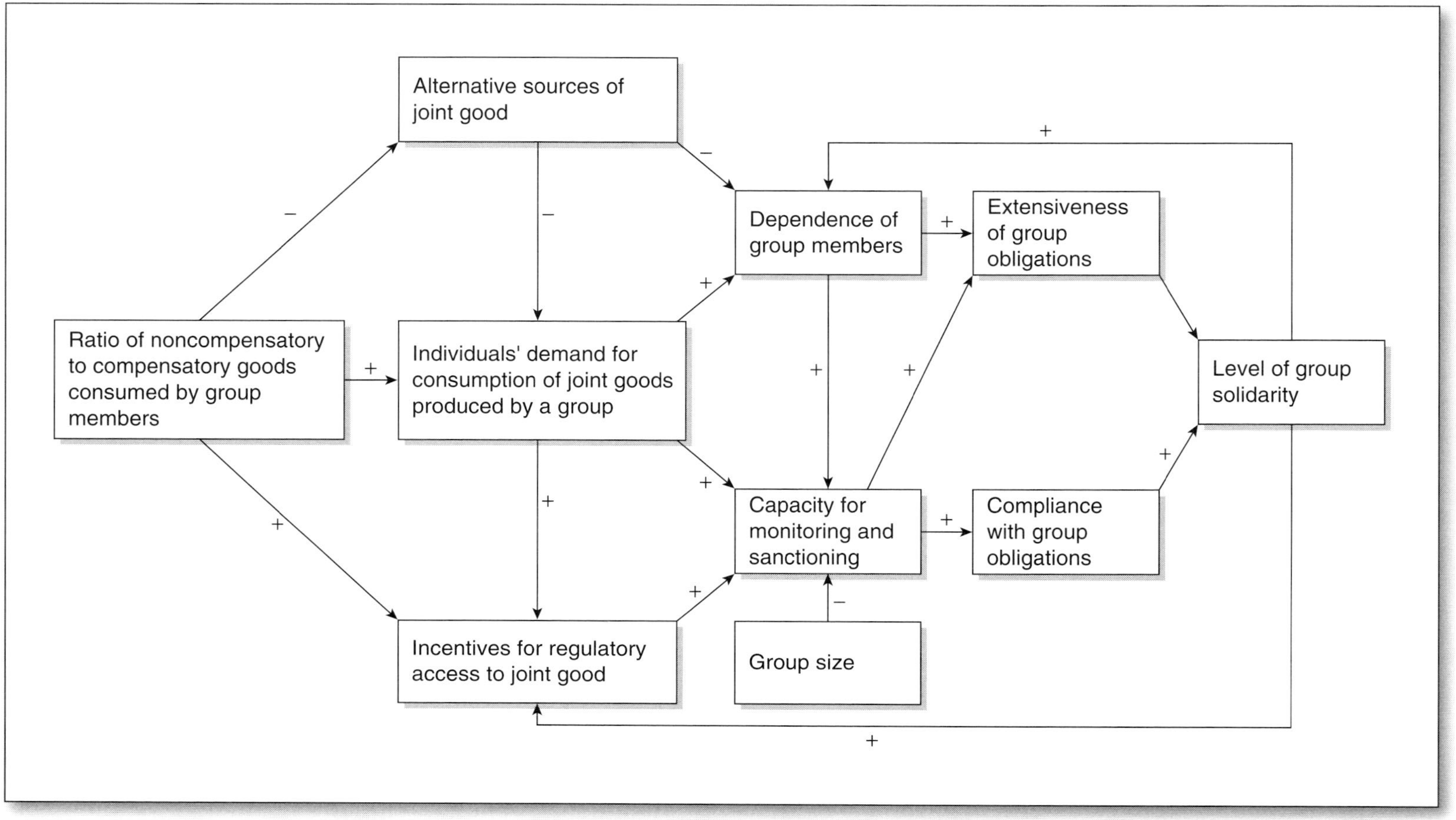

*Source:* Adapted, but extensively revised, from Michael Hechter, "Rational Choice Foundations of Social Order," in *Theory Building*, ed. J. H. Turner (Newbury Park, CA: Sage, 1988).

**517**

added a variable that is perhaps more typical of many human groupings: the ratio of consumption to compensation. That is, many groupings involve a mixture of extrinsic compensation for the production of goods consumed by others and goods consumed by members. For example, groups composed of members working for a salary in an organization often develop solidarity because they also produce joint goods—friendship, approval, assistance, and the like. Indeed, at times, solidarity develops around obligations that run counter to the official work norms of the organization.

We need to conceptualize groups not so much as two polar types, but as mixtures of (1) external compensation for goods jointly produced by and consumed by others and (2) internal consumption of goods jointly produced and consumed by members. The greater the proportion of compensation is to internal consumption, the less likely are the processes depicted in Figure 23.1 to operate; conversely, the less the ratio of compensation to internal consumption is, the more likely these processes are to be activated in ways that produce solidarity. This proposition does not violate the intent of Hechter's typology because he argues that control capacity of compensatory groups increases if such groups also produce a joint good for their members' own consumption.

A larger-scale social system, such as an organization, community, or society, is a configuration of obligatory and compensatory groups. Solidarity will be confined mostly to obligatory groups, whereas the problems of free-riding will be most evident in compensatory groups, unless these compensatory groups also develop joint goods that are highly valued and consumed by group members. Hechter thus turns back to the basic distinctions that dominated early sociological theory—*gemeinschaft* versus *geselleschaft*, *primary* versus *secondary* groups, *mechanical* versus *organic* solidarity, *traditional* versus *rational* authority, *folk* versus *urban*—and has sought to explain these distinctions as the production of joint goods and the nature of the control process that stems from whether a joint good is consumed by members or produced for a market in exchange for extrinsic compensation. Hechter believes the nature of the joint good determines the level of dependence of individuals on the group and the control capacity of the group. High dependence and control are most likely when joint goods are consumed, and hence, solidarity is high under these conditions. A society with only compensatory groups will, therefore, reveal low solidarity. What is distinctive about Hechter's conceptualization is that it is tied to a utilitarian theory in which both high and low levels of solidarity follow from rational choices of individuals.

## Patterns of Control in Compensatory and Obligatory Groups

In a vein similar to classical sociological theory, Hechter examines the process of formalization.[8] As groups get larger, informal controls become

---

[8]Ibid., pp. 59–77, 104–24.

inadequate, even in obligatory groups. Of course, if compensatory groups proliferate or grow in size, the process of creating formal controls escalates to an even greater degree. There is, however, a basic dilemma in this process: Formal monitoring and sanctioning are costly because they involve creating special agents, offices, procedures, and roles, thereby cutting into the production of goods. Obligatory groups can put off the process of formal controls because of high dependence and control that comes from joint consumption of a good that is valued, but when obligatory groups get too large, more formal controls become necessary. Compensatory groups can try to keep formal controls to a minimum, especially if they can create consumption of joint goods that reinforce the production norms for those goods that will be externally consumed. If they get too large, however, then they must also increase formal monitoring and sanctioning. In all these cases, it is rational for actors in groups to resist imposing formal controls because they are costly and cut into profits or joint consumption. But if free-riding becomes too widespread and cuts into production, then it is rational to begin to impose formal controls.

To some extent, the implementation of formal controls can be delayed or mitigated by several forces. One is common socialization, and groups often seek members who share similar outlooks and commitments to reduce the risks of free-riding and to cut the costs of monitoring. Another is selection for altruism, especially in obligatory groups, in which unselfish members are recruited. Yet there clearly are limits to how effective these forces can be in maintaining social control, especially in compensatory groups but also in obligatory groups as they get larger.

The result of this basic dilemma between the costs of free-riding, on the one side, and formalization of control, on the other, is for groups to seek "economizing" measures for monitoring and sanctioning.[9] These are particularly visible in compensatory groups in which formal social control is more essential to production, but elements of these "economizing tactics" can be seen in obligatory groups as they get larger or as they produce a joint good that creates problems of free-riding.

Hechter lists a number of monitoring economies. One way to decrease monitoring costs is to increase the visibility of individuals in the group through a variety of techniques: designing the architecture of the group so that people are physically visible to one another, requiring members to engage in public rituals to reaffirm their commitments to the group, encouraging group decision making so that individuals' preferences are exposed to others, and administering public sanctions for behavior that exemplifies group norms. Another set of techniques for reducing monitoring costs includes those that have members share the monitoring burden, as is the case when (a) rewards are given to groups rather than individuals (under the assumption that, if your rewards depend on others, you will monitor their activity), (b) privacy is limited, (c) informants are rewarded,

---

[9]Ibid., pp. 126–46.

and (d) gossip is encouraged. A final economizing technique, which follows from socialization processes, is to minimize errors of interpretation of behavior through recruitment and training of members into a homogeneous culture.

With respect to sanctions, one technique for economizing is symbolic sanctioning through the creation of a prestige hierarchy and the differential rewarding of prestige to group members who personify group norms. Another technique is public sanctioning of deviance from group norms. A final sanctioning technique is to increase the exit costs of group members through geographical isolation from other groups, imposition of non-refundable investments on entry to the group, and limitation of extra-group affiliations.

Yet, there are limits to these monitoring and sanctioning economies, especially in compensatory groups. The result is that, at some point, a group must create formal agents and offices to monitor and control. Thus, a formal organization always reveals some of the economizing processes listed and also creates agents charged with monitoring and control—for example, comptrollers, supervisors, personnel offices, quality-control agents, and the like. Such monitoring and sanctioning are extremely costly, and so, it is not surprising that organizations try to economize here as well.

In addition to the more general techniques previously listed, a variety of mechanisms for reducing agency costs, or increasing productive efficiency and hence profitability, can be employed. For example, inside and outside contractors are often used to perform work (and to incur their own monitoring and sanctioning costs) at a set price for an organization. Standardization of tools, work flow, and other features of work is another way to reduce the need for monitoring. Assessment of only outputs (and ignoring how these are generated) is yet another technique for economizing on at least some phases of monitoring. Setting production goals for each stage in production is still another technique. And, perhaps most effective, the creation of an obligatory group within the larger compensatory organization is the most powerful economizing technique, as long as the norms of the obligatory group correspond to those of the more inclusive compensatory organization (sometimes, however, just the opposite is the case, which thereby increases monitoring costs to even higher levels).

## The Theory Summarized

In Table 23.2, Hechter's theory is stated in more formal and abstract terms than in Hechter's work. When stated in this way, the theory can be applied to a wide range of empirical processes—social class formation, ethnic solidarity, complex organization, communities, and other social units. The propositions in Table 23.2 must be seen as building on the assumptions delineated in Table 23.1. When this is done, it is clear that Hechter has tried to explain, as he phrases the matter, "the micro foundations of the macro social order."

**Table 23.2**  Hechter's Implicit Principles of Social Structure

1. The more members of a group jointly produce goods for consumption outside the group, the more their productive efforts will depend on increases in the ratio of extrinsic compensation to intrinsic compensation.

2. The more members of a group jointly produce goods for their own consumption, the more their efforts will depend on the development of normative obligations.

3. The power of the group to constrain the decisions and behaviors of its members is positively related to the dependence of these members on the group for a good or compensation, with dependence increasing when

   A. More attractive alternative sources for a good or compensation are not available

   B. Information about alternative sources for a good or compensation is not readily available

   C. The costs of exiting the group are high

   D. The moving or transfer costs to another group are high

   E. The intensity of personal ties among group members is high

4. The more a group produces a joint good for its own consumption and develops normative obligations to regulate productive activity, the more likely are conditions 3-A, 3-B, 3-C, 3-D, and 3-E to be met; conversely, the more a group produces a joint good for the consumption of others outside the group, the less likely these conditions are to be met.

5. The more a group produces a joint good for its own consumption and develops extensive normative obligations to regulate productive activity, the more likely is social control through monitoring and sanctioning to be informal and implicit and, hence, less costly.

6. The more a group produces a good for external consumption and must rely on a high ratio of extrinsic over intrinsic compensation for members, the more likely is social control through monitoring and sanctioning to be formal and explicit and, hence, more costly.

7. The larger is the size of a group, the more likely is social control to be formal and explicit and the greater will be its cost.

8. The greater is the cost of social control through monitoring and sanctioning, the more likely are economizing procedures to be employed in a group.

## Macrostructural Implications

Hechter sees the basic ideas of rational choice theory as useful in understanding more macrostructural processes among large populations of individuals. For example, the basic theory, as outlined in Figure 23.1 and

Tables 23.1 and 23.2, can be used to explain processes within nation-states. A state or government imposes relatively extensive obligations on its citizens—pay your taxes, be loyal, be willing to die in war, and so on. The reason for this capacity is that citizens are often highly dependent on government for public goods and cannot leave the society easily (because they like where they live, cannot incur the exit and transfer costs, enjoy many benefits from the joint goods produced by the citizenry, and so on). Compliance with the demands of the state involves more than dependence and extensive obligations. Compliance also hinges on the state's control capacity to monitor and sanction. But how is it possible for the state to monitor and sanction all its citizens who are organized into diverse configurations of obligatory and compensatory groups?

The answer to this question, Hechter argues, lies in economies of control. Such economies can be generated within and between groups. The key process is to get the citizens themselves monitoring and sanctioning one another within groups, and then, to link these groups together in ways that maximize dependence and control capacity.

# James S. Coleman's Theory of Group Solidarity

James S. Coleman was an early advocate of a rational choice perspective,[10] and I could have summarized his early ideas in Chapter 22 on early exchange theories. Yet, not until the 1990s did Coleman produce a general theory of social organization based on rational choice principles.[11] This more synthetic theory was published not long before Coleman's early death. Coleman believed that actors have resources and interest in the resources of others; hence, interaction and ultimately social organization revolve around transactions between those who have and those who seek resources. These transactions can occur between individuals directly; they can also occur indirectly through intermediaries or chains of resource transfer; and they can occur in markets where resources are aggregated and bought and sold according to the laws of supply and demand.

## Transferring Rights to Act

Coleman conceived of resources as *rights to act*. These rights can be given away in exchange for other rights to act. Thus, for example, authority relations consist of two types: *conjoint authority* where actors unilaterally give control of their rights to act to another because the vesting of others with authority is seen as in the best interests of all actors, and *disjoint authority*, where actors give their rights away for extrinsic compensation, such as

---

[10]See, for examples of his earlier essay, James S. Coleman, *Individual Interests and Collective Action: Selected Essays* (Cambridge: Cambridge University Press, 1986).

[11]James S. Coleman, *Foundations of Social Theory* (Cambridge, MA: Belknap, 1990).

money. The same is true for norms that, in Coleman's eye, represent the transfer of rights of control to a system of rules that are sanctioned by others. Thus, social structures and cultural norms are ultimately built by virtue of individuals giving up their rights to control resources in exchange for expected benefits.

For Coleman, then, the key theoretical questions in understanding social solidarity are the following: (1) What conditions within a larger collectivity of individuals create a demand for rational actors to give their rights of control over resources to normative rules and the sanctions associated with these rules? (2) What conditions make realization of effective control by norms and sanctions?

## The Demand for Norms and Sanctions

These two issues—(1) the demand for norms and (2) their realization through effective sanctioning—are at the core of Coleman's theory. This theory goes in many directions, but I will confine our analysis to Coleman's discussion of the conditions producing group solidarity, so as to be in a position to compare Coleman's perspective with Hechter's theory of group solidarity. Thus, given the two issues guiding his approach, Coleman asked: What basic conditions increase the demand for social norms and what makes them effective? In his answer, Coleman demonstrated how a view of actors as rational, self-interested, calculating, and resource maximizing can explain emergent phenomena such as norms and group solidarity.

What conditions, then, increase the demand for norms? One is that actors are experiencing *negative externalities*, or harmful consequences in a particular context. Another is that actors cannot successfully bargain tit-for-tat or make offers or threats back and forth to reach agreements that reduce the negative externalities. Another condition is that there are too many actors involved for successful tit-for-tat bargaining, making bargaining cumbersome, difficult, and time-consuming. And, the most important condition is free-riding, where some actors do not contribute to the production of a joint good and where tit-for-tat bargaining cannot resolve the problem. Such free-riding, Coleman argued, is most likely in those groupings using disjoint authority or extrinsic compensation for productive activity (what Hechter termed a *compensatory group*). But, ultimately in Coleman's model, negative externalities give actors an interest in elaborating social structure and cultural systems. Actors begin to see that, by giving up some of their rights of control over their resources and behaviors, they can reduce negative externalities and, thereby, increase their utilities. Free-riding can become a negative externality, to the degree that it imposes costs and harm on others.

As we will see, free-riding becomes an important dynamic in Coleman's model of solidarity. But, there can be other sources of negative externalities— threats, conflict, abusive use of authority, or any source of punishment or costly action by others. Generally, actors will first engage in tit-for-tat bargaining to resolve a problem creating negative externalities. For example, a threat might be met by a counter-threat followed by an agreement to let the matter pass. But as the size of the group increases, this kind of bargaining becomes less viable: Pairwise bargaining among larger sets of actors to reduce negative externalities becomes difficult because of time and energy consumed; bargaining can create new negative externalities for actors who must constantly negotiate and for those who are left out of bargains.

Coleman argues that the creation of markets represents one solution to problems of pairwise, tit-for-tat bargaining among larger numbers of actors. As the volume of resources to be exchanged increases, and the number of buyers and sellers expands, markets determine the price or the resources that one must give up to get another valued resource, with price being determined by the relative supply and demand for resources. Yet, markets generate their own negative externalities associated with cheating, failure to meet obligations, unavailability of credit, and many other problems, and like all negative externalities, they can create demand for norms to regulate transactions.

Thus, wherever norms emerge (and other features of social systems like authority), they do so because actors have an interest in giving up certain rights to eliminate negative externalities and, thereby, to increase their utilities. Systems of norms, trust, and authority all represent ways to organize actors when tit-for-tat bargaining is difficult or unsuccessful, when the number of people involved grows beyond the capacity to bargain face-to-face, and when markets are no longer frictionless and begin to create their own negative externalities.

Under these conditions, actors will then bestow some of their rights to control resources to create proscriptive norms, or rules that prohibit certain types of behavior, and they will impose negative sanctions on those who violate these proscriptions or prohibitions. Such proscriptions and negative sanctions represent a solution by rational actors to the *first-order free-riding problem*, where actors are not contributing to the production of a jointly produced good. But, this solution to free-riding creates a *second-order free-rider problem*: Monitoring and sanctioning others are costly in time and energy, to say nothing of emotional stress and other negatives involved; hence, rational individuals are likely to engage in free-riding on the monitoring and administration of sanctions. The solution to first-order free-riding can, therefore, generate a new set of negative externalities associated with the costs and problems of sanctioning conformity to prohibitions.

The solution to this second-order free-rider problem is to *create prescriptive norms*, or norms that indicate what is supposed to be done (as opposed to what cannot be done or is prohibited), coupled with positive sanctioning for conformity. Such positive sanctions can become, in themselves, a joint good and a source of positive externalities; indeed, receipt of positive sanctions (approval, support, congratulatory statements, esteem, and the like) increases the utilities that rational actors experience. And so, as the costs or negative externalities of the first-order free-rider problem create a demand for prescriptive norms and positive sanctions, actors can enjoy enhanced benefits and reduced costs when they give up their control of some resources and behavioral alternatives to normative prescriptions. Actors thus develop an interest in prescriptive normative control, and it becomes rational for them to do so.

The problem with systems of prescriptive norms and positive sanctions is that they are only viable in relatively small groupings and dense networks where monitoring and sanctioning can be part of the normal interaction among actors as they pursue a common goal or produce a joint good. Otherwise, the admission of positive sanctions becomes costly, as does the monitoring of conformity. High degrees of solidarity are thus only possible, Coleman argues, when relatively small numbers of actors give up control over their resources to prescriptive norms and rely heavily on positive sanctions that themselves become positive externalities that increase the utilities for actors. Yet, in the end, as groups get larger, *proscriptive norms* may also need to be introduced as mechanisms of social control.

## Principles of Group Solidarity: Synthesizing Hechter's and Coleman's Theories

As is evident, Coleman's theory arrives at the same place as Hechter's rational choice approach to solidarity. This convergence of perspectives can perhaps best be appreciated by bringing the two theories together in composite form, as is done in the principles enumerated in Table 23.3. In this table,[12] the respective vocabularies of Hechter's and Coleman's schemes are mixed together in ways that emphasize the original contributions of each. What is true for solidarity, both would argue, is true for other emergent social and cultural phenomena. But let us concentrate on the four principles of solidarity.

Proposition 1 simply states Coleman's and Hechter's views on what causes actors to have an interest in creating norms. The key conditions are commonly experienced negative externalities, high rates of free-riding, and dependence of actors on each other for the production of a joint good that gives them utility. Under these conditions, actors will give up some of their rights of control. Proposition 2 summarizes the conditions that, in Hechter's terms, create extensive regulatory norms where actors relinquish a wide range of rights of control to group norms. The basic conditions under which such extensive norms emerge include interests in creating norms (which are activated by the conditions listed in Proposition 1), the ratio of consumption to extrinsic compensation for the production of a joint good (that is, the more members themselves consume the joint good, the greater their interest is in creating extensive norms), the dependence of actors on

---

[12]See also Jonathan H. Turner, "The Production and Reproduction of Social Solidarity: A Synthesis of Two Rational Choice Theories," *Journal for the Theory of Social Behavior* 22 (1993): pp. 311–28.

**Table 23.3**  Principles of Social Solidarity

1. The level of interest in creating norms among actors who are producing a joint good increases with

   A. The intensity of negative externalities that they collectively experience

   B. The rate of free-riding in the production of the joint good

   C. The level of actors' dependence on the production of the joint good

2. The extensiveness of the norms created by actors with an interest in regulating the production of a joint good increases with

   A. The actors' level of dependence on the production of the joint good

   B. The degree to which actors consume the joint good that they produce

   C. The proportion of all actors receiving utilities for the production of the joint good

   D. The rates of communication among members engaged in the production of a joint good which, in turn, is

      1. Negatively related to the size of the group

      2. Positively related to the density of network ties among members of the group

3. The ratio of prescriptive to proscriptive content of norms regulating the production of a joint good increases with

   A. The capacity to lower the costs of monitoring conformity to normative obligations, which, in turn, is positively related to

      1. Rates of communication among actors

      2. Density of network ties

      3. Ratio of informal to formal monitoring

      4. Ratio of informal to formal sanctioning

      5. Ratio of positive to negative sanctioning

   B. The ratio of positive to negative sanctioning, which, in turn, is positively related to the ratio of informal to formal sanctioning

4. The level of solidarity among actors producing a joint good is, therefore, likely to increase when

   A. The actors' dependence on the production of the joint good is high

   B. The extensiveness of normative obligations is great

   C. The ratio of prescriptive to proscriptive content of norms is high

   D. The ratio of positive to negative sanctions is high

   E. The costs for monitoring and sanctioning are low

   F. The proportion of actors receiving utilities from the production of the joint good is high

the utilities offered by the joint good is high, the proportion of actors who receive utilities from the production of a joint good is high, and rates of communication among actors are high (with such rates being negatively related to the number of actors involved and positively related to the density of their networks).

Proposition 3 then addresses the issue of the amount of proscriptive versus prescriptive content of the norms that actors create under the conditions specified in Propositions 1 and 2. The fundamental forces increasing prescriptive content are the ability of actors to monitor each others' activities during the normal course of producing a joint good (which, in turn, is related to group size and density of networks), and the capacity to use positive instead of negative sanctions (which is related to the ability to use informal means of sanctioning).

And finally, Proposition 4 summarizes how the conditions stated in the first three propositions all come together to increase social solidarity. The basic conclusion is when the actors' dependence on the production of the joint good is high, when they develop extensive norms, when the ratio of prescriptive to proscriptive content of such norms is high, when the ratio of positive to negative sanctions is also high, and when the proportion of actors receiving utilities is high, then social solidarity will increase.

# Conclusion

Rational choice theories connect sociology to economic theory and seek to do what early sociologists once felt was impossible: to conceptualize emergent social forms and structures through the behaviors of rational, self-interest actors. The two theories examined in this chapter are among the best in meeting the challenge that sociology has posed for theories that begin with assumptions of individual rationality. Just whether or not their answer is satisfactory depends on whether one is receptive to the view that humans always behave in terms of utilities and rewards and that social organization can only be fully understood in these terms.

The two theorists examined in this chapter have been part of a broad, worldwide effort to use economic theory to explain cultural and social processes. Indeed, these rational choice approaches influence not just sociology but political science as well, and there is little doubt that they are here to stay. As sociology closed the twentieth century, then, it had re-embraced what it had rejected at the beginning of the century. And now into the second decade of the twenty-first century, rational choice theorizing remains a prominent approach in scientific explanations of the social universe.

## CHAPTER 24

# Exchange-Network Theories

The pioneering work of Richard Emerson has been extended by his colleagues and several generations of students. The result is an accumulated body of mostly experimental research findings, but findings that have been used to test the plausibility of extensions to Emerson's theoretical ideas. In this chapter, I examine three theorists and their collaborators. Yet, the basic core ideas of Emerson's theory remain at the center of these new efforts.

## Karen S. Cook's Theoretical Program

Many of the problems of concern among exchange-network theorists were formulated by Karen Cook in collaboration with Richard Emerson and later with students working with either or both of them. The topics pursued by Cook and her collaborators vary, but several stand out: (1) the conditions under which actors in exchange networks develop commitments to partners; (2) the relations among power use, equity, and justice considerations; and (3) the dynamics of restricted and generalized exchanges. Each of these areas of research is briefly examined in the following pages, where the important generalizations emerging from experimental studies will be emphasized.

### Commitment Processes in Networks

In Emerson's original formulation, imbalanced power would lead the advantaged partner in an exchange to use this power to extract more resources from another actor, to the point where balancing operations push the exchange toward equilibrium. In early work with Emerson, Cook examined the process of commitment for its effects on power use, and vice versa. The reason for studying this topic is that from a network perspective, actors do not operate in a perfectly free and competitive market; rather, they have connections to each other, and by virtue of these connections, they engage in exchange. *Commitment* to an exchange occurs when actors choose their current partners over potential alternatives, and in the case of extreme commitment, when they remain with partners who can give them less beneficial payoffs than alternative partners.[1]

From the perspective of a rational and calculating actor, it would be irrational for a more powerful actor to develop commitments to others because this commitment would decrease exploration of alternatives and the resulting ability to increase their payoffs from dependent actors. Conversely, on the surface, it would seem irrational for disadvantaged actors to develop attachments to those who are using their power to extract ever more resources from them. And yet, this is exactly what appears to happen. The early finding was that power use was inversely related to commitment: actors who develop commitments were less likely to use their power advantages against their less advantaged partners.[2] One early explanation for this tendency was that commitments reduce uncertainty; hence, as actors engage in frequent exchanges, they become more committed to the ratio of payoffs and, thereby, reduce the uncertainty inherent in exchange. Moreover, commitment tempers the use of power by the advantaged, because power-advantaged actors become less likely to seek alternatives, thereby enabling payoffs for power-disadvantaged actors to be regularized at predictable

---

[1]It should be emphasized that most of this work, and until recently, virtually all work by Cook and most exchange theorists has been on *negatively connected networks* in which exchange with one actor precludes exchanging with another. For representative examples of Cook and collaborators' work, see Karen S. Cook, Richard M. Emerson, Mary R. Gillmore, and Toshio Yamagishi, "The Distribution of Power in Exchange Networks: Theory and Experimental Results," *American Journal of Sociology* 87 (1983): pp. 275–305. More recently, Yamagishi, Gillmore, and Cook have sought to extend this line of work to positively connected networks where beneficial exchange with one partner does not preclude exchanges with others. Many of the same dynamics are revealed but with some modification: The value of resources becomes the only consideration in positively connected networks, and the locus of power shifts toward the source of supply of valued resources. See their "Network Connections and the Distribution of Power in Exchange Networks," *American Journal of Sociology* 93 (1988): pp. 833–51. See also Kazuo Yamaguchi, "Power in Networks of Substitutable and Complementary Exchange Relations: A Rational-Choice Model and an Analysis of Power Centralization," *American Sociological Review* 61 (1996): pp. 308–32. For rivals to the Cook program, also see John Skvoretz and David Willer, "Exclusion and Power: A Test of Four Theories of Power in Exchange Networks," *American Sociological Review* 58 (1993): pp. 801–18.

[2]Karen S. Cook and Richard M. Emerson, "Power, Equity, and Commitment in Exchange Networks," *American Sociological Review* 43 (1978): pp. 721–39; Karen S. Cook and Richard M. Emerson, "Exchange Networks and the Analysis of Complex Organizations," *Research on the Sociology of Organizations* 3 (1984): pp. 1–30.

costs. A subsequent interpretation by Cook emphasizes that efforts to entice commitment from power-advantaged actors is a balancing strategy to decrease power use by these advantaged actors.

Later, Peter Kollock[3] argued that under conditions of risk and uncertainty in receiving payoffs, commitment can be seen as a profit-maximizing strategy by both partners to the exchange. By establishing commitments, each actor lowers the costs associated with risk and uncertainty. Moreover, commitment itself becomes a positively valued resource that increases each actor's resource payoffs.[4] In particular, commitment can be seen as a power-balancing strategy in which lower-power actors offer a new resource—commitment—to reduce power use by advantaged actors. This point, as I will explore shortly, was extended by Edward Lawler and Jeongkoo Yoon[5] who began to see commitments as markers of emotions emerging from frequent exchanges among actors, creating an attachment to the relationship per se and thereby adding new kinds of emotional utilities among the exchange partners.

## Equity and Justice in Exchange Networks

In their early collaborative work, Emerson and Cook had discovered that concerns about *equity*—or the distribution of outcomes from bargaining in accordance with each actor's respective contribution to the outcome—became interwoven with power dynamics. If actors had knowledge of each other's payoffs and if equity considerations became salient, then power use by advantaged actors was curtailed somewhat. This finding was consistent with other research on the issue of justice in exchange—a consideration that was at the center of exchange theory from the beginning.

In subsequent work with others, primarily Karen A. Hegtvedt, Cook has examined the role of justice in social exchange.[6] One of the most important conceptual distinctions highlighted by Cook and Hegtvedt is between distributive justice and procedural justice. *Distributive justice* denotes the norms or rules by which the allocation of resources among actors occurs. There are several types of such rules, including *equality* or the allocation of the same shares to all, *equity* or the distribution of resources relative to the

---

[3]Peter Kollock, "The Emergence of Exchange Structures: An Experimental Study of Uncertainty, Commitment and Trust," *American Journal of Sociology* 100 (1994): pp. 315–45.

[4]Cook and Emerson, "Power, Equity, and Commitment in Exchange Networks" (cited in note 2).

[5]See p. 537.

[6]Karen A. Hegtvedt and Karen S. Cook, "The Role of Justice in Conflict Situations," *Advances in Group Processes* 4 (1987): pp. 109–36; Karen S. Cook and Karen A. Hegtvedt, "Distributive Justice, Equity, and Equality," *Annual Review of Sociology* 9 (1983): pp. 217–41; Karen Hegtvedt, Elaine Thompson, and Karen S. Cook, "Power and Equity: What Counts in Attributions for Exchange Outcomes," *Social Psychology Quarterly* 56 (1993): pp. 100–119.

respective inputs and contributions of actors to an outcome, or *need* or the distribution of resources to those who require them most. *Procedural justice* refers to the perceived fairness of the process of bargaining itself, rather than to the distributive outcomes that emerge from negotiations. Actors' sense of fairness in the procedures influences how they will respond to each other, thereby shaping the kinds of tactics and strategies that they will employ in bargaining.

How, then, does power influence considerations of justice? The findings are somewhat mixed, but several generalizations emerge from Cook's and Hegtvedt's experimental work as well as from their efforts to summarize the large literature on justice. One generalization is that more power-advantaged actors are, in general, likely to view the distribution of resources as fair, and these perceptions of fairness are related to their ratio of inputs to outcomes (that is, they see themselves as getting back an appropriate return on their investments and costs). Power-advantaged actors have, however, a tendency to constrain their power use when they know that their advantage rests with their structural position rather than with their abilities and talents as negotiators. In contrast, power-disadvantaged actors often tend to see situations as less fair and begin to bargain harder to overcome their low relative power.

Perceptions of equity, or the sense that payoffs correspond to one's contributions, have a somewhat greater effect on attributions of why one receives a payoff than does actual power advantage.[7] Individuals who see themselves as treated fairly are likely to have positive sentiments, and they are likely to attribute their fair outcomes to their personal characteristics (to maintain their identity in the situation) as well as to their partner's characteristics. Yet, this process of attribution is altered somewhat because those who have a power advantage (and correctly perceive that they have this advantage) are likely to attribute their success more to their personal characteristics and to the situation that gives them a power advantage than to the characteristics of their exchange partners. When weaker partners are not fully aware of their structurally based power disadvantage, they will bargain harder to overcome their lower outcomes. If they enjoy success in their efforts, they are likely to attribute this success to their personal characteristics.

The relationship between distributive justice or the allocation of benefits, on the one hand, and procedural justice, on the other hand, is far from clear. But Cook and Hegtvedt extract several generalizations from the literature.[8] One is that perceptions of unfair outcomes are almost always accompanied

---

[7]Hegtvedt, Thompson, and Cook, "Power and Equity" (cited in note 6).

[8]Hegtvedt and Cook, "The Role of Justice in Conflict Situations" and Cook and Hegtvedt, "Distributive Justice, Equity, and Equality" (cited in note 6); for a review of the justice and injustice literature, see also Karen Hegtvedt and Barry Markovsky, "Justice and Injustice," in *Sociological Perspectives on Social Psychology*, eds. K. S. Cook, G. A. Fine, and J. S. House (Boston: Allyn & Bacon, 1995).

by perceptions that the procedures leading to these outcomes were also unfair. Yet, unfair procedures do not produce a corresponding sense of unjust outcomes as long as actors receive what they believe to be a fair outcome. Thus, people tend to judge procedures by outcomes: When outcomes are high or perceived as fair, people are less likely to be critical of procedures, even when they are clearly unfair; whereas, if outcomes are low or perceived as unfair, procedures are almost always seen as unjust, even if they are fair.

Considerable work is yet to be done on this line of research, but it is a central dynamic in power. Perceptions of justice and fairness influence how power processes operate: If power use generates a sense of justice, or if it is used in accordance with accepted norms of distributive and procedural justice, then power use will produce more balanced exchanges. If power imbalance leads to actions by the advantaged actor that violate rules of justice, or if behaviors generate a perception of injustice, then power use will perpetuate imbalance, and disadvantaged actors will seek new strategies to rebalance the exchange, if they can.

## Generalized Exchange Networks

In Chapter 23 on rational choice theories, we saw that the basic problem of order is defined as the problem or dilemma of *free-riding*. That is, it is rational for actors who are trying to maximize benefits and minimize costs to avoid contributing to the production of a joint good. For example, if a set of actors is to produce a product, such as a group-written term paper that will receive a grade, it is rational for each actor to avoid the costs of contributing to the production of the paper but to enjoy the benefits that a good grade bestows, or in other words, it is rational to *free-ride* on the labor of others. The dilemma, of course, is that if everyone free-rides, the joint good will not be produced, and no one will receive the benefits of the jointly produced good. As we saw in Chapter 23, rational choice theorists argue that under conditions of free-riding, actors create systems of norms, monitoring procedures, and sanctioning systems for controlling the negative results of free-riding, thereby ensuring the production of the joint good.

In her more recent work, Cook[9] along with Toshio Yamagishi,[10] who has long worked social dilemma problems (like free-riding), have approached the same topic as rational choice theorists but from a different angle. Emerson made a distinction between (1) *elementary exchange* where

---

[9]Toshio Yamagishi and Karen S. Cook, "Generalized Exchange and Social Dilemmas," *Social Psychology Quarterly* 56 (1993): pp. 235–49.

[10]For relevant works by Yamagishi, see "The Provision of a Sanctioning System in the United States and Japan," *Social Psychology Quarterly* 51 (1988): pp. 267–70; "Seriousness of Social Dilemmas and the Provision of a Sanctioning System," *Social Psychology Quarterly* 51 (1988): pp. 32–42; "Unintended Consequences of Some Solutions to the Social Dilemmas Problem," *Sociological Theory and Method* 4 (1989): pp. 21–47.

actors directly give and take resources to enhance each actor's individual calculation of personal benefits and (2) *productive exchange* where actors exchange resources to produce more benefits from the combination of their respective resources. But Emerson's portrayal did not capture a more fundamental distinction between (1) direct exchange and (2) generalized exchange. Most studies of exchange in networks focus on *direct exchanges* in which actors pass resources back and forth in a network that, ultimately, can be seen as a series of dyadic exchanges. Indeed, most studies producing the theoretical ideas summarized in this chapter come from experiments using direct, dyadic exchanges among partners. But, as we saw in Chapter 21 on the history of exchange theory, anthropologists have long been interested in *generalized exchange* systems in which actors give resources to others but do not receive resources directly back; rather, they acquire resources indirectly via actors who are a part of a pool of actors who feel obligated to pass resources on. For example, when a person offers to help someone whose car has broken down, this helpful person might receive positive rewards like thanks and gratitude directly, but also a more generalized exchange is operating: Helpful persons expect that others will help them when they have car trouble. The early anthropologists, such as Marcel Mauss and Claude Lévi-Strauss, had assumed that such generalized exchange systems created chains of social solidarity. In reviewing these early studies, Peter Ekeh[11] reached a similar conclusion, but what is more significant, he made an important distinction between types of generalized exchanges that Cook and Yamagishi were to explore further. One basic type of generalized exchange is *group-generalized exchange*, in which group members pool their resources to receive the beneficial outcomes from this pooling. Another type is what Cook and Yamagishi prefer to label *network-generalized exchange*, in which each actor provides resources to another actor who, in turn, provides benefits for yet another actor and so on for however many actors are in the network; the original actor eventually receives resources back from one of these other actors in the network.

The group-generalized exchange comes closest to approximating what rational choice theorists postulate as the kind of situation that generates free-riding, which, in turn, leads to the emergence of norms and other systems of social control. It is rational for actors to avoid contributions of their share to the pooled resources, while enjoying the benefits of group production. If all members free-ride, however, no one receives benefits, and under these conditions, systems of norms, monitoring, sanctioning, and trust and other mechanisms emerge to limit free-riding. Yet, as Cook and Yamagishi point out, network-generalized exchange systems also present potential dilemmas for free-riding. If one

---

[11]Peter P. Ekeh, *Social Exchange Theory: The Two Traditions* (Cambridge, MA: Harvard University Press, 1974).

person in the chain of resource flows takes resources from one party but does not pass the appropriate resources on to the next person in the chain, then the original actor and perhaps all those in between the defector and the first actor in the chain receive no benefits. Hence, the network collapses. Yet, because there are direct connections among actors in network exchange, Cook and Yamagishi argue that participants are more likely to cooperate in a network-generalized exchange system than in a group-generalized exchange.

The reason for this difference is that in a group-generalized exchange, where actors pool resources, the temptation to free-ride is high because each actor does not have a direct responsibility to pass resources on to a designated actor, but equally important, as the group gets larger, any one actor's decision not to participate is less consequential and perhaps less noticeable to the total group product, thereby diffusing the responsibility for each actor's noncontribution. This same tendency occurs in generalized-network exchanges as they become large, especially if the networks overlap and intersect in ways that make the chains complex and somewhat redundant, but control is still exercised because at least one actor will know if another did not make the appropriate contribution.

As a consequence, trust is more likely to evolve in the network-generalized system. Built into the nature of the network is a certain monitoring, and because of this, actors come to expect that each will exchange in the appropriate manner. This expectation becomes translated into trust; such trust creates a normative climate for participation and cooperation in the generalized exchange of resources. This tendency for trust and cooperation is greater in network-generalized exchanges than group-generalized exchanges, but as we saw in the review of rational choice theories, free-riding can generate additional mechanisms beyond trust to ensure cooperation in group-generalized exchanges. However, these mechanisms increase the costs of producing a joint good.

The significance of this recent work in Cook's evolving program is that it connects two branches of exchange theory—rational choice approaches (examined in the last chapter) and network approaches—which have during the last two decades gone their somewhat separate ways. Once problems of free-riding and other social dilemmas for actors are introduced into a network analysis of generalized-exchange systems, the opportunities for cross-fertilization increase. The significance for networks goes beyond small-group solidarities; the nature of the paths in a network-generalized system of exchange is important in all types of social structures. For example, the number of paths, the length of chains, the redundancy and density ties, their centrality, and other characteristics of the network will influence the level of free-riding. In turn, the level of free-riding will shape the kinds of mechanisms—from simple trust to more direct forms of social control such as monitoring and sanctioning—that will be used to sustain the production of joint benefits or goods. Much of the social order is constructed from such generalized-exchange systems, so the more recent direction in Cook's and her collaborators' program is promising.[12]

# Edward J. Lawler's Network Exchange Theory

Edward J. Lawler and his collaborators have developed another line of exchange-network theory that, in just the last few years, has taken Emerson's theory into the sociology of emotions and, more generally, the process of commitment to macrosructures in societies. In my view, it is now the most important of the several extensions of Emerson's ideas.

## Commitment in Exchange Networks

In conjunction with Jeongkoo Yoon, Edward J. Lawler has sought to understand how affective commitments develop in exchange relations.[13] In their model, structural power increases exchange frequency, which then reduces uncertainty about payoffs. In turn, the reduction of uncertainty increases actors' commitments to the exchange relationship because predictability ensures expected levels of payoffs from the exchange. Lawler and Yoon, however, theorize that this presumed relationship among frequency, uncertainty-reduction, and commitment is really a proxy for underlying emotional dynamics. In their view, once these emotional forces can be isolated in experiments, the uncertainty-reduction argument would be obviated by a theory of emotional attachment. Although the uncertainty-reduction processes remain an independent force in producing commitments, Lawler and Yoon's experiments confirm most of their hypotheses.

---

[12]For examples of competitive work to that of Cook and her collaborators, see David Willer, "The Basic Concepts of the Elementary Theory," in *Networks, Exchange, and Coercion*, eds. D. Willer and B. Anderson (New York: Elsevier, 1981); "Property and Social Exchange," *Advances in Group Processes* 2 (1985): pp. 123–42; and *Theory and the Experimental Investigation of Social Structures* (New York: Gordon and Breach, 1986); David Willer, Barry Markovsky, and Travis Patton, "Power Structures: Derivations and Applications of Elementary Theory," in *Sociological Theories in Progress: New Formulations*, eds. J. Berger, M. Zelditch, and B. Anderson (Newbury Park: Sage, 1989); David Willer and Barry Markovsky, "Elementary Theory: Its Development and Research Program," in *Theoretical Research Programs: Studies in the Growth of Theory*, eds. J. Berger and M. Zelditch, Jr. (Stanford, CA: Stanford University Press, 1993); Philip Bonacich, "Power and Centrality: A Family of Measures," *American Journal of Sociology* 92 (1987): pp. 1070–82; Elisa Jayne Bienenstock and Philip Bonacich, "The Core as a Solution to Exclusionary Networks," *Social Networks* 14 (1992): pp. 231–43.

[13]Edward J. Lawler and Jeongkoo Yoon, "Commitment in Exchange Relations: A Test of a Theory of Relational Cohesion," *American Sociological Review* 61 (1996): pp. 89–108; Edward Lawler, Jeongkoo Yoon, Mouraine R. Baker, and Michael D. Large, "Mutual Dependence and Gift Giving in Exchange Relations," *Advances in Group Processes* 12 (1995): pp. 271–98; Edward J. Lawler and Jeongkoo Yoon, "Power and the Emergence of Commitment Behavior in Negotiated Exchange," *American Sociological Review* 58 (1993): pp. 465–81.

**Figure 24.1** Lawler and Yoon's Model of Commitment

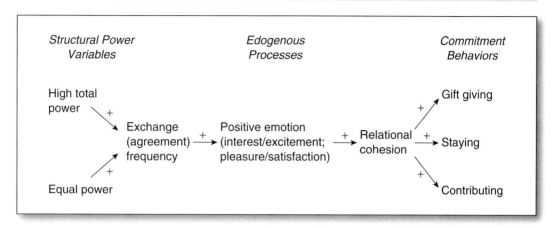

The model tested by Lawler and Yoon is presented in Figure 24.1. On the left side of the model are the structural conditions that follow from Emerson's original formulation of power-dependence. *Total power* is the degree of actor's mutual dependence on each other for resources. The greater this mutual dependence is, the higher is the total power in the relationship. Another concept that follows from Emerson's formulation is *relative power*, which is the level of inequality in the dependence of actors on each other for resources (that is, the relative power of Actor *A* is the ratio of *A*'s power over *B*'s as a proportion of both *A*'s and *B*'s power; the greater *A*'s proportion, the more is *A*'s relative power and the greater is the inequality in the relationship). As shown in Figure 24.1, Lawler and Yoon only express relative power as "equal power," but the argument is really about structural situations where there is high total power and low relative power or equality. The greater is the mutual dependence of actors on resources that they provide for each other (high total power) and the more equal are their respective dependencies for these resources (equal power or low relative power), the more *structural cohesion* is built into their power relations. As a consequence, the more frequent are exchanges and agreements in these exchanges. Thus, the effects of structural cohesion (or high total power and low relative power) on emotions and commitments operate through exchange frequency.

Emotions for Lawler and Yoon are relatively short-term positive or negative evaluative states; Lawler and Yoon emphasize mild positive emotions and their effects on commitment. Two particular types of mild emotions are emphasized: (1) interest and excitement that revolve around anticipation of payoffs that give value and (2) pleasure and satisfaction that orient actors to past and present payoffs yielding value. As the model outlines, exchange frequency under conditions of high total power and equality of power increases agreements in these exchanges, which then activate these two types of mild emotions, interest/excitement and pleasure/satisfaction.

As these emotions are activated, they increase relational cohesion. Relational cohesion is simply a combined function of the frequency of agreements in bargaining over resources and the positive emotions that are thereby aroused. Hence, the more frequent interactions and the more positive emotions generated from such interactions, the greater is the level of *relational cohesion*. Relational cohesion, in turn, produces commitment behaviors that, in the experimental settings developed by Lawler and Yoon, were divided into three types: (1) staying in the exchange relation even when attractive alternatives for resources were available; (2) giving token gifts to exchange partners unilaterally and without expectation for reciprocation; and (3) contributing to joint ventures with exchange partners, even under conditions of risk and uncertainty.

The results of the series of experiments supported the argument presented in Figure 24.1, but they did not obviate the effects of exchange frequency on uncertainty reduction in generating commitment behaviors. Thus, commitment is related to the effects of exchange frequency on uncertainty reduction and arousal of mild positive emotions, although there is good reason to believe that the two are related: uncertainty reduction probably generates positive emotions, and vice versa. In explaining their model and research findings, Lawler and Yoon introduce concepts and causal relationships not specified in the model in Figure 24.1.

One key concept is objectification of the relationship or the perception by individuals that the exchange relationship per se is an object and source of the positive emotions experienced. Such objectification becomes a "force" furthering commitment behaviors, as people stay in the relationship because the relationship per se gives value, as individuals give token gifts to symbolize the relationship, and as they undertake joint ventures in the name of the relationship.

Once the discursive discussion around the model is finished, the model in Figure 24.1 becomes more complicated. These additional complications are presented in Figure 24.2, where (a) the direct, indirect, and reverse causal forces operating in Lawler and Yoon's theorizing are delineated, (b) the uncertainty-reduction argument from Emerson and Cook's work is retained, and (c) the discussion of objectification is added. The basic arguments remain the same, even in this more robust form. High total power increases exchange frequency, whereas high relative power or inequality works against high rates of exchange agreement (as would be expected by virtue of the earlier discussion of Lawler's and various collaborators' analysis of bargaining). Thus, high mutual dependence and equality will increase exchange frequency, which then reduces uncertainty about payoffs and arouses mild positive emotions that by themselves, but also in combination, increase the level of objectification of the relationship as a gratifying entity per se, beyond the specific bargains and payoffs in any particular round of exchange. Together, objectification and relational cohesion increase attachments and commitments to the exchange relationship that, in turn, increase the level of bonding and group

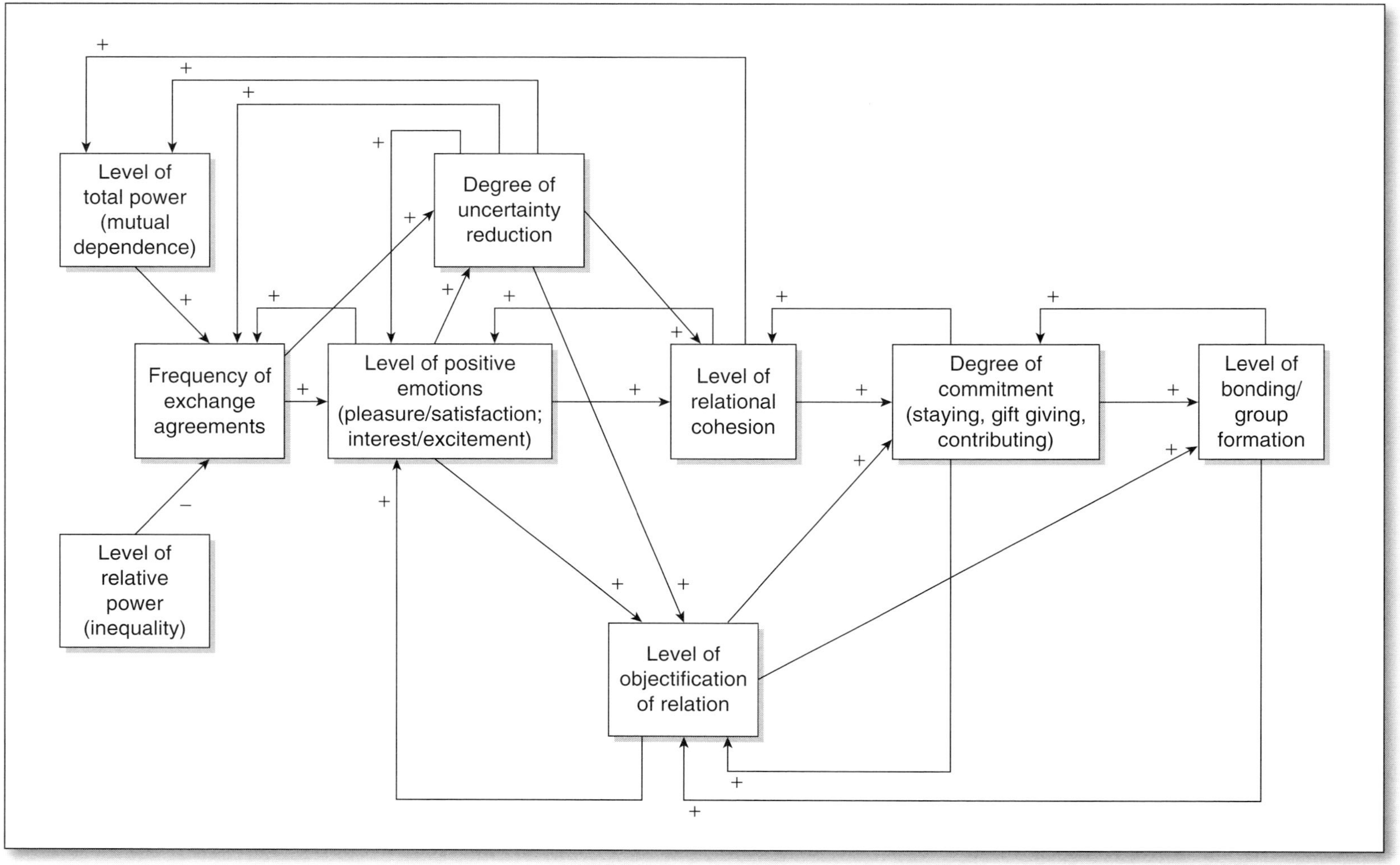

**Figure 24.2** An Extension of Lawler's Model of Relational Cohesion and Commitment

formation. Some of these causal paths are inferred from, and some represent extensions of, Lawler and Yoon's theory; what is true of the direct causal paths is even more true of the reverse causal chains that flow from right to left in the model. These paths represent elaborations and extensions of the theory, but they do so in ways consistent with the theory.

As group bonds are formed from commitment behaviors, these feed back and increase the level of objectification, which, in turn, adds an extra dose of positive emotion. Similarly, bonding, commitments, and relational cohesion all feed back, increasing positive emotions that lower uncertainty. Together, these feed back to increase frequency of exchange agreements. As uncertainty is reduced and relational cohesion increased, this escalated cohesion increases mutual dependence for valued resources that sets the commitment process in motion once again. Obviously, these positive direct, indirect, and reverse causal effects cannot go on forever, making people committed, emotional junkies, but the model emphasizes how structural conditions of high total and low relative power initiate a series of recursive processes that feed off each other and generate commitments to relationships.

In many ways, this theory on emotions converges with Émile Durkheim's analysis of emotions in *The Elementary Forms*, where proximity of individuals generates an increased sense of effervescence that, in turn, exerts a feeling of external power that needs to be symbolized. Once symbolized in totems or other means of "objectification," rituals enacted toward these symbols arouse emotions and commitments to the larger social group. Moreover, the theory also converges with Randall Collins analysis of interaction rituals. Indeed, comparing Figure 12.1 on page 251 with Figure 24.2 immediately reveals the convergence. Thus, we can see convergence among three theoretical traditions—the functionalism of Émile Durkheim, the conflict emphasis in Randall Collins theory, and now the exchange-network approach of Edward Lawler and collaborators.

## Refining the Theory of Emotions

Lawler has expanded this early theory of emotions and commitment into a more robust theory of affect.[14] He distinguishes between (1) *emotions* that are diffuse and global feelings that are arrayed along a positive-negative continuum and (2) *sentiments* directed at specific social objects, particularly task activities, self, others, and group. In introducing this distinction, Lawler argues that as individuals experience positive or negative emotions in exchange relations, they try to understand the sources and causes of their more global emotions, and from these more cognitive deliberations, they develop sentiments directed toward various social objects. And once these sentiments emerge, they feed back and affect the valences or types of negative and positive emotions experienced by persons. Table 24.1 summarizes this argument.

---

[14]Edward J. Lawler, "An Affect Theory of Social Exchange," *American Journal of Sociology* 107 (2001): pp. 321–52.

**Table 24.1**  Emotions Related to Social Objects

| Valence of Emotion | Emotion | Social Object |
|---|---|---|
| Positive | *Pleasantness* | Task |
| Negative | *Unpleasantness* | |
| Positive | *Pride* | Self |
| Negative | *Shame* | |
| Positive | *Gratitude* | Other |
| Negative | *Anger* | |
| Positive | *Affective attachment* | Social unit |
| Negative | *Affective detachment* | |

Source: E. J. Lawler, "An Affect Theory of Social Exchange," *American Sociological Review* 107 (2001): pp. 321–52. Adapted by permission.

If the global emotion is attributed (as a sentiment) to the task at hand during an exchange, persons feel *pleasantness* or *unpleasantness*. If they make the attribution to self as being responsible for the emotions, individuals will experience *pride* when the experience is positive and *shame* when it is negative. If other persons are viewed as causing the emotional experience, individuals will experience, depending upon the positive or negative feelings, either *gratitude* or *anger* toward these others. And, if the social unit in which the exchanges have occurred is viewed as the source of the emotion, people will have a sense of *affective attachment* or *affective detachment*.

In general, individuals will see themselves as responsible for positive outcomes in an exchange, while making an external attribution by blaming others or social units for failures in exchanges. Given this *distal bias* for attributions about the causes of negative feelings and the *proximal bias* toward self or immediate others for positive feelings, the interesting question is, How do people break the hold of the proximal bias and make attributions to relationships and social units for positive experiences? Lawler's answer is complex, but it revolves around two key factors: (1) the *separability* or *inseparability* of joint exchanges and (2) the type of exchange. Each of these factors is discussed below.

(1)  When a person's contribution to a joint task cannot easily be isolated from the contributions of others, this is a situation of *inseparability*. Under this condition of nonseparability of contributions to positive outcomes, individuals have difficulty taking all of the credit for exchanges that lead to successful completion of the task, nor can they easily blame others for

failures. The result is a sense of *socially mediated self-efficacy* where a person's sense of efficacy is tied to the actions of others. Perceptions of efficacy, in general, generate positive emotions like *joy, pride, elation,* whereas the absence of a sense of efficacy produces negative emotions such as *sadness, depression,* and *shame.* Lawler concludes that the "greater the nonseparability of individuals' impact on task success or failure, the greater the perception of shared responsibility" and "the greater the perception of shared responsibility for success/failure at a joint task, the more inclined actors are to attribute the resulting global and specific emotions to social units (i.e., relations, networks, or groups)."[15]

(2) Exchange relations can, Lawler concludes, be one of four basic types: (1) productive, (2) negotiated, (3) reciprocal, and (4) generalized. *Productive exchanges* revolve around the coordination of activities with others and the exchanging resources with these others to produce a *joint good* or outcome. *Negotiated exchanges* involve direct bargaining over payoffs between two or more actors and arriving at an agreement on the terms of exchange. *Reciprocal exchanges* are sequential, with one person giving of resources to another without explicit assurances that this other will reciprocate in the future. *Generalized exchanges,* as discussed earlier, involve giving resources to one member of a network (who, in turn, gives them to other members, and so on), while receiving resources from others with whom one has not engaged in direct exchange.

Lawler also develops additional propositions on how the arousal of global emotions leads to varying degrees and types of *attributions* to different social objects. Productive exchanges will reveal high nonseparability because activities are coordinated to realize a joint outcome, leading individuals to have perceptions of shared responsibility, and causing them to experience high levels of positive or negative affect depending on how successful the activities prove to be in producing a joint good valued by all. Negotiated exchanges, revolving around bargaining, will reveal: (1) a medium level of nonseparability because individuals can see their own success or failure in negotiations, (2) a high level of perception of shared responsibility (over the outcome of the negotiations), and (3) a medium-to-high emotional response to success or failure of the negotiations. Reciprocal exchanges, with unilateral giving of resources with no agreed-upon obligation to return the favor, will evidence: (1) low nonseparability because of the clear separation in time of giving and receiving, (2) low sense of shared responsibility, and (3) low arousal of global emotions.

In Lawler's view, then, productive exchange relations generate stronger global emotions than other types of exchanges because of the high level of nonseparability of each actor's contribution and the strong sense of shared responsibility. Direct exchanges between actors will generate stronger global

---

[15]Ibid., p. 334

emotions and stronger perceptions of shared responsibility than indirect or generalized exchanges. The stronger emotions for direct exchanges over indirect, generalized exchanges arise because the outcome depends upon each actor's active contribution to the negotiated agreement (disagreement) or the reciprocation (non-reciprocation) of a gift offered by another, but these positive or negative emotions will not be as intense as they are in productive exchanges where actors are closely coordinated and where their contributions are not easily separated. Indirect exchanges will generate the lowest-intensity global emotions because actors are separated and have low sense of shared responsibility for outcomes.

These dynamics also explain the nature of attributions that transform a global sense of positive or negative arousal into specific sentiments directed at objects. Lawler asks the following question: What forces increase the likelihood that actors will make attributions to relationships, networks, and groups rather than to self and others?

His answer is that relational and group attributions are most likely in productive exchanges because of the joint, nonseparability of each actor's contributions and the sense of shared responsibility for success or failure in coordinated activities to produce a valuable outcome. Negotiated exchanges can produce relational and group attributions because of the medium level of nonseparability, coupled with a high sense of shared responsibility for outcomes, but not to the extent of productive exchanges.

Reciprocal exchanges are less likely than either negotiated or productive exchanges to cause relational and group attributions because of the high separability of activities in time (between giving and its reciprocation) and the only medium-to-high level of shared responsibility. And, generalized exchanges are the least likely to cause group-level attributions because of the separability of each actor's behavior and low perceptions of shared responsibility.

When individuals who are engaged in productive exchanges make attributions to the larger structure (for example, relationship, network, or group), they subordinate self-serving tendencies to take credit for success (self-attributions) and to blame others for failure (other-attributions).

The nature of networks, whether positive or negative, also influences attributions and attachments. In *positively connected networks*, where exchange of one dyad is likely to cause exchange with others in the network, the *density* (connectedness of all persons or nodes in the network to each other) will increase over time as the positive emotions from exchange in one dyad are extended to others. When people feel good about one exchange, they typically enter another, bringing to the new exchange positive emotions that increase the likelihood of successful exchange and the positive global emotions that ensue from such success. As these dynamics radiate out across the network, the network will become denser with all individuals exchanging with each other.

Under these conditions, the network may begin to approximate a productive exchange if individuals begin to coordinate their actions, leading to network or group-level attributions that enhance positive global emotions and social solidarity. However, if dyadic exchanges activate negative emotions and if this outcome is repeated over time, group formation will be arrested and will generate networks with sparse ties. In *negatively connected networks*, where successful exchanges strength dyadic ties at the expense of ties to other actors, global emotions and specific sentiments will remain in the local exchange, thereby lowering the chances that the overall density of ties in the network will increase.

The *stability of social units* within which exchanges occur is also important in generating group level attributions and attachments. If positive global emotions emerge from successful exchanges in the group and if the group is seen by individuals as a stable source of these emotions as a result of group-level attributions, individuals' sense of efficacy increases, and they will attribute this sense to the stable structure of the group, thereby increasing their attachments to the group (what Lawler termed in Table 24.1 *affective attachment*). Conversely, when individuals see the stable structure of the group as causing negative emotional arousal, they are likely to believe that this structure will continue to arouse such emotions, leading them to feel *affective detachment* and alienation from the group.

A final consideration in Lawler's theory is the fact that social relations of exchange are *nested* in larger, more inclusive social structures. As a consequence, there is always a tension between making attributions for positive or negative global emotions to either the local exchange relationship or the larger, more inclusive social unit within which exchange relations are lodged. One implicit proposition not explicitly included in the current theory is that individuals will tend to give credit to the most immediate and proximate unit—the exchange relationship—for positive global emotions, while blaming the larger, more inclusive social unit for negative emotional arousal.

More generally, Lawler argues that since the local relationship with specific others is the locus for the exchange of resources, while being the place where the situation is defined and emotions aroused, there is a bias for attributions beyond self and other to target the relationship rather than the more distant group within which the relationship is established and maintained. Accordingly, structures of direct exchange—that is, negotiated and reciprocal exchanges—will produce relational attributions rather than group attributions for emotions. In contrast, productive and indirect (generalized exchanges) are more likely to produce group-level attributions for emotions because the focus moves out beyond any particular dyadic relationship.

## A General Theory of Commitments to Macrostructures

With this expanded version of the earlier theory of commitment in exchange relations, Lawler teamed again with Yoon and Shane Thye to extend the theory to a more general analysis of how individuals become committed to macrostructures that are far removed from their daily exchanges.[16] As Lawler's and Yoon's original theory of commitment emphasized, person-to-person ties are created by repeated interactions with others, and these ties are infused with emotions. This arousal of emotions in micro exchanges is seen as potentially generating commitments not only to others but also to larger social structures under specific conditions, especially when: (1) *joint tasks* must be coordinated and the respective contribution of each person is not easily separable, (2) *shared responsibility* for outcomes of task activities, whether successful or unsuccessful, is perceived by participants in these activities, (3) *efficacy* or control over individuals' activities and the outcomes of these activities is felt by persons, and (4) *distal attributions* for the experience of positive emotions. Many of these ideas appeared a decade ago, but they are now blended into a general theory of social commitments. The target of commitments depends upon the attributions that persons make for either positive or negative emotions. As summarized above, if individuals make self attributions for positive or negative emotions, they experience *pride* or *shame*; if they make attributions to others for their emotions, they will experience *gratitude* toward these others when the emotions experienced are positive, and *anger* towards others when the emotions aroused are negative; and if they make attributions to social units for their emotional experiences, they experience *affective attachment* when the emotions have been positive and *affective detachment* (alienation) when they have been negative.

Thus, the key to more macro-level commitments occurs when individuals begin to make external attributions to social units for positive emotional experiences, but as I have emphasized, these more distal attributions must overcome the *proximal bias* of positive emotional arousal that tends to stay local, focusing on self and others as well as the micro encounter where these emotions are aroused. Commitments must also overcome the *distal bias* of negative emotions, which tend to target others or more remote social units rather than self. And so, as Lawler emphasized a decade ago, the key question is how to overcome these biases and make external attributions to distal structures for positive emotional experiences in local exchanges.

Here is where the other conditions listed above come into play: the greater is (1) the degree of *nonseparability* of *joint tasks*, (2) the sense of *shared responsibility* for outcomes of these joint activities, and (3) the sense of *efficacy* in activities, the more likely will individuals make more distal attributions and develop commitments to more remote social structures. Under these conditions, positive emotions circulate among individuals and, as Durkheim might have argued, there is an emotional effervescence that pushes attributions outward toward social structures, which are seen as the ultimate source of positive emotional experiences.

---

[16]Edward J. Lawler, Shane R. Thye, and Jeongkoo Yoon, *Social Commitment in a Depersonalized World* (New York: Russell Sage Foundation, 2009).

The conduits for these external attributions are often along the paths of successively embedded or nested structures—from person-to-person ties lodged in groups that are embedded in organizations, from organizations located in communities, from communities to regional governments, and from regions to societies. As long as individuals are experiencing positive emotions, shared responsibility, and efficacy from their iterated interactions/exchanges, positive emotions work their way to more distal objects, including whole societies. Thus, social structures that foster structural embeddedness will evidence more potential for creating distal commitments, whereas social structures that evidence high levels of inequality will lower commitments because they reduce the sense of jointness, shared responsibility, and efficacy so essential to moving emotion to distal social units.

Other mechanisms intervene in these processes. One is simple repetition of activities; these generate positive emotions that, in turn, create demands for norms that enshrine expectations for positive affect, channel activities to ensure that positive emotions will be experienced, and provide informal sanctions to those not sharing responsibilities in collective action. Repeated interactions arousing positive emotions also generate different forms of trust: *generalized* (about humans in general), *knowledge-based* trust at specific interactions in social units, and *relational* trust in the benefits of cooperation to generate predictability and reduce uncertainty in interactions.

Yet another mechanism of social order inheres in *identity dynamics*, and here Lawler brings his exchange approach into symbolic interactionist theory (see Chapter 16). To the extent that role-, social-, and group-identities are verified in exchanges, they increase individuals' identification with the social units in which the exchanges occur. In fact, to the degree that identities of any sort are salient in an exchange, the arousal of positive emotions causes the verification of these identities. When identities are verified, this increases the sense of efficacy (of self), which enhances the arousal of positive emotions and increases the circulation of these emotions in local encounters (as would be predicted by the proximal bias). But, as positive emotions circulate, a person's sense of self becomes attached to the structures in which identities are lodged; the larger the social unit and/or social categories defining a sense of identity that is verified in exchanges, the more likely are the positive emotions experienced when these identities are verified to carry over to macro-level social units, thereby breaking the hold of the proximal bias. And, as identities are aligned with ever-more macro social units, commitments to these units increase.

In sum, from more modest beginnings in experimental laboratories, Lawler and his former students have provided a plausible answer to one of the big questions in theoretical sociology: How are the macro and micro levels of social reality to be linked? Lawler's, Thye's, and Yoon's answer is that commitment processes are built into the very nature of exchanges in groups. While some types of structures—impersonal markets, stratification of resources, and rigid/punitive organizational hierarchies—can work against the dynamics unleashed by frequency of interaction and exchange, other dynamics in exchanges operate to increase commitments to more remote social units. Frequency of interactions, shared responsibility, sense of efficacy, verification of identities, and positive emotional arousal can all begin to break the hold of the proximal bias, causing attributions to become more distal. This distal movement is more likely when social units are embedded in each other, thereby providing conduits for attributions from micro to macro social structures. The result is that commitments to macro-level sociocultural formations increase.

# Linda D. Molm's Theoretical Program

Most experimental studies employing Emerson's power-dependence ideas have focused on negotiated exchanges, where the actors seek to influence each other's contributions before distributing their resources. In contrast, in a series of theoretically informed experiments, Linda D. Molm[17] examined reciprocal exchanges, in which direct bargaining before the distribution of resources does not occur. As noted in Lawler's distinctions among types of exchange, reciprocal exchanges provide benefits for the other without knowing in advance if the other party will provide resources in return. Many exchanges are of this nature, as when a person does something beneficial for another and only afterward knows whether or not this favor is to be reciprocated. Indeed, a great portion of exchange relations in the real world involves this kind of reciprocity, where benefits or punishments are offered and received sequentially without prior negotiation over the distribution of outcomes. Thus, Molm's program examined a somewhat different kind of exchange—reciprocal rather than negotiated.[18] As we will see, reciprocal exchanges reveal dynamics that differ from those revolving around bargaining. This difference is particularly evident in Molm's analysis of punishment in exchange relations.

---

[17]For overviews of her program, see Linda D. Molm, *Coercive Power in Social Exchange* (Cambridge: University of Cambridge Press, 1997); "Risk and Power Use: Constraints on the Use of Coercion in Exchange," *American Sociological Review* 62 (1997): pp. 113–33; "Punishment and Coercion in Social Exchange," *Advances in Group Processes* 13 (1996): pp. 151–90; and "Is Punishment Effective?: Coercive Strategies in Social Exchange," *Social Psychology Quarterly* 57 (1994): pp. 79–94. For more general reviews of her work within the general context of exchange-network theory, see Linda D. Molm and Karen S. Cook, "Social Exchange and Exchange Networks," in *Sociological Perspectives on Social Psychology*, eds. K. S. Cook, G. A. Fine, and J. S. House (Boston, MA: Allyn and Bacon, 1995).

[18]Linda D. Molm, "The Structure and Use of Power: A Comparison of Reward and Punishment Power," *Social Psychology Quarterly* 51 (1988): pp. 108–22; "An Experimental Analysis of Imbalance in Punishment Power," *Social Forces* 68 (1989): pp. 178–203; "Punishment Power: A Balancing Process in Power-Dependence Relations," *American Journal of Sociology* 94 (1989): pp. 1392–428; and "Structure, Action, and Outcomes: The Dynamics of Power in Social Exchange," *American Sociological Review* 55 (1990): pp. 427–47.

## The Basic Question

The empirical findings in most research have been clear: Punitive tactics are rarely used in exchange processes, even when one actor has a clear resource advantage and could impose punishment without fear of costly retaliation. For Molm, these findings have posed the two basic questions of her research program: (1) Why would punishment tactics not be used frequently in exchange relations, even when they could be used to an actor's advantage, and (2) what conditions would increase the use of punishment strategies and make them effective? Molm argues the reason that punishment is so infrequently used in exchange is not related to its ineffectiveness; rather, the ineffectiveness of punishment is because it is so infrequently used.

In drawing this conclusion, Molm's research challenges an assumption explicitly argued by early exchange theorists—namely, that coercion is counterproductive because it leads to retaliation and a conflict spiral. Alternatively, the use of punishments reduces conciliatory bargaining tactics and impedes conflict resolution. As a result, coercive power is rarely used because of the fear of retaliation.

## The Basic Concepts

Like all power-dependence theorists, Molm begins with the assumptions and basic propositions developed by Emerson, but add additional concepts to account for punishment dynamics in exchanges. Drawing on Daniel Kahneman and Amos Tversky's theory,[19] she introduces the view that the value of outcomes from an exchange is influenced by three dynamics. One is what is termed *referential dependence*, or the tendency of actors to use the current status quo in exchange outcomes as the basic reference point for assessing gains or losses.[20] When outcomes exceed the status quo, as established by past exchanges, they are seen as gains, but when they fall below this reference point, they are seen as losses or punishments. Another key dynamic in assessing outcomes is *diminishing sensitivity*, or the impact of gains or losses as they exceed or fall below the reference point created by the status quo. The first outcomes below or above this point have far more impact on actors' assessment of whether they have gained or incurred losses than do later ones; each successive increment of gain or loss above or below the reference point will have less effect on the actors' sense of their outcomes. A third central dynamic is *loss aversion*, or the tendency of actors to

---

[19]Daniel Kahneman and Amos Tversky, "Choices, Values and Frames," *American Psychologist* 39 (1984), pp. 341–50. Their assumptions are integrated with assumptions from Emerson's original formulation. See Molm's "Risk and Power Use: Constraints on the Use of Coercion in Exchange" (cited in note 17).

[20]Linda D. Molm, "Dependence and Risk: Transforming the Structure of Social Exchange," *Social Psychology Quarterly* 57 (1994): pp. 163–76.

assign greater subjective value and weight to losses than gains. A loss has more impact than an equivalent gain, and hence, actors tend to become more concerned with avoiding losses (because they count more subjectively) than with achieving an equivalent increment of gain. As we will see, these forces influencing assessments of outcomes in exchanges are central to Molm's analysis of punishment.

Punishment is the actual act of imposing costs on others, whereas punishment power is the capacity to impose costs; this capacity is related to the extent that others depend on this actor for avoiding punishments. Conceptually, punishment power would seem to be the same as reward power, which is a function of the level of one actor's dependency on another for valued resources. Thus, both reward power and punishment power are defined by one actor's dependence on another to receive rewards or to avoid punishments. And an actor's dependence is related to the value of the resources provided by one actor to another (whether receiving rewards or avoiding punishments) and the alternative sources for a reward or for avoiding punishments. Hence, in accordance with Emerson's original formulation, a power imbalance on punishment power should lead to the use of this power advantage in the same way as actors possessing a reward power advantage. That is, rates of punishment by the resource-advantaged actor should increase as a means to extract more resources from others who depend on this actor for avoiding punishment and who do not have attractive alternatives for avoiding this punishment. But empirically, power use by punishment-advantaged actors does not occur as frequently as it does for a reward-power advantage. The question is, why?

## The Theoretical Answer

Molm's answer begins with a basic insight into the nature of power-dependence exchanges revolving around reward power. In such exchanges, power use is structurally induced: Actor A's power resides in the dependence of Actor B on it for rewards; this dependence reflects that A has alternative sources for the rewards provided by B, whereas B's alternatives for the resources provided by A are not as attractive; hence, when A looks to its alternative sources for resources, A inevitably demonstrates its power advantage over B, even if A does not want to do so. It is thus in the nature of reward-power imbalance for actors to use this advantage, whether they do so intentionally or inadvertently. The very act of exchanging with alternative actors emphasizes the advantage of one actor over another, thereby forcing the latter to increase its resource offers to the advantaged actor.

In contrast, punishment power is not structurally induced in this way. Actors must decide to punish, or impose additional costs on another who has not provided benefits that were expected. Thus, in reward-power situations, A uses power by simply shopping alternatives, forcing B to provide more rewards if B wants to continue to exchange with A, whereas in punishment-power conditions, A must strategically use punishment to impose costs on *B* who is not providing enough of what *A* wants from *B*. Thus, the use of punitive power is not so much structurally induced as it is strategically imposed when an actor feels that it is not getting what it should.

But, the question still remains: Why is the strategic use of punishment power so infrequently used compared with structurally induced use of reward power? The answer is that the strategic use of punishment power poses risks. One risk is punitive retaliation by an actor on whom punitive tactics are tried, therefore increasing the costs on the actor who initiates punitive tactics. Another risk is that punishment tactics will cause the target of punishment to withdraw and stop exchanging, thereby denying the punitive actor resources that it values. Indeed, the risks associated with losing valued rewards are far more salient than the risks associated with retaliation in deterring use of punishment.

Risk is accelerated by loss aversion, which is the tendency of actors to be more concerned about not losing what they have been receiving in the status quo rather than about increasing, at risk, their resource shares beyond the status quo. If actors are relatively satisfied, they will be reluctant to use punitive strategies to get more, especially if there are risks involved.

Still another force inhibiting the use of punitive strategies is justice. In examining justice issues, Molm adds to findings reported earlier in Cook's and Hegtvedt's work. In Molm's analysis, actors' sense of injustice increases more when punitive tactics are used against them. As a consequence, negative emotions are aroused that, in turn, make them more disposed to use punitive tactics in retaliation. The recognition by an actor that others experiencing injustice will be more likely to engage in retaliatory tactics keeps this actor from using punishment in the first place.

What forces, then, overcome the inhibitory effects of risks, loss aversion, and retaliation by those experiencing injustice? Molm's answer is that an actor will initiate a punitive-power strategy against another when its dependence on resources provided by its target is high but its receipt of resources has been low—indeed, so low that the actor has little to lose by employing punitive tactics. Thus, in Molm's studies of reciprocal exchanges, the power disadvantaged will be most likely to use coercive tactics to get what they value from a power-advantaged exchange partner. Under these conditions, where an actor has not been receiving expected rewards, it has little to lose—because it is not getting much anyhow—in initiating more coercive tactics.

In Molm's experiments, such punitive strategies will be effective if used contingently when a partner fails to provide resources and if these tactics are used consistently each time a partner fails to provide needed and expected resources. Under these conditions of (1) *contingency* and (2) *consistency*, a power-disadvantaged actor can use punishment effectively. This effectiveness increases when norms or lack of alternatives constrain the power-advantaged partner's ability to withdraw readily from a relationship.

The use of punitive tactics by the disadvantaged actor will be less effective, however, when not employed (1) contingently or (2) consistently. That is, punishment will be most effective if an actor employs coercive tactics with some regularity (consistency) when expected rewards are not forthcoming (contingency). If punitive tactics are used as a ploy to get a higher rate of return than justice norms or status quo considerations would dictate, they can be less effective in inducing an advantaged partner to provide resources. Indeed, these punitive tactics might activate negative justice sentiments and lead to withdrawal by the advantaged partner or retaliatory punishment. If the coercive power of the advantaged partner is greater than its reward power—that is, it is less costly to use coercion than to give rewards in response to punitive tactics by another—then the power-advantaged actor is more likely to retaliate with punitive tactics of its own. And the more costly it becomes for a power-advantaged actor to give rewards in response to the contingent and consistent punitive tactics by a power-disadvantaged actor, then the power-advantaged actor might resort to punitive tactics. Yet, Molm emphasizes that, even when retaliation occurs, consistent use of punishment can still be highly effective, especially if this use remains highly contingent on the targeted actor's failure to provide expected rewards.

From Molm's data, the level of positive sentiments will actually rise slightly, even from exchange relations that have been pushed to the point where the disadvantaged actor has resorted to punitive tactics to increase exchange frequency with a reluctant partner. This finding supports Lawler and Yoon's argument on effects of exchange frequency on commitment behaviors in bargaining situations, but in Molm's studies, the exchanges involved are reciprocal rather than negotiated through bargaining. More significantly, the effects of exchange frequency on emotions were generated in Molm's experiments under conditions of high relative power or inequality—thereby indicating that, in reciprocal exchanges, the emotional effects are not destroyed by inequality as they appeared to be in Lawler and Yoon's analysis of negotiated exchanges. Still, although strong and consistent use of coercion will generate more positive sentiments than will weak and sporadic use of punishment, these positive sentiments will not be as strong as those for a partner who uses no coercion at all. Thus, punishment does not increase positive sentiments to the same degree as no punishment does.

## New Theoretical Directions

Molm's analysis of punitive tactics in reciprocal exchanges supplements work by Lawler and others on bargaining in negotiated exchanges. Equally interesting, Molm's analysis converges with Lawler's more recent efforts to analyze how commitment emerges from frequently negotiated exchanges, as is modeled in Figure 24.1 on page 537. Molm has also approached the question of how exchange structures change over time, but she has sought to do so with a somewhat different model than Lawler and Yoon. She sees the emergence of commitments, trust, and normative expectations as being created by the transformation of exchange transactions from a structure of dependence to interdependence.

Structures of dependence in exchange generate greater risk, because outcomes cannot be guaranteed and, indeed, are contingent of what other actors do. Among risk-aversive actors for whom the initial gains or losses are highly salient, there is comfort in creating and sustaining a status quo where benefits are predictable—an argument that converges with Cook and Kollock's analysis of commitment as a means to reduce uncertainty.[21] One way to reduce risk and generate this comfortable status quo is to transform exchanges into structures of interdependence. This transformation involves serial dependencies in which actors' receipt of rewards depends on what they have given in the previous round of exchange. In reciprocal exchanges, actors must therefore set up mutual contingencies where each of their future payoffs depends on their partner's willingness to continue their past patterns of reward. When such serial dependencies become stabilized, they are transformed, in essence, into interdependencies. Once interdependencies are formed, the relation itself becomes a source of gratification, and in Lawler and Yoon's notion of objectification (see Figure 24.2 on page 539), the relation becomes an object outside of the exchange per se, as well as an object that has value to the actors, and thus keeps the exchanging partners in line.

Molm argues that this process of transformation is more readily achieved in the kinds of exchanges studied by Lawler and Yoon—namely, negotiated exchanges. In first bargaining over outcomes, a kind of serial dependence is created in the very structure of offer, counteroffer, and division of outcomes. As the relationship unfolds during bargaining, the actors become dependent on the relation itself to receive their benefits. If negotiated agreements become frequent, then the relation becomes even more "objectified" and, hence, more likely to be seen as a source of value in itself. In contrast, the reciprocal exchanges studied by Molm do not have the serial dependencies built into the very nature of negotiation; instead, serial dependency leading to interdependence must occur as actors sequentially give and receive benefits. The consequence is that it will be more difficult to build trust and to sustain this trust among actors that are for loss-aversive actors, especially actors for whom initial losses have high salience.

Molm argues that, because of the somewhat different ways that interdependencies are constructed in negotiated versus reciprocal exchanges, generating a ratio of exchange outcomes among actors will be more difficult in reciprocal than in negotiated exchanges. Moreover, actors will pursue less optimal and maximizing strategies in reciprocal than in negotiated exchanges. The reasons for these differences reside in the nature of bargaining as opposed to reciprocation. In bargaining, actors are constantly thinking about and calculating rewards, and the bargaining process itself keeps them engaged in exchange process. Thus, they are more likely to seek optimal solutions

---

[21]This argument is consistent with other work in power-dependence. See notes 6–8 for references on other studies by Cook, Emerson, and Kollock.

and worry less about the risks of failure because of the power of the bargaining situation to hold the participants together. In reciprocal exchanges, however, actors are far more concerned with risk aversion because they do not know if another will reciprocate until after they have offered benefits; as a result, they will be less concerned with precise calculations of utilities (which cannot be known until after the fact) and, hence, with maximization of outcomes. Rather, because of the uncertainty over reciprocation, actors will more typically try to keep outcomes at or above the status quo: a strategy that is less risky than efforts to maximize outcomes.

## The Paradoxes of Reciprocal Exchanges

There are many interesting paradoxes in Molm's theory. One is that those with less reward power are more likely to use punitive tactics against more powerful partners. The double irony is that if they do so contingently and consistently, they will increase their resource gains from a more powerful partner, at least to a point.

Still another paradox is that punishment and, in the real world, its manifestation as violence are most likely to emerge in relations that have ceased being rewarding for the less dependent actor because the more powerful partner is decreasing rates of exchange with the dependent partner. Thus, violence comes when dependencies have declined, at least on one side, forcing the more dependent and less powerful actor to try coercion to keep a more powerful partner in the exchange.

A final paradox is that the most fragile relations, where actors are both experiencing a high sense of risk and are worried about losses, are often the most likely to develop solidarities as reciprocal exchange partners seek to reduce risk by transforming serial exchanges into interdependencies in which norms, trust, and commitments can emerge to reduce risk and mitigate against actors' aversion to loss.

# Conclusions

As is evident, the original power-dependence framework provided by Richard Emerson has been taken in many directions over the last fifty years. Several generations of scholars now work in this tradition. This chapter has reviewed the most visible scholars, but their students have also contributed significantly to their work, and these students will soon become the senior scholars in this tradition. The addressed issues—power, stratified networks, commitments, justice, and emotions—are some of the fundamental properties of the social universe, and even though research is usually experimental in small group laboratories, the implications of this research for understanding societies in all their complexity are far from only micro and certainly not trivial.

# PART VI

# Structuralist and Cultural Theorizing

## CHAPTER 25

# The Rise of Structuralist and Cultural Theorizing

The notion of *social structure* or *structure* is central to sociology as an intellectual enterprise. Yet, given its centrality to sociology, it may seem surprising that the concept of structure is only vaguely theorized; it tends to be used more as a metaphor than as a precisely defined theoretical term. In the chapters to follow, I will examine a variety of theoretical approaches where the topic of structure is central to the theory rather than being an implicit metaphor that sneaks in the back door. All these approaches draw from the early masters of sociology, extracting concepts or at least theoretical images of structure from sociology's first one hundred years. As this structural tradition matured in the middle decades of the twentieth century, these images of structure from the early masters began to diverge as various scholars sought to create their own "structural" or "structuralist" program. But even as these new theory programs emerged, they still drew on the key insights of sociology's first theorists.

## Structural Elements In Karl Marx's Theories

Karl Marx's ideas penetrate just about all macro-level theoretical traditions in sociology, and so, we would expect to find Marxian concepts in structural approaches today. In particular, two key ideas appear to have been used by those developing a structural or structuralist theory program: (1) *system reproduction* and (2) *system contradiction*.[1] Let me lay out the issues.

---

[1]See Karl Marx, *A Contribution to the Critique of Political Economy* (New York: International, 1970); *The Economic and Philosophic Manuscripts of 1844* (New York: International, 1964); and *Capital: A Critical Analysis of Capitalist Production* (New York: International, 1967).

1. **Reproduction**. Marx was concerned with how patterns of inequality "reproduce" themselves. That is, how is inequality in power and wealth sustained? And how are social relations structured to maintain these inequalities? This metaphor of social reproduction has been used by many structural theorists who like to view social structures as reproduced by the repetitive social encounters among individuals.

From this metaphorical use of Marx's ideas comes a vision of social structure as the distribution of resources among actors who use their respective resources in social encounters and, in the process, reproduce social structure and its attendant distribution of resources. Thus, structure is the symbolic, material, and political resources that actors have in their encounters within organizations and communities that organize people's lives. As actors employ these resources to their advantage, they reproduce the structure of their social relations and the larger social units within which these relations are organized. Moreover, those with power also control the means of cultural production and, thus, can disproportionately determine the ideologies legitimating inequalities across all units organizing people's social relations. For example, those who can control where others are physically located, who determine their access to the means of production, who have access to coercion, who control communication channels, and who can manipulate the flow of information will be able to build up sociocultural units of organization that structure successive encounters with others who have fewer resources. In so doing, structure is reproduced, but structure is tied to the interactive encounters among individuals using their resources. It is not something out there beyond actors and their interactions in concrete situations.

2. **Contradiction**. Marx was, of course, interested in changing capitalist society, and thus, he needed to introduce a concept that could break the vicious cycle of system reproduction. His analysis of Georg Wilhelm Friedrich Hegel's dialectics gave him the critical idea of *contradiction*. Material social arrangements contain, Marx argued, patterns of social relations that are self-transforming. For example, capitalists must concentrate large pools of labor around machines in urban areas, which, ironically, allows workers to communicate grievances about their exploitation and to organize politically to change the very nature of capitalism. Thus, private expropriation of profits by capitalists *contradicts* the socially organized production process; over time, this underlying contradiction will produce social relations revolving around class conflict—that is, a revolution by workers—that changes and transforms the nature of social relations and, hence, social structure.[2]

---

[2]Karl Marx and Friedrich Engels, *The Communist Manifesto* (New York: International, 1971; originally published in 1847).

Like so many adaptations of early structural ideas, this notion of contradiction has been borrowed in a metaphorical way by contemporary theorists. It is used to introduce conflict and change into structural analysis. These theorists posit, in essence, that the distribution of resources that sustains or reproduces social relations is inherently subject to redistribution under certain conditions. The main condition is inequality. That is, structures reproduced through unequal distribution of symbolic, material, and political resources will exhibit underlying contradictions that will, in turn, generate pressures for interactions that do not reproduce the structure but instead transform it in some way through redistribution of resources.

# Émile Durkheim's Functionalism and the Emergence of Structural Sociology

No one influenced the development of all forms of structural sociology more than Émile Durkheim. His key ideas have already been examined in several places, such as Chapter 2 on the rise of functionalism and Chapter 15 on the rise of interactionist theorizing. Here, I will just concentrate on those ideas in Durkheim's work that had a significant impact on structural and structuralist sociology. Durkheim's functionalism was distinguished by its emphasis on the problem or requisite of social integration and on the mechanisms for meeting this one master requisite. In this regard, Durkheim stood directly in a long line of French thinkers, starting with Charles Montesquieu, proceeding through Jean Condorcet, Jacques Turgot, and Jean Jacques Rousseau, and then moving on to Claude-Henri de Saint-Simon and Auguste Comte. During his career, Durkheim posited four basic types of mechanisms for resolving integrative problems: (1) cultural (collective conscience, collective representations); (2) structural (interdependencies and subgroup formation); (3) interpersonal (emotion-arousing rituals and the ensuing sense of effervescence and social solidarity); and (4) cognitive (classification, modes of symbolization). In essence, Durkheimian sociology examines how systems of cultural symbols, patterns of group formation and structural interdependence, ritual performances, and systems of cognitive classification integrate variously differentiated social structures. Cultural and structural mechanisms were emphasized in Durkheim's early works, before 1900,[3] whereas interpersonal and cognitive mechanisms became increasingly prominent in his later works in the early years of the twentieth century.[4]

---

[3]Émile Durkheim, *The Division of Labor in Society* (New York: Free Press, 1947; originally published in 1893) and *The Rules of the Sociological Method* (New York: Free Press, 1938; originally published in 1895).

[4]Émile Durkheim, *The Elementary Forms of Religious Life* (New York: Free Press, 1947; originally published in 1912); Émile Durkheim and Marcel Mauss, *Primitive Classification* (London: Cohen and West, 1963; originally published in 1903).

Durkheim viewed structure in much the same way as Comte did—that is, as a form of statical analysis—but he used Montesquieu's term *social morphology*.[5] For Durkheim, as for Montesquieu, morphological analysis should focus on the "number," the "nature," and the "interrelations" of parts or "elements" that comprise a structure. This view of structure was emphasized in *The Rules of the Sociological Method*, where Durkheim viewed classification of social facts as involving attention to "the nature and number of the component elements and their mode of combination," whereas explanation "must seek separately the efficient cause (of a social fact) and the function it fulfills."[6] Durkheim's positions on classification of social facts influenced those structuralist approaches that sought to map patterns of relations among the units of social systems. Eventually, this more material approach to structure evolved into network analysis via British anthropology.

Later, Durkheim shifted emphasis to the more mental aspects of structure. Indeed, Durkheimian sociology contained an ambiguity about whether structure when broken down to its morphological components is primarily mental, interpersonal, cultural, or material. This ambiguity became more pronounced in the first decade of the twentieth century as Durkheim studied how material structures become a part of the mental structure of individuals. For example, Durkheim's early essay titled "Incest: The Nature and Origin of the Taboo"[7] along with his and Marcel Mauss' *Primitive Classification*[8] marked a clear movement to the social psychological aspects of structure. This shift became the foundation for much of Claude Lévi-Strauss' structuralism, as we will see in the next chapter, but unlike Lévi-Strauss who viewed material structures as reflection of mental categories of the mind, Durkheim always insisted that the structures of the mind reflect the material structure of actual social relations. For example, as Durkheim and Mauss noted in *Primitive Classification*:

> Society was not simply a model which classificatory thought followed; it was its own division which served as the division for the system of classification. The first logical categories were social categories; the first classes of things were classes of men, into which these things were integrated. It was because men were grouped, and thought of themselves in the form of groups, that in their ideas they grouped other things, and in the beginning the two modes of grouping were merged to the point of being indistinct. Moieties were the first genera; clans, the first species

---

[5]Charles Montesquieu, *The Spirit of the Laws* (London: Colonial, 1900; originally published in 1748).

[6]Durkheim, *The Rules of the Sociological Method* (cited in note 3), p. 96.

[7]Émile Durkheim, "Incest: The Nature and Origin of the Taboo," *Anneé Sociologique* 1 (1898): pp. 1–70.

[8]Durkheim and Mauss, *Primitive Classification* (cited in note 4).

. . . And if the totality of things is conceived as a single system, this is because society itself is seen in the same way. It is a whole, or rather it is the unique whole to which everything else is related. Thus logical hierarchy is only another aspect of social hierarchy, and the unity of knowledge is nothing else than the very unity of the collectivity, extended to the universe.[9]

Moreover, Durkheim and Mauss provided Lévi-Strauss with yet another lead for his structuralism by emphasizing the importance of mythology, especially as derived from religion, as a reliable source for decoding the "logical hierarchy" and the structure of thought. Finally, near the end of this long essay, Durkheim and Mauss introduced another element of structuralist thinking: mental structures are composed of logical connections that reflect how material and cultural "facts" are juxtaposed, merged, distinguished, and most importantly, opposed. Although they did not pursue this line of thinking, they clearly introduced Lévi-Strauss to what he was to conceptualize later as *binary oppositions*—a dominant idea in almost all cultural forms of structuralist theory. For example, Durkheim and Mauss noted:

There are sentimental affinities between things as between individuals, and they are classed according to these affinities....All kinds of affective elements combine in the representation made of it...Things are above all sacred or profane, pure or impure, friends or enemies, favourable or unfavourable; i.e., their most fundamental characteristics are only expressions of the way in which they affect social sensibility.[10]

In sum, several key elements of structuralism were evident in Durkheim's work at the turn of the century: (1) Mental structures involve the logical ordering and generation of classificatory systems that, although modeled after society, become the basis for individuals' interpretation and action in society. (2) Such structures are designed to show the connectedness of phenomena as part of a coherent, systemic whole. (3) Finally, these structures are created by the logical relations of affinities and oppositions as they are encountered in the cultural and material structure of society.

On this latter point, others in the Durkheimian circle pursued the notion that mental structures are constructed from oppositions. Most notable was Robert Hertz, who was killed in World War I, like so many of Durkheim's younger colleagues. Hertz's best-known essays were published as *Death and the Right Hand*,[11] in which the notion of binary opposition is developed

---

[9]Ibid., pp. 82–84.

[10]Ibid., pp. 85–86.

[11]Robert Hertz, *Death and the Right Hand* (London: Cohen and West, 1960; originally published in 1909).

beyond Durkheim's and Mauss' conceptualization. According to Hertz, mental structures are built up from oppositions: strong/weak, night/day, left/right, natural/social, good/bad, and so on. Yet although the critical effort in *Death and the Right Hand* is to uncover the underlying principles beneath the surface structure of observed phenomena, an ambiguity exists: Are mental categories—such as *left* and *right*—reflections of social relations, or are they generated from some underlying cognitive capacity inherent in the human brain? On the surface, Hertz took a straight Durkheimian line— that mental categories reflect social structures—but his work gives consistent hints, supported by his examples, that mental processes per se produce their own structures.

Mauss, by himself, also might have provided Lévi-Strauss with implicit suggestions for reversing Durkheim's position. Although Mauss adhered very closely to Durkheimian principles, seeing himself as the keeper of the Durkheimian tradition, his book (with Henri Beuchat) titled *Seasonal Variations of the Eskimo: A Study of Social Morphology*[12] emphasized the oppositional nature of thought—in this case the dualistic categories and behaviors created by the facts of winter and summer for the Eskimo. Moreover, in his most famous work, *The Gift*,[13] Mauss emphasized once again the search for underlying principles and practices—in this instance the principle of reciprocity—beneath surface structures and practices such as gift giving. Thus, because Lévi-Strauss read Durkheim, Mauss, and others in the Durkheimian circle, such as Hertz, the basic elements of his structuralism were readily evident. Yet the question remains, What made Lévi-Strauss reverse Durkheim's and Mauss' position and argue that the material and the cultural structure of society (for example, kinship and mythology respectively) reflect innate capacities of the human mind for generating structures? We will try to answer this question in the next chapter because it is critical not only to sociological structuralism but also to the broad structuralist movement in the humanities and other social sciences.

Structuralist sociology was also influenced by one of the last ideas Durkheim developed in *The Elementary Forms of Religious Life*:[14] the view that conceptions of the sacred as well as the totems that symbolize the sacred and the rituals that are addressed to the sacred are, actually, the worship of society. As individuals feel and sense the power of society beyond them, they have a need to represent this power in the symbols of religion and to arouse the emotion surrounding these symbols through the enactment of rituals. Thus, in enacting religious rituals, individuals in

---

[12]Marcel Mauss and Henri Beuchat, *Seasonal Variations of the Eskimo: A Study of Morphology* (London: Routledge & Kegan Paul, 1979; originally published in 1904–1905).

[13]Marcel Mauss, *The Gift: Forms and Functions of Exchange* (New York: Free Press, 1941; originally published in 1925).

[14]Durkheim, *The Elementary Forms of Religious Life* (cited in note 4).

society are not just confirming their faith in the supernatural, but they are also legitimating the structure of society. In Durkheim's view, then, religion is the worship of society and of the structures that make up people's daily lives. Thus, social structure, cognitions and beliefs, and ritual practices are seen by Durkheim as intimately interconnected. This connection among these processes became a point of emphasis in many contemporary structuralist approaches.

# Georg Simmel's Formal Structuralism

Although Durkheim was the most influential figure in the emergence of structuralism, especially structuralism revolving around the dynamics of culture, the German sociologist Georg Simmel, was almost as influential. Simmel's emphasis on discovering the underlying forms of association among individuals and groups has exerted considerable influence on some modern schools of structural sociology. Simmel believed social structure consists of "permanent interactions," and formal sociology seeks the underlying pattern of these permanent interactions. The content or substantive nature of these interactions is far less significant sociologically than their basic form. Although interactions can reveal an enormous variety of contents, the underlying form of relations might be the same. As Simmel emphasized:

> Social groups, which are the most diverse imaginable in purpose and general significance, may nevertheless show identical forms of behavior toward one another on the part of individual members. We find superiority and subordination, competition, division of labor . . . and innumerable similar features in the state, in the religious community, in a band of conspirators, in an economic association, in an art school, in the family. However diverse the interests are that give rise to these associations, the forms in which the interests are realized may yet be identical.[15]

Social structure must thus be conceptualized as forms or configurations of interaction that undergird and make possible the wide variety of substantive activities of individuals. This point makes Simmel's eclectic approach to sociology more understandable, for although he studied widely diverse substantive matters, he was always seeking the underlying form of interaction. In all Simmel's most famous essays, this is the message: Whatever the surface substance and content of social relations, there is an underlying form or structure. For example, as Simmel examined conflict, he could see that conflicts between nation-states, individual people, and small

---

[15]Georg Simmel, *Fundamental Problems of Sociology* (1918), portions of which are translated in K. W. Wolf, *The Sociology of Georg Simmel* (New York: Free Press, 1950). Quote is from p. 22 of original.

groups all reveal certain basic elements, or forms. To illustrate further, as Simmel examined the effects of increasing numbers of people in an encounter, he could argue that the geometric increase in the number of possible relations (two people can have two ties, three can have six, four can have twelve, and so on) changes the form or structure of the encounter. Furthermore, as Simmel examined the effects of money (a neutral and nonspecific medium of exchange), he could conclude that the form of social relations is fundamentally altered.[16]

Simmel's essay, *The Web of Group Affiliations*,[17] has probably exerted the most influence on more contemporary structural thinking in sociology. Here, Simmel examined the effects of social differentiation on the affiliations of individuals. In less differentiated systems, the individual is absorbed and surrounded by one or just a few groups that are lodged inside each other, and as a result, the pattern of group affiliations pulls the individual in one direction. With social differentiation, however, the individual can now have multiple group affiliations, belonging to many different groups and being pulled in many different directions. As a result, no one group can absorb the individual, and the individual only gives a portion of self to any particular group. This process of multiple group affiliations sets the person free and increases individuality because each person can, to a degree, choose and select configurations of group affiliation. At the more macro level, as differentiation encourages multiple group affiliations, it generates many cross-cutting affiliations among individuals who might find themselves in conflict in one sphere and associates in another. As a result, the polarization of society is less likely because group affiliations place individuals in diverse social structures and, thereby, prevent them from being overly mobilized by any one group or small set of groups.

## Herbert Spencer and the Superorganic

Herbert Spencer is not read today, except by persons interested in the history of ideas and by scholars outside of sociology.[18] Spencer was, in many

---

[16]Georg Simmel, *Fundamental Problems of Sociology* (1918), portions of which are translated in Wolf, *The Sociology of Georg Simmel* (New York: Free Press, 1950). Quote is from p. 22 of original.

[17]Georg Simmel, "The Intersection of Social Spheres," first published in 1890, best communicates his idea. See *Georg Simmel: Sociologist and European*, trans. Peter Laurence (New York: Barnes and Noble, 1976), but the idea is most available in *Conflict* and the *Web of Group Affiliations*, trans. Reinhard Bendix (New York: Free Press, 1955).

[18]Herbert Spencer, *The Principles of Sociology*, 4 volumes (New Brunswick, NJ: Transaction Publishers, 2002; originally published serially between 1874 and 1896). See my long introduction in this reprint of Spencer's major work.

ways, sociology's first sociologist, although he considered himself a philosopher. Yet, his major works in sociology appeared before many of the classical theorists, such as Durkheim, Simmel, and Max Weber. In these works, Spencer offered a vision of social structure, which I should at least mention here.

For Spencer, structure consists of relations among parts, whether in the physical or organic domains of the universe. Sociology is the study of superorganic systems or systems composed of relatively stable relations among organisms. Thus, sociology can study not only humans who form superorganic systems—groups, organizations, communities, societies, and inter-societal systems—but any organisms that form patterns of stable social relations—insect societies, animal packs and herds, or any superorganic system.

Structures represent solutions to fundamental problems faced by species, and in the case of humans, the problems revolved around needs to organize production, reproduction, distribution, and regulation into superorganic systems (see Chapter 2 where these functional requisites are discussed in more detail). Thus, social structures among supeorganic organisms involve cluster of relations among actors, both individuals and corporate units, that deal with the problems of (a) securing resources from the environment and converting them into usable commodities (production), (b) distributing these commodities, as well as information and persons, across members of a superorganic population organized into a society or inter-societal system, (c) reproducing members and the sociocultural formations that they have created to form a superorganic system, and finally, (d) mobilizing power and cultural systems to coordinate and control members of a superorganism (regulation). Thus, social structures are built from patterns of differentiation of individuals and the subunits that organize their activities—e.g., groups, organizations, and communities—into societal formations. Differentiation increases pressures for specialized social units for production, reproduction, distribution, and regulation; thus, superorganisms that come to form societies are differentiated in structure and culture by subassemblies of social structures addressing these problems of adaptation or functional requisites.

Spencer emphasized that differentiated systems pose problems of integration or coordination among differentiated individuals and subunits. Like Auguste Comte before him, Spencer argued that structural interdependencies through exchanges of resources in markets and consolidation of power and the symbol systems (ideologies) legitimating power are the key mechanisms by which superorganic systems among humans are integrated. Thus, much like Durkheim, but twenty years before Durkheim published *The Division of Labor in Society*, Spencer emphasized that the modes and mechanisms of integration in a society are the most critical dimension of its structure.

# Max Weber on Social Structure

Surprisingly, even Max Weber had a rather vague conception of structure and culture.[19] For Weber, social structures are composed of assemblages of individuals engaged in different types of action. He emphasized four basic substructures organizing a society: organizations, communities, stratification systems, and legitimated orders. We can roughly translate the notion of legitimated orders into what, today, we might term institutional domain (e.g., economy, polity, religion, education, law, and so on). These are regulated by systems of cultural symbols—ideologies, beliefs, norms, to employ modern terminology—and they evidence power and authority or patterns of what he termed *domination* within organizations, communities, stratification, and institutional domains. Thus, social structure consists of actions by individuals clustering into subunits—organizations, communities, social classes, and differentiated institutional orders—controlled by the prescriptions and proscriptions of cultural symbols systems and patterns of domination (by power and authority). These ideas appear in many structural and cultural theories, although their origins in Weber are often obscured.

# Conclusions

As is evident, the classical period of theorizing in sociology did not achieve much consensus over the nature of social structure. The same is true today. Still, the key elements of social structure are clear: patterns of stabilized social relations between individual and corporate actors, differentiation among these clusters by several fundamental types of structures (groups, organizations, communities, strata and classes, institutional domains, societies, and inter-societal systems), systems of cultural symbols that direct action and legitimate power, exchange relationships for distributing resources, and systems of domination through the institutionalization of power and authority. Different theories, however, emphasize varying elements from the classical tradition, with the result that the conceptual confusion over sociology's basic subject matter persists. Obviously, the cultural tradition borrows most from Durkheim and Weber in their emphasis on culture as an integrative force in societies, whereas more structural approaches emphasize interdependencies, power and authority, and at time, systems of cultural symbols.

---

[19]Max Weber, *Economy and Society*, trans./ed. G. Roth and C. Wittich (Berkeley, CA: University of California Press, 1968).

## CHAPTER 26

# Early Structural and Cultural Theories

In the decades between the classical and contemporary periods of sociological theory, structural and cultural theorizing was greatly influenced by three trends by scholars in France, England, and the United States. The French tradition was decidedly cultural, as might be expected given the long lineage from Montesquieu through Auguste Comte to Durkheim, but some rather interesting twists were added. The British also borrowed from Durkheim but less of his statements on culture and more of his morphological states about the properties of structure. Finally, the American tradition began to develop tools for mapping networks, with social structure increasingly seen as patterns and configurations of connections among nodes in a network. Except for network analysis, many of these variants faded, but elements of them can be found in almost all structural and cultural theories today. Thus, the decades between the turn into the twentieth century up to the 1950s when modern period begins were creative and productive, but the scholars working on the problem of structure did no better than those in the classical period at clarifying the properties, much less dynamics, of structure and culture.

## The French Structural Tradition of Claude Lévi-Strauss

In Chapter 21 on the rise of exchange theory, Claude Lévi-Strauss' analysis of bridal exchanges was briefly examined. In *The Elementary Structures of Kinship*,[1] Lévi-Strauss only hinted at the more philosophical view of the

---

[1]Claude Lévi-Strauss, *The Elementary Structures of Kinship* (Paris: University of France, 1949).

world that his analysis of kinship implied.[2] Most of this book examined the varying levels of social solidarity that emerge from direct and indirect bridal exchanges among kin groups. Yet in many ways, *The Elementary Structures of Kinship* was a transitional work because it began to depart from the earlier foundations provided by Durkheim and Marcel Mauss.[3] Indeed, these departures from Durkheim and Mauss signaled that Lévi-Strauss was about to turn Durkheim on his head in much the same way that Marx was to revise Georg Wilhelm Friedrich Hegel. As Durkheim and Mauss argued in *Primitive Classification,* human cognitive categories reflect the structure of society.[4] In contrast, Lévi-Strauss came to the opposite conclusion: the structure of society is but a surface manifestation of fundamental mental processes hardwired in the neurology of the human brain. Lévi-Strauss came to this position under the influence of structural linguistics, as initially chartered by Ferdinand de Saussure[5] and Roman Jakobson. De Saussure is typically considered the father both of structural linguistics[6] and of Lévi-Strauss' structuralism as well. Commentators have often viewed Lévi-Strauss' interest in linguistics as decisive in his reversal of the Durkheimian tradition. Yet, the Swiss linguist de Saussure saw himself as a Durkheimian. De Saussure's posthumously published lectures, *Course in General Linguistics,* had a decidedly Durkheimian tone: He argued that the parts of language acquire their meaning only in relation to the structure of the whole; the units of language—whether sounds or morphemes—are only points in an overall structure that transcends the individual; language is "based entirely on the opposition of concrete units"[7]; the underlying structure of language (*langue*) can be known and understood only by reference to surface phenomena, such as speech (*parole*); and the structure of language is "no longer looked upon as an organism that developed independently but as a product of the collective mind of linguistic groups."[8]

---

[2]Actually, an earlier work, "The Analysis of Structure in Linguistics and in Anthropology," *Word* 1 (1945): pp. 1–21, provided a better clue to the form of Lévi-Strauss' structuralism.

[3]Marcel Mauss, *The Gift: Forms and Functions of Exchange* (New York: Free Press, 1954; originally published in 1924) is given particular credit. It must be remembered, of course, that Mauss was Durkheim's student and son-in-law.

[4]Émile Durkheim and Marcel Mauss, *Primitive Classification* (Chicago, IL: University of Chicago Press, 1963). Originally published in 1903, this is a rather extreme and unsuccessful effort to show how mental categories directly reflect the spatial and structural organization of a population. It is a horribly flawed work, but it is the most extreme statement of Durkheim's sociologistic position.

[5]Ferdinand de Saussure, *Course in General Linguistics* (New York: McGraw-Hill, 1966); originally compiled posthumously by his students from their lecture notes in 1915.

[6]Ferdinand de Saussure, *Course in General Linguistics* (New York: McGraw-Hill, 1966; originally published in 1915).

[7]Ibid., p. 107.

[8]Ibid., p. 108.

Thus, as a contemporary of Durkheim, de Saussure was far more committed to Durkheim's vision of reality than is typically acknowledged, but he made a critical breakthrough in linguistic analysis: Speech is but a surface manifestation of more fundamental mental processes. Language is not speech or the written word; rather, it is a particular way of thinking, which, in true Durkheimian fashion, de Saussure viewed as a product of the general patterns of social and cultural organization among people. This distinction of speech as a mere surface manifestation of underlying mental processes was increasingly used as a metaphor for Lévi-Strauss' structuralism. Of course, this metaphor is as old as Plato's view that reality is a mere reflection of universal essences and as recent as Marx's dictum that cultural values and beliefs, as well as institutional arrangements, are reflections of an underlying substructure of economic relations.

Lévi-Strauss also borrowed the notion from the early-twentieth-century linguist Jakobson that the mental thought underlying language occurs as binary contrasts, such as good/bad, male/female, yes/no, black/white, and human/nonhuman. Moreover, drawing from Jakobson and others, Lévi-Strauss viewed the underlying mental reality of binary opposites as organized, or mediated, by a series of "innate codes" or rules that could be used to generate many different social forms: language, art, music, social structure, myths, values, beliefs, and so on.[9]

As Lévi-Strauss received these very Durkheimian ideas, he appeared to focus primarily on the distinction between langue and parole and on the notion of language as constructed from oppositions, while ignoring de Saussure's emphasis on the social-structural origins of langue. Yet, why did Lévi-Strauss find linguistic analysis so appealing, and why did he ignore the Durkheimian thrust of de Saussure's work? Lévi-Strauss' own self-reflective answers are not particularly revealing. For example, he claimed that he was probably born a structuralist, recalling that even when he was a two-year-old and still unable to read, he sought to decipher signs with similar groupings of letters. Another childhood influence, he claimed, was geology, in which the task was to discover the underlying geological operations for the tremendous diversity of landscapes.[10] He also constructed many genealogies, and for a time, Lévi-Strauss declared that he was an anti-Durkheimian and would embrace Anglo-American methods as an

---

[9]Actually, Jakobson simply argued that children's phonological development occurs as a system in which contrasts are critical—for example, "papa versus mama" or the contrasts that children learn between vowels and consonants. Lévi-Strauss appears to have added the jargon of information theory and computer technology. See Roman Jakobson, *Selected Writings 1: Phonological Studies* (The Hague: Mouton, 1962) and *Selected Writings 11: Word and Language* (The Hague: Mouton, 1971). For more detail, see A. R. Maryanski and Jonathan H. Turner, "The Offspring of Functionalism: French and British Structuralism," *Sociological Theory* 9 (1991): pp. 106–15.

[10]Claude Lévi-Strauss, *Myth and Meaning* (New York: Schocken, 1979).

alternative to the Durkheimian approach.[11] Still, he always kept a foot in the French tradition. For example, he dedicated his essay "French Sociology" to Mauss and emphasized:

> One could say that the entire purpose of the French school lies in an attempt to break up the categories of the layman, and to group the data into a deeper, sounder classification. As was emphasized by Durkheim, the true and only basis of sociology is social morphology, i.e., this part of sociology the task of which is to constitute and to classify social types.[12]

Lévi-Strauss' goal increasingly became one of reworking the French tradition for analyzing morphology or structure. His earlier work seemed to lie squarely in the Durkheimian tradition. In *The Elementary Structures of Kinship*[13] (certainly a very Durkheimian-sounding title), he focused on how kinship rules regulate marriage, which owes a great deal to Mauss' *The Gift*.[14] Lévi-Strauss concluded that exchange is a "common denominator of a large number of apparently heterogeneous social activities," and like Mauss before him, he posited a universal structural "principle of reciprocity." Moreover, drawing from and criticizing Durkheim's early analysis of incest,[15] whereby incest was seen as the product of rules of exogamy, Lévi-Strauss viewed rules regarding incest as ordering principles in their own right. The details here are not as important as the recognition that his work was basically Durkheimian, but there were hints of significant additions. In particular, Lévi-Strauss postulated an unconscious mind involving a blueprint or model for coding operations. For example, *reciprocity* is perhaps a universal unconscious code, lodged in the neuroanatomy of the brain and existing before the material and cultural structure of society.

Why, then, did Lévi-Strauss make this change in Durkheimian sociology? The simple answer might be that he wanted to say something new. If he merely borrowed Durkheim's idea of morphology, Mauss' and Hertz's concern with underlying structural principles, Mauss' principle of reciprocity, Durkheim's and Mauss' concern with categories of thought, mythology, and ritual, and de Saussure's as well as Jakobson's basic ideas in linguistics, what would be original about his work? His strategy was simply to turn the Durkheimian school upside down and to view mental

---

[11]Claude Lévi-Strauss, *A World on the Wane* (London: Hutchinson, 1961).

[12]Claude Lévi-Strauss, "French Sociology," in *Twentieth Century Sociology*, eds. Georges Gurvitch and Wilbert E. Moore (New York: Books for Libraries, 1945).

[13]Lévi-Strauss, *The Elementary Structures of Kinship* (cited in note 1).

[14]Mauss, *The Gift* (cited in note 3).

[15]Émile Durkheim, "Incest: The Nature and Origin of the Taboo," *Anneé Sociologique* 1 (1898): pp. 1–70.

morphology as the underlying cause of cultural and material morphology. He decided essentially to convert what Durkheim saw as "real," "a thing," and a "social fact" into an unreality. In doing so, he changed what Durkheim saw as unreal into the ultimate reality. Thus structuralism was born as the result of Lévi-Strauss' search for something new to say in the long and distinguished French lineage. All elements of the French lineage remain, but they are reversed.

Thus, during the decades of the midcentury, Lévi-Strauss' structuralism became concerned with understanding cultural and social patterns as the universal mental processes that are rooted in the biochemistry of the human brain.[16] In this sense, Lévi-Strauss' structuralism is mentalistic and reductionistic. To summarize what became the basic argument, we can say the following:[17]

1. The empirically observable must be viewed as a system of relationships among components—whether these components be elements of myths and folk tales or positions in a kinship system.

2. It is appropriate to construct "statistical models" of these observable systems to summarize the empirically observable relationships among components.

3. Such models, however, are only a surface manifestation of more fundamental forms of reality. These forms are the result of using various codes or rules to organize different binary opposites. Such forms can be visualized through the construction of mechanical models of binary oppositions.

4. The tendencies of statistical models will reflect, imperfectly, the properties of the mechanical model, but the latter is "more real."

5. The mechanical model is built from rules and binary oppositions that are innate to humans and rooted in the biochemistry and neurology of the brain.

Steps 1 and 2 are about as far as Lévi-Strauss had gone in the first publication of *The Elementary Structures of Kinship*. Subsequent work on kinship and on myths invoked at least the rhetoric of Steps 3, 4, and 5. What made structuralism distinctive, therefore, was the commitment to the

---

[16]See, for example, Claude Lévi-Strauss, "Social Structure," in *Anthropology Today*, ed. A. Kroeber (Chicago: University of Chicago Press, 1953), pp. 524–53; *Structural Anthropology* (Paris: Plon, 1958; trans. 1963 by Basic Books); and *Mythologiques: le cru et le cuit* (Paris: Plon, 1964).

[17]Mirian Glucksmann, *Structuralist Analysis in Contemporary Social Thought* (London: Routledge & Kegan Paul, 1974). A more sympathetic review of Lévi-Strauss, as well as a more general review of structuralist thought, can be found in Tom Bottomore and Robert Nisbet, "Structuralism," *A History of Sociological Analysis* (New York: Basic Books, 1978).

assumptions and strategy implied in these last steps. The major problem with this strategy is that it cannot be tested. If mechanical models are never perfectly reflected in the empirical world, how is it possible to confirm or disconfirm the application of rules to binary opposites? As Marshall Sahlins sarcastically remarked, "What is apparent is false and what is hidden from perception and contradicts it is true."[18] Yet, despite such criticisms, the imagery communicated by Lévi-Strauss, especially in Steps 1 and 3, has influenced a great deal of structural theorizing. Although the extremes of Lévi-Strauss' approach have not been adopted by many, the idea of structure as involving grammars and codes that guide actors in their actions and in the production of social structures has remained appealing to cultural theorists.

# The British Structural Tradition

## A. R. Radcliffe-Brown

A. R. Radcliffe-Brown's early works, such as his analysis of kinship among Australian tribes[19] and, more significantly, his analysis of ritual in *The Andaman Islanders*,[20] reveals many parallels to the late Durkheim's functional analysis of ritual.[21] Equally important, however, Radcliffe-Brown also developed Durkheim's views on social structure. This latter effort was particularly evident in Radcliffe-Brown's more theoretical work, especially on kinship. In his classic essay "On the Concept of Function in Social Science," Radcliffe-Brown asserted that "the concept of function . . . involves the notion of a structure consisting of a set of relations amongst unit entities, the continuity of the structure being maintained by a life-process made up of the activities of the constituent units."[22]

In Radcliffe-Brown's thinking, then, structural functionalism was to emphasize structure—that is, relations among entities—over function or the consequence of entities for system integration. Moreover, he emphasized his differences with Lévi-Strauss when he wrote to the latter:

---

[18]Marshall D. Sahlins, "On the Delphic Writings of Claude Lévi-Strauss," *Scientific American* 214 (1966): p. 134. For other relevant critiques, see Marvin Harris, *The Rise of Anthropological Theory* (New York: Crowell, 1968), pp. 464–513 and Eugene A. Hammel, "The Myth of Structural Analysis" (Addison-Wesley Module, no. 25, 1972).

[19]A. R. Radcliffe-Brown, "Three Tribes of Western Australia," *Journal of Royal Anthropological Institute of Great Britain and Ireland* 43 (1913): pp. 8–88.

[20]A. R. Radcliffe-Brown, *The Andaman Islanders* (Cambridge: Cambridge University Press, 1922; originally published in 1914).

[21]Émile Durkheim, *The Elementary Forms of Religious Life* (New York: Free Press, 1947; originally published in 1912).

[22]A. R. Radcliffe-Brown, "On the Concept of Function in Social Science," *American Anthropologist* 37 (1935): p. 396.

I use the term "social structure" in a sense so different from yours as to make discussion so different as to be unlikely to be profitable. While for you, social structure has nothing to do with reality but with models that are built up, I regard the social structure as a reality.[23]

In his last major theoretical statement, made in *A Natural Science of Society*,[24] Radcliffe-Brown echoed the sentiments in Durkheim's *The Rules of the Sociological Method*[25] and argued that social systems are an emergent natural system composed of the properties of relations among individuals. Therefore, they must be distinguished from psychological systems, which study relations within individuals. In the years between World Wars I and II, however, Radcliffe-Brown and other anthropologists were still welded to functional analysis, allowing notions of the functions of a structure to distort purely structural analysis. Yet, hints of a network approach can be found in a number of anthropological works.[26]

## S. F. Nadel and Network Analysis

S. F. Nadel's *The Theory of Social Structure*[27] was decisive for many anthropologists in separating *structure* and *function*. In so doing, Nadel proposed a mode of analysis compatible with contemporary network analysis. Nadel began his argument with the assertion that conceptions of structure in the social sciences are too vague. Indeed, we should begin with a more precise, yet general, notion of all structure: "Structure indicates an ordered arrangement of parts which can be treated as transposable, being relations invariant, while the parts themselves are variable."[28] Thus, structure must concentrate on the properties of relations rather than actors, especially on those properties of relations that are invariant and always occur.

From this general conception of all structure, Nadel proposed that "we arrive at the structure of a society through abstracting from the concrete population and its behavior the pattern or network (or system) of relationships obtaining between actors in their capacity of playing roles relative to one another."[29] Within structures exist embedded subgroups

---

[23]Quote cited in George P. Murdock, "Social Structure," in *An Appraisal of Anthropology Today*, eds. S. Tax, L. Eiseley, I. Rouse, and C. Voeglia (New York: Free Press, 1953).

[24]A. R. Radcliffe-Brown, *A Natural Science of Society* (New York: Free Press, 1948).

[25]Émile Durkheim, *The Rules of the Sociological Method* (New York: Free Press, 1938; originally published in 1895).

[26]For examples, see Raymond Firth, *Elements of Social Organization* (London: Watts, 1952); E. E. Evans-Pritchard, *The Nuer* (London: Oxford University Press, 1940); and Meyer Fortes, *The Web of Kinship among the Tallensi* (London: Oxford University Press, 1949).

[27]S. F. Nadel, *The Study of Social Structure* (London: Cohen and West, 1957).

[28]Ibid., p. 8.

[29]Ibid., p. 21.

characterized by certain types of relationships that hold people together. Thus, social structure is to be viewed as layers and clusters of networks— from the total network of a society to varying congeries of subnetworks. The key to discerning structure is to avoid what he termed "the distribution of relations on the grounds of their similarity and dissimilarity" and concentrate, instead, on the "interlocking of relationships whereby interactions implicit in one determine those occurring in others." That is, one should examine specific configurations of linkages among actors playing roles rather than the statistical distributions of actors in this or that type of role.

From these general ideas, several anthropologists, most notably J. Clyde Mitchell[30] and John A. Barnes,[31] welded the metaphorical imagery of work like Nadel's to the more specific techniques for conceptualizing the properties of networks. Coupled with path-breaking empirical studies,[32] the anthropological tradition began to merge with work in sociology and social psychology. This merger came about, however, only after network analysis had developed in the United States within social psychology.

# The American Structural Tradition in Social Psychology

At about the same time that network analysis was emerging in England in anthropology, a parallel line of development was occurring in the United States, although some figures and ideas in this American program had roots in Europe. Most of this work came from social psychology, a discipline that at the time was unique to America, where the possibilities of experiments in group settings were beginning to create considerable excitement. As we saw in Chapter 24 on exchange-network theory, this experimental tradition is very much alive today, but my concern here is with how the general network approach emerged in America within social psychological research.

## Jacob Moreno and Sociometric Techniques

A transplanted European, Jacob Moreno was an eclectic thinker; we have already encountered his ideas on role and role playing in Chapter 15, but perhaps his more enduring contribution to sociology was the development

---

[30]J. Clyde Mitchell, "The Concept and Use of Social Networks," in *Network Analysis: Studies in Human Interaction*, eds. Jeremy F. Boissevain and J. Clyde Mitchell (The Hague: Mouton, 1973).

[31]John A. Barnes, "Social Networks" (Addison-Wesley Module, no. 26, 1972). See also his "Network and Political Processes" in *Network Analysis: Studies in Human Interaction*, eds. J. F. Boissevain and J. C. Mitchell (The Hague: Mouton, 1973).

[32]Perhaps the most significant was Elizabeth Bott, *Family and Social Network: Roles, Norms, and External Relationships in Ordinary Urban Families* (London: Tavistock, 1957, 1971).

of sociograms.[33] Moreno was interested in the processes of attraction and repulsion among individuals in groups, and so he sought a way to conceptualize and measure these processes. What Moreno and subsequent researchers did was to ask group members about their preferences for associating with others in the group. Typically, group members would be asked questions about whom they liked and with whom they would want to spend time or engage in activity. Often subjects were asked to give their first, second, third, and so on, choices on these and related issues. The results could then be arrayed in a matrix (this was not always done) in which each person's rating of others in a group is recorded (see Figure 26.1 for a simplified example). The construction of such matrices became an important part of network analysis, but equally significant was the development of a sociogram in which group members were arrayed in a visual space, with their relative juxtaposition and connective lines representing the pattern of choices (those closest and connected being attracted in the direction of the arrows and those distant and unconnected being less attracted to each other). Figure 26.2 illustrates the nature of Moreno's sociograms.

This visual representation of choices, as pulled from a matrix, captures the structure of preferences or, in Moreno's terms, *the patterns of attraction*

**Figure 26.1**    An Example of an Early Matrix

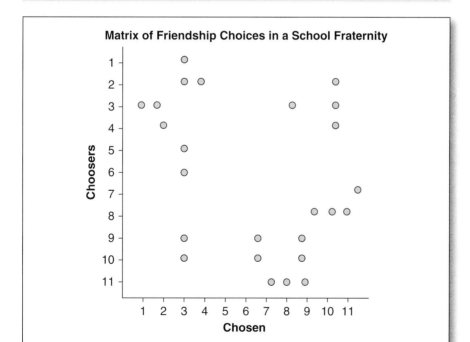

[33]Jacob L. Moreno, *Who Shall Survive?* (Washington, DC: Nervous and Mental Diseases Publishing, 1934; republished in revised form by Beacon House, New York, 1953).

**Figure 26.2** An Example of a Sociogram

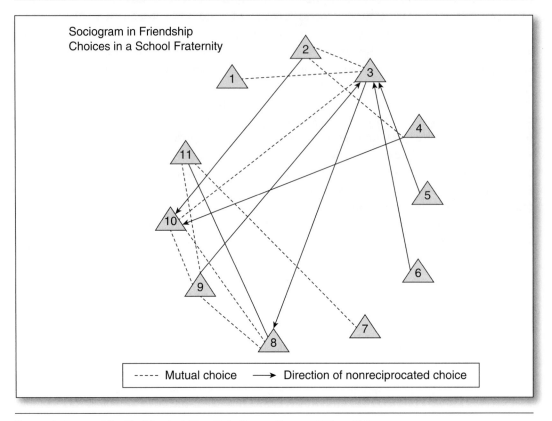

Source: J. Moreno, *Who Shall Survive?* (New York: Beacon House, 1953), p. 171.

*and repulsion* among individuals in groups. This visual array can be viewed as a network, because the connections among individuals are what is most significant. Moreover, in looking at the network, structural features emerge.

Moreno thus introduced some key conceptual ingredients of contemporary network analysis: the mapping of relations among actors in visual space to represent the structure of these relations. Yet, alongside Moreno's sociograms, other research and theoretical traditions were developing and pointing toward the same kind of structural analysis.

## Studies of Communications in Groups

Alex Bavelas[34] was one of the first to study how the structure of a network influences the flow of communication in experimental groups. Others such as

---

[34]Alex Bavelas, "A Mathematical Model for Group Structures," *Applied Anthropology* 7, no. 3 (1948): pp. 16–30.

Harold Leavitt[35] followed Bavelas' lead and also began to study how communication patterns influence the task performances of people in experimental groups. The network structure in these experiments usually involved artificially partitioning groups in such a way that messages could flow only in certain directions and through particular persons. Emerging from Bavelas' original study was the notion of *centrality*, which was evident when positions lie between other positions in a network. When communications had to flow through this central position, certain styles and levels of task performance prevailed, whereas other patterns of information flow produced different results. Figure 26.3 outlines some chains of communication flow that Bavelas originally isolated and that Leavitt later improved.

The results of these experiments are perhaps less important than the image of structure that is offered, although we should note in passing that occupying central positions, such as *C* in Figure 26.3, exerted the most influence on the emergence of leadership, task performance, and effective communication. These diagrams in Figure 26.3 resemble the sociograms, but there are some important differences that became critical in modern network analysis. First, the network is conceptualized in the communication studies as consisting of positions rather than of persons, with the result that the pattern of relations among positions is viewed as a basic or generic type of structure. Indeed, different people can occupy the same positions and the experimental results would be the same. Thus, there is a real sense that structure constitutes an emergent reality, above and beyond the individuals

**Figure 26.3**  Types in Communication Structures in Experimental Groups

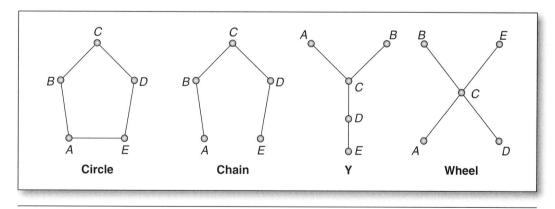

*Source:* Harold J. Leavitt, "Some Effects of Certain Communication Patterns on Group Performance," *The Journal of Abnormal and Social Psychology* 56 (1951): p. 40.

[35]Harold J. Leavitt, "Some Effects of Certain Communication Patterns on Group Performance," *Journal of Abnormal and Social Psychology* 56 (1951): pp. 38–50; Harold J. Leavitt and Kenneth E. Knight, "Most 'Efficient' Solution to Communication Networks: Empirical versus Analytical Search," *Sociometry* 26 (1963): pp. 260–67.

involved. Second, the idea that the links among positions involve flows of resources—in these studies, information and messages—anticipates the thrust of much network analysis. Of course, we could also see Moreno's sociograms as involving flows of affect and preferences among people, but the idea is less explicit and less embedded in a conception of networks as relations among positions.

Thus, these early experimental studies on communication created a new conceptualization of networks as (1) composed of positions, (2) connected by relations, and (3) involving the flows of resources.

## Early Gestalt and Balance Approaches

**Heider, Newcomb, Cartwright, and Harary.** Fritz Heider,[36] who is often considered the founder of Gestalt psychology, developed some of the initial concepts in various theories of *balance* and *equilibrium* in cognitive perceptions. In Heider's view, individuals seek to balance[37] their cognitive conceptions; in his famous POX model, Heider argued that a person will attempt to balance cognitions toward an object or entity with those of another person. If a person (*P*) has positive sentiments toward an object (*X*) and another person (*O*), but *O* has negative sentiments toward *X*, then a state of *cognitive imbalance* exists. A person has two options if the imbalance is to be resolved: (1) to change sentiments toward *X* or (2) to alter sentiments toward *O*. By altering sentiments to *X* toward the negative, cognitive balance is achieved, because *P* and *O* now reveal a negative orientation toward *X*, thereby affirming their positive feelings toward each other. Or, by altering sentiments directed to *O* toward negative, cognitive balance is achieved because *P* has a positive attitude toward *X* and negative feelings for *O*, who has a negative orientation to *X*.

Although Heider did not explicitly do so, this conception of balance can be expressed in algebraic terms, as is done in Figure 26.4 by multiplying the cognitive links in (a), that is, $(+) \times (-) \times (+) = (-)$ or imbalance. This imbalance can be resolved by changing the sign of the links toward a (−) or a (+), as is done for (b) and (c). By multiplying the signs for the lines in (b) or (c), a (+) product is achieved, indicating that the relation is now in balance.

Theodore Newcomb[38] extrapolated Heider's logic to the analysis of interpersonal communication. Newcomb argued that this tendency to seek

---

[36]Fritz Heider, "Attitudes and Cognitive Organization," *Journal of Psychology* 2 (1946): pp. 107–12. For the best review of his thought as it accumulated over four decades, see his *The Psychology of Interpersonal Relations* (New York: Wiley, 1958).

[37]The process of attribution was, along with the notion of balance, the cornerstones of Heider's Gestalt approach.

[38]Theodore M. Newcomb, "An Approach to the Study of Communicative Acts," *Psychological Review* 60 (1953): pp. 393–404. See his earlier work where these ideas took form: *Personality and Social Change* (New York: Dryden, 1943).

**Figure 26.4**   The Dynamics of Cognitive Balance

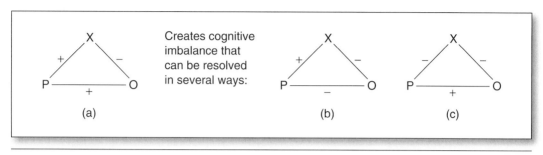

*Source*: Adapted from Fritz Heider, *The Psychology of Interpersonal Relations* (New York, Wiley: 1958), with (+) and (-) used instead of Heider's notation.

balance applies equally to interpersonal as well as to the intrapersonal situations represented by the POX model, and he constructed an ABX model to emphasize this conclusion. A person (*A*) and another (*B*) who communicate and develop positive sentiments will, in an effort to maintain balance with each other, develop similar sentiments toward a third entity (*X*), which can be an object, an idea, or a third person. However, if *A*'s orientation to *X* is very strong in either a positive or a negative sense and *B*'s orientation is just the opposite, several options are available: (1) *A* can convince *B* to change its orientation toward *X*, and vice versa, or (2) *A* can change its orientation to *B*, and vice versa. Figure 26.5 represents this interpersonal situation for A, B, and X in the same manner as Heider's POX model in Figure 26.4.

In Figure 26.5, situation (a) is in interpersonal imbalance, as can be determined by multiplying the signs (+) × (+) × (−) = (−) or imbalance. Situations (b), (c), and (d) represent three options that restore balance to the relations among *A*, *B*, and *X*. In Figure 26.5 (a), (b), and (c), the product of multiplying the signs now equals a (+), or balance.

Heider's and Newcomb's approaches were to stimulate research that would more explicitly employ mathematics as a way to conceptualize the links in interpersonal networks. The key breakthrough had come earlier[39] in the use of the mathematical theory of linear graphs. Somewhat later, in the

---

[39]For example, D. König, *Theorie der Endlichen und Unendlichen Graphen* (Leipzig, Teubner, 1936; reissued, New York: Chelsea, 1950) is, as best I can tell, the first work on graph theory. It appears that the first important application of this theory to the social sciences came with R. Duncan Luce and A. D. Perry, "A Method of Matrix Analysis of Group Structure," *Psychometrika* 14 (1949): pp. 94–116, followed by R. Duncan Luce, "Connectivity and Generalized Cliques in Sociometric Group Structure," *Psychometrika* 15 (1950): pp. 169–90. Frank Harary's Graph Theory (Reading, MA: Addison-Wesley, 1969) later became a standard reference, which had been preceded by Frank Harary and R. Z. Norman, *Graph Theory as a Mathematical Model in Social Science* (Ann Arbor: University of Michigan Institute for Social Research, 1953) and Frank Harary, R. Z. Norman, and Dorin Cartwright, *Structural Models: An Introduction to the Theory of Directed Graphs* (New York: Wiley, 1965).

**Figure 26.5**   The Dynamics of Interpersonal Balance

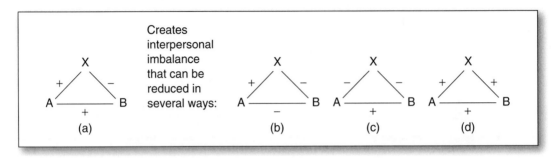

*Source*: Adapted from Theodore Newcomb, "An Approach to the Study of Communicative Arts," *Psychological Review* 60 (1953): pp. 393–404, with alterations to Newcomb's system of notation.

mid-1950s, Dorin Cartwright and Frank Harary[40] similarly employed the logic of signed-digraph theory to examine balance in larger groups consisting of more than three persons. Figure 26.6 presents a model developed by Cartwright and Harary for a larger set of actors.

The basic idea is much the same as in the POX and ABX models, but now the nature of sentiments is specified by dotted (negative) and solid (positive) lines. By multiplying the signs—(+) = solid line; (–) = dotted line—across all the lines, points of imbalance and balance can be identified. For

**Figure 26.6**   An S-graph of Eight Points

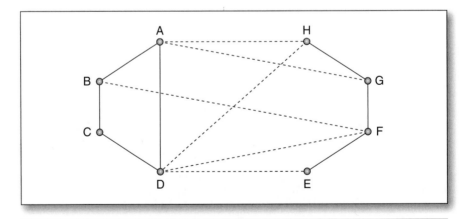

*Source*: D. Catwright and F. Harary, "Structural Balance: A Generalization of Heider's Theory," *Psychological Review* 63, no. 5 (1956), p. 286.

---

[40]Dorin Cartwright and Frank Harary, "Structural Balance: A Generalization of Heider's Theory," *Psychological Review* 63 (1956): pp. 277–93. For more recent work, see their "Balance and Clusterability: An Overview," in *Perspectives on Social Network Research*, eds. Holland and Leinhardt (New York: Academic, 1979).

Cartwright and Harary, one way to assess balance is to multiply the various cycles on the graph—for example, ABCD; ABCDEFGH; HDFG; DFE; and so on. If multiplying the signs for each connection yields a positive outcome, then this structure is in balance. Another procedure is specified by a theorem: An S-graph is balanced if and only if all paths joining the same pair of points have the same sign.

The significance of introducing graph theory into balance models is that it facilitated the representation of social relations with mathematical conventions—something that Moreno, Heider, and Newcomb had failed to do. But the basic thrust of earlier analysis was retained: Graph theory could represent directions of links between actors (this is done by simply placing arrows on the lines as they intersect with a point); graph theory could represent two different types of relations between points to be specified by double lines and arrows; it could represent different positive or negative states (the sign being denoted by solid or dotted lines); it offered a better procedure for analyzing more complex social structures; and unlike the matrices behind Moreno's and others' sociograms, graph theory would make them more amenable to mathematical and statistical manipulation. Thus, although the conventions of graph theory have not remained exactly the same, especially as adopted for network use, the logic of the analysis that graph theory facilitated was essential for the development of the network approach beyond crude matrices and sociograms or simple triadic relations to more complex networks involving the flows of multiple resources in varying directions.

# Conclusion

In Chapter 27, we will examine the effort to continue the French structuralist tradition with a more scientific stance. But the emphasis on mental and cultural process remains, although with less mysticism than Lévi-Strauss' advocacy. In Chapter 29 on contemporary network analysis, the British and American structuralist traditions remain highly visible in contemporary theorizing, as we have already seen in Chapter 24 on exchange-network analysis. In Chapter 28 on structuration theory, we can see a more synthetic blending of diverse traditions that draws from structuralism, interactionism, and other theoretical traditions as well. Thus, as structuralist theory matured, it has gone in many different directions. What is most evident in this divergence is the inability of sociological theorists to agree on their most fundamental idea—the nature of social structure and how best to conceptualize structure. Depending on each theorist's adaptation of earlier traditions—or equally important, their rejection of traditions—very different theories of structure are proposed. And so, in the end, there appears to be little consensus over what structure or culture is and what dimensions of both are to be theorized.

## CHAPTER 27

# Cultural Theories

French structuralism has exerted an enormous influence on modern social thought—from anthropology and sociology to literary criticism and many other fields of inquiry in between. These many types of structuralist analyses vary enormously, but they all have a common theme: There is a deep underlying structure to most surface phenomena, and this structure can be conceptualized as a series of generative rules that can create a wide variety of empirical phenomena. That is, empirically observable phenomena—from a literary text to a social structure—are constructed in conformity to an implicit logic and background assumptions. Some see this logic as lodged in the biology of the human brain, whereas others would view this underlying structure as a cultural product.

Purely structuralist analysis has had its greatest impact in linguistics and literary criticism, and for a time, it enjoyed considerable popularity in anthropology and sociology.[1] Over the last several decades, however, rigid

---

[1]For some general works reviewing structuralism, see Anthony Giddens, "Structuralism, Post-Structuralism and the Production of Culture," in *Social Theory Today*, eds. A. Giddens and J. H. Turner (Cambridge, UK: Polity Press, 2000); S. Clarke, *The Foundations of Structuralism* (Sussex, UK: Harvester, 1981); J. Sturrock, ed., *Structuralism and Science* (Oxford: Oxford University Press, 1979); W. G. Runciman, *"What Is Structuralism?"* in *Sociology in Its Place* (Cambridge: Cambridge University Press, 1970); Ino Rossi, *From the Sociology of Symbols to the Sociology of Signs* (New York: Columbia University Press, 1983) and Ino Rossi, ed., *Structural Sociology* (New York: Columbia University Press, 1982); Jacques Ehrmann, *Structuralism* (New York: Doubleday, 1970); Philip Pettit, *The Concept of Structuralism: A Critical Analysis* (Berkeley, CA: University of California Press, 1977); Charles C. Lemert, "The Uses of French Structuralism in Sociology" and Michelle Lamont and Robert Wuthnow, "Recent Cultural Sociology in Europe and the United States," in *Frontiers of Social Theory*, G. Ritzer, ed. (New York: Columbia University Press, 1990).

and orthodox structuralist approaches emphasizing searches for those deep and universal structures that order all phenomena have declined in sociology. In their place, several more eclectic perspectives have emerged. These theories borrow elements of structuralist analysis and blend them with other conceptual traditions, such as conflict theory, interactionism, and phenomenology. There is still an emphasis on symbolic codes and the ways in which these are produced by underlying generative rules, logics, and assumptions, but such codes are causally influenced by material conditions and are subject to interpretation by lay agents. Thus, just as Claude Lévi-Strauss turned Durkheim on his head in seeing social structure as a reflection of mental structures, many recent efforts have put Émile Durkheim back on his feet, emphasizing the ritual basis for charging up cultural symbols, while augmenting the analysis of symbol systems with Marxian conflict analysis, dramaturgy, interactionism and phenomenology, and other traditions in theoretical sociology. The result has been a revival of cultural sociology in a less ponderous guise than Parsonian functionalism. In these newer approaches, the structure of cultural codes is causally linked not only to the behavioral and interpersonal activities of individuals but also to the institutional parameters within which such activities are conducted.

Although several possible candidates can be seen as squarely in this more eclectic structuralist approach, I have selected for review here the French scholar Pierre Bourdieu and two American theorists, Robert Wuthnow and Jeffrey C. Alexander. Their work can provide a sample of what will be termed here *cultural structuralism*. Each draws from Durkheim, incorporates some of the insights of Lévi-Strauss without viewing social structure as a mere surface manifestation of cultural codes, and connects the French tradition to theories emphasizing the causal priority of material social conditions and the interpersonal processes that create, reproduce, and change cultural systems.

## Cultural Analysis: Robert Wuthnow

Even though there has been a revival of cultural analysis in sociology,[2] the nature of culture is still rather vaguely conceptualized, much as is the case for social structure. The result is that just about anything—physical objects, ideas, world views, subjective states, behaviors, rituals, thoughts, emotions, and so on—can be considered cultural. One effort to narrow somewhat the domain of cultural analysis is the work of Robert Wuthnow.

---

[2]For a review, see Robert Wuthnow and Marsha Witten, "New Directions in the Study of Culture," *Annual Review of Sociology* 14 (1988): pp. 149–67. See also Robert Wuthnow, James Davidson Hunter, Albert Bergesen, and Edith Kurzweil, *Cultural Analysis: The World of Peter L. Berger, Mary Douglas, Michel Foucault, and Jurgen Habermas* (London: Routledge & Kegan Paul, 1984).

Although most of his research has focused on religion, he has sought a more general theoretical approach.[3]

This theoretical effort preaches against positivism, incorrectly portrayed as sheer empiricism, but it nonetheless synthesizes several theoretical traditions and, in so doing, develops some general propositions on cultural processes.[4] Wuthnow's approach is, therefore, one of the more creative approaches to structuralism, primarily because it blends structuralist concerns about relations among symbolic codes with other theoretical traditions. Among these other traditions are elements of dramaturgy, institutional analysis, and subjective approaches that owe some inspiration to phenomenology.

## Cultural Structure, Ritual, and Institutional Context

In Wuthnow's view, it is wise to avoid "radical subjectivity," for the "problem of meaning may well be more of a curse than a blessing in cultural analysis."[5] It is best, he argues, to move away from an overemphasis on attitudes, beliefs, and meanings of individuals because these are difficult to measure. Instead, the structure of culture as revealed through observable communications and interactions is a more appropriate line of inquiry. In this way one does "not become embroiled in the ultimate phenomenological quest to probe and describe subjective meanings in all their rich detail."[6] Rather, the structure of cultural codes as produced, reproduced, or changed by interaction and communication is examined. Once emphasis shifts away from meaning per se to the structure of culture in social contexts and socially produced texts, other theoretical approaches become useful.

Dramaturgy is one essential supplement because of its emphasis on ritual as a mechanism for expressing and dramatizing symbols—an emphasis that clearly owes inspiration to Durkheimian theory. In a sense, individual interpersonal rituals, as well as collective rituals, express deeply held meanings, but at the same time, they affirm particular cultural structures. In so doing, ritual performs such diverse functions as reinforcing collective values,

---

[3]For examples of the work on religion, see Robert Wuthnow, *The Consciousness Reformation* (Berkeley: University of California Press, 1976) and *Experimentation in American Religion* (Berkeley: University of California Press, 1978); for a review of a more general theory, see Robert Wuthnow, *Meaning and Moral Order: Explorations in Cultural Analysis* (Berkeley, CA: University of California Press, 1987). For a review of this work, see Jonathan H. Turner, "Cultural Analysis and Social Theory," *American Journal of Sociology* 94 (July 1988): pp. 637–44.

[4]Wuthnow would seemingly not view these as laws or principles as universal, but his articulation of such laws (often implicitly) is what makes the work theoretically interesting.

[5]Wuthnow, *Meaning and Moral Order* (cited in note 3), p. 64.

[6]Ibid., p. 65.

dramatizing certain relations, denoting key positions, embellishing certain messages, and highlighting particular activities.[7]

Another important theoretical supplement is institutional analysis. Culture does not exist as an abstract structure in its own right. Nor is it simply dramatic and ritualized performances; it is also embedded in organized social structures. Culture is produced by actors and organizations that require resources—material, organizational, and political—if they are to develop systems of cultural codes, ritualize them, and transmit them to others. Once the institutional basis of cultural activity is recognized, then the significance of inequalities in resources, the use of power, and the outbreak of conflict become essential parts of cultural analysis.

In sum, Wuthnow blends a muted subjective approach with structuralism, dramaturgy, and institutional analysis. He tries to view the subjective as manifested in cultural products, dramatic performances, and institutional processes. In attempting this synthesis, Wuthnow defines his topic as *the moral order.*

## The Moral Order

Wuthnow views the moral order as involving the (1) construction of systems of cultural codes, (2) emission of rituals, and (3) mobilization of resources to produce and sustain these cultural codes and rituals. Let me examine each of these in turn.

**The Structure of Moral Codes.** A moral code is viewed by Wuthnow "as a set of cultural elements that define the nature of commitment to a particular course of behavior." These sets of cultural elements have an "identifiable structure" involving not so much a "tightly organized or logically consistent system" as some basic "distinctions" that can be used "to make sense of areas in which problems in moral obligations may be likely to arise."[8] Wuthnow sees three such distinctions as crucial to structuring the moral order: (1) moral objects versus real programs, (2) core self versus enacted social roles, and (3) inevitable constraints versus intentional options. Below, I examine each of these.

1.  The structure of a moral order distinguishes between (a) the *objects of commitment* and (b) the activities or *real programs* in which the committed engage. The objects of commitment can be varied—a person, a set of beliefs and values, a text, and so on—and the real programs can be almost any kind of activity. The critical point, Wuthnow argues, is that the objects of moral commitment and the behavior emitted to demonstrate this commitment are "connected" and, yet, "different." For example, one's object of commitment might be making a better life for one's children, which is to be

---

[7]Ibid., p. 132.

[8]Ibid., p. 66.

realized through hard work and other activities or real programs. For the structure of a moral order to be effective, it must implicitly distinguish and, at the same time, connect such objects and real programs.

2.   The structure of moral codes must also, in Wuthnow's view, distinguish between (a) the person's "real self" or "true self" and (b) the various "roles" that he or she plays. Moral structures always link self-worth and behavior but, at the same time, allow them to be distinguished so that there is a "real me" who is morally worthy and who can be separated from the roles that can potentially compromise this sense of self-worth. For example, when someone reveals "role distance," an assertion is being made that a role is beneath one's dignity or self-worth.

3.   Moral codes must also distinguish between (a) those forces that are out of people's control and (b) those that are within the realm of their will. That is, the inevitable must be distinguished from the intentional. In this way, cultural codes posit a moral evaluation of those behaviors that can be controlled through intent and will power, while forgiving or suspending evaluation for what is out of a person's control. Without this distinction, it would be impossible to know what kinds of behaviors of individuals are to be subject to moral evaluations.

Thus, the structure of a moral order revolves around three basic types of codes that denote and distinguish commitments with respect to (1) moral objects/real programs, (2) self/roles, and (3) inevitable constraint/intentional options. These three basic types of codes indicate what is desirable by separating but also by linking objects, behavior, self, roles, constraints, and intentions. Without this denotation of, and a distinction along, these three axes, a moral order and the institutional system in which it is lodged will reveal crises and will begin to break down. If objects and programs are not denoted, distinguished, and yet linked, then cynicism becomes rampant; if self and roles are confused, then loss of self-worth spreads; and if constraints and control are blurred, then apathy or frustration increases. Thus for Wuthnow:

> Morality . . . deals primarily with moral commitment—commitment to an object, ranging from an abstract value to a specific person, that involves behavior, that contributes to self-worth, and that takes place within broad definitions of what is inevitable or intentional. Moral commitment, although in some sense deeply personal and subjective, also involves symbolic constructions—codes—that define these various relations.[9]

**The Nature of Ritual.** Wuthnow believes that ritual is "a symbolic-expressive aspect of behavior that communicates something about social

---

[9]Ibid., p. 70.

relations, often in a relatively dramatic or formal manner."[10] A moral ritual "dramatizes collective values and demonstrates individuals' moral responsibility for such values."[11] In so doing, rituals operate to maintain the moral order—that is, the system of symbolic codes ordering moral objects/real programs, self/roles, and constraints/options. Such rituals can be embedded in normal interaction as well as in more elaborate collective ceremonies, and they can be privately or publicly performed.[12] But the key point is that ritual is a basic mechanism for sustaining the moral order.

However, as Wuthnow stresses, ritual is also used to cope with uncertainty in the social relations regulated by the codes of the moral order. Whether through increased options, uses of authority, ambiguity in expectations, lack of clarity in values, equivocality in key symbols, or unpredictability in key social relations, rituals are often invoked to deal with these varying bases of uncertainty. Uncertainty is thus one of the sources of escalated ritual activity. However, such uses of ritual are usually tied to efforts at mobilizing resources in institutional contexts to create a new moral order— a process that, as we will examine shortly, Wuthnow examines under the rubric of "ideology."

**Institutional Context**. For a moral order to exist, it must be produced and reproduced, and for new moral codes to emerge—that is, *ideologies*—they too must be actively produced by actors using resources. Thus systems of symbolic codes depend on material and organizational resources. If a moral order is to persist and if a new ideology is to become a part of the moral order, it must have a stable supply of resources for actors to use in sustaining the moral order, or in propagating a new ideology. That is, actors must have the material goods necessary to sustain themselves and the organizations in which they participate; they must have organizational bases that depend not only on material goods, such as money, but also on organizational know-how, communication networks, and leadership; and at times, they must also have power. Thus, the moral order is anchored in institutional structures revolving around material goods, money, leadership, communication networks, and organizational capacities.

**Ideology**. One of the central and yet ambiguous concepts in Wuthnow's analysis is his portrayal of ideology, which he defines as "symbols that express or dramatize something about the moral order."[13] This definition is very close to the one used for ritual, and so, it is somewhat unclear what

---

[10]Ibid., p. 109.

[11]Ibid., p. 140.

[12]Here Wuthnow is drawing from the late Durkheimian tradition.

[13]Wuthnow, *Meaning and Moral Order* (cited in note 3), p. 145.

Wuthnow has in mind.[14] The basic idea appears to be that an ideology is a subset of symbolic codes emphasizing a particular aspect of the more inclusive moral order. Ideologies are also the vehicles for change in the moral order because the moral order is altered through the development and subsequent institutionalization of new ideologies.

The production and institutionalization of these subsets of symbolic codes depend on the mobilization of resources (leaders, communication networks, organizations, and material goods) and the creation and emission of rituals. New ideologies must often compete with one another, and those ideologies with superior resource bases are more likely to survive and become a part of the moral order.

In sum, the moral order consists of a structure of codes, a system of rituals, and a configuration of resources that define the manner in which social relations should be constituted.[15] An important feature of the moral order is the production of ideologies, which are subsets of codes, ritual practices, and resource bases. With this conceptual baggage in hand, Wuthnow then turns to the analysis of dynamic processes in the moral order.

## The Dynamics of the Moral Order

Wuthnow employs an ecological framework for the analysis of dynamics.[16] When a moral order (1) does not specify the ordering of moral objects/real programs, self/roles, and inevitable constraints/intentional controls, (2) cannot specify the appropriate communicative and ritual practices for its affirmation and dramatization, and as a result of these conditions, (3) cannot reduce the risks associated with various activities, then ambiguity in most situations will increase, and just how individuals will behave becomes increasingly unpredictable. As a consequence, the level of uncertainty among the members of a population increases. Under conditions of uncertainty, new ideologies are likely to be produced as a way of coping. Such ideological production is facilitated by (1) high degrees of heterogeneity in the types of social units—classes, groups, organizations, and so forth—in a social system; (2) high levels of diversity in resources and their distribution; (3) high rates of change (realignment of power, redistribution of resources, establishment of new structures, creation of new types of social relations); (4) inflexibility in cultural codes (created by tight connections among a few codes); and (5) reduced capacity of political authority to repress new cultural codes, rituals, and mobilizations of resources.

---

[14]See J. H. Turner, "Cultural Analysis and Social Theory" (cited in note 3), for a more detailed critique.

[15]Wuthnow, *Meaning and Moral Order* (cited in note 3), p. 145.

[16]See Chapters 8 and 9 for other theories using such a framework. See Wuthnow, *Meaning and Moral Order* (cited in note 3) for the outline of this ecological framework, especially Chapters 5 and 6.

Wuthnow portrays these processes as an increase in "ideological variation" that results in "competition" among ideologies. Some ideologies are "more fit" to survive this competition and, as a consequence, are "selected." Such "fitness" and "selection" depend on an ideology's capacity to (1) define social relations in ways reducing uncertainty (over moral objects, programs, self, roles, constraints, options, risks, ambiguities, and unpredictability); (2) reveal a flexible structure consisting of many elements weakly connected; (3) secure a resource base (particularly money, adherents, organizations, leadership, and communication channels); (4) specify ritual and communicative practices; (5) establish autonomous goals; and (6) achieve legitimacy in the eyes of political authority and in terms of existing values and procedural rules.

The more that these six conditions can be met, the more likely is an ideology to survive in competition with other ideologies and the more likely it is to become institutionalized as part of the moral order. In particular, the institutionalization of an ideology depends on the establishment of rituals and modes of communication affirming the new moral codes within organizational arrangements that allows for *ritual dramatization* of new codes reducing uncertainty, that secures a stable resource base, and that eventually receives acceptance by political authority.

Different types of ideological movements will emerge, Wuthnow appears to argue, under varying configurations of conditions that produce variation, selection, and institutionalization.[17]

Although Wuthnow offers many illustrations of ideological movements, particularly of various kinds of religious movements as well as the emergence of science as an ideology, he does not systematically indicate how varying configurations of these general conditions produce basic types of ideological movements. Yet these variables all appear, in a rather ad hoc and discursive way, in his analysis of ideological movements. And so, there is at least an implicit effort to test the theory. In way of summary, Table 27.1 formalizes Wuthnow's theory. Wuthnow would probably reject this formalization as being too positivistic, but if his ideas are to be more explanatory and less discursive, I see formalization along these lines is desirable.

# Constructivist Structuralism: Pierre Bourdieu[18]

Pierre Bourdieu's sociology defies easy classification because it cuts across disciplinary boundaries—sociology, anthropology, education, cultural history, art, science, linguistics, and philosophy—and moves easily between

---

[17]Wuthnow offers examples in *Meaning and Moral Order*, Chapters 5–9, but the variables are woven into discursive text and rearranged in an ad hoc manner.

[18] This section is coauthored with Stephan Fuchs.

**Table 27.1** Wuthnow's Principles of Cultural Dynamics

1. The degree of stability in the moral order of a social system is a positive function of its legitimacy, with the latter being a positive and additive function of

   A. The extent to which the symbolic codes of the moral order facilitate the ordering of

      1. Moral objects and real programs

      2. Self and roles

      3. Inevitable constraints and intentional control

   B. The extent to which the symbolic codes of the moral order are dramatized by ritual activities

   C. The extent to which the symbolic codes of the moral order are affirmed by communicative acts

2. The rate and degree of change in the moral order of a social system are a positive function of the degree of ideological variation, with the latter being a positive and additive function of

   A. The degree of uncertainty in the social relations of actors, which, in turn, is an additive function of the inability of

      1. Cultural codes to order moral objects/real projects, self/roles, and constraints/options

      2. Rituals to dramatize key cultural codes

      3. Communicative acts to affirm key cultural codes

      4. Cultural codes to specify the risks associated with various activities and relations

      5. Cultural codes to reduce the ambiguity of various activities and relations

      6. Cultural codes to reduce the unpredictability of various acts and relations

   B. The level of ideological production and variation, which, in turn, is a positive and additive function of

      1. The degree of heterogeneity among social units

      2. The diversity of resources and their distribution

      3. The rate and degree of change in institutional structures

      4. The degree of inflexibility in the sets of cultural codes, which is an inverse function of

         a. The number of symbolic codes

         b. The weakness of connections among symbolic codes

      5. The inability of political authority to repress ideological production

3. The likelihood of survival and institutionization of new ideological variants is a positive and multiplicative function of

   A. The capacity of an ideological variant to secure a resource base, which, in turn, is a positive and additive function of the capacity to generate

*(Continued)*

(Continued)

---

    1. Material resources

    2. Communication networks

    3. Rituals

    4. Organizational footings

    5. Leadership

B. The capacity of an ideological variant to establish goals and pursue them

C. The capacity of an ideological variant to maintain legitimacy with respect to

    1. Existing values and procedural rules

    2. Existing political authority

D. The capacity of an ideological variant to remain flexible, which, in turn, is a positive function of

    1. The number of symbolic codes

    2. The weakness of connections among symbolic codes

---

empirical and conceptual inquiry.[19] Yet Bourdieu has characterized his work as constructivist structuralism or structuralist constructivism; in so doing, he distances himself somewhat from the Lévi-Straussian tradition:

> By structuralism or structuralist, I mean that there exists, within the social world itself and not only within symbolic systems (language, myth, etc.), objective structures independent of the consciousness and will of agents, which are capable of guiding and constraining their practices or their representations.[20]

Structures constrain and circumscribe volition, but at the same time, people use their capacities for thought, reflection, and action to construct

---

[19]Indeed, Bourdieu has been enormously prolific, having authored some twenty-five books and hundreds of articles in a variety of fields, including anthropology, education, cultural history, linguistics, philosophy, and sociology. His empirical work covers a wide spectrum of topics—art, academics, unemployment, peasants, classes, religion, sports, kinship, politics, law, and intellectuals. See Loïc J. D. Wacquant, "Towards a Reflexive Sociology: A Workshop with Pierre Bourdieu," *Sociological Theory* 7, no. 1 (Spring 1989): pp. 26–63. This article also contains a selected bibliography on Bourdieu's own works as well as secondary analyses and comments on Bourdieu.

[20]Pierre Bourdieu, "Social Space and Symbolic Power," *Sociological Theory* 7, no. 1 (Spring, 1989), p. 14.

social and cultural phenomena. They do so within the parameters of existing structures. These structures are not rigid constraints but rather materials for a wide variety of social and cultural constructions. Acknowledging his structuralist roots, Bourdieu analogizes to the relation of grammar and language in order to make this point: The grammar of a language only loosely constrains the production of actual speech; it can be seen as defining the possibilities for new kinds of speech acts. So it is with social and cultural structures: They exist independently of agents and guide their conduct, and at the same time, they also create options, possibilities, and paths for creative actions and for the construction of new and unique cultural and social phenomena. This perspective is best appreciated by highlighting Bourdieu's criticisms of those theoretical approaches from which he selectively borrows ideas.

## Criticisms of Existing Theories

**The Critique of Structuralism.** Bourdieu's critique of structuralism is similar to symbolic interactionists' attacks on Parsonian functionalism and its emphasis on norms. According to Bourdieu, structuralists ignore the indeterminacy of situations and the practical ingenuity of agents who are not mechanical rule-following and role-playing robots in standard contexts. Rather, agents use their "practical sense" (*sens pratique*) to adapt to situational contingencies within certain "structural limits" that follow from "objective constraints." Social practice is more than the mere execution of an underlying structural grammar of action, just as speech (*parole*) is more than language (*langue*). What is missing, says Bourdieu, are the variable uses and contexts of speech and action.[21] Structuralism dismisses action as mere execution of underlying principles (lodged in the human brain or culture), just as normativism forgets that following rules and playing roles require skillful adjustment and flexible improvisations by creative agents.

Most important, Bourdieu argues that structuralism hypostatizes the "objectifying glance" of the outside academic observer. The "Homo academicus" transfers a particular relation to the world, the distant and objectifying gaze of the professional academic, onto the very properties of that world.[22] As a result, the outside observer constructs the world as a mere spectacle, which is subject to neutral observation. The distant and uninvolved observer's relation to the world is not only systematic but also a passive cognition, so the world itself is viewed as consisting of cognition rather than active practices. According to Bourdieu, structuralism and other approaches that objectify the world do not simply research the empirical

---

[21]Pierre Bourdieu, *Language and Symbolic Power* (Cambridge, MA: Harvard University Press, 1989).

[22]Pierre Bourdieu, *Homo Academicus* (Stanford, CA: Stanford University Press, 1988).

world out there; rather, they construct it as an objective fact through the distancing perspective of the outside observer.

Bourdieu does not, however, reject completely structuralism and other objectifying approaches that seek, in Durkheim's words, to discover external and constraining "social facts." As we will see, Bourdieu views social classes, and factions within such classes, as social facts. As social facts, the structure of classes and class factions can be objectively observed; and as Durkheim would emphasize, they should, as social facts, be seen as external to, and constraining on, the thoughts and activities of individuals.[23] Moreover, Bourdieu at least borrows the metaphor, if not the essence, of structuralism in his efforts to discover the "generative principles" that people use to construct social and cultural phenomena—systems of classification, ideologies, forms of legitimating social practices, and other elements of "constructivist structuralism."[24]

**The Critique of Interactionism and Phenomenology.** Bourdieu is also critical of interactionism, phenomenology, and other subjectivist approaches.[25] Bourdieu believes that there is more to social life than interaction and that there is more to interaction than the "definitions of situations" in symbolic interactionism or the "accounting practices" in ethnomethodology. The *actor* of symbolic interactionism and the *member* of ethnomethodology are abstractions that fail to realize that members are always incumbents in particular groups and classes. Interactions are always *interactions-in-contexts*, and the most important of these contexts is *class location*. Even such an elementary feature of interaction as the possibility that it might even occur among particular sets of individuals varies with class background. Interaction is thus embedded in structure, and the structure constrains what is possible.

Moreover, in addition to this rather widespread critique of interactionism as "astructural," Bourdieu argues that interactionism is too cognitive in its overemphasis on the accounting and sense-making activities of agents. As a result, it forgets that actors have objective class-based interests. And, once again, the biases of Homo academicus are evident. It is in the nature of academics to define, assess, reflect, ponder, and interpret the social world; as a result of this propensity, a purely academic relation to the world is imposed on real people in social contexts. For interactionists, then, people are merely disinterested lay academics who define, reflect, interpret, and account for actions and situations. But lay interpretations, and academic portrayals of these lay interpretations, cannot accurately describe social

---

[23]Pierre Bourdieu, *Distinction: A Social Critique of the Judgement of Taste* (Cambridge, MA: Harvard University Press, 1984).

[24]See Wacquant, "Towards a Reflexive Sociology" (cited in note 19); Bourdieu, "Social Space and Symbolic Power" (cited in note 20), pp. 14–25.

[25]See Wacquant, "Towards a Reflexive Sociology" (cited in note 19).

reality for two reasons. First, as noted, these interpretations are constrained by existing structures, especially class and class factions. Second, these interpretations are themselves part of objective class struggles as individuals construct legitimating definitions for their conduct.[26]

Bourdieu then borrows from Karl Marx the notion that people are located in a class position, that this position gives them certain interests, and that their interpretative actions are often ideologies designed to legitimate these interests. People's "definitions of situations" are neither neutral nor innocent, but are often ideological weapons that are very much a part of the objective class structures and the inherent conflicts of interests generated by such structures.[27]

**The Critique of Utilitarianism.** Rational economic theories also portray, and at the same time betray, Homo academicus' relation to the social world. Like academics in general, utilitarian economic theorists[28] see humans as rational, calculating, and maximizing (*sujets ravauts*); thus, rational exchange theories mistake a model of the human actor for real individuals, thereby reifying their theoretical abstractions.

Yet Bourdieu does not replace the economic model of rational action with an interpretative model of symbolic action. He does not argue that rational action theory is wrong because it is too rationalistic or because it ignores the interpretative side of action. To the contrary, he holds that rational action theory does not realize that even symbolic action is rational and based on class interests. Thus, according to Bourdieu, the error of the economic model is not that it presents all action as rational and interested; rather, the big mistake is to restrict interests and rationality to the immediate material payoffs collected by reflective and profit-seeking individuals.[29]

Bourdieu reasons that all social practices are part of, and embedded in, individuals' (self-)interests, even if individual agents are unaware of their interests and even if the stakes of these practices are not material profits. Social practices are attuned to the conditions of particular arenas in which actions might yield profits without deliberate intention. For example, in science, it is the most "disinterested" and "pure" research that yields the highest cultural profits—that is, academic recognition and reputation. In social fields other than economic exchange, it is the structural denial of any interests that often yields the highest gains. It is not that agents cynically deny being interested to increase their gains even more; rather, innocence ensures that honest disinterestedness nevertheless is the most profitable practice.

---

[26]Bourdieu, *Outline of a Theory of Practice* (Cambridge: Cambridge University Press, 1977), pp. 22 ff. and *Distinction* (cited in note 23).

[27]Same as above.

[28]See the brief summary of utilitarianism in Chapter 21.

[29]See Wacquant, "Towards a Reflexive Sociology" (cited in note 19), p. 43.

For example, gift exchange economies—the subject of Bourdieu's early anthropological research[30]—might illustrate this complex idea. Gift exchange economies are typically embedded in larger social relations and solidarities so that exchange is not purely instrumental and material but has a strong *moral* quality to it. Economic exchanges are expected to follow the social logic of solidarity and group memberships at least as much as they follow the economic logic of material gain. From the narrow economic perspective of rational-action theory, the logic of solidarity would seem like an intrusion of "nonrational" forces, such as tradition or emotion, into an otherwise purely rational system of exchange. Yet, the logic of solidarity points to those processes by which *symbolic* and *social capital* are accumulated—a "social fact" that is missed by the narrow economic determinism of rational-action theory. But, once the notion of capital is extended to include symbolic and social capital, apparently "irrational" practices can now be seen to follow their own (self-)interested logic, and contrary to initial impressions, these practices are not irrational at all. The denial of narrowly economic interests in gift-exchange economies conceals the fact that, as the social and economic capital are increased, the more will the purely instrumental aspects of exchange move into the background. For instance, birthday and Christmas presents are socially more effective when they appear less material and economic; those who brag about the high costs of their presents do not understand the nature of gift exchanges and, as a consequence, are considered rude, thereby losing symbolic and social capital.

Thus, in broadening economic exchange to include social and symbolic resources, as all sociological exchange theories eventually do,[31] Bourdieu introduces a central concept in his approach: capital.[32] Those in different classes reveal not only varying levels or amounts of capital but also divergent types and configurations of capital. Bourdieu's view of capital recognizes that the resources individuals possess can be material, symbolic, social, and cultural; moreover, these resources reflect class location and are used to further the interests of those in a particular class position.

## Bourdieu's Cultural Conflict Theory

Although Bourdieu has explored many topics, the conceptual core of his sociology is a vision of social classes and the cultural forms associated with these classes.[33] In essence, Bourdieu combines a Marxian theory of objective

---

[30]Bourdieu, *Outline of a Theory of Practice* (cited in note 26).

[31]See Chapters 20 and 22.

[32]Pierre Bourdieu, "The Forms of Capital," in *Handbook of Theory and Research in the Sociology of Education*, ed. J. G. Richardson (New York: Greenwood, 1986). See also Michele Lamont and Annette P. Larreau, "Cultural Capital: Allusions, Gaps, and Glissandos in Recent Theoretical Developments," *Sociological Theory* 6, no. 2 (Fall 1988), pp. 153–68.

[33]Bourdieu, *Distinction* and *Outline of a Theory of Practice* (cited in notes 23 and 26).

class position in relation to the means of production with a Weberian analysis of status groups (lifestyles, tastes, prestige) and politics (organized efforts to have one's class culture dominate). The key to this reconciliation of Karl Marx's and Max Weber's views of stratification is the expanded conceptualization of *capital* as more than economic and material resources, coupled with elements of French structuralism.

**Classes and Capital**. To understand Bourdieu's view of classes, it is first necessary to recognize a distinction among four types of capital:[34] (1) *economic capital*, or productive property (money and material objects that can be used to produce goods and services); (2) *social capital*, or positions and relations in groupings and social networks; (3) *cultural capital*, or informal interpersonal skills, habits, manners, linguistic styles, educational credentials, tastes, and lifestyles, and (4) *symbolic capital*, or the use of symbols to legitimate the possession of varying levels and configurations of the other three types of capital.

These forms of capital can be converted into one another, but only to a certain extent. The degree of convertibility of capital on various markets is itself at stake in social struggles. The over-production of academic qualifications, for example, can decrease the convertibility of educational into economic capital ("credential inflation"). As a result, owners of credentials must struggle to get their cultural capital converted into economic gains, such as high-paying jobs. Likewise, the extent to which economic capital can be converted into social capital is at stake in struggles over control of the political apparatus, and the efforts of those with economic capital to buy cultural capital can often be limited by their perceived lack of taste (a type of cultural capital).

The distribution of these four types of capital determines the objective class structure of a social system. The overall class structure reflects the total amount of capital possessed by various groupings. Hence the dominant class will possess the most economic, social, cultural, and symbolic capital; the middle class will possess less of these forms of capital; and the lower classes will have the least amount of these capital resources.

The class structure is not, however, a simple lineal hierarchy. Within each class are *factions* that can be distinguished by (1) the composition or configuration of their capital and (2) the social origin and amount of time that individuals in families have possessed a particular profile or configuration of capital resources.

---

[34]Bourdieu, "The Forms of Capital" (cited in note 32). For another cultural approach to analyzing classes, see Michelle Lamont, *Money, Morals and Manners: The Culture of the French and American Upper-Middle Class* (Chicago, IL: Univeristy of Chicago Press, 1992); "Symbolic Boundaries and Status," in *Cultural Sociology*, ed. Lyn Spillman (Malden, MA and Oxford: Blackwell, 2002), pp. 98–119; *The Dignity of Working Men: Morality and the Boundaries of Race, Class, and Immigration,* (Cambridge: Harvard University Press and New York: Russell Sage Foundation, 2002).

**Table 27.2** Representation of Classes and Class Factions in Industrial Societies

### Dominant Class: Richest in All Forms of Capital

**Dominant faction**: Richest in economic capital, which can be used to buy other types of capital. This faction is composed primarily of those who own the means of production—that is, the classical bourgeoisie.

**Intermediate faction**: Some economic capital, coupled with moderate levels of social, cultural, and symbolic capital. This faction is composed of high-credential professionals.

**Dominated faction**: Little economic capital but high levels of cultural and symbolic capital. This faction is composed of intellectuals, artists, writers, and others who possess cultural resources valued in a society.

### Middle Class: Moderate Levels of All Forms of Capital

**Dominant faction**: Highest in this class in economic capital but having considerably less economic capital than the dominant faction of the dominant class. This faction is composed of petite bourgeoisie (small business owners).

**Intermediate faction**: Some economic, social, cultural, and symbolic capital but considerably less than the intermediate faction of the dominant class. This faction is composed of skilled clerical workers.

**Dominated faction**: Little or no economic capital and comparatively high social, cultural, and symbolic capital. This class is composed of educational workers, such as schoolteachers, and other low-income and routinized professions that are involved in cultural production.

### Lower Class: Low Levels of All Forms of Capital

**Dominant faction**: Comparatively high economic capital for this general class. Composed of skilled manual workers.

**Intermediate faction**: Lower amounts of economic and other types of capital. Composed of semi-skilled workers without credentials.

**Dominated faction**: Very low amounts of economic capital. Some symbolic capital in uneducated ideologues and intellectuals for the poor and working person.

*Note:* We have had to make inferences from Bourdieu's somewhat rambling text, but the table captures the imagery of Bourdieu's analysis. He probably would not like this layered (like a cake) imagery in the table, but the critical point is that individuals and families in factions of different classes often have more in common than individuals and families at different factions within a class. This makes stratification a much more complex phenomenon than is typically portrayed by sociologists.

Table 27.2 represents schematically Bourdieu's portrayal of the factions in three classes. The top faction within a given class controls the greatest proportion of economic or productive capital typical of a class; the bottom faction possesses the greatest amount of cultural and symbolic capital for a class; and the middle faction possesses an intermediate amount of economic, cultural, and symbolic capital. The top faction is the dominant faction within a given class, and the bottom faction is the dominated faction for that class, with the middle faction being both superordinate over the dominated faction and subordinate to the top faction. As factions engage in struggles to control resources and legitimate themselves, they mobilize social capital to form groupings and networks of relations, but their capacity to form such networks is limited by their other forms of capital. Thus, the overall distribution of social capital (groups and organizational memberships, network ties, social relations, and so forth) for classes and their factions will correspond to the overall distribution of other forms of capital. However, the particular forms of groupings, networks, and social ties will reflect the particular configuration of economic, cultural, and symbolic capital typically possessed by a particular faction within a given class.

Bourdieu borrows Marx's distinction between a class *for itself* (organized to pursue its interests) and one *in itself* (unorganized but having common interests and objective location in a class and class-faction). Then he argues that classes are not real groups but only "potentialities." As noted earlier, the objective distribution of resources for Bourdieu relates to actual groups as grammar relates to speech: It defines the possibilities for actors but requires actual people and concrete settings to become real. And, it is the transformation of class and class-faction interests into actual groupings that marks the dynamics of a society.

Such transformation involves the use of productive material, cultural, and symbolic capital to mobilize social capital (groups and networks); even more important, class conflict tends to revolve around the mobilization of symbols into ideologies that legitimate a particular composition of resources.[35] Much conflict in human societies, therefore, revolves around efforts to manipulate symbols to make a particular pattern of social, cultural, and productive resources seem the most appropriate. For example, when intellectuals and artists decry the "crass commercialism," "acquisitiveness," and "greed" of big business, this activity involves the mobilization of symbols into an ideology that seeks to mitigate their domination by the owners of the means of production.

But class relations involve more than a simple pecking order. There are also homologies among similarly located factions within different classes. For example, the rich capitalists of the dominant class and the small business owners of the middle class are equivalent in their control of productive resources and their dominant position relative to other factions in their respective classes.[36] Similarly, intellectuals, artists, and other cultural elites in the dominant class are equivalent to schoolteachers in the middle class because of their reliance on cultural capital and because of their subordinate

---

[35]Pierre Bourdieu, "Social Space and the Genesis of Groups," *Theory and Society* 14 (November 1985): pp. 723–44.

[36]Bourdieu makes what in network analysis (see Chapter 29) is termed *regular structural equivalence.* That is, those incumbents in positions that stand in an equivalent (similar) relation to other positions will act in a convergent way and evidence common attributes.

position in relation to those who control the material resources of their respective classes.

These homologies in class factions across different classes make class conflict complex, because those in similar objective positions in different classes—say, intellectuals and schoolteachers—will mobilize symbolic resources into somewhat similar ideologies—in this example, emphasizing learning, knowledge for its own sake, and life of the mind and, at the same time, decrying crass materialism. Such ideologies legitimate their own class position and attack those who dominate them (by emphasizing the importance of those cultural resources that they have more of). At the same time, their homologous positions are separated by the different amounts of cultural capital owned: The intellectuals despise the strained efforts of schoolteachers to appear more sophisticated than they are, whereas the schoolteachers resent the decadent and irresponsible relativism of snobbish intellectuals. Thus, ideological conflict is complicated by the simultaneous convergence of factions within different classes and by the divergence of these factions by virtue of their position in different social classes.

Moreover, an additional complication stems from people sharing similar types and amounts of resources but having very different origins and social trajectories. Those who have recently moved to a class faction—say, the dominant productive elite or intermediate faction of the middle class—will have somewhat different styles and tastes than those who have been born into these classes, and these differences in social origin and mobility can create yet another source of ideological conflict. For example, the "old rich" will often comment on the "lack of class" and "ostentatiousness" of the "new rich"; or, the "solid middle class" will be somewhat snobbish toward the "poor boy who made good" but who "still has a lot to learn" or who "still is a bit crude."

All those points of convergence and divergence within and between classes and class factions make the dynamics of stratification complex. Although there is always an objective class location, as determined by the amount and composition of capital and by the social origins of capital holders, the development of organizations and ideologies is not a simple process. Bourdieu often ventures into a more structuralist mode when trying to sort out how various classes, class factions, and splits of individuals with different social origins within class factions generate categories of thought, systems of speech, signs of distinction, forms of mythology, modes of appreciation, tastes, and lifestyle.

The general argument is that objective location—(1) class, (2) faction within class, and (3) social origin—creates interests and structural constraints that, in turn, allow different social constructions.[37] Such constructions might

---

[37]Bourdieu is not very clear about the issue of how the structural potentialities of a given objective class location become transformed into actual social groups capable of historical action. Like Lévi-Strauss, Bourdieu pursues the formal analogies between deep structures and actual practices, but he lacks a theory about how and when the transformations are going to be made, and made successfully.

involve the use of formal rules (implicitly known by individuals with varying interests) to construct cultural codes that classify and organize things, signs, and people in the world. This kind of analysis by Bourdieu has not produced a fine-grained structuralist model of how individuals construct particular cultural codes, but it has provided an interesting analysis of "class cultures." Such class cultures are always the dependent variable for Bourdieu, with objective class location being the independent variable and with rather poorly conceptualized structuralist processes of generative rules and cultural codes being the "intervening variables." Yet the detailed description of these class cultures is perhaps Bourdieu's most unique contribution to sociology and is captured by his concept of *habitus*.

**Class Cultures and Habitus**. Those within a given class share certain modes of classification, appreciation, judgment, perception, and behavior. Bourdieu conceptualizes this mediating process between class and individual perceptions, choices, and behavior as habitus.[38] In a sense, habitus is the "collective unconscious" of those in similar positions because it provides cognitive and emotional guidelines that enable individuals to represent the world in common ways and to classify, choose, evaluate, and act in a particular manner.

The habitus creates syndromes of taste, speech, dress, manner, and other responses. For example, a preference for particular foods will tend to correspond to tastes in art, ways of dressing, styles of speech, manners of eating, and other cultural actions among those sharing a common class location. There is, then, a correlation between the class hierarchy and the cultural objects, preferences, and behaviors of those located at particular ranks in the hierarchy. For instance, Bourdieu devotes considerable attention to *taste*, which is seen as one of the most visible manifestations of the habitus.

Bourdieu views taste in a holistic and anthropological sense to include appreciation of art, ways of dressing, and preferences for foods.[39] Although taste appears as an innocent, natural, and personal phenomenon, it co-varies with objective class location: The upper class is to the working class what an art museum is to television; the old upper class is to the new upper class what polite and distant elegance is to noisy and conspicuous consumption; and the dominant is to the dominated faction of the upper class what opera is to avant-garde theater. Because tastes are organized in a cultural hierarchy that mirrors the social hierarchy of objective class location, conflicts between tastes are class conflicts.

Bourdieu roughly distinguishes between two types of tastes, which correspond to high versus low overall capital, or high versus low objective class

---

[38]Bourdieu, *Distinction* (cited in note 23).

[39]Ibid.

position.[40] The taste of liberty and luxury is the taste of the upper class; as such, it is removed from direct economic necessity and material need. The taste of liberty is the philosophy of art for its own sake. Following Immanuel Kant, Bourdieu calls this aesthetic the "pure gaze." The pure gaze looks at the sheer form of art and places this form above function and content. The upper-class taste of luxury is not concerned with art illustrating or representing some external reality; art is removed from life, just as upper-class life is removed from harsh material necessity. Consequently, the taste of luxury purifies and sublimates the ordinary and profane into the aesthetic and beautiful. The pure gaze confers aesthetic meaning to ordinary and profane objects because the taste of liberty is at leisure to relieve objects from their pragmatic functions. Thus, as the distance form basic material necessities increases, the pure gaze or the taste of luxury transforms the ordinary into the aesthetic, the material into the symbolic, the functional into the formal. And, because the taste of liberty is that of the dominant class, it is also the dominant and legitimate taste in society.

In contrast, the working class cultivates a "popular" aesthetic. Their taste is the taste of necessity, for working-class life is constrained by harsh economic imperatives. The popular taste wants art to represent reality and despises formal and self-sufficient art as decadent and degenerate. The popular taste favors the simple and honest rather than the complex and sophisticated. It is downgraded by the "legitimate" taste of luxury as naive and complacent, and these conflicts over tastes are class conflicts over cultural and symbolic capital.

Preferences for certain works and styles of art, however, are only part of tastes as ordered by habitus. Aesthetic choices are correlated with choices made in other cultural fields. The taste of liberty and luxury, for example, corresponds to the polite, distant, and disciplined style of upper-class conversation. Just as art is expected to be removed from life, so are the bodies of interlocutors expected to be removed from one another and so is the spirit expected to be removed from matter. Distance from economic necessity in the upper-class lifestyle not only corresponds to an aesthetic of pure form but also entails that all natural and physical desires are to be sublimated and dematerialized. Hence, upper-class eating is highly regulated and disciplined, and foods that are less filling are preferred over fatty dishes. Similarly, items of clothing are chosen for fashion and aesthetic harmony rather than for functional appropriateness. Distance from necessity is the motif underlying the upper-class lifestyle as a whole, not just aesthetic tastes as one area of practice.

Conversely, because they are immersed in physical reality and economic necessity, working-class people interact in more physical ways, touching one another's bodies, laughing heartily, and valuing straightforward outspokenness more than distant and false politeness. Similarly, the working-class

---

[40]Ibid. Actually, Bourdieu makes more fine-tuned distinctions, but we focus only on the main oppositions here.

taste favors foods that are more filling and less refined but more physically gratifying. The popular taste chooses clothes and furniture that are functional, and this is so not only because of sheer economic constraints but also because of a true and profound dislike of that which is formal and fancy.

In sum, Bourdieu has provided a conceptual model of class conflict that combines elements of Marxian, Weberian, and Durkheimian sociology. The structuralist aspects of Bourdieu's conceptualization of habitus as the mediating process between class position and individual behavior have been underemphasized in this review, but clearly Bourdieu places Durkheim back on his feet by emphasizing that class position determines habitus. But the useful elements of structuralism—systems of symbols as generative structures of codes—are retained and incorporated into a theory of class conflict as revolving around the mobilization of symbols into ideologies legitimating a class position and the associated lifestyle and habitus.

## Jeffrey C. Alexander on Cultural Pragmatics

As theorizing about cultural dynamics has gained traction in sociology once again, some have advocated a "strong program" in cultural sociology. To many cultural sociologists, much analysis of culture is part of a "weak program" where culture is seen as something that emerges out of structural arrangements and that can only be theorized in reference to social structures. A strong program, in contrast, would make culture the principle topic rather than an adjunct or, in Marx's works, a superstructure to material social-structural conditions. Moreover, this program would involve thick descriptions of symbolic meanings and the mechanisms by which such meanings are constructed. Culture would be seen as texts with themes, plotlines, moral evaluations, traditions, frameworks, and other properties that make culture an autonomous realm, separated from social structure.[41] Much of the work in such a strong program would be empirical, examining specific types of cultural formations and analyzing them in detail. And, only after such a strong program existed for a time could the relationship between culture and social structure be examined through such processes as rituals and interactions. To a degree, both Wuthnow's and Bourdieu's theories evidence some elements of a strong program, but I would imagine that they could be criticized for devoting too much effort at connecting cultural

---

[41]See, for example: Jeffrey C. Alexander, Ron Eyerman, Bernard Giessen, and Neil J. Smelser, *Cultural Trauma and Collective Identity* (University of California Press, 2004); Jeffrey Alexander, Bernard Giessen, and Jason Mast, *Social Performance: Symbolic Action, Cultural Pragmatics, and Ritual* (Cambridge, UK: Cambridge University Press, 2006); Philip Smith and A. T. Riley, *Cultural Theory*, 2nd ed. (Oxford, UK: Blackwell); Jeffrey C. Alexander, *The Civil Sphere* (Oxford University Press, 2006); Jeffrey Alexander, *The Meaning of Social Life: A Cultural Sociology* (New York: Oxford University Press, 2005); Jeffrey Alexander, Ronald Jacobs, and Philip Smith, *The Oxford Handbook of Cultural Sociology* (New York: Oxford University Press, 2012).

processes to social-structural dynamics, thus giving short shrift to culture as a distinctive realm of social reality.

Jeffrey Alexander and his colleagues at Yale and other key centers of cultural theorizing have been part of the movement pushing for a strong program. Even though not all cultural sociologists go this far, most cultural sociologists have been influenced by the call for the analysis of culture per se and by the need to engage in rich and thick empirical descriptions of cultural processes. Of course, description does not always lead to theorizing about why the culture described exists and operates the way it does. Thus, even a strong program must eventually begin to explain cultural dynamics more than simply describe empirical manifestations of these dynamics. Alexander's work on cultural pragmatics[42] is a good illustration of moving beyond description to explain at least a limited range of cultural processes.

In pursuing the goal to develop theories about culture, Alexander blends a heavy dose of Émile Durkheim's analysis of ritual and emotion in *The Elementary Forms of the Religious Life* (see pp. 321–322 in Chapter 15) with Erving Goffman's dramaturgy (see Chapter 19). This mix makes sense because one of the most conspicuous strands of cultural theorizing revolves around rituals and performances that arouse emotions which bring background collective representations, implicit scripts, and themes to the foreground of interaction with audiences of others.

## History of Ritualized Performances

Alexander draws from Durkheim's distinction between mechanical and organic solidarity to present, to say the least, a condensed history of ritualized performances. In simple, homogenous societies, all of the elements of performances are fused together and seamless so that culture is always in the foreground, making individuals experience rituals as personal, immediate, and iconographic. The cultural script, texts, collective representations, stage, props, actors, audience, means for symbolic production, and social powers of individuals are, as he puts it, *fused* together, allowing interaction to seem not only seamless but authentic as individuals engage in ritual performances to immediate audiences.

With the differentiation of societies, however, there is (1) a separation of foreground texts and background symbolic representations, (2) an estrangement of the symbolic means of production from the mass of social actors, and (3) a disconnect between elites who carry out symbolic actions and their mass audiences. The result is that successful performances are no longer automatic but something that takes skill and effort to *refuse* the elements of background representations with *texts* that are used in the foreground, on a stage, through ritual performances in front of audiences. Rituals

---

[42]Jeffrey C. Alexander, "Cultural Pragmatics: Social Performances Between Ritual and Strategy," *Sociological Theory* 22 (2004): pp. 512–74.

become the means by which the disparate elements of culture are re-assembled through effort and performances.

At times in primary groups, refusion is not so necessary even in complex societies; interaction rituals proceed smoothly and seamlessly as background comes to foreground in an emotionally gratifying way. Still, the dramatic increase in the number and scale of social spaces and the vast public sphere in modern, complex societies inevitably cause separation among the elements of performances. As a consequence, it is always problematic as to how to refuse them through ritual performances among people. The cultural world is fragmented and detached from many performances, giving the modern world problems of cultural integration and meaning in social situations—very old themes that go back to the founding of sociology.

Alexander has, with a different vocabulary, rephrased the basic problem that Durkheim emphasized in his earlier work in *The Division of Labor in Society*. How can performances be made in ways that refuse what inevitably gets decomposed with structural and cultural differentiation in a society? For Alexander, a successful performance that refuses background to foreground stands or falls upon individuals and collective actions to achieve what he terms (1) *cultural extension* of the background representations and their interpretation in a text to the audience and (2) *psychological* (and emotional) *identification* of the audience with performances and its interpretation of the background representations as text. Only in this way can the fragmentation of complex societies be overcome in performances. Alexander's theory is thus about the steps and strategies of actors in successfully refusing culture during their performances. I will come back to these shortly, but let me now backtrack to outline some of the basic assumptions that Alexander makes in developing his theory of cultural pragmatics.

## Assumptions About Actors and Performances

Alexander assumes that actors are motivated by moral concerns and that they seek to bring both background representations and scripts of culture to the forefront of action and interaction with audiences. In realizing this fundamental goal, Alexander emphasizes several key properties of refusing:

1. Actors convert background representation of culture and scripts into *texts* that decode and interpret these background elements of culture.

2. To bring off a successful performance, they must also achieve *cathexis*, or some kind of emotional attachment to the text as it has been decoded.

3. With interpretations of background representations and scripts that are emotionally valenced, individuals and potentially collective actors are in a better position to engage in cultural extension of the text to

the audience; if successful, the audience will psychologically identify with the performance and the underlying text, script, and background representations.

4. In making a performance to an audience, actors always assess the means of symbolic reproduction, or the stage and props that are available for a performance.

5. The dramatic presentation of text thus involves physical and verbal gestures on a stage and the use of props.

6. Performances like all actions are constrained by power, which can delimit, limit, or facilitate access to text as well as the availability of stages, staging props, actors who can engage in performances, and audiences that these actors can reach in interpreting and decoding background cultural elements into a text.

As is evident, the dramatic metaphor is central to cultural pragmatics, which perhaps makes it a part of dramaturgy. Moreover, much like dramaturgy summarized in Chapter 19, there is an emphasis on *strategic* elements in just how to go about (a) reaching or achieving *cultural extension* to an audience and (b) getting the members of the audience to *identify* with the performance and the cultural text.

## Challenges and Strategies Employed in Performances

Refusing always poses challenges that, in turn, lead actors to adopt various strategies for achieving cultural extension and audience identification with a performance and its underlying text. First, in order to give a successful performance, an effective *script* must be created that compresses background cultural meanings and intensifies these meanings in ways that facilitate an effective performance. Alexander lists several techniques for doing so: (a) *cognitive simplification* of background representations so that audiences do not need to deal with too much complexity, (b) *time-space compression* that collapse elements in time and space so that the elements are highlighted and less dependent upon contextual interpretations, (c) *moral agonism* whereby representations are stated as dichotomies such as good vs. evil, conflicts against enemies, and challenges that must overcome obstacles, and (d) *twistings and turnings* in the plot line that keep audiences engaged.

Second, refusing involves a script, action, and performances as actors "walk and talk" in space. This process in more engaging when writers of scripts leave room for dramatic inventions and interpretations and when directors of staged actions allow for some dramatic license on the part of performers. When scripts, direction, and staging are too tightly orchestrated, performances come off as stiff, artificial and less engaging than when actors are seen as authentically brining to an audience emotionally charged background elements of culture.

Third, refusing always involves the use of social power. This power must be mobilized on at least three fronts: (a) the appropriation of relevant symbolic means of production, such as the right venues and stages where a performance can be most effective and reach the right audience; (b) the appropriation of the means of symbolic distribution in which the background representations can be secured and then through performances distributed to audiences; and (c) the appropriation of some control over the subsequent debate, discourse, and criticism of a performance.

Fourth, actors are always in a double refusing situation. They have to connect with the (a) text and, then, (b) the audience. The best way to bring off this "double refusion" is through giving a performance that seems natural and as part of the ongoing flow of the situation, whereas disjointed performances will only exacerbate the process of refusing. This problem is aggravated in complex societies as individuals play different roles in highly diverse social context; under these conditions, it is often difficult to give a performance in all stages that is natural rather than somewhat disjointed. The result is that refusing will fail, or partially fail, thereby reducing the extension of culture and audience identification.

And fifth, there is the challenge of refusing audience with the performance text because, in complex societies, audiences are frequently diverse, larger, and separated in time and space from actors, as is especially the case with performances that are given through various media. This reality of the stages and audiences in complex societies places enormous demands on actors, directors, and scriptwriters to pull off an effective performance. Some of the strategies listed above—cognitive simplification, time-space compression, moral agonism, and twists and turns are one set of means for overcoming the problems of appealing the larger, more diverse, and separated audiences. These strategies simplify, decontextualize to a degree, moralize, and make engaging the text and performance in ways that extend the culture to the audience and emotionally pull them in to the point of identifying with the performance and text.

## Why Pragmatics?

I have stated Alexander's argument abstractly, as he does, but without examples. The point of the theory, I believe, is to emphasize that fusing of background cultural elements with performances is a generic and universal process that has been made more difficult and challenging in complex, highly differentiated societies. Yet, if background culture of a society cannot be fused with actors' performances, the problems of integration in complex societies become that much greater. In simple, homogeneous societies of the past, performances were naturally fused, but with complexity, refusing must occur. This refusing, I believe Alexander intends to argue, can occur at many different levels and among different types of actors. The process is perhaps easiest at the level of encounters of face-to-face interaction, but if those interacting are strangers to each other and from different backgrounds, then the interaction will often be awkward and stilted because the script, direction, staging, use of props, and acting in front of the audience are disjointed or unclear. At the other extreme are dramatic performances by (political, economic, religious) actors to large audiences given through mass media, and here the same problems exist. The actors confront a large, diverse, and spatially disconnected audience where the script, performance, text, and staging must somehow pull in diverse audiences who are asked to emotionally identify with the performance and text being brought forward. Relatively few actors can pull this off in natural settings, although good actors in movies and the stage are often able to pull audiences into their performances, but these successful performances only highlight the difficulty of doing so in real life situations. In between encounters of individuals and media presentations are performances at all the intervening levels of society—groups, organizations, civic meeting, lectures, rallies, protest events, revolutions, and other stages[43]—where actors confront audiences of varying sizes and backgrounds and where they must give a performance that extends culture and pulls the audience into the performance and text so that they identify emotionally with both. Again, only relatively few actors can bring these kinds of performances off and achieve full refusion. And yet, the viability of complex societies depends upon some degree of success in such performances.

Thus, ritual performances that connect audience with texts that decode background cultural representations are a key dynamic, in Alexander's view, in all social situations. Yet, many situations in complex societies have been subject to defusion as a simple consequence of the scale and differentiation of society. In these defused situations, the importance of performance rituals becomes ever-more evident because performances are not automatic, nor do they seamlessly unfold. Whether it be one person in an encounter writing the script, decoding background representations in a text, appropriating stages and props, and giving the performance or a large team of actors coordinating the writing, directing, staging, marketing, and securing actors and audiences, the dynamics are the same; moreover, they are critical to the integration of societies.

Only when a strong program in cultural sociology, Alexander seems to argue, would this need to bring cultural representations from background to the front stage be seen as critical. Without a prior understanding of the dynamics of culture per se, the ritual performances needed to make it salient, relevant, and engrossing to audiences would not be appreciated and, hence, theorized.

---

[43]For example, the titles of the following books by Alexander reveal that more macro-level effects of performance dynamics: *Performative Revolution in Egypt: An Essay on Cultural Power* (New York: Oxford University Press, 2011); *The Performance of Politics: Obama's Victory and The Democratic Struggle for Power* (New York: Oxford University Press, 2010); and *Peformance of Power* (Cambridge, UK: Polity Press, 2011).

# Conclusion

With the conflict critique on functional theories in the 1960s and 1970s, especially the approach of Talcott Parsons who did emphasize culture dynamics, sociological attention shifted to the material bases of society as they generated conflicts of interests that, under various conditions, would lead to varying types of conflict. Culture was not irrelevant in this conceptual shift, but it was relegated to the analysis of beliefs and ideologies as they aroused parties to conflict or legitimated oppressive social structures. Just as conflict theory reacted to functionalism, I suspect that the new cultural sociology emerged as a reaction to the simplification of cultural analysis when it was seen as the sidekick of conflict dynamics, ultimately generated by the material conditions of societies.

There were intellectual traditions, such as phenomenology and hermeneutics, that remained viable during this period, but they did not explore culture in all of its manifestations; these were specialized theories that were often more cognitive than cultural. It is obvious, but surprisingly underappreciated, that everything humans do when they act and organize is cultural. Ideas are expressed with language, not just words but the language of emotions; ideas take hold when they are used by interacting persons and collective actors to build up social structures, reproduce such structures, or tear them down, only to rebuild them in another form. But, culture is more—new cultural theories appear to argue—because it is a domain of reality where symbols are organized and stored and then brought into use in dramatic performances. They are not simple superstructures to material social structures, but an autonomous set of dynamics that need to be theorized and, eventually, connected to the structural properties of social reality. The notion of *performances* seems to be one wedge for recognizing the autonomous dynamics of culture per se and necessity of bringing culture to stages and props in social settings that are part of social structures. It is the capacity to extend cultural representations to audiences and to get audiences to emotionally identify with these representations through scripts, direction, texts, staging, and acting that culture exerts its power. This power is exerted over actions of both persons and corporate units as they build up, reproduce, dismantle, and built up new social structures.

In somewhat different ways, Wuthnow, Bourdieu, and Alexander have sought to highlight the properties of culture and how culture is used in social settings. Each explicitly, or more implicitly in the case of Bourdieu, sees ritual and performances as critical in generating the emotions necessary to give culture its power to influence how people behave and how social structures are created, reproduced, or changed. Yet, when theorized by these scholars and others, the conceptualization of culture becomes a bit vague— *moral order, habitus, cultural and symbolic capital, background representations, texts, scripts,* and the like. These are not precise conceptualizations.

They are evocative, to be sure, but they are not denotative in any precise sense. From empirical descriptions of these in real empirical contexts, perhaps it will be possible to isolate the properties and dynamics of each of these evocative terms, which I think would represent a much stronger program in cultural sociology.

## CHAPTER 28

# Structuration Theory

During the last forty years, Anthony Giddens has been one of the most prominent critics of the scientific pretensions of sociology. Yet, at the same time, he has developed a relatively formal abstract conceptual scheme for analyzing the social world. In his *The Constitution of Society*,[1] Giddens brought elements of his advocacy together into a theoretical synthesis under the rubric of earlier "structuration theory." This theory represents one of more creative theoretical efforts of the second half of the twentieth century. Although Giddens has developed theoretical interests in modernity and, indeed, has become an important contributor to the debate about modernity and postmodernity,[2] his theoretical contribution still resides primarily in the more formal statement of structuration theory. Thus, in this chapter, I will briefly review Giddens' critique of positivists' natural science view of sociology and, then, devote most of my efforts to summarizing the key ideas in structuration theory.

---

[1]Anthony Giddens, The *Constitution of Society: Outline of the Theory of Structuration* (Oxford: Polity, 1984) and *Central Problems in Social Theory* (London: Macmillan, 1979). The University of California Press also has editions of these two books. For an excellent overview, both sociologically and philosophically, of Giddens' theoretical project, see Ira Cohen, *Structuration Theory: Anthony Giddens and the Constitution of Social Life* (London: Macmillan, 1989). For a commentary and debate on Giddens' work, see J. Clark, C. Modgil, and S. Modgil, eds., *Anthony Giddens: Consensus and Controversy* (London: Falmer, 1990). For a selection of readings, see *The Giddens Reader*, ed. Philip Cassell (Stanford, CA: Stanford University Press, 1993).

[2]See, for examples, Anthony Giddens, *The Consequences of Modernity* (Stanford, CA: Stanford University Press, 1990); Ulrich Beck, Anthony Giddens, and Scott Lash, *Reflexive Modernization* (Stanford, CA: Stanford University Press, 1994); Anthony Giddens, *Modernity and Self-Identity* (Stanford, CA: Stanford University Press, 1991).

# Giddens' Critique of "Scientific" Social Theory

Anthony Giddens reasoned that there never can be any universal and timeless sociological laws, like those in physics or the biological sciences. Humans have the capacity for agency, and hence, they can change the very nature of social organization—thereby obviating any laws that are proposed to be universal. At best, "the concepts of theory should for many research purposes be regarded as sensitizing devices, nothing more."[3] Giddens buttresses this conclusion with two points of argument.

First, Giddens asserts that social theorizing involves a *double hermeneutic.* Stripped of its jargon, this means that the concepts and generalizations used by social scientists to understand social processes can be employed by lay persons as agents who can alter these social processes. We must recognize, Giddens contends, that ordinary actors are also "social theorists who alter their theories in the light of their experience and are receptive to incoming information."[4] Thus, social science theories are not often news to individuals; when they are, such theories can be used to transform the very order they describe. Within the capacity of humans to be reflexive—that is, to think about their situation—is the ability to change the culture and structure of the situation.[5]

Second, social theory is by its nature social criticism. Social theory often contradicts the reasons that people give for doing things and is, therefore, a critique of these reasons and the social arrangements that people construct in the name of these reasons. Sociology does not, therefore, need to develop a separate body of critical theory, as others have argued; it *is* critical theory by its very nature and by virtue of the effects it can have on social processes.

The implications, Giddens believes, are profound. We need to stop imitating the natural sciences. We must cease evaluating our success as intellectuals by whether or not we have discovered "timeless laws." We must recognize that social theory does not exist "outside" our universe. We should accept that what sociologists and lay actors do is, in a fundamental sense, very much the same. And, we must redirect our efforts to developing "sensitizing concepts" that allow us to understand the active processes of interaction among individuals as they produce and reproduce social structures while being guided by these structures.

---

[3]Giddens, *The Constitution of Society* (cited in note 1), p. 326.

[4]Ibid., p. 335.

[5]See, in particular, Anthony Giddens, *Profiles and Critiques in Social Theory* (London: Macmillan, 1982) and *New Rules of Sociological Method: A Positive Critique of Interpretative Sociologies*, 2nd ed. (Stanford, CA: Stanford University Press, 1993).

# The "Theory of Structuration"

Because Giddens does not believe that abstract laws of social action, interaction, and organization exist, his theory of structuration is not a series of propositions. Instead, as Giddens' critique of science would suggest, his "theory" is a cluster of sensitizing concepts, linked together discursively. The key concept is *structuration*, which is intended to communicate the duality of structure.[6] That is, social structure is used by active agents; in so using the properties of structure, they transform or reproduce this structure. Thus the process of structuration requires a conceptualization of the nature of structure, of the agents who use structure, and of the ways that these are mutually implicated in each other to produce varying patterns of human organization.

## Reconceptualizing Structure and Social System

Giddens believes structure can be conceptualized as "rules" and "resources" that actors use in interaction contexts that extend across space and over time. In so using these rules and resources, actors sustain or reproduce structures in space and time.

**Rules**. *Rules* are "generalizable procedures" that actors understand and use in various circumstances. Giddens posits that a rule is a methodology or technique that actors know about, often only implicitly, and that provides a relevant formula for action.[7] From a sociological perspective, the most important rules are those that agents use in the reproduction of social relations over significant lengths of time and across space. These rules reveal certain characteristics: (1) they are frequently used in (a) conversations, (b) interaction rituals, and (c) the daily routines of individuals; (2) they are tacitly grasped and understood and are part of the "stock knowledge" of competent actors; (3) they are informal, remaining unwritten and unarticulated; and (4) they are weakly sanctioned through interpersonal techniques.[8]

The thrust of Giddens' argument is that rules are part of actors' "knowledgeability." Some can be normative in that actors can articulate and explicitly make reference to them, but many other rules are more implicitly understood and used to guide the flow of interaction in ways that are not easily expressed or verbalized. Moreover, actors can transform rules into new combinations as they confront and deal with one another and the contextual particulars of their interaction.

---

[6]See *The Constitution of Society* (cited in note 1), pp. 207–13.

[7]Ibid., pp. 20–21.

[8]Ibid., p. 22.

**Resources.** As the other critical property of structure, *resources* are facilities that actors use to get things done. For, even if there are well-understood methodologies and formulas—that is, rules—to guide action, there must also be the capacity to perform tasks. Such capacity requires resources, or the material equipment and the organizational ability to act in situations. Giddens visualizes resources as what generate *power*.[9] Power is not a resource, as much social theory argues. Rather, the mobilization of other resources is what gives actors power to get things done. Thus, power is integral to the very existence of structure: As actors interact, they use resources, and as they use resources, they mobilize power to shape the actions of others.

Giddens visualizes rules and resources as "transformational" and as "mediating."[10] What he means by these terms is that rules and resources can be transformed into many different patterns and profiles. Resources can be mobilized in various ways to perform activities and achieve ends through the exercise of different forms and degrees of power; rules can generate many diverse combinations of methodologies and formulas to guide how people communicate, interact, and adjust to one another. Rules and resources are mediating in that they are what tie social relations together. They are what actors use to create, sustain, or transform relations across time and in space. And, because rules and resources are inherently transformational—that is, generative of diverse combinations—they can lace together many different patterns of social relations in time and space.

Giddens developed a typology of rules and resources that is rather vague and imprecise.[11] He sees the three concepts in this typology—domination, legitimation, and signification—as "theoretical primitives," which is perhaps an excuse for defining them imprecisely. The basic idea is that resources are the stuff of domination because they involve the mobilization of material and organizational facilities to do things. Some rules are transformed into instruments of legitimation because they make things seem correct and appropriate. Other rules are used to create signification, or meaningful symbolic systems, because they provide people with ways to see and interpret events. Actually, the scheme makes more sense if the concepts of domination, legitimation, and signification are given less emphasis and the elements of his discussion are selectively extracted to create the typology presented in Figure 28.1.

In the left column of Figure 28.1, structure is viewed by Giddens as composed of rules and resources. Rules are transformed into two basic types of

---

[9]Ibid., pp. 14–16.

[10]Here Giddens seems to be taking what is useful from structuralism and reworking these ideas into a more sociological approach. Giddens remains, however, extremely critical of structuralism; see his "Structuralism, Post-structuralism and the Production of Culture" in *Social Theory Today*, eds. A. Giddens and J. Turner (Cambridge, England: Polity, 2000).

[11]*The Constitution of Society*, p. 29 and *Central Problems in Social Theory*, pp. 97–107 (both works cited in note 1).

**Figure 28.1** Social Structure, Social System, and the Modalities of Connection

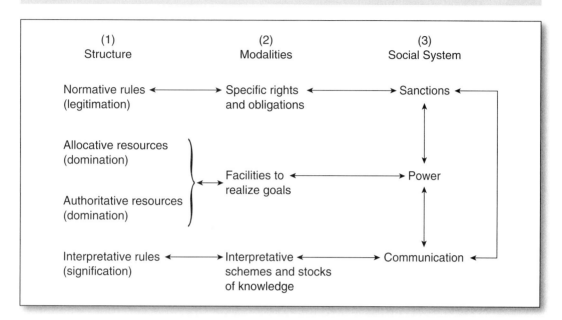

mediating processes: (1) *normative*, or the creation of rights and obligations in a context, and (2) *interpretative*, or the generation of schemes and stocks of taken-for-granted knowledge in a context. Resources are transformed into two major types of facilities that can mediate social relations: (1) *authoritative resources*, or the organizational capacity to control and direct the patterns of interactions in a context, and (2) *allocative resources*, or the use of material features, artifacts, and goods to control and direct patterns of interaction in a context.

Giddens sees these types of rules and resources as mediating interaction via three modalities, as is portrayed in Column 2 of Figure 28.1: rights and obligations, facilities, and interpretative schemes. The figure deviates somewhat from Giddens' discussion, but the idea is the same: the three modalities connect rules and resources to interaction. These modalities are then used to (a) generate the power that enables some actors to control others, (b) affirm the norms that, in turn, allow actors to be sanctioned for their conformity or nonconformity, and (c) create and use the interpretative schemes that make it possible for actors to communicate with one another.

Giddens also stresses that rules and resources are interrelated, emphasizing that the modalities and their use in interaction are separated only analytically. In the actual flow of interaction in the real empirical world, they exist simultaneously, thereby making their separation merely an exercise of analytical decomposition. Thus, power, sanctions, and media of communication are interconnected, as are the rules and resources of social structure. In social systems, where people are co-present and interact, power is used to secure a particular set of rights and obligations as well as a system of communication; conversely, power can be exercised only through communication and sanctioning.

Giddens, sees social structure as something used by actors, not as some external reality that pushes and shoves actors around. Social structure is defined as the rules and resources that can be transformed as actors use them in concrete settings. But, the question arises: How is structure to be connected to what people actually do in interaction settings, or what Giddens terms *social systems*? The answer is the notion of modalities, whereby rules and resources are transformed into power, sanctions, and communication. Thus, structure is not a mysterious system of codes, as Claude Lévi-Strauss and other structural idealists imply, nor is it a set of determinative parameters and external constraints on actors. In Giddens' conceptualization, social structure is transformative and flexible, it is part of actors in concrete situations, and it is used by them to create patterns of social relations across space and through time.

Moreover, this typology allows Giddens to emphasize that, as agents interact in social systems, they can reproduce rules and resources (via the modalities) or they can transform them. Thus, social interaction and social structure are reciprocally implicated. Structuration is, therefore, the dual processes in which rules and resources are used to organize interaction across time and in space and, by virtue of this use, to reproduce or transform these rules and resources.

## Reconceptualizing Institutions

Giddens believes that institutions are systems of interaction in societies that endure over time and that distribute people in space. Giddens uses phrases like "deeply sedimented across time and in space in societies" to express the idea that, when rules and resources are reproduced over long periods of time and in explicit regions of space, then institutions can be said to exist in a society. Giddens offers a typology of institutions showing the weights and combinations of rules and resources that are implicated in interaction.[12] If signification (interpretative rules) is primary, followed respectively by domination (allocative and authoritative resources) and then legitimization (normative rules), a "symbolic order" exists. If authoritative domination, signification, and legitimization are successively combined, political institutionalization occurs. If allocative dominance, signification, and legitimization are ordered, economic institutionalization prevails. And if legitimization, dominance, and signification are rank ordered, institutionalization of law occurs. Table 28.1 summarizes Giddens' argument.

In this conceptualization of institutions, Giddens seeks to avoid a mechanical view of institutionalization in several senses. First, systems of interaction in empirical contexts are a mixture of institutional processes.

---

[12] *The Constitution of Society*, p. 31 and *Central Problems in Social Theory*, p. 107 (both works cited in note 1).

**Table 28.1  The Typology of Institutions**

| Type of Institution | | Rank Order of Emphasis on Rules and Resources |
|---|---|---|
| 1. Symbolic orders, or modes of discourse, and patterns of communication | are produced and reproduced by | the use of interpretative rules (signification) in conjuction with normative rules (legitimation) and allocative as well as authoritative resources (domination). |
| 2. Political institutions | are produced and reproduced by | the use of authoritative resources (domination) in conjuction with interpretative rules (signification) and normative rules (legitimation). |
| 3. Economic institutions | are produced and reproduced by | the use of allocative resources (domination) in conjuction with interpretative rules (signification) and normative rules (legitimation). |
| 4. Legal institutions | are produced and reproduced by | the use of normative rules (legitimation) in conjuction with authoritative and allocative resources (domination) and interpretative rules (signification). |

Economic, political, legal, and symbolic orders are not easily separated; there is usually an element of each in any social system context. Second, institutions are tied to the rules and resources that agents employ and thereby reproduce; they are not external to individuals because they are formed by the use of varying rules and resources in actual social relations. Third, the most basic dimensions of all rules and resources—signification, domination, and legitimation—are all involved in institutionalization; it is only their relative salience for actors that gives the stabilization of relations its distinctive institutional character across time and in space.

## Structural Principles, Sets, and Properties

The extent and form of institutionalization in societies are related to what Giddens terms structural principles.[13] These are the most general principles that guide the organization of societal totalities. These are what stretch systems across time and space, and they allow for system integration,

---

[13] *The Constitution of Society* (cited in note 1), pp. 179–93.

or the maintenance of reciprocal relations among units in a society. For Giddens, "structural principles can thus be understood as the principles of organization which allow recognizably consistent forms of time-space distanciation on the basis of definite mechanisms of societal integration."[14] The basic idea seems to be that rules and resources are used by active agents in accordance with fundamental principles of organization. Such principles guide just how rules and resources are transformed and employed to mediate social relations.

On the basis of their underlying structural principles, three basic types of societies have existed: (1) "tribal societies," which are organized by structural principles that emphasize kinship and tradition as the mediating force behind social relations across time and in space; (2) "class-divided societies," which are organized by an urban/rural differentiation, with urban areas revealing distinctive political institutions that can be separated from economic institutions, formal codes of law or legal institutions, and modes of symbolic coordination or ordering through written texts and testaments; and (3) "class societies," which involve structural principles that separate and yet inter-connect all four institutional spheres, especially the economic and political.[15]

Structural principles are implicated in the production and reproduction of structures or structural sets. These structural sets are rule and resource bundles, or combinations and configurations of rules and resources, which are used to produce and reproduce certain types and forms of social relations across time and space. Giddens offers the example of how the structural principles of class societies (differentiation and clear separation of economy and polity) guide the use of the following structural set: *private property-money-capital-labor-contract-profit.* The details of his analysis are less important than the general idea that the general structural principles of class societies are transformed into more specific sets of rules and resources that agents use to mediate social relations. This structural set is used in capitalist societies and, as a consequence, is reproduced. In turn, such reproduction of the structural set reaffirms the more abstract structural principles of class societies.

As these and other structural sets are used by agents and as they are thereby reproduced, societies develop *structural properties,* which are "institutionalized features of social systems, stretching across time and space."[16] That is, social relations become patterned in certain typical ways. Thus the structural set of *private property-money-capital- labor-contract-profit* can mediate only certain patterns of relations; that is, if this is the rule and resource bundle with which agents must work, then only certain forms of relations can be produced and reproduced in the economic sphere. Hence

---

[14]Ibid., p. 181.

[15]For an extensive discussion of this typology, see Giddens' *A Contemporary Critique of Historical Materialism: Power, Property and the State* (London: Macmillan, 1981).

[16]*The Constitution of Society* (cited in note 1), p. 185.

the institutionalization of relations in time and space reveals a particular form, or in Giddens' terms, structural property.

## Structural Contradiction

Giddens always emphasizes the inherent "transformative" potential of rules and resources. Structural principles, he argues, "operate in terms of one another but yet also contravene each other."[17] In other words, they reveal contradictions that can be either primary or secondary. A "primary contradiction" is one between structural principles that are formative and constitute a society, whereas a "secondary contradiction" is one that is "brought into being by primary contradictions."[18] For example, there is a contradiction between structural principles that mediate the institutional-ization of private profits, on the one hand, and those that mediate socialized production, on the other. If workers pool their labor to produce goods and services, it is contradictory to allow only some to enjoy profits of such socialized labor.

Contradictions are not, Giddens emphasizes, the same as conflicts. Con-tradiction is a "disjunction of structural principles of system organization," whereas conflict is the actual struggle between actors in "definite social practices."[19] Thus, the contradiction between private profits and socialized labor is not, itself, a conflict. It can create situations of conflict, such as struggles between management and labor in a specific time and place, but such conflicts are not the same as contradiction.

For Giddens, the institutional patterns of a society represent the creation and use by agents of very generalized and abstract principles. These prin-ciples represent the development of particular rules and the mobilization of certain resources; such principles generate more concrete "bundles" or "sets" of rules and resources that agents actively use to produce and repro-duce social relations in concrete settings; in addition, many of these prin-ciples and sets contain contradictory elements that can encourage actual conflicts among actors. In this way, structure "constrains" but is not disem-bodied from agents. Rather, the "properties" of total societies are not exter-nal to individuals and collectivities but are persistently reproduced through the use of structural principles and sets by agents who act. Let us now turn to Giddens' discussion of these active agents.

## Agents, Agency, and Action

As is evident, Giddens visualizes structure as a duality, as something that is part of the actions of agents. Thus in Giddens' approach, it is essential to

---

[17]Ibid., p. 193.

[18]Ibid.

[19]Ibid., p. 198.

understand the dynamics of human agency. He proposes a "stratification model," which is an effort to synthesize psychoanalytic theory, phenomenology, ethnomethodology, and elements of action theory. This model is depicted in the lower portions of Figure 28.2. For Giddens, *agency* denotes the events that an actor perpetrates rather than intentions, purposes, ends, or other states. Agency is what an actor actually does in a situation that has visible consequences (not necessarily intended consequences). To understand the dynamics of agency requires analysis of each element on the model.

As drawn, the model in Figure 28.2 actually combines two overlapping models in Giddens' discussion, but his intent is reasonably clear: humans "reflexively monitor" their own conduct and that of others; in other words, they pay attention to, note, calculate, and assess the consequences of

**Figure 28.2**   The Dynamics of Agency

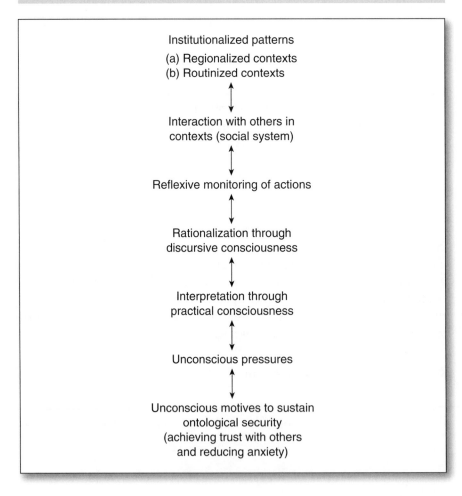

actions.[20] Monitoring is influenced by two levels of consciousness.[21] One is *discursive consciousness*, which involves the capacity to give reasons for or rationalize what one does (and presumably to do the same for others' behavior). *Practical consciousness* is the stock of knowledge that one implicitly uses to act in situations and to interpret the actions of others. This knowledgeability is constantly used, but rarely articulated, to interpret events—one's own and those of others. Almost all acts are indexical in that they must be interpreted by their context, and this implicit stock of knowledge provides these contextual interpretations and frameworks.

There are also unconscious dimensions to human agency. There are many pressures to act in certain ways, which an actor does not perceive. Indeed, Giddens argues that much motivation is unconscious. Moreover, motivation is often much more diffuse than action theories portray. That is, there is no one-to-one relation between an act and a motive. Actors might be able to rationalize through their capacity for discursive consciousness in ways that make this one-to-one relationship seem to be what directs action. But much of what propels action lies below consciousness and, at best, provides very general and diffuse pressures to act. Moreover, much action might not be motivated at all; an actor simply monitors and responds to the environment.

In trying to reintroduce the unconscious into social theory, Giddens adopts Erik Erikson's psychoanalytic ideas.[22] The basic force behind much action is an unconscious set of processes to gain a sense of trust in interaction with others. Giddens terms this set of processes *the ontological security system of an agent.* That is, one of the driving but highly diffuse forces behind action is the desire to sustain ontological security or the sense of trust that comes from being able to reduce anxiety in social relations. Actors need to have this sense of trust. How they go about reducing anxiety to secure this sense is often unconscious because the mechanisms involved are developed before linguistic skills emerge in the young and because psychodynamics, such as repression, might also keep these fundamental feelings and their resolution from becoming conscious. In general, Giddens argues that ontological security is maintained through the routinization of encounters with others, through the successful interpretation of acts as practical or stock knowledge, and through the capacity for rationalization that comes with discursive consciousness.

As the top portions of Figure 28.2 emphasize, institutionalized patterns have an effect on, while being a consequence of, the dynamics of agency.

---

[20]Ibid., pp. 5–7; see also *Central Problems in Social Theory* (cited in note 1), pp. 56–59.

[21]His debt to Alfred Schutz and phenomenology is evident here, but he has liberated it from its subjectivism. See Chapter 15 on the rise of interactionist theorizing.

[22]*The Constitution of Society* (cited in note 1), pp. 45–59.

As we will see shortly, unconscious motives for ontological security require routinized interactions (predictable, stable over time) that are regionalized (ordered in space). Such regionalization and routinization are the products of past interactions of agents and are sustained or reproduced through the present (and future) actions of agents. To sustain routines and regions, actors must monitor their actions while drawing on their stock knowledge and discursive capacities. In this way, Giddens visualizes institutionalized patterns implicated in the very nature of agency. Institutions and agents cannot exist without each other, for institutions are reproduced practices by agents, whereas the conscious and unconscious dynamics of agency depend on the routines and regions provided by institutionalized patterns.

## Routinization and Regionalization of Interaction

Both the ontological security of agents and the institutionalization of structures in time and space depend on routinized and regionalized interaction among actors. Routinization of interaction patterns is what gives them continuity across time, thereby reproducing structure (rules and resources) and institutions. At the same time, routinization gives predictability to actions and, in so doing, provides a sense of ontological security. Thus, routines become critical for the most basic aspects of structure and human agency. Similarly, regionalization orders action in space by positioning actors in places relative to one another and by circumscribing how they are to present themselves and act. As with routines, the regionalization of interaction is essential to the sustenance of broader structural patterns and ontological security of actors, because it orders people's interactions in space and time, which in turn reproduces structures and meets an agent's need for ontological security.

**Routines.** Giddens sees routines as the key link between the episodic character of interactions (they start, proceed, and end), on the one hand, and basic trust and security, on the other hand.[23] Moreover, "the routinization of encounters is of major significance in binding the fleeting encounter to social reproduction and thus to the seeming 'fixity' of institutions."[24] In a very interesting discussion in which he borrows heavily from Erving Goffman (but with a phenomenological twist), Giddens proposed several procedures, or mechanisms, that humans use to sustain routines: (1) opening and closing rituals, (2) turn taking, (3) tact, (4) positioning, and (5) framing.[25] Each of these is discussed below.

---

[23]Ibid., pp. 60–109.

[24]Ibid., p. 72.

[25]This list has been created from what is a much more discursive text.

1. Because interaction is serial—that is, it occurs sequentially—there must be *symbolic markers of opening and closing*. Such markers are essential to the maintenance of routines because they indicate when in the flow of time the elements of routine interaction are to begin and end. There are many such interpersonal markers—words, facial gestures, positions of bodies—and there are physical markers, such as rooms, buildings, roads, and equipment, that also signal when certain routinized interactions are to begin and end. (Note, for example, the interpersonal and physical markers for a lecture, which is a highly routinized interaction that sustains the ontological security of agents and perpetuates institutional patterns.)

2. *Turn taking* in a conversation is another process that sustains a routine. All competent actors contain in their practical consciousness, or implicit stock of knowledge, a sense of how conversations are to proceed sequentially. People rely on "folk methods" to construct sequences of talk; in so doing, they sustain a routine and, hence, their psychological sense of security and the larger institutional context. (Think, for example, about a conversation that did not proceed smoothly in conversational turn taking; recall how disruptive this was for your sense of order and routine.)

3. *Tact* is, in Giddens' view, "the main mechanism that sustains 'trust' or 'ontological security' over long time-space spans." By tact, Giddens means "a latent conceptual agreement among participants in interaction" about just how each party is to gesture and respond and about what is appropriate and inappropriate. People carry with implicit stocks of knowledge that define for them what would be tactful and what would be rude and intrusive. And they use this sense of tact to regulate their emission of gestures, their talking, and their relative positioning in situations to remain tactful, thereby sustaining their sense of trust and the larger social order. (Imagine interactions in which tact is not exercised—how they disrupt our routines, our sense of comfort, and our perceptions of an orderly situation.)

4. Giddens rejects the idea of *role* as very useful and substitutes the notion of *position*. People bring to situations a position or "social identity that carries with it a certain range of prerogatives and obligations," and they emit gestures in a process of mutual positioning, such as locating their bodies in certain points, asserting their prerogatives, and signaling their obligations. In this way, interactions can be routinized, and people can sustain their sense of mutual trust as well as the larger social structures in which their interaction occurs. (For example, examine a student/student or professor/student interaction for positioning and determine how it sustains a sense of trust and the institutional structure.)

5. Much of the coherence of positioning activities is made possible by *frames*, which provide formulas for interpreting a context. Interactions tend to be framed in the sense that there are rules that apply to them, but these are not purely normative in the sense of precise instructions for

participants. Equally important, frames are more implicitly held, and they operate as markers that assert when certain behaviors and demeanors should be activated. (For example, compare your sense of how to comport yourself at a funeral, at a cocktail party, in class, and in other contexts that are "framed.")

In sum, social structure is extended across time by these techniques that produce and reproduce routines. In so stretching interaction across time in an orderly and predictable manner, people realize their need for a sense of trust in others. In this way, then, Giddens connects the most basic properties of structure (rules and resources) to the most fundamental features of human agents (unconscious motives).

**Regionalization.** Structuration theory is concerned with the reproduction of relations not only across time but also in space. With the concept of regionalization of interaction, Giddens addresses the intersection of space and time.[26] For interaction is not just serial, moving in time; it is also located in space. Again borrowing from Goffman and also from time and space geography, Giddens introduces the concept of *locale* to account for the physical space in which interaction occurs as well as the contextual knowledge about what is to occur in this space. In a locale, actors are not only establishing their presence in relation to one another but they are also using their stocks of practical knowledge to interpret the context of the locale. Such interpretations provide them with the relevant frames, the appropriate procedures for tact, and the salient forms for sequencing gestures and talk.

Giddens classifies locales by their *modes.* Locales vary in (1) their physical and symbolic boundaries, (2) their duration across time, (3) their span or extension in physical space, and (4) their character, or the ways they connect to other locales and to broader institutional patterns. Locales also vary in the degree to which they force people to sustain high public presence (what Goffman termed *frontstage*) or allow retreats to back regions where public presence is reduced (Goffman's *backstage*).[27] They also vary in how much disclosure of self (feelings, attitudes, and emotions) they require, some allowing "enclosure" or the withholding of self and other locales requiring "disclosure" of at least some aspects of self.

Regionalization of interaction through the creation of locales facilitates the maintenance of routines. In turn, the maintenance of routines across time and space sustains institutional structures. Thus, it is through routinized and regionalized systems of interaction that the reflexive capacities of agents reproduce institutional patterns.

---

[26]Ibid., pp. 110–44.

[27]See Erving Goffman, *The Presentation of Self in Everyday Life* (Garden City, NY: Doubleday, 1959); see also Chapter 19 on dramaturgical theorizing.

# Conclusion

Figure 28.3 represents one way to visualize Giddens' conceptual scheme. In a rough sense, as one moves from left to right, the scheme gets increasingly micro, although Giddens would probably not visualize his theory in these macro versus micro terms. But the general message is clear: Rules and resources are used to construct structures; these rules and resources are also a part of structural principles that include structural sets; these structural properties are involved in institutionalization of systems of interaction; such interaction systems are organized by the processes of regionalization and routinization; and all these processes are influenced by practical and discursive consciousness that, in turn, are driven by unconscious motives, especially needs for ontological security.

Giddens would not consider his theory anything more than a conceptual scheme for describing, analyzing, and interpreting empirical events. Moreover, he would not see this scheme as representing timeless social processes, although the reason his works are read and respected is because these do seem like basic and fundamental processes that transcend time, context, and place.

**Figure 28.3**   Key Elements of "Structuration Theory"

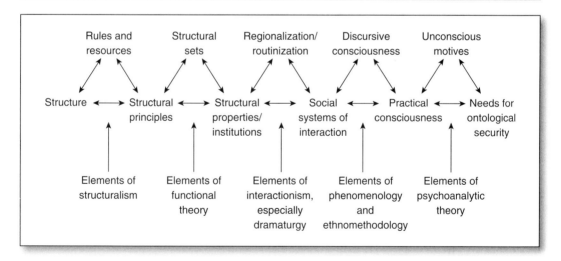

## CHAPTER 29

# Network Analysis

During the last forty years, work within anthropology, psychology, social psychology, sociology, communications, geography, and political science has converged on the conceptualization of structure as *social networks*. During this period, rather metaphorical and intuitive ideas about networks have been reconceptualized in various types of algebra, graph theory, and probability theory. This convergence has, in some ways, been a mixed blessing. On the one hand, grounding concepts in mathematics can give greater precision and provide a common language for pulling together a common conceptual core from the overlapping metaphors of different disciplines. On the other hand, the extensive use of mathematics and computer algorithms far exceeds the technical skills of most social scientists. More importantly, the use and application of quantitative techniques per se have become a preoccupation among many who seem less and less interested in explaining how the actual social world operates.

Nonetheless, despite these drawbacks, the potential for network analysis as a theoretical approach is great because such network analysis captures an important property of social structure—patterns of relations among social units, whether people, collectivities, locations, or status positions. As Georg Simmel emphasized, at the core of any conceptualization of social structure is the notion that structure consists of relations and links among entities. Network analysis forces us to conceptualize carefully the nature of the entities and relations, as well as the properties and dynamics that inhere in these relations.[1]

---

[1]For some readable overviews on network analysis, see Barry Wellman, "Network Analysis: Some Basic Principles," *Sociological Theory* (1983), pp. 155–200; Jeremy F. Boissevain and J. Clyde Mitchell, eds., *Network Analysis* (The Hague: Mouton, 1973) and *Social Networks in Urban Situations* (Manchester: Manchester University Press, 1969); J. A. Barnes, "Social Networks" (Addison-Wesley Module, no. 26, 1972); Barry S. Wellman and S. D. Berkowitz,

# Basic Theoretical Concepts In Network Analysis

## Points and Nodes

The units of a network can be persons, positions, corporate or collective actors, or virtually any entity that can be connected to another entity. In general, these units are conceptualized as *points* or *nodes*, and they are typically symbolized by letters or numbers. In Figure 29.1, a very simple network is drawn with each letter representing a point or node in the network. One goal of network analysis, then, is to array in visual space a pattern of connections among the units that are related to each other. In a mathematical sense, it makes little difference what the points and nodes are, and this has great virtue because it provides a common set of analytical tools for analyzing very diverse phenomena. Another goal of network analysis is to explain the dynamics of various patterns of ties among nodes, although this goal is often subordinated to developing computer algorithms for representing the connections among points and nodes in more complex networks than the one portrayed in Figure 29.1.

## Links, Ties, and Connections

The letters in Figure 29.1 represent the nodes or points of a structure. The lines connecting the letters indicate that these points are attached to each other in a particular pattern. The concept of *tie* is the most frequent way to denote this property of a network, and so in Figure 29.1, there are ties between *A* and *B*, *A* and *C*, *A* and *D*, *B* and *E*, *C* and *D*, and *D* and *E*. We

**Figure 29.1**    A Simple Network

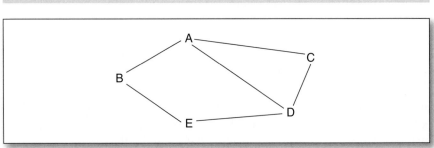

*Social Structures: A Network Approach* (Cambridge: Cambridge University Press, 1988). Somewhat more technical summaries of recent network research can be found in Samuel Leinhardt, ed., *Social Networks: A Developing Paradigm* (New York: Academic, 1977); Paul Holland and Samuel Leinhardt, eds., *Perspectives in Social Network Research* (New York: Academic, 1979); Ronald S. Burt, "Models of Network Structure," *Annual Review of Sociology* 6 (1980): pp. 79–141; Peter Marsden and Nan Lin, eds., *Social Structure and Network Analysis* (Newbury Park, CA: Sage, 1982). For advanced research on networks, consult recent issues of the journal *Social Networks*.

not only need to know that points in a network are connected, but we also must have some idea of what it is that connects these points. That is, what is the nature of the tie? What resources flow from node to node? From the point of view of graph theory, it does not make much difference, but when the substantive concerns of sociologists are considered, it is important to know the nature of the ties. As we saw in Chapter 15 on the early sociograms constructed by Jacob Moreno, the ties involved emotional states such as liking and friendship, and the nodes themselves were individual people. But the nature of the tie can be diverse: the flow of information, money, goods, services, influence, emotions, deference, prestige, and virtually any force or resource that binds actors to each other.

Often, as we saw in Chapter 24 on exchange-network theory, the ties are conceptualized as resources. When points or nodes are represented by different letters, this denotes that actors are exchanging different resources, such as prestige for advice, money for services, deference for information, and so on. Conversely, if they were exchanging similar resources, the nodes would be represented by the same letter and subscripted numbers, such as $A_1$, $A_2$, and $A_3$. But this is only one convention; the nature of the tie can also be represented by different kinds of lines, such as dotted, dashed, or colored lines. In graph theory, the lines can also reveal direction, as indicated by arrows. Moreover, if multiple resources are connecting positions in the graph, multiple lines (and, if necessary, arrows specifying direction) would be used. Thus, the graph represented in Figure 29.1 is obviously very simple, but it communicates the basic goal of network analysis: to represent in visual space the structure of connections among units.

One way to rise above the diversity of resources examined in network analysis is to visualize resource flows in networks for three generic types: materials, symbols, and emotions. That is, what connects persons, positions, and corporate actors in the social world is the flow of (1) symbols (information, ideas, values, norms, messages, etc.), (2) materials (physical things and perhaps symbols, such as money, that give access to physical things), and (3) emotions (approval, respect, liking, pleasure, and so forth). In non-sociological uses of networks, the ties or links can be other types of phenomena, but when the ties are social, they exist along material, symbolic, and emotional dimensions.

The configuration of ties can also be represented as a matrix, and in most network studies, the matrix is created before the actual network diagram. Moreover, when large numbers of nodes are involved, the matrix is often a better way to grasp the complexity of connections than a diagram, which would become too cumbersome to be useful. Figure 29.2 presents the logic of a matrix, using the very simple network represented in Figure 29.1. The mathematics of such matrices can become very complicated, but the general point is clear: to cross-tabulate which nodes are connected to each other (as is done inside the triangular area of the matrix in Figure 29.2). If possible, once the matrix is constructed, it can be used to generate a graph, something like the one in Figure 29.1. With the use of sophisticated

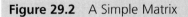

**Figure 29.2**  A Simple Matrix

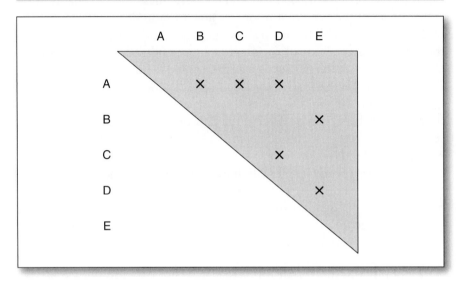

computer algorithms in network analysis, the matrix is the essential step for subsequent analysis; an actual diagram might not be drawn because the mathematical manipulations are too complex. Yet, most matrices will eventually be converted in network analysis into some form of visual representation in space—perhaps not a network digraph but some other technique, such as three dimensional bar graphs or clusters of points, will be used to express in visual space the relations among units.

# Patterns and Configurations of Ties

From a network perspective, social structure is conceptualized as the form of ties among positions or nodes. That is, what is the pattern or configuration among what resources flowing among what sets of nodes or points in a graph? To answer questions like this, network sociology addresses several properties of networks. The most important of these are number of ties, directedness, reciprocity of ties, transitivity of ties, density of ties, strength of ties, bridges, brokerage, centrality, and equivalence.

### Number of Ties

An important piece of information in performing network analysis is the total number of ties among all points and nodes. Naturally, the number of potential ties depends on the number of points in a graph and the number of resources involved in connecting the points. Yet, for any given number of points and resources, it is important to calculate both the actual and potential number of ties that are (and can be) generated. This information can then be used to calculate other dimensions of a network structure.

## Directedness

It is important to know the direction in which resources flow through a network; so, as indicated earlier, arrows are often placed on the lines of a graph, making it a *digraph*. As a consequence, a better sense of the structure of the network emerges. For example, if the lines denote information, we would have a better understanding of how the ties in the network are constructed and maintained, because we could see the direction and sequence of the information flow.

## Reciprocity of Ties

Another significant feature of networks is the reciprocity of ties among positions. That is, is the flow of resources one way, or is it reciprocated for any two positions? If the flow of resources is reciprocated, then it is conventional to have double lines with arrows pointing in the direction of the resource flow. Moreover, if different resources flow back and forth, this too can be represented. Surprisingly, conventions about how to represent this multiplicity of resource flows are not fully developed. One way to denote the flow of different resources is to use varying-colored lines or numbered lines; another is to label the points with the same letter subscripted (that is, $A_1$, $A_2$, $A_3$, and so forth) if similar resources flow and with varying letters (that is, $A$, $B$, $C$, $D$) if the resources connecting actors are different. But, whatever the notation, the extent and nature of reciprocity in ties become an important property of a social network.

## Transitivity of Ties

A critical dimension of networks is the level of transitivity among sets of positions. *Transitivity* refers to the degree to which there is a *transfer* of a relation among subsets of positions. For example, if nodes $A_1$ and $A_2$ are connected with positive affect, and positions $A_2$ and $A_3$ are similarly connected, we can ask, will positions $A_1$ and $A_3$ also be tied together with positive affect? If the answer to this question is "yes," then the relations among $A_1$, $A_2$, and $A_3$ are transitive. Discovering patterns of transitivity in a network can be important because it helps explain other critical properties of a network, such as density and the formation of cliques.

## Density of Ties

A significant property of a network is its degree of connectedness, or the extent to which nodes reveal the maximum possible number of ties. The more the actual number of ties among nodes approaches the total possible number among a set of nodes, the greater is the overall *density* of a network.[2]

---

[2]There are other ways to measure density; this definition is meant to be illustrative of the general idea.

Figure 29.3 compares the same five-node network under conditions of high and low density of ties.

Of even greater interest are subdensities of ties within a larger network structure. Such subdensities, which are sometimes referred to as *cliques*, reveal strong, reciprocated, and transitive ties among a particular subset of positions within the overall network.[3] For example, in Figure 29.4, there are three clusters of dense ties in the network, thus revealing three distinct cliques within the larger network.

## Strength of Ties

Yet another crucial aspect of a network is the volume and level of resources that flow among positions. A weak tie is one where few or sporadic amounts of resources flow among positions, whereas a strong tie evidences a high level of resource flow. The overall structure of a network is significantly influenced by clusters and configurations of strong and weak ties. For example, if the ties in the cliques in Figure 29.4 are all strong, the network is composed of cohesive subgroupings that have relatively sparse ties to one another. On the other hand, if the ties in these subdensities are weak, then the subgroupings will involve less intense linkages,[4] with the

**Figure 29.3**   High- and Low-Density Networks

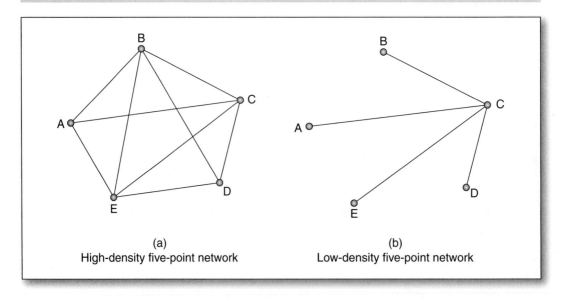

(a)
High-density five-point network

(b)
Low-density five-point network

---

[3]The terminology on subdensities varies. *Clique* is still the most prominent term, but *alliances* has been offered as an alternative. Moreover, the old sociological standbys *group* and *subgroup* seem to have made a comeback in network analysis.

[4]At one time, *intensity* appears to have been used in preference to *strength*. See Mitchell, "The Concept and Use of Social Networks." It appears that Granovetter's classic article shifted usage in favor of *strength* and *weakness*. See note 5.

**Figure 29.4**   Network with Three Distinct Cliques

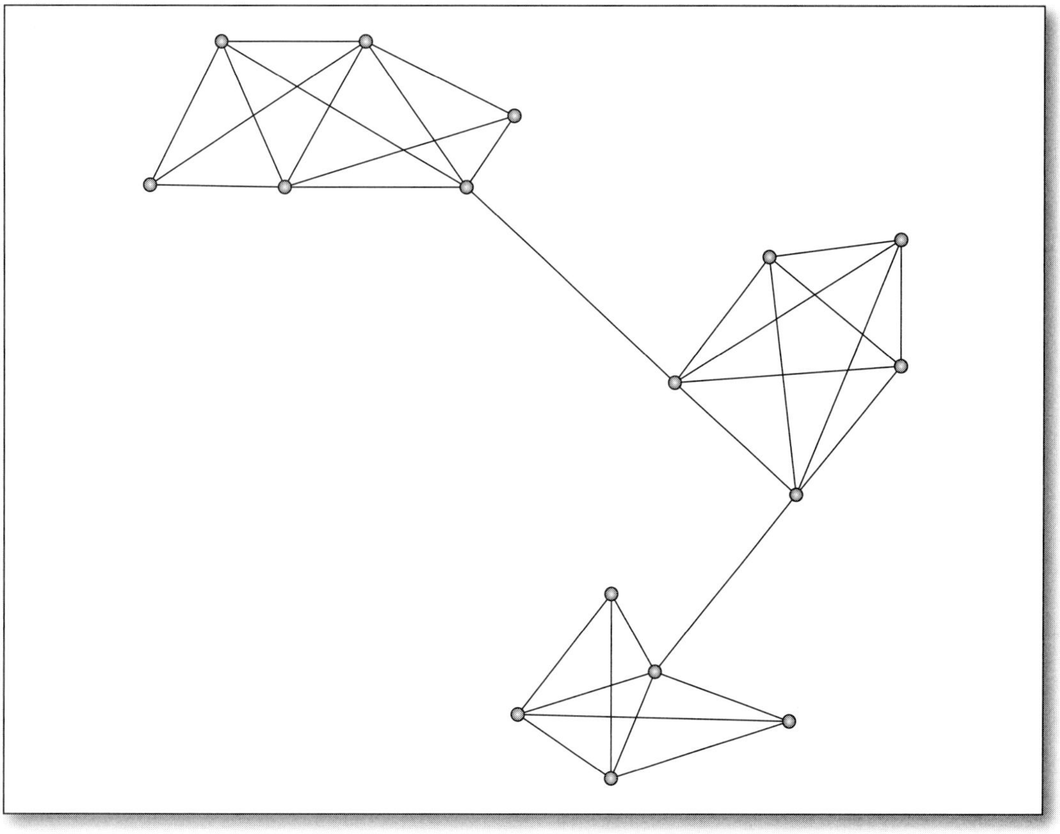

result that the structure of the whole network will be very different than would be the case if these ties were strong.

## Bridges

When networks reveal subdensities, it is always interesting to know which positions connect the subdensities, or cliques, to one another. For example, in Figure 29.4, those ties connecting subdensities are bridges and are crucial in maintaining the overall connectedness of the network. Indeed, if one removed one of these positions or severed the tie, the structure of the network would be very different—it would become three separate networks. These bridging ties are typically weak,[5] because each position in the bridge is

---

[5]See Mark Granovetter, "The Strength of Weak Ties," *American Journal of Sociology* 78 (1973): pp. 1360–80 and "The Strength of Weak Ties: A Network Theory Revisited," *Sociological Theory* (1983), pp. 201–33. The basic network "law" from Granovetter's original study can be expressed as follows: *The degree of integration of a network composed of highly dense subcliques is a positive function of the extensiveness of bridges, involving weak ties, among these subcliques.*

more embedded in the flow of resources of a particular subdensity or clique. But, nonetheless, such ties are often crucial to the maintenance of a larger social structure; it is not surprising that the number and nature of bridges within a network structure are highlighted in network analysis.

## Brokerage

At times, a particular position is outside subsets of positions but is crucial to the flow of resources to and from these subsets. This position is often in a brokerage situation because its activities determine the nature and level of resources that flow to and from subsets of positions.[6] In Figure 29.5, position $A_7$ is potentially a broker for the flow of resources from subsets consisting of positions $A_1$, $A_2$, $A_3$, $A_4$, and $A_5$ to $B_1$, $B_2$, $B_3$, $B_4$, $B_5$, and $B_6$. Position $A_7$ can become a broker if (1) the distinctive resources that pass to, and from,

**Figure 29.5**   A Network with Brokerage Potential

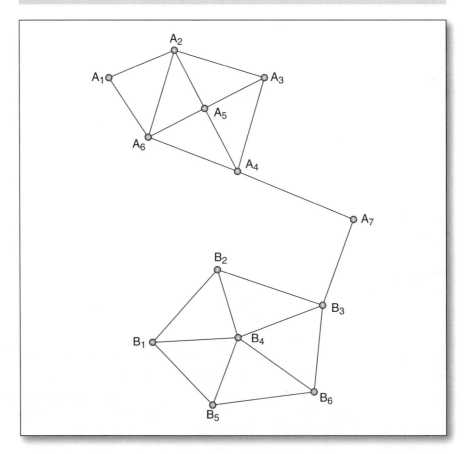

---

[6]Ronald S. Burt has, perhaps, done the most interesting work here. See, for example, his *Toward a Structural Theory of Action* (New York: Academic, 1982) and "A Structural Theory of Interlocking Corporate Directorships," *Social Networks* 1 (1978–1979): pp. 415–35.

these two subsets are needed or valued by at least one of these subsets, and (2) direct ties, or bridges, between the two subsets do not exist. Indeed, a person or actor in a brokerage position often seeks to prevent the development of bridges (like those in Figure 29.4) and to manipulate the flow of resources such that at least one, and if possible both, subsets are highly dependent on its activities.

## Centrality

An extremely important property of a network is *centrality*, as was noted in Chapter 26 for Bavelas' and Leavitt's studies of communication in experimental groups. There are several ways to calculate centrality:[7] (1) the number of other positions with which a particular position is connected, (2) the number of points between which a position falls, and (3) the closeness of a position to others in a network. Although these three measures might denote somewhat different points as central, the theoretical idea is fairly straightforward: Some positions in a network mediate the flow of resources by virtue of their patterns of ties to other points. For example, in Figure 29.3 (b), point *C* is central in a network consisting of positions *A, B, C, D,* and *E*. Or, to take another example, points $A_5$ and $B_4$ in Figure 29.5 are more central than other positions because they are directly connected to all, or to the most, positions and because a higher proportion of resources will tend to pass through these positions. A network can also reveal several nodes of centrality, as is evident in Figure 29.6. Moreover, patterns of centrality can shift over time. Thus many of the dynamics of network structure revolve around the nature and pattern of centrality.

## Equivalence

When positions stand in the same relation to another position, they are considered *equivalent*. When this idea was first introduced into network analysis, it was termed *structural equivalence* and restricted to situations in which a set of positions is connected to another position or set of positions in exactly the same way.[8] For example, positions $C_2$, $C_3$, and $C_4$ in Figure 29.6 are structurally equivalent because they reveal the same relation to position $C_1$.

---

[7]The definitive works here are Linton C. Freeman, "Centrality in Social Networks: Conceptual Clarification," *Social Networks* 1 (1979): pp. 215–39 and Linton C. Freeman, Douglas Boeder, and Robert R. Mulholland, "Centrality in Social Networks: Experimental Results," *Social Networks* 2 (1979): pp. 119–41. See also Linton C. Freeman, "Centered Graphs and the Structure of Ego Networks," *Mathematical Social Sciences* 3 (1982): pp. 291–304 and Philip Bonacich, "Power and Centrality: A Family of Measures," *American Journal of Sociology* 92 (1987); pp. 1170–82.

[8]François Lorrain and Harrison C. White, "Structural Equivalence of Individuals in Social Networks," *Journal of Mathematical Sociology* 1 (1971): pp. 49–80; Harrison C. White, Scott A. Boorman, and Ronald L. Breiger, "Social Structure from Multiple Networks: I. Block Models of Roles and Positions," *American Journal of Sociology* 8 (1976): pp. 730–80.

**Figure 29.6**   Equivalence in Social Networks

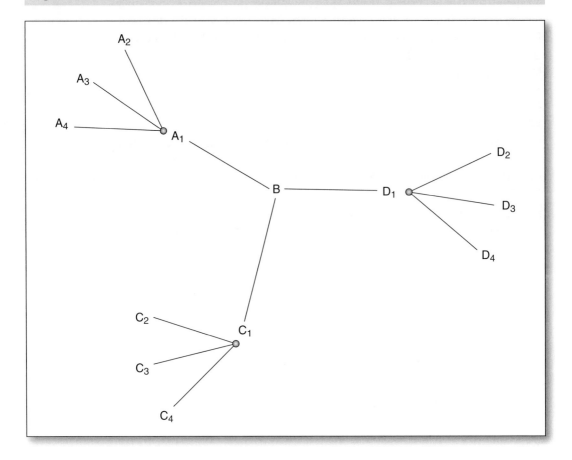

Figure 29.6 provides another illustration of structural equivalence, as well. $A_2$, $A_3$, and $A_4$ are structurally equivalent to $A_1$; similarly, $D_2$, $D_3$, and $D_4$ are equivalent to $D_1$; and $A_1$, $C_1$, and $D_1$ are structurally equivalent to $B$.

This original formulation of equivalence was limited, however, in that positions could be equivalent only when *actually connected to the same position*. We might also want to consider all positions as equivalent when they are connected to different positions but in the same form, pattern, or manner. For instance, in Figure 29.6, $A_2$, $A_3$, $A_4$, $D_2$, $D_3$, $D_4$, $C_2$, $C_3$, and $C_4$ can all be seen as equivalent because they bear the *same type* of relation to another position—that is to $A_1$, $D_1$, and $C_1$, respectively. This way of conceptualizing equivalence is termed *regular equivalence*[9] and, in a sense, subsumes the

---

[9]Lee Douglas Sailer, "Structural Equivalence," *Social Networks* 1 (1978): pp. 73–90; John Paul Boyd, "Finding and Testing Regular Equivalence," *Social Networks* 24 (2002): pp. 315–31; John Paul Boyd and Kai J. Jonas, "Are Social Equivalences Ever Regular? Permutation and Exact Tests," *Social Networks* 32 (2001): pp. 87–123; Katherine Faust, "Comparison of Methods for Positional Analysis: Structural Equivalence and General Equivalence," *Social Networks* 10 (1988): pp. 313–41.

original notion of *structural equivalence.* That is, structural equivalence, wherein the equivalent *positions must actually be connected to the same position in the same way,* is a particular type of a more general equivalence phenomenon. These terms, *structural* and *regular,* are awkward, but they have become conventional in network analysis, so we are stuck with them. The critical idea is that the number and nature of equivalent positions in a network have important influences on the dynamics of the network.[10] The general hypothesis is that actors in structurally equivalent or regularly equivalent positions will behave or act in similar ways.

# Conclusion

The mathematics of network analysis can become quite complicated, as can the computer algorithms used to analyze data sets of the processes outlined above. This listing of concepts is somewhat metaphorical because it eliminates the formal and quantitative thrust of much network analysis. Indeed, much network analysis bypasses the conversion of matrices into graphs like those in the various figures presented and, instead, performs mathematical and statistical operations on just the matrices themselves. Yet, if network analysis is to realize its full theoretical (as opposed to methodological) potential, it might be wise to use concepts, at least initially, in a more verbal and intuitive sense.

Few would disagree with the notion that social structure is composed of relations among positions. But is this all that social structure is? Can the concepts denoting nodes, ties, and patterns of ties (number, strength, reciprocity, transitivity, bridges, brokerage, centrality, and equivalence) capture all the critical properties of social structure?

The answer to these questions is probably "no." Social structure probably involves other crucial processes that are not captured by these concepts. Yet a major property of social structure *is* its network characteristics, as Georg Simmel was perhaps the first to really appreciate. For, whatever other dimensions social structure might reveal—cultural, behavioral, ecological, temporal, psychological, and so forth—its backbone is a system of interconnections among actors who occupy positions relative to one another and who exchange resources. And so, network analysis has great potential for theories of social structure. Has this potential been realized? Probably not, for several reasons.

First, as just noted, network analysis is overly methodological and concerned with generating quantitative techniques for arraying data in matrices and then converting the matrices into descriptions of particular networks (whether as graphs or as equations). As long as this is the case, network sociology will remain primarily a tool for empirical description.

---

[10] In many ways, Karl Marx's idea that those who stand in a common relationship to the means of production have common interests is an equivalence agreement. Thus, the idea of equivalence is not new to sociology—just the formalism used to express it is new.

Second, there has been little effort to develop principles of network dynamics per se. Few[11] seem to ask theoretical questions within the network tradition itself. For example, how does the degree of density, centrality, equivalence, bridging, and brokerage influence the nature of the network and the flow of relations among positions in the network? There are many empirical descriptions of events that touch on this question but few actual theoretical laws or principles.[12]

Third, network sociology has yet to translate traditional theoretical concerns and concepts into network terminology in a way that highlights the superiority, or at least the viability, of using network theoretical constructs for mainstream theory in sociology. For example, power, hierarchy, differentiation, integration, stratification, conflict, and many other concerns of sociological theory have not been adequately reconceptualized in network terms, and hence it is unlikely that sociological theory will adopt or incorporate a network approach until this translation of traditional questions occurs.

All these points, however, need to be qualified because numerous sociologists have actually sought to develop laws of network processes and to address traditional theoretical concerns with network concepts. Although these efforts are far from constituting a coherent theory of network dynamics, they do illustrate the potential utility of network sociology, as we saw, for example, in the review of network exchange theory in Chapter 24.

---

[11]There are, of course, some notable exceptions to this statement. For an example, John Martin Levi Martin, *Social Structures* (Princeton, NJ: Princeton University Press, 2009); "Structures of Power in Naturally Occurring Communities," *Social Networks* 20 (1998): pp. 197–225, and "Formation and Stabliziation of Vertical Hierarchies among Adolescents," *Social Psychology Quarterly* (2010); Ronald S. Burt, *Toward a Structural Theory of Action* (cited in note 6); *Structural Holes: The Social Structure of Competition* (Cambridge, MA: Harvard University Press, 1992); Noah E. Friedkin, *A Structural Theory of Social Influence* (Cambridge, UK: Cambridge University Press, 1998).

[12]Mark Granovetter, "The Theory-Gap in Social Network Analysis" in *Perspectives on Social Network Research*, eds. P. Holland and S. Leinhardt (New York: Academic, 1979).

**PART VII**

# The Challenge of Critical Theorizing

## CHAPTER 30

# The Rise of Critical Theory

## Lines of Critical Theorizing in Europe

Virtually all early sociologists were influenced by a broad intellectual movement, often termed the Enlightenment, which grew out of both the Renaissance and, later, the Age of Science in the seventeenth century.[1] As we have seen for the emergence of most theoretical perspectives in sociology, the Enlightenment still inspires thinkers in at least two respects. First, the social universe has often been seen as *progressing*, moving from one stage of development to another. To be sure, theorists have disagreed about the stages, and many have had doubts about the notion of *progress*, but it would be hard to deny that sociologists see directional movement of society or world systems as a central theme. A second legacy from the Enlightenment has been the belief that science can be used to further social progress. As with the idea of progress, this faith in science has not been universal, but even those who have doubted that science is the key to social progress still tend to believe that scientific analysis of the human condition and its pathologies can be used for human betterment.

These two points of emphasis from the Enlightenment were part of a more general effort to come to terms with what is often called *modernity* or the transformations associated with the rise of commerce and industrial capitalism from the debris of the old feudal order. Indeed, the central problem for all early sociologists was to understand the dramatic transformations of the social order being caused by the expansion of commerce and markets, the industrialization of production, the urbanization

---

[1]Jonathan H. Turner, "Founders and Classics: A Canon in Motion" in *The Student Sociologist's Handbook*, ed. C. Middleton, J. Gubbay, and C. Ballard (Oxford: Blackwell, 1997).

of labor, the decline of cohesive and local communities, the rise of the bureaucratic state, the decreasing salience of sacred symbols as a result of expanding secular law and science, the conflicts among new social classes, and many other disruptive transformations. These were changes that early theorists sought to comprehend. Some were pessimistic and worried about what was occurring; others were optimistic about the new modern age; still others believed that things would get better after the current turmoil subsided. But no one, who was considered a serious social thinker, could ignore modernity.

Critical theorizing in all its forms enters this old debate about modernity from a number of different directions. As the name implies, most theorists in this *critical* tradition view industrial capitalism in negative terms, and some have even posited a new stage of history, *postmodernity*, which is similarly viewed in a negative light. Almost all critical theorists disparage the optimism of the Enlightenment, seeing the use of science for constructing a better society as naive, as pursuit of an illusion, or even as harmful. For most, science is part of a broader culture of commerce and capitalism, which, to critical theorists, are the cause of the problems in the modern or postmodern era, not part of their solution. Yet, ironically, these very same critics often appear to be figures of the Enlightenment because they address the very same problems of the earlier Enlightenment-inspired theorists, because they use analysis and reason to pronounce the problems of the modern or postmodern era, and because they often propose solutions to the ills of the current era, even as they drown their pronouncements in pessimism. True, most critical theorists maintain a hearty disdain for science and the implicit Enlightenment projects of theories examined in earlier chapters, but they have not escaped the mood, tone, and problematic of the Enlightenment.

## The Critical Thrust of Karl Marx's Analysis of Capitalism

In 1846, Karl Marx and Friedrich Engels completed *The German Ideology*, which was initially rejected by the publisher.[2] Much of this work is an attack on the Young Hegelians, who were advocates of the German philosopher Georg Hegel, and is of little interest today. Yet this attack contained certain basic ideas that have served as the impetus behind *critical theory*, or the view that social theory must be critical of oppressive arrangements and propose emancipatory alternatives. This theme exists, of course, in all of Marx's work,[3] but the key elements of contemporary critical theory are most evident in this first statement.

---

[2]Karl Marx and Friedrich Engels, *The German Ideology* (New York: International, 1947; written in 1846).

[3]Karl Marx, *Capital: A Critical Analysis of Capitalist Production*, vol. 1 (New York: International, 1967; originally published in 1867); Karl Marx and Friedrich Engels, *The Communist Manifesto* (New York: International, 1971; originally published in 1848).

Marx criticized the Young Hegelians severely because he had once been one of them and was now making an irrevocable break. Marx saw the Hegelians as hopeless idealists, in the philosophical sense. That is, they saw the world as reflective of ideas, with the dynamics of social life revolving around consciousness and other cognitive processes by which ideal essences work their magic on humans. Marx saw this emphasis on the *reality of ideas* as nothing more than a conservative ideology that supports people's oppression by the material forces of their existence. His alternative was to stand Hegel on his head, but in this early work there is still an emphasis on the relation between consciousness and self-reflection, on the one hand, and social reality, on the other. This dualism became central to contemporary critical theory.

Actually, Marx's standing of Hegel on his head has been reversed by some contemporary theorists who, in essence, have put Hegel back on his feet. Indeed, for many who commented on the condition of modernity or postmodernity (see Chapter 32) in the first decades of the twenty-first century, the world has been transformed into a sea of symbols that have lost anchorage in material conditions and that have, as a result, changed the very nature of society from one driven by control of the means of material production to one dominated by signs and texts symbolizing little but themselves. For critical theorists schooled in the Marxian tradition, even those who call themselves postmodernists, such arguments go too far, but there can be little doubt that Marx's dismissal of Hegel and the Young Hegelians was not the final word on the place of ideas, symbols, and signs in societal evolution.

Marx was a modernist, not a postmodernist, and so he went a different direction. For Marx, humans are unique by virtue of their conscious awareness of themselves and their situation; they are capable of self-reflection and, hence, assessment of their positions in society. Such consciousness arises from people's daily existence and is not a realm of ideas that is somehow independent of the material world, as much German philosophy argued or as later versions of postmodernism implied. For Marx, people produce their ideas and conceptions of the world because of social structures in which they are born, raised, and live.

The essence of people's lives is the process of production. For Marx, human "life involves, before anything else, eating and drinking, a habitation, clothing, and many other material things."[4] To meet these contingencies of life, production is necessary, but as production satisfies one set of needs, new needs arise and encourage alterations in the ways that productive activity is organized. The elaboration of productive activity creates a division of labor, which, in the end, is alienating because it increasingly deprives humans of their capacity to control their productive activities. Moreover, as people work, they are exploited in ways that generate private

---

[4]Marx and Engels, *The German Ideology* (cited in note 2), p. 15.

property and capital for those who enslave them. Thus, as people work as alienated cogs in the division of labor, they produce that which enslaves them: private property and profits for those who control the modes and means of production. Marx provided a more detailed discussion of the evolution of productive forces to this capitalist stage, and like any Enlightenment thinker, he argued that this capitalist stage would lead to a new era of human organization.

Marx believed that the capacity to use language, to think, and to analyze their conditions would enable humans to alter their environment. People do not merely have to react to their material conditions in some mechanical way; they can also use their capacities for thought and reflection to construct new material conditions and corresponding social relations. Indeed, the course of history involved such processes as people actively restructured the material conditions of their existence. The goal of social theory, Marx implicitly argued, is to use humans' unique facility to expose those oppressive social relations and to propose alternatives. Marx's entire career was devoted to this goal, and this emancipatory aspect of Marx's thought forms the foundation for critical theory, even in some of its postmodern manifestations.

Marx used the somewhat ambiguous term *praxis* to describe this blending of theory and action. The basic notion is that action to change social conditions generates increased knowledge that can then be used to mount more effective change-producing action. Thus, the interplay between action and theoretical understanding can eventually lead individuals to a better social life. Although those with power can impose their ideologies on subordinates and, thereby, distort the latter's perceptions of their true interests, Marx had typical Enlightenment-inspired faith that subordinates possessed the capacity for praxis and that they would eventually use their capacities for agency to change the nature of modernity.

Today, contemporary critical theorists appear somewhat divided on the question of whether analysis of modernity and postmodernity can be used to improve the human condition. As we will see shortly, many confronted Max Weber's pessimism about the ever tightening "steel enclosure" or what Talcott Parsons posed as "the iron cage" of rational-legal authority and state domination. Others sustained the emancipatory faith of Marx's belief in praxis.

Still others emphasized an inherent force articulated in Marx's analysis of capitalism—the capacity of money-driven markets to *commodify* all things, symbols, and ideals—as a basis for a renewed pessimism about the human condition. To commodify means that symbols, signs, objects, cultures, relationships, and virtually anything can be turned into a marketable thing, to be bought and sold for a price stated in terms of money and subject to Adam Smith's laws of supply and demand. Hence, as capitalists seek profits, they buy and sell not just the material objects necessary for human survival, but they produce and sell symbols and signs that, as commodities, lose their power to provide meaning to human life.

Coupled with information technologies that Marx could never have visualized, as well as markets for services and cultural symbols that Marx did not fully anticipate, the social world is now dominated by the production and distribution of signs, symbols, texts, and other cultural commodities. This transformation has changed the very nature of humans' capacities to understand and respond to their conditions.

## Weber's Pessimism and the Basic Problem for Early European Theory

Max Weber was concerned with the historical transition to modern capitalist societies, and his description and explanation of this transition represent a devastating critique of Marx's optimism about revolutionary movements toward a new utopian society. Weber's analysis is complex, and the historical detail that he presented to document his case is impressive, but his argument is captured by the concept of *rationalization*.[5] Weber argued that the rationality that defines modern societies is *means/ends rationality* and, hence, involves a search for the most efficient means to achieve a defined end. The process of rationalization, Weber felt, involves the ever-increasing penetration of means/ends rationality into more spheres of life, thereby destroying older traditions. As bureaucracies expand in the economic and governmental sphere and as markets allow individuals to pursue their personal ends rationally, the traditional moral fabric is broken. Weber agreed with Georg Simmel that this rationalization of life brings individuals a new freedom from domination by religious dogmatism, community, class, and other traditional forces, but in their place, it creates a new kind of domination by impersonal economic forces, such as markets and corporate bureaucracies, and by the vast administrative apparatus of the ever-expanding state. Human options were, in Weber's view, becoming ever-more constrained by the "iron cage" of rational and legal authority. Unlike Marx, Weber did not see such a situation as rife with revolutionary potential; rather, he saw the social world as increasingly administered by impersonal bureaucratic forces.

This pessimistic view seemed, by the early 1930s, to be a far more reasonable assessment of modernity than was Marx's utopian dream. Indeed, the communist revolution in Russia had degenerated into Stalinism and bureaucratic totalitarianism by the Communist Party; in the West, particularly the United States, workers seemed ever-more willing to sell themselves in markets and work in large-scale organizations; and political fascism in Germany and Italy was creating large authoritarian bureaucracies. How, then, was the first generation of critical theorists to reconcile Weber's more accurate assessment of empirical trends with Marx's optimistic and emancipatory vision? This became the central question of early critical theory.

---

[5]Max Weber, *Economy and Society*, trans. G. Roth (Berkeley: University of California Press, 1978).

## Simmel's Defense of Modernity and Implicit Attack on Marx

Many of Georg Simmel's ideas represent an important qualification to Marx's reasoning and, to a lesser extent, to Weber's as well. Marx's more emancipatory side saw capitalism as producing the conditions that would lead to a revolution, ushering in a new form of human organization in which individuals are freed from the capitalists' domination. Thus, as capitalism expands, the division of labor makes workers appendages to machines, concentrates workers in urban areas, quantifies social relations through money and markets, and forces workers to be mere role players (rather than fully involved participants) in social relations. In so doing, capitalism generates the personal alienation and resentments as well as the social structural conditions that will lead subordinates to become aware of their domination and to organize in an effort to change their plight.

Simmel challenged much of Marx's analysis in his *The Philosophy of Money*.[6] This critique revolves around one of the themes in Marx's writing: Capitalism quantifies social life with money and, in so doing, makes exchanges in markets paramount; the result is that human social relations are increasingly commodified. Such commodification is personified in the labor market, where workers sell themselves as a thing, and coupled with the growing division of labor, workers become mere cogs in an impersonal organizational machine. Such processes, Marx believed, would be so oppressive as to initiate revolutionary pressures for their elimination.

Simmel, however, looked at these forces much differently. Although a certain level of alienation from work and commodification of relations through the use of money are inevitable with increasing differentiation and expansion of productive forces and markets, Simmel saw these forces of modernity as liberating individuals from the constraints of tradition. In Simmel's Enlightenment-oriented view, people have more options about how they spend their money and what they do; they can move about with more freedom and form new and varied social relations; they can live lifestyles that reflect their tastes and values; and, in general, they are more liberated than their counterparts in less complex, traditional societies.

This critique of Marx was, however, rejected by the early critical theorists who did not want to visualize modern societies as liberating. And yet, these theorists were confronted with the failure of Marx's predictions about the communist revolution and the coming emancipation of society. By the end of the twentieth century, they would also have to confront the triumph of world-level capitalism over socialism. In an attempt to reconstruct Marx's vision of humans' capacity to make history, they were forced to accept Weber's highly pessimistic view of the constraints of modern society and to reject Simmel's more optimistic diagnosis. But, in so doing, they became

---

[6]Georg Simmel, *The Philosophy of Money*, trans. T. Bottomore and D. Frisbie (Boston: Routledge & Kegan Paul, 1978; originally published in 1907).

trapped in a dilemma: If capitalism is not self-transforming as Marx's revolutionary model indicates, if modern life is not so liberating as Simmel felt, and if Weber's analysis of increasing constraint in societies must therefore be accepted as true, then how is liberation to occur? What force will drive people's emancipation from domination? Early critical theorists would not accept Simmel's judgment—that is, people are more *free* than in traditional societies—and so they conceptually retreated into a contemplative subjectivism. They viewed the liberating force as somehow springing from human nature and its capacity for conscious reflection—a kind of watered down, even impotent, sense of praxis.

# The Rise of The Frankfurt School of Critical Theory

## The Frankfurt School and the Cultural Turn

The spirit of Georg Wilhelm Friedrich Hegel (1770–1831) could not be exorcised by much twentieth-century critical theory. Key elements of the Marxian scheme—such as the dialectical view of history, the concept of alienation, or the notion of praxis, for example—came from Hegel. Karl Marx converted these basic ideas to a materialism emphasizing that the alienation created by inequalities in material relations of production generated an inherent dialectic of history led by humans who possessed the capacities for agency and praxis and who, thereby, would move human society to its final state of communism. In contrast with Hegel, Marx believed that ideas, politics, and other institutional systems were *superstructures* reflecting and, indeed, being controlled by a *substructure* lodged in the patterns of organization and ownership of economic production.

More than any Enlightenment-inspired sociologist of his time, Marx saw that the critique of existing relations of domination, the emergence of class conflict, the emancipation of humans, and the progress of society were all interwoven. The critique was to begin with attacks on the inequalities generated by the economic system and, then, on the political and ideological superstructures that legitimated the means and modes of production. Yet, by the third decade of the twentieth century, even the Great Depression had not produced the predicted revolution by the proletariat, nor was it possible to see humans as progressing. Even when times were better after World War II, capitalism was not collapsing but, if anything, gaining converts. And China's "communist revolution" and subsequent "cultural revolution" had begun to look very much like the Stalin purges in Russia.

The collapse of communism in the 1990s forced further adjustments by critical theory.[7] Indeed, criticism moved from one revolving around the

---

[7]See, for examples, David Hoy and Thomas McCarthy, *Critical Theory* (Oxford: Blackwell, 1994) or Stephen Regan, ed., *The Year's Work in Critical and Cultural Theory* (Oxford: Blackwell, 1995). Earlier reviews and analyses of critical theory and sociology include Paul

*immiseration* of the population to its tasteless overconsumption and manipulation by the symbols of advertising. In the end, critical theory and postmodernism began to blend together as concerns with symbols, signs, culture, and ideology seemed to hold sway over older Marxian views about the economic substructure. Or, at the very least, critical theorists were working very hard to find problems in the cultural products of mature capitalist systems and the developing capitalist world order. Marx was perhaps turning over in his grave, but Hegelian themes were nonetheless reemerging.

I will pause, therefore, and offer a few representative samples of how the critical theorists working in the decades before the twentieth century's midpoint were trying to keep their Marxian faith given a reality that was no longer on its Marxian trajectory. In so doing, Marxian materialism and Hegelian idealism were put back together in an uneasy accommodation.

Thus, the first generation of critical theorists, who are frequently referred to as the Frankfurt School because of their location in Germany and their explicit interdisciplinary effort to interpret the oppressive events of the twentieth century, confronted a real dilemma: how to reconcile Marx's emancipatory dream with the stark reality of modern society as conceptualized by Max Weber.[8] Indeed, when the Frankfurt Institute for Social Research was founded in 1923, there seemed little reason to be optimistic about developing a theoretically informed program for freeing people from unnecessary domination. The defeat of the left-wing working-class movements, the rise of fascism in the aftermath of World War I, and the degeneration of the Russian Revolution into Stalinism had, by the 1930s, made it clear that Marx's analysis needed drastic revision. Moreover, the expansion of the state, the spread of bureaucracy, and the emphasis on means/ends rationality through the application of science and technology all signaled that Weber's analysis had to be confronted.

---

Connerton, ed., *Critical Sociology* (New York: Penguin Books, 1970); Raymond Geuss, *The Idea of a Critical Theory* (New York: Cambridge University Press, 1981); David Held, *Introduction to Critical* Theory (Berkeley: University of California Press, 1980); Trent Schroyer, *The Critique of Domination: The Origins and Development of Critical Theory* (New York: Braziller, 1973); Albrecht Wellmer, *Critical Theory of Society* (New York: Seabury, 1974); Ellsworth R. Fuhrman and William E. Snizek, "Some Observations on the Nature and Content of Critical Theory," *Humboldt Journal of Social Relations* 7 (Fall–Winter 1979–1980): pp. 33–51; Zygmunt Bauman, *Towards a Critical Society* (Boston: Routledge & Kegan Paul, 1976); Robert J. Antonio, "The Origin, Development and Contemporary Status of Critical Theory," *Sociological Quarterly* 24 (Summer 1983): pp. 325–51; Jim Faught, "Objective Reason and the Justification of Norms," *California Sociologist* 4 (Winter 1981): pp. 33–53.

[8]For descriptions of this activity, see Martin Jay, *The Dialectical Imagination* (Boston: Little, Brown, 1973), and "The Frankfurt School's Critique of Marxist Humanism," *Social Research* 39 (1972): pp. 285–305; David Held, *Introduction to Critical Theory* (Berkeley: University of California Press, 1980): pp. 29–110; Robert J. Antonio, "The Origin, Development, and Contemporary Status of Critical Theory," *Sociological Quarterly* 24 (Summer 1983): pp. 325–51; Phil Slater, *Origin and Significance of the Frankfurt School* (London: Routledge & Kegan Paul, 1977).

The members of the Frankfurt School wanted to maintain Marx's views on praxis—that is, a blending of theory and action or the use of theory to stimulate action, and vice versa. And they wanted theory to expose oppression in society and to propose less constrictive options. Yet, they were confronted with the spread of political and economic domination of the masses. Thus modern critical theory in sociology was born in a time when there was little reason to be optimistic about realizing emancipatory goals.

Three members of the Frankfurt School are most central: György Lukács, Max Horkheimer, and Theodor Adorno.[9] Lukács' major work appeared in the 1920s,[10] whereas Horkheimer[11] and Adorno[12] were active well into the 1960s. In many ways, Lukács was the key link in the transition from Marx and Weber to modern critical theory, because Horkheimer and Adorno were reacting to much of Lukács analysis and approach. All these scholars are important because they directly influenced the intellectual development and subsequent work of Jürgen Habermas, the most prolific contemporary critical theorist whose work is examined in the next chapter.[13]

**György Lukács.** Lukács blended Marx and Weber together by seeing a convergence of Marx's ideas about commodification of social relations through money and markets with Weber's thesis about the penetration of rationality into ever more spheres of modern life. Borrowing from Marx's analysis of the "fetishism of commodities," Lukács employed the concept of *reification* to denote the process by which social relationships become "objects" that can be manipulated, bought, and sold. Then, reinterpreting

---

[9]Other prominent members included Friedrich Pollock (economist), Erich Fromm (psychoanalyst, social psychologist), Franz Neumann (political scientist), Herbert Marcuse (philosopher), and Leo Loenthal (sociologist). During the Nazi years, the school relocated to the United States, and many of its members never returned to Germany.

[10]György Lukács, *History and Class Consciousness* (Cambridge, MA: MIT Press, 1968; originally published in 1922).

[11]Max Horkheimer, *Critical Theory: Selected Essays* (New York: Herder and Herder, 1972) is a translation of essays written in German in the 1930s and 1940s; *Eclipse of Reason* (New York: Oxford University Press, 1947; reprinted by Seabury in 1974) was the only book by Horkheimer originally published in English. It takes a slightly different turn than earlier works, but it does present ideas that emerged from his association with Theodor Adorno. See also Horkheimer, *Critique of Instrumental Reason* (New York: Seabury, 1974). See David Held, *Introduction to Critical Theory* (cited in note 7), pp. 489–91, for a more complete listing of Horkheimer's works in German.

[12]Theodor W. Adorno, *Negative Dialectics* (New York: Seabury, 1973; originally published in 1966) and with Max Horkheimer, *Dialectic of Enlightenment* (New York: Herder and Herder, 1972; originally published in 1947).

[13]See Held, *Introduction to Critical Theory* (cited in note 7), pp. 485–87, for a more complete listing of his works. See also: "From Lukács to Adorno: Rationalization as Reification," pp. 339–99 in Jürgen Habermas, *The Theory of Communicative Action*, vol. 1 (Boston: Beacon, 1984) contains Habermas' critique of Lukács, Horkheimer, and Adorno.

Weber's notion of rationalization to mean a growing emphasis on the process of calculation of exchange values, Lukács combined Weber's and Marx's ideas. As traditional societies change, he argued, there is less reliance on moral standards and processes of communication to achieve societal integration; instead, there is more use of money, markets, and rational calculations. As a result, relations are coordinated by exchange values and by people's perceptions of one another as "things."[14]

Lukács painted himself into a conceptual corner, however. If indeed such is the historical process, how is it to be stopped? Lukács' answer was to resurrect a contrite Hegel; that is, rather than look to contradictions in material conditions or economic and political forces, one must examine the dialectical forces inherent in human consciousness. There are limits, Lukács argued, to how much reification and rationalization people will endure. Human subjects have an inner quality that keeps rationalization from completely taking over.[15]

This emphasis on the process of consciousness is very much a part of critical theory that borrows much from the early Marx[16] and that, at the Frankfurt School, had a heavy dose of Freud and psychoanalytic theory. As a result, unlike its sources of inspiration, Marx and Weber, early critical theory was subjectivist and failed to analyze *intersubjectivity*, or the ways people interact through mutually shared conscious activity. Emphasizing the inherent resistance of subjects to their total reification, Lukács could only propose that the critical theorist's role is to expose reification at work by analyzing the historical processes that have dehumanized people. As a consequence, Lukács made critical theory highly contemplative, emphasizing that the solution to the problem of domination resides in making people more aware and conscious of their situation through a detailed, historical analysis of reification.

**Max Horkheimer and Theodor Adorno.** Both Horkheimer and Adorno were highly suspicious of Lukács' Hegelian solution to the dilemma of reification and rationalization. These processes do not imply their own critique, as Hegel would have suggested. Subjective consciousness and material reality cannot be separated. Consciousness does not automatically offer resistance to those material forces that commodify, reify, and rationalize. Critical theory must, therefore, actively (1) describe historical forces that

---

[14]Lukács, *History and Class Consciousness* (cited in note 10).

[15]Ibid., pp. 89–102. In a sense, Lukács becomes another Young Hegelian whom Marx would have criticized. Yet, in Marx's own analysis, he sees alienation per se as producing resistance by workers to further alienation by the forces of production. This is the image that Lukács seems to take from Marx.

[16]Karl Marx and Friedrich Engels, *The German Ideology* (New York: International, 1947; originally written in 1846).

dominate human freedom and (2) expose ideological justifications of these forces. Such is to be achieved through interdisciplinary research among variously trained researchers and theorists who confront one another's ideas and use this dialogue to analyze concrete social conditions and to propose courses of ameliorative action. This emphasis on praxis—the confrontation between theory and action in the world—involves developing ideas about what oppresses and what to do about it in the course of human struggles. As Horkheimer argued, "[The] value of theory is not decided alone by the formal criteria of truth . . . but by its connection with tasks, which in the particular historical moment are taken up by progressive social forces."[17] Such critical theory is, Horkheimer claimed, guided by a "particular practical interest" in the emancipation of people from class domination.[18] Thus, critical theory is tied, in a sense that Marx might have appreciated, to people's practical interests.

As Adorno and Horkheimer interacted and collaborated, their positions converged (although Horkheimer had seemingly rejected much of his earlier work by the late 1950s). Adorno was more philosophical and, yet, more research oriented than Horkheimer; Adorno's empirical work on the authoritarian personality had a major impact on research in sociology and psychology, but his theoretical impact came from his collaboration with Horkheimer and, in many ways, through Horkheimer's single-authored work.[19] Adorno was very pessimistic about the chances of critical theory making great changes, although his essays were designed to expose patterns of recognized and unrecognized domination of individuals by social and psychological forces. At best, his "negative dialectics" could allow humans to tread water until historical circumstances were more favorable to emancipatory movements. The goal of negative dialectics was to sustain a constant critique of ideas, conceptions, and conditions. This critique could not by itself change anything, for it operates only on the plane of ideas and concepts. But it can keep ideological dogmatisms from obscuring conditions that might eventually allow emancipatory action.

Both Horkheimer and Adorno emphasized that humans' subjective side is restricted by the spread of rationalization. In conceptualizing this process, they created a kind of dualism between the subjective world and the realm of material objects, seeing the latter as oppressing the former. From their viewpoint, critical theory must expose this dualism, and it must analyze

---

[17]Max Horkheimer, "Zum Rationalismusstreit in der gegenwartigen Philosophie," originally published in 1935; reprinted in *Kritische Theorie*, vol. 1, ed. A. Schmidt (Frankfurt: Fischer Verlag, 1968), pp. 146–47. This and volume 2 represent a compilation of many of the essays Horkheimer wrote while at the Institute in Frankfurt.

[18]Habermas used this idea, but he extended it in several ways.

[19]Theodor W. Adorno, Else Frenkel-Brunswick, Daniel Levinson, and R. Nevitt Sanford, *The Authoritarian Personality* (New York: Harper & Row, 1950).

how this "instrumental reason" (means/ends rationality) has invaded the human spirit. In this way, some resistance can be offered to these oppressive forces.

Within the Frankfurt School, then, the idealism of Lukács had been brought partially back into a more orthodox Marxian position, but not completely so. The damage had been done to pure Marxian materialism, and outside of the narrow confines of Frankfurt, critical theory once again turned to idealism, even among those critical Marxists who had emigrated to America from Frankfurt during the rise of Nazism.[20]

**Gramsci's Theory of Ideological Hegemony.** Antonio Gramsci was an Italian Marxist who, obviously, cannot be considered part of the Frankfurt School. Yet, he is a key figure in continuing what the Frankfurt School emphasized: Criticism acknowledging that the capitalist systems of the twentieth century's midpoint were generating prosperity and that the working classes in these systems did not seem particularly disposed to revolution. Gramsci completed the turning of Marx's ideas back into a more Hegelian mode.[21] Marx believed that ideology and the "false consciousness" of workers were ideological obfuscations created and maintained by those who controlled the material (economic) substructure. Marx had argued— see Chapter 10 for more details about how this idea was carried forward in the twentieth century—that those who control the means and modes of production also control the state that, in turn, generates ideologies justifying this control and power. In this way, the proletariat is kept, for a time until the full contradictions of capitalism are manifest, from becoming a class for themselves ready to pursue revolutionary conflict with their oppressors. Gramsci simply turned this argument around: The superstructure of state and ideology drives the organization of society and the consciousness of the population.

Gramsci believed the ruling social class is *hegemonic*, controlling not only property and power, but ideology as well. Indeed, the ruling class holds onto its power and wealth by virtue of its ability to use ideologies to manipulate workers and all others. The state is no longer a crude tool of coercion, nor an intrusive and insensitive bureaucratic authority; it has become the propagator of culture and the civic education of the population, creating and controlling key institutional systems in more indirect, unobtrusive and, seemingly, inoffensive ways. Thus, the views of capitalists become the dominant views of all, with workers believing in the appropriateness of the market-driven systems of competition; the commodification of objects, signs, and symbols; the buying and selling of their labor; the use of law to enforce contracts favoring the interests of the wealthy; the encouragement

---

[20]See note 8.

[21]Antonio Gramsci, *Selections from the Prison Notebooks* (New York: International, 1971; originally published in 1928).

of private charities, the sponsorship of clubs and voluntary organizations; the state's conceptions of a "good citizen"; the civics curriculum of the schools; and virtually all spheres of institutional activity that are penetrated by the ideology of the state. Culture and ideology are, in Albert Bergesen's words, "no longer the thing to be explained but . . . now a thing that does the explaining."[22] A dominant material class rules, to be sure, but it does so by cultural symbols, and the real battle in capitalist societies is over whose symbols will prevail. Or, more accurately, can subordinates generate alternative ideologies to those controlled by the state?

This view of critical theory takes much of the mechanical menace out of Weber's "iron cage" metaphor, because the state's control is now "soft" and "internal." It has bars that bend flexibly around those whose perceptions of the world it seeks to control. The Marxian view of emancipation is still alive in Gramsci's theories, because the goal of theory is to expose the full extent to which ideology has been effectively used to manipulate subordinates. Moreover, the recognition that systems of symbols become the base of society is a theme that resonated well with later postmodernists (see Chapter 32) and structuralists (see Chapter 26) who began to conceptualize modernity as the production of signs and symbols.

**Althusser's Structuralism.** Initially, Louis Althusser seems more strictly orthodox in his Marxism than Gramsci;[23] yet, he was also a French scholar in a long line of structuralists whose emphasis is on the logic of the deeper, underlying structure of surface empirical reality.[24] Althusser remains close to Marx in this sense: The underlying structure and logic of the economy is ultimately determinative. But, having said this, he then developed a theory of the "Ideological State Apparatus,"[25] which gave prominence to the state's use of ideology to sustain control within a society.

For Althusser, economic, political, and ideological systems reveal their own structures, hidden beneath the surface and operating by their own logics. The economic might be the dominant system, circumscribing the operation of political and ideological structures, but these latter have a certain autonomy. History is, in essence, a reshuffling of these deep structures, and the individual actor becomes merely a vessel through which the inherent properties of structures operate. Individual actions, perceptions, beliefs, emotions, convictions, and other states of consciousness are

---

[22]Albert Bergesen, "The Rise of Semiotic Marxism," *Sociological Perspectives* 36 (1993): p. 5.

[23]Louis Althusser, *For Marx* (New York: Pantheon, 1965); *Lenin and Philosophy* (New York: Monthly Review Press, 1971); Louis Althusser and Etienne Balabar, *Reading Capital* (London: New Left, 1968).

[24]See Chapters 25, 26, and 27 for examples of this French lineage of structuralism.

[25]"Ideology and Ideological Status Apparatus," in Althusser, *Lenin and Philosophy* (cited in note 23).

somehow less real than the underlying structure that cannot be directly observed. To analogize the structuralist theories from which Althusser drew inspiration, social control comes from individuals perceiving that they are but words in a grammatical system generated by an even more fundamental structure. Each actor is at a surface place in the economic and political structures of a society, and their perceptions of these places also put them within an ideological or cultural sphere. But these places and spheres are only one level of reality; people also see themselves as part of a deeper set of structures that, in essence, defines who and what they are. Under these conditions, ideology has even more power because it is doing much more than blinding the subjects to some other reality, such as their objective class interests. Ideology is also defining actors' places in a reality beyond their direct control and a reality operating by its own logic of structure.

Thus, unlike Marx or Gramsci who believe ideology is a tool—an invidious and insidious one—used by those in power, Althusser sees the Ideological State Apparatus as more controlling because it is perceived not just as conventions, rules, mores, traditions, and beliefs, but instead as the essence of order and persons' placed in this order. The subject is thus trapped in the deeper logics of economic, political, and ideological systems that erode human capacities for praxis and agency.

## The Transformation of Marx's Project

In sum, by the middle of the twentieth century when the contemporary period of sociological theory began, Marx's emancipatory project had been turned into something very different than he had visualized. His and Engel's *The Communist Manifesto* was a call to arms, based on a view of the inherent contradictions in the nature of capitalist systems. Within one hundred years of this call, critical theory had become decidedly more philosophical. Indeed, Marx's dismissal of the Young Hegelians in *The German Ideology* had apparently not worked; they were back in different forms and guises, but they increasingly dominated critical theorizing in the twentieth century. The Young Hegelians so viciously criticized by Marx and Engels had considered themselves revolutionaries, but Marx saw them as more concerned with ideas about reality than with reality itself. They were accused of "blowing theoretical bubbles" about ideals and essences, and it could be imagined that he and Engels might make the very same criticisms of the critical theories that developed in the second half of the twentieth century, especially as these theories began to merge with postmodernism, as we will see in Chapter 32.

# American-Style Critical Theory

From its very beginnings, American sociology was less concerned with the big issues of modernity that dominated European sociology. Instead, American sociology was interwoven with various ameliorative social movements,[26] beginning with the abolitionist movement and working its way through the women's suffrage and social welfare movements of the early twentieth century. Compared to their European counterparts, the first generation of sociologists was not trained in science or even the social sciences. The result was concern with what today can be called social problems—racism, discrimination, poverty, and plight of immigrants, to list a few such perceived problems. Concern was with solving these problems and making society more just and fair. Not all sociologists were so persuaded but probably a majority were, with the result that the critical wing of the discipline was, for much of the twentieth century, different in tone and scholarship than was the case in Europe. Only after European critical theorists immigrated to the United States, mostly from the Frankfurt School, did more European-style critical theorists emerge and, like their European counterparts, American theorists became concerned with the problems of modernity and postmodernity as much as they were interested in the issues of discrimination and injustices against select subpopulations, such as ethnic minorities and women.

The two great social movements in the second half of the twentieth century—the civil rights movement for minorities and the feminist movement for women—are the sources of a critical approach that emphasizes the continued existence of racism and sexism and, more broadly, that criticizes the failure of civil rights approaches to eliminate both subtle and obvious forms of discrimination. These approaches were institutionalized in academia not only in many sociology departments but also in various types of ethnic and women studies departments/programs within academia. Yet, this institutionalization only began in the 1960s; indeed, the critical period of American sociology is not part of the early sociological canon. True, racism and poverty, especially during the Great Depression were part of American sociology, which for the most part operated under the ideology of amelioration that was less critical than American critical theory would become several decades later. Thus, I will only briefly mention American critical theory in this chapter because, in essence, it is an outgrowth of social movements in the 1960s and 1970s and is more a part of contemporary sociological theory than early sociological theory.

The feminist movement was the inspiration for feminist theorizing, and as American academia incorporated the women's movement—its ideology and substantive advocacy—into women's study departments and into tracks within humanities departments (e.g., history, English) and social science departments (primarily sociology), a unique brand of scholarship coupled with political advocacy emerged. Similarly, critical race theory emerged from the creation of ethnic studies departments and programs, often broken down into specific ethnic categories, such as Chicano studies, Black studies, and Asian-American studies programs and departments.

---

[26]Stephen P. Turner and Jonathan H. Turner, *The Impossible Science: An Institutional Analysis of American Sociology* (Newbury Park, CA: Sage, 1990).

Some of this incorporation of the broader civil rights movement is an extension of early American sociologists' concerns with amelioration, but over the second half of the twentieth century, critical race theorists became, first and foremost, ever-more vocal critics of such ameliorative efforts to extend civil rights because, it was argued, they have led to continued discrimination in new, more subtle forms. While there can be Marxist ideals as well as elements of all who have theorized about stratification in these critical approaches, they have adopted many other methodological and theoretical (and philosophical) approaches to understanding the wide spectrum of ways and contexts in which racism continues to operate.

While these new American critical approaches are theoretical, they are more focused and less concerned with the bigger picture of modernity, as have been most European critical theorists. Indeed, American critical theorists often challenge social science in general and sociological theory in particular as simply "part of the problem," as we will see in Chapter 33.

## CHAPTER 31

# Critical Theories of the Frankfurt School

The German philosopher-sociologist Jürgen Habermas undoubtedly has been the most prolific descendant of the original Frankfurt School. As with the earlier generation of Frankfurt School social theorists, Habermas' work revolves around several important questions: (1) How can social theory develop ideas that keep Karl Marx's emancipatory project alive and, at the same time, recognize the empirical inadequacy of his prognosis for advanced capitalist societies? (2) How can social theory confront Max Weber's historical analysis of rationalization in a way that avoids his pessimism and thereby keeps Marx's emancipatory goals at the center of theory? (3) How can social theory avoid the retreat into subjectivism of earlier critical theorists, such as György Lukács, Max Horkheimer, and Theodor Adorno, who increasingly focused on states of subjective consciousness within individuals and, as a consequence, lost Marx's insight that society is constructed from, and must therefore be emancipated by, the processes that sustain social relations among individuals? (4) How can social theory conceptualize and develop a theory that reconciles the forces of material production and political organization with the forces of intersubjectivity among reflective and conscious individuals in such a way that it avoids (a) Weber's pessimism about the domination of consciousness by rational economic and political forces,[1] (b) Marx's naive optimism about inevitability of class consciousness and revolt, and (c) early critical theorists' retreat into the subjectivism of Hegel's dialectic, where oppression mysteriously mobilizes its negation through increases in subjective consciousnesses and resistance?

At different points in his career, Habermas has focused on one or another of these questions, but all four have always guided his approach, at

[1]That is, the spread of means/end rationality into ever-more spheres of life.

least implicitly. Habermas has been accused of abandoning the critical thrust of his earlier works, but this conclusion is too harsh. For, in trying to answer the above questions, he has increasingly recognized that mere critique of oppression is not enough. Such critique becomes a "reified object itself." Although early critical theorists knew this, they never developed conceptual schemes that accounted for the underlying dynamics of societies. For critique to be useful in liberating people from domination, it is necessary, Habermas seems to say, for the critique to discuss the fundamental processes integrating social systems. In this way, the critique has some possibility of suggesting ways to create new types of social relations. Without theoretical understanding about how society works, critique is only superficial debunking and becomes an exercise in futility. This willingness to theorize about the underlying dynamics of society, to avoid the retreat into subjectivism, to reject superficial criticism and to base critique on reasoned theoretical analysis instead, and to incorporate ideas from many diverse theoretical approaches make Habermas' work theoretically significant.[2]

## Jürgen Habermas' Analysis of "The Public Sphere"

In his first major publication, *Structural Transformation of the Public Sphere,* Habermas traced the evolution and dissolution of what he termed the *public sphere.*[3] This sphere is a realm of social life where people can discuss matters of general interest; where they can discuss and debate these issues without recourse to custom, dogma, and force; and where they can resolve differences of opinion by rational argument. To say the least, this conception of a public sphere is rather romanticized, but the imagery of free and open discussion that is resolved by rational argumentation became a central theme in Habermas' subsequent approach. Increasingly throughout his career, Habermas came to see emancipation from domination as possible through "communicative action," which is a reincarnation of the public sphere in more conceptual clothing.

In this early work, however, Habermas appeared more interested in history and viewed the emergence of the public sphere as occurring in the eighteenth century, when various forums for public debate—clubs, cafés, journals, newspapers—proliferated. He concluded that these forums helped erode the basic structure of feudalism, which is legitimated by religion and custom rather than by agreements that have been reached

---

[2]Jürgen Habermas, *The Theory of Communicative Action* (Boston: Beacon, 1981, 1984). Some useful reviews and critiques of Habermas' work include John B. Thompson and David Held, eds., *Habermas: Critical Debates* (London: Macmillan, 1982); David Held, *An Introduction to Critical Theory,* Chap. 9–12 (London: Hutchinson, 1980).

[3]Jürgen Habermas, *Struckturwandel der Offentlichkeit* (Neuwied, Germany: Luchterhand, 1962).

through public debate and discourse. The public sphere was greatly expanded, Habermas argued, by the extension of market economies and the resulting liberation of the individual from the constraints of feudalism. Free citizens, property holders, traders, merchants, and members of other new sectors in society could now be actively concerned about the governance of society and could openly discuss and debate issues. But, in a vein similar to Weber's analysis of rationalization, Habermas argued that the public sphere was eroded by some of the very forces that stimulated its expansion. As market economies experience instability, the powers of the state are extended in an effort to stabilize the economy; with the expansion of bureaucracy to ever-more contexts of social life, the public sphere is constricted. And, increasingly, the state seeks to redefine problems as technical and soluble by technologies and administrative procedures rather than by public debate and argumentation.

The details of this argument are less important than the fact that this work established Habermas' credentials as a critical theorist. All the key elements of critical theory are there—the decline of freedom with the expansion of capitalism and the bureaucratized state, as well as the seeming power of the state to construct and control social life. The solution to these problems is to resurrect the public sphere, but how is this to be done given the growing power of the state? Thus, in this early work, Habermas had painted himself into the same conceptual corner as his teachers in the Frankfurt School. The next phase of his work extended this critique of capitalist society, but he also tried to redirect critical theory so that it does not have to retreat into the contemplative subjectivism of Lukács, Horkheimer, and Adorno. Habermas began this project in the late 1960s with an analysis of knowledge systems and a critique of science.

# The Critique of Science

In *The Logic of the Social Sciences*[4] and *Knowledge and Human Interest*,[5] Habermas analyzes systems of knowledge in an effort to elaborate a framework for critical theory. The ultimate goals of this analysis is to establish the fact that science is but one type of knowledge that exists to meet only one set of human interests. To realize this goal, Habermas posits three basic types of knowledge that encompass the full range of human reason: (1) There is *empirical/analytic* knowledge, which is concerned with understanding the lawful properties of the material world. (2) There is *hermeneutic/historical*

---

[4]Jürgen Habermas, Zur Logik der Sozialwissenschaften (Frankfurt: Suhrkamp, 1970).

[5]Jürgen Habermas, *Knowledge and Human Interest*, trans. J. Shapiro (London: Heinemann, 1970; originally published in German in 1968). The basic ideas in *Zur Logik der Sozialwissenschaften* and *Knowledge and Human Interest* were stated in Habermas' inaugural lecture at the University of Frankfurt in 1965 and were first published in "Knowledge and Interest," *Inquiry* 9 (1966): pp. 285–300.

knowledge, which is devoted to the understanding of meanings, especially through the interpretations of historical texts. (3) There is *critical* knowledge, which is devoted to uncovering conditions of constraint and domination.

These three types of knowledge reflect three basic types of human interests: (1) a technical interest in the reproduction of existence through control of the environment, (2) a practical interest in understanding the meaning of situations, and (3) an emancipatory interest in freedom for growth and improvement. Such interests reside not in individuals but in more general imperatives for reproduction, meaning, and freedom that presumably are built into the species as it has become organized into societies. These three interests create, therefore, three types of knowledge. The interest in material reproduction has produced science or empirical/analytic knowledge, the interest in understanding of meaning has led to the development of hermeneutic/historical knowledge, and the interest in freedom has required the development of critical theory.

These interests in technical control, practical understanding, and emancipation generate different types of knowledge through three types of media: (1) "work" for realizing interests in technical control through the development of empirical/analytic knowledge, (2) "language" for realizing practical interests in understanding through hermeneutic knowledge, and (3) "authority" for realizing interests in emancipation through the development of critical theory. There is a kind of functionalism in this analysis: needs for "material survival and social reproduction," "continuity of society through interpretive understanding," and "utopian fulfillment" create interests. Then, through the media of work, language, and authority, these needs produce three types of knowledge: the scientific, hermeneutical, and critical.

This kind of typologizing is, of course, highly reminiscent of Weber and is the vehicle through which Habermas makes the central point: Positivism and the search for natural laws constitute only one type of knowledge, although the historical trend has been for the empirical/analytic to dominate the other types of knowledge. Interests in technical control through work and the development of science have dominated the interests in understanding and emancipation. And so, if social life seems meaningless and cold, it is because technical interests in producing science have dictated what kind of knowledge is permissible and legitimate. Thus Weber's rationalization thesis is restated with the typological distinction among interest, knowledge, and media. Table 31.1 summarizes Habermas' argument.

This typology allowed Habermas to achieve several goals. First, he attacked the assumption that science is value free because, like all knowledge, it is attached to a set of interests. Second, he revised the Weberian thesis of rationalization in such a way that it dictates a renewed emphasis on hermeneutics and criticism. These other two types of knowledge are being driven out by empirical/analytic knowledge, or science. Therefore, it is

**Table 31.1**   Types of Knowledge, Interests, Media (and Functional Needs)

| Functional Needs | Interests | Knowledge | Media |
|---|---|---|---|
| Material survival and social reproduction generate pressures for | technical control of the environment, which leads to the development of | empirical/analytic knowledge, which is achieved through | work |
| Continuity of social relations generates pressures for | practical understanding through interpretations of other's subjective states, which leads to the development of | hermeneutic and historical knowledge, which is achieved through | language |
| Desires for utopian fulfillment generate pressures for | emancipation from unnecessary domination, which leads to the development of | critical theory, which is achieved through | authority |

necessary to reemphasize these neglected types of knowledge. Third, by viewing positivism in the social sciences as a type of empirical/analytic knowledge, Habermas associated it with human interests in technical control. He therefore visualized social science as a tool of economic and political interests.

Science thus becomes an ideology; actually, Habermas sees it as the underlying cause of the *legitimation crises* of advanced capitalist societies (more on this shortly). In dismissing positivism in this way, he oriented his own project to hermeneutics with a critical twist. That is, he visualized the major task of critical theory as the analysis of those processes by which people achieve interpretive understanding of one another in ways that give social life a sense of continuity and meaning. Increasingly, Habermas came to focus on the communicative processes among actors as the theoretical core for critical theorizing. Goals of emancipation cannot be realized without knowledge about how people interact and communicate. Such an emphasis represents a restatement in a new guise of Habermas' early analysis of the public sphere, but now the process of public discourse and debate is viewed as the essence of human interaction in general. Moreover, to understand interaction, it is necessary to analyze language and linguistic processes among individuals. Knowledge of these processes can, in turn, give critical theory a firm conceptual basis from which to launch a critique of society and to suggest paths for the emancipation of individuals. Yet, to justify this emphasis on hermeneutics and criticism, Habermas must first analyze the crises of capitalist societies through the overextension of empirical/analytic systems of knowledge.

## Legitimation Crises in Society

As Habermas had argued in his earlier work, there are several historical trends in modern societies: (1) the decline of the public sphere, (2) the increasing intervention of the state into the economy, and (3) the growing dominance of science in the service of the state's interests in technical control. These ideas are woven together in *Legitimation Crisis.*[6]

The basic argument in *Legitimation Crisis* is that, as the state increasingly intervenes in the economy, it also seeks to translate political issues into "technical problems." Issues thus are not topics for public debate; rather, they represent technical problems that require the use of technologies by experts in bureaucratic organizations. As a result, there is a "depoliticization" of practical issues by redefining them as technical problems. To do this, the state propagates a "technocratic consciousness" that Habermas believed represents a new kind of ideology. Unlike previous ideologies, however, it does not promise a future utopia, but like other ideologies, it is seductive in its ability to veil problems, to simplify perceived options, and to justify a particular way of organizing social life. At the core of this technocratic consciousness is an emphasis on *instrumental reason,* or what Weber termed means/ends rationality. That is, criteria of the efficiency of means in realizing explicit goals increasingly guide evaluations of social action and people's approach to problems. This emphasis on instrumental reason displaces other types of action, such as behaviors oriented to mutual understanding. This displacement occurs in a series of stages: Science is first used by the state to realize specific goals; then, the criterion of efficiency is used by the state to reconcile competing goals of groupings; next, basic cultural values are themselves assessed and evaluated for their efficiency and rationality; finally, in Habermas' version of the brave new world, decisions are completely delegated to computers, which seek the most rational and efficient course of action.

This reliance on the ideology of technocratic consciousnesses creates, Habermas argues, new dilemmas of political legitimation. Habermas believes that capitalist societies can be divided into three basic subsystems: (1) *the economic,* (2) *the politico-administrative,* and (3) *the cultural* (what he later calls *lifeworld*). From this division of societies into these subsystems, Habermas then posits four points of crises: (1) an *economic crisis* occurs if the economic subsystem cannot generate sufficient productivity to meet people's needs; (2) a *rationality crisis* exists when the politico-administrative

---

[6]Jürgen Habermas, *Legitimation Crisis,* trans. T. McCarthy (London: Heinemann, 1976; originally published in German in 1973).

subsystem cannot generate a sufficient number of instrumental decisions; (3) a *motivation crisis* exists when actors cannot use cultural symbols to generate sufficient meaning to feel committed to participate fully in the society; and (4) a *legitimation crisis* arises when actors do not possess the "requisite number of generalized motivations" or diffuse commitments to the political subsystem's right to make decisions. Much of this analysis of crises is described in Marxian terms but emphasizes that economic and rationality crises are perhaps less important than either motivational or legitimation crises. For, as technocratic consciousness penetrates all spheres of social life and creates productive economies and an intrusive state, the crisis tendencies of late capitalism shift from the inability to produce sufficient economic goods or political decisions to the failure to generate (a) diffuse commitments to political processes and (b) adequate levels of meaning among individual actors.

In *Legitimation Crisis*, there is an early form of what becomes an important distinction: *Systemic* processes revolving around the economy and the politico-administrative apparatus of the state must be distinguished from *cultural* processes. This distinction will later be conceptualized as system and lifeworld, respectively, but the central point is this: In tune with his Frankfurt School roots, Habermas is shifting emphasis from Marx's analysis of the economic crisis of production to crises of meaning and commitment; if the problems or crises of capitalist societies are in these areas, then critical theory must focus on the communicative and interactive processes by which humans generate understandings and meanings among themselves. If instrumental reason, or means/ends rationality, is driving out action based on mutual understanding and commitment, then the goal of critical theory is to expose this trend and to suggest ways of overcoming it, especially because legitimation and motivational crises make people aware that something is missing from their lives and, therefore, receptive to more emancipatory alternatives. So the task of critical theory is to develop a theoretical perspective that allows the restructuring of meaning and commitment in social life. This goal will be realized, Habermas argues, by further understanding of how people communicate, interact, and develop symbolic meanings.

## Early Analyses of Speech and Interaction

In 1970, Habermas wrote two articles that marked a return to the idea of the public sphere, but with a new, more theoretical thrust. They also signaled an increasing emphasis on the process of speech, communication, and interaction. In his "On Systematically Distorted Communication," Habermas outlined the nature of undistorted communication.[7] True to Habermas'

---

[7]Jürgen Habermas, "On Systematically Distorted Communication," *Inquiry* 13 (1970): pp. 205–18.

Weberian origins, this outline is an ideal type. The goal is to determine the essentials and essence of undistorted communication so that those processes that distort communication, such as domination, can be better exposed. What, then, are the features of undistorted communication? Habermas lists five: (1) expressions, actions, and gestures are noncontradictory; (2) communication is public and conforms to cultural standards of what is appropriate; (3) actors can distinguish between the properties of language per se and the events and processes that are described by language; (4) communication leads to and is the product of intersubjectivity, or the capacity of actors to understand one another's subjective states and to develop a sense of shared collective meanings; and (5) conceptualizations of time and space are understood by actors to mean different things when externally observed and when subjectively experienced in the process of interaction. The details of his analysis on the distortion of communication are less essential than the assertions about what critical theory must conceptualize. For Habermas, the conceptualization of undistorted communication is used as a foil for mounting a critique against those social forces that make such idealized communication difficult to realize. Moreover, as his subsequent work testifies, Habermas emphasizes Condition 4, or communication and intersubjectivity among actors.

This emphasis became evident in his other 1970 article, "Toward a Theory of Communicative Competence."[8] The details of this argument are not as critical as the overall intent, especially because his ideas undergo subsequent modification. Habermas argues that, for actors to be competent, they must know more than the linguistic rules of how to construct sentences and to talk; they must also master "idealogue-constitutive universals," which are part of the "social linguistic structure of society." Behind this jargon is the idea that the meaning of language and speech is contextual and that actors use implicit stores or stocks of knowledge to interpret the meaning of utterances. Habermas then proposes yet another ideal type, "the ideal speech situation," in which actors possess all the relevant background knowledge and linguistic skills to communicate without distortion.

Thus, in the early 1970s, Habermas begins to view the mission of critical theory as emphasizing the process of interaction as mediated by speech. But such speech acts draw on stores of knowledge—rules, norms, values, tacit understandings, memory traces, and the like—for their interpretation. These ideals of the speech process represent a restatement of the romanticized public sphere, where issues were openly debated, discussed, and rationally resolved. What Habermas has done, of course, is to restate this view of what is good and desirable in more theoretical and conceptual terms, although it could be argued that there is not much difference between the romanticized portrayal of the public sphere and the ideal-typical conceptualization of speech. But with this conceptualization, the goal of critical

---

[8]Jürgen Habermas, "Toward a Theory of Communicative Competence," *Inquiry* 13 (1970): pp. 360–75.

theory must be to expose those conditions that distort communication and that inhibit realization of the ideal speech situation. Habermas' utopia is thus a society where actors can communicate without distortion, achieve a sense of one another's subjective states, and openly reconcile their differences through argumentation that is free of external constraint and coercion. In other words, he wants to restore the public sphere but in a more encompassing way—that is, in people's day-to-day interactions.

Habermas moved in several different directions in trying to construct a rational approach for realizing this utopia. He borrows metaphorically from psychoanalytic theory as a way to uncover the distortions that inhibit open discourse,[9] but this psychoanalytic journey is far less important than his growing concentration on the process of communicative action and interaction as the basis for creating a society that reduces domination and constraint. Thus, by the mid-1970s, he labels his analysis *universal pragmatics,* whose centerpiece is the "theory of communicative action."[10] This theory will be discussed in more detail shortly, but let us briefly review its key elements.

Communication involves more than words, grammar, and syntax; it also involves what Habermas terms *validity claims.* There are three types of claims: (1) those asserting that a course of action as indicated through speech is the most effective and efficient means for attaining ends; (2) those claiming that an action is correct and proper in accordance with relevant norms; and (3) those maintaining that the subjective experiences as expressed in a speech act are sincere and authentic. All speech acts implicitly make these three claims, although a speech act can emphasize one more than the other two. Those responding to communication can accept or challenge these validity claims; if challenged, then the actors contest, debate, criticize, and revise their communication. They use, of course, shared stocks of knowledge about norms, means/ends effectiveness, and sincerity to make their claims as well as to contest and revise them. This process (which restates the public sphere in yet one more guise) is often usurped when claims are settled by recourse to power and authority. But if claims are settled by the giving of reasons for and reasons against the claim in a mutual give-and-take among individuals, then Habermas sees it as rational discourse. Thus, built into the very process of interaction is the potential for rational discourse that can be used to create a more just, open, and free society. Such discourse is not merely means/ends rationality, for it involves adjudication of two other validity claims: those concerned with normative appropriateness and those concerned with subjective sincerity. Actors thus

---

[9]Habermas sometimes calls this aspect of his program *depth hermeneutics.* The idea is to create a methodology of inquiry for social systems that parallels the approach of psychoanalysis—that is, dialogue, removal of barriers to understanding, analysis of underlying causal processes, and efforts to use this understanding to dissolve distortions in interaction.

[10]For an early statement, see "Some Distinctions in Universal Pragmatics: A Working Paper," *Theory and Society* 3 (1976): pp. 155–67.

implicitly assess and critique one another for effectiveness, normative appropriateness, and sincerity of their respective speech acts; so the goal of critical theory is to expose those societal conditions that keep such processes from occurring for all three types of validity claims.

In this way, Habermas moves critical theory from Lukács', Horkheimer's, and Adorno's emphasis on subjective consciousness to a concern with *intersubjective* consciousness and the interactive processes by which intersubjectivity is created, maintained, and changed through the validity claims in each speech act. Moreover, rather than viewing the potential for liberating alternatives as residing in subjective consciousness, Habermas could assert that emancipatory potential inheres in each and every communicative interaction. Because speech and communication are the basis of interaction and because society is ultimately sustained by interaction, the creation of less restrictive societies will come about by realizing the inherent dynamics of the communication process.

## Habermas' Reconceptualization of Social Evolution

All critical theory is historical in the sense that it tries to analyze the long-term development of oppressive arrangements in society. Indeed, the central problem of critical theory is to reconcile Marx's and Weber's respective analyses of the development of advanced capitalism. It is not surprising, therefore, that Habermas produces a historical/evolutionary analysis, but in contrast with Weber, he sees emancipatory potential in evolutionary trends. Yet, at the same time, he wants to avoid the incorrect prognosis in Marx's analysis, while retaining the emancipatory thrust of Marx's approach. Habermas' first major effort to effect this reconciliation appeared in his "The Reconstruction of Historical Materialism,"[11] parts of which have been translated and appear in *Communication and the Evolution of Society*.[12]

Habermas' approach to evolution pulls together many of the themes discussed earlier, and so, a brief review of his general argument can set the stage for an analysis of his most recent theoretical synthesis, *The Theory of Communicative Action*.[13] In many ways, Habermas reintroduces traditional functionalism into Marx's and Weber's evolutionary descriptions, but with both a phenomenological and a structuralist emphasis.

As have all functional theorists, he views evolution as the process of structural differentiation and the emergence of integrative problems. He

[11]Jürgen Habermas, *Zur Rekonstruktion des Historischen Materialismus* (Frankfurt: Suhrkamp, 1976).

[12]Jürgen Habermas, *Communication and the Evolution of Society*, trans. T. McCarthy (London: Heinemann, 1979).

[13]For an earlier statement, see Jürgen Habermas, "Towards a Reconstruction of Historical Materialism," *Theory and Society* 2, no. 3 (1975): pp. 84–98.

also borrows from Herbert Spencer, Talcott Parsons, and Niklas Luhmann when he argues that the integration of complex systems leads to an adaptive upgrading, increasing the capacity of the society to cope with the environment.[14] That is, complex systems that are integrated are better adapted to their environments than less complex systems. The key issue, then, is the following: What conditions increase or decrease integration? For, without integration, differentiation produces severe problems.

Habermas' analysis of system integration argues that contained in the world views or stocks of knowledge of individual actors are learning capacities and stores of information that determine the overall learning level of a society. In turn, this learning level shapes the society's steering capacity to respond to environmental problems. At times, Habermas refers to these learning levels as organization principles. Thus, as systems confront problems of internal integration and external contingencies, the stocks of knowledge and world views of individual actors are translated into organization principles and steering capacities, which, in turn, set limits on just how a system can respond. For example, a society with only religious mythology will be less complex and less able to respond to environmental challenges than a more complex society with large stores of technology and stocks of normative procedures determining its organization principles. But societies can "learn"[15] that, when confronted with problems beyond the capacity of their current organization principles and steering mechanisms, they can draw upon the "cognitive potential" in the world views and stocks of knowledge of individuals who reorganize their actions. The result of this learning creates new levels of information that allow the development of new organization principles for securing integration despite increased societal differentiation and complexity.

The basis for societal integration lies in the processes by which actors communicate and develop mutual understandings and stores of knowledge. To the extent that these interactive processes are arrested by the patterns of economic and political organization, the society's learning capacity is correspondingly diminished. One of the main integrative problems of capitalist societies is the integration of the material forces of production (economy as administered by the state), on the one side, and the cultural stores of knowledge that are produced by communicative interaction, on the other side. Societies that differentiate materially in the economic and political realms without achieving integration on a normative and cultural level (that is, shared understandings) will remain unintegrated and experience crises.

Built into these dynamics, however, is their resolution. The processes of communicative interaction that produce and reproduce unifying cultural

---

[14]He borrows from Niklas Luhmann here (see Chapter 5 in this work), although much of Habermas' approach is a reaction to Luhmann.

[15]Habermas analogizes here to Jean Piaget's and Lawrence Kohlberg's analysis of the cognitive development of children, seeing societies as able to learn as they become more structurally complex.

symbols must be given equal weight with the labor processes that generate material production and reproduction. At this point, Habermas developed his more synthetic approach in *The Theory of Communicative Action.*

# The Theory of Communicative Action

The two-volume *The Theory of Communicative Action* pulls together into a reasonably coherent framework various strands of Habermas' thought.[16] Yet, true to his general style of scholarship, Habermas wandered over a rather large intellectual landscape. In Thomas McCarthy's words, Habermas develops his ideas through "a somewhat unusual combination of theoretical constructions with historical reconstructions of the ideas of 'classical' social theorists."[17] Such thinkers as Marx, Weber, Durkheim, Mead, Lukács, Horkheimer, Adorno, and Parsons are, for Habermas, "still very much alive" and are treated as "virtual dialogue partners."[18] As a consequence, the two volumes meander through selected portions of various thinkers' work critiquing and yet using key ideas. After the dust settles, however, the end result is a very creative synthesis of ideas into a critical theory.

Habermas' basic premise is summarized near the end of volume 1:

If we assume that the human species maintains itself through the socially coordinated activities of its members and that this coordination is established through communication—and in certain spheres of life, through communication aimed at reaching agreement—then the reproduction of the species also requires satisfying the conditions of a rationality inherent in communicative action.[19]

In other words, intrinsic to the process of communicative action, where actors implicitly make, challenge, and accept one another's validity claims, is a rationality that can potentially serve as the basis for reconstructing the social order in less oppressive ways. The first volume of *The Theory of Communicative Action* thus focuses on action and rationality in an effort to reconceptualize[20] both processes in a manner that shifts emphasis from the subjectivity and consciousness of the individual to the process of symbolic

---

[16]Jürgen Habermas, *The Theory of Communicative Action*, 2 vols. (cited in note 2). The subtitle of volume 1, *Reason and the Rationalization of Society*, gives some indication of its thrust. The translator Thomas McCarthy has done an excellent service in translating very difficult prose. Also, his "Translator's Introduction" to volume 1, pp. v–xxxvii, is the best summary of Habermas' recent theory that I have come across.

[17]Thomas McCarthy, "Translator's Introduction" (cited in note 16), p. vii.

[18]Ibid.

[19]Jürgen Habermas, *The Theory of Communicative Action* (cited in note 16), vol. 1, p. 397.

[20]Recall that its subtitle is *Reason and the Rationalization of Society*.

interaction. In a sense, volume 1 is Habermas' microsociology, whereas volume 2 is his macrosociology. In the second volume, Habermas introduces the concept of *system* and tries to connect it to micro processes of action and interaction through a reconceptualization of the phenomenological concept of lifeworld.

## The Overall Project

Let me begin by briefly reviewing the overall argument, and then return to volumes 1 and 2 with a more detailed analysis. There are four types of action: (1) teleological, (2) normative, (3) dramaturgical, and (4) communicative. Only communicative action contains the elements whereby actors reach intersubjective understanding. Such communicative action—which is, actually, interaction—presupposes a set of background assumptions and stocks of knowledge, or in Habermas' terms, a *lifeworld*. Also operating in any society are *system processes*, which revolve around the material maintenance of the species and its survival. The evolutionary trend is for system processes and lifeworld processes to become internally differentiated and differentiated from each other. The integration of a society depends on a balance between system and lifeworld processes. As modern societies have evolved, however, this balance has been upset as system processes revolving around the economy and the state (also law, family, and other reproductive structures) have "colonized" and dominated lifeworld processes concerned with mutually shared meanings, understandings, and intersubjectivity. As a result, modern society is poorly integrated.

These integrative problems in capitalist societies are manifested in crises concerning the "reproduction of the lifeworld"; that is, the acts of communicative interaction that reproduce this lifeworld are displaced by "delinguistified media," such as money and power, that are used in the reproduction of system processes (economy and government). The solution to these crises is a rebalancing of relations between lifeworld and system. This rebalancing is to come through the resurrection of the public sphere in the economic and political arenas and in the creation of more situations in which communicative action (interaction) can proceed uninhibited by the intrusion of system's media, such as power and money. The goal of critical theory, therefore, is to document those facets of society in which the lifeworld has been colonized and to suggest approaches whereby situations of communicative action (interaction) can be reestablished. Such is Habermas' general argument, and now we can fill in some of the details.

## The Reconceptualization of Action and Rationality

In volume 1 of *The Theory of Communicative Action*, Habermas undertakes a long and detailed analysis of Weber's conceptualization of action and rationalization. He wants to reconceptualize rationality and action in ways that allow him to view rational action as a potentially liberating rather than imprisoning force. In this way, he feels, he can avoid the pessimism of Weber and the retreat into subjectivity of Lukács, Adorno, and Horkheimer. There are, Habermas concludes, several basic types of action:[21]

1. *Teleological* action is behavior oriented to calculating various means and selecting the most appropriate ones to realize explicit goals. Such action becomes strategic when other acting agents are involved in one's calculations. Habermas also calls this action "instrumental" because it is concerned with means to achieve ends. Most importantly, he emphasizes that this kind of action is too often considered to be "rational action" in previous conceptualizations of rationality. As he argues, this view of rationality is too narrow and forces critical theory into a conceptual trap: if teleological or means/ends rationality has taken over the modern world and has, as a consequence, oppressed people, then how can critical theory propose rational alternatives? Would not such a rational theory be yet one more oppressive application of means and ends rationality? The answers to these questions lie in recognizing that there are several types of action and that true rationality resides not in teleological action but in communicative action.

2. *Normatively regulated* action is behavior that is oriented to common values of a group. Thus, normative action is directed toward complying with normative expectations of collectively organized groupings of individuals.

3. *Dramaturgical action* is action that involves conscious manipulation of oneself before an audience or public. It is ego-centered in that it involves actors mutually manipulating their behaviors to present their own intentions, but it is also social in that such manipulation is done in the context of organized activity.

4. *Communicative action* is interaction among agents who use speech and nonverbal symbols as a way of understanding their mutual situation and their respective plans of action to agree on how to coordinate their behaviors.

These four types of action presuppose different kinds of worlds. That is, each action is oriented to a somewhat different aspect of the universe, which can be divided into the (1) *objective or external world* of manipulable objects; (2) *social world* of norms, values, and other socially recognized expectations; and (3) *subjective world* of experiences. Teleological action is concerned primarily with the objective world; normatively regulated action with the social; and dramaturgical with the subjective and external. But only with communicative action do actors "refer simultaneously to things in the objective, social, and subjective worlds in order to negotiate common definitions of the situation."[22]

---

[21]Jürgen Habermas, *The Theory of Communicative Action* (cited in note 16), pp. 85–102.

[22]Ibid., p. 95.

Such communicative action is therefore potentially more rational than all of the others because it deals with all three worlds and because it proceeds as speech acts that assert three types of validity claims. Such speech acts assert that (1) statements are true in propositional content, or in reference to the external and objective world; (2) statements are correct with respect to the existing normative context, or social world; and (3) statements are sincere and manifest the subjective world of intention and experiences of the actor.[23] The process of communicative action in which these three types of validity claims are made, accepted, or challenged by others is inherently more rational than other types of action. If a validity claim is not accepted, then it is debated and discussed in an effort to reach understanding without recourse to force and authority.[24] The process of reaching understanding through validity claims, their acceptance, or their discussion takes place against the background of a culturally ingrained pre-understanding. This background remains unproblematic as a whole; only that part of the stock of knowledge that participants make use of and thematize at a given time is put to the test. To the extent that definitions of situations are negotiated by participants themselves, this thematic segment of the lifeworld is at their disposal with the negotiation of each new definition of the situation.[25]

Thus, in the process of making validity claims through speech acts, actors use existing definitions of situations or create new ones that establish order in their social relations. Such definitions become part of the stocks of knowledge in their lifeworlds, and they become the standards by which validity claims are made, accepted, and challenged. Thus, in reaching an understanding through communicative action, the lifeworld serves as a point of reference for the adjudication of validity claims, which encompass the full range of worlds—the objective, social, and subjective. And so, in Habermas' eyes, there is more rationality inherent in the very process of communicative interaction than in means/ends or teleological action.[26] As Habermas summarizes:

> We have . . . characterized the rational structure of the processes of reaching understanding in terms of (a) the three world-relations of actors and the corresponding concepts of the objective, social, and subjective worlds; (b) the validity claims of propositional truth, normative rightness, and sincerity or authenticity; (c) the concept of a rationally motivated agreement, that is, one based on the intersubjective recognition of criticizable validity claims; and (d) the concept of

---

[23]Ibid., p. 99.

[24]Recall Habermas' earlier discussion of nondistorted communication and the ideal speech act. This is his most recent reconceptualization of these ideas.

[25]Ibid., p. 100.

[26]Ibid., p. 302.

reaching understanding as the cooperative negotiation of common definitions of the situation.[27]

Thus, as people communicatively act (interact), they use and at the same time produce common definitions of the situation. Such definitions are part of the lifeworld of a society; if they have been produced and reproduced through the communicative action, then they are the basis for the rational and non-oppressive integration of a society. Let us now turn to Habermas' discussion of this lifeworld, which serves as the court of appeals in communicative action.

## The Lifeworld and System Processes of Society

Habermas believes the lifeworld is a "culturally transmitted and linguistically organized stock of interpretative patterns." But what are these "interpretative patterns" about? What do they pertain to? His answer, as one expects from Habermas, is yet another typology. There are three different types of interpretative patterns in the lifeworld: There are interpretative patterns with respect to culture, or systems of symbols; there are those pertaining to society, or social institutions; and there are those oriented to personality, or aspects of self and being. That is, (1) actors possess implicit and shared stocks of knowledge about cultural traditions, values beliefs, linguistic structures and their use in interaction; (2) actors also know how to organize social relations and what kinds and patterns of coordinated interaction are proper and appropriate; and (3) actors understand what people are like, how they should act, and what is normal or aberrant.

These three types of interpretative patterns correspond, Habermas asserts, to the following functional needs for reproducing the lifeworld (and, by implication, for integrating society): (1) reaching understanding through communicative action transmits, preserves, and renews cultural knowledge; (2) communicative action that coordinates interaction meets the need for social integration and group solidarity; and (3) communicative action that socializes agents meets the need for the formation of personal identities.[28]

Thus, the three components of the lifeworld—culture, society, personality—meet corresponding needs of society—cultural reproduction, social integration, and personality formation—through three dimensions along with communicative action is conducted: reaching understanding, coordinating interaction, and effecting socialization. As Habermas summarizes in volume 2:

---

[27]Ibid., p. 137.

[28]We are now into volume 2, ibid., pp. 205–40, titled *System and Lifeworld: A Critique of Functionalist Reason*, which is a somewhat ironic title because of the heavily functional arguments in volume 2. But, as noted earlier, Habermas' earlier work has always had an implicit functionalism.

In coming to an understanding with one another about their situation, participants in communication stand in a cultural tradition which they use and at the same time renew; in coordinating their actions via intersubjective recognition of criticizable validity claims, they rely upon their membership in groupings and at the same time reenforce their integration; through participating in interaction with competent persons, growing children internalize value orientations and acquire generalized capacities for action.[29]

These lifeworld processes are interrelated with system processes in a society. Action in economic, political, familial, and other institutional contexts draws on, and reproduces, the cultural, societal, and personality dimensions of the lifeworld. Yet, evolutionary trends are for differentiation of the lifeworld into separate stocks of knowledge with respect to culture, society, and personality and for differentiation of system processes into distinctive and separate institutional clusters, such as economy, state, family, and law. Such differentiation creates problems of integration and balance between the lifeworld and system.[30] And therein reside the dilemmas and crises of modern societies.

## Evolutionary Dynamics and Societal Crises

In a sense, Habermas blends traditional analysis by functionalists on societal and cultural differentiation with a Marxian dialectic whereby the seeds for emancipation are sown in the creation of an ever more rationalized and differentiated society. Borrowing from Durkheim's analysis of mechanical solidarity, Habermas argues that "the more cultural traditions pre-decide which validity claims, when, where, for what, from whom, and to whom must be accepted, the less the participants themselves have the possibility of making explicit and examining the potential groups in which their yes/no positions are based."[31] But "as mechanical solidarity gives way to organic solidarity based upon functional interdependence," then "the more the worldview that furnishes the cultural stock of knowledge is decentered" and "the less the need for understanding is covered in advance by an interpreted lifeworld immune from critique," and therefore, "the more this need has to be met by the interpretative accomplishments of the participants themselves." That is, if the lifeworld is to be sustained and reproduced, it becomes ever more necessary with growing societal complexity for social actions to be based on communicative processes. The result is that there is greater potential for rational communicative action because less and less of

---

[29]Ibid., p. 208

[30]This is the old functionalist argument of "differentiation" producing "integrative problems," which is as old as Spencer and which is Parsons reincarnated with a phenomenological twist.

[31]All quotes here are from p. 70 of volume 1.

the social order is preordained by a simple and undifferentiated lifeworld. But system processes have reduced this potential, and the task of critical theory is to document how system processes have colonized the lifeworld and thereby arrested this potentially superior rationality inherent in the speech acts of communicative action.

How have system processes restricted this potential contained in communicative action? As the sacred and traditional basis of the lifeworld organization has dissolved and been replaced by linguistic interaction around a lifeworld differentiated along cultural, social, and personality axes, there is a countertrend in the differentiation of system processes. System evolution involves the expansion of material production through the greater use of technologies, science, and "delinguistified steering mechanisms" such as money and power to carry out system processes.[32] These media do not rely on the validity claims of communicative action; when they become the media of interaction in ever more spheres of life—markets, bureaucracies, welfare state policies, legal systems, and even family relations—the processes of communicative action so essential for lifeworld reproduction are invaded and colonized. Thus, system processes use power and money as their media of integration, and in the process they "decouple the lifeworld" from its functions for societal integration.[33] There is an irony here because differentiation of the lifeworld facilitated the differentiation of system processes and the use of money and power,[34] so "the rationalized lifeworld makes possible the rise of growth of subsystems which strike back at it in a destructive fashion."[35]

Through this ironical process, capitalism creates market dynamics using money, which in turn spawn a welfare state employing power in ways that reduce political and economic crises but that increase those cries revolving around lifeworld reproduction. For the new crises and conflicts "arise in areas of cultural reproduction, of social integration and of socialization."[36]

## Conclusion: The Goal of Critical Theory

Habermas has now circled back to these initial concerns and those of early critical theorists. He has recast the Weberian thesis by asserting that true rationality inheres in communicative action, not teleological (and strategic

---

[32]Here Habermas is borrowing from Simmel's analysis in *The Philosophy of Money* (see Chapter 21 of this work) and from Parsons' conceptualization of generalized media (see Chapter 3).

[33]Volume 2 of *The Theory of Communicative Action*, pp. 256–76.

[34]Habermas appears in these arguments to borrow heavily from Parsons' analysis of evolution (see Chapter 4 of this work).

[35]Volume 2 of *The Theory of Communicative Action*, p. 227.

[36]Ibid., p. 576.

or instrumental) action, as Weber claimed. And he has redefined the critical theorist's view on modern crises; they are not crises of rationalization, but crises of colonization of those truly rational processes that inhere in the speech acts of communicative action, which reproduce the lifeworld so essential to societal integration. Thus, built into the integrating processes of differentiated societies (not the subjective processes of individuals, as early critical theorists claimed) is the potential for a critical theory that seeks to restore communicative rationality despite impersonal steering mechanisms. If system differentiation occurs in delinguistified media, like money and power, and if these reduce the reliance on communicative action, then crises are inevitable. The resulting collective frustration over the lack of meaning in social life can be used by critical theorists to mobilize people to restore the proper balance between system and lifeworld processes. Thus, crises of material production will not be the impetus for change, as Marx contended. Rather, the crises of lifeworld reproduction will serve as the stimulus to societal reorganization. And returning to his first work, Habermas sees such reorganization as involving (1) the restoration of the public sphere in politics, where relinguistified debate and argumentation, rather than delinguistified power and authority, are used to make political decisions (thus reducing "legitimation crises") and (2) the extension of communicative action back into those spheres—family, work, and social relations—that have become increasingly dominated by delinguistified steering media (thereby eliminating "motivational crises").

The potential for this reorganization inheres in the nature of societal integration through the rationality inherent in the communicative actions that reproduce the lifeworld. The purpose of critical theory is to release this rational potential.

## CHAPTER 32

# Postmodern Critical Theories

The label *postmodern* encompasses many divergent points of view, but the term contains two common themes: (1) a critique of sociology as a science and (2) a decisive break with modernity in which cultural symbols, media-driven images, and other forces of symbolic signification have changed the nature of social organization and the relation of individuals to the social world.

## The Postmodern Critique of Science

The Age of Science, as it emerged from the Enlightenment, posited that it would be possible to use language to denote key properties of the universe and to communicate among scientists the nature and dynamics of these properties. Indeed, it was believed that, as testing general theories against empirical cases ensues, knowledge is accumulated; and as a science matures, ever-more formal languages, such as mathematics, can be used by theorists, and ever-more precise measuring instruments can be developed by experimental researchers. In this manner, the accumulation of knowledge about properties and dynamics of the universe would accelerate. For such accumulation to occur, the degree of correspondence between theories stated in languages and the actual nature of the universe would have to increase. No scientist assumed, of course, that there could ever be a perfect correspondence, but there was a faith that the use of more precise languages and measuring instruments calibrated for these languages could make representations of the universe increasingly accurate.

---

*This chapter was coauthored with Kenneth Allan.

This faith in science was one of the cornerstones of *modernism* in at least this sense: Scientific knowledge could be used to forge a better society. As knowledge about the world accumulated, it could be used to increase productivity, democracy, and fairness in patterns of social organization. As with all critical approaches, postmodernism attacks modernity's faith in science. Furthermore, postmodernism poses three interrelated problems associated with human knowledge.

First is the problem of representation. Postmodernists often question the view that science could be used to demystify the world by discovering and using the law-like principles governing its operation. Undergirding this modern belief was the notion that there is a single best mode—scientific theory and research findings—for expressing "truth" about the world. Postmodernists typically challenge this assumed correspondence between the signs of scientific language and obdurate reality. Does the language of science, or any language, provide a direct window through which we can view reality? That is, does language simply represent reality? Or, is language a social construction that by its very existence distorts the picture of reality? To the degree that language is a social construction, and thus related to social groups and their interests, the assumption of the direct representation of language is rendered problematic.

Second are the related problems of power and vested interests. Though some postmodernists may concede that the physical world might operate by laws, the very process of discovering these laws creates culture that, in turn, is subject to interests, politics, and forms of domination. For example, law-like knowledge in subatomic physics has reflected political interests in war making or the laws of genetics can be seen to serve the interests of biotechnology firms. What is true of the laws of the physical and organic worlds is even more true of social laws whose very articulation reflects moral, political, economic, and other interests within the social sphere. From a postmodernist's point of view, truth in science, especially social science, is not a correspondence between theoretical statements and the actual social universe, but a cultural production like any other sign system. Science cannot, therefore, enjoy a privileged voice because it is like all cultural texts.

Third is the problem of continuity. Postmodernists question the view that knowledge can be used to advance society and that it accumulates in ways that increase continuity among understandings about the world. This faith in knowledge was a hallmark of modernity, but to postmodernists, who see discontinuities in knowledge as tied to shifts in the interests of dominant factions in society, such faith in the progressing continuity of knowledge and culture is not only misguided but empirically wrong. Postmodernists argue that, because there is not a truth that exists apart from the ideological interests of humans, discontinuity of knowledge is the norm, and a permanent pluralism of cultures is the only real truth that humans must continually face.

In the end, the postmodern philosophical attack on science denies privileged status to any knowledge system, including its own "because any place of arrival is but a temporary station. No place is privileged, no place better than another, as from no place the horizon is nearer than from any other."[1] Postmodernism emphasizes that, as a human creation, knowledge is relative to, and contingent on, the circumstances in which it was generated. Because knowledge is ultimately a system of signs, or a language of human expression, it is about itself as much as an external world "out there."

This critique has many of the same elements as expressed by the first critical theorists examined in Chapter 30, but it adds new twists and takes new turns. We should, thereby, examine this shift in emphasis within the postmodern critique, but we should pursue the more general argument further by examining the key founding thinkers and contemporary figures in the postmodern intellectual movement.

## Jean-François Lyotard

Jean-François Lyotard built much of his critique of science[2] on a notion borrowed from Ludwig Wittgenstein: language as a game.[3] Wittgenstein had posited an analogous relationship between the manner in which language functions and the way games are played. He argued that language, like a game, is an autonomous creation that requires no justification for its existence other than itself and is subject only to its own rules. With the term *language*, Wittgenstein was denoting not simply words and their syntactical arrangements but rather all that is wrapped up in the presentation, reception, and enactment of human expression. And this expression exists for no other reason than itself and is subject to no other rules than its own.

Lyotard, using Wittgenstein's analogy, proposes a comparison between the narrative form of knowledge, on the one side, and the denotative, scientific form of knowledge, on the other. Narrative is a form of expression that is close to the social world of real people; it is expressed within a social circle for the purpose of creating and sustaining this social circle. In this view of narratives, Lyotard means something akin to the oral histories of small familial-based groups in which there are internal rules concerning who has the right to speak and who has the responsibility to listen. Verification of the knowledge created in such a narrative is reflexive because such verification of the narrative refers to its own rules of discourse.

In contrast, the denotative, scientific form of knowledge does not originate from social bonds, but rather, science proposes to simply represent what is in the physical universe, thereby subjugating the narrative form of knowledge. Lyotard argues that narrative and tradition are no longer needed in science because theory and research will reveal the true nature of

[1]Zygmunt Bauman, *Intimations of Postmodernity* (London and New York: Routledge, 1992).

[2]Jean-François Lyotard, *The Postmodern Condition* (Minneapolis: University of Minnesota Press, 1979, 1984).

[3]Ludwig Wittgenstein, *Philosophical Investigations* (New York: Macmillan, 1936–1949, 1973).

the universe. Yet, there is a problem with science: To be heard, science must appeal to a form of narrative knowledge—in this case a grand narrative. This grand narrative is based on the Enlightenment's promise of human emancipation and encompasses the vision of progress most clearly expressed by Georg Hegel. Lyotard maintains that postmodernism is defined by a diffuse sense of doubt concerning any such grand narrative and that this need to appeal to a narrative reveals science to be a language game like any other. Thus, science has no special authority or power to supervise other language games. According to Lyotard's vision, dissension must now be emphasized rather than consensus; heterogeneous claims to knowledge, in which one voice is not privileged over another, are the only true basis of knowledge.

## Richard Rorty

The philosopher Richard Rorty pushes the philosophical critique of science further to the extreme—indeed, to the point of appearing to assert that there is no external, obdurate reality "out there." Science argues, of course, that there is a reality out there, that languages can be used in increasingly precise ways to denote and understand its properties and dynamics, that language can be used to communicate the discoveries of science to fellow scientists and others as well, that truth is the degree of correspondence between theory and data, and that efforts to increase this correspondence make science self-correcting. Hence, science does use language in ways that make it a more "objective" representation of the external world, ensuring that certain languages are more objective than others. But, Rorty asserts, the issue can never be which language is more objective or scientific because the use of language is always directed toward pragmatic ends. Underlying every claim that one language brings a better understanding to a phenomenon than another is the assumption that it is more useful for a particular purpose. As Rorty claims, "vocabularies are useful or useless, good or bad, helpful or misleading, sensitive or coarse, and so on; but they are not 'more objective' or 'less objective' nor more or less 'scientific.'"[4]

In addition, even if there is a true reality and a true language with which to represent that reality, the moment humans use a language, it becomes evaluative. Thus, discovering the "true nature" of reality is not the goal of language use, scientific or otherwise, but rather, this use is directed at practical concerns, and such pragmatic concerns are always value based. Social scientists can tell stories that converge and reflect their common value concerns, thereby increasing their sense of solidarity and community as social scientists. Social scientists can also tell stories of power or of forces that divide them, thereby revealing the discordant features of any collective. But these stories are about this community of individuals more than about any real world out there.

---

[4]Richard Rorty, "Method, Social Science, and Social Hope," in *Consequences of Pragmatism* (Minneapolis: University of Minnesota Press, 1982).

What, then, is left for social analysts? Rorty's answer is typical of many postmodernists: Deconstruct texts produced by communities of individuals using language for some value-laden, practical purpose. *Deconstruction* refers to the process of taking apart the elements of a text, and in Rorty's view, such deconstruction can be (a) critical, exposing the interests and ideology contained in the text, or (b) affirming, revealing elements of a text to enlighten and inform.

As becomes evident then, Lyotard and Rorty would take sociological theory in a very different direction. Emphasis would be on language and texts,[5] and scientific explanations of an obdurate social reality would be seen as yet another form of text. This new direction—which represents a philosophical assault on scientific sociological theory—can be further appraised with illustrative examples of sociologists who have used the thrust of this philosophical critique in their more explicitly sociological works.

## Illustrative Elaborations and Extensions Within Sociology

**Richard Harvey Brown's "Society as Text."** Richard Harvey Brown[6] specifically applies the philosophical critique of postmodernism to social science, positing that social and cultural realities, and social science itself, are linguistic constructions. Brown advocates an approach termed *symbolic realism*[7] in which the universe is seen as existing for humans through communicative action. Moreover, each act of communication is based on previously constructed communicative actions—modes and forms of discourse, ideologies, world views, and other linguistic forms. Hence the search for the first or ultimate reality is a fruitless endeavor. Indeed, the "worlds" that are accepted as "true" at any one point in human history are constituted through normative, epistemological, political, aesthetic, and moral practices which, in turn, are themselves symbolic constructions. Symbolic realism is thus a critical approach that seeks to uncover the ideologies surrounding the premises on which knowledge, senses of self, and portrayals of realities are constructed.

---

[5]For the postmodernist, all cultural expressions are to be understood as language. But the use of linguistic systems as a basis for understanding all social phenomena is not new with postmodernism. For example, this linguistic equivalence model is central to the work of Claude Lévi-Strauss. But, postmodernism has, building on the poststructuralist work of Jacques Derrida and Michel Foucault.

[6]Richard Harvey Brown, *Society as Text; Essays on Rhetoric, Reason, and Reality* (Chicago: The University of Chicago Press, 1987); *Social Science as Civic Discourse: Essays on the Invention, Legitimation, and Uses of Social Theory* (Chicago: The University of Chicago Press, 1989); "Rhetoric, Textuality, and the Postmodern Turn in Sociological Theory," *Sociological Theory* 8 (1990): pp. 188–97.

[7]Brown, *Social Science as Civic Discourse* (cited in note 6), pp. 49–54.

In this critical vein, Brown concludes that sociological theories themselves are "practices through which things take on meaning and value, and not merely as representations of a reality that is wholly exterior to them."[8] Theory in sociology ought to be critical and reflexive, with theorists recognizing that their own theories are themselves rhetorical constructions and, thus, texts constructed in time, place, and context, as well as through linguistic conventions. This kind of approach to social theory as rhetoric sees its own discourse as not being about society—that is, as an effort to construct "true" representations on the nature of society—but, rather, as being simply part of what constitutes society, particularly its forms of textual discourse and representation.[9]

**Charles C. Lemert's Emphasis on Rhetoric.** For Charles Lemert,[10] all social theory is inherently discursive, stated in loose languages and constructed within particular social circles. What discursive theoretical texts explain—that is, "empirical reality"—is itself a discursive text, constructed like any text and subject to all the distorting properties of any text production. That theoretical text depends on empirical texts, and vice versa, for their scientific value increases science's discursiveness. Each scientific portrayal of reality—whether from the theory or research findings side—is a text and, actually, a kind of "text on top of another text." This compounding of texts has implications for social scientific explanations: Social science explanations are often less adequate to understanding reality than are ordinary discursive texts that are less convoluted and compounded.

This understanding of the primacy of language leads to the use of irony in social theory. But the social theorist's use of irony is more than a literary device; it is a position from which the theorist views reality and its relationship to language. The physical universe is known to humans only through representation, culture, or language. Thus, reality shifts in response to different modes of representation. For example, in the eyes of humanity, the earth has shifted from being the center of the universe to being simply one of many planets circling one of a multitude of stars. But this position of the theorist also views language as humanity's certainty: Language is certain, and in that sense real, because the fundamental qualities and meanings of a

---

[8]Ibid., p. 188.

[9]In the postmodern literature, a distinction is often made between social and sociological theory. Social theory is generally understood to be a text that is self-consciously directed toward improving social conditions through entering the social discourse, whereas sociological theory is a denotative text that is abstracted from social concerns and involvement. In the view of postmodernism, social theory is preferred to sociological theory.

[10]Charles C. Lemert, "The Uses of French Structuralisms in Sociology," *Frontiers of Social Theory: The New Syntheses*, ed. George Ritzer (New York: Columbia University Press, 1990), pp. 230–54. Charles C. Lemert, "General Social Theory, Irony, Postmodernism," *Postmodernism and Social Theory*, eds. Steven Seidman and David G. Wagner (Cambridge, MA: Blackwell, 1990), pp. 17–46.

linguistic system are known, valid, and replicable within itself. Because language is certain, theorists can make general statements concerning the properties of the physical universe, but the certitude of those statements rests in language and not in the physical reality or even the assumed relationship between culture and reality. The only position, then, for a social theorist is an ironic one: General theoretical statements can be made but with a tongue-in-cheek attitude because the author of such statements is reflexively aware that the only certitude of the statements rests in the linguistic system and not in the physical or social reality.

**Mark Gottdiener's and Steven Seidman's Critique**. Steven Seidman[11] adopts Rorty's distinction between enriching and critical forms of text deconstruction. And, along with Mark Gottdiener,[12] and many others as well, Seidman questions any social theory that posits a foundationalism, or the view that knowledge accumulates such that one level of knowledge can serve as the base on which ever-more knowledge is built. Foundationalism is, of course, at the very core of science, so this critique is truly fundamental for the activities that intellectuals can pursue. For Seidman and Gottdiener, however, foundationalism is just another effort to impose a grand narrative as a privileged voice.

Gottdiener sees foundationalism in sociological theory as an ideology, based on a *logocentrism* where "the classics" in theory are seen as the base on which a theoretical position is built. Such logocentrism is nothing more than a political ploy by established theorists to maintain their privileged position. Thus, sociological theory is about language and power games among theorists, seeking to construct a grand narrative that also sustains their privilege and authority within an intellectual community.[13]

If such is the case, Seidman argues, the hope of human emancipation through sociological theory must be replaced by "the more modest aspiration of a relentless defense of immediate, local pleasures and struggles for justice."[14] But Gottdiener sees this position as akin to Rorty's concern with the use of vocabularies to sustain communities of scholars. Because of the inherent and ultimate privileging of one morality over another in such communities—not all moralities, even local ones, are commensurable one with another—theory does not become sufficiently critical. Instead, Gottdiener advocates a continuous, critical, and reflexive cycle of

---

[11]Steven Seidman, "The End of Sociological Theory," in *The Postmodern Turn: New Perspectives on Social Theory*, ed. Steven Seidman (Cambridge: Cambridge University Press, 1994), pp. 84–96.

[12]Mark Gottdiener, "The Logocentrism of the Classics," *American Sociological Review* 55 (June 1990): pp. 460–63; "Ideology, Foundationalism, and Sociological Theory," *Sociological Quarterly* 34 (1993): pp. 653–71.

[13]Gottdiener, "Ideology, Foundationalism, and Sociological Theory" (cited in note 12), p. 667.

[14]Seidman, "The End of Sociological Theory" (cited in note 11), p. 120.

evaluation relative to the relationship between power and knowledge for evaluating all theories—postmodern or otherwise—that seek some grand narrative or self-legitimating tradition.

In sum, these representative commentaries offer a sense for the postmodern critique of science. Yet, postmodernism is much more than a philosophical critique. If this were all that postmodernists had to offer, there would be little point in examining these criticisms. Moreover, not all postmodernist theorists accept the philosophical critique just outlined, although most are highly suspicious of the hard-science view of sociological theory.[15] Indeed, most are committed to analysis of contemporary societies, especially the effects that dramatic changes in distribution, transportation, and information systems have had on the individual self and patterns of social organization. We can begin with "economic postmodernists" who generally employ extensions of Karl Marx's ideas and who, to varying degrees, still retain some of Marx's emancipatory zeal or, if not zeal, guarded hope that a better future that may lie ahead.

# Economic Postmodernism

Economic postmodernists are concerned with *capital*, especially its *over-accumulation* (that is, overabundance), as well as its level of dispersion and rapid movement in the new world system of markets driven and connected by information technologies. Moreover, culture or systems of symbols are seen to emerge from economic processes, but they exert independent effects on not only the economy but also every other facet of human endeavor. Indeed, for some economic postmodernists, advanced capitalism has evolved into a new stage of human history[16] that, like earlier modernity, is typified by a series of problems, including the loss of a core or essential sense of self, the use of symbolic as much as material means to control individuals, the increased salience of cultural resources as both tools of repression and potential resistance, the emotional disengagement of individuals from culture, and the loss of national identities and a corresponding shift to local and personal identities. This list, and other "pathologies" of the postmodern era, sound much like those that concerned early sociologists when they worried about such matters as anomie and egoism (Émile Durkheim), alienation (Marx), marginal and fractured self (Georg Simmel), ideological control and manipulation by the powerful (Marx and, later, Antonio

---

[15]For example, Lemert, *Sociology After the Crisis*, (Boulder, CO: Westview, 1995), p. 78 makes a distinction between radical postmodernism and strategic postmodernism. Radical postmodernists disavow any possibility of truth or reality whereas strategic postmodernists attempt to undercut the authority that modernist knowledge claims while preserving the language and categories that modernist knowledge uses. Strategic postmodernists, according to Lemert, still maintain the modernist hope of emancipation.

[16]See, for example, Stephen Crook, Jan Pakulski, and Malcolm Waters, *Postmodernization* (London: Sage, 1992).

Gramsci and Louis Althusser), political-ideological mobilization as resistance (Marx), over-differentiation and fragmentation of social structure (Adam Smith, Herbert Spencer, and Durkheim), rationalization and domination by over-concerns with efficiency (Max Weber), and so on. Thus, economically oriented postmodernists evidence many of the same analytical tendencies of those who first sought to theorize about modernity.

## Fredric Jameson

Among the central figures in economic postmodernism, Fredric Jameson is the most explicitly Marxist.[17] Although his theory is about the complex interplay among multinational capitalism, technological advance, and the mass media, "the truth of postmodernism . . . [is] the world space of multinational capital."[18] He posits that capitalism has gone through three distinct phases, with each phase linked to a particular kind of technology. Early-market capitalism was linked to steam-driven machinery; mid-monopoly capitalism was characterized by steam and combustion engines; and late-multinational capitalism is associated with nuclear power and electronic machines.

Late-multinational capitalism is the subject of postmodern theory. In particular, the nature of praxis, or the use of thought to organize action to change conditions and the use of experiences in action to reexamine thought, is transformed and confounded by the changed nature of signification that comes when the machines of symbolic reproduction—cameras, computers, videos, movies, tape recorders, fax machines—remove the direct connection between human production and its symbolic representation. These machines generate sequences of signs on top of signs that alter the nature of praxis—that is, how can thought guide action on the world, and vice versa, when concepts in such thought are so detached from material conditions?

Drawing from Marx's philosophy of knowledge, Jameson still attempts to use the method of praxis to critique the social construction of reality in postmodernity. Marx argued that reality did not exist in concepts, ideas, or reflexive thought but in the material world of production. Indeed, he broke with the Young Hegelians over this issue, seeing them as "blowing theoretical bubbles" about the reality of ideas. But, like the earlier generation of critical theorists in the first decades of the twentieth century (see Chapter 30), those of the late twentieth century begin to sound even more Hegelian. According to Jameson, the creation of consciousness through production was unproblematically represented by the aesthetic of the machine in earlier phases of capitalism, but in multinational capitalism, electronic machines

---

[17]Fredric Jameson, *The Postmodern Condition* (Minneapolis: University of Minnesota Press, 1984).

[18]Ibid., p. 92.

like movie cameras, videos, tape recorders, and computers do not have the same capacity for signification because they are machines of reproduction rather than of production.

Thus, the foundation of thought and knowledge in postmodernity is not simply false, as Marx's view of "false consciousness" emphasized; it is nonexistent. Because the machines of late capitalism reproduce knowledge rather than produce it and because the reproduction itself is focused more on the medium than on the message, the signification chain from object to sign has broken down. Jameson characterizes this breakdown as the schizophrenia of culture. Based on de Saussure's notion that meaning is a function of the relationship between signifiers (see Chapters 25 and 26), the concept of a break in the signification chain indicates that each sign stands alone, or in a relatively loose association with fragmented groups of other signs, and that meaning is free-floating and untied to any clear material reality.

Moreover, in a postmodern world dominated by machines of reproduction, language loses the capacity to ground concepts to place, to moments of time, or to objects in addition to losing its ability to organize symbols into coherent systems of concepts about place, time, and object. As language loses these capacities, time and space become disassociated. If a sign system becomes detached and free-floating and if it is fragmented and without order, the meaning of concepts in relation to time and space cannot be guaranteed. Indeed, meaning in any sense becomes problematic. The conceptual connection between the "here-and-now" and its relation to the previous "there-and-then" has broken down, and the individual experiences "a series of pure and unrelated presents in time."[19]

Jameson goes on to argue that culture in the postmodern condition has created a fragmented rather than alienated subject. Self is not so much alienated from the failure to control its own productive activities; rather, self is now a series of images in a material world dominated by the instruments of reproduction rather than production. In addition, the decentering of the postmodern self produces a kind of emotional flatness or depthlessness "since there is no longer any self to do the feeling . . . [emotions] are now free-floating and impersonal."[20] Subjects are thus fragmented and dissolved, having no material basis for consciousness or narratives about their situation; under these conditions, individuals' capacity for praxis—using thought to act and using action to generate thought—is diminished. Of course, this capacity for praxis is not so diminished that Jameson cannot develop a critical theory of the postmodern condition, although the action side of Marx's notion of praxis is as notably absent, if not impotent, as it was for the first generation of Frankfurt critical theorists.

---

[19]Ibid., p. 72.

[20]Ibid., p. 64.

# David Harvey

Like Jameson, David Harvey[21] posits that capitalism has brought about significant problems associated with humans' capacity to conceptualize time and space. Yet for Harvey, the cultural and perceptual problems associated with postmodernism are not new. Some of the same tendencies toward fragmentation and confusion in political, cultural, and philosophical movements occurred around the turn into the twenty-first century. And, in Harvey's view, the cultural features of the postmodern world are no more permanent—as many postmodernists imply—than were those of the modernity that emerged in the nineteenth and early twentieth century.

Unlike Jameson, Harvey does not see the critical condition of postmodernity as the problem of praxis—of anchoring signs and symbols in a material reality that can be changed through thought and action but rather as a condition of *overaccumulation*, or the modes by which too much capital is assembled and disseminated. All capitalist systems—as Marx recognized—have evidenced this problem of overaccumulation, because capitalism is a system designed to grow through exploitation of labor, technological innovation, and organizational retrenchment. At some point, there is overabundance: too many products to sell to nonexistent buyers, too much productive capacity that goes unused, or too much money to invest with insufficient prospects for profits.

This overaccumulation is met in a variety of ways, the most common being the business cycle where workers are laid off, plants close, bankruptcies increase, and money is devalued. Such cycles generally restore macro-level economic controls (usually by government) over money supply, interest rates, unemployment compensation, bankruptcy laws, tax policies, and the like. But Harvey emphasizes another response to overaccumulation: absorption of surplus capital through temporal and spatial displacement. Temporal displacement occurs when investors buy "futures" on commodities yet to be produced, when they purchase stock option in hopes of stock prices rising, when they invested in other financial instruments (mortgages, long-term bonds, government securities), or when they pursue any strategy for using time and the swings of all markets to displace capital and reduce overaccumulation. Spatial displacement involves moving capital away from areas of overaccumulation to new locations in need of investment capital. Harvey argues that displacement is most effective when both its temporal and spatial aspects are combined, as when money raised in London is sent to Latin America to buy bonds (which will probably be resold again in the future) to finance infrastructural development.

The use of both spatial and temporal displacement to meet the issue of overaccumulation can contribute to the more general problem of time and space displacement. Time and space displacement occurs because of four

---

[21]David Harvey, *The Conditions of Postmodernity: An Inquiry into the Origins of Cultural Change* (Oxford: Blackwell, 1989).

factors: (1) advanced communication and transportation technologies, (2) increased rationalization of distribution processes, (3) meta- and world-level money markets that accelerate the circulation of money, and (4) decreased spatial concentration of capital in geographical locations (cities, nations, regions). These changes create a perceived sense of time and space compression that must be matched by changes in beliefs, ideologies, perceptions, and other systems of symbols. As technologies combine to allow us to move people and objects more quickly through space—as with the advent of travel by rail, automobile, jet, rocket—space becomes compressed; that is, distance is reduced and space is not as forbidding or meaningful as it was at one time. Ironically, as the speed of transportation, communication, market exchanges, commodity distribution, and capital circulation increases, the amount of available time decreases, because there are more things to do and more ways to do them. Thus, our sense of time and space compresses in response to increases in specific technologies and structural capacities. If these technological and structural changes occur gradually, then the culture that renders the resulting alterations in time and space understandable and meaningful will evolve along with the changes. But, if the changes in structure and technology occur rapidly, as in postmodernity, then the modifications in symbolic categories will not keep pace, and people will be left with a sense of disorientation concerning two primary categories of human existence, time and space. The present response to overaccumulation, "flexible capitalism," helps create a sense of time and space compression as capital is rapidly moved and manipulated on a global scale in response to portfolio management techniques.

In addition, because the new mode of accumulation is designed to move capital spatially and temporally in a flexible and thus ever-changing manner, disorientation ensues as the mode of regulation struggles to keep up with the mode of accumulation. For example, if capital sustaining jobs in one country can be immediately exported to another with lower-priced labor, beliefs among workers about loyalty to the company, conceptions about how to develop a career, commitments of companies to local communities, ideologies of government, import policies, beliefs about training and retraining, conceptions of labor markets, ideologies of corporate responsibility, laws about foreign investment, and many other cultural modes for regulating the flow of capital will all begin to change. Thus, in postmodernity, physical place has been replaced by a new social space driven by the new technologies of highly differentiated and dynamic markets, but cultural orientations have yet to catch up with this pattern of time and space compression.

As with most economic postmodernists, Harvey emphasizes that markets now distribute services as much as they deliver commodities or "hard goods", and many of the commodities and services that are distributed concern the formation of an image of self and identity. Cultural images are now market driven, emphasizing fashion and corporate logos as well as other markers of culture, lifestyle, group membership, taste, status, and virtually anything that individuals can see as relevant to their identity. As boredom, saturation, and imitation create demands for new images with which to define self, cultural images constantly shift—being limited only by the imagination of people, advertisers, and profit-seeking producers. As a result, the pace and volatility of products to be consumed accelerates, and producers for markets as well as agents in markets (such as advertisers, bankers, investors) search for new images to market as commodities or services.

Given a culture that values instant gratification and easy disposability of commodities, people generally react with sensory block, denial, a blasé attitude, myopic specialization, increased nostalgia (for stable old ways), and an increased search for eternal but simplified truths and collective or personal identity. To the extent that these reactions are the mark of postmodernity, Harvey argues that they represent the lag between cultural responses to new patterns of capital displacement over time and place. Eventually, culture and people's perceptions will catch up to these new mechanisms for overcoming the latest incarnation of capital overaccumulation.

## Scott Lash and John Urry

Like David Harvey, Scott Lash and John Urry argue that a postmodern disposition occurs with changes in advanced capitalism that shift time and space boundaries.[22] In their view, shifting conceptualizations of time and space are associated with changes in the distribution of capital. Moreover, like most postmodern theorists, they stress that postmodern culture is heavily influenced by the mass media and advertising. Yet, revealing their Marxian roots, they add that the postmodern disposition is particularly dependent on the fragmentation of class experience and the rise of the service class. With their emphasis on capital and the class structure, the focus of Lash and Urry's analysis is thus Marxian, but their method is Weberian: They disavow causal sequences, preferring to speak in terms of preconditions and ideal types. Thus, they see the postmodernism forms outlined by Lyotard, Jameson, and as we will see, Baudrillard as an ideal type against which different systems of culture can be compared.

Like Harvey, Lash and Urry do not see postmodern culture as entirely new, but unlike Harvey, they are less sure that it is a temporary phase waiting for culture to catch up to changed material conditions. Lash an Urry believe that postmodern culture will always appeal to certain audiences with "postmodern dispositions." These dispositions emerge in response to three forces: First, the boundary between reality and image must become blurred as the media, and especially advertising, present ready-made rather than socially constructed cultural images. Second, the traditional working class must be fractured and fragmented; at the same time, a new service class

[22]Scott Lash and John Urry, *The End of Organized Capitalism* (Madison, WI: University of Wisconsin Press, 1987); *Economies of Signs and Space* (Newbury Park, CA: Sage, 1994).

oriented to the consumption of commodities for their symbolic power to produce, mark, and proclaim distinctions in group memberships, taste, lifestyle, preferences, gender orientation, ethnicity, and many other distinctions must become prominent. And third, the construction of personal and subjective identities must increasingly be built from cultural symbols detached from physical space and location, such as neighborhood, town, or region; as this detachment occurs, images of self become ever-more transitory. As these three forces intensify, a postmodern disposition becomes more likely, and these dispositions can come to support a broader postmodern culture where symbols marking difference, identity, and location are purchased by the expanding service class.

Although Lash and Urry are reluctant to speak of causation, it appears that at least four deciding factors bring about these postmodern conditions. The first factor involves the shift from Taylorist or regimented forms of production, such as the old factory assembly line, to more flexible forms of organizing and controlling labor, such as production teams, "flex-time" working hours, reduced hierarchies of authority, and deconcentration of work extending to computer terminals at home. Like Harvey, Lash and Urry believe that these shifts cause and reflect decreased spatial concentration of capital, and expanded communication and transportation technologies, spatial dispersion, deconcentration of capital, and rapid movement of information, people, and resources are the principle dynamics of change. The second factor concerns large-scale economic changes—the globalization of a market economy, the expansion of industry and banking across national boundaries, and the spread of capitalism into less developed countries. A third factor is increased distributive capacities that accelerate and extend the flow of commodities from the local and national to international markets. This increased scope and speed of circulation can empty many commodities of their ethnic, local, national, and other traditional anchors of symbolic and affective meaning. This rapid circulation of commodities increases the likelihood that many other commodities will be made and purchased for what they communicate aesthetically and cognitively about ever-shifting tastes, preferences, lifestyles, personal statements, and new boundaries of prestige and status group membership. And, a fourth factor is really a set of forces that follows from the other factors: (a) the commodification of leisure as yet one more purchased symbolic statement; (b) the breakdown of, and merger among, previously distinct and coherent cultural forms (revolving around music, art, literature, class, ethnic, or gender identity, and other cultural distinctions in modernism); (c) the general collapse of social space, designated physical locations, and temporal frames within which activities are conducted and personal identifications are sustained; and (d) the undermining of politics as tied to traditional constituencies (a time dimension) located in physical places like neighborhoods and social spaces such as classes and ethnic groups.

Together, these factors create a spatially fragmented division of labor, a less clear-cut working class, a larger service class, a shift to symbolic rather than material or coercive domination, a use of cultural more than material resources for resistance, and a level of cultural fragmentation and pluralism that erodes nationalism. But Lash and Urry argue, in contrast with Jameson, this emptying out process is not as deregulated as it might appear. They posit that new forms of distribution, communication, and transportation all create networks in time, social spaces, and physical places. Economic governance occurs where the networks are dense, with communications having an increasingly important impact on the difference between core and peripheral sites. Core sites are heavily networked communication sites that function as a "wired village of noncontiguous communities."[23]

All these economic postmodernists clearly have roots in Marxian analysis, both the critical forms that emerged in the early decades of the century (see Chapter 30) and the world-system forms of analysis that arose in the 1970s and continue to the present day (see Chapter 13). Early critical theorists had to come to terms with the Weberian specter of coercive and rational-legal authority as crushing emancipatory class activity, but this generation of postmodern critics has had to reconcile their rather muted emancipatory goals to the spread of world capitalism as the preferred economic system; the prosperity generated by capitalism; the breakdown of the proletariat as a coherent class (much less a vanguard of emancipation); the commodification of everything in fluid and dynamic markets; the production and consumption of symbols more than hard goods (as commodities are bought for their symbolic value); the destruction of social, physical, and temporal boundaries as restrictions of space and time are changed by technologies; the purchase of personal and subjective identities by consumer-driven actors; and the importance of symbolic and cultural superstructures as driving forces in world markets glutted with mass media and advertising images. Given these forced adaptations of the Marxian perspective, it is not surprising that many postmodernists have shifted their focus from the economic base to culture.

# Cultural Postmodernism

All postmodern theories emphasize the fragmenting character of culture and the blurring of differences marked by symbols. Individuals are seen as caught in these transformations, participating in, and defining self from, an increasing array of social categories, such as race, class, gender, ethnicity, or status, while being exposed to ever-increasing varieties of cultural images as potential markers of self. At the same time, individuals lose their sense of being located in stable places and time frames. Many of the forces examined by economic postmodernists can account for this fragmentation of culture, decline in the salience of markers of differences, and loss of identity in time, place, and social space, but cultural postmodernists place particular

---

[23]Lash and Urry, *Economies of Signs and Space* (cited in note 22), p. 28.

emphasis on mass media and advertising because these are driven by markets and information technologies.

## Jean Baudrillard

The strongest postmodern statement concerning the effects of the media on culture comes from Jean Baudrillard,[24] who sees the task before the social sciences today as challenging the "meaning that comes from the media and its fascination."[25] In contrast with philosophical postmodernism, Baudrillard's theory is based on the assumption that there is a potential equivalence or correspondence between the sign and its object, and based on this proposition, Baudrillard posits four historical phases of the sign.

In the first phase, the sign represented a profound reality, with the correlation and correspondence between the sign and the obdurate reality it signified being very high. In the next two phases, signs dissimulated or hid reality in some way: In the second phase, signs masked or counterfeited reality, as when art elaborated or commented on life, whereas in the third phase, signs masked the absence of any profound reality, as when mass commodification produced a plethora of signs that have no real basis in group identity but have the appearance of originating in group interaction.

The second phase roughly corresponds to the period of time from the Renaissance to the Industrial Revolution, whereas the third phase came with the Industrial Age, as production and new market forces created commodities whose sign values marking tastes, style, status, and other symbolic representations of individuals began to rival the use value (for some practical purpose) or exchange-value (for some other commodity or resource like money) of commodities. In Baudrillard's view, then, the evolution of signs has involved decreasing, if not obfuscating, of their connection to real objects in the actual world.

The fourth stage in the evolution of the sign is the present postmodern era. In this age, the sign "has no relation to any reality whatsoever: It is its own pure simulacrum."[26] Signs are about themselves and, hence, are simulations or simulacrums of other signs with little connection to the basic nature of the social or material world. Baudrillard's prime example of simulacrum is Disneyland. Disneyland presents itself as a representation of Americana, embodying the values and joys of American life. Disneyland is offered as imagery—a place to symbolically celebrate and enjoy all that is good in the real world. But Baudrillard argues that Disneyland is presented as imagery

---

[24]Jean Baudrillard, *For a Critique of the Political Economy of the Sign* (St. Louis: Telos, 1972, 1981); *The Mirror of Production* (St. Louis: Telos, 1973, 1975); *Simulacra and Simulation* (Ann Arbor: University of Michigan Press, 1981, 1994); *Symbolic Exchange and Death* (Newbury Park, CA: Sage, 1993).

[25]Baudrillard, *Simulacra and Simulation* (cited in note 24), p. 84.

[26]Ibid., p. 6.

to hide the fact that it is American reality itself. Life in the surrounding "real" communities, for example, Los Angeles and Anaheim, consists simply of emulations of past realities: People no longer walk as a mode of transportation; rather, they jog or power walk. People no longer touch one another in daily interaction; rather, they go to contact-therapy groups. The essence of life in postmodernity is imagery; behavior is determined by image potential and is thus simply image. Baudrillard depicts Los Angeles as "no longer anything but an immense scenario and a perpetual pan shot."[27] Thus, when Disneyland is presented as a symbolic representation of life in America, when life in America is itself an image or simulation of a past reality, then Disneyland becomes a simulation of a simulation with no relationship to any reality whatsoever, and it hides the nonreality of daily life.

Baudrillard argues that the presentation of information by the media destroys information. This destruction occurs because there is a natural entropy within the information process; any information about a social event is a degraded form of that event and, hence, represents a dissolving of the social. The media is nothing more than a constant barrage of bits of image and sign that have been removed an infinite number of times from actual social events. Thus, the media does not present a surplus of information, but on the contrary, what is communicated represents total entropy of information and, hence, of the social world that is supposedly denoted by signs organized into information. The media also destroys information because it stages the presentation of information, presenting it in a prepackaged meaning form. As information is staged, the subjects are told what constitutes their particular relationship to that information, thereby simulating for individuals their place and location in a universe of signs about signs.

Baudrillard argues that the break between reality and the sign was facilitated by advertising. Advertising eventually reduces objects from their use-value to their sign-value; the symbols of advertisements become commodities in and of themselves, and image more than information about the commodity is communicated. Thus, advertisements typically juxtapose a commodity with a desirable image—for example, a watch showing one young male and two young females with their naked bodies overlapping one another—rather than providing information about the quality and durability of the commodity. So, that what is being sold and purchased is the image rather than the commodity itself. But, further, advertising itself can become the commodity sought after by the consuming public rather than the image of the advertisement. In the postmodern era, the form of the advertisement rather than the advertisement itself becomes paramount. For example, a currently popular form of television commercials is what could be called the "MTV style." Certain groups of people respond to these commercials not because of the product and not simply because of the images contained

---

[27]Ibid., p. 13.

within the advertisements, but because they respond to the overall form of the message and not to its content at all. Thus, in postmodernity, the medium is the message, and what people are faced with, according to Baudrillard, are simulations of simulations and an utter absence of any reality.

## Further Elaborations of Cultural Postmodernism

**Kenneth Gergen**. The self is best understood, in Kenneth Gergen's view,[28] as the process through which individuals categorize their own behaviors. This process depends on the linguistic system used in the physical and social spaces that locate the individual at a given time. Because conceptualizations of self are situational, the self generally tends to be experienced by individuals as fragmented and sometimes contradictory. Yet, people are generally motivated to eliminate inconsistencies in conceptualizations, and though Gergen grants that other possible factors influence efforts to resolve inconsistencies, people in Western societies try to create a consistent self-identity because they are socialized to dislike cognitive dissonance in much the same way they are taught to reason rationally. Gergen thus sees an intrinsic relationship between the individual's experience of a self and the culture within which that experience takes place, a cultural stand that he exploits in his understanding of the postmodern self.

Gergen argues that the culture of the self has gone through at least three distinct stages—the romantic, modern, and current postmodern phase. During the romantic period, the self as an autonomous individual and agent was stressed as individuals came out from the domination of various institutions including the church and manorial estate; during the modern period, the self was perceived as possessing essential or basic qualities, such as psychologically defined inherent personality traits. But the postmodern self consists only of images, revealing no inherent qualities, and most significantly, has lost the ability as well as desire to create self-consistency. Further, because knowledge and culture are fragmented in the postmodern era, the very concept of the individual self must be questioned and the distinction between the subject and the object dropped. According to Gergen, the very category of the self has been erased as a result of postmodern culture.

Thus, like Baudrillard, Gergen sees the self in postmodern culture as becoming saturated with images that are incoherent, communicating unrelated elements in different languages. And corresponding to Baudrillard's death of the subject, Gergen posits that the category of the self has been eradicated because efforts to formulate consistent and coherent definitions of who people are have been overwhelmed by images on images, couched in diverse languages that cannot order self-reflection.

---

[28]Kenneth J. Gergen, *The Saturated Self* (New York: Basic Books, 1991); *The Concept of Self* (New York: Holt, Rinehart and Winston, 1971).

**Norman Denzin and Douglas Kellner**. In contrast with Baudrillard's claim that television is simply a flow of incessant disjointed and empty images, both Norman Denzin[29] and Douglas Kellner[30] argue that television and other media have formed people's ideas and actions in much the same way as traditional myth and ritual: These media integrate individuals into a social fabric of values, norms, and roles. In the postmodern culture and economy, media images themselves are the basis from which people get their identities—in particular, their identities of race, class, and gender.

In addition, Denzin and Kellner advocate a method of social activism: a critical reading of the texts from media presentations to discover the under-lying ideologies, discourses, and meanings that the political-economy produces. The purpose of these critical readings is to "give a voice to the voice-less, as it deconstructs those popular culture texts which reproduce stereo-types about the powerless."[31] Both theorists disavow any grand narrative, and like more radical postmodernists, neither advocates a centerpoint, ultimate hope, and grand or totalizing discourse. Yet, like critical theorists before them, they both hold out the hope of forming new solidarities and initiating emancipatory conflicts through the exposé of the political-economy of signs.

But Denzin, unlike Kellner, takes issue with Baudrillard's and Jameson's views on self as an incoherent mirage of signs and symbols and as incapable of ordering images into some coherence. Denzin argues that the "lived experience" itself has become the final commodity in the circulation of capital and that the producers of postmodern culture selectively choose which lived experiences will be commodified and marketed to members of a society. Postmodern culture only commodifies those cultures that present a particular aesthetic picture of race, class, and gender relations, but because culture has become centrally important in postmodernity, this process of commodification has a positive value for giving individuals a sense of identity and for enabling them to act in the material world on the basis of this identity.

**Mark Gottdiener**. Like Denzin and Kellner, Mark Gottdiener wants to maintain a critical postmodern stand but also to argue that an objective referent is behind the infinite regress of meaning. In contrast with Denzin and Kellner, Gottdiener sees the effects of media and markets as trivializing

---

[29]Norman K. Denzin, "Postmodern Social Theory," *Sociological Theory* 4 (1986): pp. 194–204; *Images of Postmodern Society: Social Theory and Contemporary Cinema* (London: Sage, 1991); *Symbolic Interactionism and Cultural Studies* (Oxford: Blackwell, 1992).

[30]Douglas Kellner, "Popular Culture and the Construction of Postmodern Identities," in *Modernity and Identity*, eds. Scott Lash and Jonathan Friedman (Oxford: Blackwell, 1992); *Media Culture; Cultural Studies, Identity and Politics Between the Modern and the Postmodern* (London: Routledge, 1995).

[31]Denzin, *Images of Postmodern Society* (cited in note 29), p. 153.

the culture of postmodernity.[32] According to Gottdiener, signs in techno-logically advanced societies can circulate between the levels of lived experi-ence and the level where the sign is expropriated by some center of power, including producers and marketers of symbols.

Capitalizing on Baudrillard's notion of sign-value, Gottdiener argues that there are three separate phases of interaction wherein a sign can be endowed with meaning. In the first stage, economically motivated produc-ers create objects of exchange-value for money and profit, an intent that is decidedly different from the goals of those who purchase the objects for their use-value. In the second stage, these objects become involved in the everyday life of the social groups that use them. During this stage, users might "transfunctionalize" the object from its use-value into a sign-value to connect the object to their subgroup or culture (for example, a type of denim jacket is personalized to represent a group, such as the Hell's Angels). The third stage occurs if and when the economic producers and retailers adopt these personalized and transfunctionalized objects and commodify them (for instance, the Hell's Angels' style of jacket can now be bought by any suburban teenager in a shopping mall). This third stage involves a "sym-bolic leveling" or "trivialization" of the signed object.[33]

**Thomas Luckmann.** Although Thomas Luckmann[34] recognizes the impor-tance of the media and advertising in creating a postmodern culture, he focuses on the process of de-institutionalization as it pushes people into the cultural markets found in the mass media. The basic function of any institu-tion, Luckmann argues, is to provide a set of predetermined meanings for the perceived world and, simultaneously, to provide legitimation for these mean-ings. Religion, in particular, provides a shield of solidarity against any doubts, fears, and questions about ultimate meaning by giving and legitimating an ultimate meaning set. Yet, modern structural differentiation and specialization has, Luckmann contends, made the ultimate meanings of religion structurally unstable because individuals must confront a diverse array of secular tasks and obligations that carry alternative meanings. This structural instability has, in turn, resulted in the privatization of religion. This privatization of religion is, however, more than a retreat from secular structural forces; it is also a response to forces of the sacralization of subjectivity found in mass culture.

Because of the effects of structural differentiation, markets, and mass culture, consciousness within individuals is one of immediate sensations

---

[32]Mark Gottdiener, "Hegemony and Mass Culture: A Semiotic Approach," *American Journal of Sociology* 90 (1985): pp. 979–1001; *Postmodern Semiotics: Material Culture and the Forms of Postmodern Life* (Oxford: Blackwell, 1995).

[33]Gottdiener, "Hegemony and Mass Culture" (cited in note 32), p. 996.

[34]Thomas Luckmann, "The New and the Old in Religion," *Social Theory for a Changing Society*, eds. Pierre Bourdieu and James S. Coleman (Boulder, CO: Westview, 1991).

and emotions. As a consequence, consciousness is unstable, making acceptance of general legitimating myths, symbols, and dogmas problematic—Lyotard's "incredulity toward grand narratives." Yet, capitalist markets have turned this challenge into profitable business. The individual is now faced with a highly competitive market for ultimate meanings created by mass media, churches and sects, residual nineteenth-century secular ideologies, and substitute religious communities. The products of this market form a more or less systematically arranged meaning set that refers to minimal and intermediate meanings but rarely to ultimate meanings. Under these conditions, a meaning set can be taken up by an individual for a long or short period of time and combined with elements from other meaning sets. Thus, just as early capitalism and the structural forces that it unleashed undermined the integrative power of religion, so advanced capitalism creates a new, more postmodern diversity of commodified meaning sets that can be mass produced and consumed by individuals in search of cultural coherence that can stave off their anxieties and fears in a structurally differentiated and culturally fragmented social world.

**Zygmunt Bauman**. Like Luckmann, Zygmunt Bauman[35] examines the effects of de-institutionalization on meanings about self in chaotic, often random, and highly differentiated systems. Within these kinds of systems, identity formation consists of self constitution with no reference point for evaluation or monitoring, no clear anchorage in place and time, and no lifelong and consistent project of self formation. People thus experience a high degree of uncertainty about their identity, and as a consequence, Bauman argues, the only visible vehicle for identity formation is the body.

Thus, in postmodernity, body cultivation becomes an extremely important dynamic in the process of self-constitution. Because the body plays such an important role in constituting the postmodern-self, uncertainty is highest around bodily concerns, such as health, physique, aging, and skin blemishes; these issues become causes of increased reflexivity, evaluation, and thus, uncertainty.

Bauman, like Luckmann, argues that the absence of any firm and objective evaluative guide tends to create a demand for a substitute. These substitutes are symbolically created, as other people and groups are seen as "unguarded totemic poles which one can approach or abandon without applying for permission to enter or leave."[36] Individuals use these others as reference points and adopt the symbols of belonging to the other. The availability of the symbolic tokens depends on their visibility, which, in turn, depends on the use of the symbolic tokens to produce a satisfactory self-construction. In the end, the efficacy of these symbols rests on either expertise in some task or mass following.

---

[35]Zygmunt Bauman, *Modernity and Ambivalence* (Ithaca NY: Cornell University Press, 1991); *Intimations of Postmodernity* (London and New York: Routledge, 1992).

[36]Bauman, *Intimations of Postmodernity* (cited in note 35), p. 195.

Bauman also argues that accessibility of the tokens depends on an agent's resources and increasingly is understood as knowledge and information. So, for example, people might adopt the symbols associated with a specific professional athlete—wearing the same type of shoe or physically moving in the same defining manner—or individuals might assume all the outward symbols and cultural capital associated with a perceived group of computer wizards. The important issue for Bauman is that these symbols of group membership can be taken up or cast off without any commitment or punitive action because the individuals using the symbols have never been an interactive part of these groups' or celebrities' lives.

The need for these tokens results in "tribal politics," defined as self-constructing practices that are collectivized.[37] These tribes function as imagined communities and, unlike premodern communities, exist only in symbolic form through the shared commitments of their members.[38] For example, a girl in rural North Carolina might pierce various body parts, wear mismatched clothing three sizes too large, have the music of Biohazard habitually running through her mind, and see herself as a member of the grunge or punk community but never once interact with group members. Or, an individual might develop a concern for the use of animals in laboratory experiments, talk about it to others, wear proclamations on T-shirts and bumper stickers, and attend an occasional rally, and thus, might perceive himself as a group member but not be part of any kind of social group or interaction network. These quasi groups function without the powers of inclusion and exclusion that earlier groups possessed; indeed, these "neotribes" are created only through the repetitive performance of symbolic rituals and exist only as long as the members perform the rituals.

Neo-tribes are thus formed through concepts rather than through face-to-face encounters in actual social groups. They exist as "imagined communities" through self-identification and persist solely because people use them as vehicles for self-definition and as "imaginary sediments."[39] Because the persistence of these tribes depends on the affective allegiance of the members, self-identifying rituals become more extravagant and spectacular. Spectacular displays, such as body scarring or extreme or random violence, are necessary because, in postmodernity, public attention is the true scarce resource on which self and other are based.

# Conclusion

Any assessment of postmodernism that will not simply have the characteristics of a polemic will have to be based on some common ground. That

---

[37]Ibid., pp. 198–99.

[38]See Benedict Anderson, *Imagined Communities* (London: Verso, 1983).

[39]See H. Mehan and H. Wood, *Reality of Ethnomethodology* (New York: John Wiley, 1975) and Niklas Luhmann, "Society, Meaning, Religion—Based on Self-Reference," *Sociological Analysis* 46 (1985): pp. 5–20.

common ground is provided by the general properties of language, culture, and knowledge. Postmodernism is based on a critique of science against which postmodernism itself cannot stand firmly. All culture and language is distanced from the physical world. Such abstraction is a necessary condition of culture and language because, without some degree of removal from the physical world, there would only be the thing-in-itself and no human meaning as we understand it. Because language and meaning are not moored in the physical world but are, actually, representations of the world, they are inherently contingent and unstable and, thus, must be reified and stabilized in some way. In addition, because culture is by its very nature abstract and contingent, it is self-referential and is undergirded by incorrigible propositions or unchallenged beliefs about the world. Reification of ideas into reality, stabilization, and the protection of incorrigible assumptions occur principally through (1) the structuring or institutionalization of collective activities and (2) the investment of emotions by individuals—both of which are tied to group processes and identity.

The function of all cultural knowledge, particularly language and theory, is to call attention to some elements in the world, both social and physical, while excluding others. The process of inclusion and exclusion is a fundamental way in which meaning is created. As Max Weber indicated, culture is the process of singling out from "the meaningless infinity of the world process" a finite portion that is in turn infused with meaning and significance. And the incorrigible propositions undergirding any knowledge system also function through inclusion and exclusion: A system cannot simultaneously be based on pragmatism and mysticism.

Thus, postmodernists are in a sense correct in their critique of science: Science, like any knowledge system, is based on incorrigible assumptions, is an abstraction from physical reality, is in need of reification and stabilization through the processes of institutionalization and emotional investment, and is bent on systematically subjugating other knowledge systems to assert its own reality. But, what postmodernists have missed—despite disclaimers about having no privileged voice—is that their own knowledge systems are subject to the same properties. In creating a system of knowledge, postmodernists must reify and stabilize their knowledge through the same processes of institutionalization, emotional investment, and exclusion—or be subject to the nihilism of endless regression.

Mark Gottdiener and early critical theorists are correct when they assert that knowledge, beliefs, and group interests are inseparable. What he and most other critical theorists fail to understand, however, is that their own knowledge systems function in the same way as science and are open to the same critique. The battle over the definition of science, knowledge, and theory is a cultural war for legitimization on which turns the allocation of institutional and material resources. Based on a generalized understanding of how culture functions within and between groups, the behavior of both postmodernists and social scientists is fairly predictable, especially because most of the protagonists are situated within academia.

Postmodernism is premised on a fundamental error that originated with structuralism (see Chapters 25 and 26): The structure of the sign system is posited to be the dynamic on which human action and interaction depends. This prejudicial favoring of culture over other properties and processes in social life might be one defining characteristic of postmodernism. Even those who appear to want to consider other factors, such as Denzin, Kellner, and Gottdiener, end up simply analyzing cultural artifacts such as film or billboards and then imputing their findings to the social actors who might or might not interpret the artifact in the same manner or use the culture in the way the researcher supposes. This error has resulted in a general over-emphasis on culture, the signification system, and the problem of representation to the neglect of human agency and interaction. Even if culture is as fragmented and free-floating as postmodernists claim, it will have little effect on people until it becomes the focus of their interactions. And in micro-level interaction there are processes that tend to mitigate the problems of free-floating signifiers and emotionally flat symbols, as the theories of interaction presented in the chapters of Part IV document. People respond to the contingent nature of culture at the micro level by producing a Goffmanian type of interaction equilibrium and natural rituals to emotionally infuse symbols (see Chapters 19 and 27).

This fundamental error has also produced some questionable assertions by postmodernists concerning the self. For the category of the self to be obliterated or to be fragmented, as postmodernists claim, culture must be exclusively determinative, and it is not. The creation and organization of the self is informed and constrained by culture, but it is not a direct function of the sign system. From a sociological point of view, the self is a process that is the joint work of individuals and groups in relation to their social environment. The self is an internalized structure of meanings that has as its source the process of role taking in real groups and with real people in a person's particular biographical history. Media images can inform the interaction through which the self is constituted, but the interaction itself determines how those images will be used and what meanings will be attached to them.

It appears that postmodernism is moving toward a more moderated position. Each of the founders of postmodern thought posited a radical break with modernity and a universal problem of meaning and signification, but most subsequent postmodern thinkers have made attempts at grounding their analyses in the material world. Thus, the intellectual crisis is not as deep as was first supposed. The economic postmodernists, in particular, are using more generalized principles and processes to explain social phenomena. If postmodernism is to have a substantial voice beyond a critical stand against social science, it must move toward these more moderated positions.

## CHAPTER 33

# American-Style Critical Theories

This chapter on American versions of critical theorizing is also the last chapter of the book. It may appear strange for me, as one committed to the epistemology of science, to end on this note, but most of the book is about scientific theorizing. And so, perhaps by ending on a more activist note, I can give due emphasis to the chapters that I have put at the tail end of the book. Critical theories are driven by a moral vision of what "the good society" *should* be, and one of the reasons that students, in America at least, take sociology courses and become majors is that they share this vision. Sociology is about the social organization of people in all of its manifestations; if the problems of society inhere in these dynamics of social organization, then sociology is the best discipline for understanding these problems and, more importantly, for doing something about them. Many of the first generation of American sociologists, beginning in the late 1800s, founded sociology with this motivation—to make a better society—at the same time that they espoused the virtues of science. Auguste Comte in Europe gave sociology a name with the same goal, although he felt that science was the path to human salvation. Most early American sociologists, in contrast, did not know much about science, despite their rhetorical support of it.

In American sociology today, critical theory is not only an artifact of this long history of activist motivations among sociologists but also the consequence of internalizing external social movements into departments and programs within academia. Thus, for example, the civil rights, feminists, and gay and lesbian social movements in the broader society have become

---

*This chapter is primarily authored by Patricia R. Turner, with my contributions being relatively minor.

part of the academic mission of universities that have hired within departments or created new departments and programs to include scholarship
about the issues, history, and forces that pushed people to mobilize collectively in the name of justice and fairness for categories of persons who have
been subject to discrimination.

As a starting point for founding of academic programs, it was inevitable
that these critical theories would not only be critical of existing conditions
in a society but that they would be activist in their intentions to change
these conditions. Sociology is an obvious place for activist fueled by beliefs
about what is wrong and what must be in a just society; thus, it should not
be surprising that even theorizing should be influenced by these beliefs and
motivations. There will always be tension between science as one kind of
belief system and ideology as another kind of belief system (see Figure 1.1
on page 5), and this tension reverberates throughout academia and the
broader society as well. This is a tension that will simply have to be endured
because it is endemic to sociology and, now, to academia more generally.

In this chapter, feminism will be given the most attention because it has
evolved a powerful critique and complex set of theoretical arguments that
are only rivaled by Marxist-inspired class analysis and European critical
theories. A much less coherent intellectual movement can be found in
critical theories about race and ethnicity, but over the last few decades, these
critical theories have gained some prominence, although there is still much
less active theorizing in these areas than is the case with feminist theories.
These two critical approaches to theory are uniquely American in tone and
style and are thus worthy of attention in a book devoted to contemporary
sociological theorizing.

# The Feminist Critique of Sociological
# Theory: Gender, Politics, and Patriarchy

Since the early 1970s, one of the most sustained challenges to mainstream
sociological theory has come from critical feminist theorists. Appearing
shortly after the beginning of the second wave of the women's movement in
the mid-to-late 1960s, the first feminist critiques focused on the underrepresentation of women and women's experiences within sociology, both as
the subjects of research and the producers of theory. Concurrently, feminist
theorists examined the construction of gender and sex roles in modern
society to demonstrate the existence of a "female world" that sociology had
hitherto ignored.[1] Subsequent critiques went further, as feminists used the
concepts of gender and patriarchy to reveal masculine (or androcentric)
stances in social research methodologies and in sociological theory. These

---

[1] Jessie Bernard, *The Female World* (New York: Free Press, 1981); Ann Oakley, *The Sociology
of Housework* (New York: Pantheon, 1974).

more radical critiques questioned the capacity of sociological research and theory, as a body of knowledge constructed from the experiences of men, to address the experiences of women.

Critical feminist theorists proposed alternative methodological approaches, including the construction of a "feminist standpoint" or women's sociology that would begin with the social universe of women and reflect women's perspectives on society.[2] In the past decade, several radical feminist theorists have also used the epistemological issues inherent in feminist methodologies to critique the "positivistic" foundations of sociological understanding and to lay the groundwork for a "feminist epistemology."[3]

The feminist critique, like much of sociological theory at present, does not form a coherent paradigm. There is little consensus among critical feminist theorists about what constitutes the feminist critique or about how sociological understandings should be restructured to obviate the criticisms of feminists. Nevertheless, several common threads distinguish the feminist position from other forms of critical theory. What the critical feminist theorists share with their more scientifically oriented colleagues is the conviction that gender represents a fundamental form of social division within society. They also share a commitment to analyzing the sources of oppression and inequality for women, the most important being the patriarchal structure of society and its institutions. Still, the feminist theorists examined in this chapter have focused on gender and forms of patriarchy to criticize social research practices and the production of sociological theory itself.[4] Indeed, they have questioned the legitimacy and objectivity of these "scientific" methods by exploring the ways in which they embody androcentric (male-oriented) modes of thought. Finally, these critical feminist theorists are often self-consciously aware of the political and practical implications of their attacks for feminist politics and the status of women. As Mary Jo Neitz stated, "the critical questions for feminist scholarship

---

[2]Dorothy Smith, "Women's Perspective as a Radical Critique of Sociology," *Sociological Inquiry* 44 (1974): pp. 7–15; "Sociological Theory: Methods of Writing Patriarchy," in *Feminism and Sociological Theory* (Newbury Park, CA: Sage, 1989), pp. 34–64; *The Everyday World as Problematic: A Feminist Sociology* (Boston: Northeastern University Press, 1987). Also Nancy Hartsock, *Money, Sex, and Power* (New York: Longman, 1983).

[3]For example, see Chris Weedon, *Feminist Practice & Poststructuralist Theory* (New York: Basil Blackwell, 1987); Judith Butler, "Contingent Foundations: Feminism and the Question of Post-Modernism," in *The Postmodern Turn: New Perspectives on Social Theory* (Cambridge: Cambridge University Press, 1994), pp. 152–70; Susan Hekman, *Gender and Knowledge: Elements of a Postmodern Feminism* (Boston: Northeastern University Press, 1990); Sondra Farganis, "Postmodernism and Feminism," in *Postmodernism and Social Inquiry* (New York: Guilford, 1994); and Thomas Meisenhelder, "Habermas and Feminism: The Future of Critical Theory," in *Feminism and Sociological Theory*, ed. Ruth A. Wallace (Newbury Park, CA: Sage, 1989), pp. 119–34.

[4]This has led some to question whether many feminist critiques should properly be called theory. See Mary Jo Neitz, "Introduction to the Special Issue Sociology and Feminist Scholarship," *The American Sociologist* 20 (1989): p. 5.

came out of the women's movement, not out of the disciplines."[5] Consequently, most critical feminist theorists want to preserve the emancipatory dimension of feminist theory—that is, its ability to serve, like Marxism, as "both a mode of understanding and a call to action."[6] This self-conscious conflation of theory, method, politics, and praxis, combined with a focus on gender and patriarchy as the primary sources of oppression and inequality, constitutes the common denominators distinguishing the feminist critique of sociological theory.

## Representation and the Construction of Gender

**Early Challenges to Social Science.** Early feminist critiques of sociological research and theory were concerned primarily with the issue of representation, especially with respect to:[7]

1. Omission and underrepresentation of women as research subjects

2. Concentration on masculine-dominated sectors of social life

3. Use of paradigms, concepts, methods and theories that more faithfully portray men's than women's experiences

4. Use of men and male lifestyles as the norms against which social phenomena were interpreted

One of the most influential early works that addressed all of these issues is Ann Oakley's survey of housewives and their opinions of housework. Oakley argued that discrimination against women in society is mirrored by

---

[5]Ibid., p. 4.

[6]Sondra Farganis, "Social Theory and Feminist Theory: The Need for Dialogue," *Social Inquiry* 56 (1986): p. 56.

[7]Kathryn Ward and Linda Grant, "The Feminist Critique and a Decade of Published Research in Sociology Journals," *The Sociological Quarterly* 26 (1985): p. 140. On the issue of inadequate representation of women as the subjects of research, see Arlie Russell Hochschild, "A Review of Sex Role Research," *American Journal of Sociology* 78 (1973): pp. 1011–29 and Cynthia Fuchs Epstein, "A Different Angle of Vision: Notes on the Selective Eye of Sociology," *Social Science Quarterly* 55 (1974): pp. 645–56. Critiques on the neglect of female-dominated social sectors include Ann Oakley, *Sociology of Housework* (New York: Pantheon, 1974) and Jessie Bernard, "My Four Revolutions: An Autobiographical History of the ASA," *American Journal of Sociology* 78 (1973): pp. 773–91. For early critiques of sociological methods and their failure to reflect women's experiences and perspectives, see Dorothy Smith, "Women's Perspective as a Radical Critique of Sociology," *Sociological Inquiry* 44 (1974): pp. 7–15 and Arlie Russell Hochschild, "The Sociology of Feeling and Emotion: Selected Possibilities," in *Another Voice: Feminist Perspectives on Social Life and Social Science* (New York: Octagon, 1976), pp. 280–307. Finally, among the early feminist theorists to criticize the use of men and their lifestyles as "normative" were Joan Acker, "Women and Social Stratification: A Case of Intellectual Sexism," *American Journal of Sociology* 78 (1973): pp. 936–45 and Jessie Bernard, "Research on Sex Differences: An Overview of the State of the Art," in *Women, Wives, Mothers* (Chicago: Aldine Publishing Company, 1975), pp. 7–29.

sexism in sociology, and she used the academic neglect of housework *as work* to address the broader issue of sexual bias within sociological research and theory in general.[8] Oakley stated that women's invisibility in sociology can be found in all the major subject areas of sociology. In the subject area of deviance, for example, Oakley argued that until the mid-1970s very little data had been collected on women and that "theories of deviance may include some passing reference to women, but interpretations of female behavior are uncomfortably subsumed under the umbrella of explanation geared to the model of masculine behavior."[9] She also questioned whether or not standard definitions of deviance consider patterns of behavior that are gender related or associated only with women.[10] With regard to social stratification theory, to take an example from another prominent subject area of sociology, Oakley posited that the following untested assumptions about class membership effectively render women invisible and irrelevant: (1) The family is the unit of stratification; (2) the social position of the family is determined by the status of the man in it; and (3) only in rare circumstances is a woman's social position not determined by the men to whom she is attached by marriage or family of origin.[11] Oakley argued that these assumptions often do not reflect social reality, because many people do not live in families, many families are headed by women, and many husbands and wives do not have identical social status rankings. The problematics of these assumptions would be revealed, according to Oakley, if the significance of gender as a criterion for social differentiation and stratification is recognized by sociologists. Without such recognition, women's roles and position in the social stratification system would continue to be hidden and misrepresented.[12]

Oakley attributed the inherent sexism in sociological theory and research to the male-oriented attitudes of sociology's "founding fathers,"[13] the paucity of

---

[8]Oakley, *Sociology of Housework* (cited in note 1), p. 2.

[9]Ibid., p. 5.

[10]Ibid., p. 8.

[11]Ibid., pp. 8–9. In a similar critique of social stratification literature, Joan Acker adds two assumptions: "(a) Women determine their own social status only when they are not attached to a man and (b) women are unequal to men in many ways, are differentially evaluated on the basis of sex, but this is irrelevant to the structure of stratification systems." See Acker, "Women and Social Stratification: A Case of Intellectual Sexism," *American Journal of Sociology* 78 (1973): p. 937.

[12]Oakley, *Sociology of Housework* (cited in note 1), pp. 12–13.

[13]Ibid., p. 21. Oakley argues that of the five "founding fathers" of sociology—Marx, Comte, Spencer, Durkheim, and Weber—only two, Marx and Weber, had "emancipated views" about women. Terry Kandal, in a more recent analysis of the "woman question" in classical sociological theory, offers a less condemnatory accounting, asserting that there were "complex and contradictory variations in the writings about women by different classical theorists." See *The Woman Question in Classical Sociological Theory* (Miami: Florida International University Press, 1988): p. 245.

women social researchers and theorists, and the pervasiveness of ideologies advocating gender roles within contemporary societies. The ideology of gender, she argued, contains stereotypical assumptions about women's social status and behavior that are uncritically reproduced within sociology, and these stereotypes will only be overcome if women's experiences are made the focus of analysis and are viewed from their perspective.[14]

Most of these early critiques of sociological research and theory shares with Oakley two related assumptions about the primacy and construction of gender: First, gender is a fundamental determinant of social relations and behavior, and second, gender divisions in a society shape the experiences and perspectives of each sex, with the result that women's experiences are distinctly different from those of men. Some feminist scholars went further than Oakley and began to argue that society is gendered in ways that segregate men and women into distinct and often exclusionary homosocial worlds. Building on Georg Simmel's insight that "women possess a world of their own which is not comparable with the world of men,"[15] Jessie Bernard argued in *The Female World* that society is divided into "single-sex" worlds. Sociology and other disciplines in the humanities and human sciences have dealt heretofore almost exclusively with the male world. Bernard sought to correct this imbalance by tracing the historical development of the female world and the uniquely female experiences and perspectives that have emerged from it. She has argued that the female world differs subjectively and objectively from that of men, and hence, the female world must be examined "as an entity in its own right, not as a byproduct of the male world."[16] The neglect of the female world and women's experiences by sociology and other disciplines, Bernard has asserted, deprives public debate of perspectives that might provide innovative solutions and approaches to contemporary problems.[17]

Other feminist theorists have used the concept of gendered social spheres to explore more specifically the stratification of sex roles and the social construction of gender. Jean Lipman-Blumen proposed a homosocial theory of sex roles to account for the traditional barriers that restrict women's entry into male spheres—such as politics, military, and major league sports—and that often confine women to the domestic sphere.[18] She hypothesized that men are socialized to be attracted to, and to be interested in, other men. This attraction is reinforced and perpetuated by patriarchal social institutions that traditionally value men over women and give to men nearly exclusive control of

---

[14]Ibid., pp. 21–28.

[15]As quoted in opening epigraphs in Jessie Bernard's *The Female World* (New York: Free Press, 1981).

[16]Ibid., p. 3.

[17]Ibid., pp. 12–15.

[18]See, for example, Jean Lipman-Blumen, "Toward a Homosocial Theory of Sex Roles: An Explanation of the Sex Segregation of Social Institutions," *Signs* (1976): pp. 15–31.

resources.[19] With the important exceptions of reproductive and sexual needs, men look to men for support, whereas women are forced to transform themselves into sex objects to acquire resources and support from men. Lipman-Blumen argued the preeminence of men in the exchange and protection of resources creates "dominance hierarchies" that persist even when technology eliminates the need for the differentiation and stratification of sex roles.[20]

In her highly influential book, *The Reproduction of Mothering: Psychoanalysis and the Sociology of Gender*, Nancy Chadorow theorized that women's responsibility for childrearing (and the collateral absence of male domestic roles) has profound consequences for the construction of gender identity and the sexual division of labor. Chadorow posits, "all societies are constituted around a structural split, growing out of women's mothering, between the private, domestic world of women and the public, social world of men."[21] This structural split is created by a sexual division of labor that is itself reproduced each generation by gender personality differences between men and women. These behavioral differences or "intrapsychic structures" are not biological; rather, they stem from the distinct social relationships girls and boys develop with their mothers. Girls learn to be women and to mother by identifying with their mothers, whereas boys must develop a masculine gender identification in opposition to their mothers and often in the absence of affective, ongoing relationships to a father figure. This results in different "relational capacities" and "senses of self" in men and women that prepare them "to assume the adult gender roles which situate women primarily within the sphere of reproduction in a sexually unequal society."[22]

## A Sociology for Women: Feminist Methodologies, Epistemologies, and "Standpoint" Theories

Efforts in the late 1970s and 1980s to devise a sociology for women arose from a growing conviction among more radical critical feminist theorists that to simply refocus the discipline's theoretical and methodological lenses on gender and women's domains would do little to correct the androcentric (male) biases and patterns of patriarchal thought inhering in sociological work. Because of these biases, traditional forms of explanation within sociology were increasingly seen as fundamentally incapable of representing accurately a social world in which, many feminist critics began to assert, all social relations are gendered.[23] Recognizing the link between feminist

---

[19]Ibid., p. 16.

[20]Ibid., p. 17.

[21]Nancy Chadorow, *The Reproduction of Mothering: Psychoanalysis and the Sociology of Gender* (Berkeley: University of California Press, 1978), pp. 173–74.

[22]Ibid., p. 173.

[23]Joan Acker, "Making Gender Visible," in *Feminism and Sociological Theory*, ed. R. A. Wallace (Newbury Park, CA: Sage, 1989), p. 73.

thought and politics, John Shotter and Josephine Logan argue that only by finding a "new voice" can feminist scholars and the women's movement as a whole escape the "pervasiveness of patriarchy":

> The women's movement must of necessity develop itself within a patriarchal culture of such a depth and pervasiveness that, even in reacting to or resisting its oppressive nature, the women's movement continually "reinfects" or "contaminates" itself with it. All of us, women and men alike, are "soaked" in it.... Patriarchy is enshrined in our social practices, in our ways of positioning and relating ourselves to one another, and in the resources we use in making sense of one another.... We must find a different voice, a new place currently unrecognized, from which to speak about the nature of our lives together.[24]

This kind of more radical attack on the sociology of knowledge was fueled by a growing frustration among feminist critics in general about what they saw as a continued resistance within sociology—and sociological theory in particular—to study gender and to draw out the conceptual and theoretical implications of this research. In their analysis of articles published in ten sociological journals between 1974 and 1983, Grant and Ward found that the number of theoretical papers, reviews, and critiques focusing on gender in mainstream journals was still relatively small compared with other traditional topics—an indication, they feel, that journal editors continue to view gender as a peripheral in contemporary sociology.[25]

Other feminist critics have echoed Grant and Ward's concerns. Acker's review of stratification literature asserts that, aside from Rae Lesser Blumberg's landmark book,[26] stratification texts still do not "successfully integrate women into the analysis and generally evade the problem by including brief descriptions of sex-based inequality generally ungrounded in a conceptualization of societal-wide stratification."[27] Judith Stacey and Barrie Thorne conclude that although feminist scholars have made valuable contributions to numerous traditional branches of sociological research (for example, organizations, occupations, criminology, deviance and stratification) and have pioneered work in many others (for example, sexual

---

[24]John Shotter and Josephine Logan, "The Pervasiveness of Patriarchy: On Finding a Different Voice," in *Feminist Thought and the Structure of Knowledge* (New York: New York University Press, 1988), pp. 69–70.

[25]Linda Grant and Kathryn Ward, "Is There an Association Between Gender and Methods in Sociological Research?" *American Sociological Review* 52 (1987): p. 861.

[26]Rae Lesser Blumberg, *Stratification: Social, Economic and Sexual Inequality* (Dubuque, IA: William C. Brown, 1978).

[27]Joan Acker, "Women and Stratification: A Review of Recent Literature," *Contemporary Sociology* 9 (1980): p. 26.

harassment, feminization of poverty), they had yet to effect significant conceptual transformations in the field.[28] Feminist scholars in sociology—unlike their counterparts in anthropology, history, and literary criticism—have not succeeded in influencing the discipline to the point where women are being put regularly at the center of analysis. Instead, Stacey and Thorne argue that "feminist sociology seems to have been both co-opted and ghettoized, while the discipline as a whole and its dominant paradigms have proceeded relatively unchanged."[29]

Feminist scholars propose a variety of explanations to account for the "ghettoization" of gender issues within sociological research and theory. In their study of women's involvement in theory production, Ward and Grant emphasize that the relative lack of theorizing on gender might be partly because of the scarcity and low profile of women theorists. Compared with their male colleagues, Ward and Grant found that women sociologists (1) affiliate with the American Sociological Association's theory section less, (2) self-identify as theorists less, (3) write fewer textbooks and journal articles, (4) receive less visibility in textbooks and popular teaching materials, and (5) serve less frequently as editors or board members of theory journals.[30] As possible explanations for the "peculiar eclipsing" of women as theorists, Ward and Grant cite (1) the comparatively high status of theory production, which, in turn, can lead to higher barriers against the entry of women and (2) the fragmentation of contemporary sociological theory into multiple and competing paradigms that can restrict the spread of feminist thought.

Ward and Grant also speculate that differences in how women sociologists approach their research subjects might decrease the likelihood of their work on gender being accepted for publication. They have found that there are "systematic links" between gender and methods within sociology, with women scholars publishing in major sociological journals employing qualitative methods more often than their male colleagues.[30] Many feminist theorists argue that qualitative methods (for example, intensive interviews and participant observation) are more appropriate for exploring gender and women's issues, which tend to be more private, context bound, and hence, less easily quantifiable.[31] Yet Grant and Ward have failed to find a

---

[28]Judith Stacey and Barrie Thorne, "The Missing Feminist Revolution in Sociology," *Social Problems* 32 (1985): pp. 301–16.

[29]Ibid., p. 302.

[30]Grant and Ward, "Is There an Association Between Gender and Methods in Sociological Research?" (cited in note 25), pp. 856–62.

[31]See Marlene Mackie, "Female Sociologists' Productivity, Collegial Relations, and Research Style Examined through Journal Publications," *Social and Social Research* 69 (1985): pp. 189–209; Ellen Carol Dubois, ed., *Feminist Scholarship: Kindling in the Groves of Academe* (Urbana: University of Illinois Press, 1985); and Rhoda Unger, "Through the Looking Glass: No Wonderland Yet! The Reciprocal Relationship between Methodology and Models of Reality," *Psychology of Women* Quarterly 8 (1983): pp. 9–32.

correlation between gender and methods in published research on gender among mainstream sociological journals. In gender articles, both sexes preferred quantitative methods, leading Grant and Ward to speculate that "qualitative papers on gender might have presented double nonconformity, reducing the likelihood of acceptance for publication."[32] Finally, they also refer to Judith A. Howard's contention that the influence of feminist perspectives is limited by "the inability of extant social theories (including Marxism) to conceptualize gender as a major organizing principle of society and culture and by the predominance of positivist epistemological traditions that encourage emphasis on gender as a variable rather than a concept."[33]

Acker takes a different tack, suggesting that sociological theory "continues in a prefeminist mode" because of both institutional resistance within the discipline and the underdevelopment of feminist alternatives to mainstream theoretical concepts and methodologies.[34] Sociology, Acker argues, shares with other academic disciplines:

> A particular connection to power in society as a whole or to the relations of ruling: The almost exclusively male domain of academic thought is associated with abstract, intellectual, textually mediated processes through which organizing, managing and governing are carried out.... The perspectives that develop their concepts and problematics from within what is relevant to the relations of ruling are successful.[35]

Acker questions whether critical feminist theories can ever effect a paradigm shift within sociological theory as long as societal institutions remain patriarchally structured and power relations continue to be dominated by men.[36] Yet, Acker also holds feminist theory accountable for its relative lack of influence within mainstream sociological theory. Feminist scholars, she argues, "have not, as yet, been able to suggest new ways of looking at things that are obviously better than the old ways for comprehending a whole

---

[32]Grant and Ward, "Is There an Association Between Gender and Methods in Sociological Research?" (cited in note 25), p. 861.

[33]See J. A. Howard, "Dilemmas in Feminist Theorizing: Politics and the Academy," *Current Perspectives in Social Theory* 8 (1987): pp. 279–312.

[34]Joan Acker, "Making Gender Visible" (cited in note 23), pp. 65–81.

[35]Ibid., pp. 68–69. As Acker readily acknowledges, her analysis of sociology's relationship to ruling power structures owes much to Dorothy Smith. See note 2: Smith, *The Everyday World as Problematic.*

[36]Ibid., Acker, p. 78.

range of problems."[37] Acker outlines her vision of a feminist paradigm capable of competing with or supplanting established theoretical positions. Such a paradigm would[38]

1. Provide a better understanding of class structure, the state, social revolution, and militarism, as well as a better understanding of the sex segregation of labor, male dominance in the family, and sexual violence

2. Place women and their lives in a central place in understanding social relations as a whole, while creating a more accurate and comprehensive account of industrial, capitalist society

3. Contain a methodology that produces knowledge for, rather than of, women in all their diverse situations

Implicit in Acker's proposal for a feminist paradigm is a radical critique of the very concepts, methodologies, and epistemological assumptions that form the foundation of sociological understandings of the social universe. As espoused by feminist theorists such as Dorothy Smith, Sandra Harding, and Evelyn Fox Keller, feminist theorists have failed thus far to transform prevailing mainstream theoretical paradigms because the underlying epistemologies and methodologies give privilege to the male experience.[39]

Dorothy Smith, one of the first feminist critical theorists to call for a "woman-centered" sociology, asserts that sociological thought has been "based on and built up within the male social universe,"[40] and as a consequence, sociology contains unexamined androcentric (male) modes of thought that serve the interests of men and that are by definition gender biased and exclusionary of women's perspectives.[41] She argues that as long as feminist scholars work within forms of thought made or controlled by men, women will be constrained to view themselves not as subjects but as the "other" and their experience will be marginalized accordingly.[42] It is not enough, she claims:

To supplement an established sociology by addressing ourselves to what has been left out, overlooked, or by making sociological issues

---

[37]Ibid., Acker, p. 72.

[38]Ibid., Acker, p. 67.

[39]Dorothy Smith, *The Everyday World as Problematic* (cited in note 2). Also see Sandra Harding, *The Science Question in Feminism* (Ithaca, NY: Cornell University Press, 1986); Evelyn Fox Keller, "Feminism and Science," *Signs* 7 (1982): pp. 589–602.

[40]Smith, "Women's Perspective" (cited in note 2), p. 7.

[41]Stacey and Thorne, "The Missing Feminist Revolution" (cited in note 28), p. 309.

[42]Smith, *The Everyday World as Problematic* (cited in note 2), p. 52.

of the relevances of the world of women. That merely extends the authority of the existing sociological procedures and makes of a women's sociology an addendum.[43]

This radical feminist critique has taken three main forms. First, it criticizes standard methodological practices and proposes to replace them with feminist methodologies. Second, it questions the epistemological assumptions of "positivistic" science because science, like the broader society, is gendered, and therefore, new epistemologies need to be developed that eliminate gender bias while recognizing the primacy of gender and its implications for knowledge production. Finally, radical feminist theorists propose the construction of an independent feminist standpoint that can avoid both the androcentric biases inherent in social research practices and the positivistic epistemological foundations of mainstream sociological theory.[44]

One of the first detailed feminist critiques of contemporary social methodology was a volume of essays edited by sociologists Marcia Millman and Rosabeth Moss Kanter.[45] Viewing the various critiques collectively, Millman and Moss identify six standard methodological practices that can lead to gender bias in social research. During the past thirty years, these practices have remained central to the feminist critique of social methodology:[46]

1. The use of conventional field-defining models that overlook important areas of social inquiry

2. The focus by sociologists on public, official, visible role players to the neglect of unofficial, supportive, private, and invisible spheres of social life and organization that are equally important

3. The assumption in sociology of a "single society," in which generalizations can be made that will apply equally to men and women

4. The neglect in numerous fields of study of sex as an important explanatory variable

5. The focus in sociology on explaining the status quo, which tends to provide rationalizations for existing power relations

[43]Smith, "Women's Perspective" (cited in note 2), p. 7. A similar criticism is made by Liz Stanley and Sue Wise in their book *Breaking Out: Feminist Consciousness and Feminist Research* (London: Routledge, 1983), p. 28.

[44]Shotter and Logan, "The Pervasiveness of Patriarchy" (cited in note 24), pp. 69–86. Also, see Dorothy Smith, "A Sociology for Women," in *The Prism of Sex* (Madison: University of Wisconsin Press, 1979), pp. 135–88.

[45]Marcia Millman and Rosabeth Moss Kanter, eds., *Another Voice: Feminist Perspectives on Social Life and Social Science* (New York: Octagon, 1976).

[46]Ibid., pp. ix–xvii.

6. The use of certain methodological techniques, often quantitative, and research situations that might systematically prevent the collection of certain kinds of data

First, Millman and Kanter argue that sociologists' reliance on models of social structure and action has led to a "systematic blindness to crucial elements of social reality."[47] For example, they assert that the sociological focus on Weberian rationality as an explanation for human action and social organization effectively removes the equally important element of emotion from consideration. They also question the veracity of sociological models that do not focus on the individual and his or her subjective experience as the center of analysis and instead emphasize issues of agency.[48] Bernard had earlier made a distinction between "agency," which emphasizes variables, and "communion," which focuses on individuals:

> Agency operates by way of mastery and control; communion with naturalistic observation, sensitivity to qualitative patterning, and greater personal participation by the investigator. . . . The specific processes involved in agentic [*sic*] research are typically male preoc-cupations. . . . The scientist using this approach creates his own controlled reality. He can manipulate it. He is master. He has power. The communal approach is much humbler. It disavows control, for control spoils the results. Its value rests precisely on the absence of controls.[49]

Millman and Kanter make the point that research based exclusively on agentic quantitative methods fails to represent accurately crucial segments of the social world.[50]

Second, sociology overlooks important arenas of social life by focusing only on "official actors and actions," and ignoring private, unofficial, and local social structures where women often predominate.[51] Millman, for example, posits that research on deviance and social control often empha-sizes locations such as courtrooms and mental hospitals, but fails to recog-nize "the importance of studying everyday, interpersonal social control and

---

[47]Ibid., p. ix.

[48]See Arlie Russell Hochschild's essay "The Sociology of Feeling and Emotion: Selected Possibilities," in *Another Voice: Feminist Perspectives on Social Life and Social Science*, eds. Marcia Millman and Rosabeth Moss Kanter (New York: Octagon, 1976), pp. 280–307.

[49]Jessie Bernard, "My Four Revolutions" (cited in note 7), p. 785. For more discussion of agency and communion approaches to research see David Bakan, "Psychology Can Now Kick the Science Habit," *Psychology Today* 5 (1972): pp. 26, 28, 86–88; and Rae Carlson, "Sex Differences in Ego Functioning: Exploratory Studies of Agency and Communion," *Journal of Consulting and Clinical Psychology* 37 (1971): pp. 267–77.

[50]Millman and Kanter, eds., *Another Voice* (cited in note 46), p. x.

[51]Ibid., p. xi.

the subtle, continuous series of maneuvers that individuals use to keep each other in line during ordinary mundane activities."[52]

Third, the assumption by sociologists that all humans inhabit a "single society" runs counter to evidence collected by feminist sociologists such as Bernard and Oakley that men and women often inhabit their own social worlds.[53] Focusing on a more narrow issue, Thelma McCormack posits that voting studies have erroneously assumed that men and women inhabit a single political culture, with the result that women tend to appear more conservative or apathetic.[54]

Fourth, Millman and Kanter cite several studies that demonstrate the failure of social researchers to consider sex as an explanatory variable. The studies include Sarah Lightfoot's analysis of the sociology of education, in which she asserts that researchers do not consider issues raised by the fact that most teachers are women.[55]

Fifth, Millman and Kanter argue that by seeking to explain the status quo, sociologists need to be more sensitive to the ways in which their research might also legitimate existing social relations and institutions. They argue that researchers should focus more attention on social transformation.[56] Arlene Daniels goes further to assert that research on women should not only concern itself with revealing the sources of women's oppression but should also engage in exploring the concrete ways in which their status and lives can be improved.[57]

Finally, Millman and Kanter point out that unquestioned methodological assumptions and techniques can adversely affect findings and conclusions. They cite David Tresemer's analysis of statistical studies of sex differences. Tresemer asserts that most of these studies are misleading because they improperly use bipolar, unidimensional continuous, normal distributions that have the effect of exaggerating differences.[58] Although this particular problem might best be corrected by adopting another less biased quantitative method, Millman and Kanter claim that in many cases qualitative techniques might be more suitable and yield more balanced results than the standard quantitative approaches.[59]

---

[52]Ibid.

[53]Ibid. See also note 1: Bernard, *The Female World*, and Oakley, *The Sociology of Housework*.

[54]Millman and Kanter, eds., *Another Voice*, p. xiii. See also Thelma McCormack, "Toward a Nonsexist Perspective on Social and Political Change," *Another Voice* (cited in note 45), pp. 1–33.

[55]Millman and Kanter, eds., *Another Voice*, p. xiv.

[56]Ibid., p. xv.

[57]Ibid. Also see Arlene Daniels, "Feminist Perspectives in Sociological Research," *Another Voice* (cited in note 45), pp. 340–80.

[58]Millman and Kanter, eds., Another Voice, p. xv. See also David Tresemer, "Assumptions Made About Gender Roles," *Another Voice* (cited in note 45), pp. 308–39.

[59]Millman and Kanter, eds., *Another Voice*, p. xvi.

Critical feminist theorists have developed several methodological approaches designed to address the topic of gender asymmetry and to avoid the possible gender biases in standard sociological practices. Judith Cook and Mary Fonow assert that feminist methodologies frequently employ the following seven research strategies and techniques:[60]

1. Visual techniques, such as photography and videotaping to collect or elicit data

2. Triangulation, or the use of more than one research technique simultaneously

3. The use of linguistic techniques in conversational analysis

4. Textual analysis as a means to identify gender bias

5. Refined quantitative approaches to measure phenomena related to sexual asymmetry and women's worlds

6. Collaborative strategies or collective research models to enhance feedback and promote cooperative, egalitarian relations among researchers

7. Situation-at-hand research practices that use an already existing situation as a focus for sociological inquiry or as a means of collecting data

Cook and Fonow stress that none of these techniques is explicitly or exclusively feminist; however, their innovative character is revealed in their application and in the degree to which they incorporate and are informed by five basic principles that govern the production of feminist knowledge.[61] Cook and Fonow identify these principles as follows:[62]

1. The necessity of continuously and reflexively attending to the significance of gender relations as a basic feature of social life, including the conduct of research

2. The centrality of consciousness-raising as a specific methodological tool and as a "way of seeing"

3. The need to challenge the norm of "objectivity" that assumes a dichotomy between the subject and object of research

4. The concern for the ethical implications of research

5. An emphasis on the transformation of patriarchy and the empowerment of women

---

[60]Judith Cook and Mary Fonow, "Knowledge and Women's Interests: Issues of Epistemology and Methodology in Feminist Sociological Research," *Sociological Inquiry* 56 (1986): pp. 2–29.

[61]Ibid., p. 14.

[62]Ibid., p. 2.

Feminist standpoint theories, as espoused by Dorothy Smith, Hilary Rose, Nancy Hartsock, and others, build on these epistemological and methodological principles by explicitly focusing on women and their direct experience as the center of analysis. Standpoint theorists argue that they can use women's experience to analyze social relations in ways that overcome the androcentric dichotomies of Enlightenment "positivism"—such as culture versus nature, rational mind versus irrational emotions, objectivity versus subjectivity, public versus private—that have structured knowledge production in the social and natural sciences.[63] Smith asserts that "women's perspective discredits sociology's claim to constitute an objective knowledge independent of the sociologist's situation."[64]

Feminist standpoint theorists articulate a feminist methodology that at once privileges the feminist standpoint as more inherently objective, challenges "mainstream" sociological inquiry, and provides a paradigmatic alternative. Smith disputes that such a paradigm shift would entail a "radical transformation of the subject matter."[65] Rather, she argues that what is involved is the restructuring of the relationship between the sociologist and the object of her research:

> What I am suggesting is more in the nature of a re-organization which changes the relation of the sociologist to the object of her knowledge and changes also her problematic. This re-organization involves first placing the sociologist where she is actually situated, namely at the beginning of those acts by which she knows or will come to know; and second, making her direct experience of the everyday world the primary ground of her knowledge.[66]

Critical theorists also suggest that a feminist standpoint methodology rooted in women's experience would elucidate the epistemological connections among the production of knowledge, everyday experiences, and political praxis that "positivistic" epistemologies often deny. Rose asserts in "Women's Work: Women's Knowledge" that human knowledge and consciousness "are not abstract or divorced from experience or 'given' by some process separate from the unitary material reality of the world. Human knowledge . . . comes from practice, from working on and changing the world."[67]

Viewed collectively, feminist empiricism—in the form of feminist methodologies, epistemologies, and standpoints—challenges key tenets of

---

[63]Sandra Harding, *The Science Question in Feminism* (Ithaca: Cornell University Press, 1986), pp. 136–62.

[64]Smith, "Women's Perspective" (cited in note 2), p. 11.

[65]Ibid.

[66]Ibid.

[67]Hilary Rose, "Women's Work: Women's Knowledge" in *What is Feminism*, eds. Juliet Mitchell and Ann Oakley (New York: Pantheon, 1986), p. 161.

traditional empiricism embodied in positivistic science. Sandra Harding argues that feminist empiricism specifically questions three central assumptions:[68]

1.  The assumption that the social identity of the observer is irrelevant to the "goodness" of the results of research, asserting that the androcentrism of science is both highly visible and damaging. It argues that women as a social group are more likely than men as a social group to select problems for inquiry that do not distort human social experience.

2.  The assumption that science's methodological and sociological norms are sufficient to eliminate androcentric biases by suggesting that the norms themselves appear to be biased insofar as they have been incapable of detecting androcentrism.

3.  The assumption that science must be protected from politics. Feminist empiricism argues that some politics—the politics of movement for emancipatory social change—can increase the objectivity of science.

## Critiquing the Critique: Challenges to Critical Feminist Theories

Feminist methodologies, epistemologies, and standpoint theories have received their own share of criticism. The most formidable of these have come from feminist critics themselves, who use feminist concepts and positions to, in effect, critique the critique. What links many of these counter critiques is an emphasis on the role of ideology in the structuring of feminist theory, epistemology, and practice.

The foundation for all critical feminist theory is the belief in the primacy of gender as a fundamental division that structures social relations. Sarah Matthews questions the importance of gender dichotomy, arguing that "this dichotomy does not match social reality as closely as assumed."[69] The existence of gender identities coded masculine and feminine does not, she asserts, necessarily mean that gender is the critical variable determining social behavior:[70]

All of these [feminist] critiques have in common as their beginning point the assumption that distinguishing between two genders is the appropriate foundation from which to build research questions and theory. To say that women have been excluded from sociological research; that research on women must be done to parallel research on men; that different methodologies must be utilized to understand

---

[68]Harding (cited in note 63), p. 162.

[69]Sarah Matthews, "Rethinking Sociology through a Feminist Perspective," *The American Sociologist* 17 (1982): p. 29.

[70]Ibid.

women in society; that boys and girls are socialized differently; and that women as a group are oppressed, is to accept and to re-enforce the taken-for-granted assumption that there are in fact two gender categories into which it is important to sort all human beings.[71]

Matthews goes on to argue that gender or sex is not "an immutable fact" and that feminist research and theory can be interpreted as supportive of this position. That this support has not been acknowledged, she asserts, is due to the ideological basis of feminism that is committed to seeing two genders.[72] She concludes by positing that sociologists can overcome sexual bias in research by developing paradigms "that do not include gender as having a priori significance."[73]

Attempts to construct feminist methods that espouse a privileged position for an independent "women's standpoint" have also been criticized by feminist critics such as Elizabeth Spelman. Spelman sees the phrase "as a woman" as "the Trojan horse of feminist ethnocentrism" because it embodies the assumption that "gender identity exists in isolation from race and class identity."[74] She argues that the feminist perspective or standpoint "obscures the heterogeneity of women"[75] and hence serves as little more than a methodological means of privileging white, middle-class women's experience. Spelman, in particular, challenges the following five assumptions inherent in feminist discussions of gender:[76]

1. Women can be talked about "as women."

2. Women are oppressed "as women."

3. Gender can be isolated from other elements of identity that affect one's social, economic, and political position such as race, class, ethnicity; hence, sexism can be isolated from racism and classism.

4. Women's situation can be contrasted with men's.

5. Relations between men and women can be compared with relations between other oppressor/oppressed groups, and hence, it is possible to compare the situation of women with the situation of blacks, Jews, the poor, and others.

---

[71]Ibid., p. 30.

[72]Ibid., p. 29.

[73]Ibid.

[74]Elizabeth Spelman, *Inessential Woman: Problems of Exclusion in Feminist Thought* (Boston: Beacon, 1988), p. x.

[75]Ibid., p. ix.

[76]Ibid., p. 165.

## Conclusion: Two or More Sociologies of Gender?

Critical feminism has been highly critical of specific forms of scientific theorizing[77] in sociology and, perhaps surprisingly, to other forms of critical theorizing as well.[78] There are, of course, powerful scientific theories of gender dynamics[79] that explicitly seek to develop propositions that can explain gender discrimination and stratification. The development of these theories is driven by much the same motivation as critical theorizing: to understand the dynamics of gender stratification so that this understanding can be used to reduce, if not eliminate, gender inequalities. Yet, these theories are not drawn from ideologies but from an assessment of the generic social processes that historically and today systematically generate gender inequalities.

For critical feminist theorizing, such scientific theories do not go far enough. They do not advocate change, and they assume that gender differences can be understood with the same tools as all other phenomena are to be understood, ignoring the differences in the social universes of men and

---

[77]See, for example, the following essays in Paula England, ed., *Theory on Gender/Feminism on Theory* (New York: Aldine de Gruyter, 1993); Lynn Smith-Lovin and J. Miller McPherson, "You are Who You Know: A Network Approach to Gender," pp. 223–51; Dana Dunn et al., "Macrostructural Perspectives on Gender Inequality," pp. 69–90; Miriam Johnson, "Functionalism and Feminism: Is Estrangement Necessary?" pp. 115–30; Debra Friedman and Carol Diem, "Feminism and the Pro-(Rational-)Choice Movement: Rational-Choice Theory, Feminist Critiques and Gender Inequality," pp. 91–114. Other works include Miriam Johnson, "Feminism and the Theories of Talcott Parsons," in *Feminism and Sociological Theory*, ed. R. C. Wallace (Newbury Park, CA: Sage, 1989), pp. 101–18; Marian Lowe and Ruth Hubbard, "Sociobiology and Biosociology: Can Science Prove the Biological Bias of Sex Differences in Behavior," in *Genesis and Gender* (New York: Gordian, 1979): pp. 91–112; Arlie Russell Hochschild, "The Sociology of Feeling and Emotion: Selected Possibilities," in *Another Voice: Feminist Perspectives on Social Life and Social Science,* eds. Marcia Millman and Rosabeth Moss Kanter (New York: Octagon, 1976), pp. 280–307; Paula England, "A Feminist Critique of Rational-Choice Theories: Implications for Sociology," *The American Sociologist* 20 (1989): pp. 14–28; and Paula England and Barbara Kilbourne, "Feminist Critique of the Separative Model of the Self: Implications for Rational Choice Theory," *Rationality and Society* 2, no.2: pp. 156–71.

[78]In addition to the work cited at the beginning of this chapter, for Foucault and post-structuralism, see Caroline Ramazanoglu, ed., *Up Against Foucault: Explorations of Some Tensions between Foucault and Feminism* (New York: Routledge, 1993. For critical feminist analyses of Marxist theory and the connections between it and feminist theory, see Catherine MacKinnon, "Feminism, Marxism, Method, and the State: An Agenda For Theory," *Signs* 7 (1982): pp. 515–44; Mia Campioni and Elizabeth Grosz, "Love's Labours Lost: Marxism and Feminism," in *A Reader in Feminist Knowledge* (New York: Routledge, 1991), pp. 366–97; Beth Anne Shelton and Ben Agger, "Shotgun Wedding, Unhappy Marriage, No-Fault Divorce? Rethinking Feminism-Marxism Relationship," in *Theory on Gender/Feminism on Theory*, pp. 25–42.

[79]For examples, see: Janel Saltzman Chafetz, *Gender Equity: An Integrated Theory of Stability and Change,* (Newbury Park, CA: Sage, 1990). See also her *Feminist Sociology: An Overview of Contemporary Theories,* (Itasca, IL: Peacock, 1988). Rae Lesser Blumberg, *Stratification: Socio-Economic and Sexual Inequality,* (Dubuque, IW: William C. Brown, 1978).

women. Thus, in the end, critical and scientific theories of gender will remain at odds.

# Critical Theories on Race and Ethnicity

From its very beginnings in the United States, sociology has been concerned with the pervasiveness of racial and ethnic discrimination. Indeed, the ameliorative thrust of much early American sociology was devoted to documenting and then explaining racial and ethnic discrimination. Some of these explanations were couched in more theoretical terms, others in explicitly ideological terms, but they were all critical in at least this sense: discrimination and inequality emerging from such discrimination is seen to be morally wrong and, moreover, dysfunctional for a society. Sociological knowledge should, therefore, be employed to expose racial oppression and to mount attacks on the institutional systems by which such oppression is carried out. In the modern era of sociology, this goal revolved around supporting the legal attack on ethnic discrimination, particularly discrimination against African-Americans, during the 1950s, and later in the 1960s as the civil rights movement achieved at least one of its key goals: a series of civil rights acts in the federal codes that made discrimination on the basis of race and other categoric distinctions (e.g., gender, religious affiliation) illegal.

## Critical Race Theory

Critical race theory emerged out of critical approaches that developed in legal scholarship. The basic conclusion was that the civil rights movement and the laws that it inspired were no longer effective in addressing long-term discrimination against "people of color" in the United States. [80] The civil rights movement had lost its momentum, and compared to the feminist movement that was just gearing up in the 1970s, the civil rights movement seemed rather tame and uncritical of persisting ethnic/racial discrimination and stratification in America.

---

[80]Adalberto Aguirre, "Academic Sorytelling: A Critical Race Theory Story of Affirmative Action," *Sociological Perspectives* 43 (2000): pp. 319–26; Kimberle Crenshaw, Neil Gotanda, Gary Peller, and Kendall Thomas, eds., *Critical Race Theory: The Key Writings That Formed the Movement*, (New York: New Press, 1995); Richard Delgado, "The Ethereal Scholar: Does Critical Legal Sudies Have What Minorities Want?" *Harvard Critical Legal Studies Law Review* 22 (1987): pp. 301–22; Richard Delgado, ed., *Critical Race Theory: The Cutting Edge* (Philadelphia, PA: Temple University Press, 1995); Mari J. Matsuda, Charles R. Lawrence, Richard Delgado, and Kimberle Crenshaw, *Words That Wound: Critical Race Theory, Assaultive Speech, and the First Amendment*, (Boulder, CO: Westview Press, 1993); Carlos J. Nan, "Adding Salt to the Wound: Affirmative Action and Critical Race Theory," *Law and Inequality: A Journal of Theory and Practice* 12 (1994): pp. 553–72; Enid Trucios-Haynes, "Why Race Matters: LatCrit Theory of Lantina/o Racial Identity," *La Raza Law Journal* 12, (2001): pp. 1–42.

Some of the themes in critical race theory were similar to those emerging in the feminist movement. There was a parallel to feminist standpoint theorizing in the emphasis on the need to understand the lived experiences of people of color in their local circumstances as these were imposed upon them by patterns of institutionalized racism. The story of what people had to endure became a major preoccupation as ethnographic data, accounts, parables, and histories of people actually experiencing discrimination were assembled. It was implicit in this emphasis that whites and more affluent sectors of Americans are in a very poor position to understand the plight of people of color. They should not, therefore, be on the vanguard of enacting laws and enforcing laws and establishing programs of amelioration because they could not understand what it was like to be living in circumstances created and sustained by prejudicial beliefs and overt as well as subtle patterns of discrimination. A number of important themes follows from this basic theme in much critical race theory, including the following:[81]

(1) Racism is normal, not an aberration. As a result, it is not so easy to eliminate because it is built into not only the way that that individuals categorize and respond to each other but is also part of a process by which prejudice and discrimination are built up in the culture and social structure of society.

(2) Racism and the inequalities that it systematically generates persist because they promote the interests of whites, and whites only support reform when it is in their interests.

(3) There is little incentive by whites in all classes to get rid of racism because it provides benefits, such as the following:

    (a) Employers have a low-wage pool of desperate workers to exploit and to threatened working class whites if their wage demands are too high.

    (b) If working-class whites can split the labor market and confine people of color to a limited range of low-wage, low-benefit jobs, they can protect their better-wage, better-benefit jobs.

(4) Law cannot be neutral when their enactment is constrained by (1), (2), and (3) above. Law is, therefore, inherently political and supportive of the interests of those with power and money.

(5) Race is a social construction in this sense: it can be changed and adapted to new circumstances, and "racialization" of targeted sub-populations can be adjusted to sustain oppression.

(6) Racialization is inherently intersectional, which, in turn, fractures racial identities (and the potential for unified world views) because social categories, such as class, gender, sexual orientation, and politics

---

[81]Matsuda et al., *Words That Wound* (cited in note 80).

that partition a population all intersect with social constructions of race, making it less likely that all people of color will perceive that they have common interests in eliminating racism.

(7) The seeming fairness of using merit and credentials as a means for sorting persons into various slots in society (carrying varying levels of resources) is a smokescreen for giving the middle classes a leg up in competition for jobs and other resources. Merit is defined by white culture and is supportive of their interests against the interests of people of color. For instance, test scores on standardized aptitude and achievement tests portray a white cultural world, making it difficult for those not exposed to this world to compete, thereby giving whites the false perception that the "playing field" where competition of life chances is level and that those who cannot meet these standards are less worthy. Continued racial oppression can occur because all people have had an "equal opportunity," again disadvantaging and stigmatizing those who have not grown up within white culture.

(8) The call for diversity and the constant commentary of its benefits serves white interests (say, the qualify for research grants from the federal government) more than the interests of people of color, who are stigmatized by affirmative-action programs as being less able to meet standards through normal recruitment routes. Moreover, this call for diversity does not generally meet the needs of people, while masking the fact that many people of color cannot qualify for many programs because of the barriers imposed by having to live under the conditions generated systematically by racism and patterns of discrimination. To have, for example, a diversity program for college students does little for those who have dropped out of high school and their parents, both of whom have different needs and interests from college students who qualify for diversity programs. Yet, diversity programs offer the illusion that the effects of discrimination have been addressed, while stigmatizing those who have not qualified for such programs.

For at least these reasons, legal theory and social science theorizing, particularly that in sociology, have not adequately conceptualized the dynamics of racism. Of course, the points above represents assertions and, in many ways, fail to appreciate the explanatory power of many existing theories of ethnic and racial discrimination. Yet, because these points are fueled by ideologies and designed to criticize, if not inflame, they implicitly portray the existing state of theories of discrimination as never having considered the forces listed above. In actual fact, this assertion is not true,[82] but these lists mostly target law as an effective tool in eliminating racism.

---

[82]See Adalberto Aguirre and Jonathan H. Turner, *American Ethnicity: The Dynamics and Consequences of Ethnic Discrimination*, 7th ed. (New York: McGraw-Hill, 2010) for a review of theories and for a more synthetic scientific theory that does take into account many of the points made by critical race theorists.

## Critical Theories of Race and Racism

Some scholars identified with critical race theory also seem to imply a variant and perhaps a somewhat less inflammatory alternative to this theory. As Bonilla-Silva emphasizes,[83] the notion of society becoming "color blind" and only concerned with merit and accomplishment is a smokescreen to perpetuate subtle and invidious forms of discrimination. He proposes instead an assault on this kind of "new racism." There is a more academic flavor to these approaches. For example, Patricia Hill Collins,[84] who shares many of the percepts of critical race theory, offers a list of guidelines that critical theories of race and racism should follow:

(1) The focus theory should be on social inequalities rather than race per se; emphasis should be on the processes by which social justice can be achieved by all those subject to discriminatory practices.

(2) Research and theorizing should be interdisciplinary.

(3) The dynamics of intersectionality should be emphasized so that the relations among race, class, ethnicity, nation, and communities are examined.

(4) The material basis of inequality as much as cultural processes, especially political and economic dynamics, should be central to analysis of race and racism.

(5) Race and racism in global context should also be central to analysis.

(6) The many manifestations of power and its dynamics in diverse setting should be emphasized in the analysis of race and racism.

Some of these points overlap with those listed under critical race theory, but there is an obvious difference in tone. Moreover, these points emphasize how the analysis of race and racism should proceed, rather than making blanket critique of existing programs administered by law and social welfare programs.

## Conclusions

Theorizing on the dynamics of discrimination has always been split between those theories that are more value neutral and those that are explicitly ideological. At times, the same theorists have produced both kinds of theories, but there is—much like feminist theories—a significant difference between critical and scientific theories. In critical theories, there is often an indictment of scientific theories as "part of the problem" whereas

---

[83]Eduardo Bonilla-Silva, *Racism without Racists: Color-Blind Racism and the Persistence of Racial Inequality in the United States* (Lanham, MD: Rowman and Littlefield, 2003).

[84]This list taken from Collins' website and class syllabi.

in scientific theories, the goal is to avoid the emotion-arousing effects of ideologies and, instead, to provide a more dispassionate analysis of the conditions under which prejudicial beliefs and institutionalized patterns of discrimination increase or decrease. Like all critical theories, one goal of critical race theories is to expose persistent and often invidious patterns of racism and discrimination; in so doing, plans of action (as opposed to explanation) to change social systems can be formulated. Scientific theorists often have the same goal, but critical theorists will generally see them as too sedate and as supporting the status quo. Like feminism, then, there will be at least "two sociologies" of race and ethnicity—a situation that has been part of American sociology since its beginnings and clearly is not about to go away in the second decade of the twenty-first century.

# General Conclusion

There is an obvious difference in emotional tone and subject matter of European and American critical theories. They often overlap, and Americans have contributed to the European canon probably more than the reverse because American critical theory tends to be somewhat nation-centric, especially critical race theory compared to critical feminist theory. European theory still focuses on the conditions and problems of modernity, in all its manifestations, whereas feminism and race theories are about the dynamics revolving around unfairly devalued social categories of persons who have been the victims of discrimination, prejudices, and unjust treatment. European theories are clearly more academic and flow from academia to the lay-intellectual world, whereas American critical theories are the result of social movements in the broader society that have been brought into academia and, in many respects, stay in academia.

It is clear that my biases—despite a substantial amount of activist work on my part, especially in my younger years—lie with science. I am much like Auguste Comte—only more sane, I should hope—in the view that by discovering the laws of social dynamics, we can use these laws to make a better world. As I discovered in my own early work, when sociological analysis is driven by ideology, it becomes highly distorted by the emotion and passion about what I thought should and ought to be. Now, I am more circumspect; I try to figure out why certain social arrangement exists not by positing evil but by trying to figure out, dispassionately, what forces are driving the formation and operation of these dynamics. The models and laws that emerge from such analysis will, I believe, provide better guidance to social amelioration than my earlier works that were driven by ideological fervor. Critical theorists would disagree with my statements above, and often passionately so, as I have learned. Thus, the divide that has been woven through American sociology from its inception and, to a lesser extent, European sociology as well is still with us, with little chance of abating. In the end, each sociologists must discover which is the better path to take. I have taken both in my career, but even in the early, more activist period, I was disquieted by the fact that when doing science, I found that my conclusions came into conflict with my ideology. I wanted social arrangements that were often not attainable given the forces in play. To some, this is "to sell out" to the evil powers that be, and it is a justification for the status quo. To me, however, it is a better way to try to develop policies for change that actually have a chance of working rather than hurting people. Again, many would disagree. A book on contemporary sociological theory must accept the divide, unless we wish to have two types of contemporary theory books: those espousing primacy of science and those espousing the primacy of doing something about the problems of the social world. And, maybe there are two sociologies: scientific sociology and humanistic sociology. I do not think that these are a contradiction. But alas, some would disagree.

# Index

# About the Author

**Jonathan H. Turner** (PhD, Cornell University) is Distinguished Professor of sociology at the University of California at Riverside and University Professor for the University of California. He is the author of 37 books, which have been published in twelve different languages, and many research articles in journals and books.

# ⑤SAGE research**methods**

The essential online tool for researchers from the world's leading methods publisher

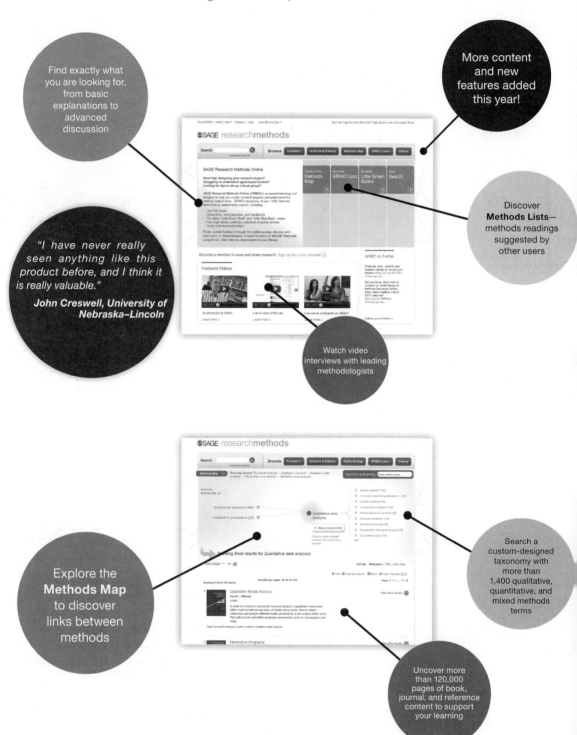

Find exactly what you are looking for, from basic explanations to advanced discussion

More content and new features added this year!

"I have never really seen anything like this product before, and I think it is really valuable."

*John Creswell, University of Nebraska–Lincoln*

Discover **Methods Lists**— methods readings suggested by other users

Watch video interviews with leading methodologists

Explore the **Methods Map** to discover links between methods

Search a custom-designed taxonomy with more than 1,400 qualitative, quantitative, and mixed methods terms

Uncover more than 120,000 pages of book, journal, and reference content to support your learning

# Find out more at
# www.sageresearchmethods.com